SUPERTALL | MEGATALL

HOW HIGH CAN WE GO?

ORO Editions
Publishers of Architecture, Art, and Design
Gordon Goff: Publisher

www.oroeditions.com
info@oroeditions.com

Published by ORO Editions

FOLLOW ONLINE
smithgill.com
smithgill.blog
Facebook @smithgillarch
Instagram @asggarch
Twitter @smithgillarch

10 9 8 7 6 5 4 3 2 1 First Edition

ISBN: 978-1-954081-37-6

Color Separations and Printing: ORO Group Ltd.

Printed in China.

ORO Editions makes a continuous effort to minimize the overall carbon footprint of its publications. As part of this goal, ORO Editions, in association with Global ReLeaf, arranges to plant trees to replace those used in the manufacturing of the paper produced for its books. Global ReLeaf is an international campaign run by American Forests, one of the world's oldest nonprofit conservation organizations. Global ReLeaf is American Forests' education and action program that helps individuals, organizations, agencies, and corporations improve the local and global environment by planting and caring for trees.

CONTENTS

FOREWORD

SUPERTALL | MEGATALL: HOW HIGH CAN WE GO?

The number of tall, supertall, and megatall buildings being designed and constructed has grown in unprecedented fashion in the first two decades of the 21st Century, driven by the forces of urbanization, finance, and the human desire for iconic structures.

These two decades have seen more tall building construction than in all previous history. In Supertall Megatall: How High Can We Go? master architect Adrian Smith and his collaborative design partner Gordon Gill at Adrian Smith + Gordon Gill Architecture describe how these feats of architecture and engineering are conceived and come to fruition. It makes a fascinating tale.

The architectural concept of a building must respond to the aesthetic sense, local historical and cultural influences, and the need to provide functional and attractive working or living spaces. The building must at the same time be structurally efficient, energy efficient, comfortable, and well able to withstand the forces of nature such as wind and earthquake. Following 9/11 the need to consider vulnerability to terrorist attacks also became apparent. The taller the building, the greater the challenge, especially from wind forces. Understanding and quantifying wind forces is important, not only from the perspective of structural strength but also for the comfort of the occupants. Wind tunnel testing is often done at the conceptual stage of design so that aerodynamic shaping can be incorporated right from the start. My own personal involvement has been in these wind studies, including wind tunnel tests, meteorological investigations, and the use of damping systems to control wind-induced motions.

This has provided me with a window into the work of numerous other specialists who all contribute to the successful completion of a tall building project. For the investors in supertall and megatall towers the technical decisions made by the design team are critical to their commercial success. The safety and comfort of the occupants are also critically dependent on the right technical decisions being made. The book gives a great depiction of the decision-making process.

The list of specialists needed for a supertall or mega-tall project is very long: architects, structural engineers, mechanical-electrical-plumbing (MEP) consultants, geotechnical consultants, wind consultants, snow and ice experts, wall systems specialists, elevator companies, landscape architects, interior designers, noise and acoustics consultants, construction contractors, specialty fabricators, damping systems specialists; The list goes on. Rather like the conductor of an orchestra, the architect coordinates the efforts of the whole team so that ideally, they all work in harmony and produce an inspiring result. Adrian Smith and Gordon Gill have accumulated an impressive portfolio of supertall and megatall buildings, a tribute not only to their inspiring architecture but also to their ability to successfully manage large teams working on very complex projects.

Specific projects are described in a variety of countries including the UAE, the USA, China, Saudi Arabia, South Korea, India, and the Chechen Republic. Each of these projects has their interesting aspects but of special note is Jeddah Tower in Saudi Arabia at over 1000 m tall, which is under construction at the present time. The tapered form of the Jeddah Tower was influenced by Adrian Smith's experience on the existing world's tallest building, Burj Khalifa (828 m) in Dubai, while he was at SOM Chicago. Another noteworthy project is 1 Dubai Atrium City, which is conceived as three mega-towers linked at several levels by sky bridges. The bridges are used not only to enable travel between the towers at several above-ground levels but also to transfer wind loading between the towers, making them more wind resistant.

Sustainability in the form of conserving energy and water while reducing CO2 and landfill waste, is a recurring theme throughout the book. It is a central issue in a discussion with Adrian Smith at the end of the book where he also discusses the limiting factors on height and how a tall building needs to be viewed in the context of the city around it, not in isolation. His views of the future of cities will be of interest to a broad audience.

Peter Irwin, CM, PhD, PEng, FASCE, FSEI, FCSCE, FEIC, FCAE
Founding Partner and Past President
RWDI, Guelph, Ontario, Canada
July 26, 2021

CHAPTER I. INNOVATIVE SYSTEMS

STRUCTURALLY INTEGRATED CONFIGURATIONS

The most important aspect in the design of supertall towers is to skillfully integrate architecture and structure. These disciplines cannot be separated and both benefit from total integration. Unlike most structures where gravity is the initial criteria for design, supertall towers have other horizontal forces that influence the overall design process.

It is both beneficial and cost efficient to design supertall buildings at the early concept stage to take advantage of the primary loads affecting the building's performance. Architects and engineers collaborate on multiple iterations to refine and sculpt the overall design.

With early and accurate knowledge of a tower's site conditions and context, architects and engineers work together to develop breakthrough ideas that result in structures that are extraordinary human accomplishments and transformative landmarks.

The overall goal is to devise a design that complements and enhances the architecture, the function, the buildability, the durability, and the sustainability, while creating the most efficient design for the client. By using an integrated parametric approach and collaborating with wind testing scientists and structural engineers, architects can look at the formal design issues of the tower, along with programmatic concerns, wind performance, structural optimization, occupant comfort and usability, material efficiency, space utilization, and the performance and interconnectedness between these variables.

The building's structure must be designed to maximize its efficiency while minimizing its disruption to the intended uses of the tower; all within acceptable initial and long-term cost and operating parameters. It is not enough to design efficient and usable structures, they must also be buildable, as well as durable, resilient, and environmentally responsible.

+ 1 PARK AVE
+ CHENGDU GREENLAND TOWER
+ WUHAN GREENLAND CENTER
+ YONGSAN DANCING DRAGONS
+ LAKESIDE RESIDENTIAL TOWERS
+ SKY SAIL
+ BURJ 2020
+ ZA'ABEEL COMMERCIAL TOWER

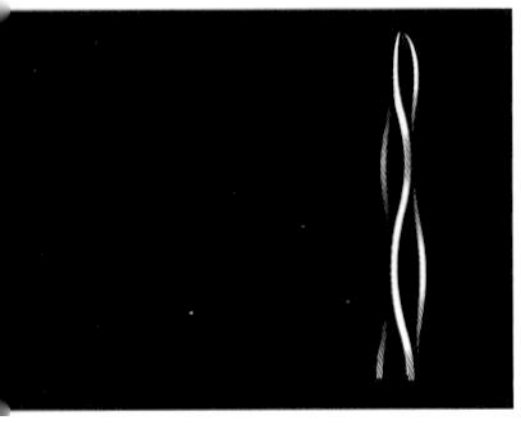

1 PARK AVENUE

DUBAI, UNITED ARAB EMIRATES, 2008

500M

1 Park Avenue has ambitious sustainability goals and was conceived as a net-zero energy tower that integrates wind-turbine power generation and solar power generation, with a wide array of passive technologies.

Advanced building technologies and climate appropriate systems are integrated to create onsite power generation that reduces or eliminates the need to draw energy from the grid. Proposed sustainable systems include a climate wall, radiant heating and cooling systems, geothermal systems, solar collection, rain water and gray water collection, and controlled daylighting.

The design proceeded through schematic design into design development with a Dubai-based client, however, the 2008 economic downturn caused the project to go on hold. Although it remains unrealized, the graceful design has informed much of our work and remains an inspiring, thoughtful architectural vision.

+ CONTEXT
+ PROGRAM
+ FORM
+ RESEARCH + DEVELOPMENT
+ FACADE
+ PERFORMANCE
+ STRUCTURE

CONTEXT

The tower's flowing form translates its curves to a horizontal form. The fluid form symbolizes Dubai's relationship to water, drawing parallels to the movements of the Gulf that defines the city.

The tower and podium's smooth, rounded figure further recalls and embraces the history of Dubai's pearl industry. Like a strand of pearls, which have been harvested and traded in the Arabian Gulf for generations, the tower shimmers in the sun.

PROGRAM

1 Park Avenue's site is situated in the northeast portion of the East Park District of the Jumeirah Garden City Master Plan, at the intersection of South Boulevard and 11th Street. The total planned plot size is approximate 66,485 sm. The tower is oriented to take advantage of the triangular shape of the site and to maximize access from the proposed perimeter roads.

The approximately 600,000 sm mixed-use complex includes premium offices, condominiums, and service apartments, along with the world's highest luxury hotel with a multi-story atrium. Three podium buildings, which range from six to nineteen stories, provide offices and support for the hotel in a park-like setting. The tower's auxiliary space at the top includes two restaurants and a club/observatory with a 20-story-high dome.

Other facilities and amenities include a business center in the tower's residential zone, a health club, an Olympic-sized swimming pool, several ballrooms and meeting rooms in the podium buildings, lush landscaping with fountains and other water features throughout the development, and four levels of underground parking.

SITE PLAN SKETCH, 2008

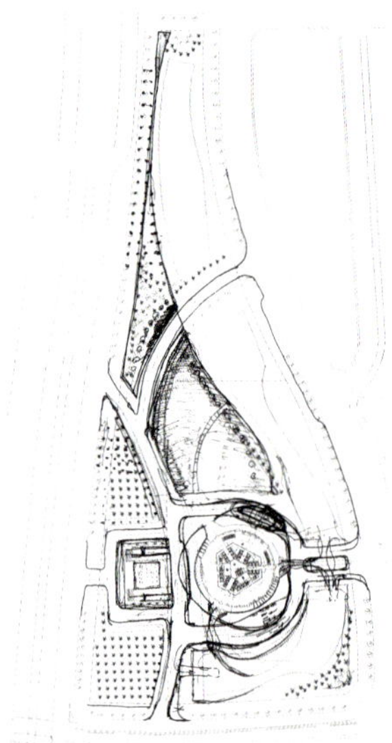

PROGRAM

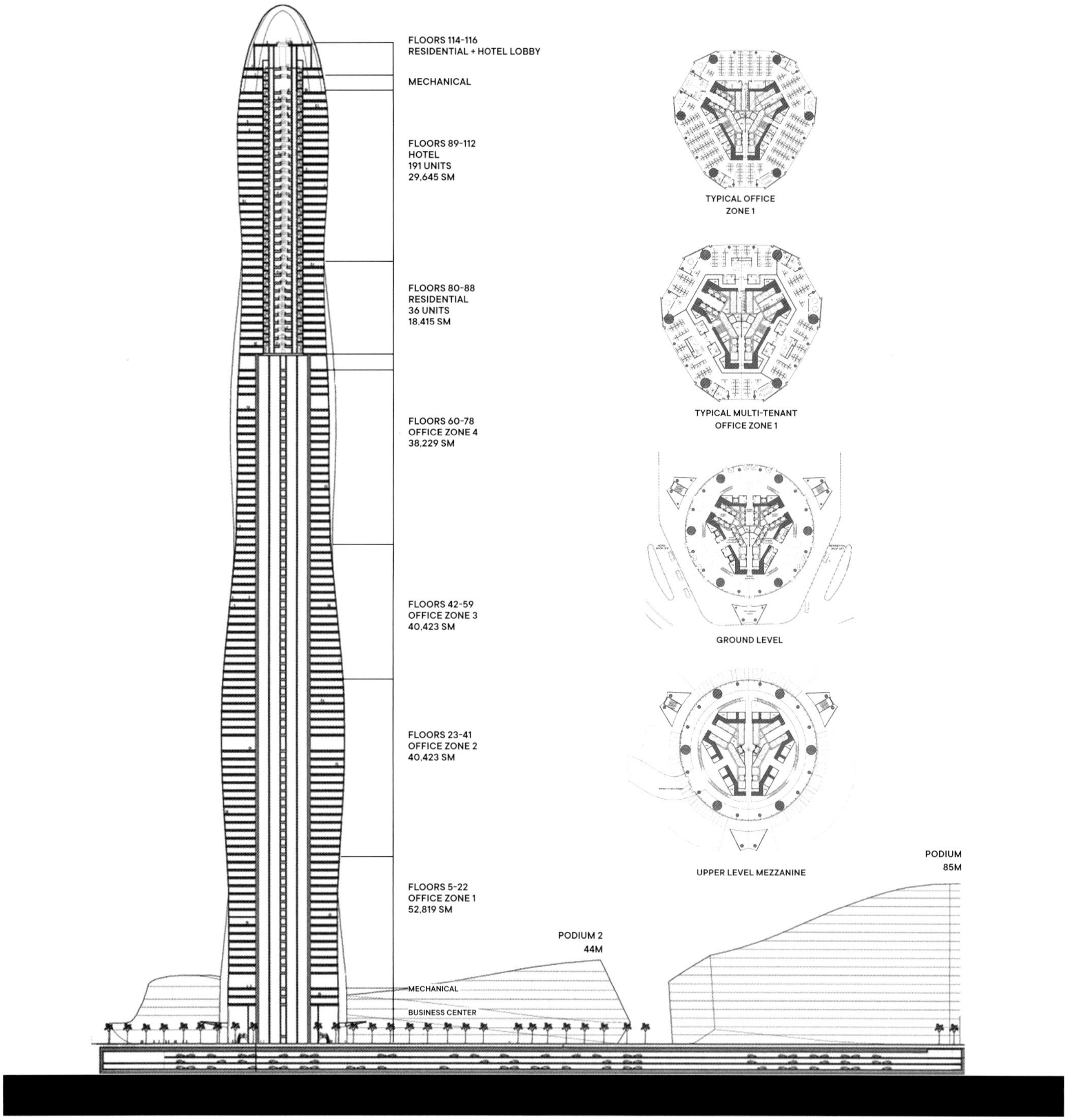

FLOORS 114-116
RESIDENTIAL + HOTEL LOBBY
MECHANICAL
FLOORS 89-112
HOTEL
191 UNITS
29,645 SM
FLOORS 80-88
RESIDENTIAL
36 UNITS
18,415 SM
FLOORS 60-78
OFFICE ZONE 4
38,229 SM
FLOORS 42-59
OFFICE ZONE 3
40,423 SM
FLOORS 23-41
OFFICE ZONE 2
40,423 SM
FLOORS 5-22
OFFICE ZONE 1
52,819 SM
MECHANICAL
BUSINESS CENTER
PODIUM 2
44M
PODIUM
85M
TYPICAL OFFICE
ZONE 1
TYPICAL MULTI-TENANT
OFFICE ZONE 1
GROUND LEVEL
UPPER LEVEL MEZZANINE

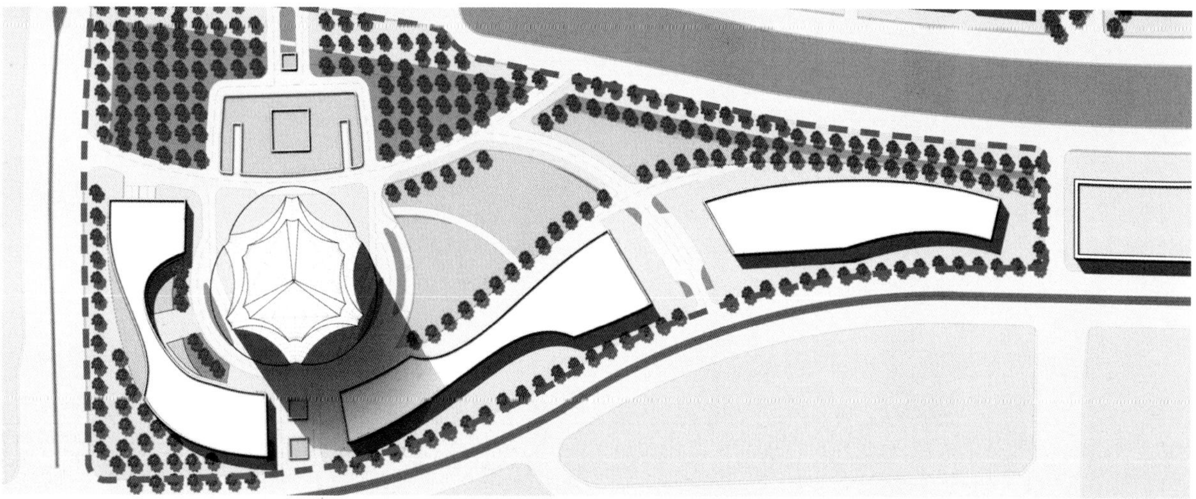

FORM

As designed, the tower is one of the most advanced skyscrapers in the world and has the potential to be one of Dubai's most poetic and evocative structures. The undulating form is biomorphic, with proportions that taper from the bottom to the top, giving it an almost-human figure. The tower comes alive as you walk around it; its graceful symmetry shifting and moving depending on the angle from which it is viewed.

Each floor plate is unique because of the varying forms of the tower, although all floors are tri symmetrical. While some floor plates are nearly round, others resemble a triangle imposed within a circle. Each floor has ample access to views and daylight because of the unique configuration.

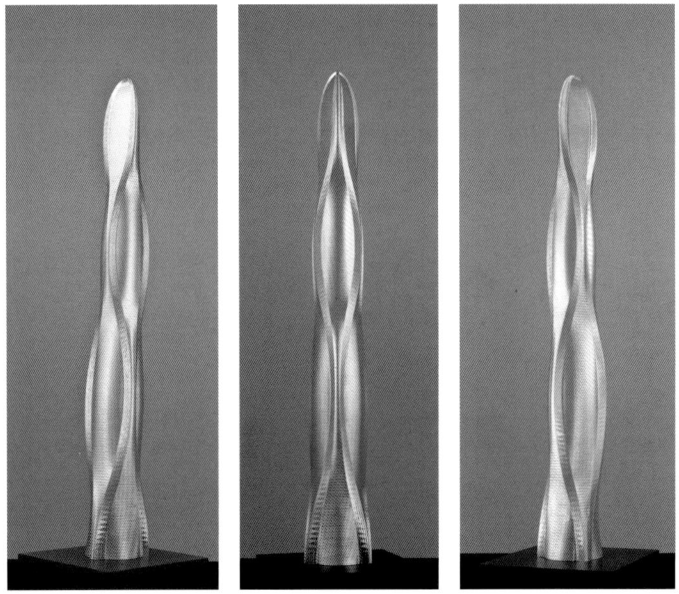

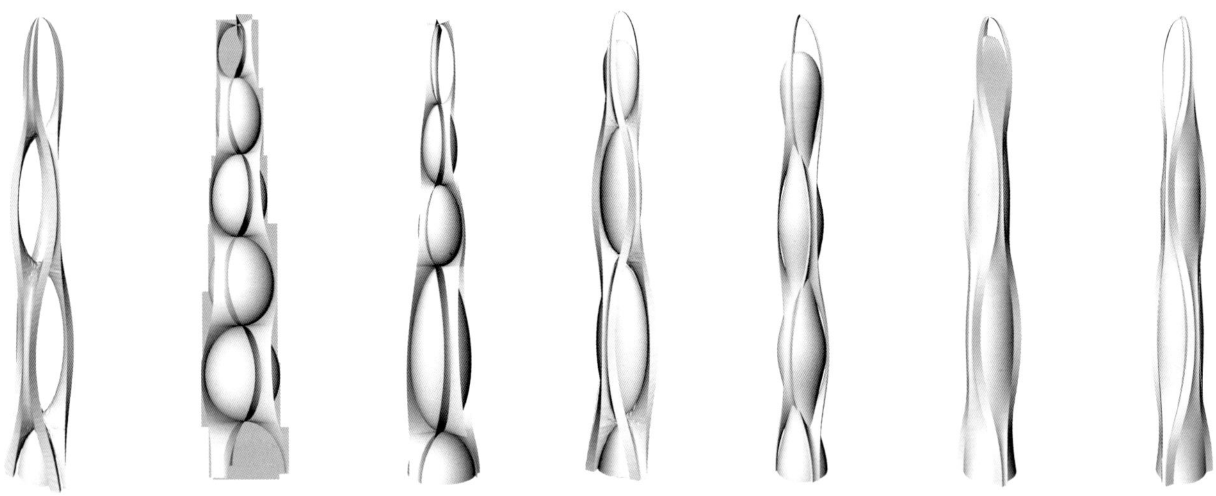

During the design of the 1 Park Avenue, the shape was sculpted with wind performance in mind. The undulation of the tower works to reduce vortex shedding and therefore the structural wind loads imposed on the tower. This would potentially reduce structural cost and increase overall efficiency of the tower in terms of its behavior, and occupant comfort in high wind situations.

Additionally, various configurations for wind turbines were explored conceptually. At the top of the tower, it was envisioned that the wind turbines could be located between the main body of the tower and the structural outside frame that creates the form.

Further massing tests were done to create circular holes in the top of the tower where wind turbines could be located, and viewed from the observation area. In all cases, the placement of these turbines was carefully done so as not to cause visual impact or vibrations in sensitive residential areas of tower, but rather to be a feature at the top where the turbines would be most efficient.

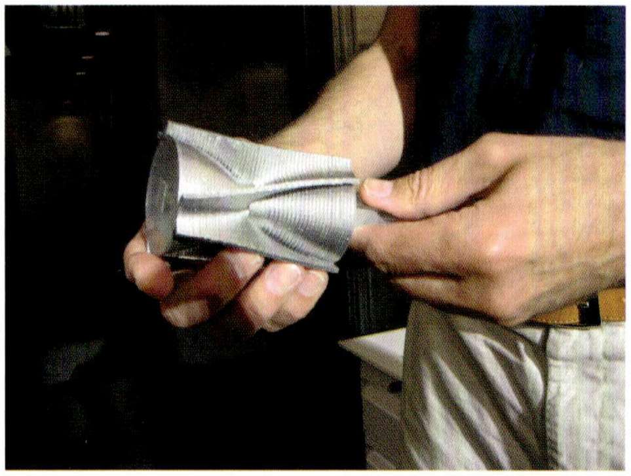

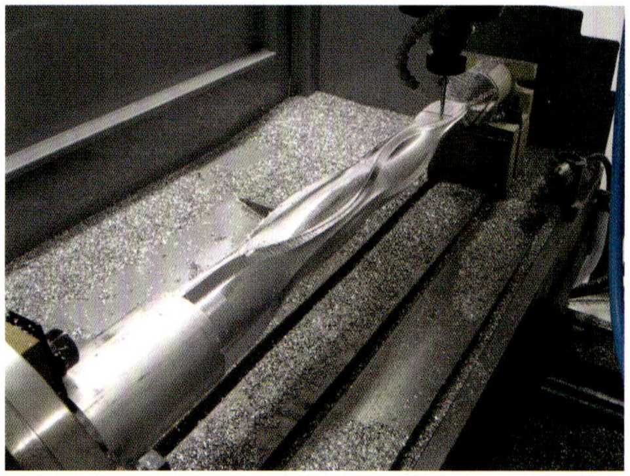

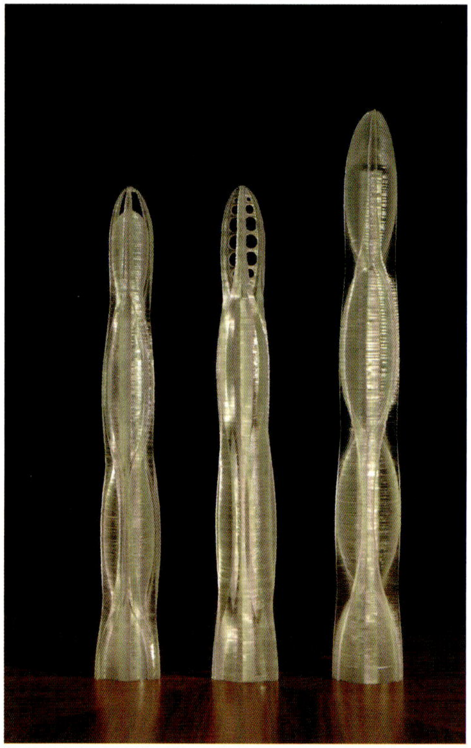

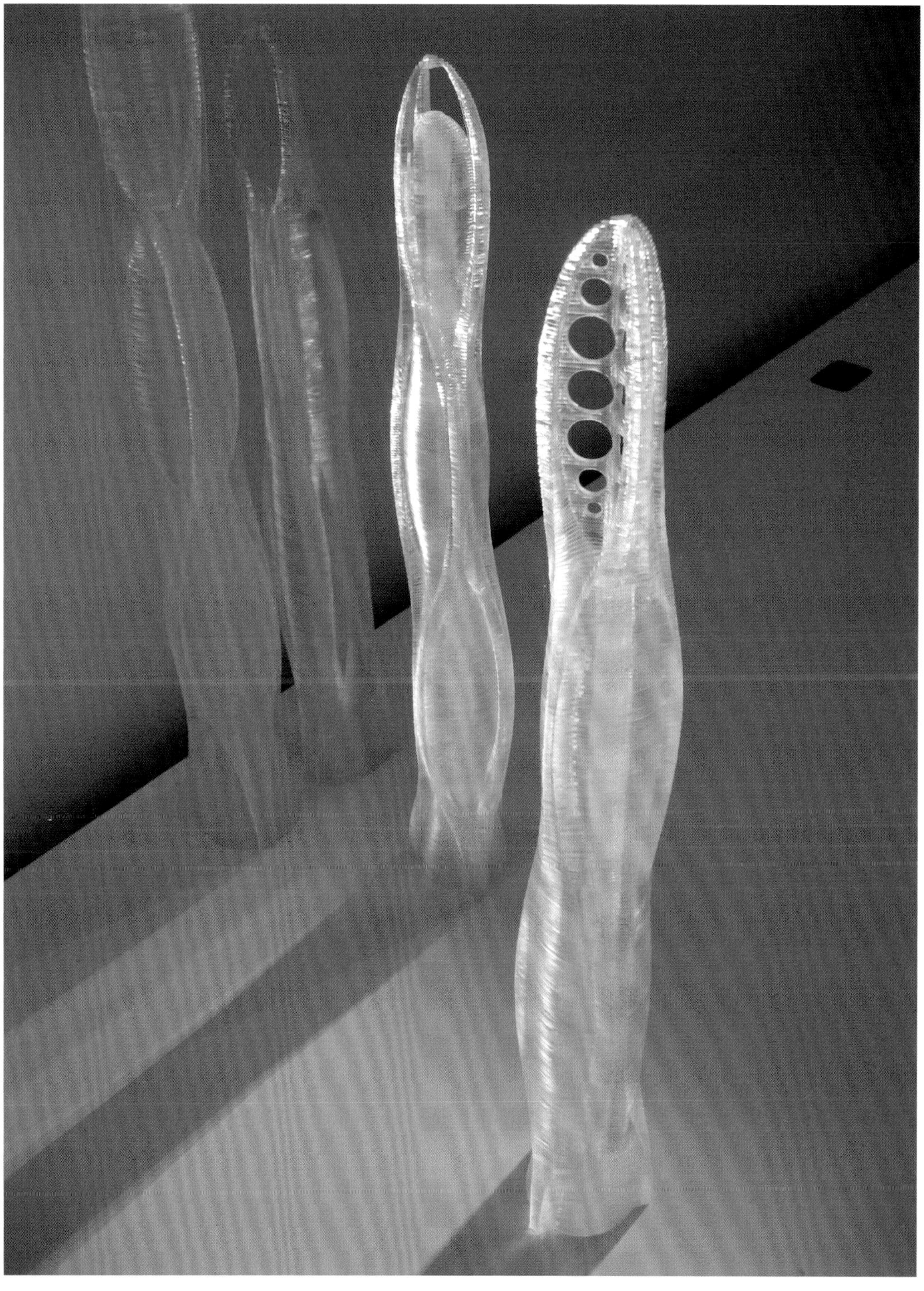

FACADE

Climate concerns dictate the building's skin, prioritizing shading against the region's strong solar gain. The transparent high-performance exterior wall controls the transfer of heat and light with the help of a high-tech system of light shelves and light-sensor-activated shades. Shading fins extend above each floor, which shades the glass beneath and allows for a more transparent curtain wall. Integrated photovoltaic cells will harvest solar energy.

The office levels exterior wall has custom high-performance unitized systems. A double curtain-wall system integrates with the building HVAC system to reuse energy captured in the ventilated cavity. The wall's exterior light shelves and shading fins are approximately 600 mm deep, three per floor, with integrated photovoltaic surfaces. Each sun-shading device also has LED strip lights for low-cost lighting. The exterior wall incorporates interior automatic/manual vertical shades connected to light sensors for glare control.

The facade surface has a stepped profile with like-sized panels that follow the shape of the tower's geometry. Alternate methods of geometric rationalization, such as sloped trapezoidal glazing, were part of the schematic design studies to improve efficiency.

The glazing is a four-sided butt-glazed system, structurally glazed to sub-frames. Strips of stainless-steel cladding cover 70 percent of the main ribbon columns—or mega-columns—and 30 percent of the glazing area, reducing the overall window-to-wall ratio for better energy performance. Special mullion profiles and custom fabricated stainless-steel and aluminum mullions adapt to the tower form.

The hotel's exterior wall is also proposed as a single-wall system. Glass is high-performance insulated glazing with a light transmission of 36 percent, which is high compared to glass typically used in the Middle East, but was possible because of the sunshades.

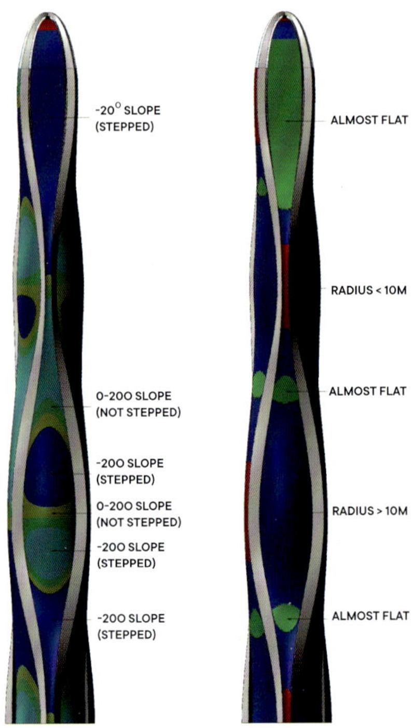

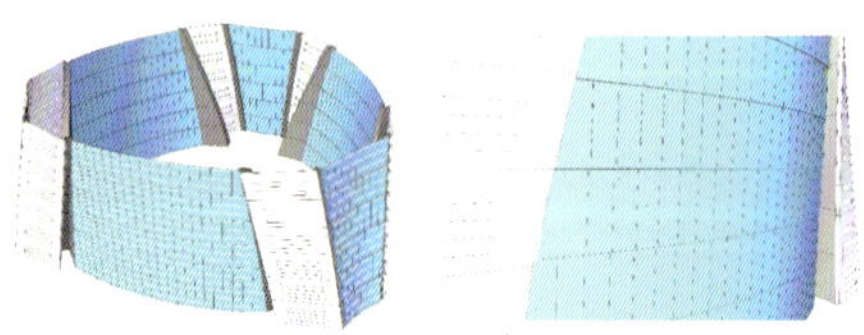

TRAPEZOIDAL RATIONALIZATION

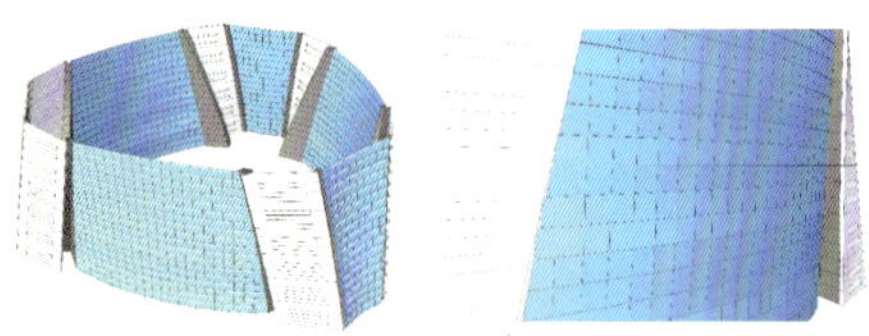

STEPPED SLOPING RATIONALIZATION

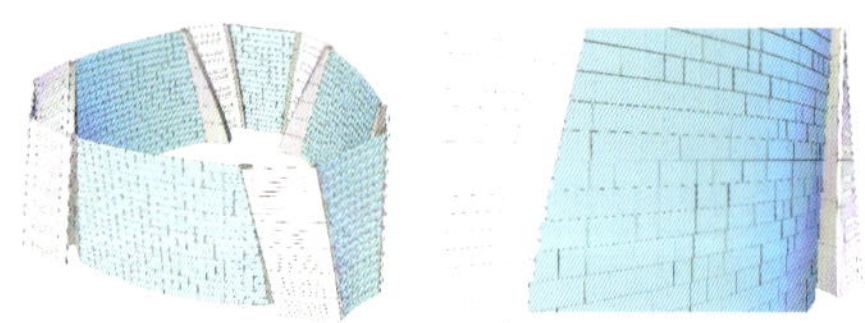

STEPPED VERTICAL RATIONALIZATION

The sky lobby has a cable-wall system with canopies made of stainless steel that have integrated photovoltaic panels, as well as delicately fritted skylights.

The exterior braced mega-columns are reinforced-concrete and it is envisioned that a steel frame will be embedded within each mega-column. These steel frames will serve a dual purpose: first they will assist with erection by providing a framework for attaching the concrete formwork. Second, they will provide a positive connection of the diaphragm bracing members between the core and the mega-columns.

Because the mega-columns curve around the exterior of the building, horizontal diaphragm tie forces between the core and the mega-columns exist at each floor level. The floor framing and the minor exterior gravity columns can be framed in either concrete or steel. Preliminary studies of the two framing options indicate that steel columns and steel floor framing with composite metal deck slab would be the preferred option.

PERFORMANCE

Twelve vertical-axis wind turbines are contained within each of the three slots between the mega-columns and the dome at the top of the tower. Maintenance access to the turbines is via ladder cages inside the mega columns. The location of the turbines was studied and optimized using CFD modeling; the shape of the structure allows wind to be channeled into the turbine area, so the turbines are placed near the top of the tower, where they have the highest wind speeds and minimize any vibration issues or disruption to the building occupants. The turbines are a visible representation of the futuristic design and the sustainable aspirations of the tower as 21st-century structure.

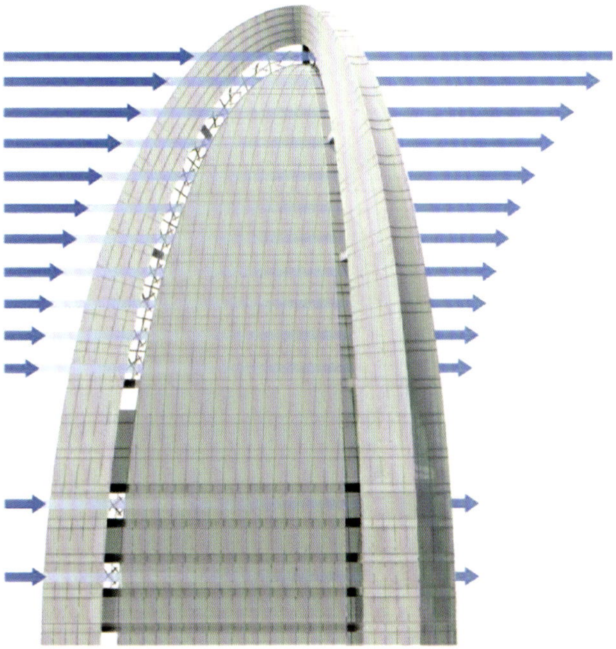

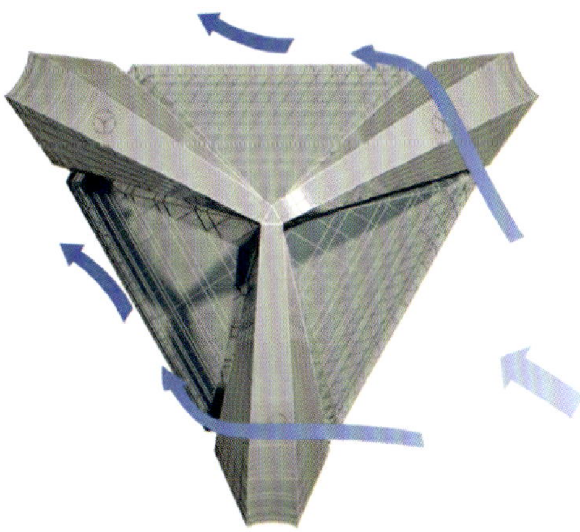

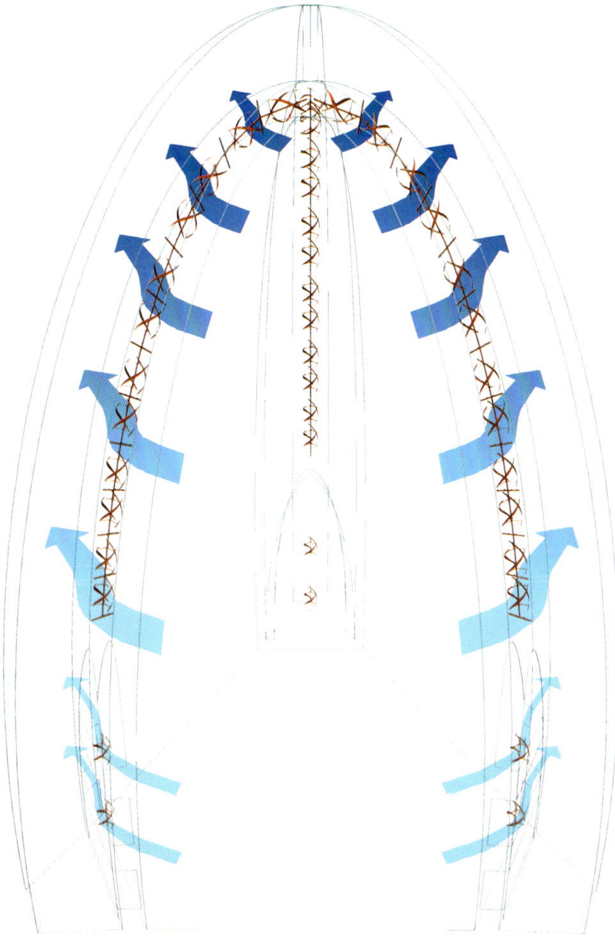

PERFORMANCE

HALVORSON & PARTNERS, STRUCTURAL ENGINEER

The wind climate in Dubai is moderate, with a base wind speed of 38m/s per the Dubai Municipal Code. Although the magnitude of the wind pressure is important, the shape of the building and the dynamic properties of the building can be as important when designing for wind loads.

The architectural form of the concept building tapers from the base of the building to the top with the cross sectional dimensions at the top of the building being 75 percent that of the base. With respect to the wind induced dynamic loads on the building, the tapered shape is beneficial because it will reduce the organized shedding of wind vortices.

Although the cross-section at any particular plan may be circular or nearly triangular, shapes which are prone to regular vortex shedding. The orientation of the triangular plans vary over the height which will also reduce the organized wind vortices.

In optimizing the lateral load resisting system, three principles exist: Design the structure so that gravity load and wind load are resisted by the same elements; place the gravity elements as far apart as possible; and, link the gravity elements together with "links" that are as rigid as possible. The logic behind these principles is simple:

- By carrying the wind overturning forces on elements that are already carrying large gravity loads, the axial stiffness inherent in the gravity element is also used in resisting overturning forces and in reducing lateral drifts.

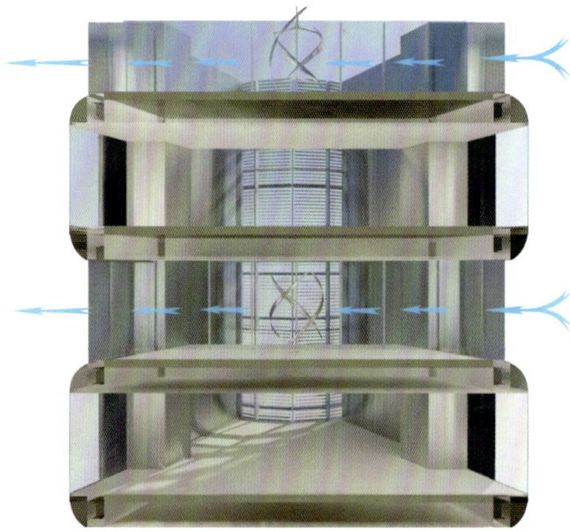

BUILDING INTEGRATED WIND TURBINES

- By locating the gravity elements as far apart as possible, the wind overturning forces are proportionately reduced, much as a table with legs at the corners is more stable than one with the legs inboard.

- The lateral drift at the top of a building can be thought of as comprised of two components: "cantilever deflections" caused by column shortening and lengthening resulting from wind overturning forces; and, "shear racking" caused by distortions of the structure in between the columns. The stiffer the structure between columns, the "links", then the less material is required in the columns. Since column quantities can exceed half the total material quantities in a tower, reducing that quantity is very beneficial.

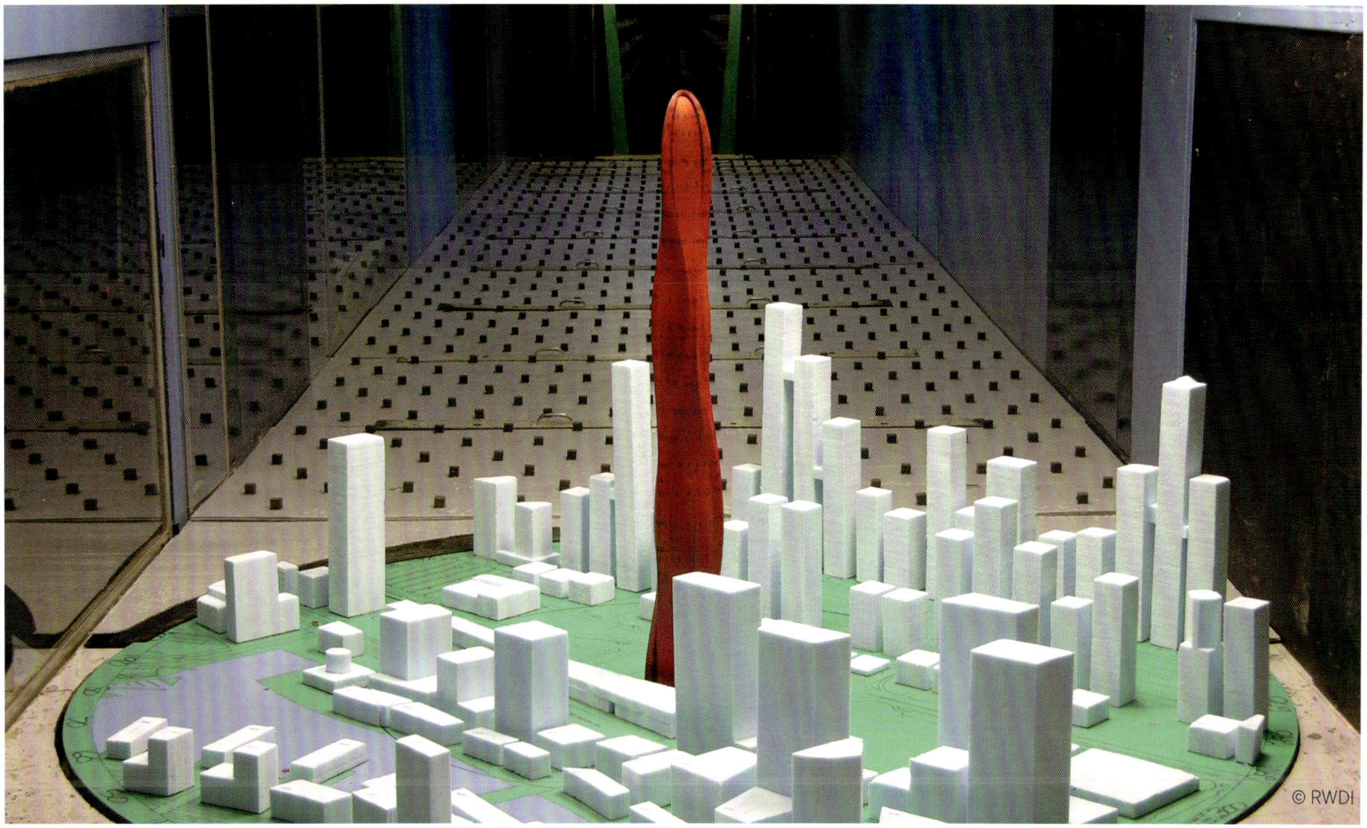

WIND TUNNEL TESTING

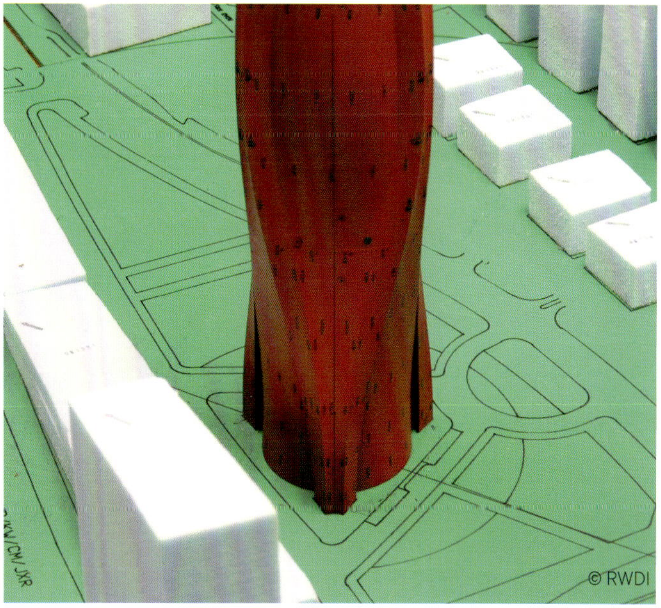

PERFORMANCE

HALVORSON & PARTNERS, STRUCTURAL ENGINEER

A building with such a unique and complex architectural appearance would imply that the structural system must also be unique and complex. However, the envisioned lateral system for this tower is, in its simplest form, a combination of a core and outrigger system with an exterior braced mega-column frame. The core and outrigger structural system has been used extensively for tall building designs and a variation is used here to integrate the structural design into the desired architectural form.

The proposed structural concept consists of a central hexagonal concrete core that is tied to the exterior braced mega-column frame at three outrigger zones, with each zone consisting of four levels. The outriggers in each zone can be concrete walls or steel trusses. Approximately 50 percent of the gravity loads are carried by the central core and 50 percent are carried by the exterior mega-columns. The central core and the mega-columns work together to resist the wind and seismic lateral loads.

PERFORMANCE

SYSKA HENNESSEY, MEP ENGINEER

Water Efficient Plumbing Fixtures

Water efficiency begins with the devices that are ultimately the end users. Dual flush toilets and flush valves, low-flow and no-flow urinals, and low-flow showers and sinks dramatically reduce the water consumption of the building, by as much as 40 percent.

Water Collection and Reuse System

Water will be collected from a number of sources on the site: rain water, cooling coil condensate waste, showers, sinks and laundry, stored and filtered for reuse. This captured and filtered water can then be used for cooling tower operation, irrigation, and potentially in the buildings flush toilets.

Ground Coupled Pre-Cooling

Both the ground and the adjacent canal provide an opportunity to implement passive means of energy exchange to reduce the reliance on mechanical heating and cooling equipment. Flexible water piping is designed in the building foundation elements—caissons, slabs, and perimeter retaining walls—to provide condenser water heat rejection before passing through the cooling towers. This strategy provides the opportunity to reduce the energy and water consumption requirements of the cooling tower by as much as 50 percent.

High-Performance HVAC

High-performance HVAC begins with a well-integrated, high-performance building envelope. The double-wall curtain-wall system is integrated with the building HVAC system so that energy captured in the ventilated cavity can be collected and used for pre-heating of outdoor air in winter and assisting with dehumidification of outdoor air in summer. As part of the sustainable, high performance design, waste energy is recovered and reused wherever and whenever possible to minimize the need for mechanical refrigeration and heating.

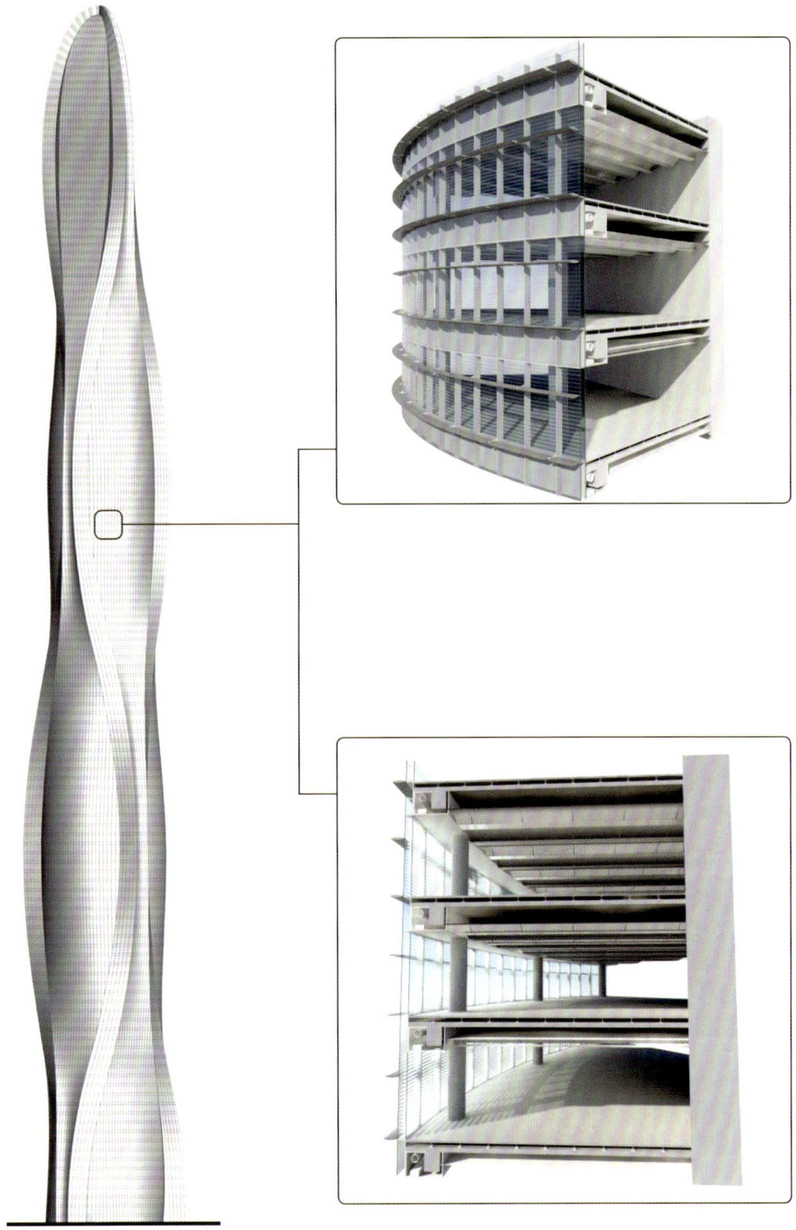

Office levels use ventilated chilled beams as the means of providing flexible, local cooling and heating that provides energy-efficient comfort cooling locally controlled to the office occupants. Perimeter chilled beams will be provided with heating coils to minimize heat loss during winter conditions.

Service apartments and hotel rooms will be provided with super efficient fan coil units with local controls to provide quick response heating and cooling to these areas. Radiant heating will be provided at floor level in specific areas of the apartments and hotel rooms to provide comfort to occupants during winter. Recovery of energy from exhaust and relief air paths that can then be transferred to incoming outdoor ventilation air will allow for higher quantities of ventilation air to each space than a conventional building, without the normal energy penalty. Monitoring of indoor air contaminants also provide the ability to adjust the ventilation air volumes to maintain superior indoor air quality for the building occupants.

The design for the ground-coupled pre-cooling system incorporates condenser water piping embedded in the building's foundation elements to pre-cool condenser water and reduce reliance on the cooling towers to reject heat to outdoors. This strategy will also dramatically reduce the water consumption of the cooling towers: typically the most water-intensive use of large buildings. Combined with a high-efficiency chiller system and natural gas-fired boiler system utilizing variable speed pumping, significant annual energy savings will be realized.

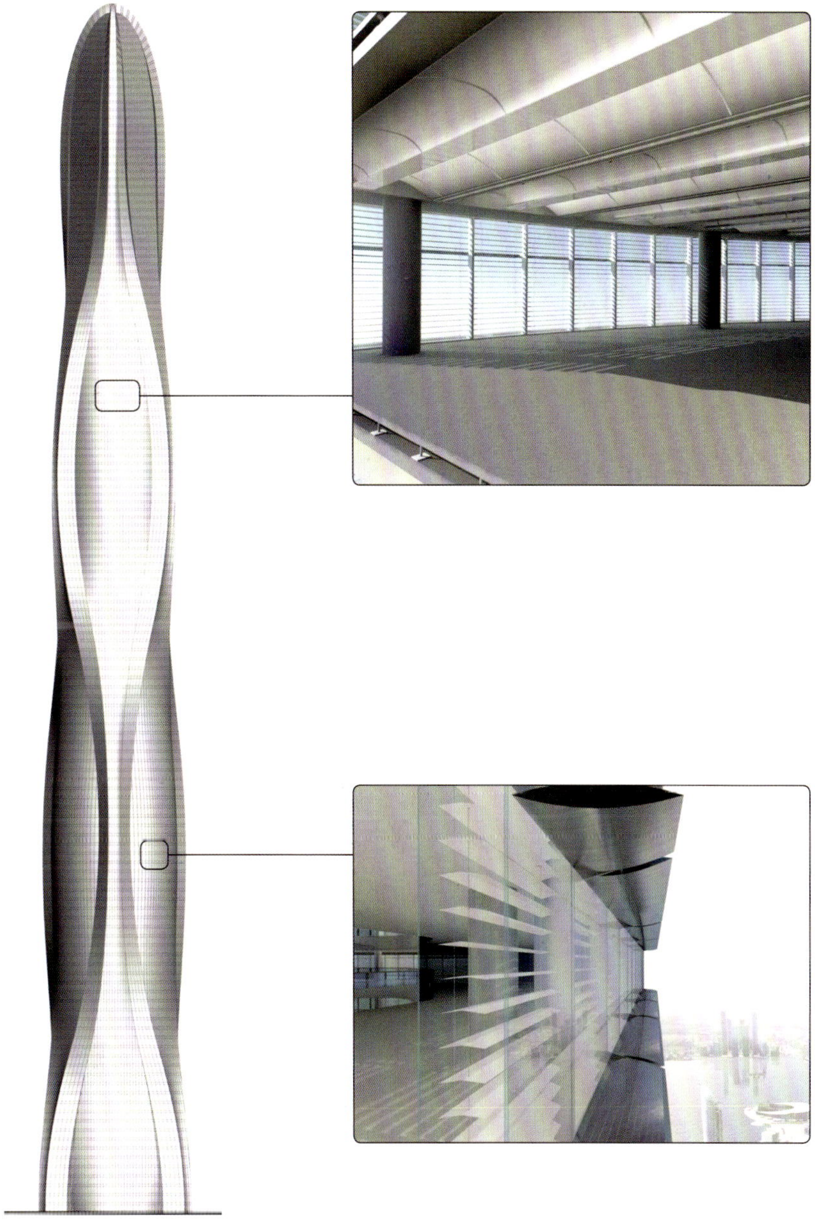

PERFORMANCE

SYSKA HENNESSY, MEP ENGINEER

Electrical Systems: Lighting control systems for office levels will be provided to respond to natural light levels by dimming or shutting off lights when not needed. Occupancy sensors will be used where appropriate to shut off lights in rooms of variable occupancy.

On-site renewable-energy generation will be used in the form of building-integrated photovoltaics, building-integrated wind turbines, and on-site co-generation systems using fuel cells, micro-turbines or bio-gas generators to minimize the reliance on environmentally damaging power plants.

An integrated, intelligent building system will be provided that provides the interface for the HVAC controls, lighting controls, building management system, security system and other building operating systems.

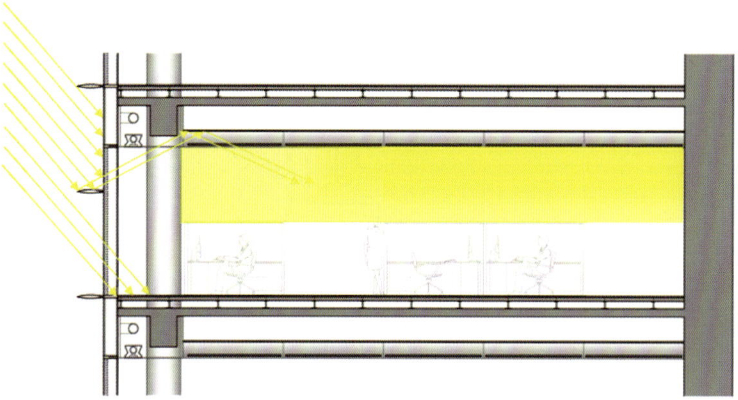

EXTERIOR SHADING AND IMPROVED NATURAL LIGHTING

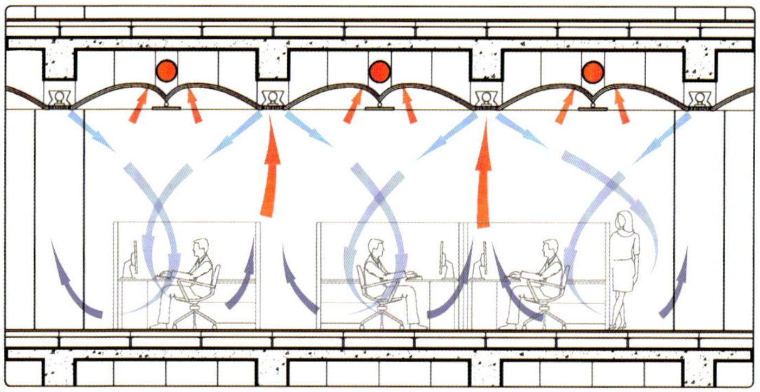

HVAC SYSTEM

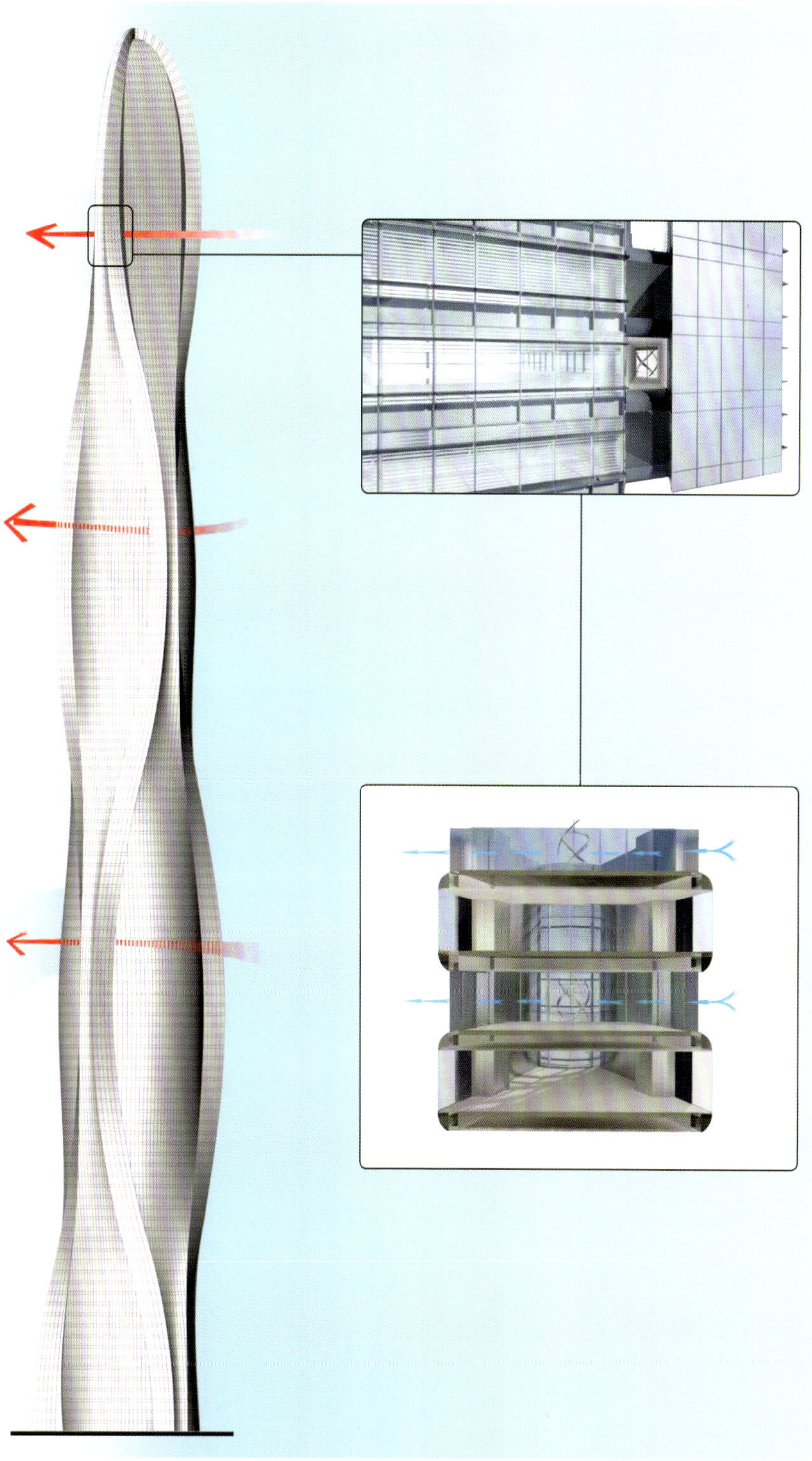

PERFORMANCE

SYSKA HENNESSY, MEP ENGINEER

The design of the tower aspires to be a net-zero energy building. The sustainable strategies are comprehensive, starting with aggressive energy reductions to allow the building to perform well enough where it would be possible for on-site power generation to provide for the needs of the building, without use of the electrical grid.

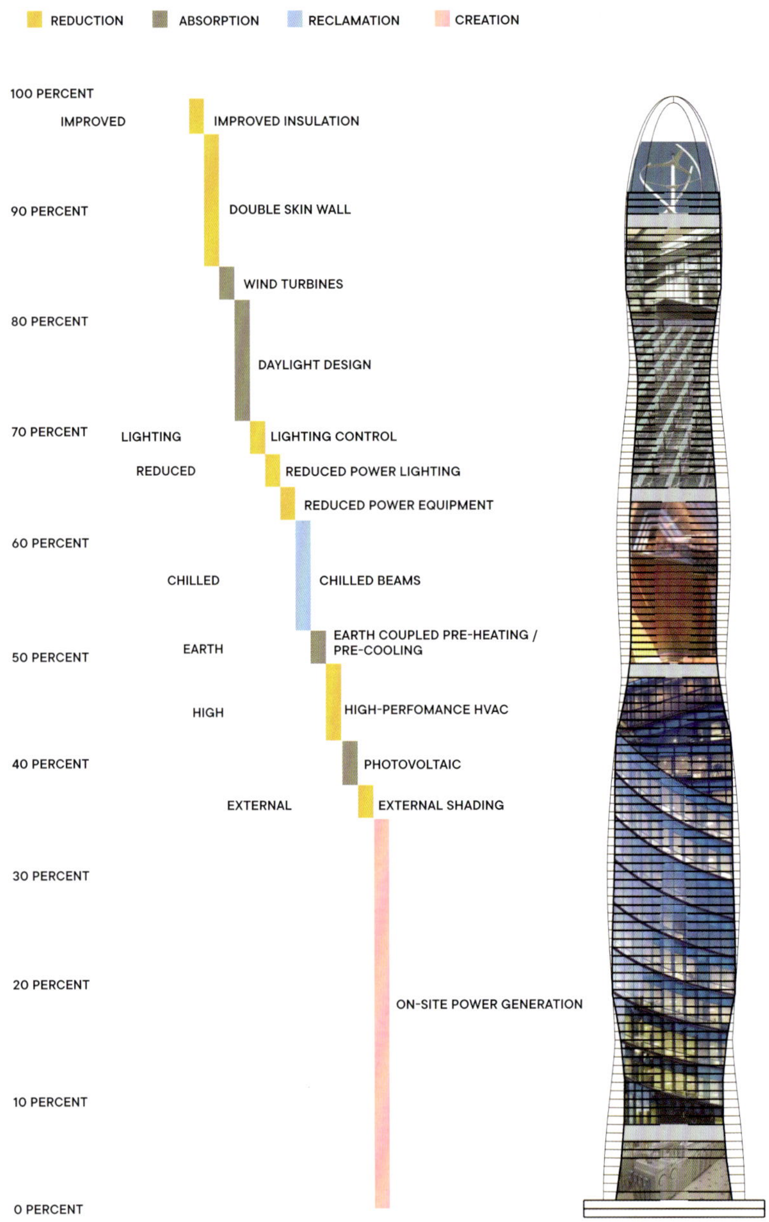

STRUCTURE

HALVORSON & PARTNERS, STRUCTURAL ENGINEER

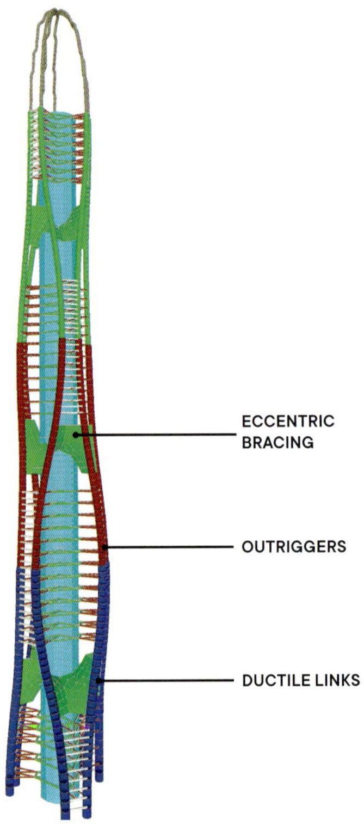

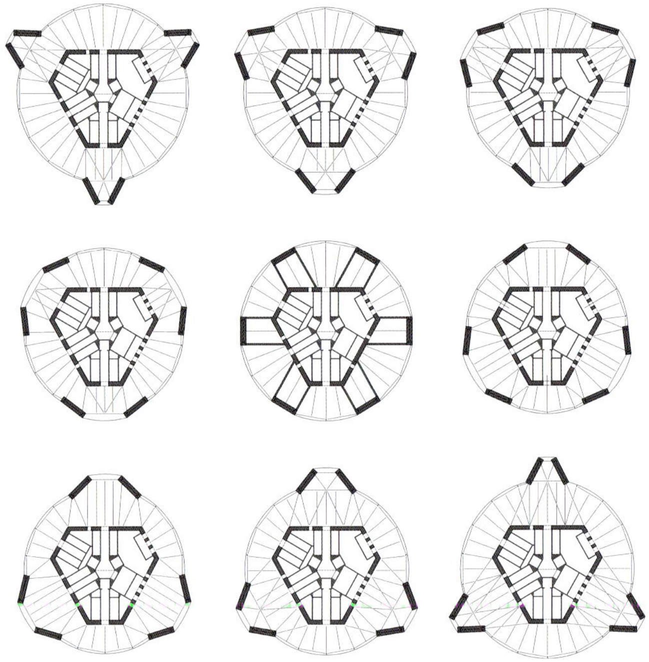

The structural concept is based on achieving the highest efficiency and functionality. By placing the core elements in the center of the building the perimeter is open to views and light. The structure is also concentrated within the core, and around the perimeter, to leave floor areas without obstructions.

Although the core is an efficient location for structure, the dimensions of the core are not adequate for the entire lateral load strength and stiffness required for the height so a structure around the perimeter is required. The most efficient type of perimeter structure is a braced tube, which is a series of columns with diagonal bracing, typically made of structural steel, like those found in the John Hancock Tower in Chicago.

However over the last decade, the tallest buildings in the world have utilized either concrete or composite—a mixture of steel and concrete—construction for economic reasons.

Therefore, a system employing concrete diagonals is appealing. While concentric bracing—the stiffest form that intersects at nodes—has little ductility, we wanted to ensure that 1 Park Avenue had exceptional ductility to resist seismic events. A form of "eccentric" bracing using reinforced-concrete was developed in which the diagonals do not intersect at points, but instead are separated by a few meters where they converge.

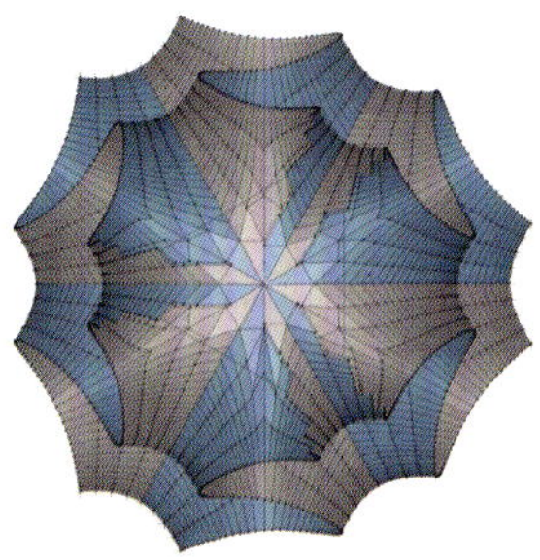

CONCRETE WALLS

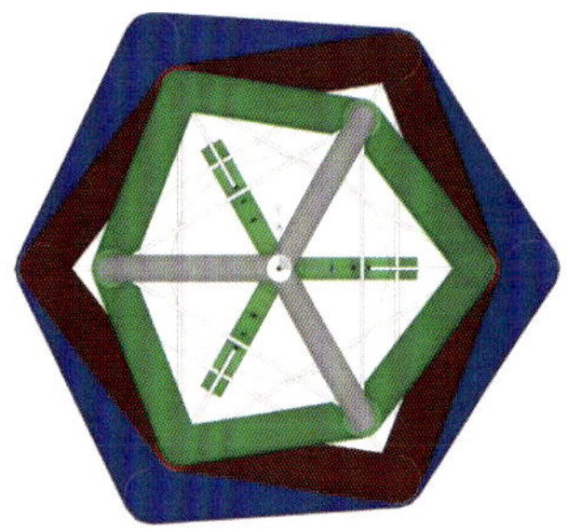

STRAIGHT FRAME ELEMENTS

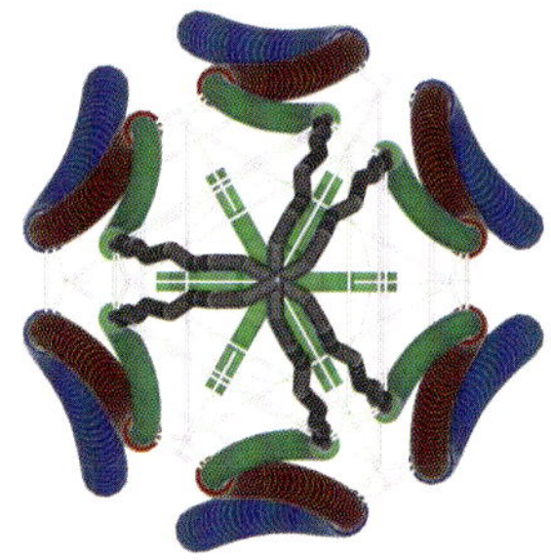

CURVED FRAME ELEMENTS

CONCRETE WALL SCHEME

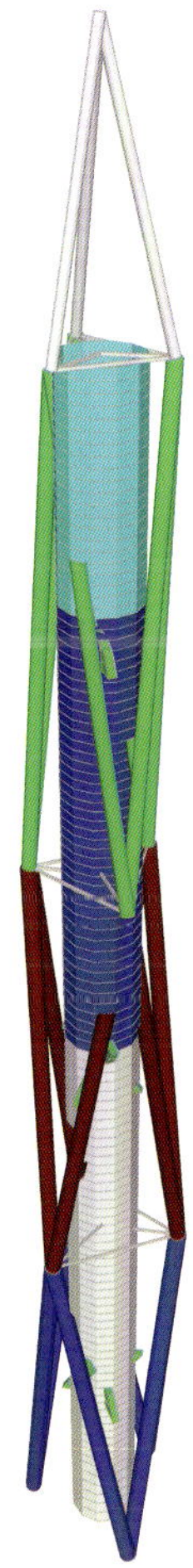

STRAIGHT FRAME SCHEME

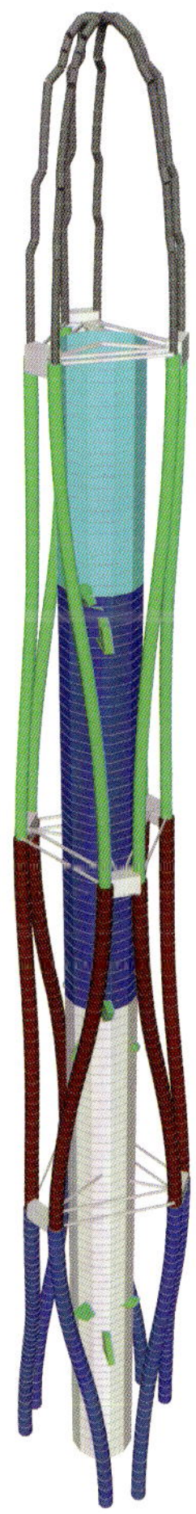

CURVED FRAME SCHEME

STRUCTURE

HALVORSON & PARTNERS, STRUCTURAL ENGINEER

In this zone, where the diagonals are close together, ductile links are provided between the diagonals in the form of reinforced-concrete special moment resisting spandrel beams.

To ensure that the tower is rigidly tied together so that it acts as one unit—and to achieve ultimate efficiency—outriggers are provided at every three levels. These diagonalized steel members are designed to add to the overall stiffness, strengthening the tower, and providing added damping and ductility for seismic events.

Floor framing is envisioned as steel beams and girders that support a composite metal deck and concrete floor. A concrete floor system is also a viable option; however, the steel floor system has more advantages. Because all the exterior columns lean inward toward the core, and the mega-columns curve along the perimeter, structural steel allows for a variable geometry to be easily achieved by linking structural design software to the fabricator's detailing and fabrication software.

Detailing tension ties between the exterior frame and the core walls are simpler with strong positive ties made through steel to steel connections. Steel framing and composite metal deck slabs provide a lighter floor system with longer spans that offer larger lease spans in office space.

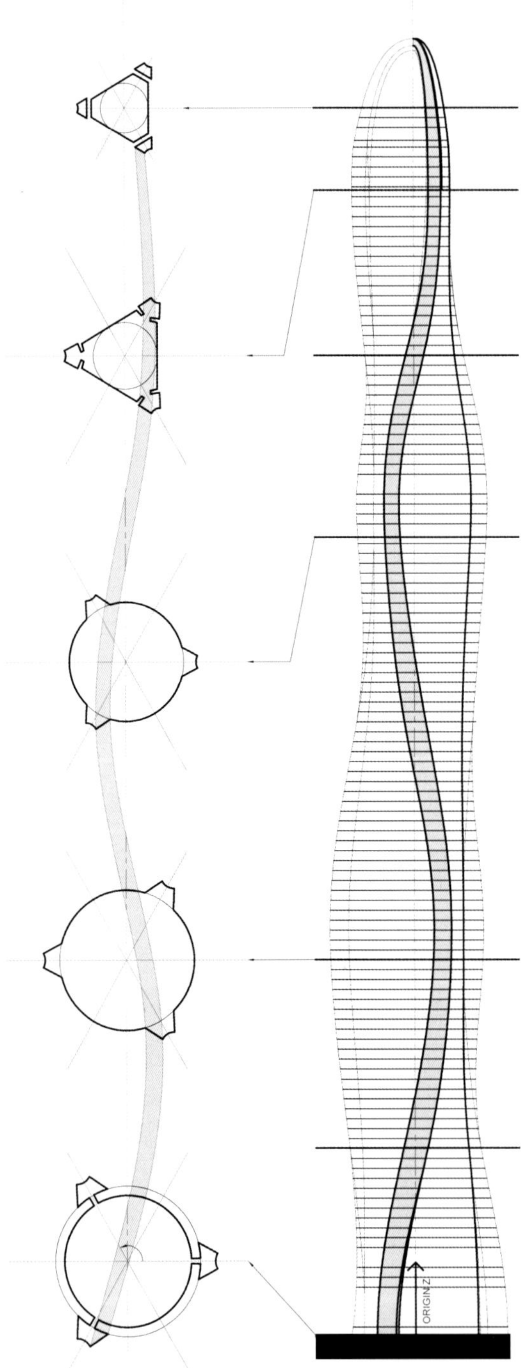

CHENGDU GREENLAND TOWER

CHENGDU, CHINA, 2011
460M

Chengdu is the second-largest region in the southwest of China, situated in the Sichuan plain surrounded by the Mount Siguniang to the west. Chengdu Greenland Tower is now under construction in Dongcun, the center of Chengdu's booming business district and conveniently adjacent to the subway public transportation.

At 468 meters tall, the tower will be the tallest in the region. It interprets and integrates Chengdu's urban structure, local culture, and Chinese traditional Feng Shui theory into a modern form.

The design creates a comfortable garden city with a convenient traffic pattern for vehicular, pedestrian, and the metro transportation. The complex serves as a comprehensive urban hub for the modern experience with retail, office, residential, entertainment, and conference functions.

The design considers the structural nature of building in a high-seismic zone by using a geometrical plan and tapered form with a high-performance bracing system that ensures higher stability and efficiency for the structure.

- CONTEXT
- SITE
- PROGRAM
- PODIUM
- PERFORMANCE
- FACADE
- CROWN
- RESEARCH + DEVELOPMENT
- STRUCTURE
- CONSTRUCTION

CONTEXT

The design was inspired by the unique ice mountain topography around Chengdu. The mountain is a powerful symbol of Chengdu's enterprising spirit and promising future. Like the mountain ridges that reflect light from the sky and the valleys that reflect light from the earth, the tower performs as a light sculpture. At night the tower will display a 360-degree light performance, creating a connection between the sky and the earth.

CONTEXT

The form was developed through various iterations, from an initial organic concept to a rationalized geometry. The facets of the "ice tower" have symmetry but they also taper from the length of the tower. Finding the ideal taper, to fit the program and to create the best proportion, was a challenge that caused many explorations by the design team.

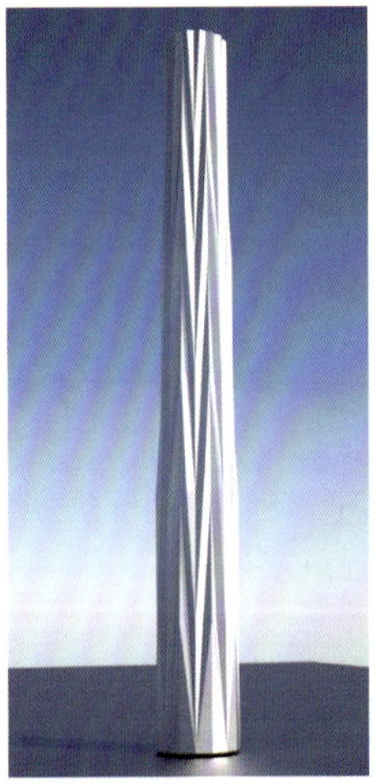

OPTION 1

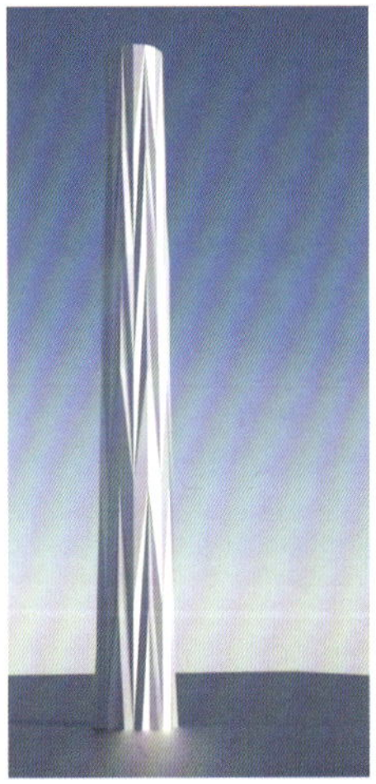

OPTION 2

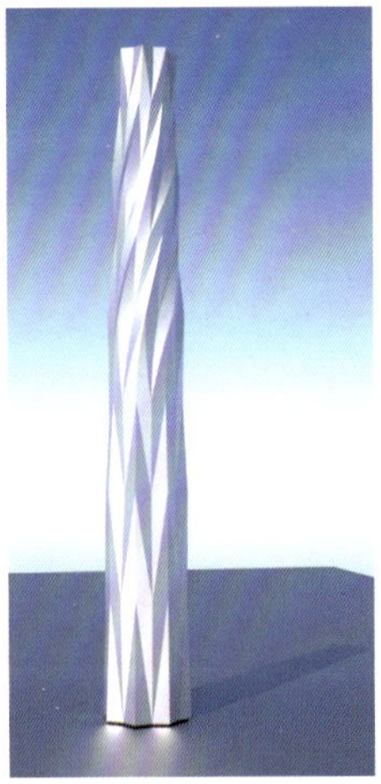

OPTION 3

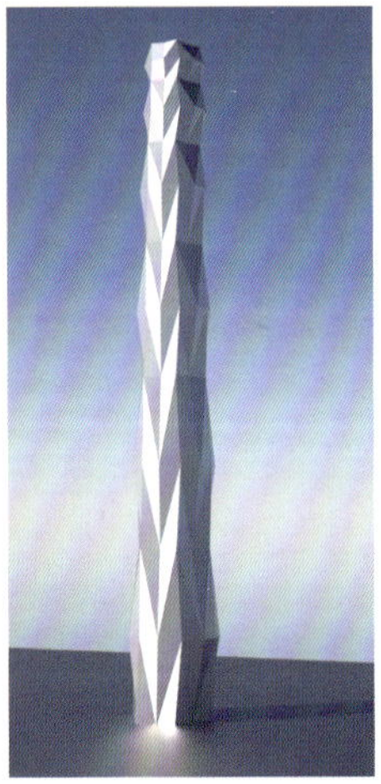

OPTION 4

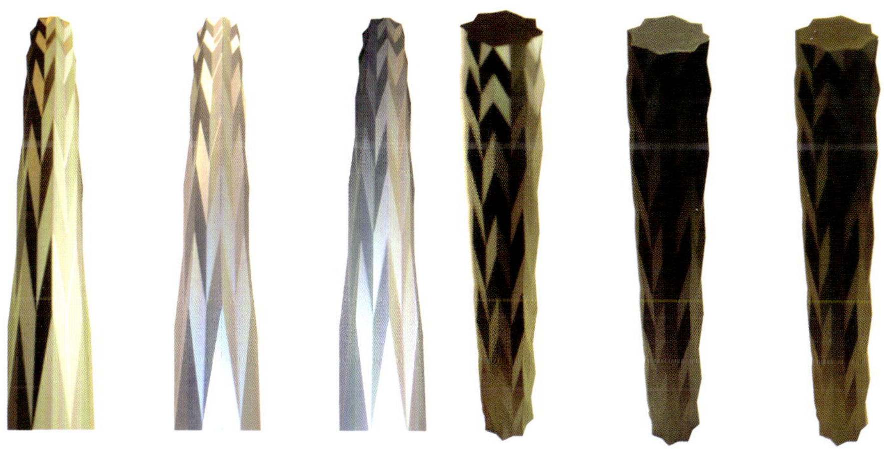

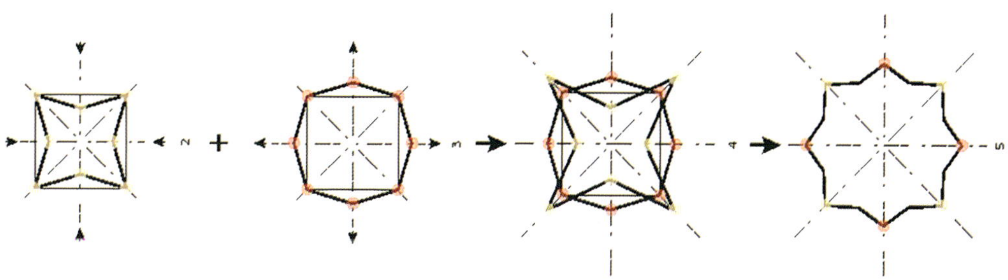

SITE

Greenland Tower Chengdu is located at the north gateway of the Chengdu Dongcun District Core area, west of central green spine, extending to Yidu Avenue to the north, to Yinmu Road along the green spine to the east, to Dujian Street on the south, and to Chunshu Street on the west. The overall building site area is 24,530 sm.

The topography has its highest elevation at east Yinmu Street, then slopes down to north Yidu Avenue, and reaches its lowest elevation along west Chunshu street. The average site elevation difference from east to west is approximately 7 m.

The site access was challenging because of the elevation change in the ground plane, which is about two stories, and the need to have separate entrances for the different programs.

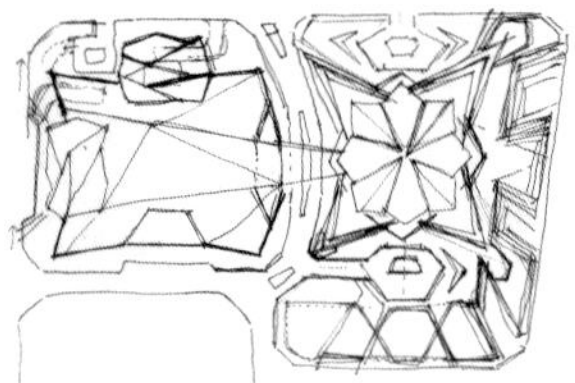

SITE PLAN SKETCH, 2011

SITE PLAN

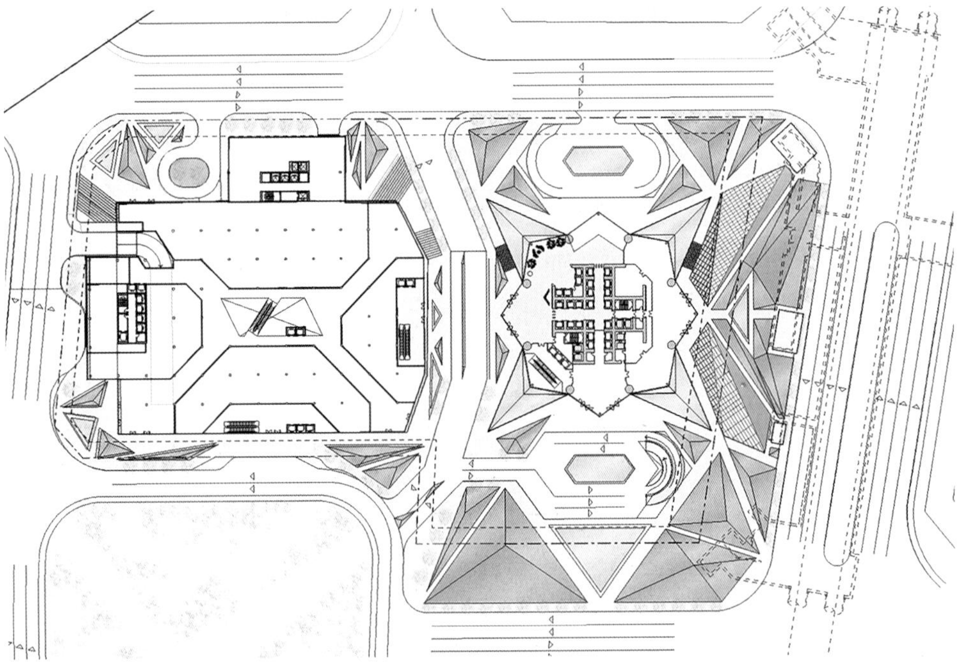

PROGRAM

The Greenland Tower complex is comprised of Tower 1 (T1), a mixed-used supertall tower to the north of the site, Tower 2 (T2) and Tower 3 (T3) are both hotel apartment towers that are located southwest and south of the site, and the podium and conference center at the southeast side.

T1, the main tower, is programed with Class-A office space, CEO executive suites, and a five-star hotel with a sky club at the tower's top. The large entry canopies cover the drop-off areas glass sky-lit spaces, allowing natural light through while protecting occupants from the elements.

The main entrance and lobby is located at lower ground with a direct connection to the hotel ground lobby. The ground lobby is located at the south of the tower with a coffee shop that is internally connected to the office ground lobby.

The office floors span 119,000 sm over four major zones, reaching from levels 6-49. These office floors are grouped into several zones: Zone 1A Levels 6-10; Zone 1B Levels 11-15; Zone 2 Levels 15-24; Zone 3A Levels 29, 31-35; Zone 3B Levels 29, 35-39; Zone 4 floors 30, 39-49.

The executive suites are a relatively new program typology that mixes high-end office space with luxury residential accommodations in 200 sm-700 sm suites. These suites are located over approximately 50,000 sm within two zones from Levels 55-71 and have a designated sky lobby and amenity space at Level 55.

The five-star hotel is just over 50,000 sm with 470 rooms on levels 82-104. The design team was challenged to provide standardized hotel room sizes within the unique design shape of the floor plans. The plans were extensively studied and although the room modules do vary, they are within an acceptable range to the hotel operator and become an asset to the types of rooms that can be offered.

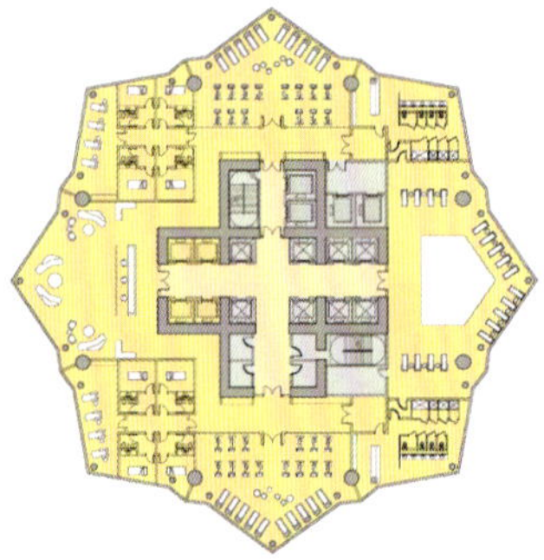

TYPICAL CEO OFFICE

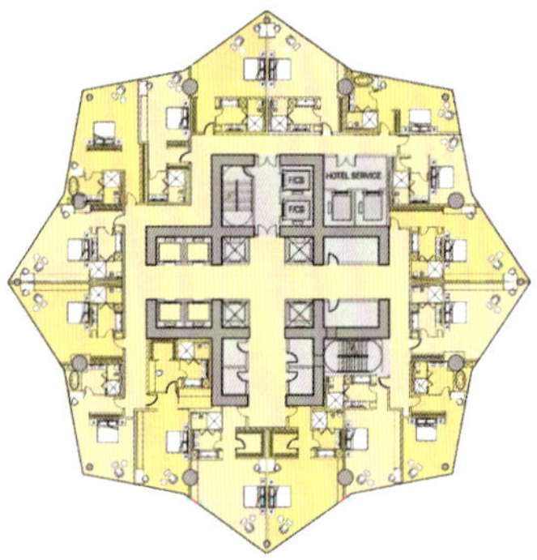

TYPICAL HOTEL

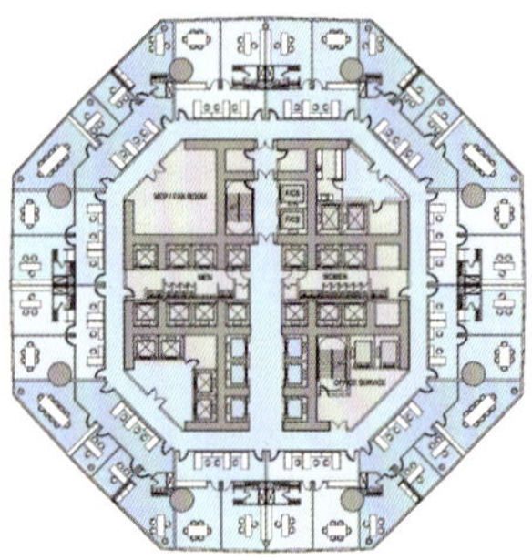

TYPICAL OFFICE

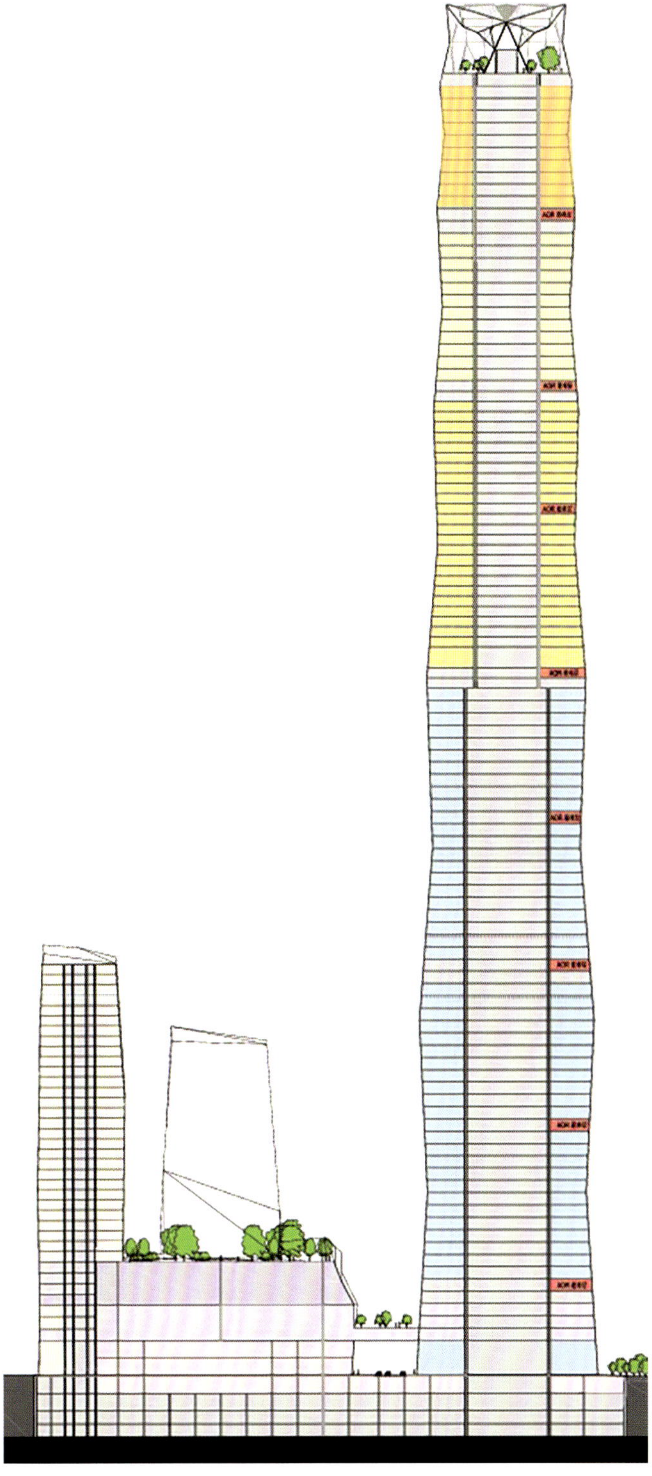

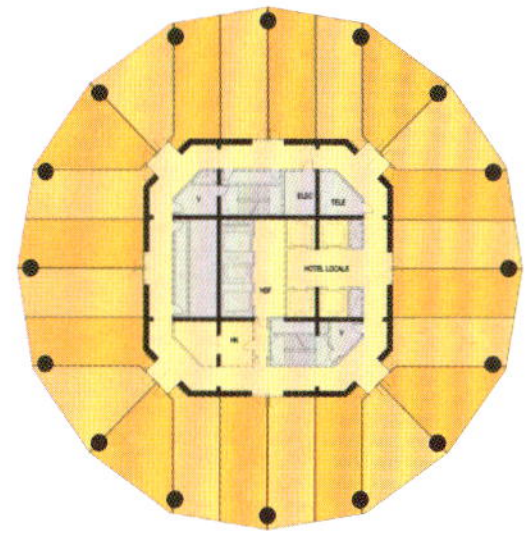

LEVEL 85

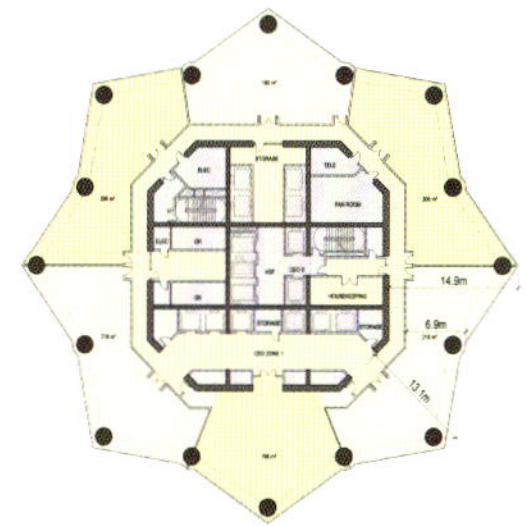

LEVEL 55

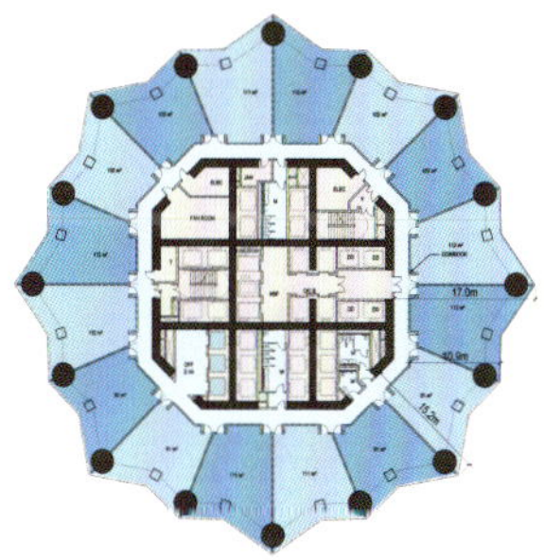

LEVEL 7

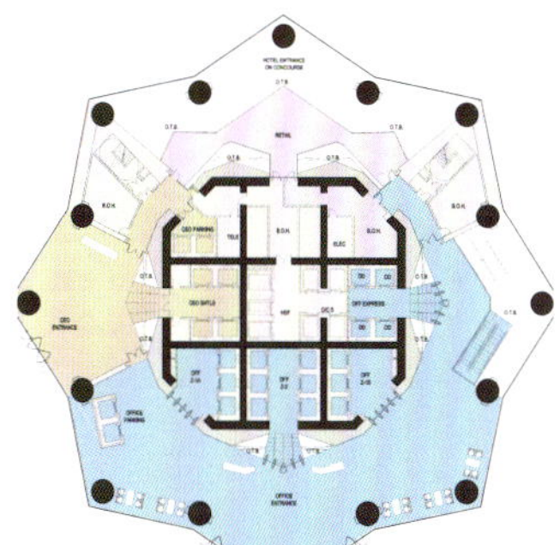

GROUND LEVEL

PROGRAM

The hotel also has a designated sky lobby with restaurant amenities, as well as a full-service spa, gym, swimming pools, and health center on Levels 76–80.

There is a 3,764 sm sky club on Levels 108–109, at the top of the tower, which will be open to tenants and visitors and consists of meeting, dining, and entertainment opportunities.

The tower will be a multi-modal transportation hub that offers commuters several travel options. Underground parking spaces are available to tenants and there are shuttles that run from the basement level to the upper-ground lobby to provide drivers with easy access to the offices and executive suites. The building is further connected to public transportation options with escalators that give commuters easy access to subway connections. These access points are further enhanced by lower-ground retail programing.

The mechanical floors are spread out throughout the building to serve all floors. They are separated by 20 floors, located at Levels 3–6, 25–27, 50–52, 72–74, 105–106. Areas of refuge are separated by a maximum 45m, as required by Chinese Code. They are located on Levels 6, 15, 25, 30,40, 50,53,63, 72, 73, 84, 94, and 105.

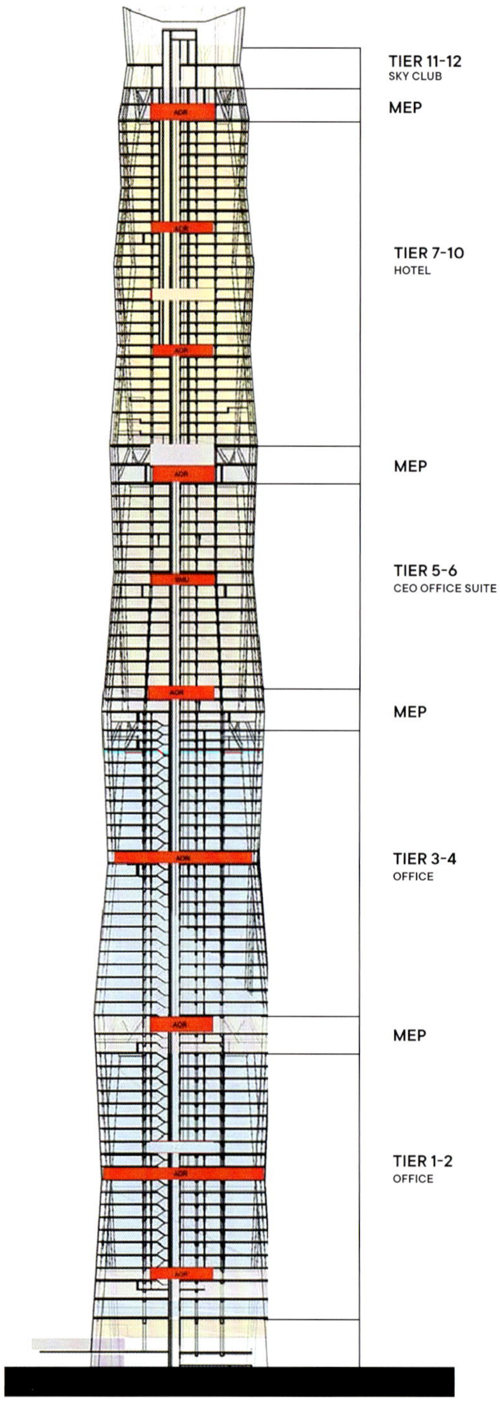

PODIUM

The 30,000 sm podium piece is connected to the tower by a glass bridge and canopy. The design shares the tower's faceted glass, but it is presented in a more refined way with larger facets encompassing the higher levels and smaller facets giving scale to the entry levels.

The first two floors consist of high-end retail, conference space with small meeting rooms, and a 1,000 sm ballroom. A long span flexible exhibition space, a larger conference facility, and 3,000 sm ballroom are available on Level three. Access to several rooftop gardens with usable outdoor space is also reached at Level three.

The two auxiliary towers, T2 and T3, are 30-story Soho apartments that are physically and stylistically connected to the podium and tower. The podium's rooftop garden is used by the Soho apartments as a shared amenity. T2 and T3 share a design language with T1 but like the podium, the faceted geometry is stylistically simpler than the supertall icon. In this way, the four buildings of the complex work together toward one architectural vision.

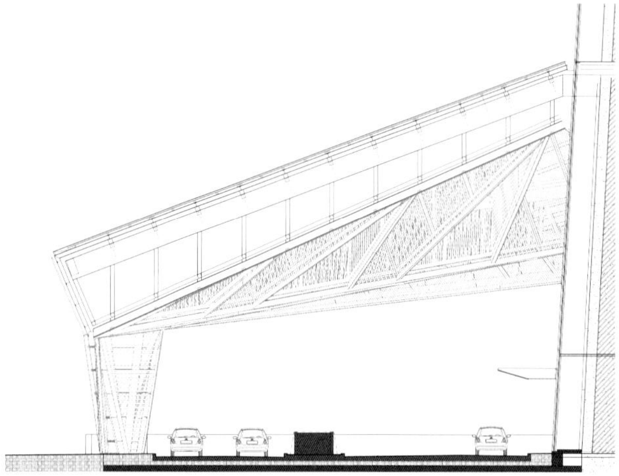

PODIUM SECTION

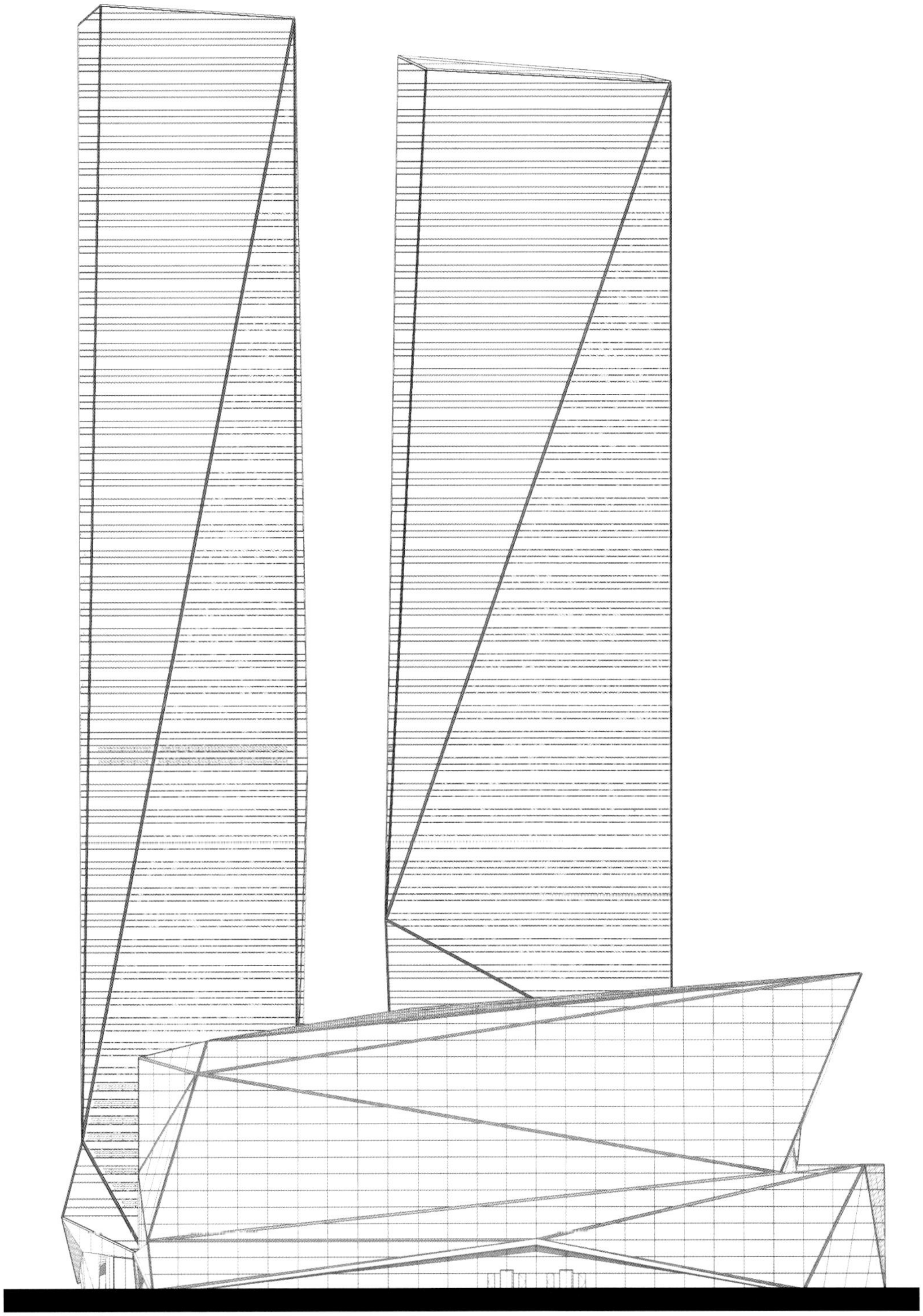

PERFORMANCE

The exterior wall of the tower was designed to be highly efficient in both cost and energy performance. The panel sizes and types were studied to optimize minimal variations for efficient construction. The exterior wall's defining features are exterior round stainless steel pipes, designed to capture the sunlight as it hits the tower. Various configurations were studied before deciding upon the final design.

Another important aspect of the exterior wall is the detailing that reinforces the unique geometry of the tower. The panel joints are carefully designed and incorporate metal reveals where the joints come together at the building's facets. Here, integrated lighting allows the tower to transform into a festival of lights at night, following the facets of the design shape.

EXTERIOR WALL DIAGRAMS

EXTERIOR WALL MODEL

EXTERIOR WALL MOCK UP, 2015

PERFORMANCE

THORNTON TOMASETTI + RWDI

When designing a structure at this height, a variety of practical issues need to be considered and adopted into the architectural form. One key element is how the tower's structure will respond to wind loading. The tower's overall form is essentially a tapered, faceted, cylinder. This shape helps to confuse the wind, preventing large vortices from shedding in a coherent pattern.

It is the well-correlated vortices that can produce a high dynamic response, which results in both high-inertial wind loads and elevated motions, perceivable by occupants. Compared to a more traditionally shaped box or rectangular building, Greenland Tower has superior aerodynamic performance because it disrupts the wind more efficiently over the tower height.

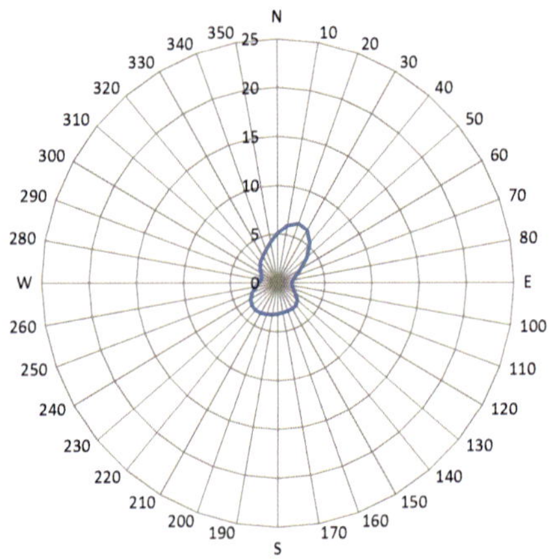

COMMON WINDS

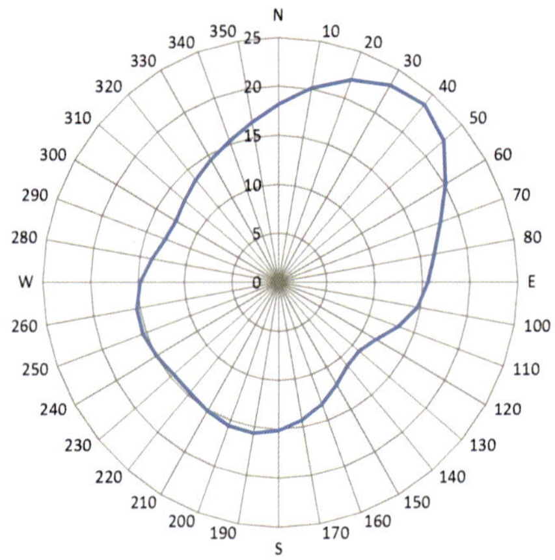

DESIGN WINDS

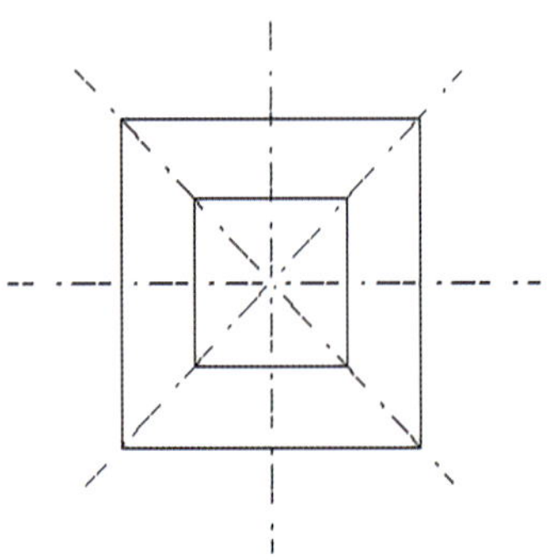

SQUARE PLAN

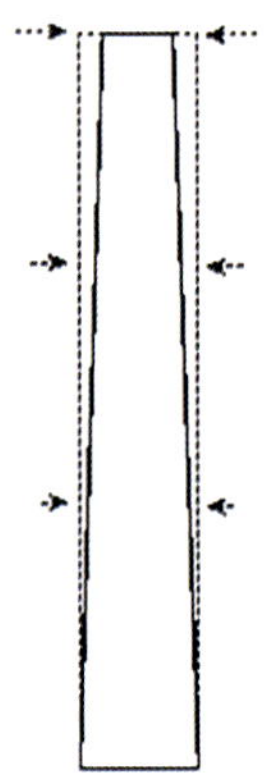

ELEVATION

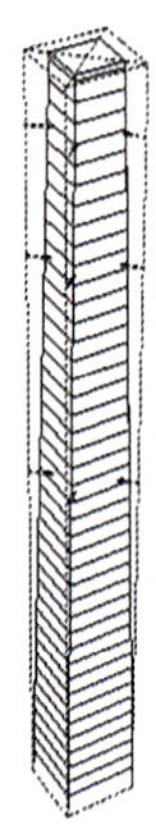

TAPERED FORM

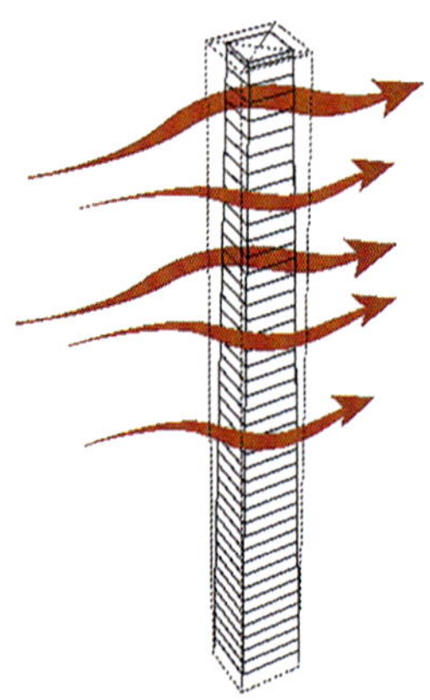

REDUCE WIND LOAD

WIND TUNNEL TESTING

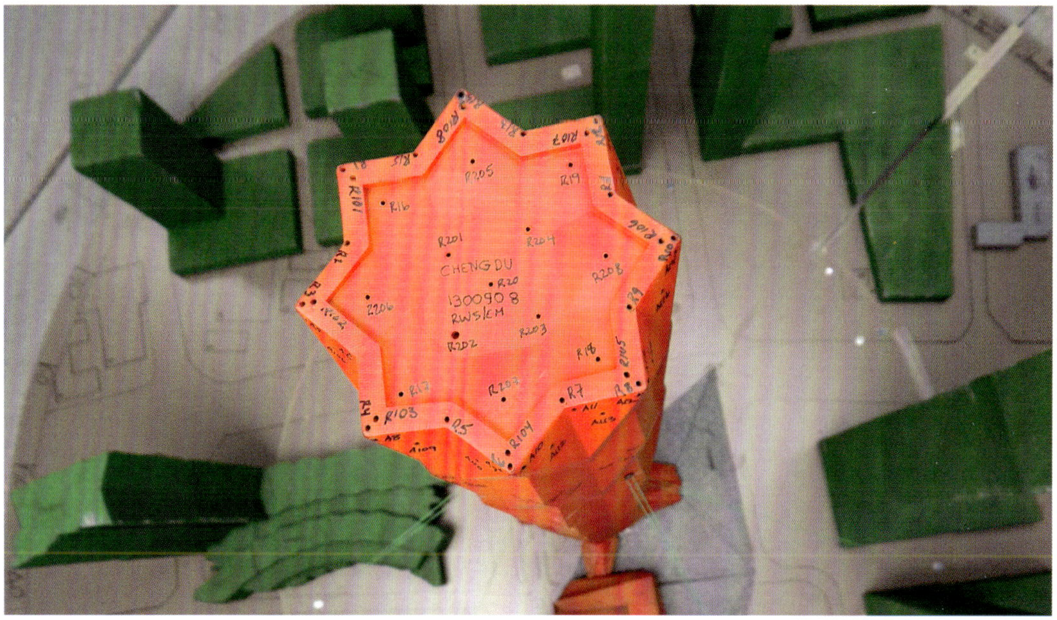

FACADE

LERCH BATES, FACADE ACCESS

The windows washing is accomplished with an articulating gondola that has access to the length of the vertical facades and telescopes horizontally, as required to safely negotiate the building geometry and the multifaceted facades. Once the gondola is outboard of the crown, the first set of intermittent stabilization anchors are engaged by the operators controlling the gondola.

As the gondola descends, the automated BMU lengthens the jib. This allows the suspension wire ropes connecting the gondola to the JIB to remain perpendicular to the facade. At the same time, the gondola articulates to keep it in contact with the building face.

These functions are computer controlled by the BMU and allow workers to fully descend the building while cleaning the glass. Once the gondola reaches the bottom of the tower, the process reverses and the gondola ascends following the same path.

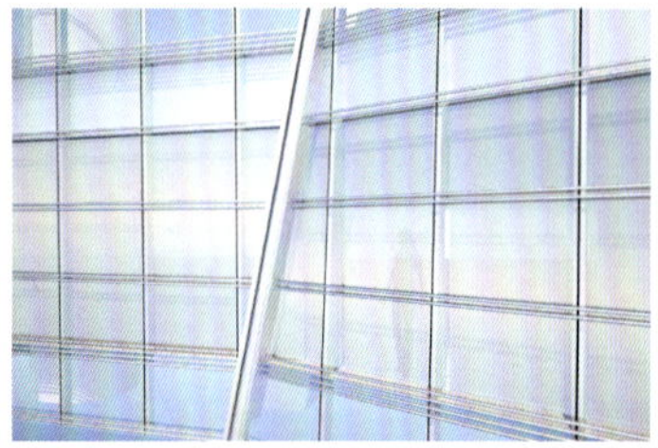

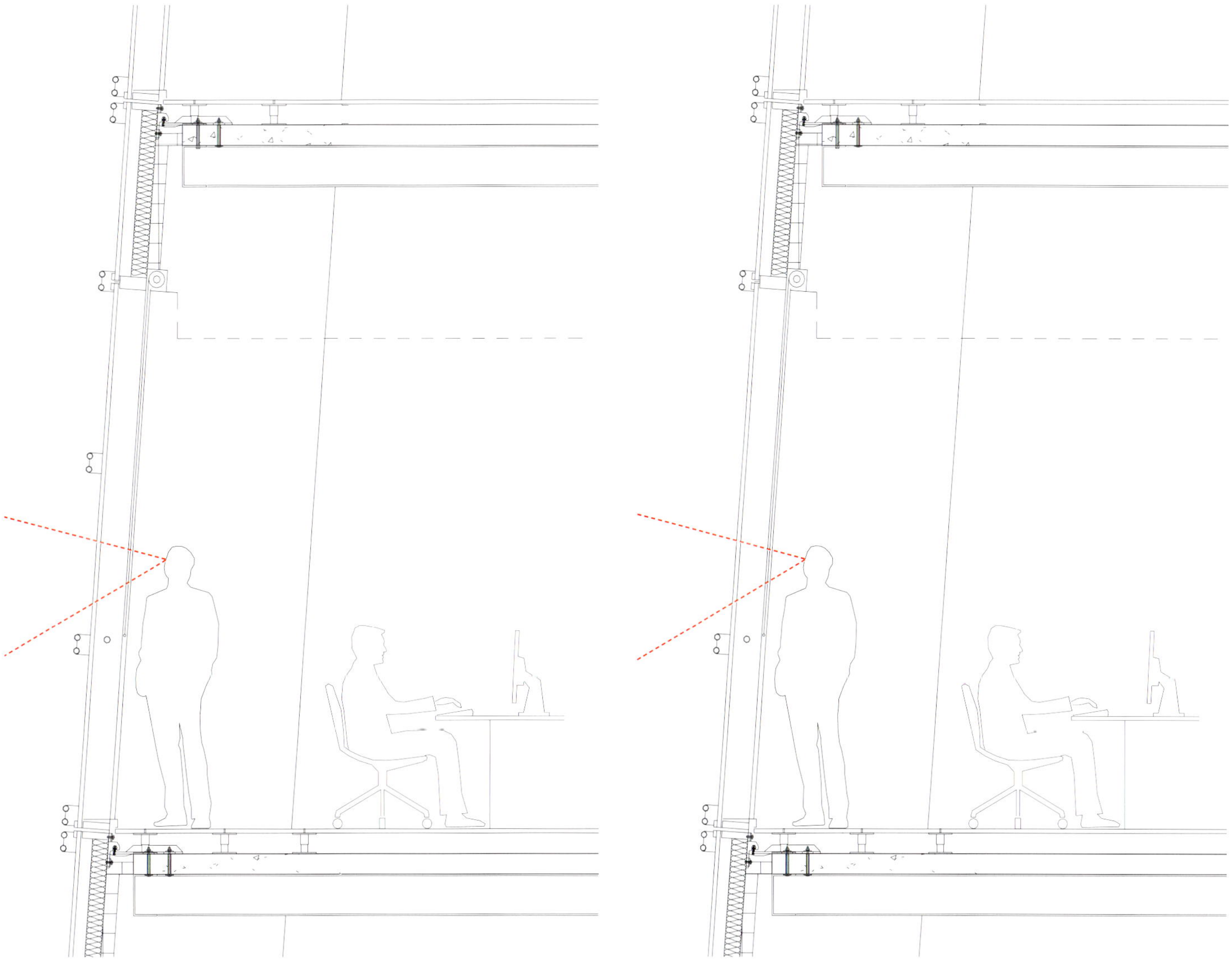

EXTERIOR WALL DETAIL

CROWN

Greenland Tower's crown is a sky club and amenity space for the building's occupants with 360-degree views of Chengdu and the surrounding mountain scenery. The multi-story atrium space and core of the building is clad with faceted wall panels that play off the tower's exterior geometry.

The lighting scheme traces the tower's form and will be able to change color and brightness in subtle waves up and down the tower. The lighting will allow the tower to be an important landmark not just in the daytime, but also have a special place on the night-time skyline.

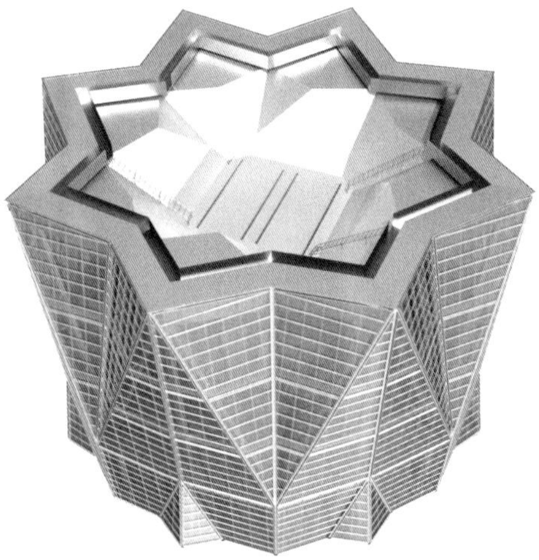

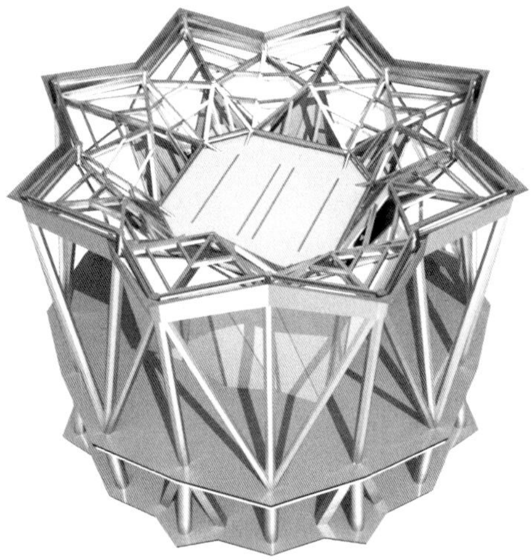

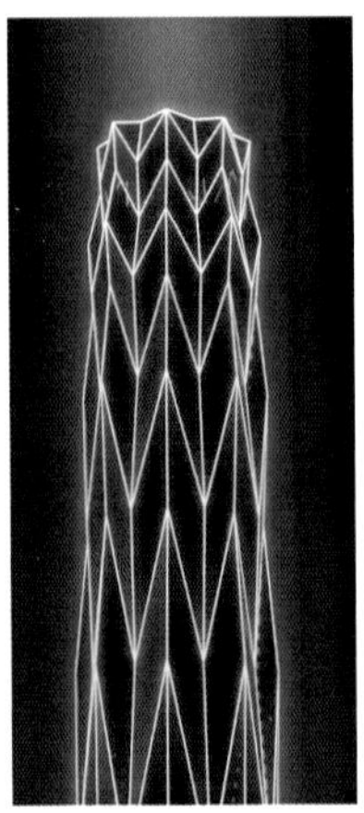

TOP STUDY
ORIGINAL MASSING

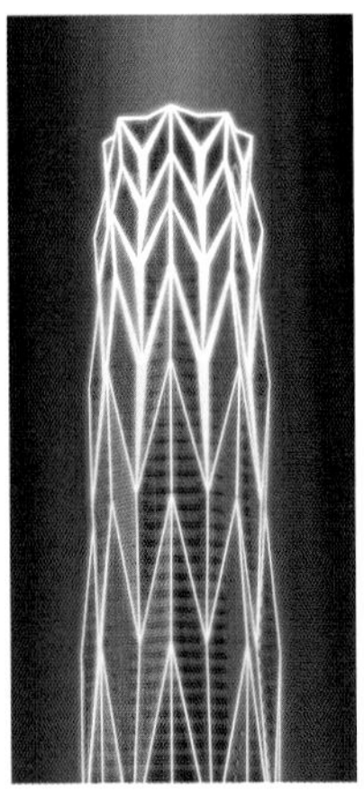

TOP STUDY
3M CROWN

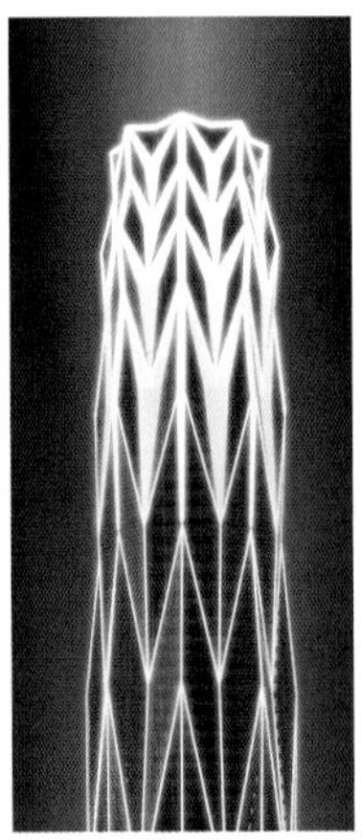

TOP STUDY
6M CROWN

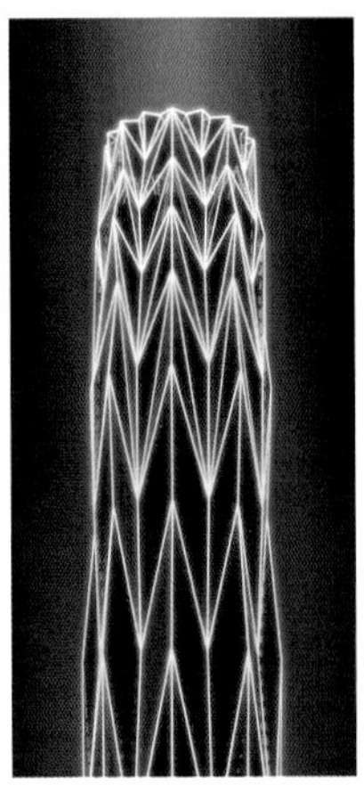

TOP STUDY
DENSE FACET OPT. 1

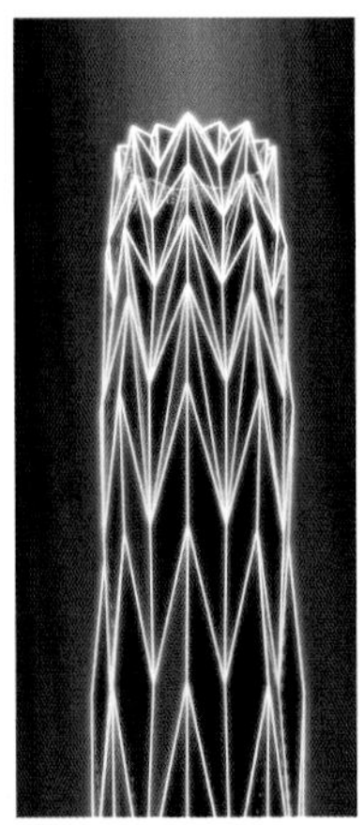

TOP STUDY
DENSE FACET OPT. 2

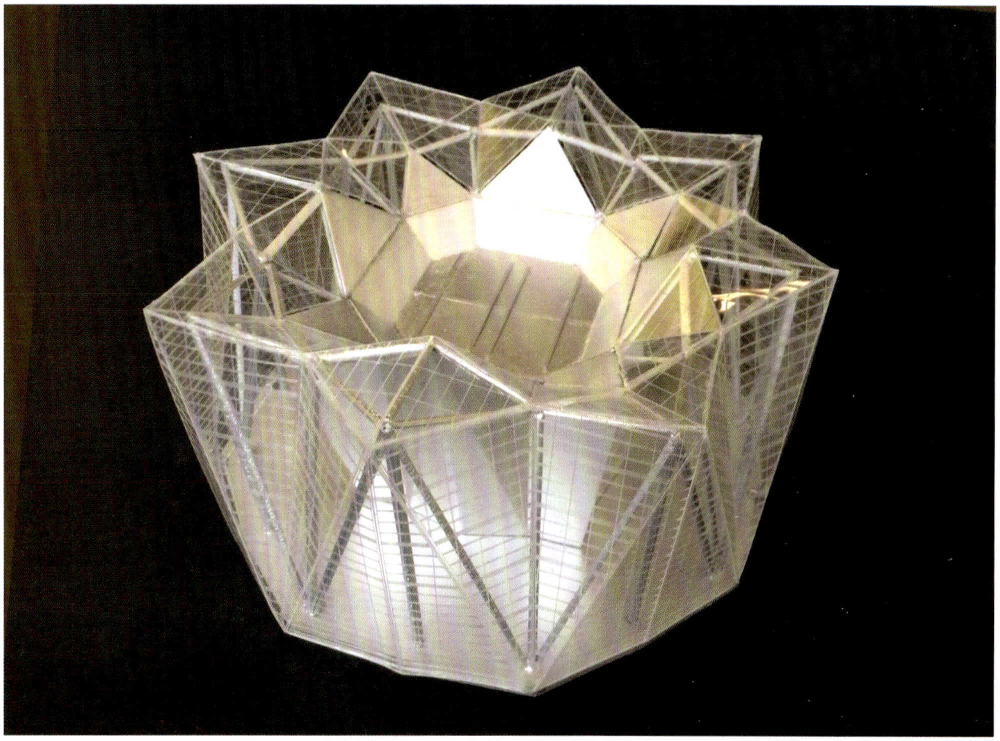

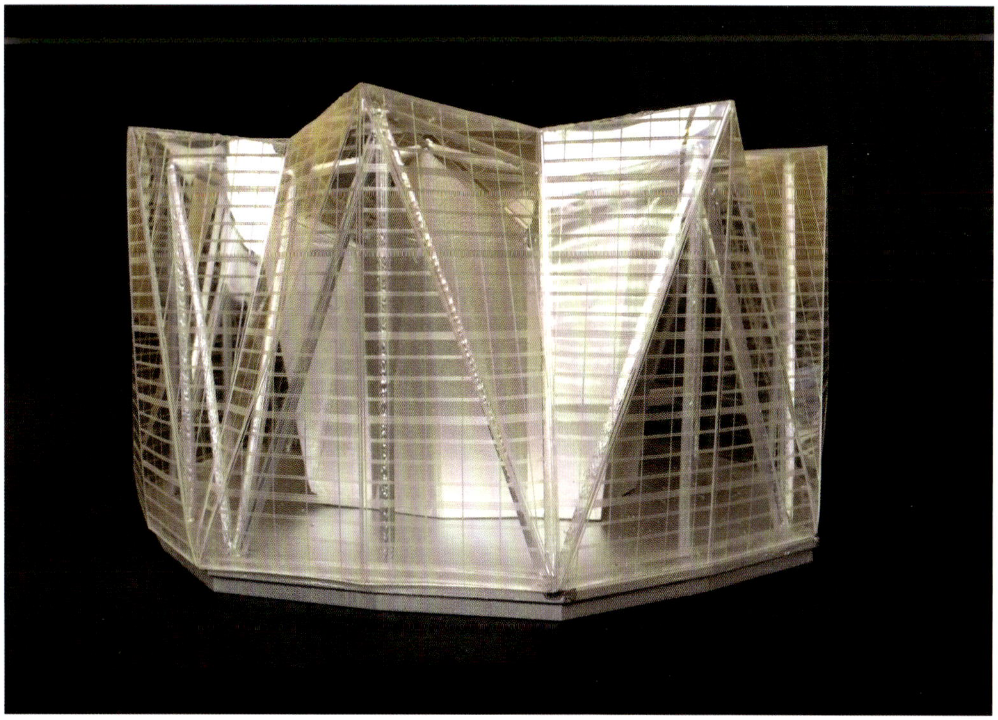

RESEARCH + DEVELOPMENT

The sculpted form of the tower creates a unique reflective effect that gives the tower its overall design character. However, the technical issues of resolving such a complicated shape in the curtain wall posed challenges.

The most difficult detail was the point in which the tips of the geometry intersect. To solve this, the design included a stainless steel clad channel reveal that served several purposes. The first, is to facilitate the installation of the glass joints that are necessary with several panels coming together at once. These reveals allowed for detailing that would ensure proper protection against water infiltration and excessive movement in the facade panels.

The second purpose was to provide a location where festive lighting could be installed, but hidden from view from the inside of the tower. The geometry of these reveals repeated around the tower but they do taper as the tower reduces in size from bottom to top. The tapering form of the Chengdu tower serves also serves multiple purposes. In a mixed-use tower, it is important that the floor plates are the proper size for the program they house and so the taper allows upper floors to be smaller to accommodate hotel and corporate suite uses efficiently. The taper also increases the performance of the tower under wind load as a tower which is wider at the top would have more vortex shedding and wind force than one which tapers.

Finally, the subtle taper is used to add elegance to the tower as it is viewed in perspective, to keep the top from appearing overly heavy.

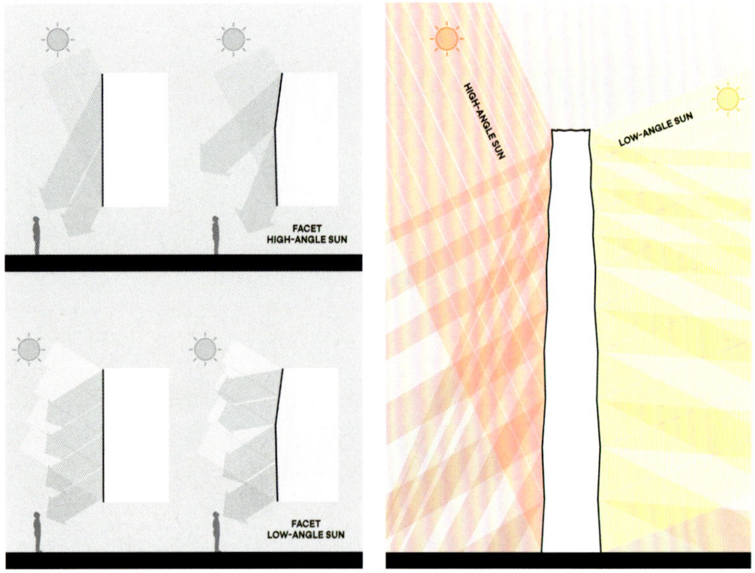

FACADE SOLAR STUDIES

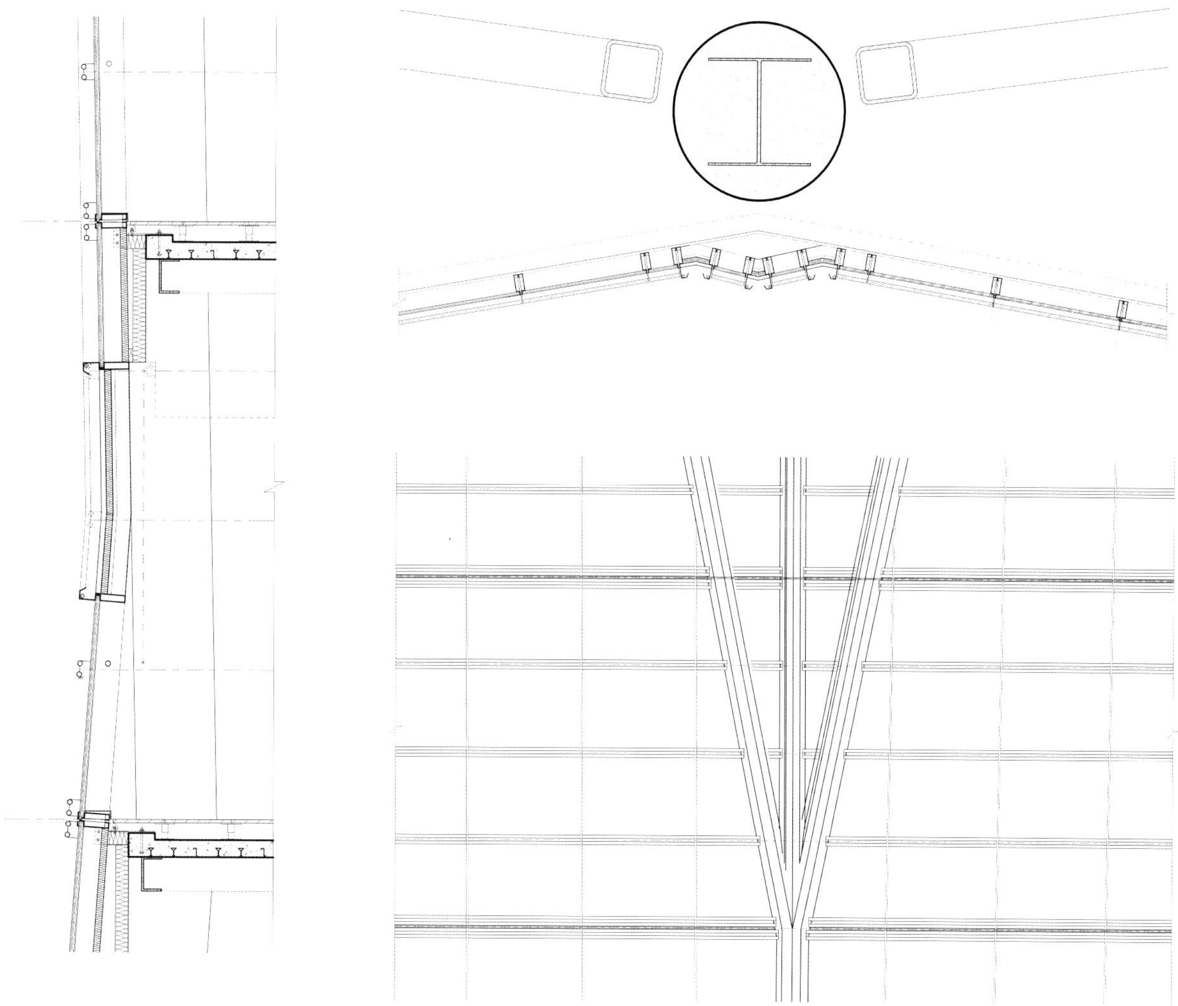

EXTERIOR WALL DETAILS

STRUCTURE

THORNTON TOMASETTI, STRUCTURAL ENGINEER

Greenland Tower has a unique shape, similar to the configuration of a pyramid distributed along the building height and symmetrical in the center. Each floor plan is slightly different, although the plans can be separated into three groups: octagon, 16-side polygon, and 32-side polygon. The 16-side polygon is the basic form, while the octagon and 32-side polygon are mutated versions that fit inside the original.

To integrate with the architectural profile, one composite column is placed at each corner of a 16-side polygon. Each composite column, which contributes to the tower's overall lateral stiffness when the columns connect to the core, slopes at five degrees from the vertical line. Following an alternate pattern, the composite columns slope toward and away from the core. This creates the unique building profile.

According to the architectural plan, the main tower includes a gravity system and a lateral system. Some structural members belong only to the gravity system or the lateral system, but it is also common that some structural members—like the core wall—are key components of both the gravity system and lateral system. From a structureal point of view, any tall building is a cantilever element.

Under lateral loads (wind and seismic load), the overturning moment on the tower increases proportionally to the square of the building's height, while the tower deflection increases proportionally to building height by the fourth power. The lateral system elements include the core wall, composite columns, outrigger trusses, and the exterior diagonal bracing.

The core dimension for the plan is about 28m x 28m from the base to Level 54. From Level 54 to Level 65, the flange wall slopes inward and the core dimension reduces gradually. At Level 65 and above, the core dimension for the plan is about 24m x 24m. The thickness of the flange wall at the bottom is 1m, reducing to 0.4m at the top. The web wall thickness is 0.8m at the bottom and reducing to 0.4m at the top.

SHEAR WALL

LATERAL LOAD RESISTING SYSTEM

STRUCTURE

FACADE

Coinciding with the mechanical floor locations, four sets of outrigger truss levels are located at Levels 25–29, 50–54, 72–76, and 105–108. Each outrigger truss is three-stories tall. There are eight outrigger trusses in the plan at each outrigger level.

Vertical diagonal braces are placed between the composite columns, totaling 16 braces on each floor. Along the building height, the braces are divided into multiple zones, with each zone having five to 12 levels to match the building profile.

The major function of the vertical diagonal braces is to connect the composite columns to form a system similar to a braced frame.

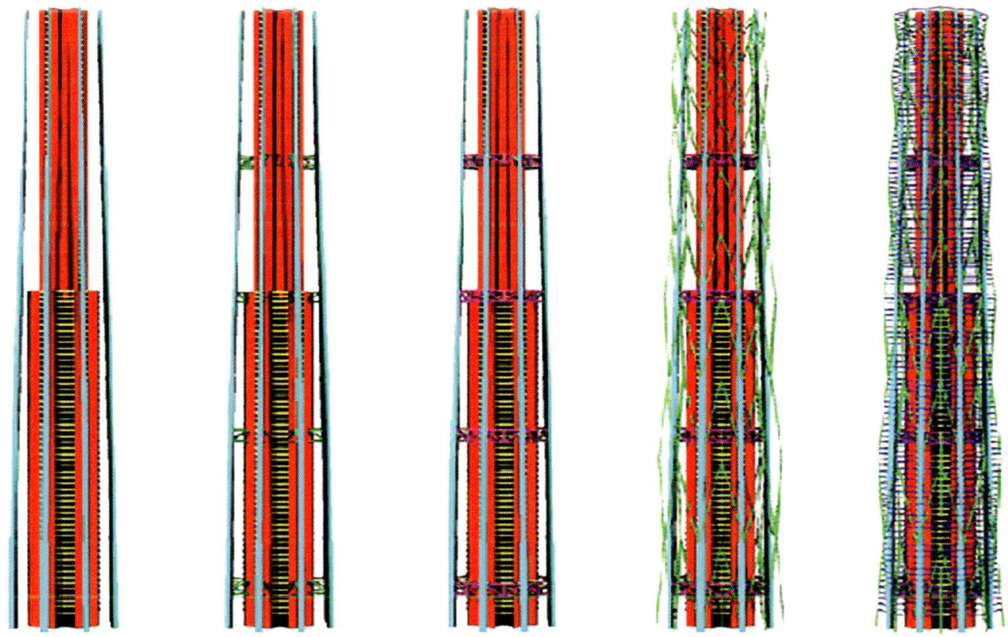

STRUCTURE

THORNTON TOMASETTI, STRUCTURAL ENGINEER

As compared to the classical "Mega Frame," composing of column-and-belt truss, the introduction of vertical diagonal braces dramatically enhances both the lateral stiffness and shear resistance of the perimeter frame. The structural analysis results clearly show that the perimeter-braced mega frame takes a large proportion of the total story shear and overturning moment.

As an important part of the lateral system, vertical-diagonal braces take some gravity load as well. The brace connects to the perimeter composite columns at the ends, transferring the load in the brace into the composite columns. This helps avoid the condition where braces take on too many loads and the negative impact on the architectural building profile is due to large diagonal braces.

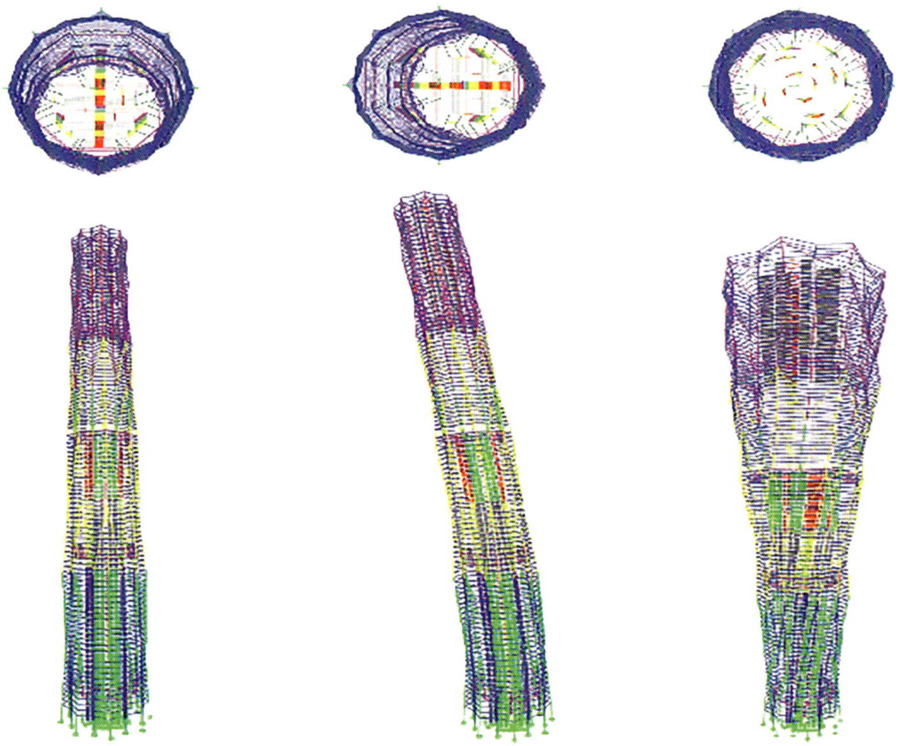

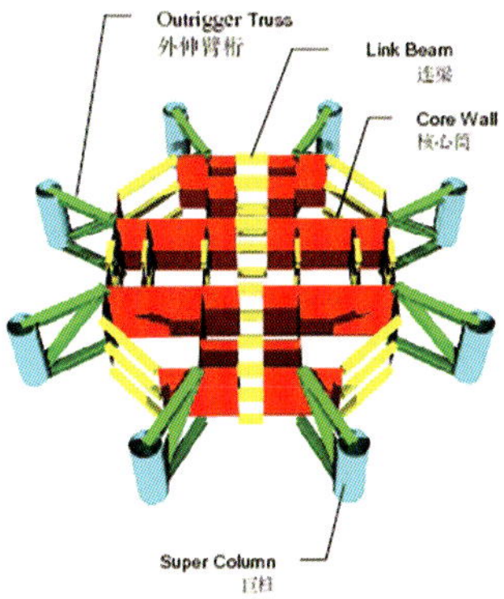

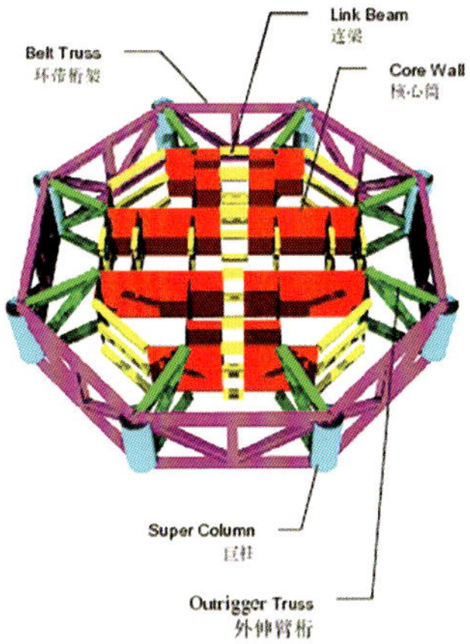

© Greenland Group

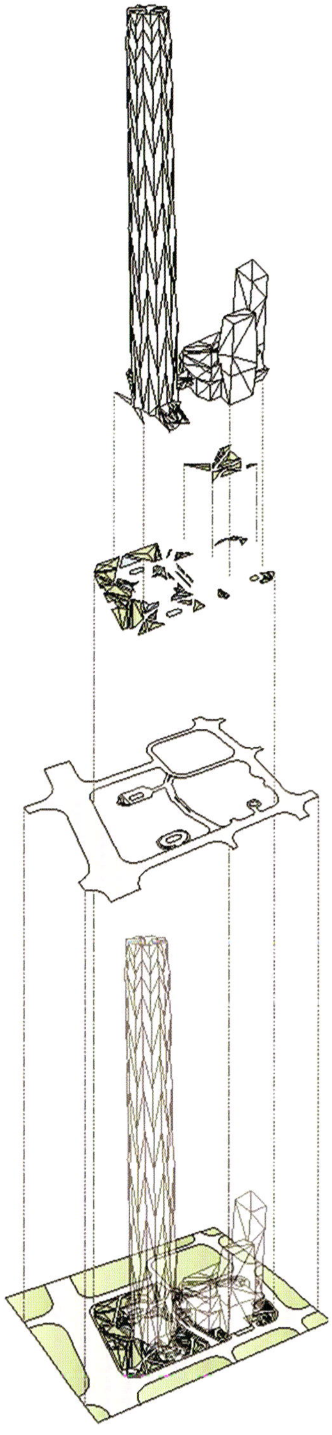

Construction began on Greenland Tower Chengdu in the Fall of 2014. These in-progress construction photographs show the tower facade's glass facets that follow the geometry of the architectural expression.

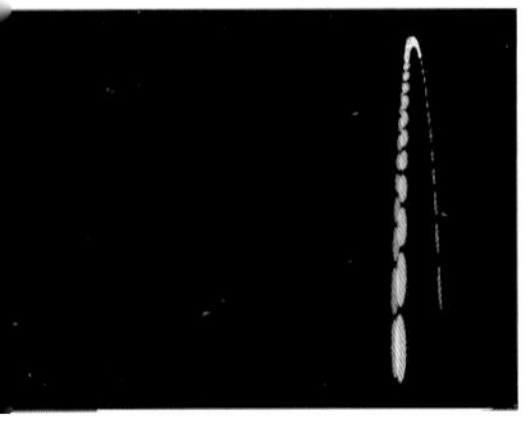

WUHAN GREENLAND CENTER

WUHAN, CHINA, 2010

636M

The design for the 636-meter-tall, 125-story, 320,000 sm, mixed-use Wuhan Greenland Center is now under construction in Wuhan, China. The original program included 200,000 sm of office space, 60,000 sm of residential space, and a 45,000 sm hotel.

The tower is a purposeful approach to design with a unique blend of the art and the science of architecture. The design represents a combination of the formal relationships of performance (the art) and technical aspects of performance (the science), which we refer to as *Form Follows Performance*.

The streamlined form combines three key shaping concepts—a tapered body, softly rounded corners, and a domed top—to reduce wind resistance and vortex action that builds up around supertall towers. The building's efficient aerodynamic performance also allows it to minimize the amount of structural material, and the associated embodied carbon, needed for construction.

The tower is a powerful new icon for Wuhan's skyline and, as designed, would be the third tallest building in the world when completed in 2022.

- CONTEXT
- PROGRAM
- FORM
- PERFORMANCE
- RESEARCH + DEVELOPMENT
- INTERIOR
- CROWN
- STRUCTURE
- CONSTRUCTION

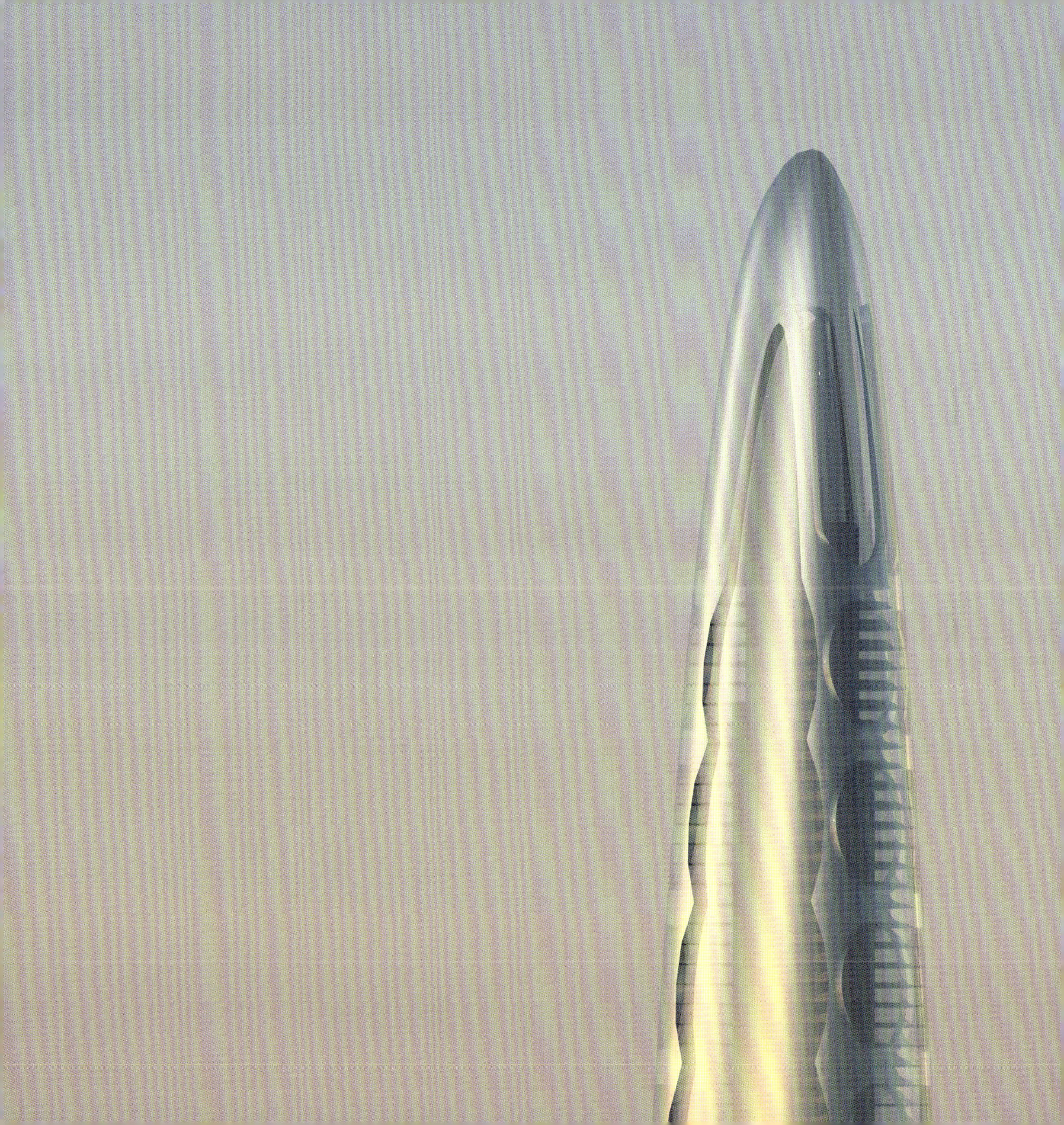

CONTEXT

Wuhan, the capital city of Hubei Province in central China, is located on the Jianghan Plain, which joins the Han River and the Yangtze River. Divided by the Yangtze, Wuhan is known as the "Three Towns of Wuhan," with Hankou and Hanyang on the west bank and Wuchang on the east.

The three tapered sides of Wuhan Greenland Center represent the three townships and two rivers that intersect to form one unified city. The corners rise from its tripod-shaped base and taper upward, culminating in an arched tip above the dome at the top.

The corners are distributed smooth curved glass, contrasting markedly with the more textured curtain wall cladding the body of the tower.

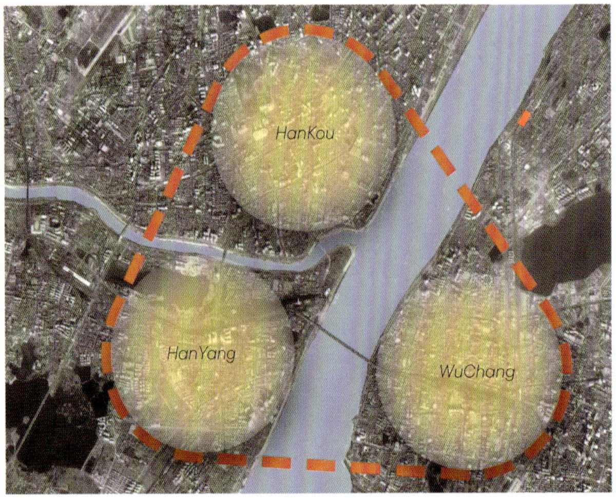

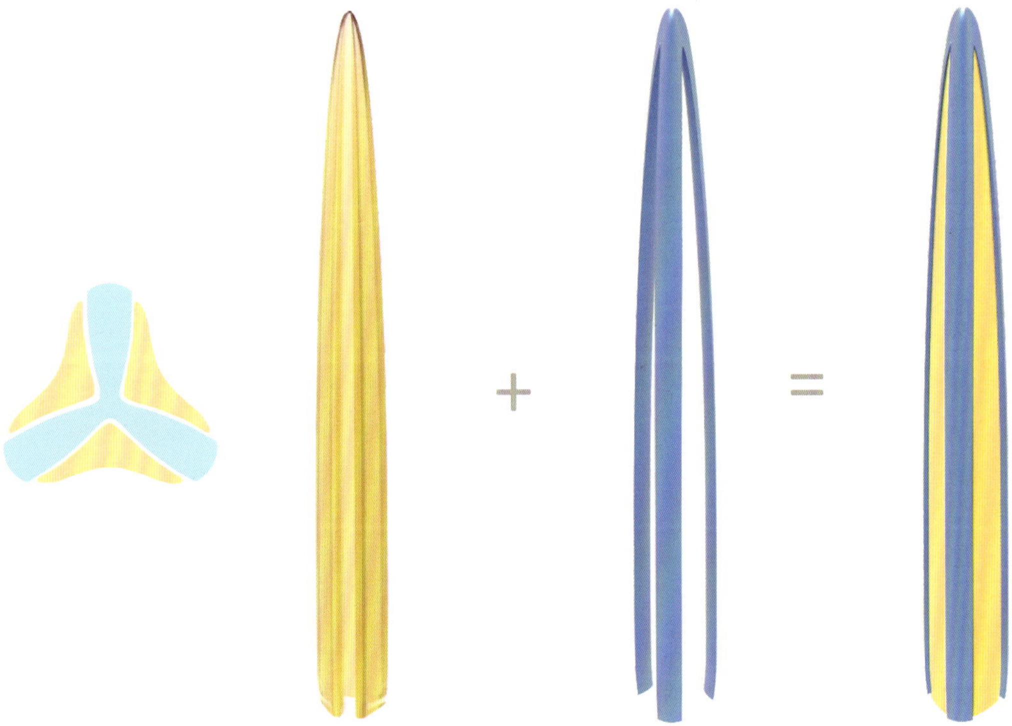

PROGRAM

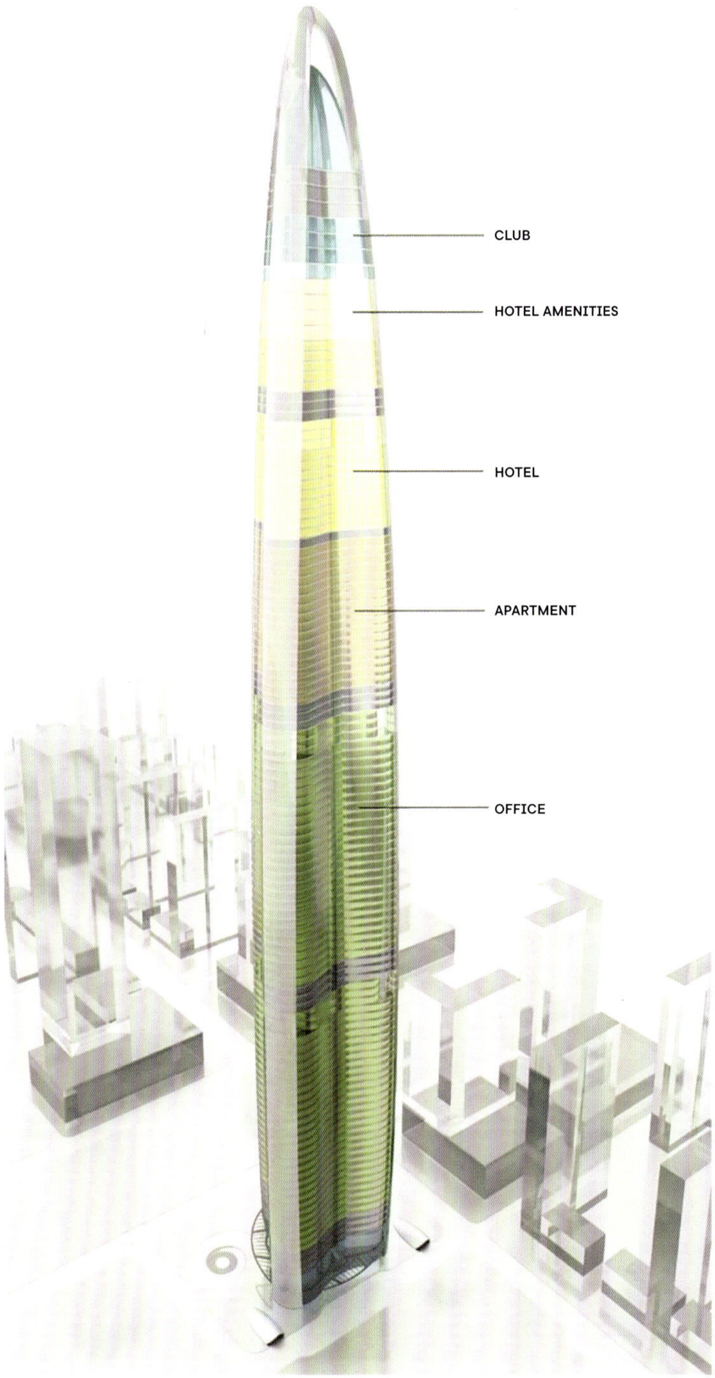

Wuhan Greenland Center is comprised of 320,000 sm of gross floor area with 200,000 sm of offices, 60,000 sm of luxury apartments and condominiums, and a 60,000 sm five-star hotel. There is also a 5,000 sm, 27-meter-tall private club with spectacular views at the tower's top level.

During the competition phase a more triangular form was envisioned with a hexagonal core but as the project and program developed a more elongated Y-shaped form emerged for both the tower core as well as overall form.

COMPETITION

FINAL

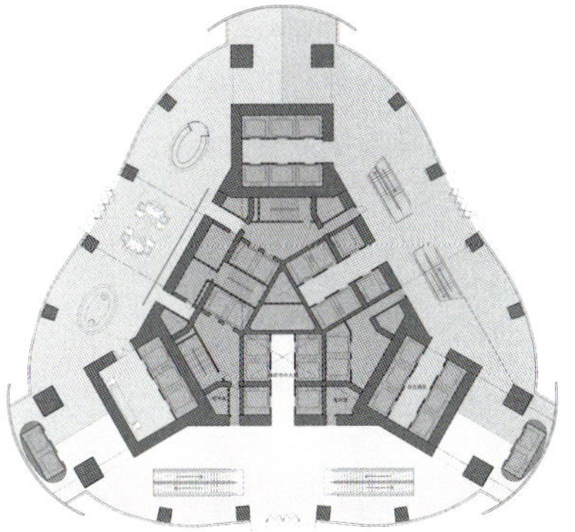

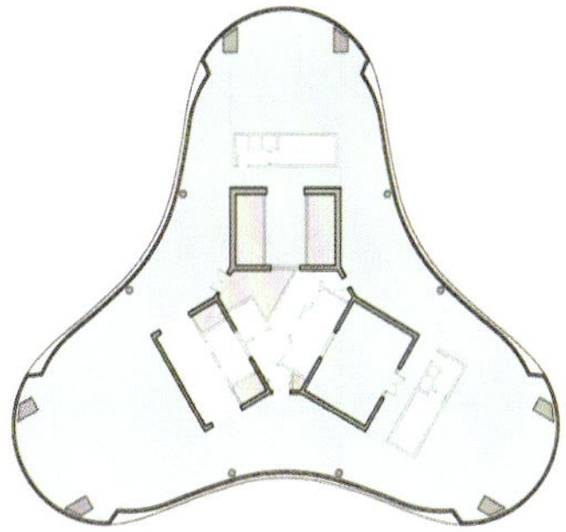

GROUND LEVEL

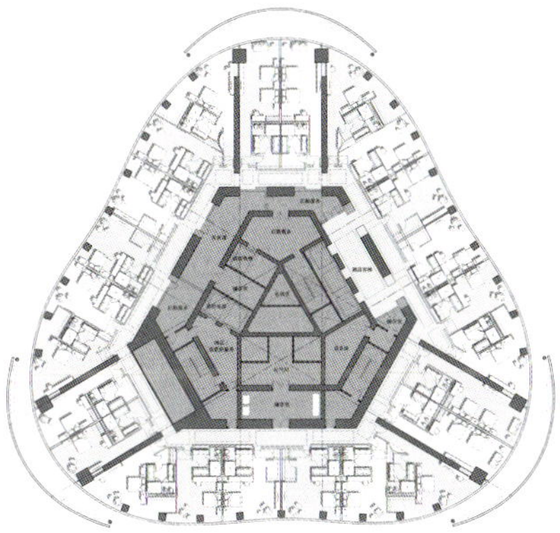

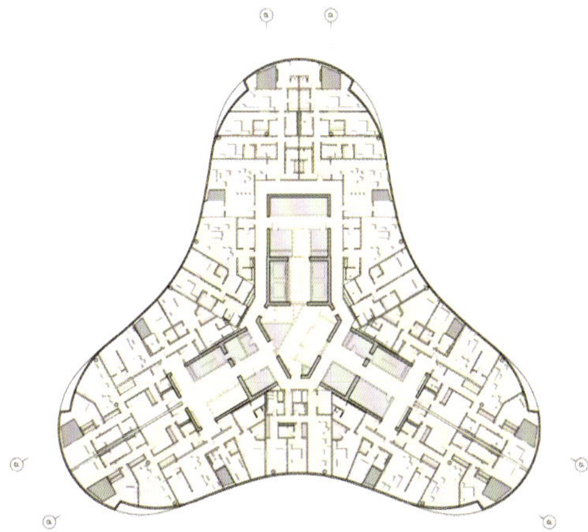

TYPICAL HOTEL

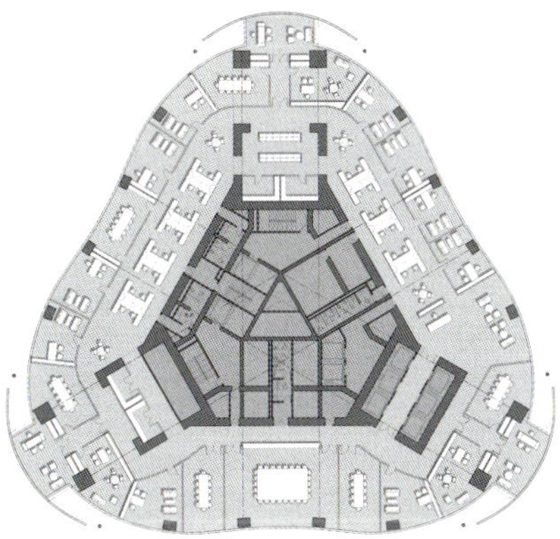

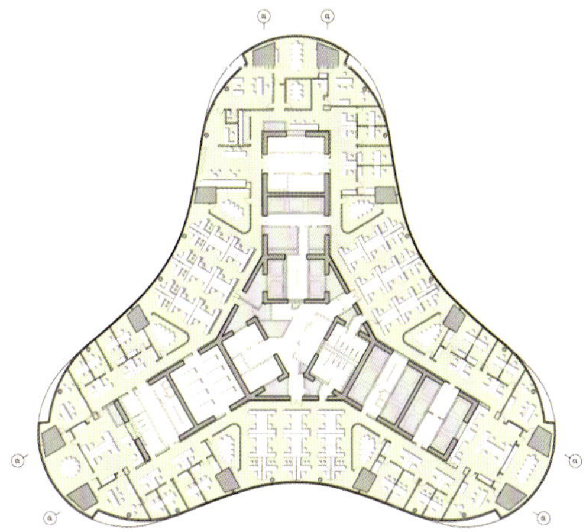

TYPICAL OFFICE

FORM

During the design phase, the tower's form was a dynamic element that, in addition to the client's program requirements, had multidisciplinary input that impacted the tower design. An integrated digital model assembled the parameters and requirements from various team members to form one, shared 3D design space. The model was used to coordinate with wind and structural engineers, consolidate the client program, and evaluate the design parameters in a continual feedback loop. This process was essential to the execution of the tightly integrated tower design.

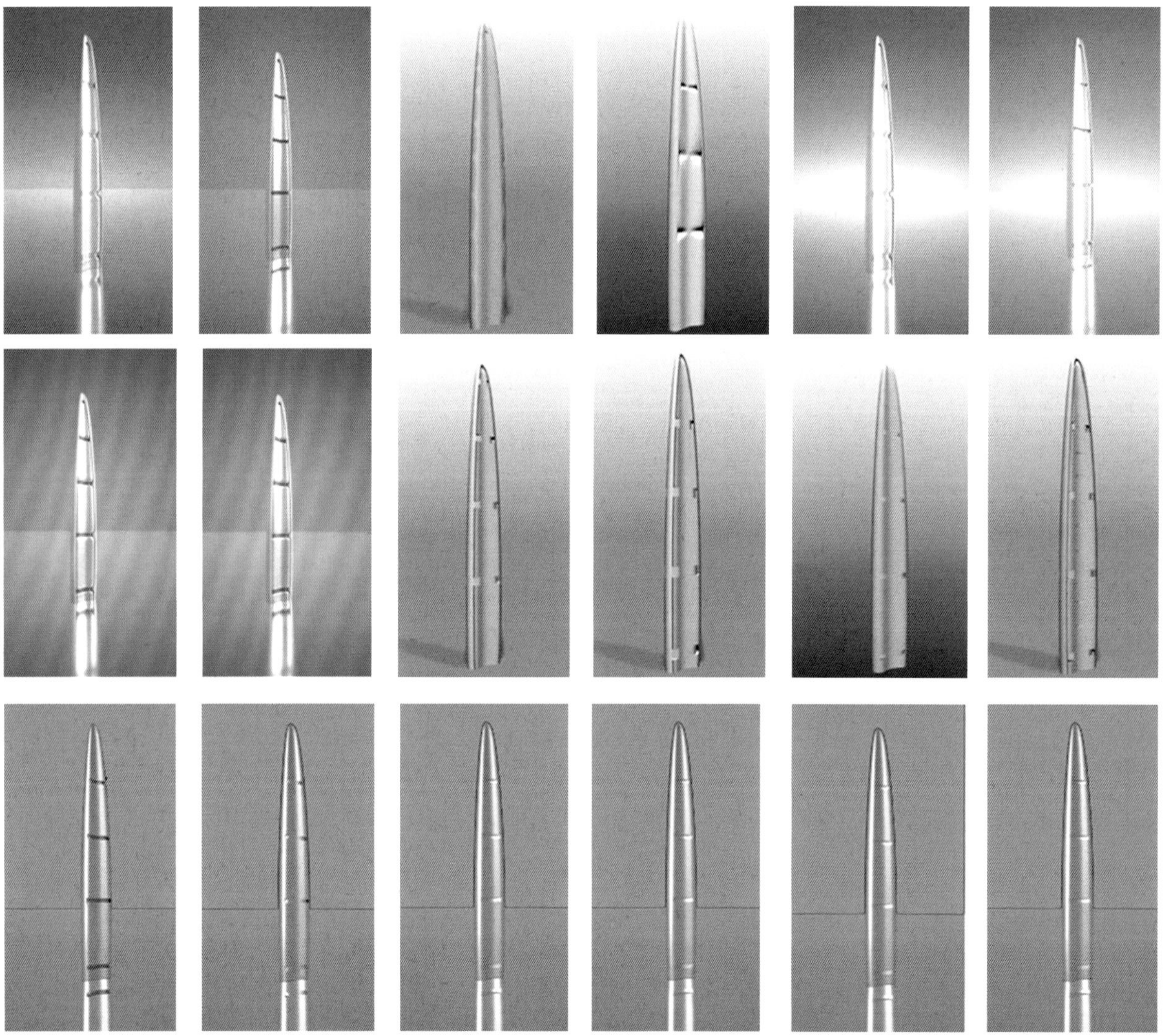

ORIGINAL COMPETITION ENTRY
OCTOBER 2010

FINAL DESIGN DEVELOPMENT
OCTOBER 2014

PERFORMANCE

The tower is comprised of two main exterior wall types, which accentuate the tower's formal expression: a shaded, textured main body and a reflective, smooth, curved shield. The main body of the tower's exterior wall is made up of both vertical polished stainless-steel fins and perforated aluminum horizontal sun-shading devices that will protect the interior from both strong mid-day and afternoon solar conditions.

Glare is controlled by an exterior metal sunshade that also filters and diffuses sunlight. Integrated smart shading systems are incorporated into each unit, giving the users and building owners control of the shades. Floor-to-ceiling glass windows also provide unobstructed views to the surrounding city.

By reducing incident solar radiation and therefore building cooling loads, daytime energy consumption is greatly reduced.

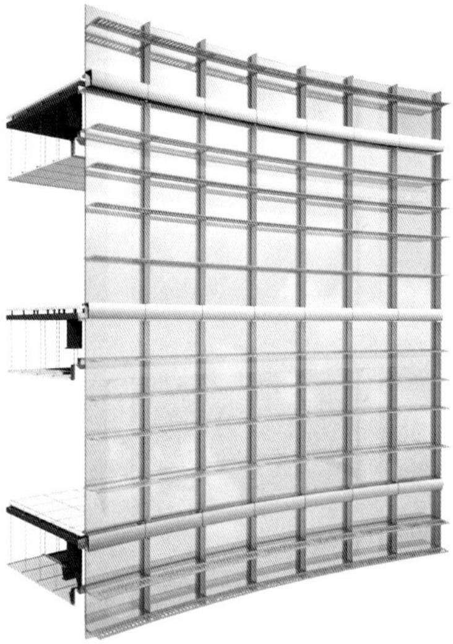

TYPICAL EXTERIOR WALL

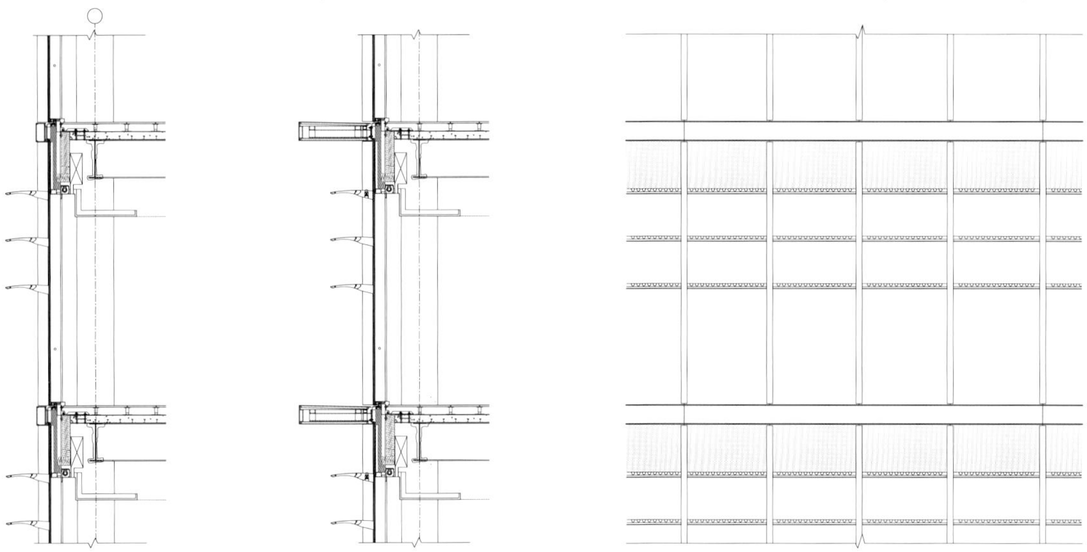

PERFORMANCE

By using custom parametric modeling tools that evaluated the formal design of the tower along with programmatic concerns, wind performance, and structural optimization, the designers established relationships between different design performance criteria such as geometric optimization, programmatic efficiency, and reduction of material.

This process determined the building's aerodynamic features, such as the overall tapering of the tower, the rounding and separation of the top, and a series of wind-relief notches that increase structural efficiency and consequently reduce the materials, cost, and associated embodied carbon used for construction by approximately 15 percent compared to a similar building without those features.

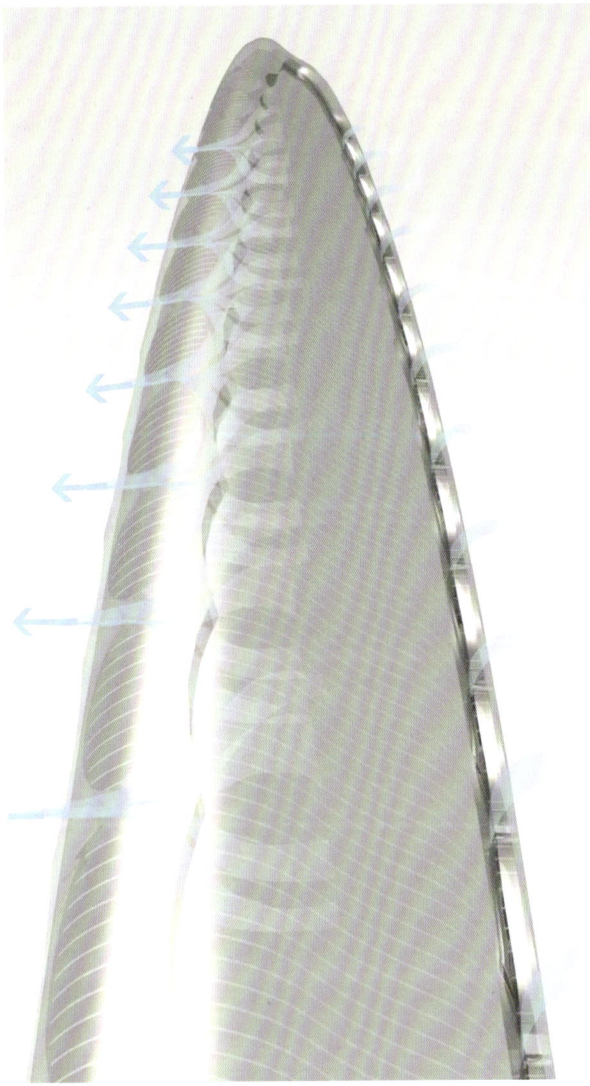

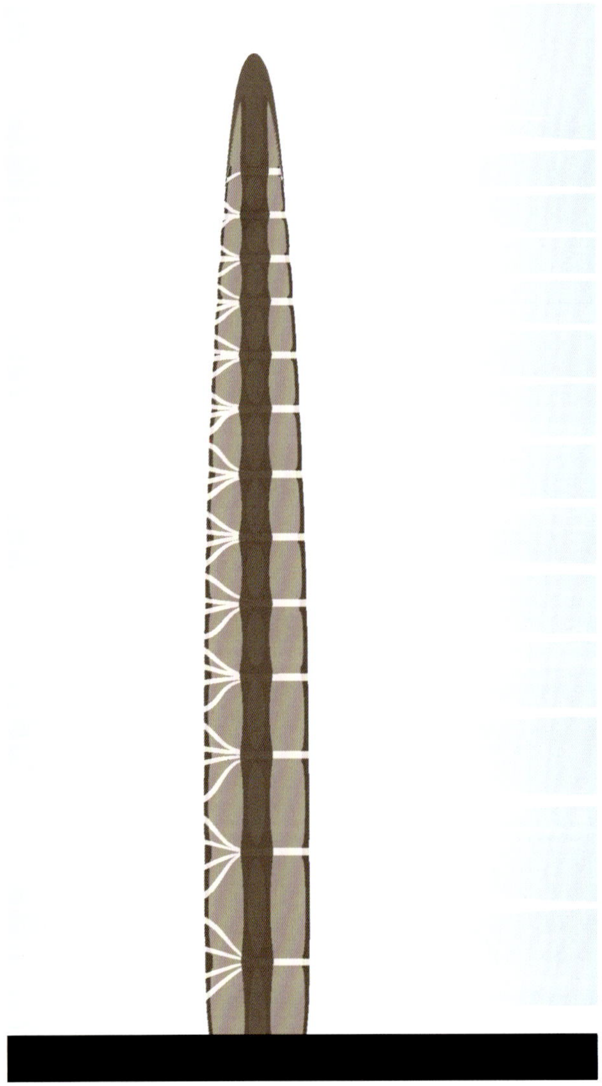

SOFT CORNERS

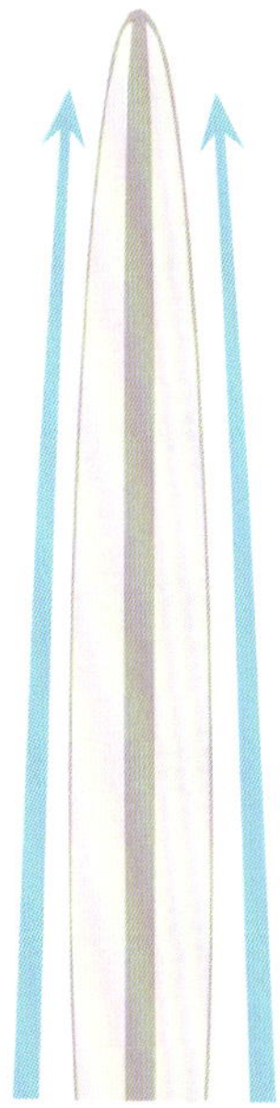

TAPERING

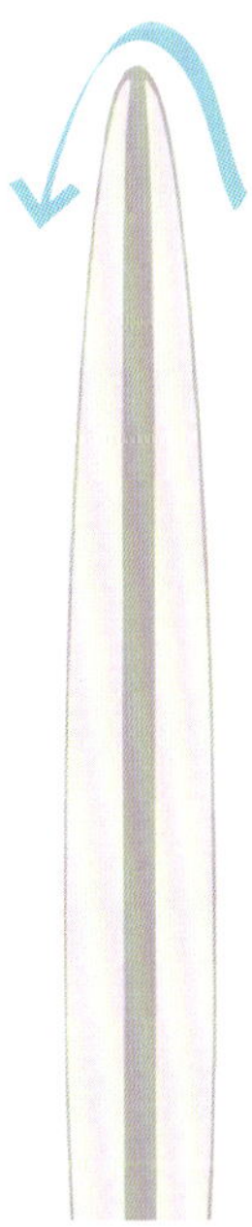

ROUND TOP

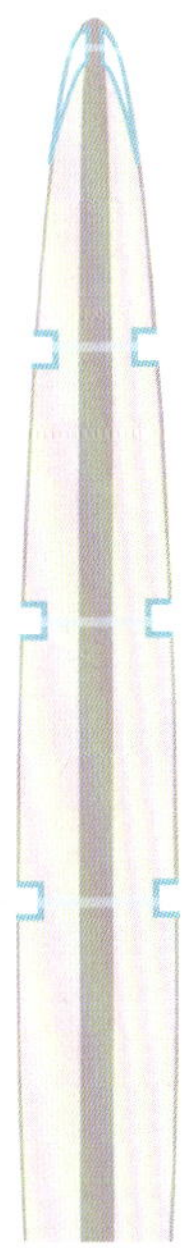

WIND RELIEF

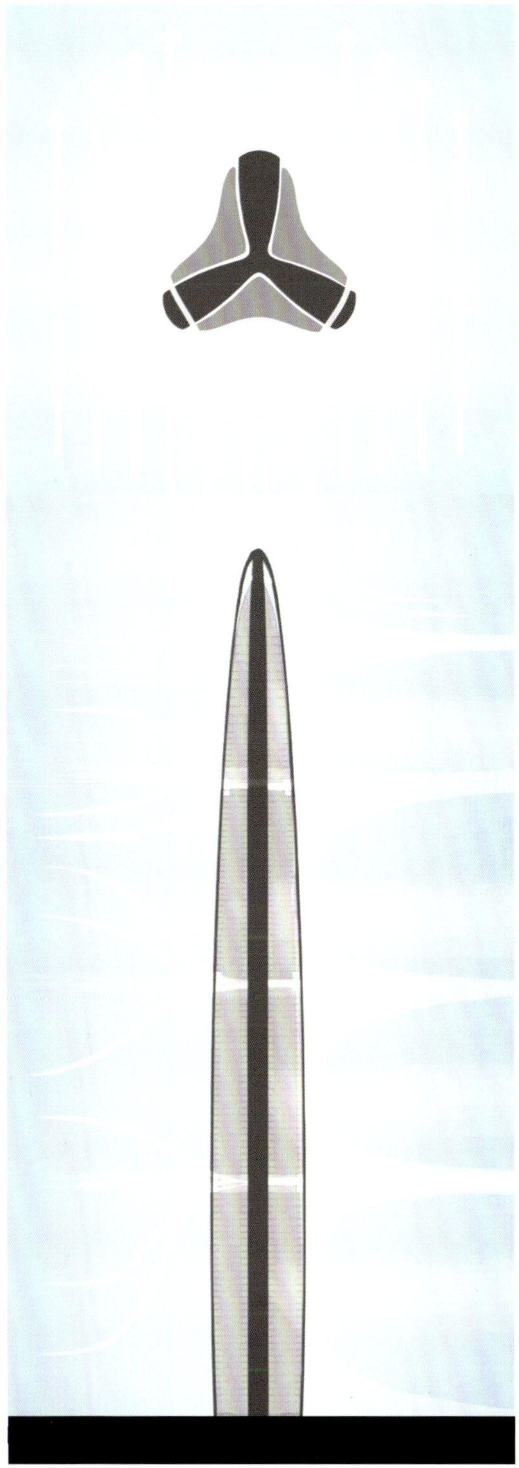

PERFORMANCE

In architecture, vortex shedding is when winds spread in a cyclical manner on the sides of a building as airflow separates off the building's face. Supertall buildings are highly susceptible to these wind forces and accelerations, which are influenced by the shape of the building. It is therefore important to consider the building's site conditions when designing its form.

Structural wind loading, perpendicular to the direction of the flow stream, causes dynamic loading due to vortex shedding. When the force of the vortex shedding is large, and the frequency of the shedding is close to the natural frequency of the building in the same direction, the effects can be significant and detrimental.

At higher elevations, the wind pressures are even greater. By tapering the building's form the force on the building is greatly reduced. Tapering also disorganizes the wind and reduces its vortex-shedding load effect, disrupting the frequency of the vortices, which differ as the floor plates vary.

Innovative wind vents increase wind performance at vertical quarter sections. The notch floors hold various functional program elements such as areas for mechanical and building maintenance equipment. On the hotel levels, the notches act as active program space as semi-enclosed, outdoor terraces. The hotel lounge space spills out onto a unique exterior space approximately 450 m in the air.

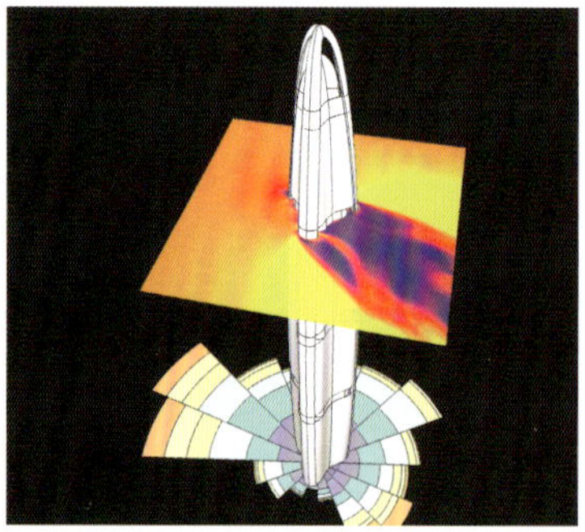

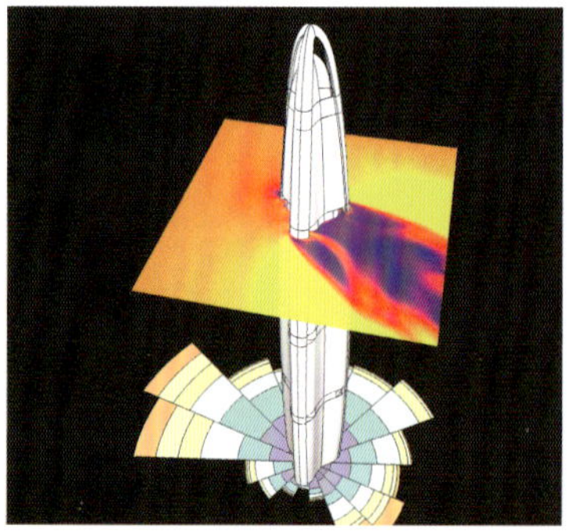

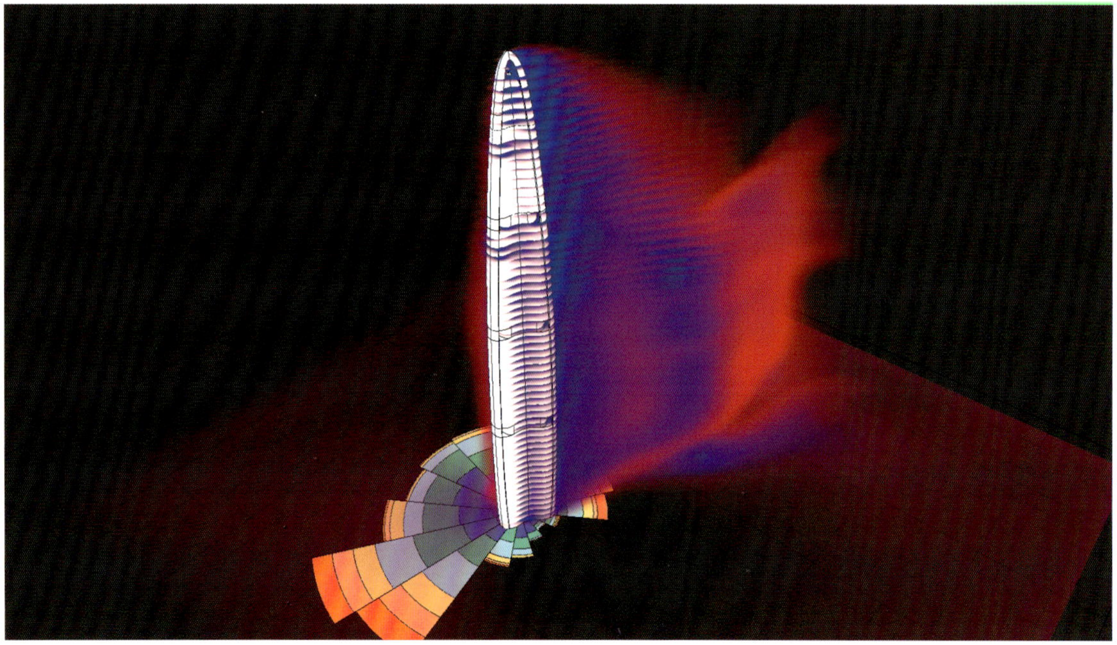

PERFORMANCE

The form of the tower was designed, and wind-tunnel tested, so that the overall wind load, as well as the cross-wind loading due to vortex shedding, was reduced. Initially, a vortex-shedding strategy of vented corner screen walls on each of the tower's three sides was suggested. Openings between the screen wall and the structure spanned the length of the building, directing wind around the corner to the back face of the building. Further studies consolidated the continuous vents into larger openings, which were tested and compared with strategies and a baseline tower with no openings. A significant reduction in wind loading was achieved, which translated into a substantial structural savings.

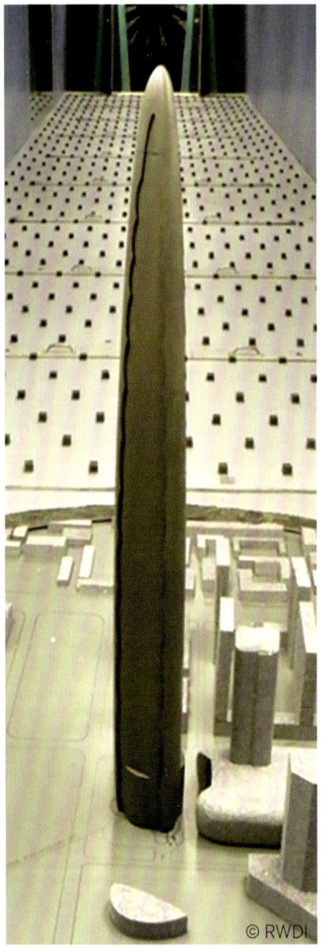

CONTINUOUS CORNER VENTS

A continuous corner vent was designed to promote vortex shedding and reduce the cross-wind forces.

LARGE OPENINGS

Consolidating the continuous vent into three-story openings reduced the overall wind loads on the tower.

SOLID FORM

As the design was developed texture was introduced to further promote vortex shedding.

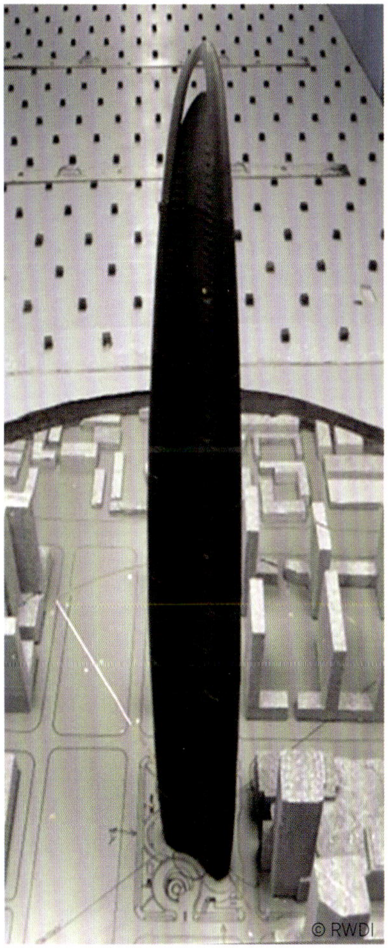

ADD TEXTURE

The initial strategies were compared against a solid form as a baseline for the wind-load reduction.

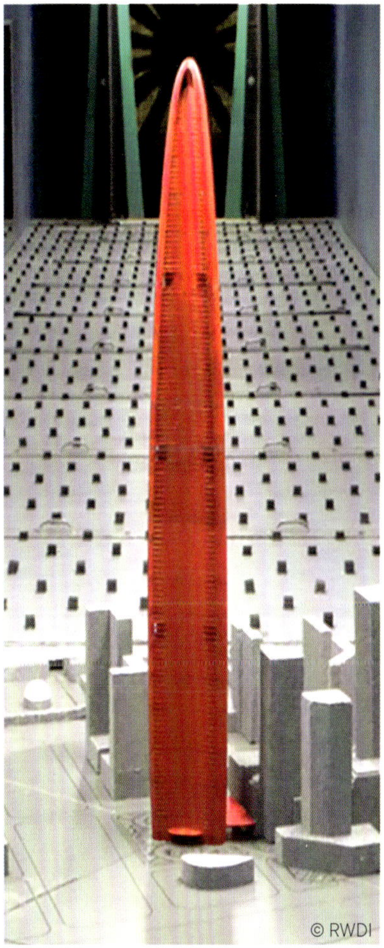

CONFIGURATION TESTING

The final design was tested in the wind tunnel.

FINAL DESIGN

PERFORMANCE

DETAIL ELEVATION

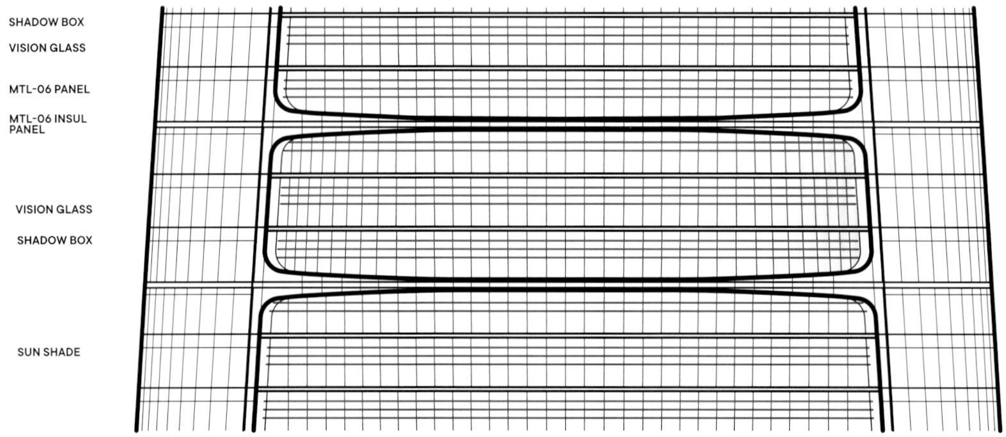

NOTCH DETAILS

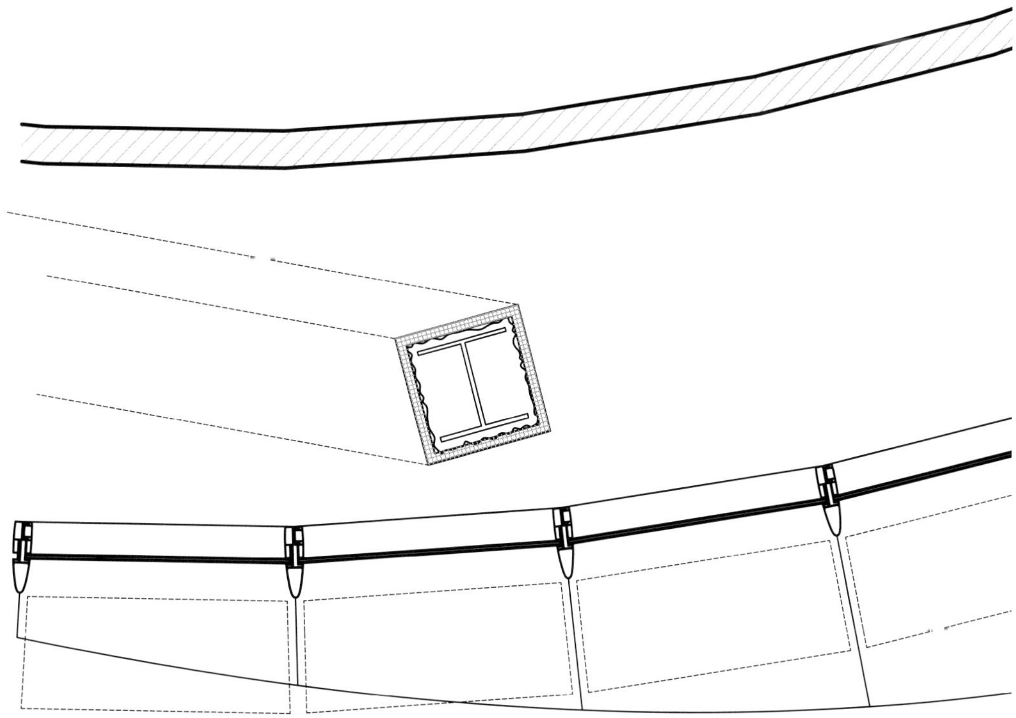

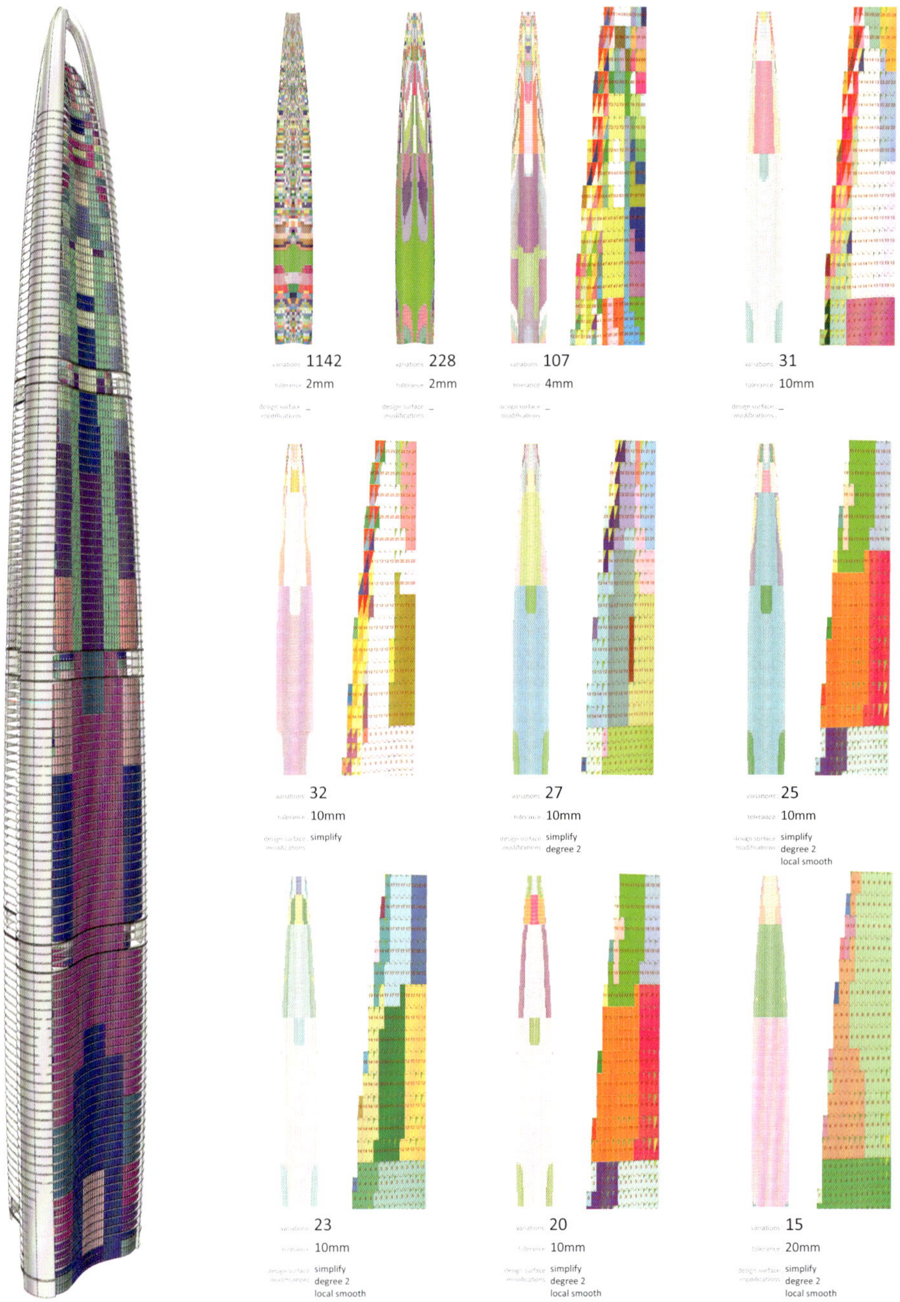

PANELIZATION STUDIES

CONSTRUCTION, 2018 © Whhb123

INTERIOR

The tower's sculpted interior public spaces reflect the tower's exterior silhouette. The conical silhouette is visibly echoed in the entrances to the primary elevator bank from the main lobby, as well as in the shapes of the elevator cabs and other public spaces. The lobbies have full height glass walls that maximize transparency, allowing views from inside toward the entry-canopy drop-off areas and establishing a seamless relationship between the interior and the exterior.

The design of the feature wall in the office lobby is a light Corian® material that diffuses and bounces incoming daylight. A detail of the wall is a dimple that registers the sunlight and shadows as they move across the space throughout the year, areas with shadowing have a smaller dimple and those receiving full sun have a large dimple. During the evening hours the wall is backlit and the dots glow from behind.

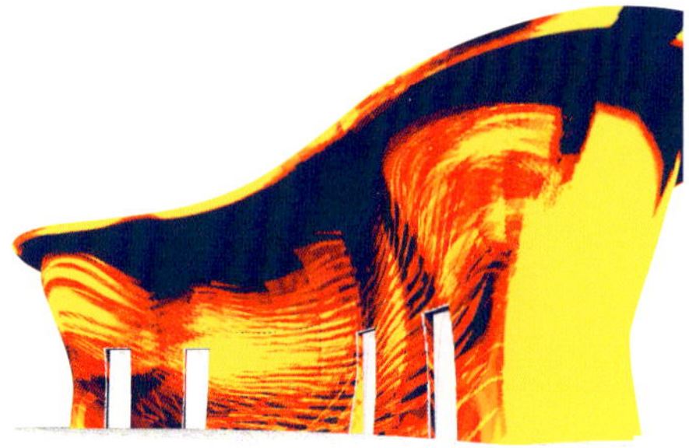

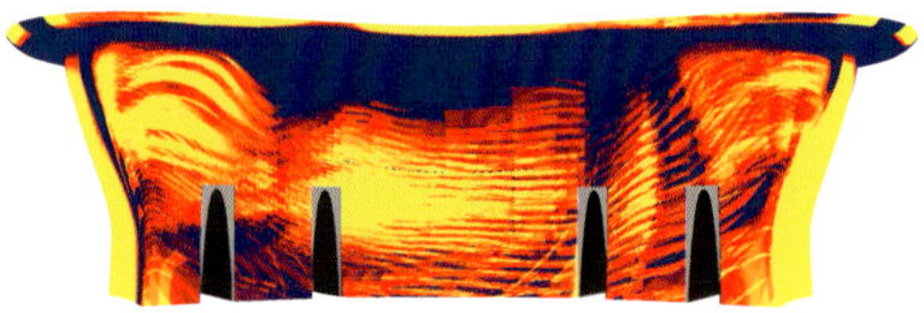

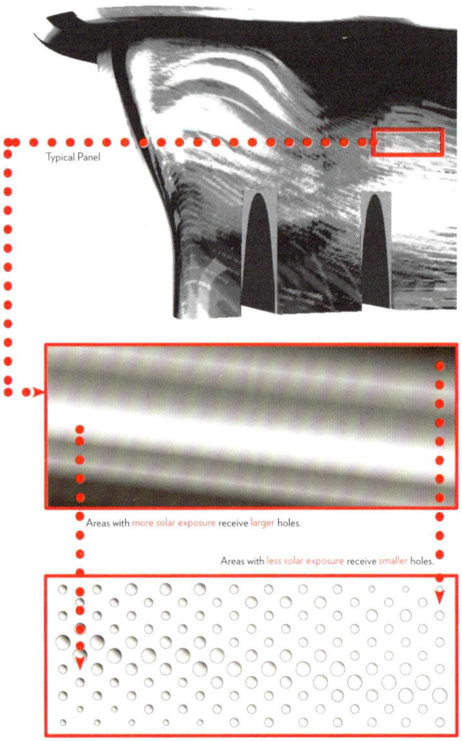

CONSTRUCTION, 2018 © Greenland Group

CROWN

The tower's top structure is a unique feature and poses a design challenge to the engineers because of the advanced geometry and large wind loads. The crown is located above Level 125, with an overall height of 61 m. It contains a large tripod supporting structure and a 36 m dome, which has a triangular shaped floor. The crown space is currently programed as a private club space with a bar and small restaurant. Because of its unique shape the space offers unique 360-degree views of the Yangtze River and the City of Wuhan.

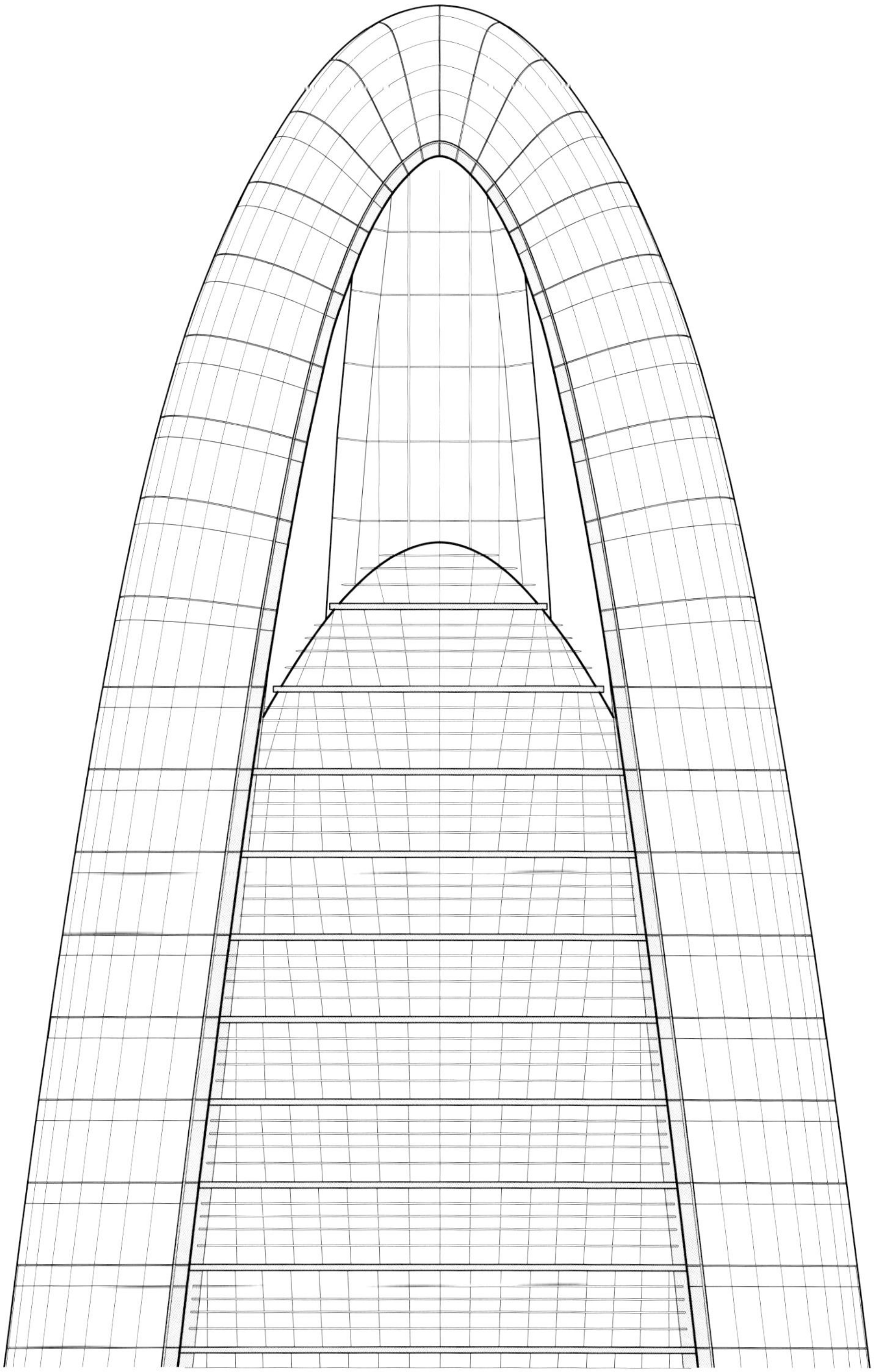

CROWN

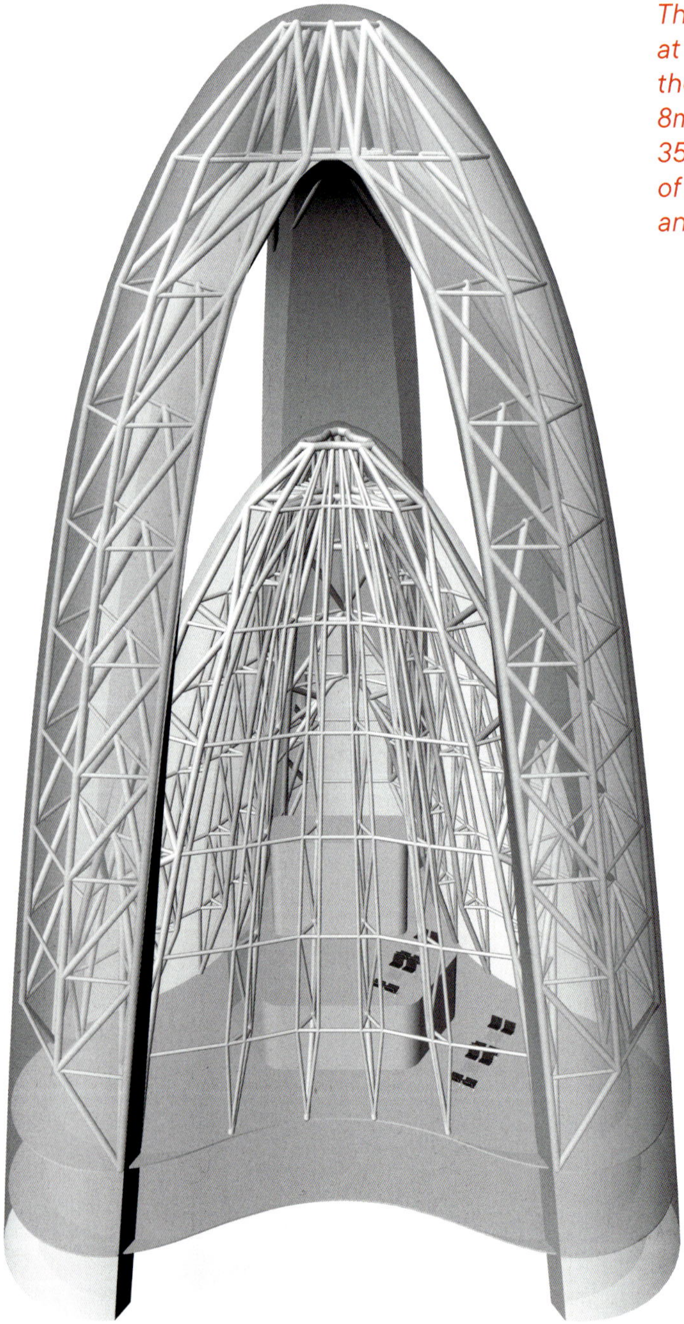

The dome connects to the tripod at the base and separates from the tripod at the height of about 8m. The top of the dome is about 35m above Level 125 and consists of a crown tripod, a dome tripod, and a facade-supporting frame.

STRUCTURE

THORNTON TOMASETTI, STRUCTURAL ENGINEER

The structural height of the building is 575 m, with the building aspect ratio of 8.5. The tower has a triangle shape on plan and taper as it rises from the ground level to the top of the building. Super columns (SC1) are be located at the corners to maximize the building lateral stiffness.

To enhance the ductility and reduce the column sizes, built-up steel members are encased in concrete super columns. The steel ratio is approximately 4 to 5 percent, considering the structural strength, ductility, and economic requirements. The following aspects were considered when selecting the lateral system:

1. Strucutral layout maximizes the efficiency of a lateral system
2. Architectural function
3. Constructability
4. Materials

The core takes most of the overturning moment and base shear. Steel plates can be added to the core wall at the bottom levels to decrease the compression ratio and improve the ductility and strength. The embedded plates also help facilitate the connect truss to the core wall.

The super column at the corner resists an overturning moment by the connection of the outrigger truss. Ductility is considered when designing the outrigger trusses because they can dissipate the energy and protect the critical vertical members, such as the core and super columns.

The tower's lateral structural system is a core + outrigger truss + super frame, highlighted by fully utilizing the best merits of steel and concrete. The combination satisfies the architectural and mechanical functions, and is an effective, efficient, and safe solution.

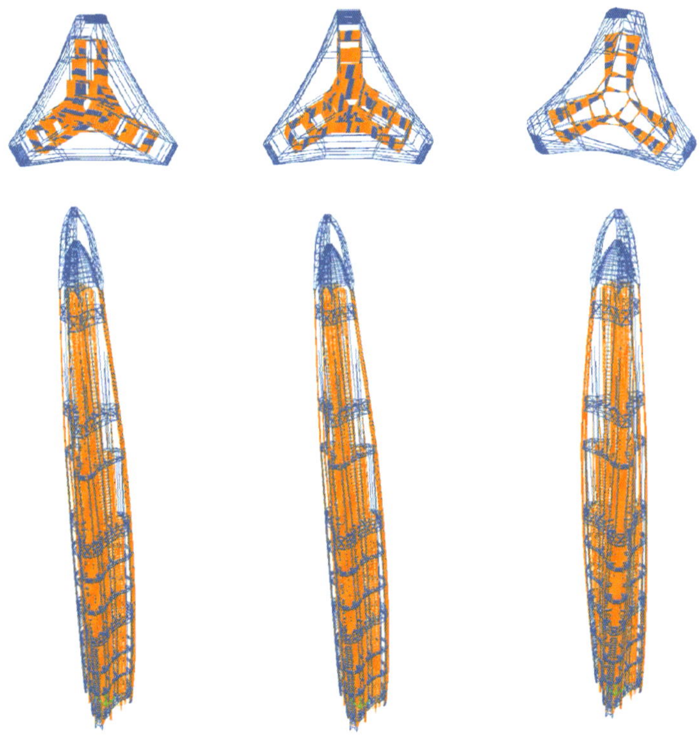

X TRANSLATION
T1 = 8.44 SECOND

Y TRANSLATION
T2 = 8.40 SECOND

Z TORSION
T3= 4.49 SECOND

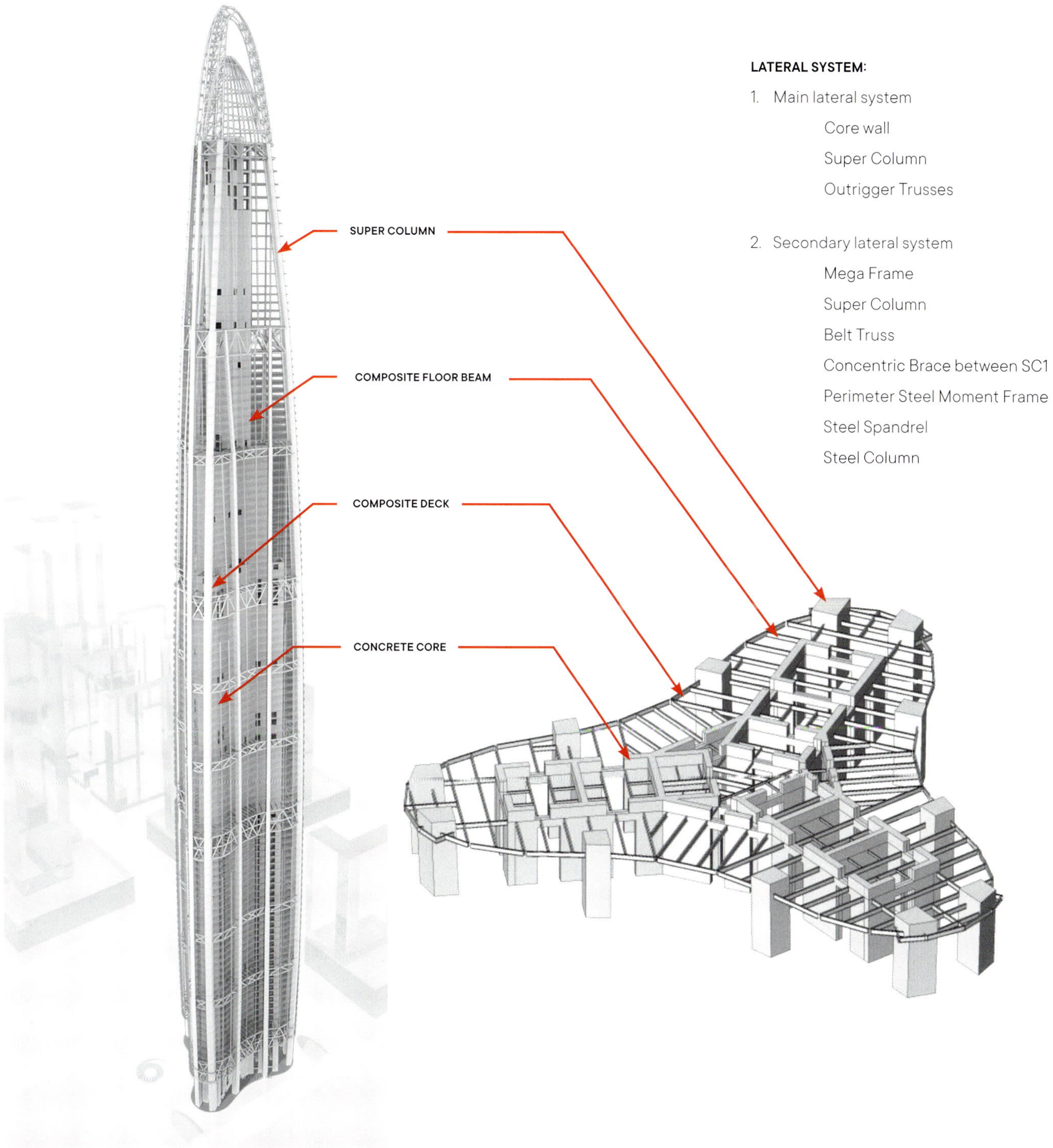

LATERAL SYSTEM:
1. Main lateral system
Core wall
Super Column
Outrigger Trusses
2. Secondary lateral system
Mega Frame
Super Column
Belt Truss
Concentric Brace between SC1
Perimeter Steel Moment Frame
Steel Spandrel
Steel Column
SUPER COLUMN
COMPOSITE FLOOR BEAM
COMPOSITE DECK
CONCRETE CORE

CONSTRUCTION

The tower is now under construction and is anticipated to be complete in 2021 with occupancy at the beginning in 2022. As of spring 2021, the structure has topped off and the exterior wall is close to being completed.

© Whhb

After Wuhan Greenland Center had been under construction for several years, the height was reduced to 476m. The reason for this is related to the airspace planning and restrictions. Since the height reduction happened after construction was well underway, the body of the tower and exterior wall was completed according to the design drawings, but the top of the building was changed.

© Whhb123

YONGSAN DANCING DRAGONS

SEOUL, KOREA, 2011

450M

In 2011, AS+GG designed two towers for the Yongsan International Business District in Seoul, Korea. The district's name, Yongsan, means "dragon hill" in Korean.

The mixed-use development was to be home to 20 new skyscrapers, including towers designed by Renzo Piano, Daniel Liebskind, Jahn, KPF, BIG, and many other world-renowned architects. The towers were programed as Officetel, small residential units that may be purchased and used as live-work studios.

Early iterations of the design included several proposals, including a curved 'wave tower' and another with a triangular, twisting design that featured a central atrium. The final design was informed by the architectural overhangs on ancient Korean temples. Although the towers share an architectural language, they are not identical.

Honoring the developments name, Dancing Dragons is also inspired by the tower's unique "breathable" skin and the way the towers form a composition that plays off each another, adding movement and variety to the skyline.

The tower's facade features openings that are placed at intervals of approximately 15-20 floors that improve the wind performance of the building.

These "cutouts" are clad in glass, providing an abundance of natural light to the units, and creating dramatic skylights at the highest level and exciting transparent floors at the lower levels. Unique details such as these create superior, high-value penthouse units that have a 360-degree views of downtown Seoul and the adjacent Han River.

- CONTEXT
- SITE
- PROGRAM
- PERFORMANCE
- INTERIOR
- RESEARCH + DEVELOPMENT
- STRUCTURE

CONTEXT

The design concept for the Dancing Dragons explores a new typology for supertall buildings in which the main tower consists of a "bundle" of four tower masses around a central core and structure. The cruciform structure leaves the corners devoid of major columns for breaks in the massing; the forms seem to float where the tower is cut. The bundled design allows the geometry to be cut away in a dramatic way, allowing areas of living space to reach beyond the structure for unique views.

This strategy maximizes column-free views at the perimeter - where conventional supertall structure typically have a multitude of columns- and present a high spatial flexibility at the corners, while still maintaining a rigorous planning module. When the vertical bars are interrupted, there are unique duplex units. At the top of the building, the bars become independent of the core and contain luxurious penthouse units with 360-degree views of Seoul. The areas in between create dramatic roof decks and multi-story amenity spaces. The overall form evokes the thrust of plant stalks shooting out from the ground. The cantilever structure is a thoroughly modern interpretation of the traditional stone pagoda eave.

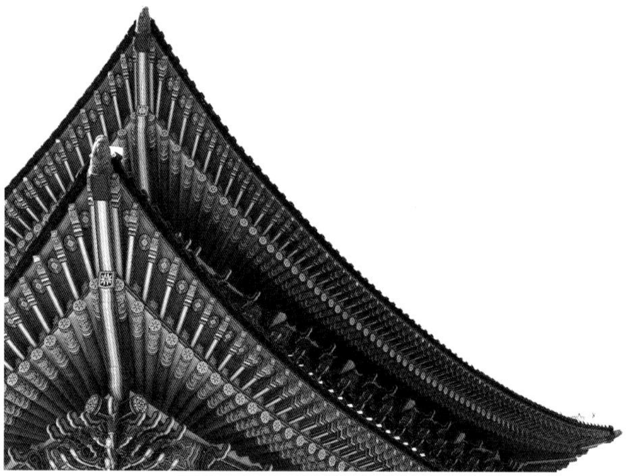

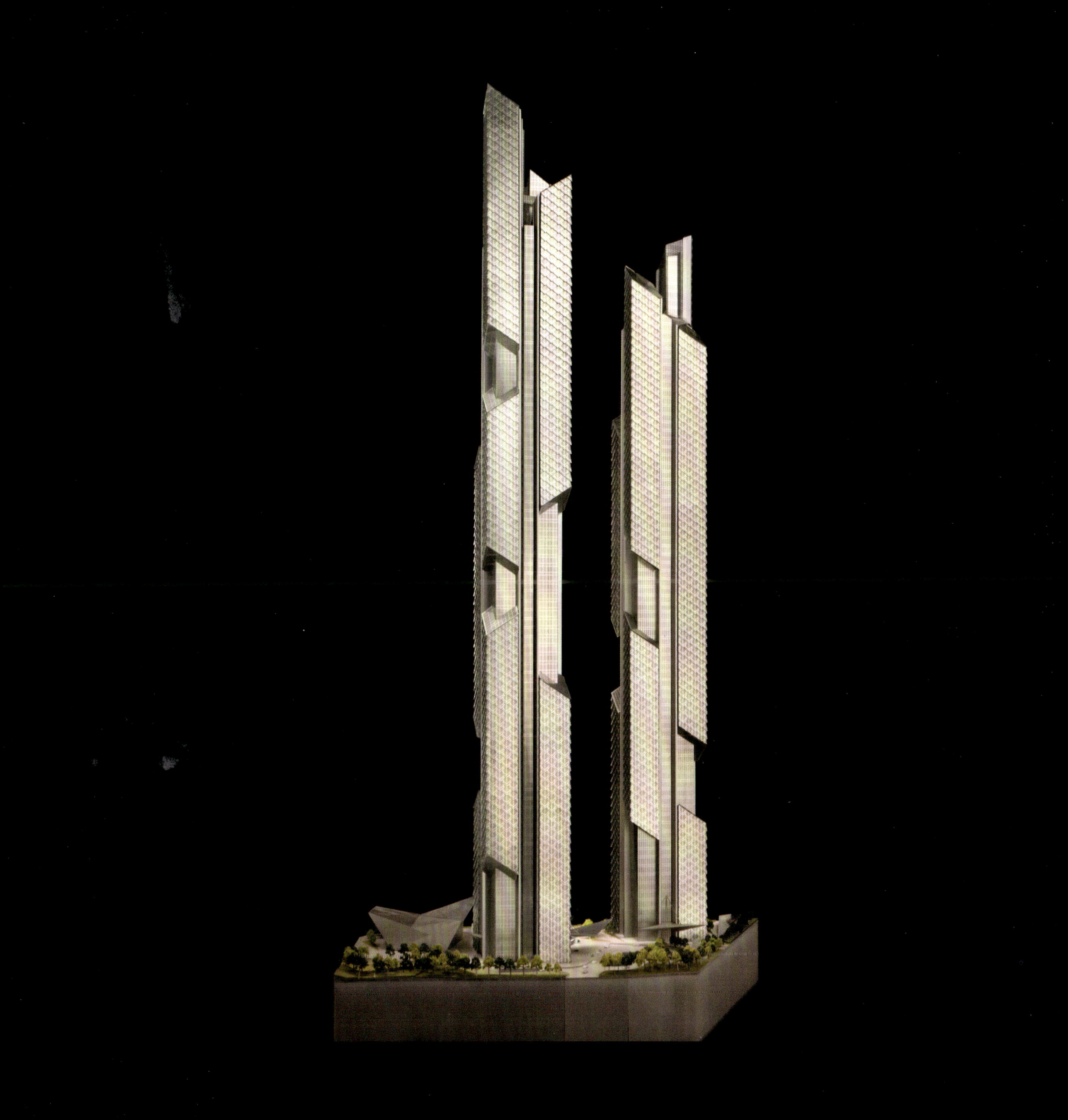

SITE

The towers share the landscaped plaza that meets the podium and are slightly staggered to maximize views and daylight. The triangulation of the facade is translated onto the ground plane by three-dimensionally forming programed and landscaped spaces that are defined activity zones to gather, play, relax, and participate. The taller tower's 18-meter-deep sunken garden provides a gradual and charming access to the underground retail zone, while providing daylight into those spaces.

The site plan is organized by a pedestrian path that reaches from the west side to the east and closely matches the location of the main circulation path in the underground retail. Public art and water features along the main pedestrian area define an inviting pedestrian path that will experience an abundance of foot traffic toward Yongsan Station. The site's lighting strategy strengthens the wayfinding by delineating routes throughout, including the main pedestrian access. Robust local plantings guide or buffer, while enhancing the site's sustainability and ecology.

The podium provides direct access to the underground retail zone and serves as a dazzling object that anchors the busiest corner of the site. Cooling towers serving both towers are hidden under the envelope of the podium. Water features and a wetland biotope capture the site's stormwater runoff for treatment and reuse in the cooling towers.

SITE PLAN

PROGRAM

The towers' officetel program features a mix of units that range from a one-room studio to a three-bedroom duplex. The amenity program was developed to support the units in each tower to maintain the highest standard of luxury and includes a swimming pool, fitness center, business center, and lounge with restaurant and bar.

The taller of the two towers, T1, is 88 stories with 95 levels in total. The second tower, T2, has 77 stories with 83 levels, including technical floors. Both towers are split into two tiers, each with a group of four elevators. The penthouse units in T1, which are in the corners where the building massing drops off at the top, are dedicated to serve the pinnacle.

The high-rise zone elevators serve the multi-story top amenity spaces, which are programed with functions including a gym, restaurant, and pool. There are a set of three parking shuttles that give access to the parking floors and the public retail mall located on the lower levels of the site.

TYPICAL FLOOR PLANS

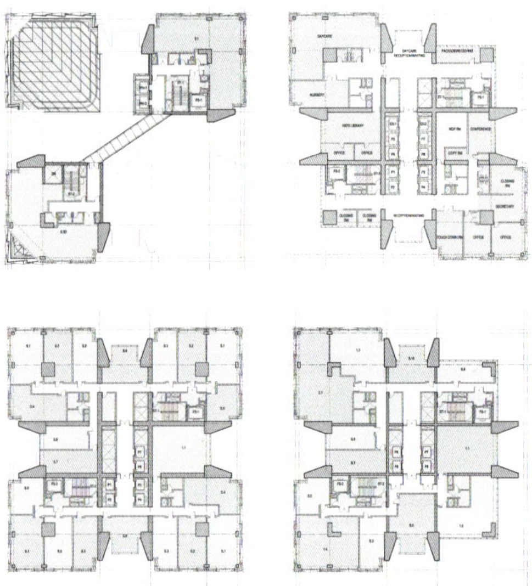

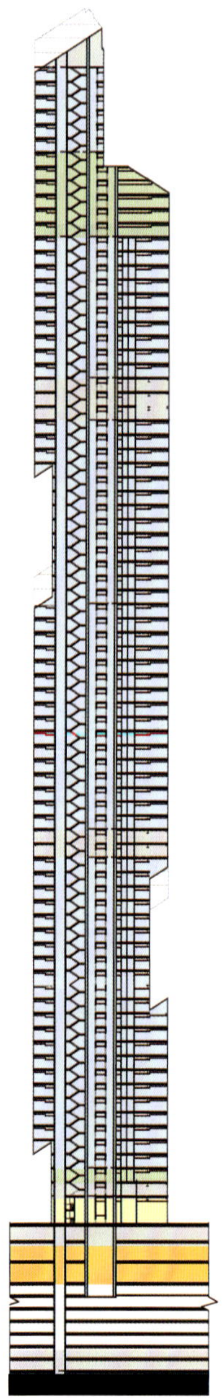

SECTION A

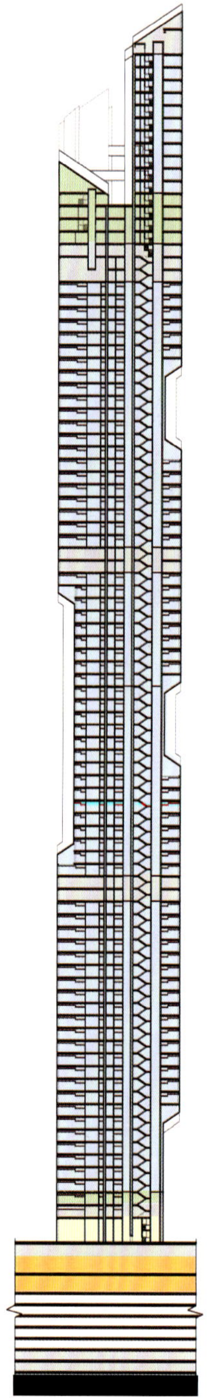

SECTION B

PLAN VARIATIONS

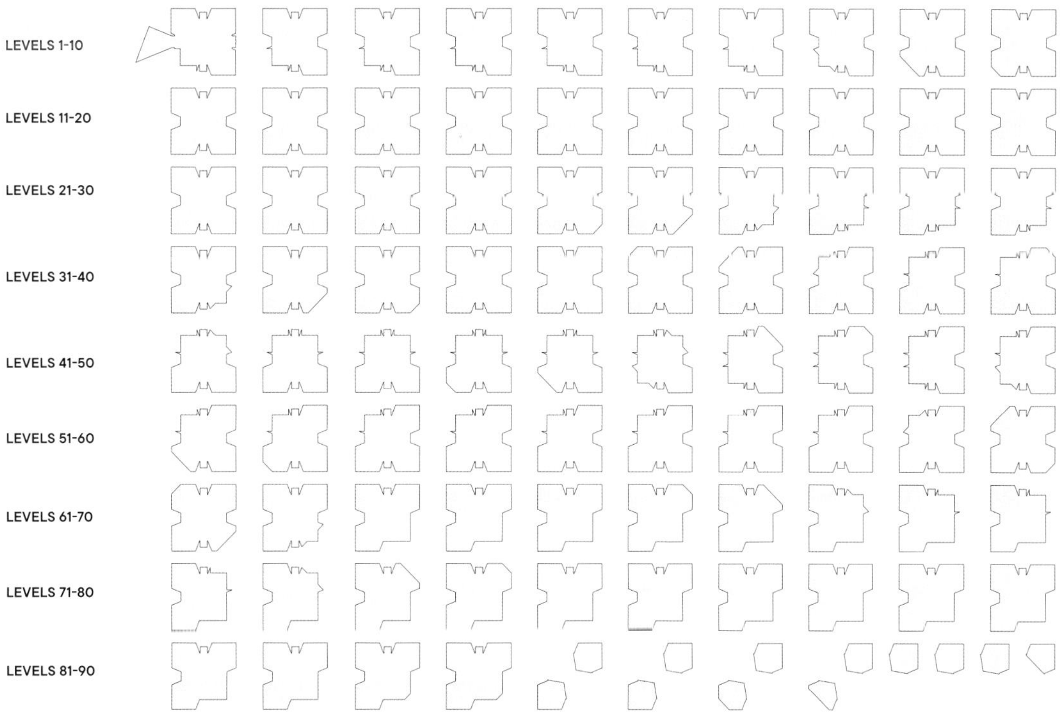

PERFORMANCE

The exterior wall enhances the overall design concept by creating the "breathable skin" of the building. The facade is formed with overlapping shingled glazed panels that intake air at the bottom and exhaust air higher up, using natural convection. The shingles act as shields so high wind speeds near the top of the tower do not create uncomfortable conditions for occupants when the facade is in the open position.

The climate in Seoul is pleasant for much of the spring and fall, therefore full use of the system can save significant amounts of energy that would otherwise be used for artificial ventilation. The facade is designed to be tuned to the Building Management System or can operate automatically.

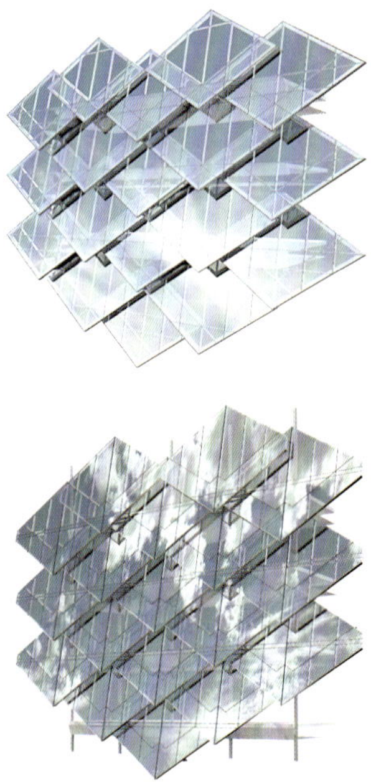

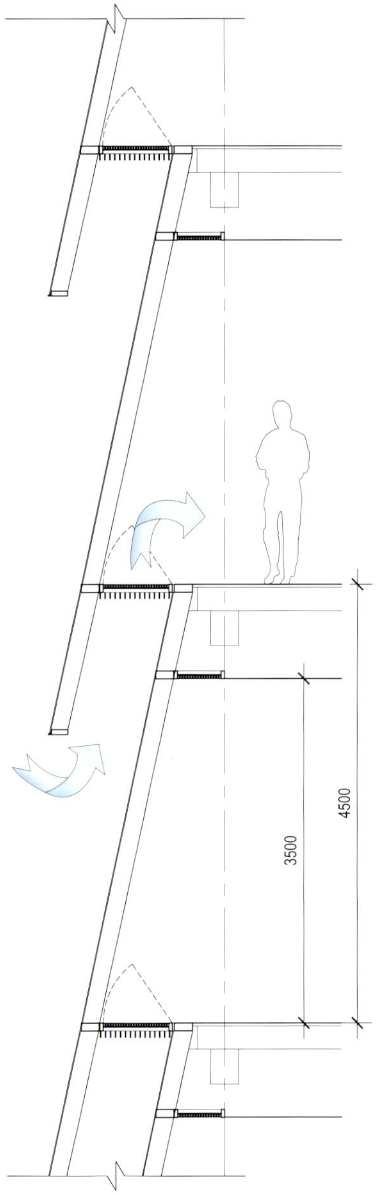

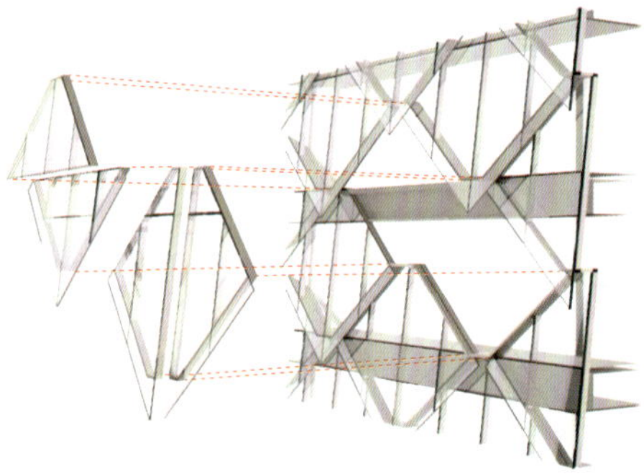

Panels are orientated diagonally to create a texture on the cantilevered parts of the building, but left smooth on the main mass of the building core. This pattern accentuates the massing moves of the tower and provides extra solar protection where it is needed most.

INTERIOR

The ground-floor lobby design is a warm and inviting space with polished and sealed concrete floors and textured warm-toned venetian plaster walls. A key design feature is the ceiling, which is composed of low-iron clear glass facets that are set below a mirrored-glass layer, creating an interactive, kaleidoscope affect that activates the lobby and sets the tone for other spaces such as the elevator lobby, the elevator cabs, and corridors. Public spaces are punctuated with a trademark color, red or yellow, used for visual excitement that will also help way finding. Specialty local art pieces are featured throughout, emphasizing a local, contemporary design concept.

LOBBY

ROOFTOP BAR AND RESTAURANT (RIGHT)

INTERIOR

In general, officetel units tend to be small, so there are multiple occupant amenities. Well-being is a key goal of the design. Residents of both towers have full access to a business center, two levels of gym and spa services, an indoor and an outdoor pool, and a rooftop club that features an indoor-outdoor sky lounge and bar with dramatic views of the new Yongsan Business District and Seoul. A party room is also accessible to the upper roof deck, which creates a lively space for residents' guests.

The program was developed so that residents can meet many of their needs without leaving the building, using the social spaces and amenities over multiple floors. Quintessential for the modern urbanite, officetel planning focuses on luxurious, gracious, and flexible design suitable for the young professional lifestyle.

Units offered include studio, one, two, and three bedrooms, all with generous storage space, transformable built-in cabinetry, integrated mechanical systems, and custom interior shades. Each

UNIT AS RESIDENCE

UNIT AS OFFICE

INTERIOR

DECK BAR

VIEW FROM LOWER CUTS

INDOOR POOL AND
AMENITY SPACE (RIGHT)

RESEARCH + DEVELOPMENT

The design team extensively studied massing cuts to the tower to create the most ideal composition, both between the two towers and on the skyline as a whole.

The study also included ways to find the most ideal layouts for the officetel units and to achieve the client's program for the proper mix of the units. Upward-facing massing cuts yield units with skylights, and downward-facing cuts yield units with tilted windows.

These strategic moves greatly affect the spaces, as each cut spans across several units.

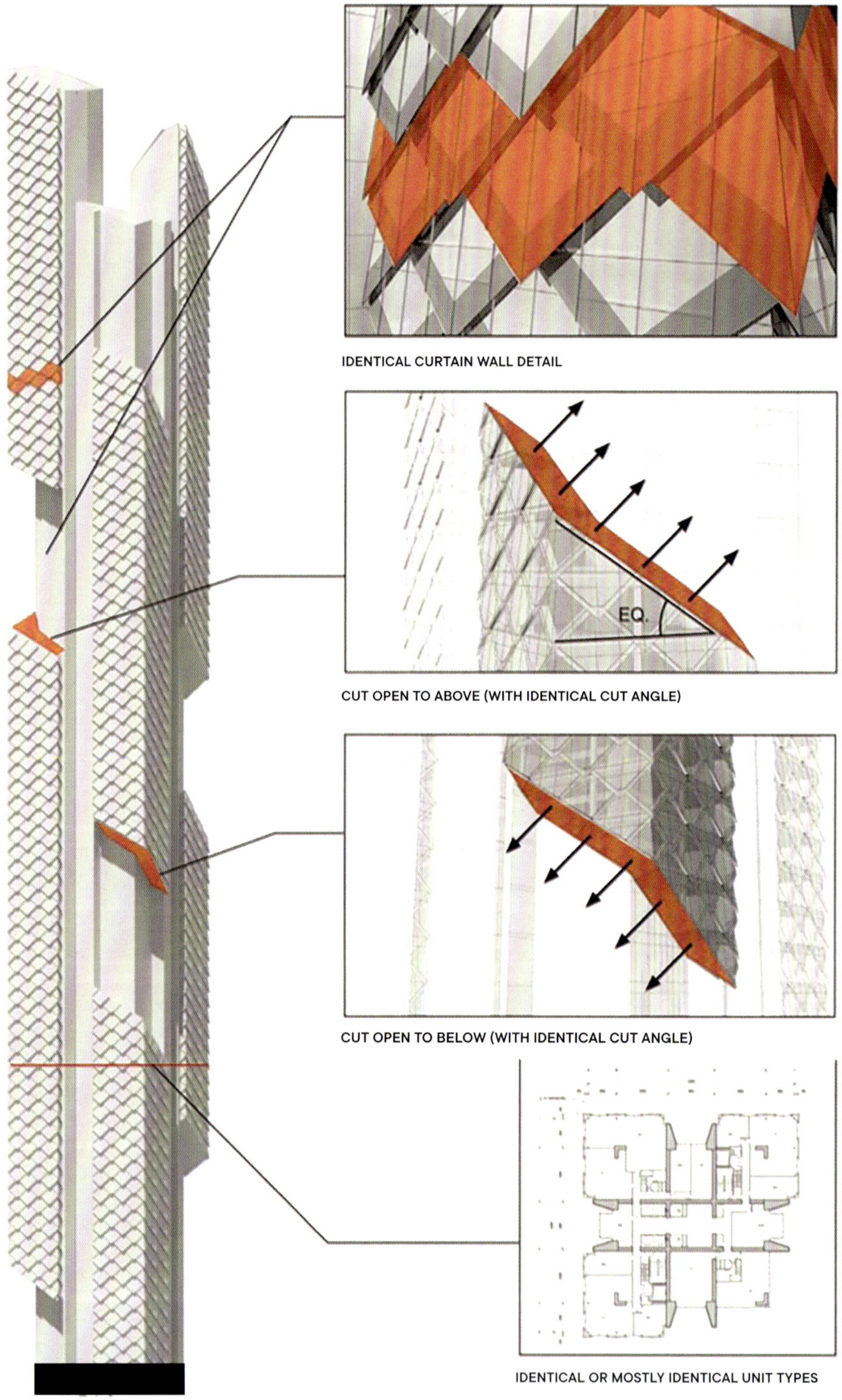

IDENTICAL CURTAIN WALL DETAIL

CUT OPEN TO ABOVE (WITH IDENTICAL CUT ANGLE)

CUT OPEN TO BELOW (WITH IDENTICAL CUT ANGLE)

IDENTICAL OR MOSTLY IDENTICAL UNIT TYPES

IDENTICAL CURTAIN WALL DETAIL

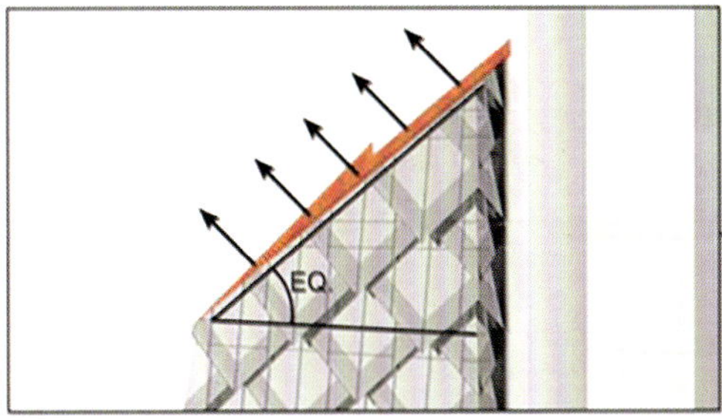

CUT OPEN TO ABOVE (WITH IDENTICAL CUT ANGLE)

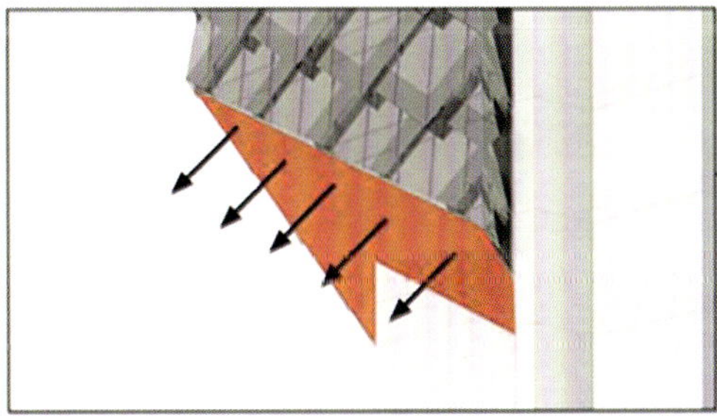

CUT OPEN TO BELOW (WITH IDENTICAL CUT ANGLE)

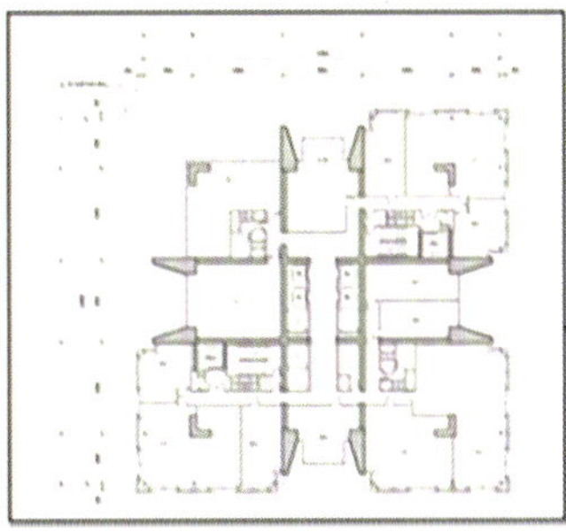

IDENTICAL OR MOSTLY IDENTICAL UNIT TYPES

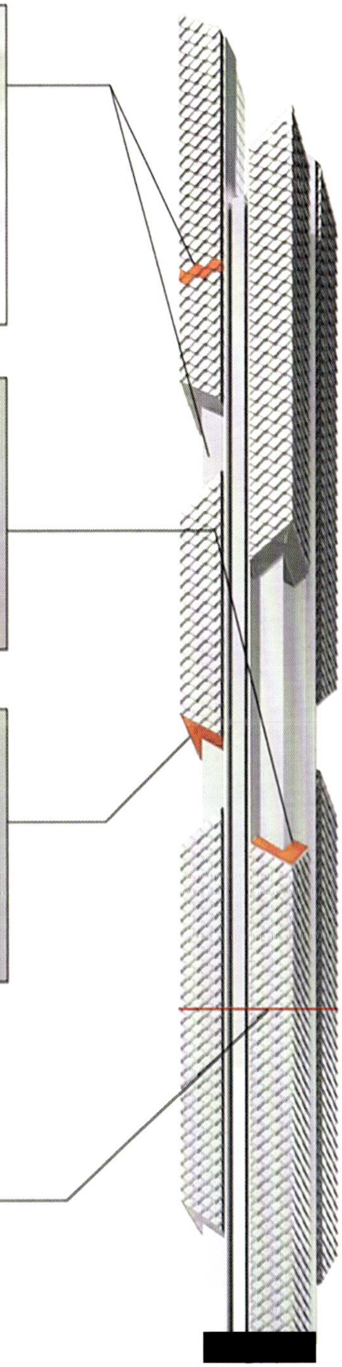

STRUCTURE

WERNER SOBEK, STRUCTURAL ENGINEER

A customized structural design was required so that the overall performance and stability of the towers was not compromised by the massing cuts. While most towers of a similar height have large columns at the corners, this was not possible for Dancing Dragons. Instead, a lateral bracing system that will withstand wind and seismic loads is assured by H-shaped reinforced-concrete core walls in combination with eight mega columns linked to the core.

The columns are located at the third-points of the tower to open up the corners, so the massing can start and stop. The columns at the end of the "H" frame act as both structural elements and large architectural features, creating a strong reveal up the sides of the tower. The core walls and mega columns run continuously over the complete height of the buildings. Four corner columns are also activated for the lateral bracing via belt trusses connected to the core walls and mega columns in the MEP levels, as well as via frame girders connected to the mega columns in each level. The edges of the slabs are vertically supported via steel elements and tied back to the core at the mechanical levels to allow the cut-outs of the slabs over the building elevation

The same number of stories support each diagonal opposite side to achieve a balanced system and to avoid additional moments onto the bracing system. The slab system of the outer slabs and the corner areas of the inner slabs is a composite deck on steel beams. The inner slab areas between the core walls are reinforced-concrete slabs, with support beams were required. Both towers are founded on a raft with piles.

As the basement structure beneath the towers is exposed to uplift forces due to the high groundwater table additional tension piles may be required in this area.

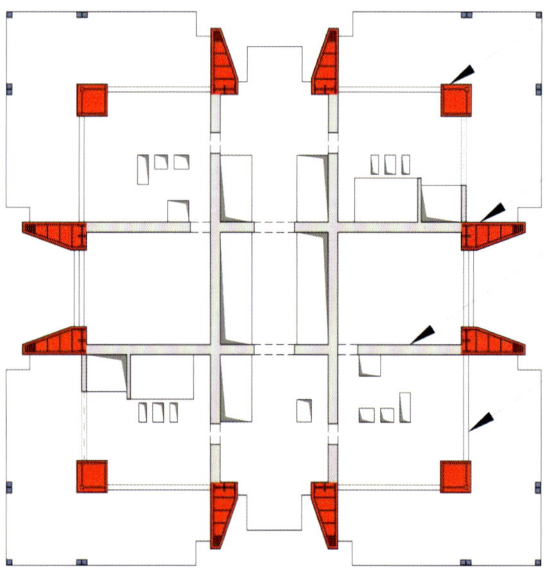

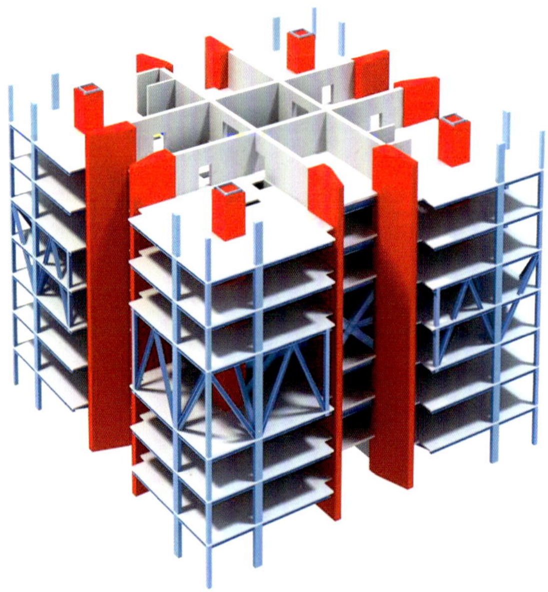

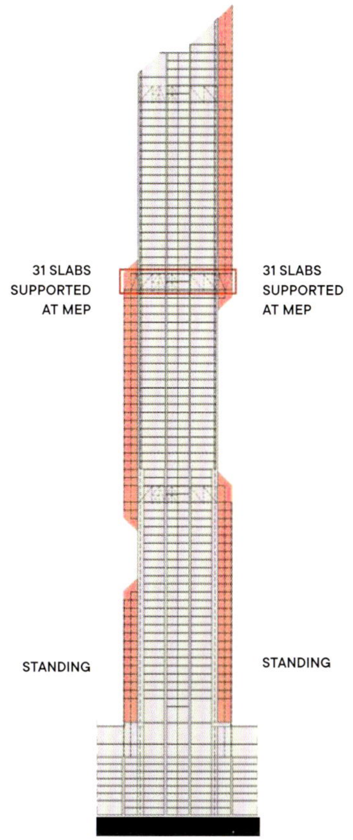
31 SLABS
SUPPORTED
AT MEP
31 SLABS
SUPPORTED
AT MEP
STANDING
STANDING

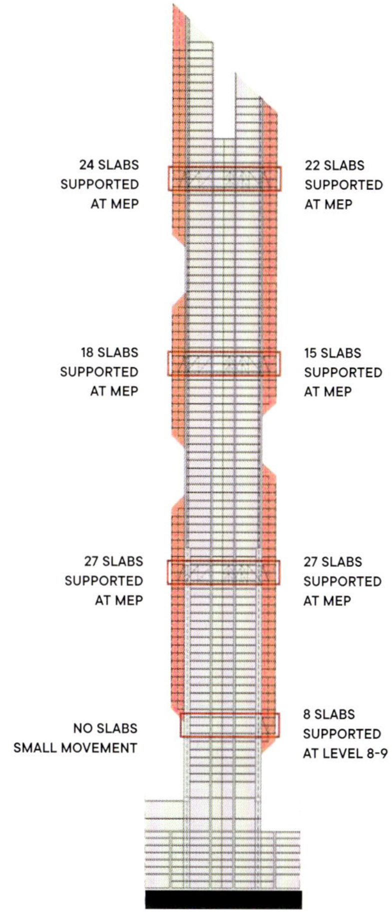
24 SLABS
SUPPORTED
AT MEP
22 SLABS
SUPPORTED
AT MEP
18 SLABS
SUPPORTED
AT MEP
15 SLABS
SUPPORTED
AT MEP
27 SLABS
SUPPORTED
AT MEP
27 SLABS
SUPPORTED
AT MEP
NO SLABS
SMALL MOVEMENT
8 SLABS
SUPPORTED
AT LEVEL 8-9

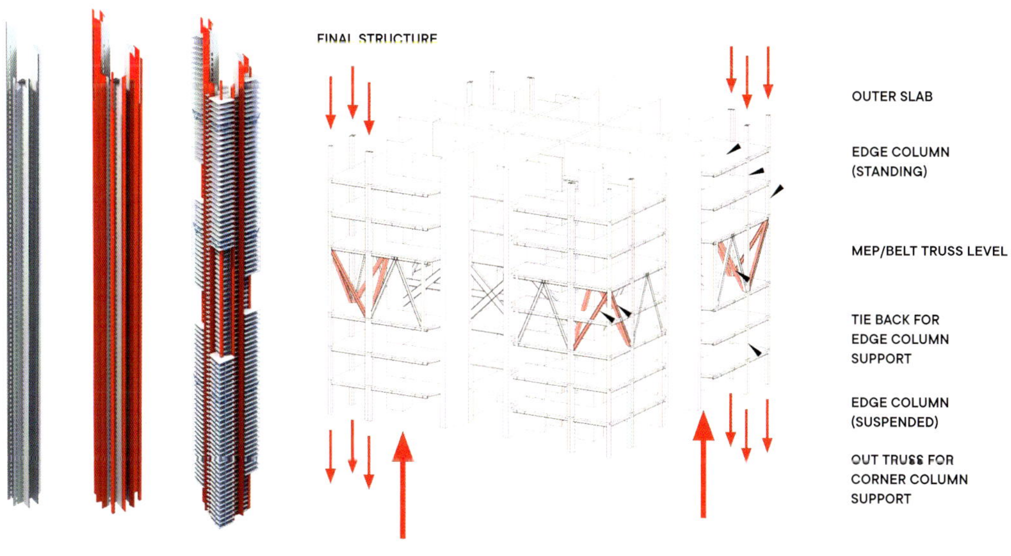
FINAL STRUCTURE
OUTER SLAB
EDGE COLUMN
(STANDING)
MEP/BELT TRUSS LEVEL
TIE BACK FOR
EDGE COLUMN
SUPPORT
EDGE COLUMN
(SUSPENDED)
OUT TRUSS FOR
CORNER COLUMN
SUPPORT

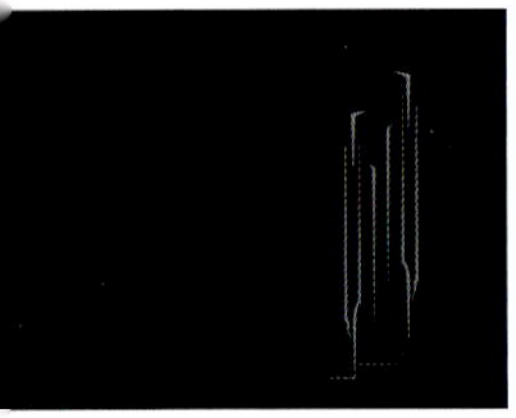

LAKESIDE RESIDENTIAL TOWERS

CHICAGO, USA, 2015

450M

The competition design for Lakeside Residential Towers at 400 N. Lakeshore Drive was completed for Related Midwest after they acquired the previous site for Santiago Calatrava's Chicago Spire. The site was left with existing foundations for the unbuilt 450m tower, which included a basement that went several stories below grade with caissons designed to support the tower.

The site has the potential to redefine urban living in Chicago by transforming the skyline and propelling real-estate values into the 21st century. AS+GG's design focused on the prime location, situated at Lake Michigan and the Chicago River, by using the existing tower foundations and Lake Shore Drive ramps to fully maximize the value.

Setting a benchmark for urban living, the primary goal of the design was to create a premier residential address that was also cozy and comfortable, with the tag line Coming Home.

A variety of residential unit typologies that can cater to various city lifestyles are included. Part of the proposal included fast-track design and construction process with advanced occupancy.

- + CONTEXT
- + SITE
- + PROGRAM
- + PERFORMANCE
- + STRUCTURE

CONTEXT

The design contributes to the architectural heritage of Chicago, building on this tradition by delivering a scheme that is grounded in AS+GG's firm philosophy, *Form Follows Performance*.

An initial design goal was to create a form that was memorable—simple enough that a child could draw it. A shape that is instantly recognizable to become a new icon for Chicago's already impressive skyline. We also recognized the high-profile project, would have an impact in terms of the city's context and the lingering controversies with the previous design.

To keep costs low, the design reuses the existing structure, adding building extrusions without wall or column cantilevers. The building shape creates fully occupiable corners and unique view opportunities.

The low position of horizontal mullions and the off-corner columns create special character. Residential units become more generous in size and offer a feeling of being home in the sky. Most units have commanding views perched above the city and across the horizon.

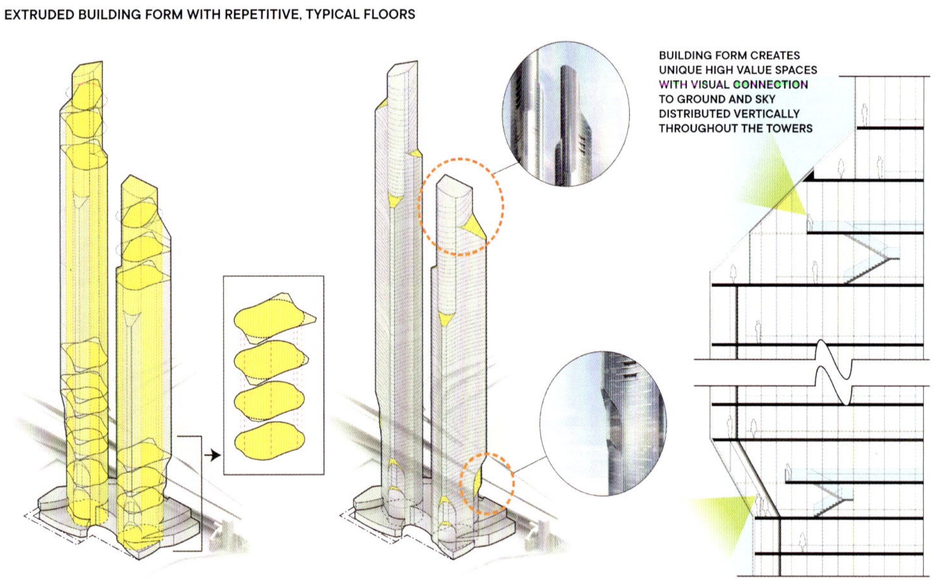

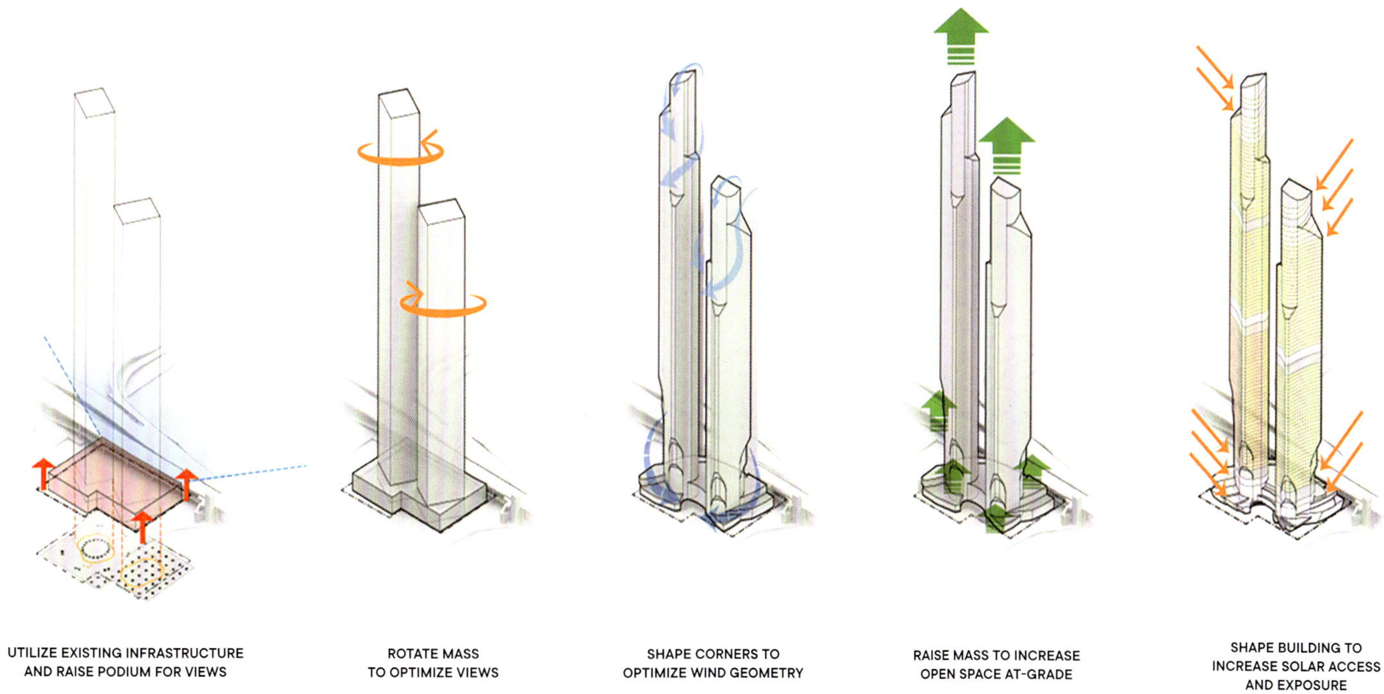
UTILIZE EXISTING INFRASTRUCTURE
AND RAISE PODIUM FOR VIEWS
ROTATE MASS
TO OPTIMIZE VIEWS
SHAPE CORNERS TO
OPTIMIZE WIND GEOMETRY
RAISE MASS TO INCREASE
OPEN SPACE AT-GRADE
SHAPE BUILDING TO
INCREASE SOLAR ACCESS
AND EXPOSURE

SITE

The project was designed to become part of a cohesive neighborhood unit with the tower base resembling a park-like setting with welcoming edges that connect neighbors to the Chicago River, Ogden Slip, and DuSable Park, while mitigating perceived impacts of vehicular traffic.

The prominence of the site required a look at the entire master plan vision to determine how connections to the lakefront park system and the Chicago Riverwalk could be achieved.

The setting emulates the Chicago city-in-the-park motto 'Urbs in Horto," translated as City in the Garden. The expression encourages city residents to rethink the way that people live in the city. Although surrounded by concrete, city dwellers are more connected to nature than they might expect. The towers have panoramic lake and river views that connect each unit with its natural surroundings, creating a sense of personal well-being for the residents.

SITE PLAN SKETCH, 2018

The tower is conveniently accessed for arrivals by foot, bike, or car. It also has a clearly demarcated circulation for both apartment and condominium residents. A major design movement was to create an exceptional arrival experience for residents. This was accomplished by raising the tower mass so that the lobbies are elevated above Lake Shore Drive to deliver spacious views of Lake Michigan.

EFFICIENT FLOOR PLATE SIZING = ± 13,000 SF

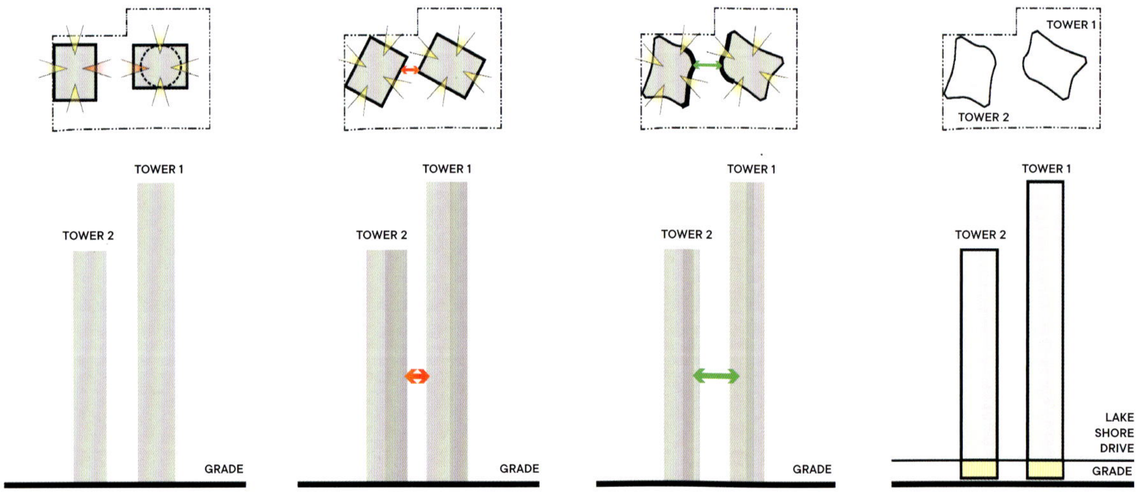

LOCATE TOWER 1 ON EXISTING FOUNDATIONS

ROTATE BUILDINGS TO MAXIMIZE VIEWS

SHAPE BUILDINGS TO MAXIMIZE DISTANCE BETWEEN TOWERS

TOWERS AT-GRADE HAVE ENTRANCES FACING THE UNDERBELLY OF LAKE SHORE DRIVE

PROGRAM

The primarily residential towers have both rental apartments and condominiums. This combination of unit types ensures a diverse resident mix including urban professionals, empty nesters, and families. Low-rise units focus on views of the river, streets, and trees, connecting the user with the energy of the city. Mid-tier units enjoy long views of the lake, river, and skyline that are accentuated with window walls in bay-shaped configurations. Top-tier duplex penthouse condominiums combine luxury, space, and open views to the sky above to create one-of-a-kind, unique living experiences. Penthouse views are punctuated with outdoor terraces that are protected with wind screens to ensure comfortable indoor and outdoor living.

Amenities are designed to be resort-like with a world-class fitness facility, a series of lounges, sports rooms, private dining rooms, a screening room, a technology room, exterior grills and cabanas, private sun decks, pools, and gardens. The amenities are situated in close proximity to views of the river and the city beyond and are tiered for each level of residential living.

Sustainable design strategies enhance the program and occupants comfort including rainfall harvesting and condensate recovery with graywater collection, treatment, and storage. The reclaimed water is used in landscape irrigation and in common areas for toilet flushing. On site water is also be used to facilitate the rejection of heat from the central chilled water plant.

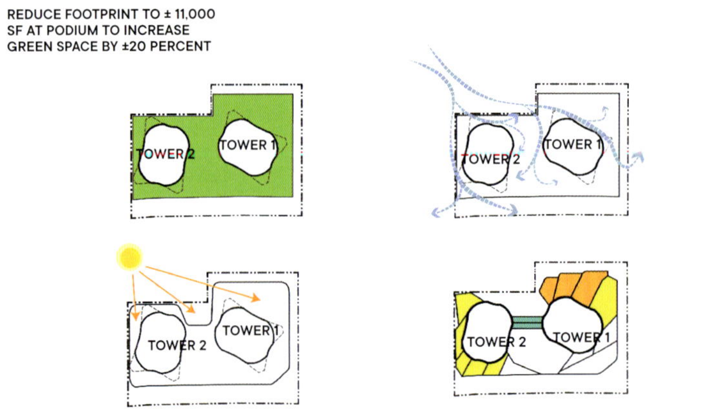

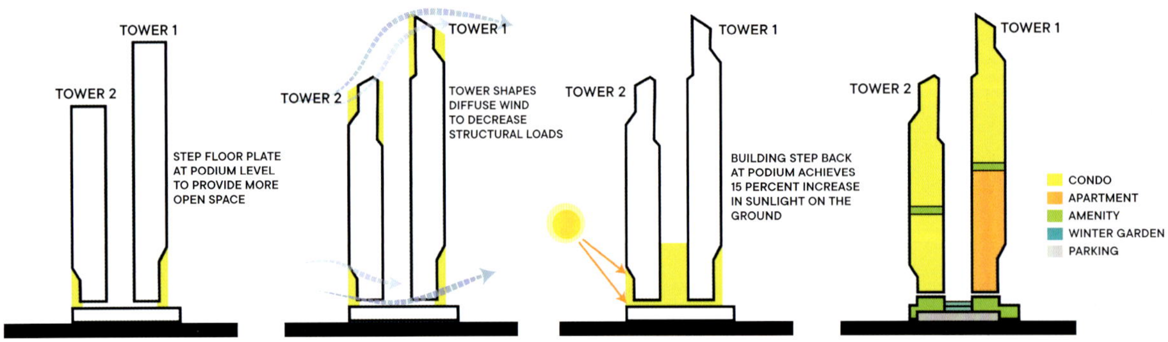

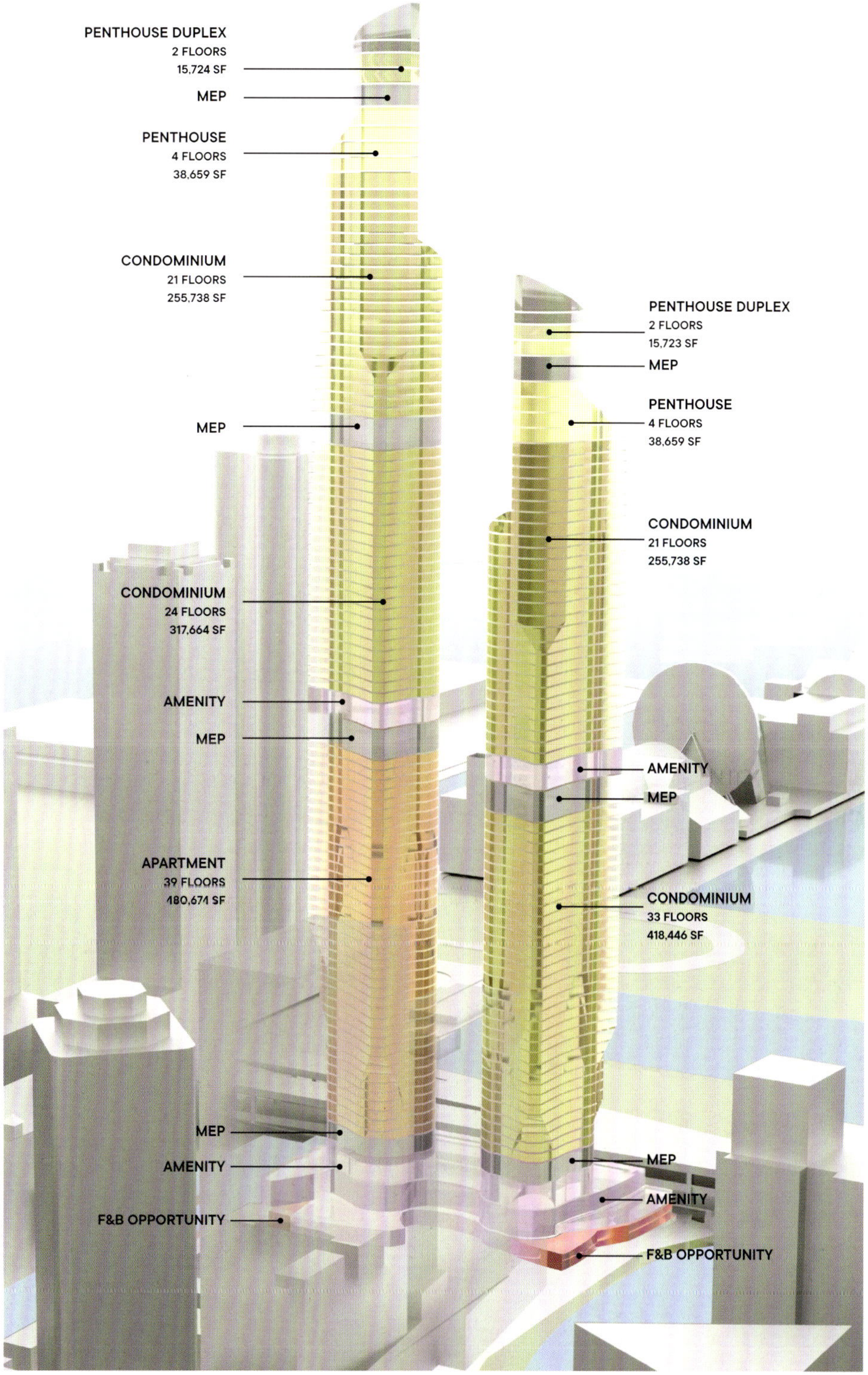
PENTHOUSE DUPLEX
2 FLOORS
15,724 SF
MEP
PENTHOUSE
4 FLOORS
38,659 SF
CONDOMINIUM
21 FLOORS
255,738 SF
MEP
CONDOMINIUM
24 FLOORS
317,664 SF
AMENITY
MEP
APARTMENT
39 FLOORS
480,674 SF
MEP
AMENITY
F&B OPPORTUNITY
PENTHOUSE DUPLEX
2 FLOORS
15,723 SF
MEP
PENTHOUSE
4 FLOORS
38,659 SF
CONDOMINIUM
21 FLOORS
255,738 SF
AMENITY
MEP
CONDOMINIUM
33 FLOORS
418,446 SF
MEP
AMENITY
F&B OPPORTUNITY

PERFORMANCE

THORNTON TOMASETTI, STRUCTURAL ENGINEER

At the outset of the competition the design team understood that wind-tunnel testing was critical to understanding the feasibility of a towers' massing and proposed structural system. RWDI was commissioned to perform two complete High Frequency Force Balance (HFFB) tests on T1 and T2.

Wind-tunnel testing indicates a very significant phenomenon. At their current height, either one of the towers alone would require a Tuned Mass Damper (TMD), however, when both towers are adjacent, neither of them require a TMD. Their wind-dynamic interaction and the shielding they create together mitigates the effects of organized vortex shedding over their height.

The massing of the tower was also studied and the removal of the corners at the base reduces the design forces by 5–10 percent. The softening of the massing edges from the chamfering of the floor plans also is beneficial. It was important to ensure the project could be efficiently realized so the constructability of the dual tower concept was a significant area of study during the competition.

The structure of both towers is comprised of cast-in-place reinforced-concrete walls, coupling beams, and conventionally reinforced—or post-tensioned flat-plate concrete floor framing. The structure contains no outriggers.

Due to the continuous and uninterrupted vertical nature of the shear walls for the tower, a highly efficient jump-form or slip-form system, can be used. Formwork for the floor slabs also can be reused due to the highly repetitive geometry of the tower. The faces of the shear walls are vertical, with the exception of the fin wall ends, which taper to follow the form of the tower.

The asymmetric starting/stopping of the corners, the chamfering of the corner tips, and the degradation of the massing of the tower top also contributes to the reduction of wind loads due to vortex shedding. Sloped corner columns require reusable temporary steel supports or working platforms until the corner-column ties are installed.

The basement/podium structure and foundation construction utilize top-down and up-down techniques to reduce the construction schedule and minimize the settlements of the adjacent properties.

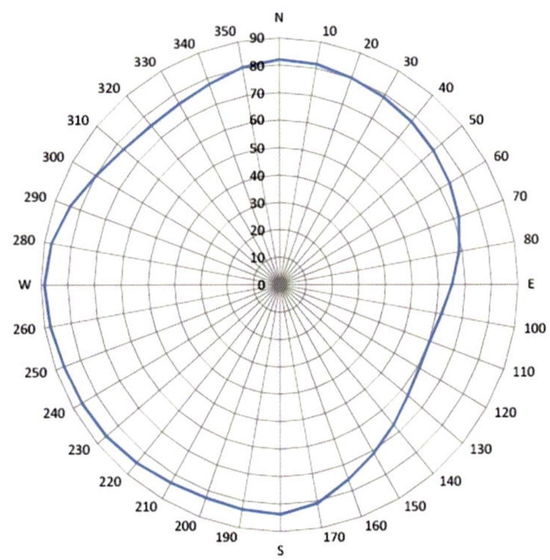

COMMON WINDS

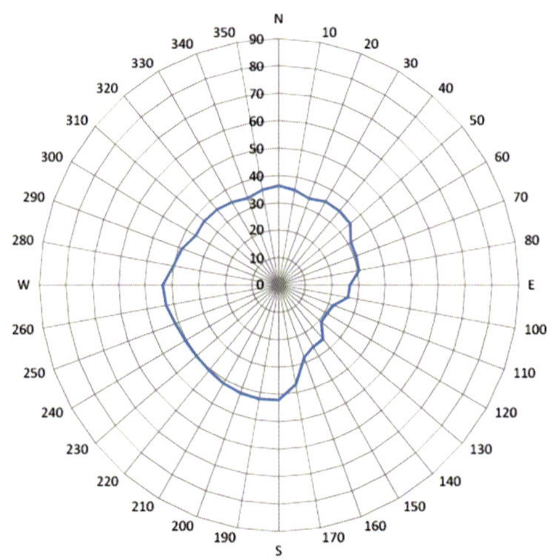

EXTREME WINDS

WIND TUNNEL TESTING

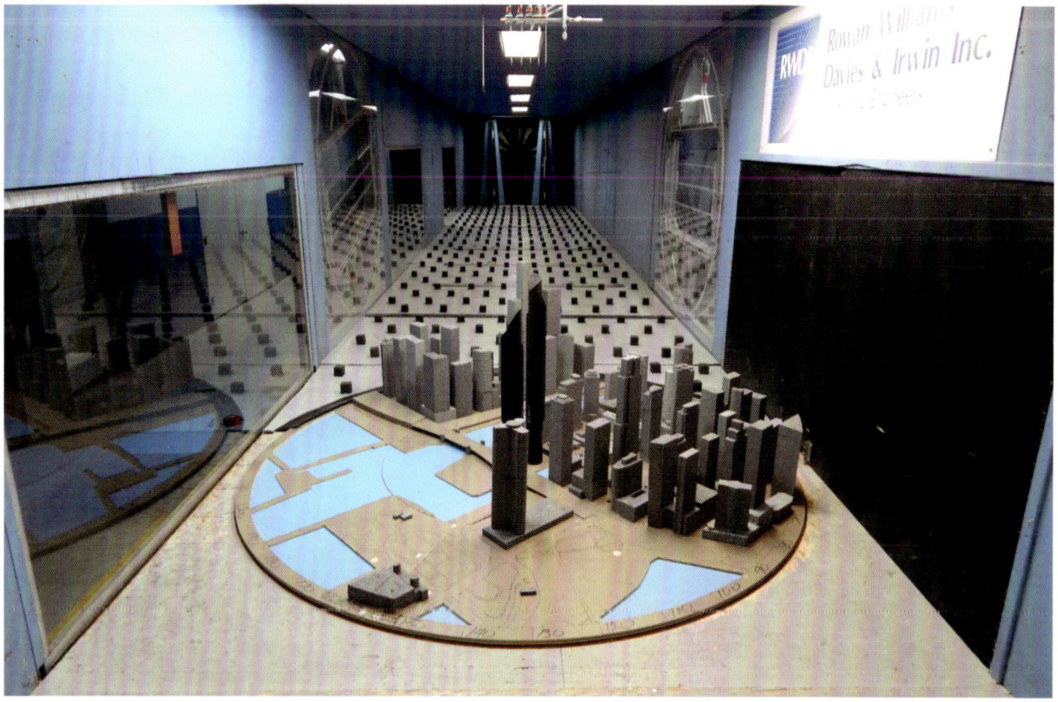

STRUCTURE

THORNTON TOMASETTI, STRUCTURAL ENGINEER

The T1 foundations were designed to utilize the existing rock caissons and existing cofferdam from the previously stalled project. T1 is centered directly in the excavated "hole." Because the tower is centered on the existing ring of 20 rock caissons there is enough strength to resist the gravity and wind-tunnel test loads induced by T1 in both phases. However, the major challenge is transferring the load in the tower structure to the circular ring of foundations. T1 would be one of the only, if not the only, supertall tower that does not have foundations installed directly below the tower superstructure elements, i.e. columns and walls.

The floor construction in T1 and T2 utilizes an 8-inch post-tensioned (PT) flat-plate concrete system, typical, where the PT steel is predominately used for minimizing slab deflections. Typical unsupported spans in both towers range from 25–28 ft. Slab cambering reduces the long-term vertical deflection.

DESIGN SKETCH, 2018

Fin walls provide additional efficiencies in the towers' floor framing by providing additional restraint in the slabs. This additional restraint allows further optimization of the reinforcement, both mild-steel reinforcing bar and post-tensioning steel.

At the penthouse levels, a 9-inch flat-plate, conventionally reinforced, concrete system allows for future flexibility. As the tower rises, the structure grows outwards at the corners of the massing.

These corners are structured by the installation of sloped reinforced-concrete columns. The slopes occur over two to three stories to keep the column vertically manageable and constructible. The slope on these columns creates a horizontal force outward that is restrained at the floor where the kink in the column occurs. This force is manageable, as a series of in-floor beams provide restraint by utilizing high-strength steel ties that are attached to the core.

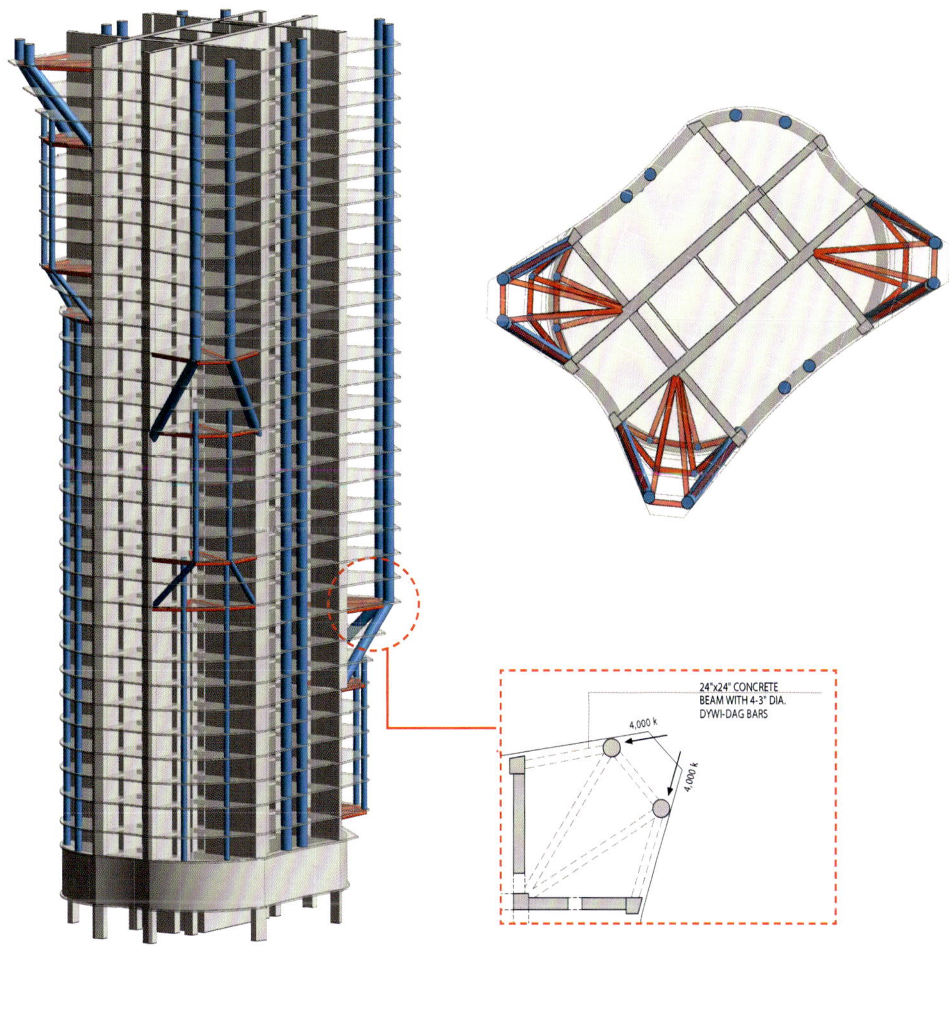

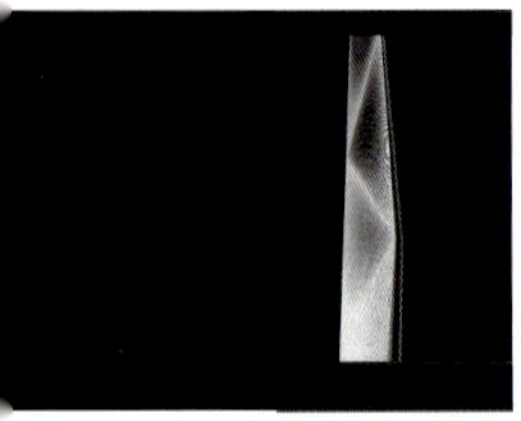

SKY SAIL

SUZHOU, CHINA, 2012

718M

Sky Sail was designed to be a self-sustaining, integrated, and intelligent structure that combines optimal performance with aesthetic beauty. Design considerations included cultural and contextual inspiration, views, thermal comfort, daylighting, and wind behavior.

Like a sailboat pushed across the early morning water by a slow breeze, Sky Sail tapers as it rises to meet the oncoming wind.

The building was designed as a symbol of Suzhou's relationship to the water, a testament to the new commercial and economic force amid the waters of the Yangtze River Delta.

Sky Sail, was inspired by the traditional sailboats that have moved through the waterways within Suzhou for centuries. The design takes the cultural heritage of the classic sailboat and reinterprets it for the 21st-century as a performance-driven tower.

+ SITE
+ PROGRAM
+ PERFORMANCE
+ FACADE
+ CROWN
+ RESEARCH + DEVELOPMENT
+ STRUCTURE

NORTH WITH RESIDENTIAL

WEST WITH HOTEL

PROGRAM

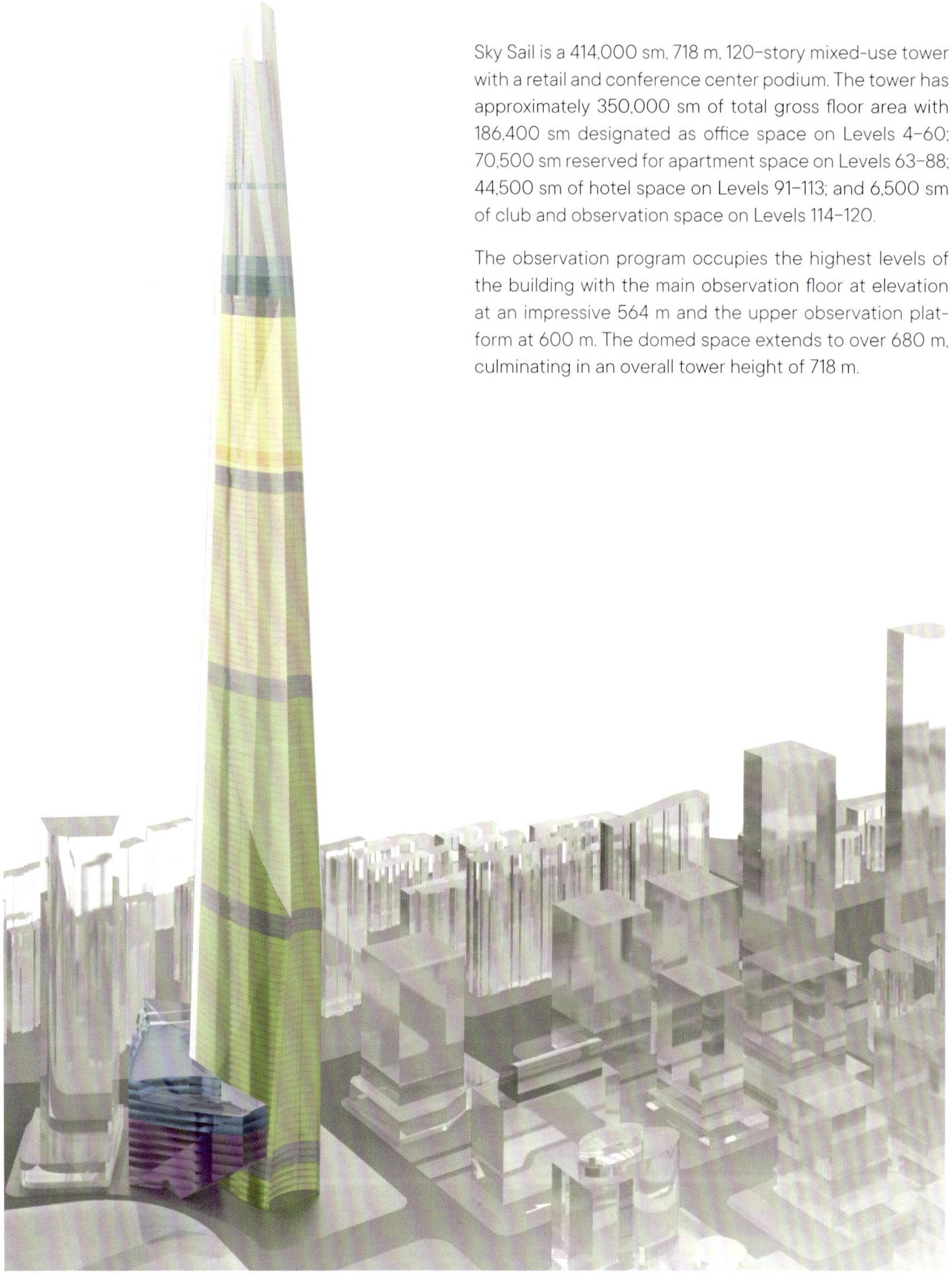

Sky Sail is a 414,000 sm, 718 m, 120-story mixed-use tower with a retail and conference center podium. The tower has approximately 350,000 sm of total gross floor area with 186,400 sm designated as office space on Levels 4–60; 70,500 sm reserved for apartment space on Levels 63–88; 44,500 sm of hotel space on Levels 91–113; and 6,500 sm of club and observation space on Levels 114–120.

The observation program occupies the highest levels of the building with the main observation floor at elevation at an impressive 564 m and the upper observation platform at 600 m. The domed space extends to over 680 m, culminating in an overall tower height of 718 m.

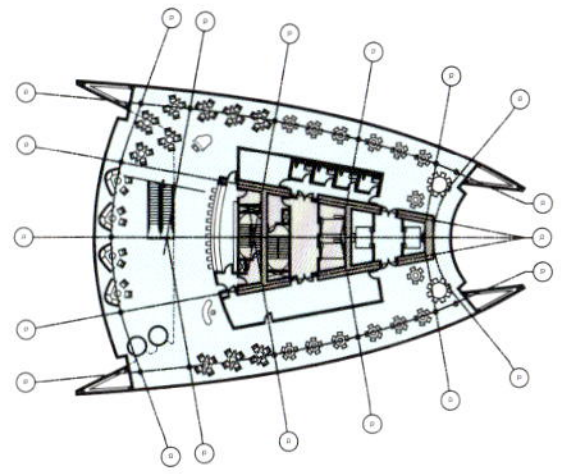

OBSERVATION

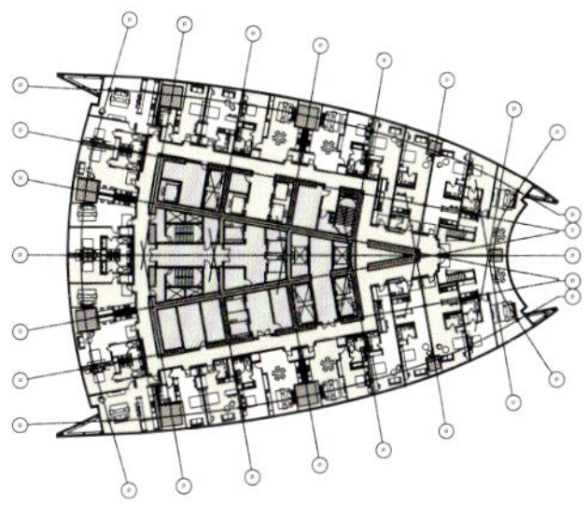

TYPICAL APARTMENT

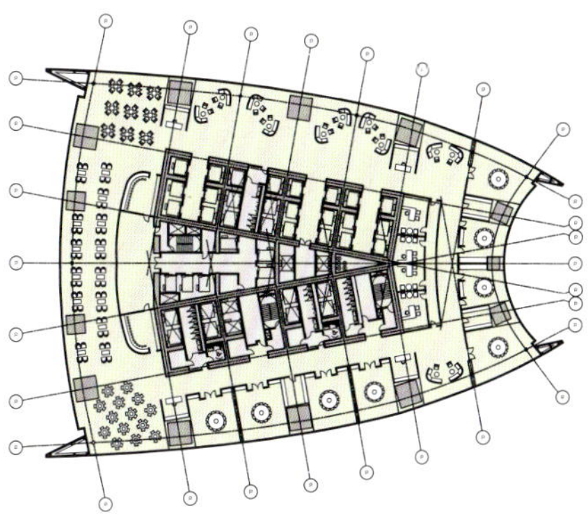

TYPICAL OFFICE

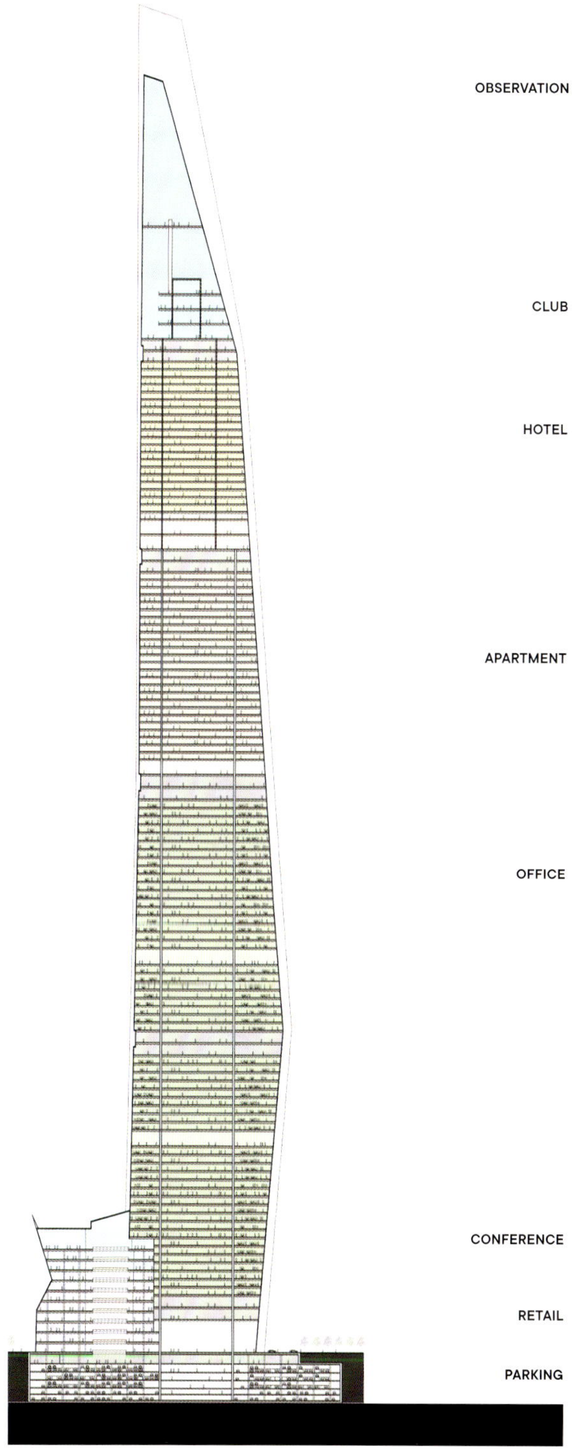

PERFORMANCE

There are several features that limit the impact of the wind on the overall structure, including a tapering form, a textured facade to break up the vortex shedding, and a wind slot at the top that allows for air to pass over the building.

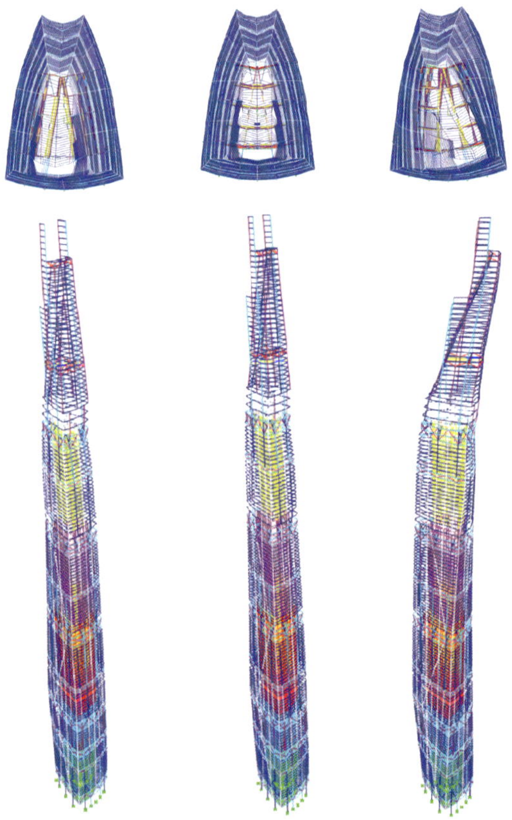

MODE 1
X TRANSLATION
T1 = 9.56S

MODE 2
Y TRANSLATION
T2 = 8.20S

MODE 3
Z TORSION
T3 = 4.26S

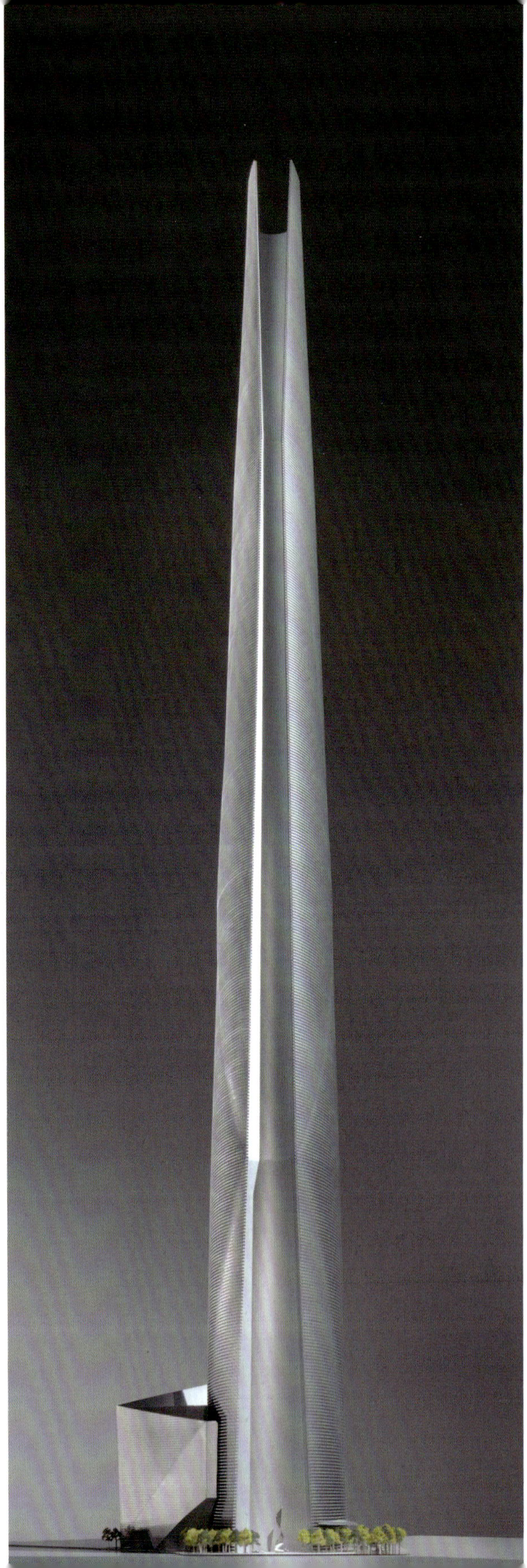

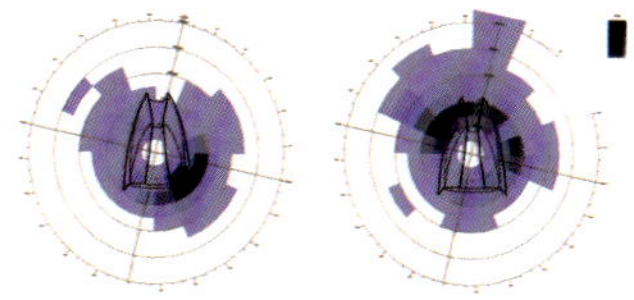

SUMMER AND WINTER
SITE WIND ROSE

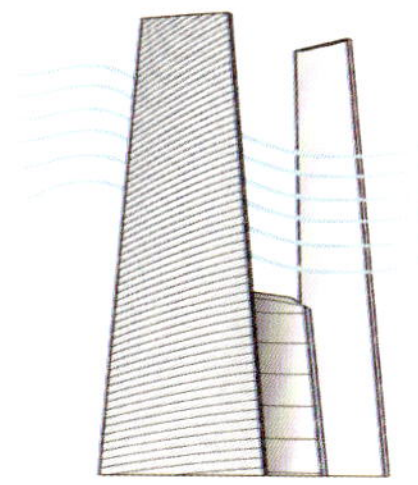

TOWER TOP
WIND LOADING

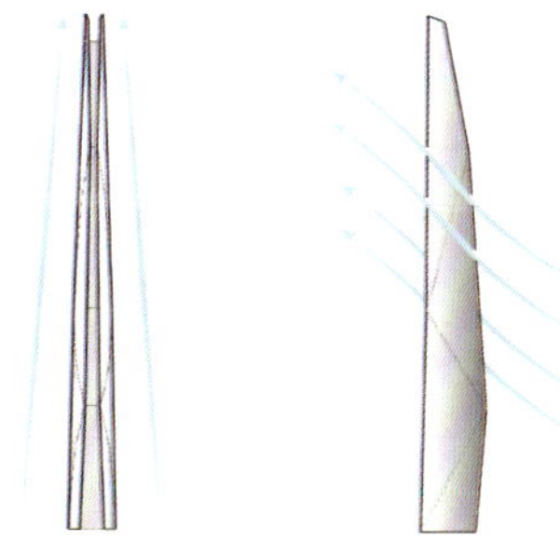

TOWER WIND
EXPOSURE ELEVATION

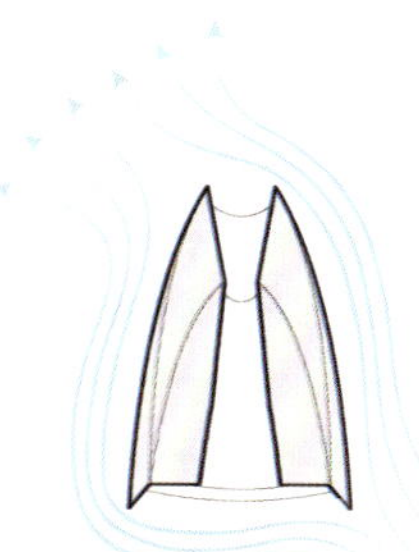

TOWER WIND
EXPOSURE PLAN

FACADE

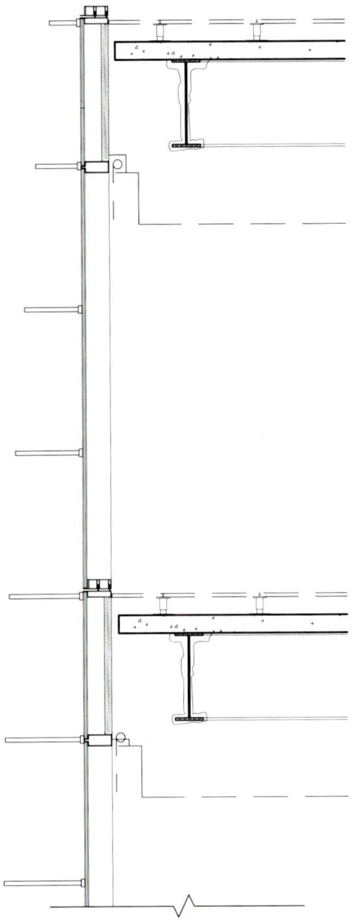

EXTERIOR WALL SHADING SYSTEM

CROWN

Supertall buildings have the unique opportunity to provide the occupants and visitors a view of the city from a new vantage point. One of the team's major goals was to design a form that maximized views without compromising the thermal performance of the building. This was achieved by creating a north-pointing triangular form, which gives the observation area uninterrupted views while minimizing the direct solar exposure to the east and west.

The observation zone is envisioned as a public space that is accessed by a glass elevator and rises to 600 m. At this height, Sky Sail's most significant views look east to Jinji Lake and west to the Suzhou's Old City.

RESEARCH + DEVELOPMENT

This project used parametric design to optimize the form based on several variables which contributed to the analysis by the design team. Inputs included solar radiation, wind, orientation, and views. The form was found with the help of an algorithm which was developed to optimize its performance.

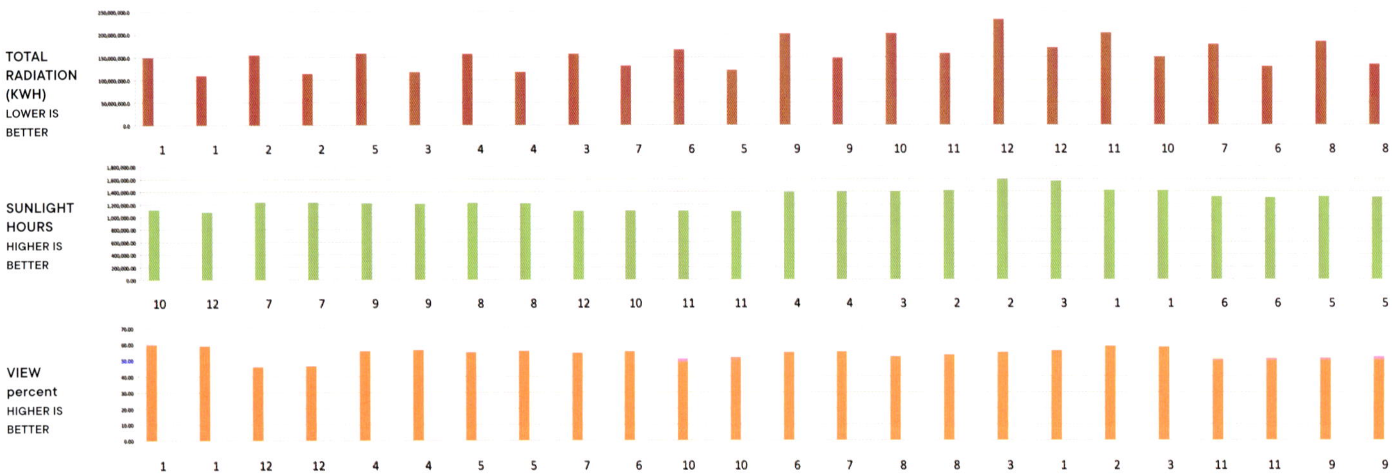

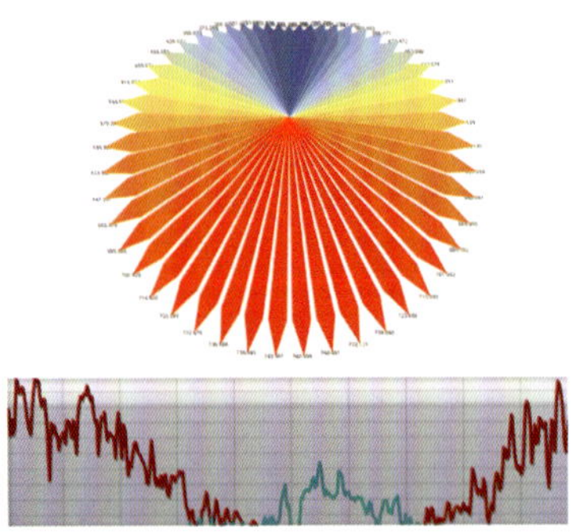

ANNUAL RADIATION ROSE

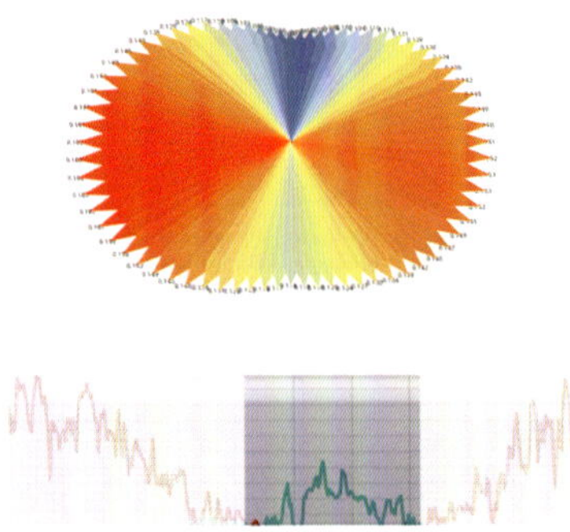

SUMMER RADIATION ROSE

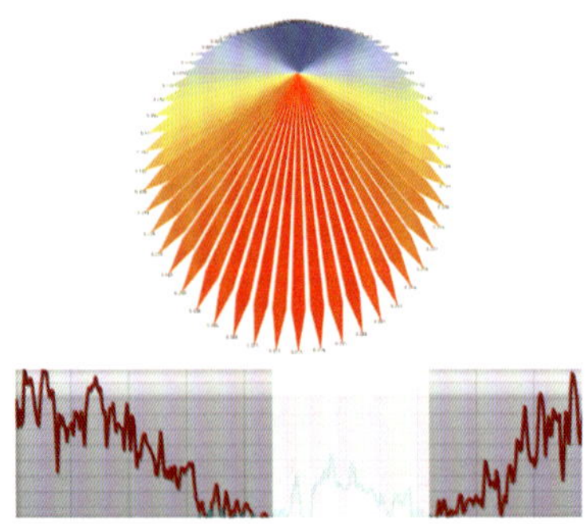

WINTER RADIATION ROSE

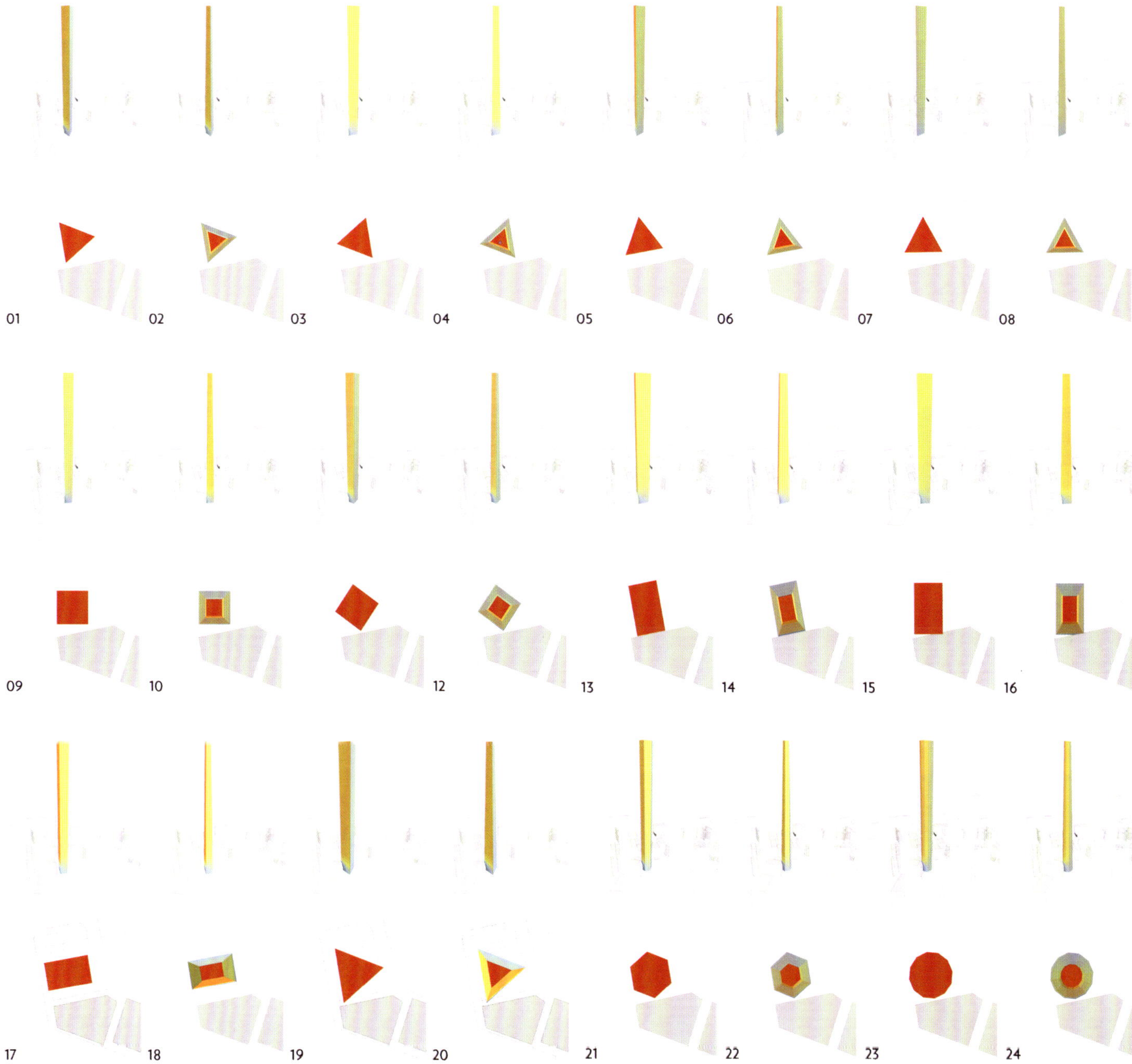
01
02
03
04
05
06
07
08
09
10
12
13
14
15
16
17
18
19
20
21
22
23
24

STRUCTURE

THORNTON TOMASETTI, STRUCTURAL ENGINEER

The tower has a gravity system and lateral system that are not independent of each other. Although some structural members belong to either the gravity system or lateral system, many structural members in this design, like the super columns and core wall, are key components of both the gravity system and lateral system.

The lateral system is a core wall mega braced frame outrigger truss system, suitable for supertall buildings over 300 m. This system is cost effective compared with similar systems and is efficient in resisting lateral loads.

When selecting a lateral system, there are a few architectural constraints and preferences. First, the tower should be a trapezoid shape in plan and the core at the center of the building will house the elevators and MEP spaces, as well as a system of shear walls linking all core structures.

The outrigger truss and belt truss will be effective on limited floors. Additionally, it is possible to avoid large columns at the building's corners. It is also important to reduce the structural beam height on typical office floors.

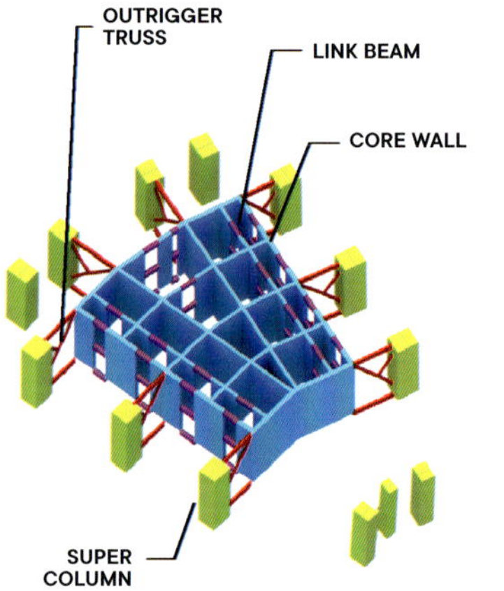

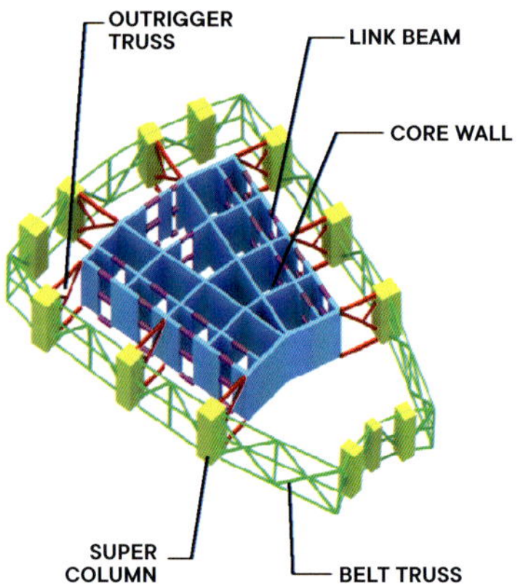

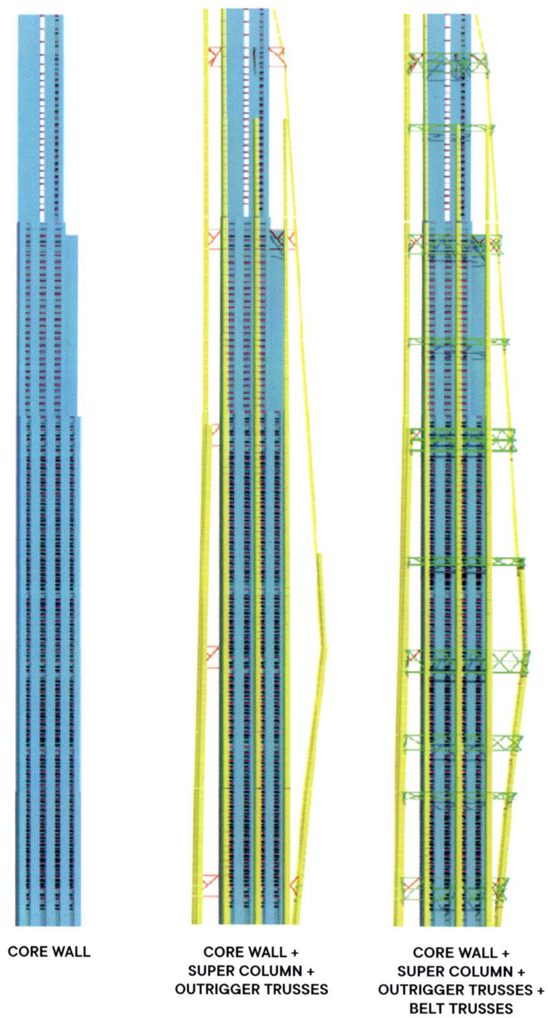

© Thornton Tomasetti

BURJ 2020

DUBAI, UAE, 2014

711M

The Burj 2020 District establishes a 21st century landmark, signifying Dubai's next generation of growth. Anchored by a 700-meter-tall commercial tower, the district is a new southern gateway to the city, as seen from Dubai World Central and Al Maktoum International Airport, as well as the city's approach from Abu Dhabi, Jebel Ali, and the Arabian Gulf.

The Burj 2020 complex will also serve as the southern gateway into the city and the Dubai Multi Commodities Centre Company (DMCC), the client for the project. The goal was to enhance DMCC's global profile as a destination for commodities trading and to set a new standard for Class-A office buildings in Dubai.

The project is intended to be self-sustaining, combining optimal performance with aesthetic beauty; a progressive, environmental complex that integrates advanced technology to enhance the performance of the building. Burj 2020 will be a transformative, iconic addition to Dubai's skyline standing in harmony with the Burj Khalifa on the north side of the city.

+ CONTEXT
+ SITE
+ PROGRAM
+ FORM
+ PERFORMANCE
+ OBSERVATION
+ STRUCTURE

CONTEXT

The design inspiration for the Burj 2020 district reflects DMCC's important trade mission. As a global hub for the flow of highly-valued goods, DMCC is recognized in financial markets as the gateway organization that enables international commerce in the UAE and the Middle East. The trade of diamonds is one of DMCC's most acclaimed successes and is a source of inspiration for the physical design of Burj 2020.

As one of the earth's most precious resources, diamond's are the hardest natural material known to man. They blend beauty with strength to create an enduring value. Like diamonds, beauty, strength, value, and endurance also inspire the design and enable the creation of a landmark district featuring the tower that is now coined "The Dubai Diamond," which once completed will be one of the tallest commercial towers on earth.

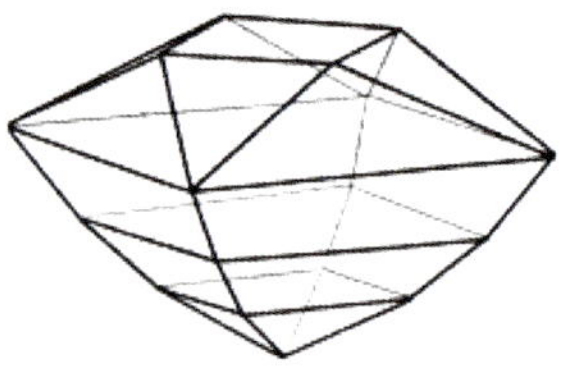

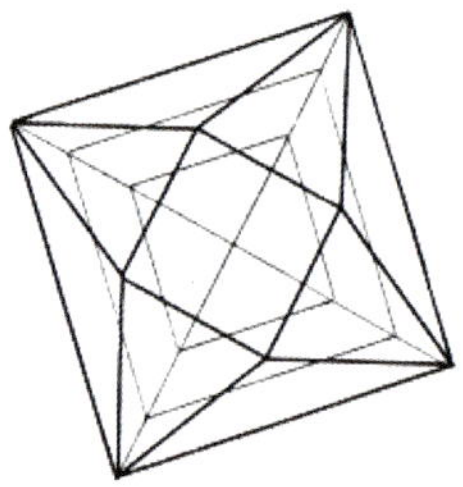

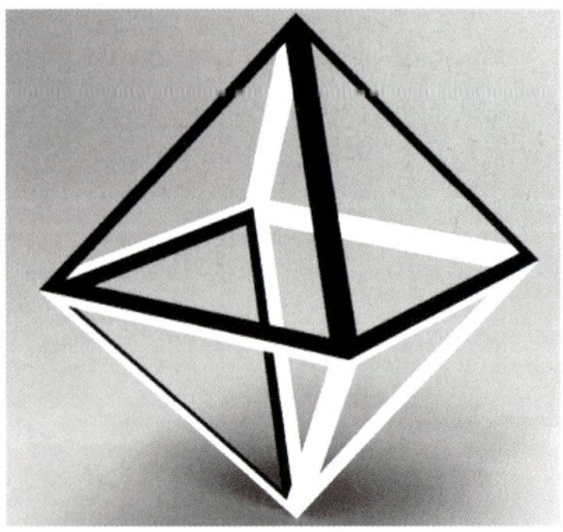

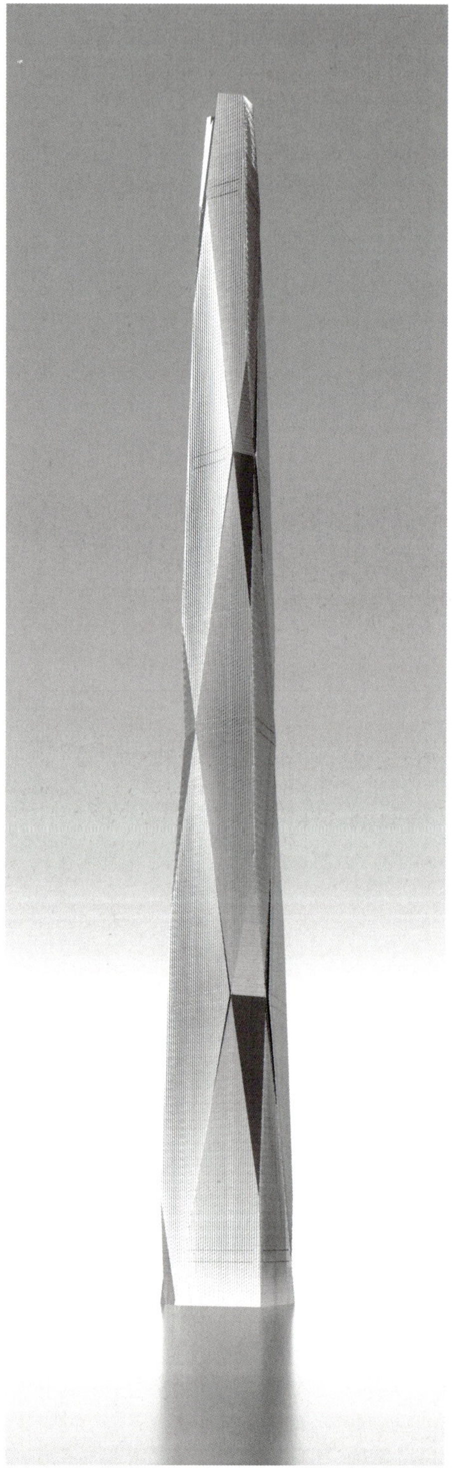

SITE

The site is one of the most commercially viable and visited places in Dubai. The design establishes a dynamic mixed-use environment with state-of-the-art, world-class business accommodations for regional and multinational companies, as well as the DMCC Headquarters. The district will be an optimal setting for trade and enterprise by blending high-quality office space with retail, cultural, entertainment, hotel, and residential functions.

The public realm expands on the site's signature identity, defined as an urban park that integrates landscape, hardscape, water features, and art installations. Other important principles include creating an urban plaza of international significance; providing amenities for multiple uses; creating convenient arrival and drop off sequences, access to parking and other services; and connecting the district to existing public transportation options.

PROGRAM

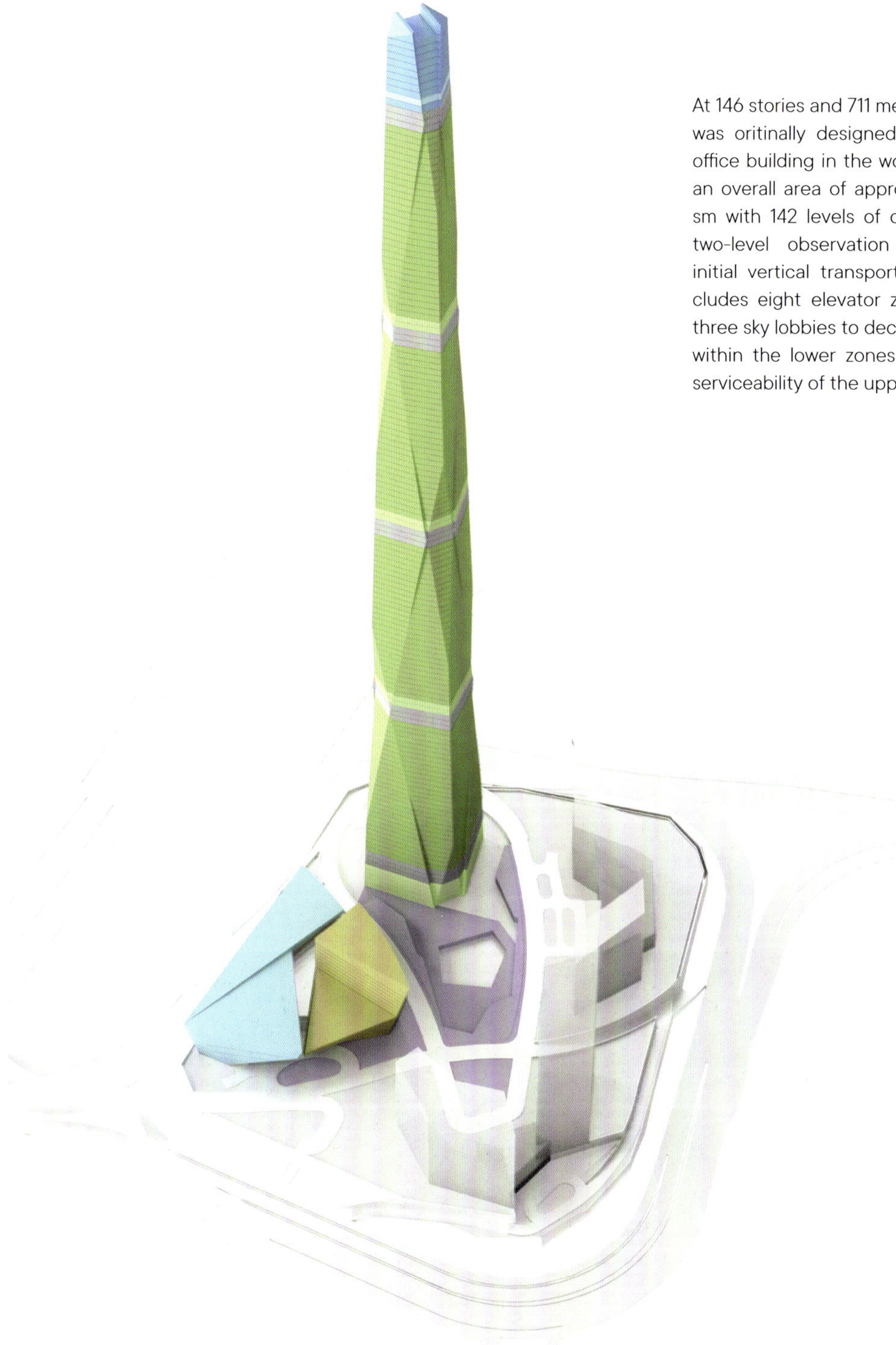

At 146 stories and 711 meters tall, Burj 2020 was oritinally designed to be the tallest office building in the world. The tower has an overall area of approximately 340,000 sm with 142 levels of office space and a two-level observation experience. The initial vertical transportation concept includes eight elevator zones divided with three sky lobbies to decrease the core size within the lower zones and increase the serviceability of the upper office zones.

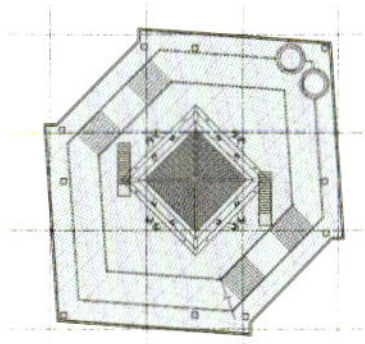

OBSERVATION

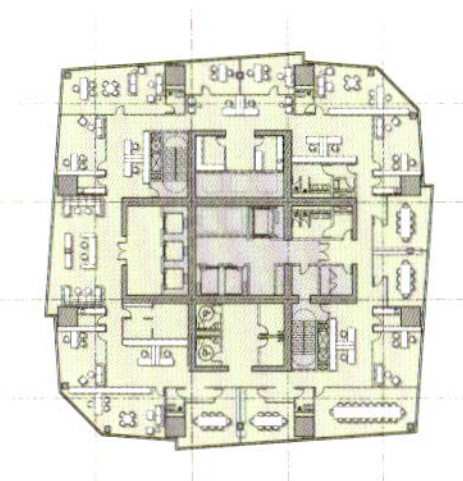

ZONE 7

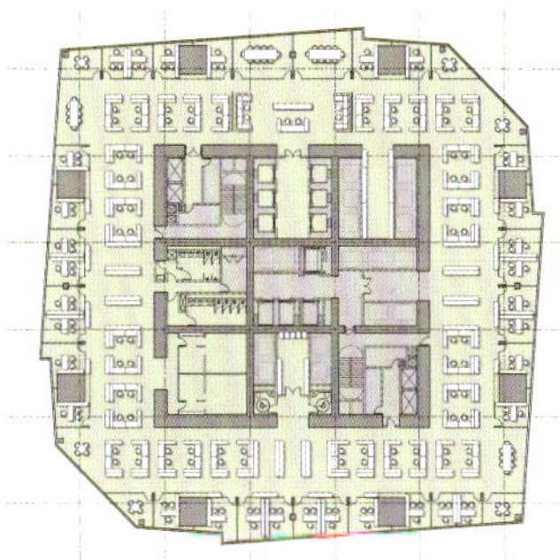

ZONE 3

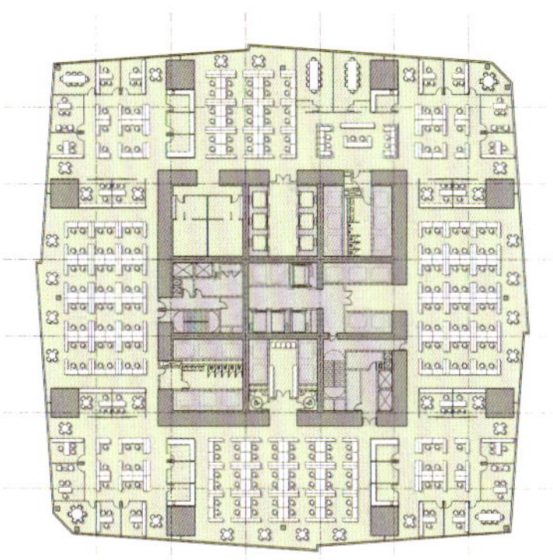

ZONE 1

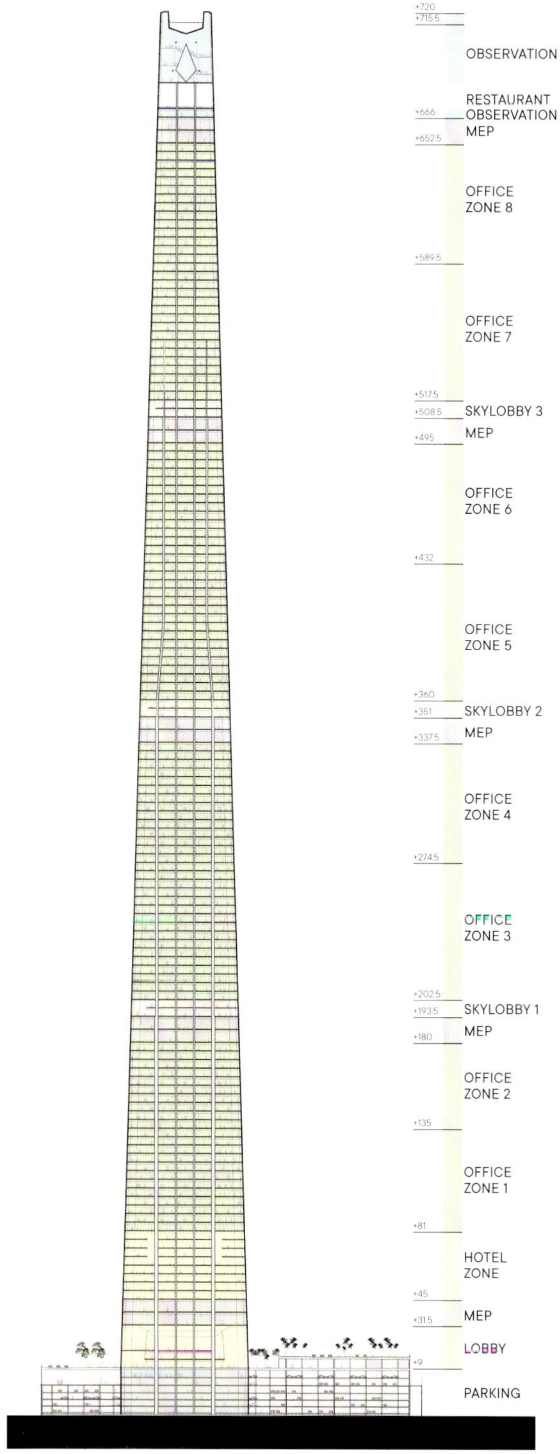

FORM

Burj 2020 is an architectural form that balances efficiency, occupant comfort, and sustainability. The form was developed to be aerodynamic and efficient in its floor plate and in its structure and environmental system performance.

By combining efficiency and comfort with aerodynamic forms, the building is more cost effective, user friendly, and easier to maintain then other buildings of a comparable size and height. Functionally, the building has a square floor plate that maximizes floor efficiency and maintains a standardized lease span throughout each level.

As the building tapers equally from all sides, the core reduces in size, allowing the lease space and efficiencies to be maintained while mitigating or reducing the wind vortices. In supertall buildings, the wind forces and acceleration of movement can be mitigated through tapering, stepping or sloping the tower's sides, and creating irregular corner notches.

Burj 2020's distinct form also responds to the constraints of the site. The building appears slenderer than a rectangular block of the equivalent size. This slimming of its profile toward the base helps maximizes the public realm at the street level.

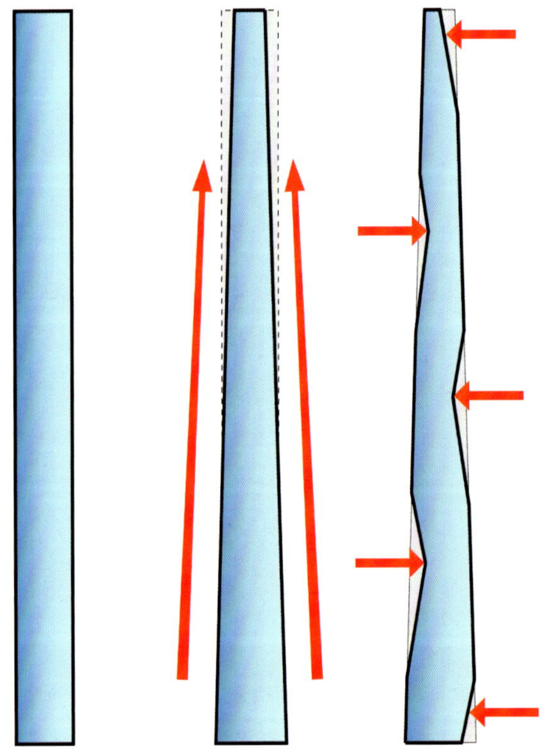

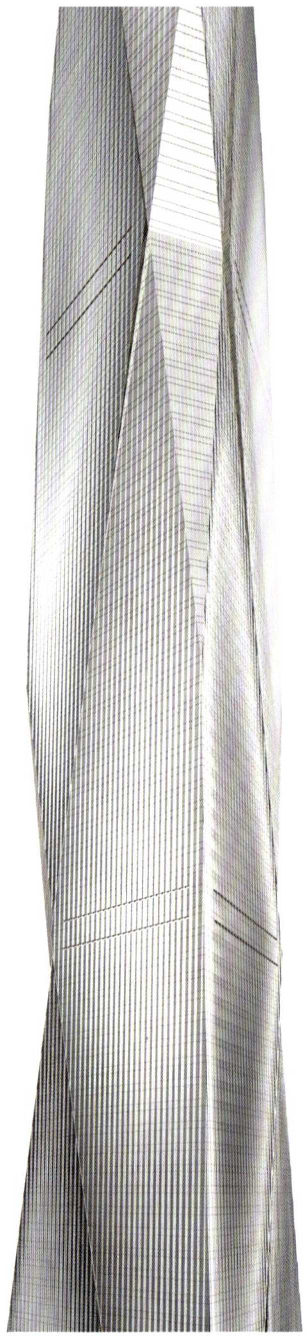

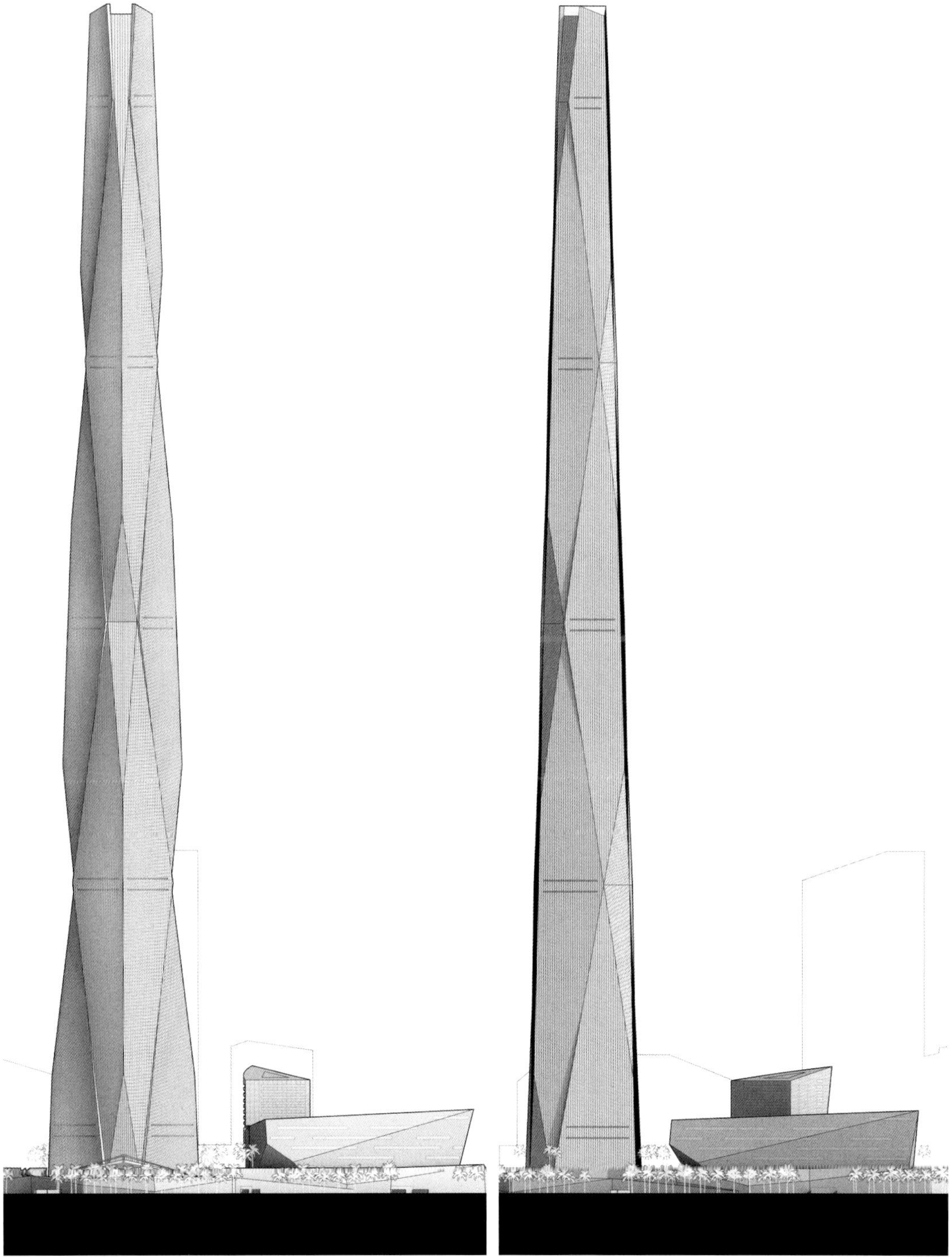

PERFORMANCE

The design of the facade is a key component of the building's high-performance response. It was engineered to reduce heating and cooling loads, control daylighting, reduce the occurrence of glare, and improve thermal comfort for building occupants. The design is based on a 1.5-meter module, the standard module for most modern office buildings.

On the exterior of the building, vertical sunshades protect from harsh solar conditions and help mitigate glare. The sunshades, or vertical fins, also serve an important architectural function by helping emphasize the building's verticality and give the tower a glistening appearance during the early morning and late afternoons.

Daylight is a useful source of visual comfort and energy savings. Using daylighting increases occupants' comfort and productivity while decreasing the energy used by reducing the need for artificial lighting and cooling loads generated by lighting fixtures.

Dubai has intense sunlight throughout the year, with external daylight levels ranging from 75,000–100,000 lux, while the lighting levels required inside the office spaces are 300–2,000 lux. While the vertical shading devices of the building reduce direct sunlight and solar heat gain, the selection of glazing type is crucial to achieve adequate daylight levels and minimize glare potential.

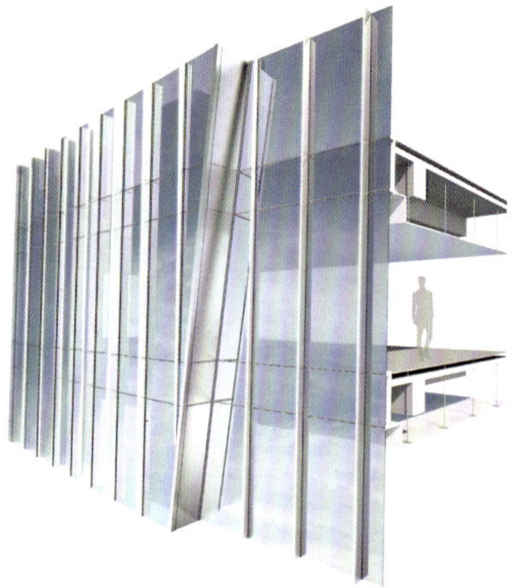

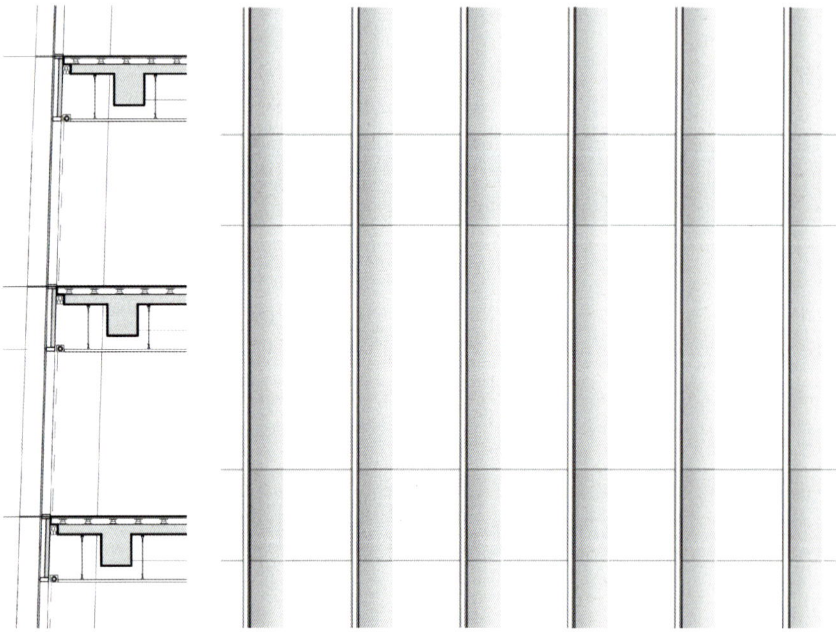

TYPICAL EXTERIOR WALL

PERFORMANCE

An early High Frequency Force Balance (HFFB) wind-tunnel analysis for the tower was studied to evaluate the structural wind loads for following critical items including assessment of the site and Dubai's wind climate, the effects of tapering the tower shape, the effects of notching the tower's shape, the effects of tower rotation on the loads, and the assessment of the tower's peak motions.

The HFFB model tested had two configurations: without corner notches and with corner notches. It was determined that the notches contributed to an approximate 20 percent reduction in wind loading on the tower, in addition to the 75 percent wind-reduction effect of the tapered shape of the tower when compared to a square prism.

Tower rotation sensitivity studies also indicated that the preliminary rotation of the tower is close to the optimal rotation for minimizing wind loading on the tower. The results of the wind-tunnel test indicated that the tower wind forces and motions are dominated by a cross-wind directional response.

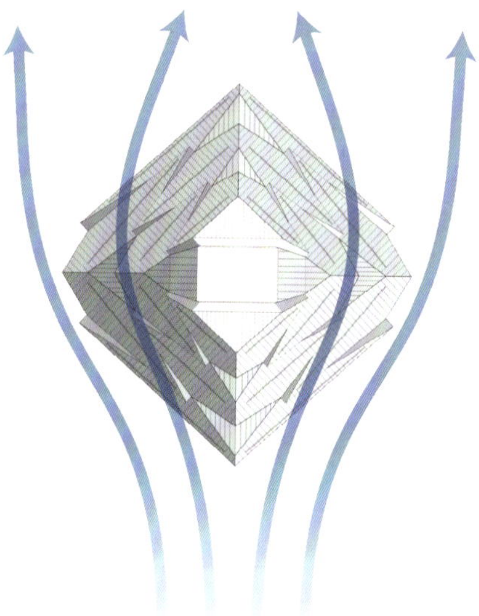

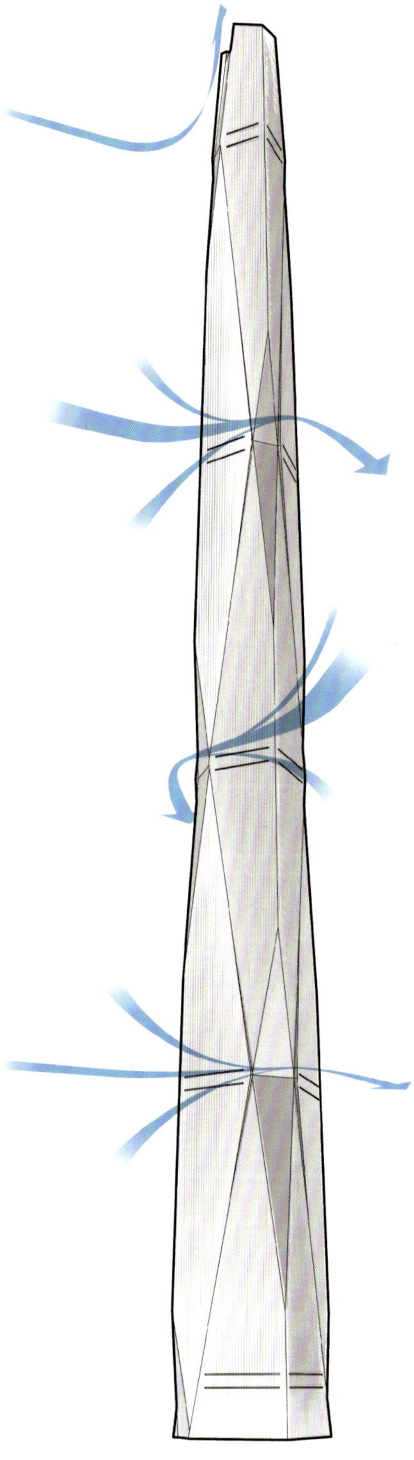

© RWDI

WIND TUNNEL MODEL

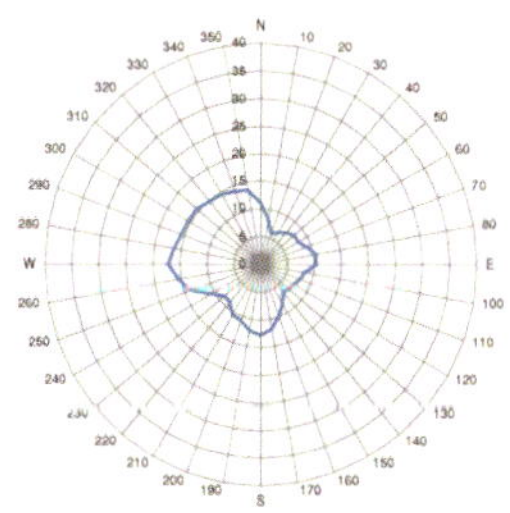

COMMON WINDS

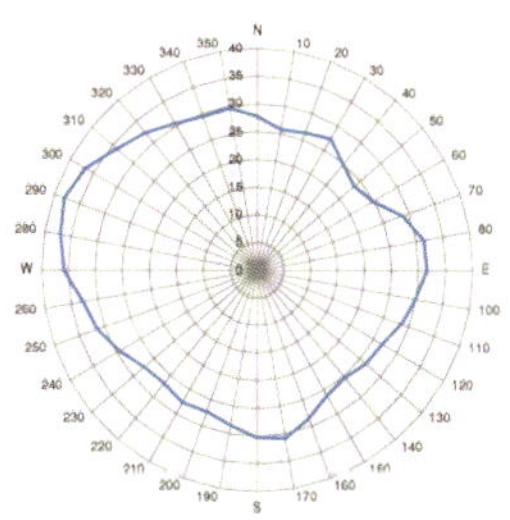

DESIGN WINDS

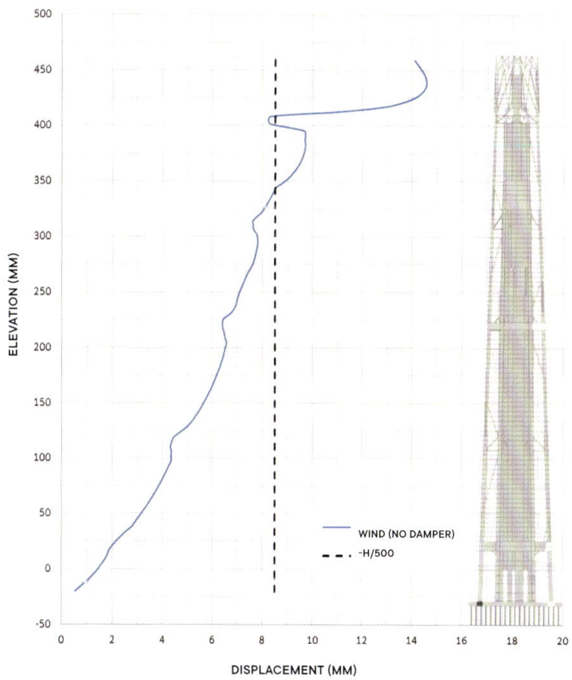

OBSERVATION

The observation experience occupies two levels in the top 50 meters of the tower and several concepts were explored that would maximize the value of the space. Various attractions were considered to capitalize on the tower's title as world's tallest occupied floor as well as the emerging appeal of the observation entertainment experience.

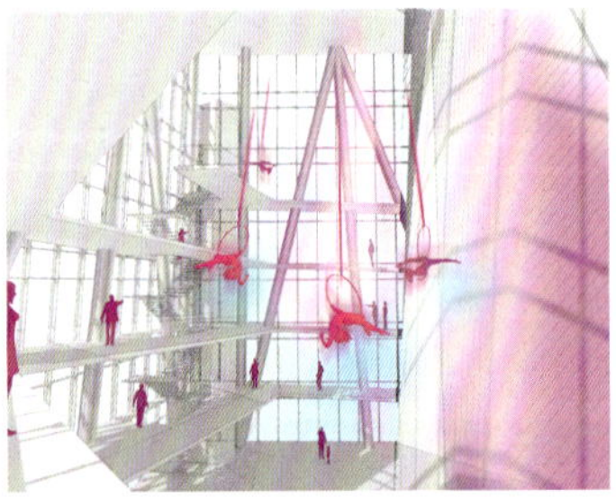

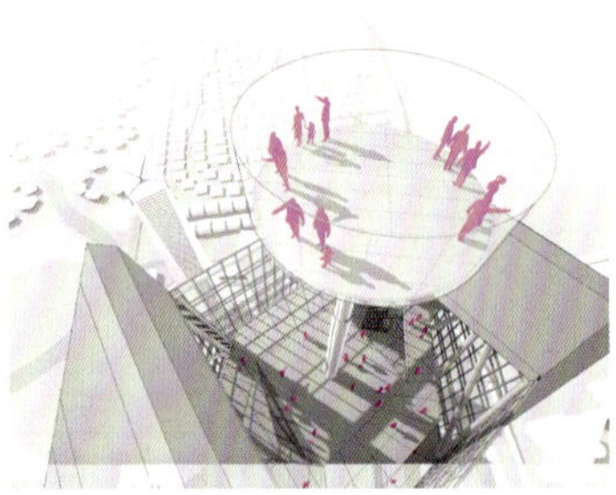

STRUCTURE

THORNTON TOMASETTI, STRUCTURAL ENGINEER

The structural system is comprised of an assembly of concrete elements that address the stringent design requirements of a supertall building, concentrating on the tower's strength and stiffness in resisting lateral loading, both wind and seismic. Resistance to lateral load is provided by a reinforced-concrete core that is augmented by eight reinforced-concrete mega columns that are linked to the core with two-story deep reinforced-concrete outriggers and belt walls located at the mechanical levels. The eight columns have a constant linear slope over the full height of the tower, maximizing structural efficiency and constructability.

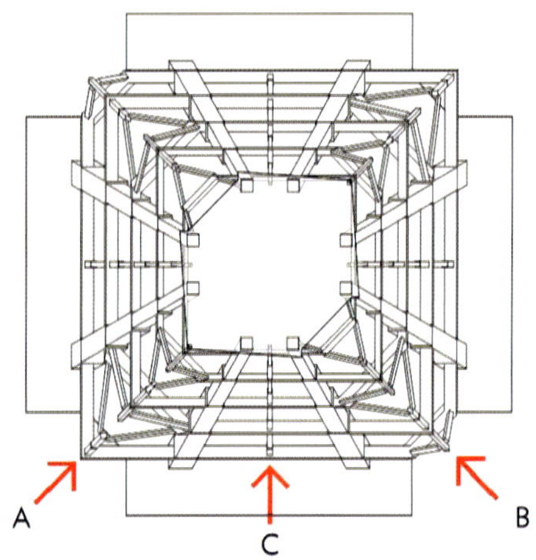

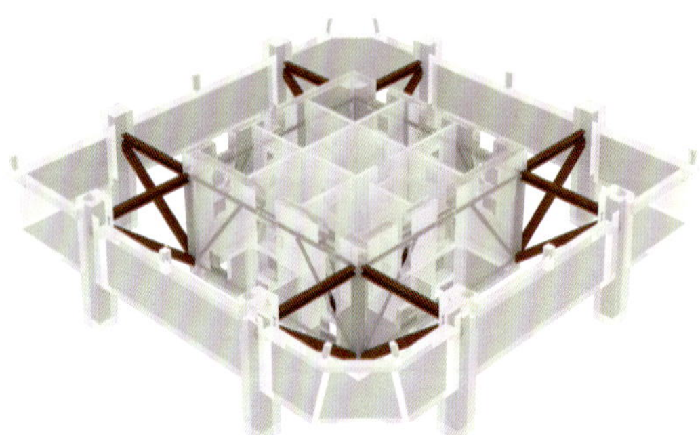

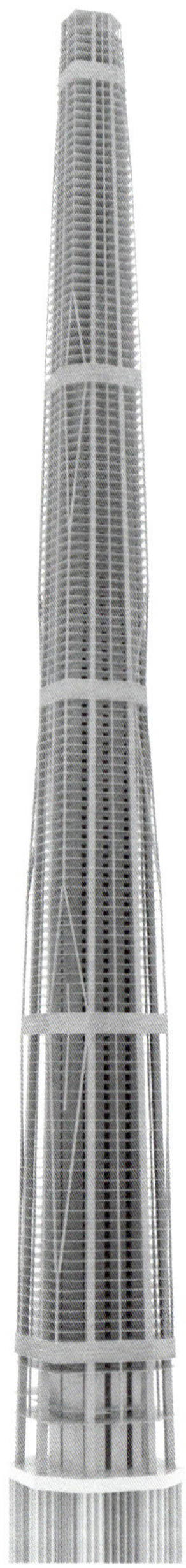

STRUCTURAL REVIT MODEL

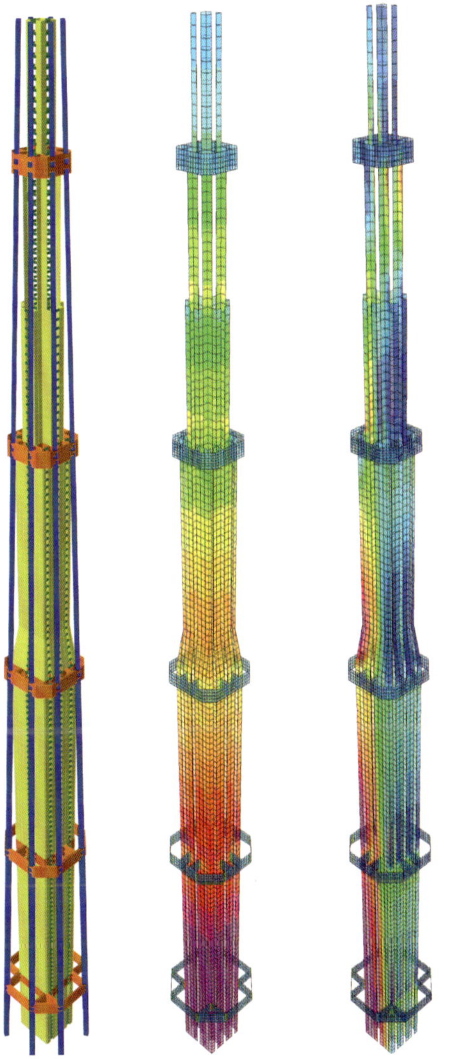

OVERALL MODEL | GRAVITY WALL STRESSES | WIND AND SEISMIC WALL STRESSES

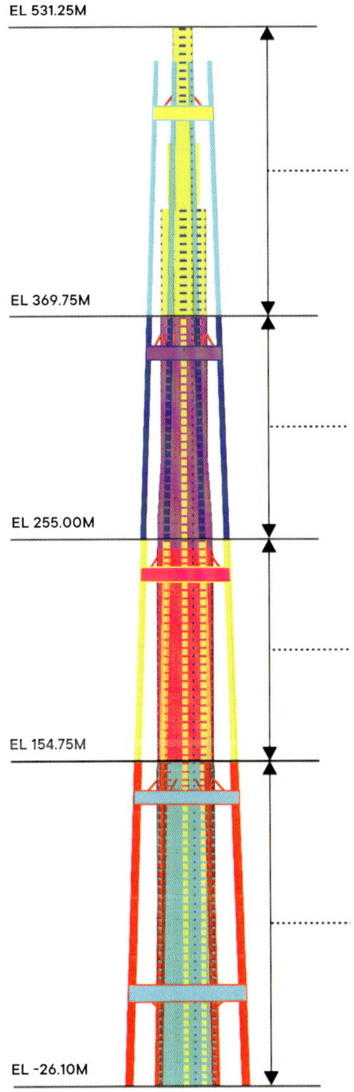

Typical floor-to-floor heights are 4.5 meters throughout the tower program and floor framing is arranged to promote floor-by-floor repetition over each level. Concrete compressive cube strengths required are not expected to exceed 115 MPa, and 60 to 80 MPa at significant heights. Advances in concrete-mix designs and concrete-pumping technology will be brought to place high strength concrete in the upper portions of the tower.

The perimeter belt walls also act as a transfer wall for the secondary columns required along the tower's perimeter. This minimizes the accumulation of load for the secondary columns, keeping their sizes small and helping move the gravity load to the mega columns, which aids in the resistance to lateral overturning forces. The outrigger and perimeter belt walls also provide redundancy for the tower, as it creates a secondary system for column load redistribution.

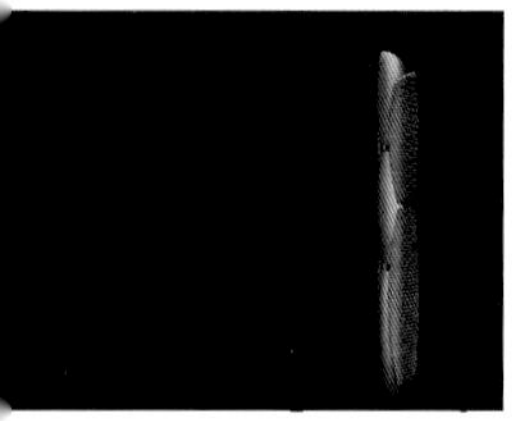

ZA'ABEEL COMMERCIAL TOWER

DUBAI, UAE, 2008

394M

The Za'abeel Commercial Tower is an office building that was designed as part of the conceptual Energy City Master Plan in Dubai.

The main design concept was to achieve a unique circular form that responds to the local environment with solar protection on the south, east, and west sides. The north-facing exterior has a smooth appearance, contrasting with the integrated building PVs on the other sides.

The non-directional shape of the building's footprint provides the design basis for the tower. When extruded, the circle becomes a cylinder, which features the highest volume to surface to area ratio, making it the most efficient building typology to clad.

A structural solution allows the floors to be primarily cantilevered with slender perimeter columns, so the office spaces can be as open as possible.

+ CONTEXT
+ PROGRAM
+ PERFORMANCE
+ STRUCTURE

CONTEXT

Each side of a leaf performs different functions. The top receives the sun's rays for photosynthesis while protecting the light-sensitive underside that is responsible for carbon dioxide uptake. The tower reflects a similar symbiosis.

There is a performative outer shell that receives direct sunlight and converts it into energy with photovoltaic panels that also protects the interior of the building from solar radiation.

The southern "shell" of the tower mimics the protective properties found in nature. Creatures with shells are typically slow-moving or stationary animals that have developed a shell as a safeguard against the elements and/or predators. Buildings are stationary so the development of protective measures becomes an opportunity for innovation.

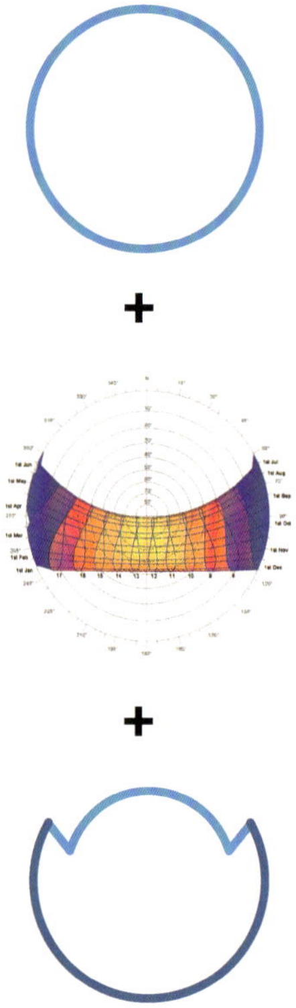

The form's circular shape creates a complex and dynamic relationship to the sun. In a desert climate like Dubai, protection from the sun becomes as critical as conserving energy. The diagram below shows the path of the sun in Dubai from July to December.

To achieve maximum efficiency, the circle is divided into two parts: the southern shell that protects the building from direct solar radiation and the northern face, which protected and therefore allowed for taking full advantage of views without any need for sun-shading devices.

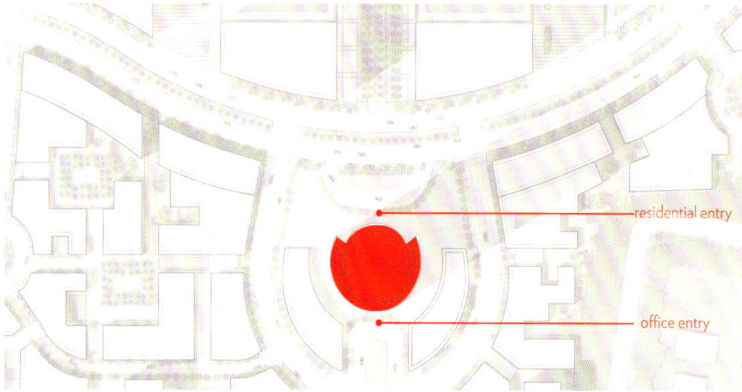

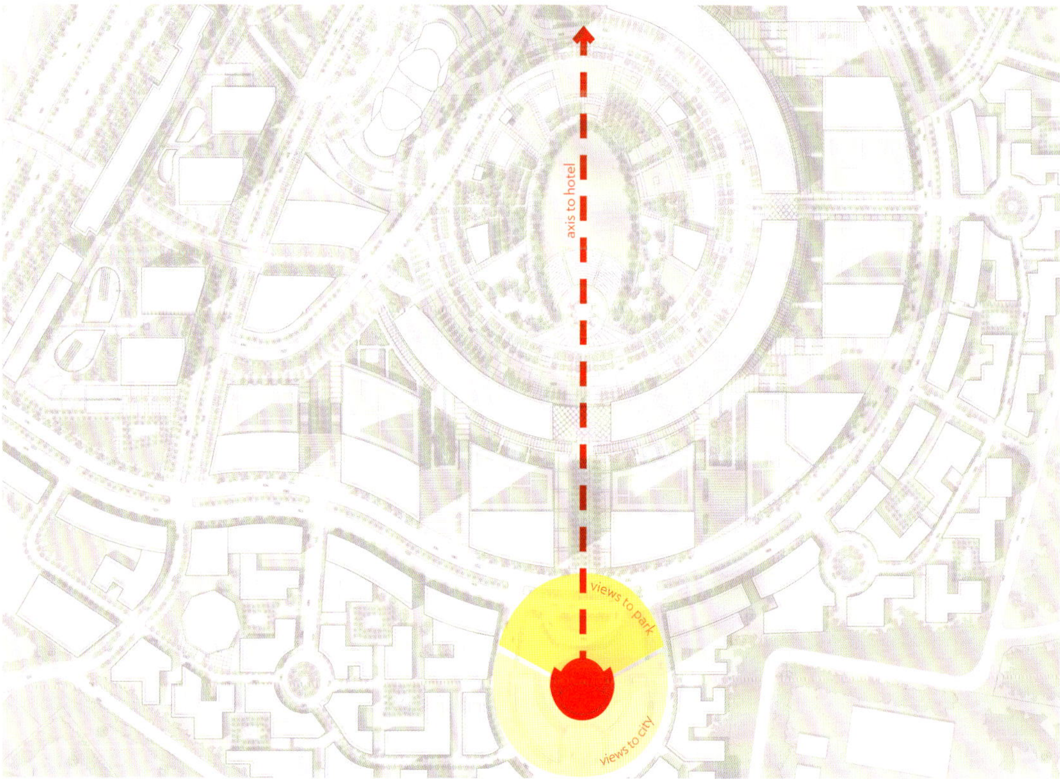

PROGRAM

The mixed-use tower has office spaces on the lower levels and residential floors in the top half of the tower where the massing is smaller. A club area is located at the crown of the building where the massing sets back.

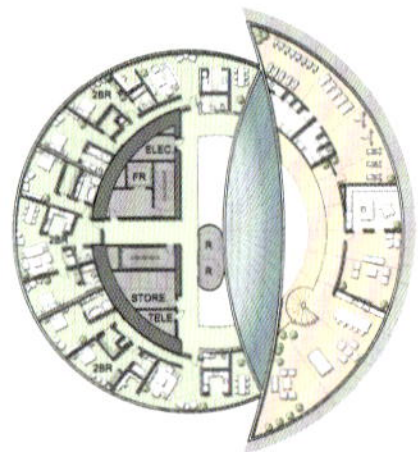

RESIDENTIAL TIER 3

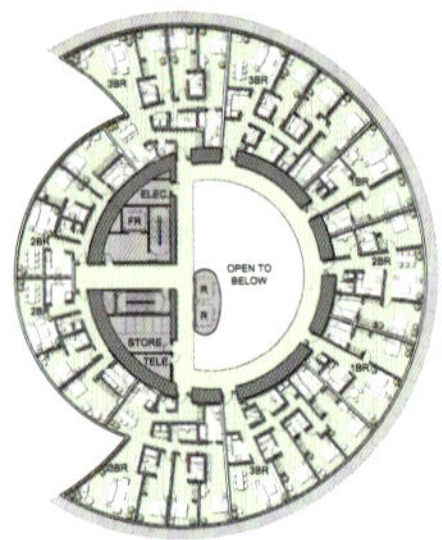

RESIDENTIAL TIER 2

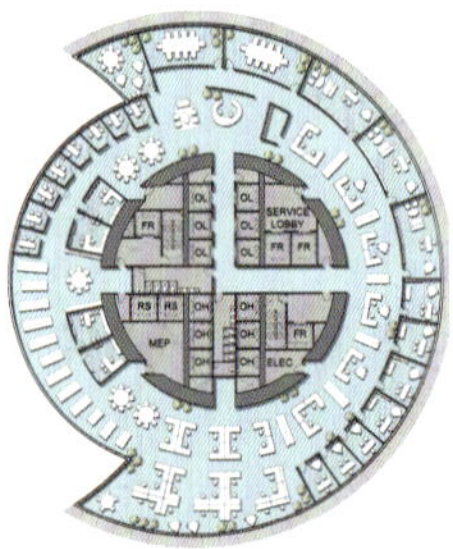

OFFICE TIER 1

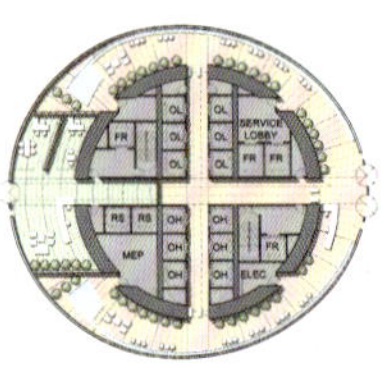

LOBBY

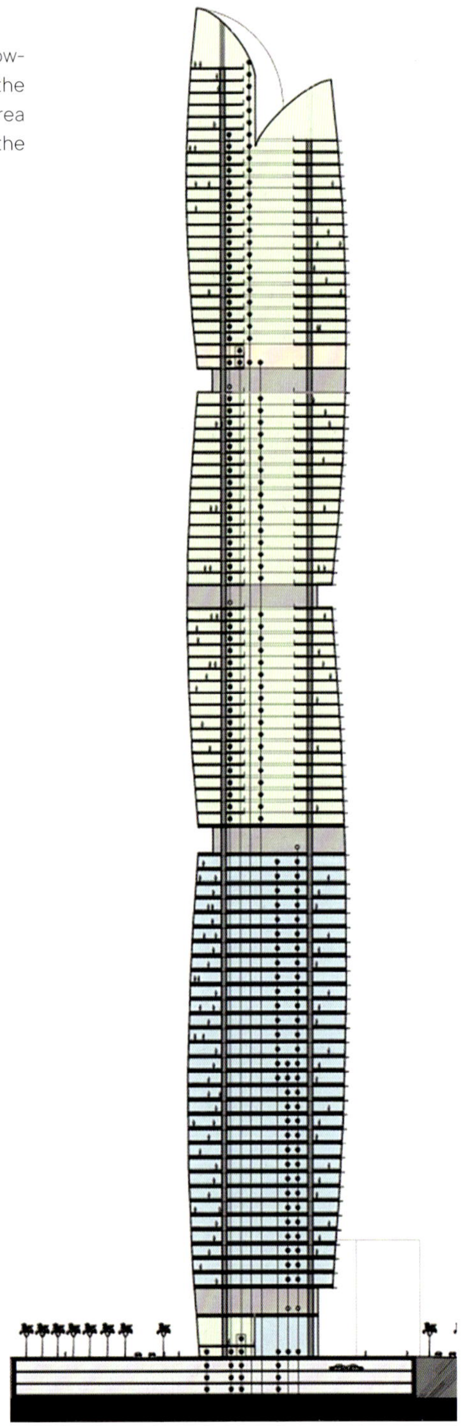

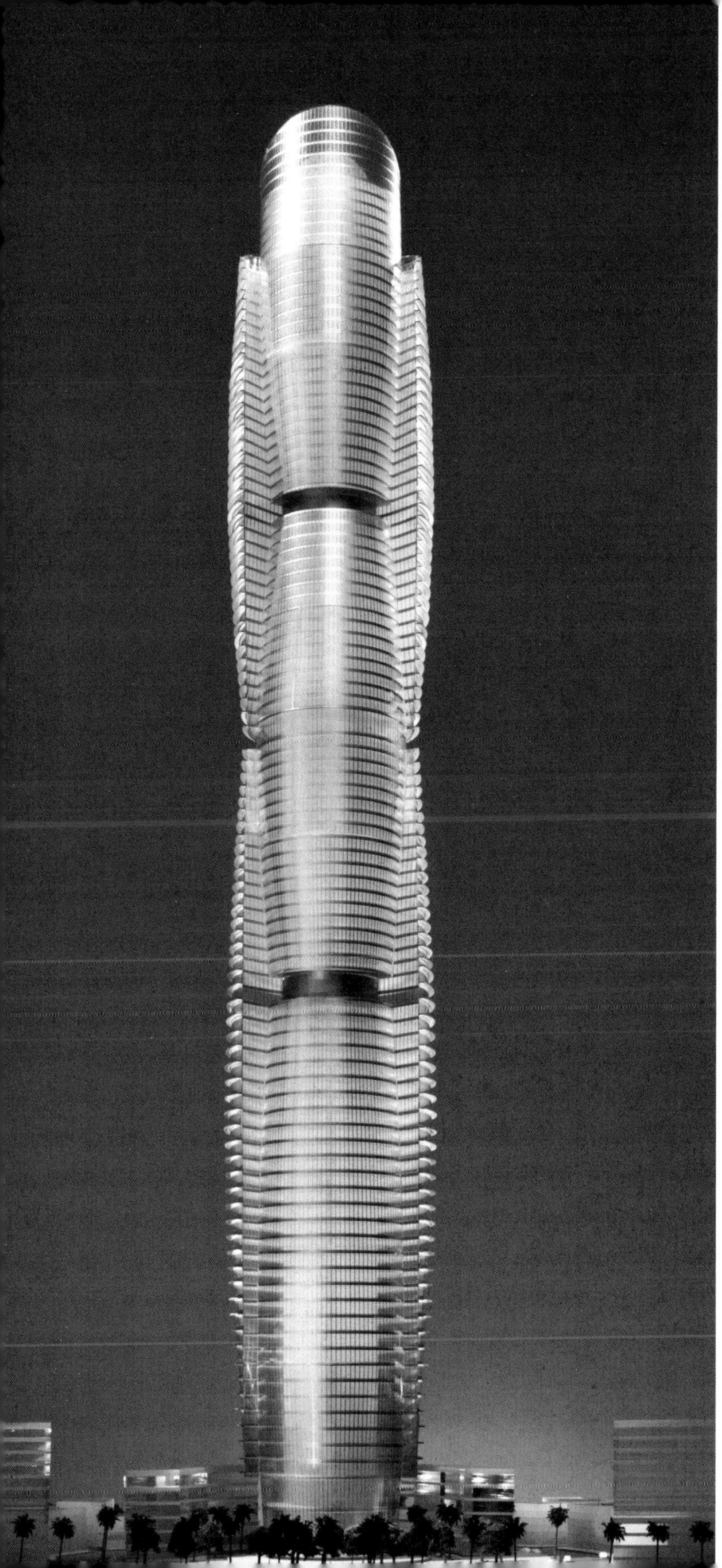
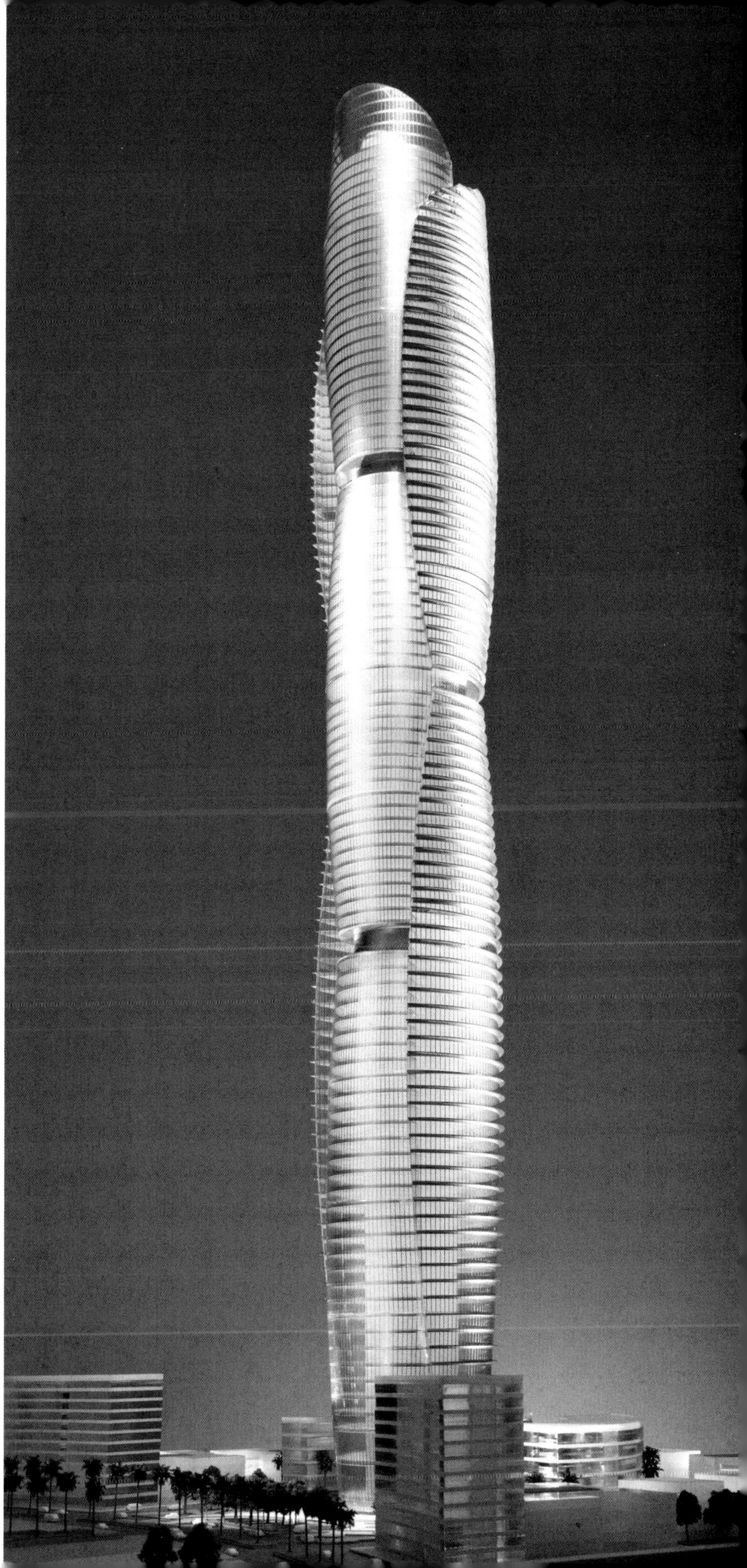

PERFORMANCE

The shading scheme is designed so that solar gain is reduced on the south, east, and west faces of the tower. Horizontal sunshades are also integrated into the facade, optimally tilted to shade occupants and reduce glare. The upper part of these shades have integrated photovoltaics that capture sunlight for energy production. Sunshades are not required on the north side of the tower, which is smooth with breaks at the mechanical floors where the air intakes are expressed.

SOLAR ANALYSIS DIAGRAMS

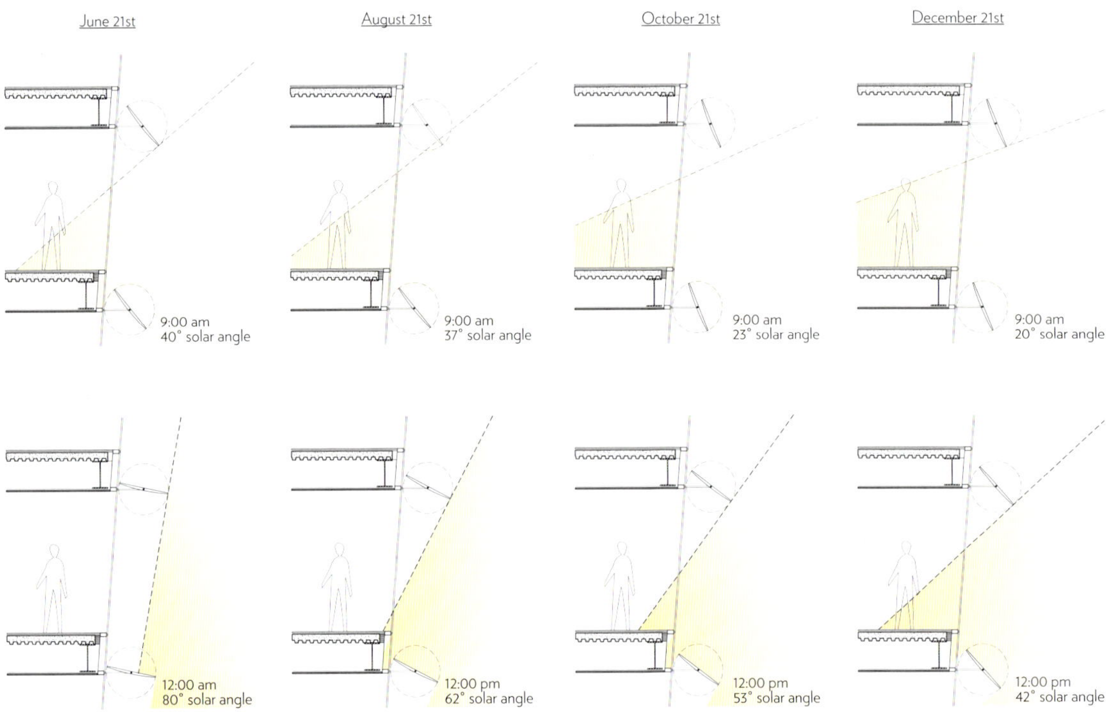

STRUCTURE

THORNTON TOMASETTI, STRUCTURAL ENGINEER

The structural system is an efficient assembly of steel and concrete elements designed to provide the superior versatility and structural performance required to accommodate the tower's unique profile. The centerpiece of the system is a robust concrete core that resists the wind and earthquake loads.

The core also resists gravity loads, allowing the omission of the traditional perimeter columns. Instead, each floor is supported by a series of tapered cantilevered plate girders that extend radially from the core. The length of the cantilevered girders is different at each floor, reflecting the tower's geometry. The contours are easily accommodated because perimeter columns are not utilized.

Typical office and residential floors consist of a composite steel deck with cast-in-place concrete slabs. The deck rests on the structural beams configured in concentric circles about the core, which frame into the tapered girders. Each girder frames into an embedded steel column within the core. Minimal structure is required along the building perimeter because the ends of the girders are tied together with small steel tubes. These slender elements reduce floor vibrations for the comfort of occupants. It is anticipated that a piled raft foundation system will support the core wall.

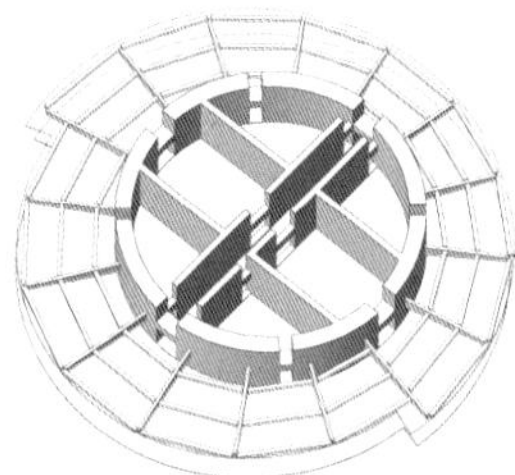

TYPICAL FLOOR FRAMING

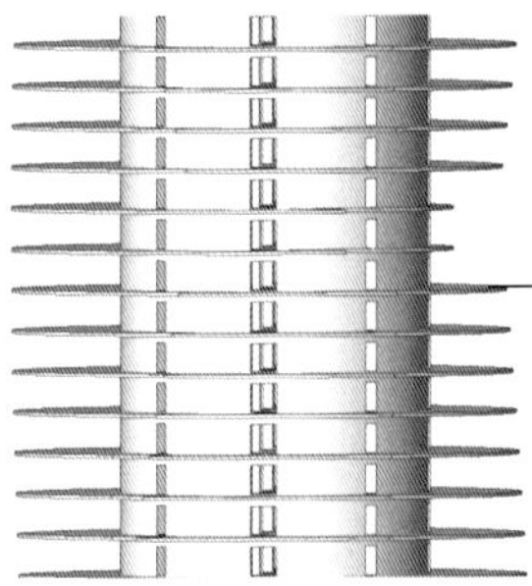

SLAB EDGES AT PROFILE SETBACK

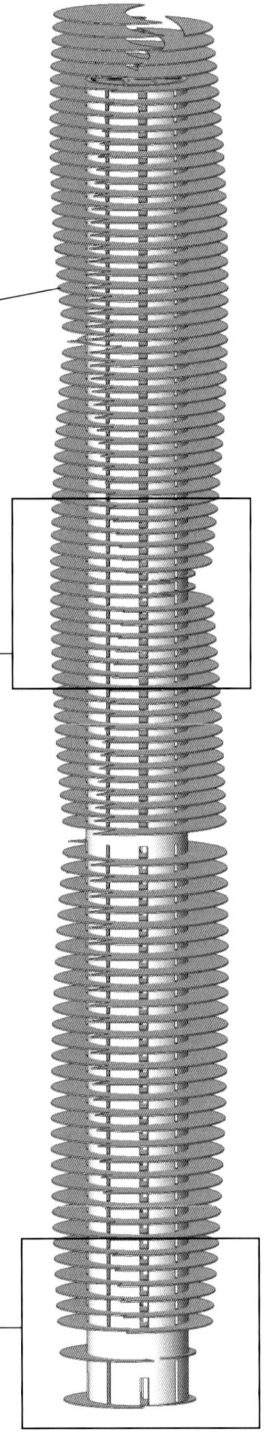

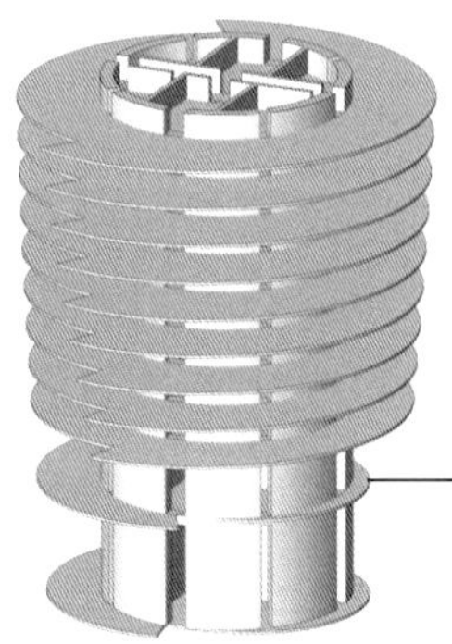

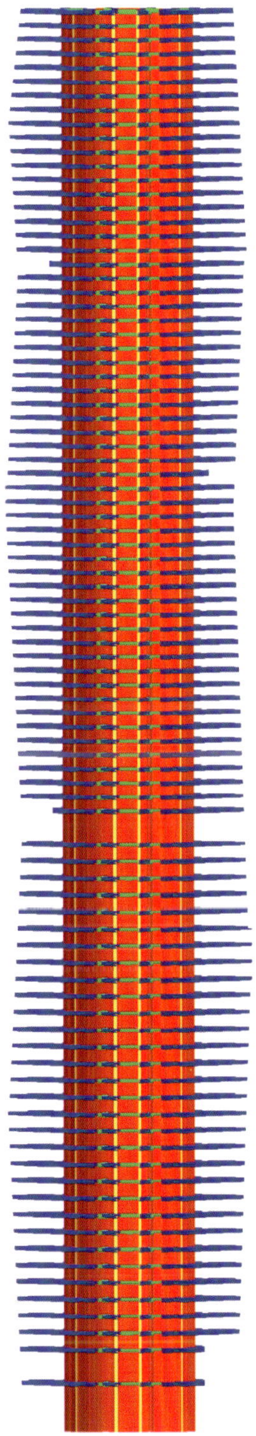

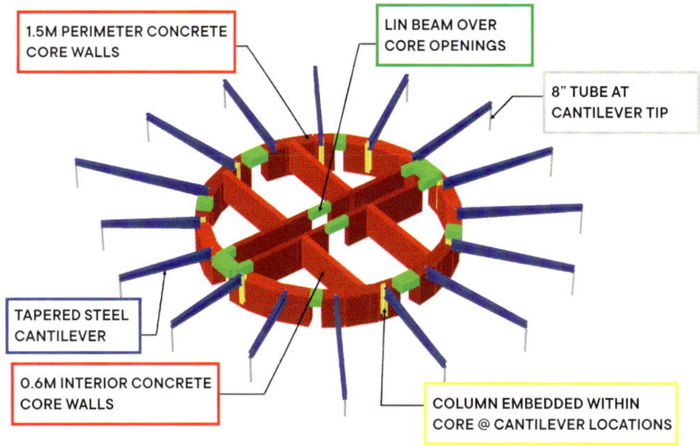
1.5M PERIMETER CONCRETE CORE WALLS
LIN BEAM OVER CORE OPENINGS
8" TUBE AT CANTILEVER TIP
TAPERED STEEL CANTILEVER
0.6M INTERIOR CONCRETE CORE WALLS
COLUMN EMBEDDED WITHIN CORE @ CANTILEVER LOCATIONS

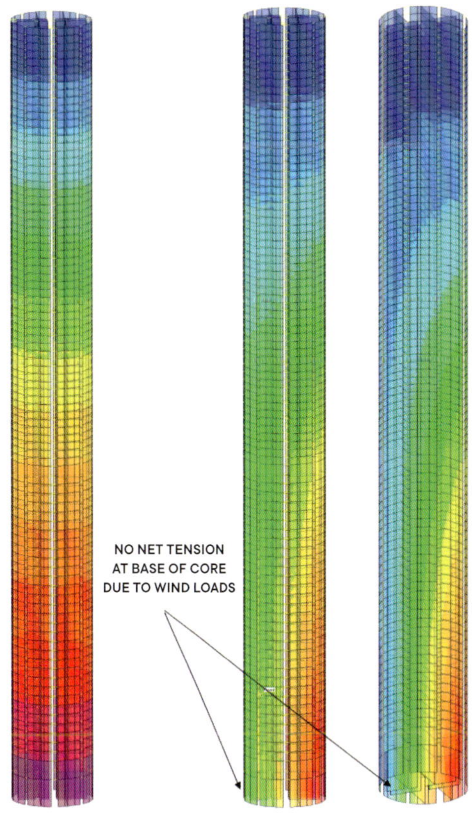
NO NET TENSION AT BASE OF CORE DUE TO WIND LOADS

CHAPTER II. HARNESSING ENERGIES

INTEGRATED SOLAR AND WIND POWER

The construction of a tall tower demands a wide range of resources. There is an inherent requirement for innovation to create a lasting, iconic, sustainable, and resilient structure. By utilizing natural energies such as wind or solar power, that vary by region, a tower can capitalize on available resources and incorporate them to design a more efficient structure.

Supertall construction offers unique challenges to overcome, as well as opportunities to innovate and create concepts that have not yet been considered. Each project presents a chance to discover more about this typology, existing at the very edge of architecture and structural engineering. The projects contained in this chapter were designed to harness wind and solar power by virtue of their form. In these Supertalls, form strictly follows performance.

Openings for wind and solar panels are strategically placed at the proper orientation, while the tower itself is formed to enhance these features. These towers represent the next generation of supertall design, with the goal that someday they will power themselves with their own renewable energy.

+ CLEAN TECH TOWER
+ MERAAS TOWER
+ ZA'ABEEL SIGNATURE TOWER I
+ XIAN GREENLAND TOWER
+ ZA'ABEEL HOTEL

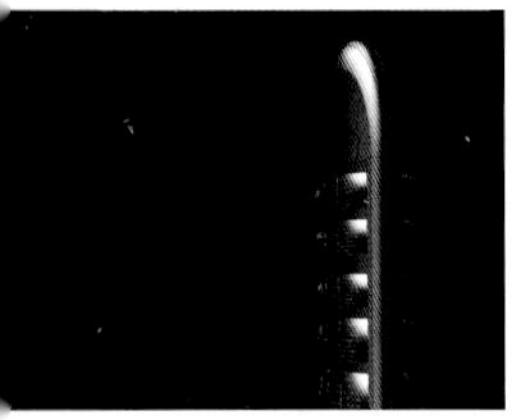

CLEAN TECH TOWER

CHICAGO, USA, 2007

300M

The proposed Clean Technology Tower at 321 South Wacker represents the next generation of high-performance architecture: a skyscraper that absorbs its environmental context to go beyond net-zero and provide excess energy, establishing a new international standard for high-performance buildings. The scheme remains unbuilt, although it influenced numerous other projects since its design in 2006.

Building on the principles of biomimicry, the tower utilizes advanced technologies and climate-appropriate building systems to foster a symbiotic relationship with its local environment. The tower is sited and formed to harness the power of natural forces at its site, as it refines the conventional methods of capturing those natural forces to significantly increase efficiency.

The primary strategy is to place the wind turbines at the building's corners to captures wind as it accelerates around the tower. Using the facade area as a collection device to capture the wind, the turbines become increasingly dense as the tower ascends and wind speeds increase.

At the apex, where wind speeds are at a maximum, a domed, double-roof cavity wind farm captures air, using negative pressures at the top to pull air upward from the shafts of the building to help ventilate the interior spaces. The dome is shaded by photovoltaic cells that minimize heat gain while capturing the energy of the southern sun.

Inspired by the clean technology concept the wind turbines are part of the tower's distinct architecture. The double-skinned facade with integrated shading devices acts like a thermos which protects the building from the cold climate.

+ CONTEXT
+ PROGRAM
+ PERFORMANCE
+ RESEARCH + DEVELOPMENT

CONTEXT

The tower's facade was designed as a double-skinned wall with a one-meter cavity between the two layers. Although less common in the US, double-wall facades are widely used in Europe due to more stringent energy codes. It is estimated that the double wall could save 15–20 percent of total energy cost in this tower.

Chicago is a cold-intensive climate, therefore the building's double wall creates a "thermos bottle" effect that keeps out the cold climate. The facade also integrates shading devices between the two facades to help with heat gain during the summer months.

The exterior wall's fritted glass pattern is strategic, letting in the light and views where needed and shading the spaces that have the highest heat gain, at the pinnacle and the ground level. To further protect the interior spaces, a high-performance Low-E coating is used on the glass.

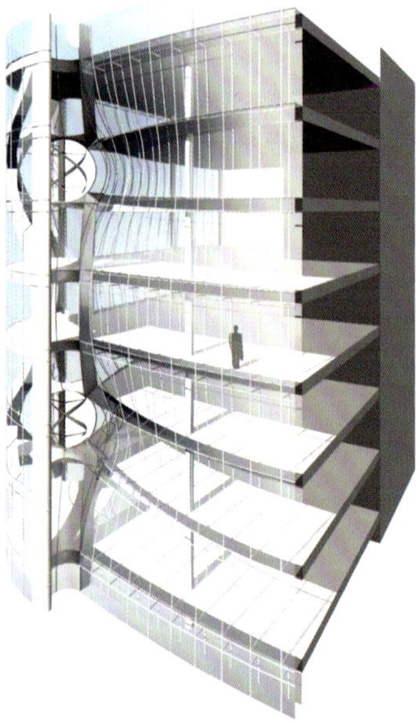

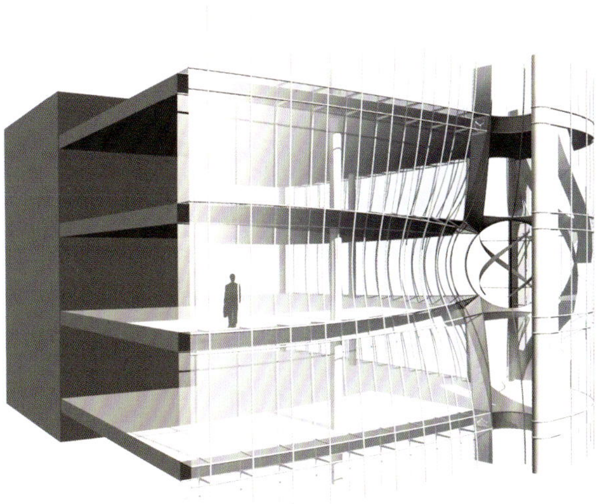

Although office buildings in Chicago are not required to have operable windows it is thought that occupant comfort is increased with a direct connection to the outside. When used effectively, operable winds can reduce heating and cooling loads during the fall and spring months by introducing fresh air when the temperature is pleasant. Operable windows integrated into the Clean Tech Tower's double wall cavity on the south elevation are naturally ventilated and heated by the sun within the cavity.

Electronically tinted glass responds automatically to the sun, helping save energy by blocking solar gain and glare or increasing daylighting during cooler months, further improving human comfort levels. Sunshades installed in the cavity between the double wall can be linked to the building's maintenance system to automatically track the sun and change position as required.

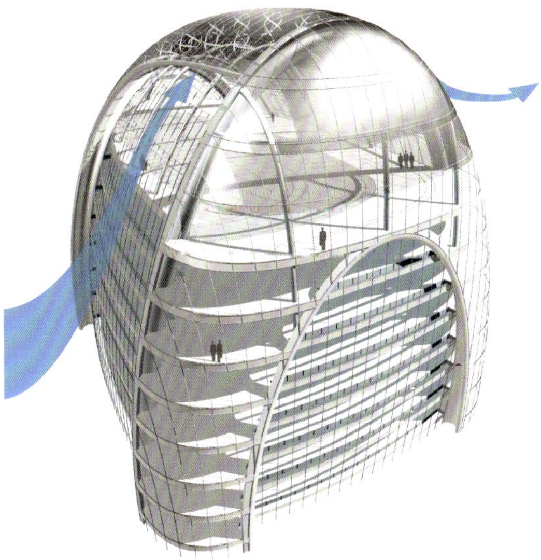

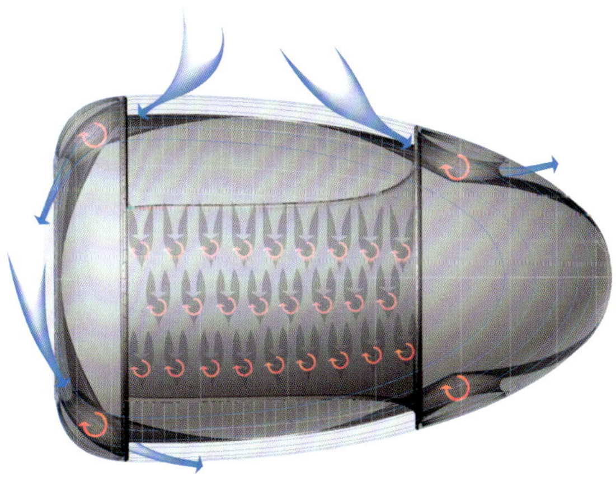

PROGRAM

The design for Clean Tech Tower has over 1.8 million sf of office space and a 300,000 sf hotel, a spa, and street-level retail. The tower's domed observation offers unrestricted skyward views, creating a truly modern, grand atrium space and garden. A plaza and park at the north side enhances the tower's connection with the surrounding neighborhood with a public gathering space for tenants. The plaza complements the tower's winter garden, strengthening the connection with the existing retail.

Office space is located on the highest floors to maximize the views and take advantage of the direct natural daylight. Hotel and office lobbies have dedicated street entrances and vehicle pick-up and drop-off locations on Van Buren Street and Upper Wacker Drive. Service access to the building is located below grade on Lower Wacker Drive. The tower is accessible via public and private transportation and below-grade parking is also directly accessible to the tower.

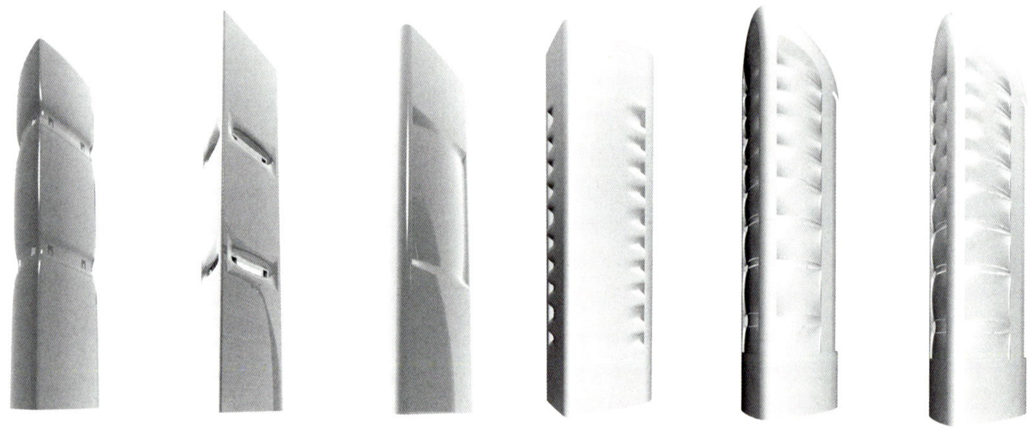

OPTIONS EXPLORED TO MAXIMIZE HARVESTING OF WIND TO ENERGY

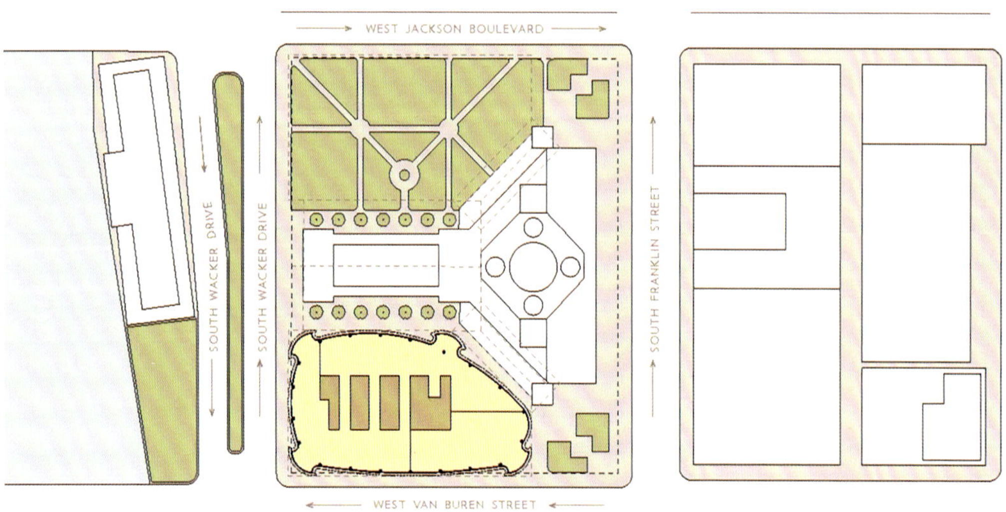

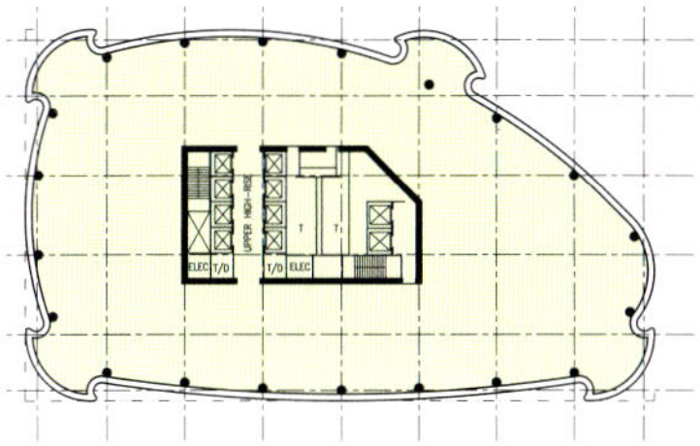

HIGH-RISE
OFFICE PLAN

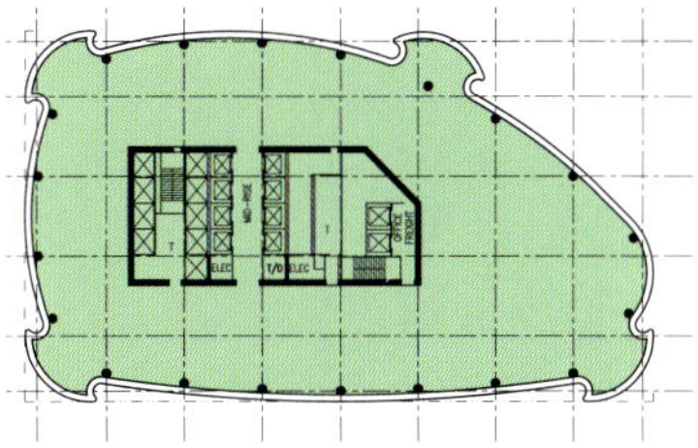

MID-RISE
OFFICE PLAN

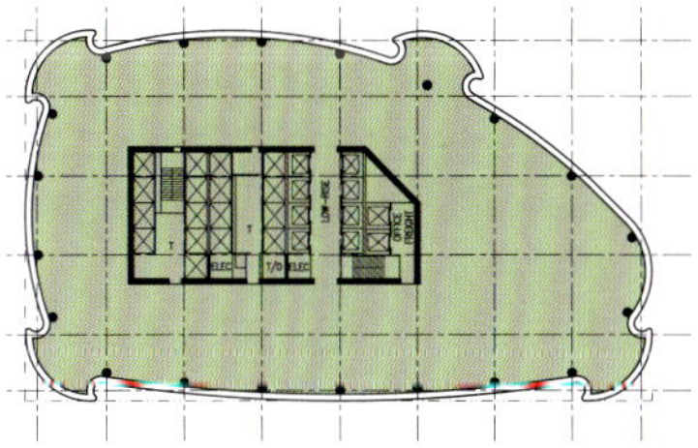

LOW-RISE
OFFICE PLAN

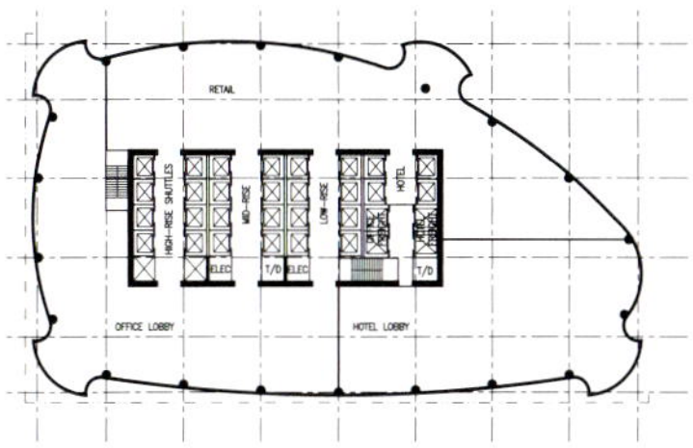

GROUND FLOOR
LOBBY PLAN

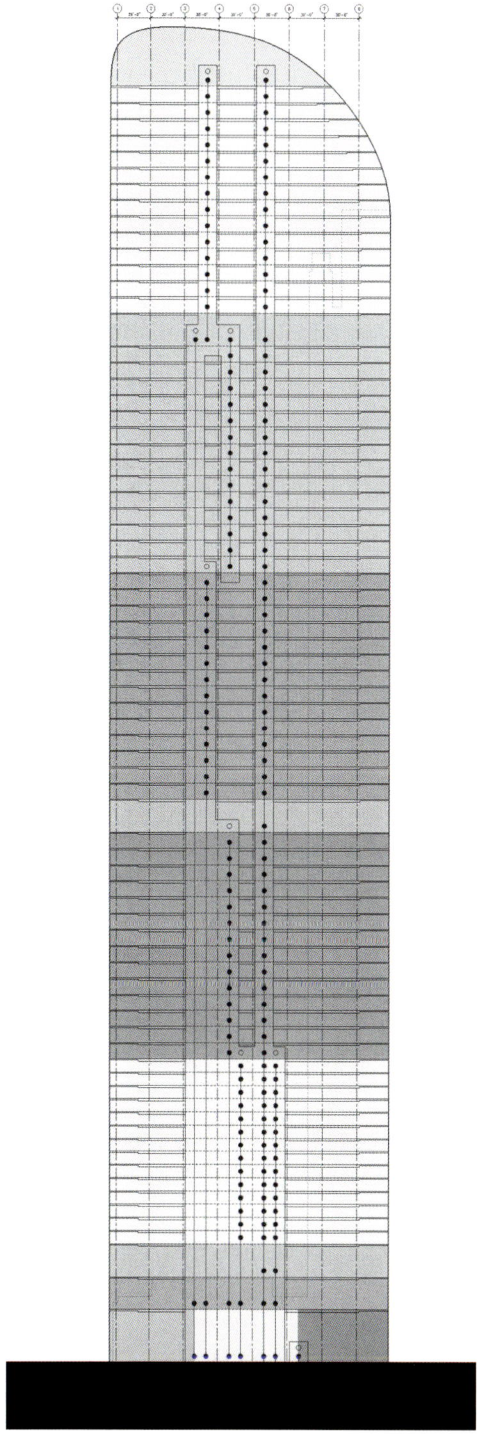

PERFORMANCE

Clean technology incorporates a broad range of industries, including energy, water, manufacturing, advanced materials, and transportation. Examples include wind and solar energy, water filtration, industrial process controls, and hydrogen fuel cells. Clean technology buildings use energy, water, materials, and other inputs more efficiently than traditional high-rises. They are designed to create less waste while delivering equal or superior performance, improving client profitability through cost reduction and/or increased revenues.

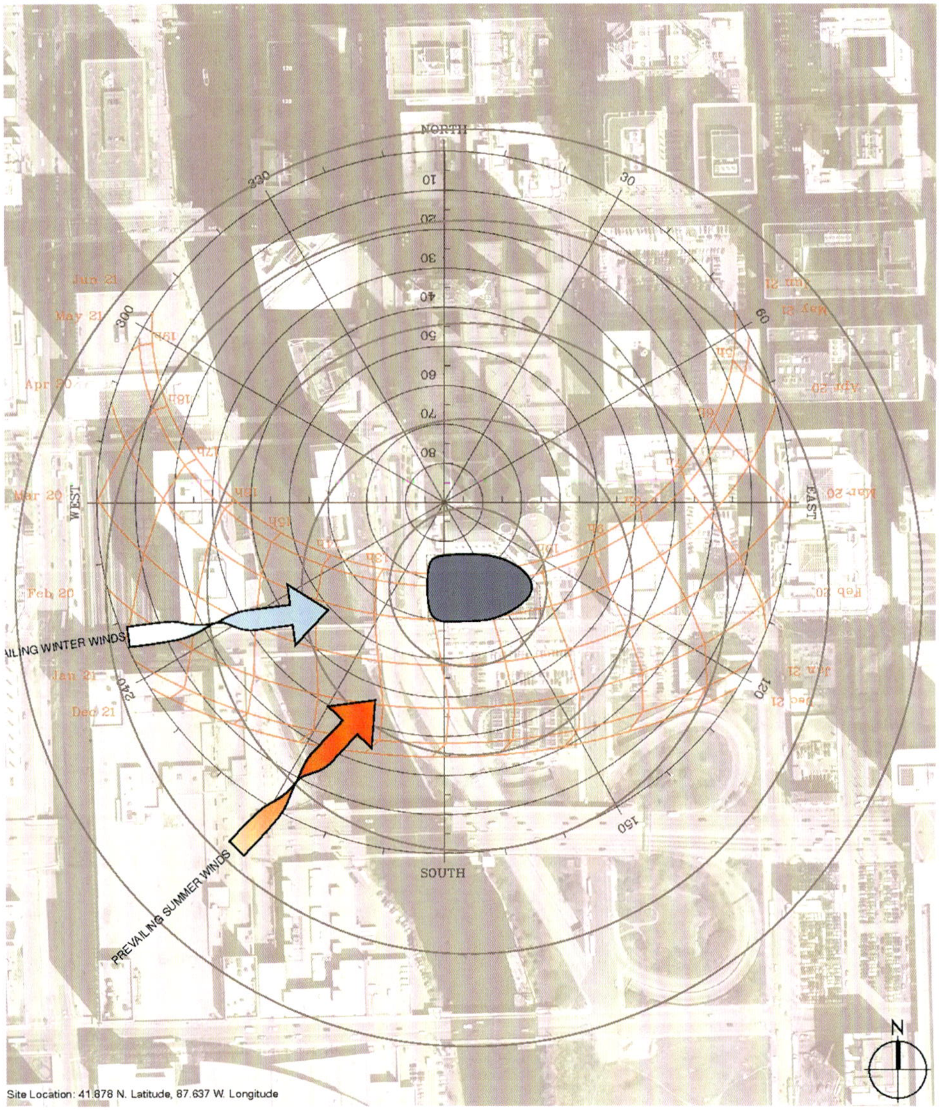

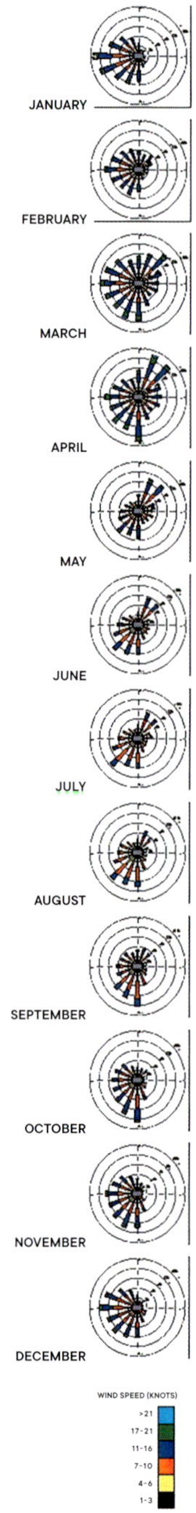

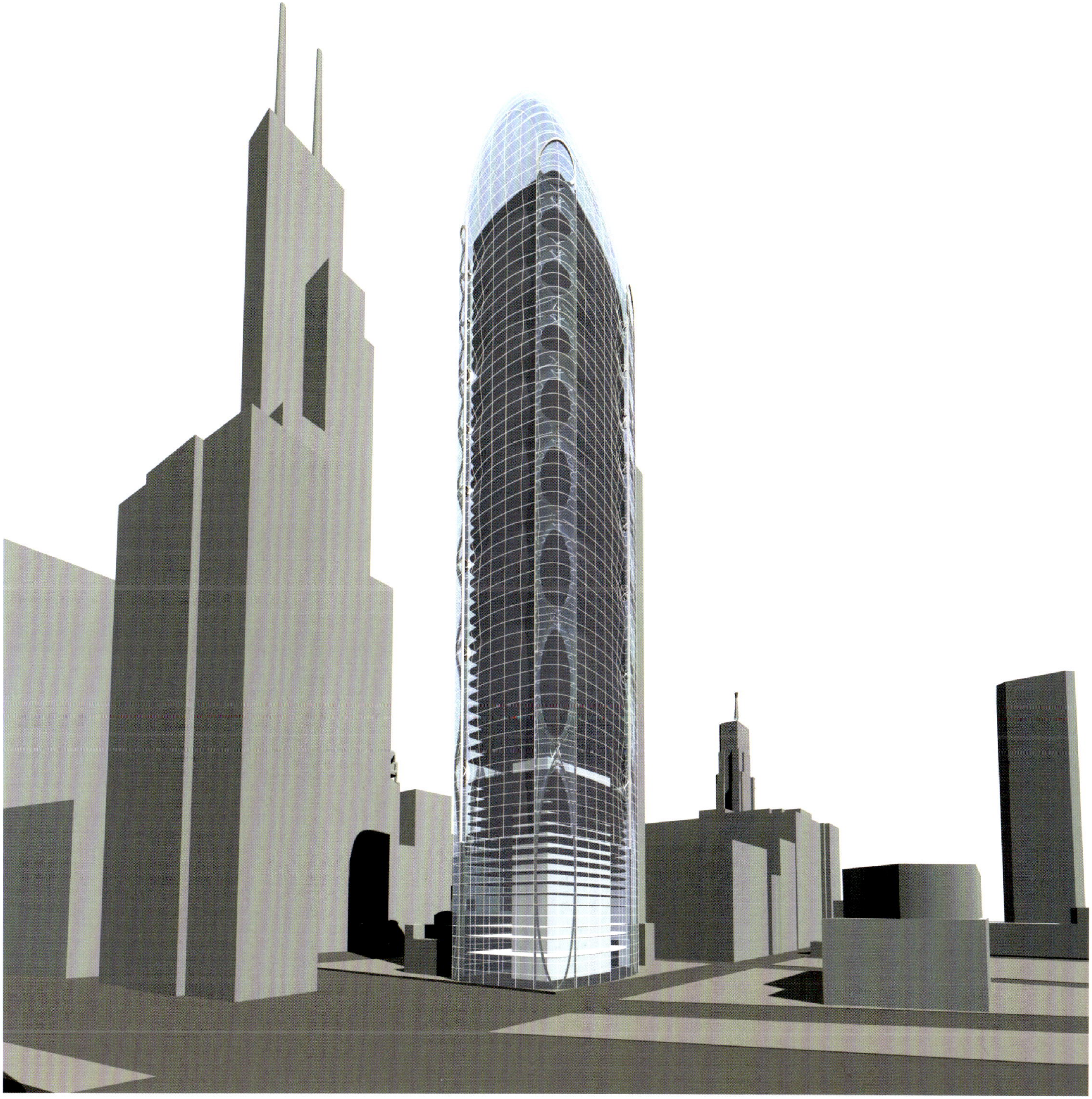

Several measures were proposed to save energy in the MEP systems such as high-efficiency chillers, modulating boilers, premium efficiency motors, waterside economizers, variable frequency drives, and airside energy recovery. Technologies in elevator systems include twin elevators to reduce shaft space, destination service control to reduce trips, and the latest energy-efficient elevator drives.

Geothermal heating and cooling via tubes in the tower foundations are proposed, as well as the study of geothermal earth ducts to pre-cool air for the lower levels. Fuel cells can recover heat from other systems and introduce the ability to save energy through storage, with the potential to sell it back to the grid.

Measures to reduce water usage include collection of rainwater for irrigation, low-flow high-efficiency fixtures, and, if allowed by code, a graywater system with on-site treatment and re-use.

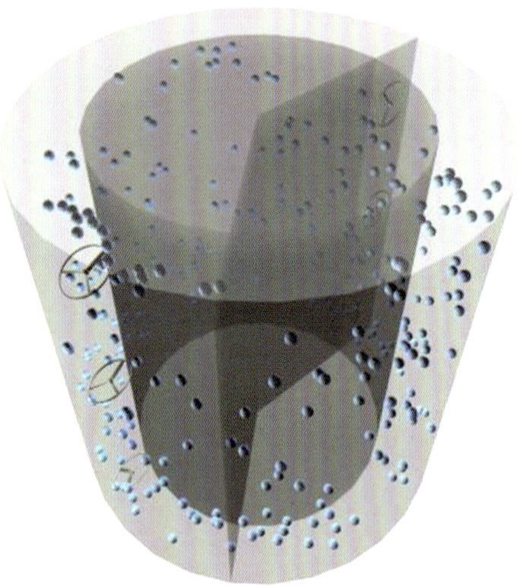

THERMOS BOTTLE CONCEPT

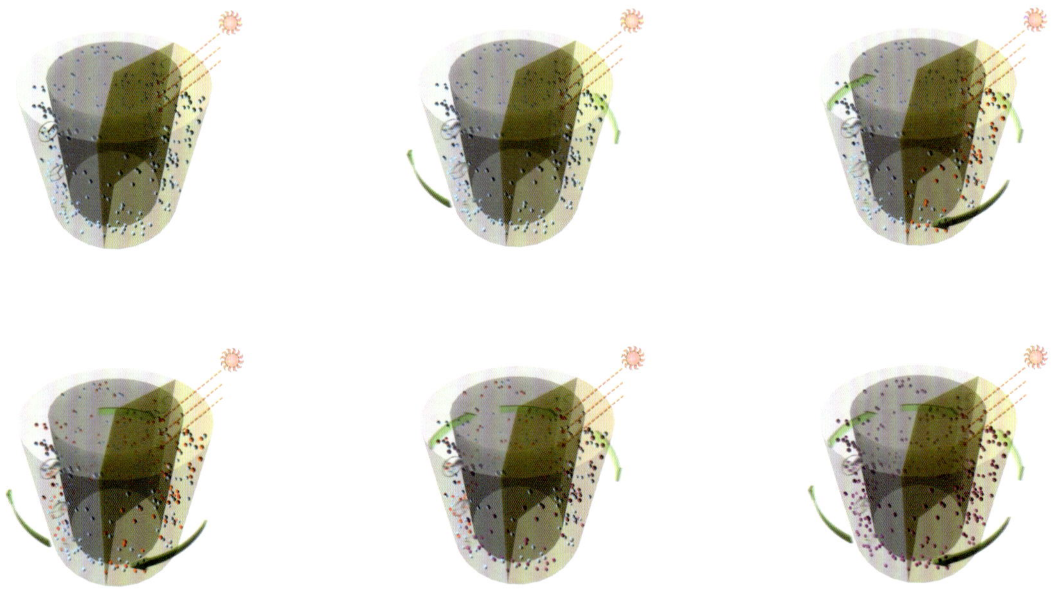

MERAAS TOWER

DUBAI, UAE, 2008

526M

Meraas Tower combines simple geometric principles with new and emerging technologies to create a modern, soaring "tower of light" in Dubai. Exposing the intermediate floors gives the illusion that the building is composed of four smaller towers stacked on top of one another, creating a vertical city.

The 526-meter, mixed-use tower has a total gross constructed area of approximately 290,904 sm with an additional below-grade ballroom facility and parking spaces. The building's orientation is optimized to maximize solar and wind energy capturing and is designed as positive energy.

Like a prism, the tower has a series of faceted surfaces that increase the light and air traveling through the building. The facets are visually interesting and purposefully performative. They maximize the energy derived from the building integrated photovoltaic panels (BIPV) and help balance the natural light in the building's interior with 360-degree views.

These facets also create ventilated sky gardens that activate the form as the building ascends. The opening floors at various height of the tower help to reduce the lateral wind load on structure.

- \+ SITE
- \+ PROGRAM
- \+ INTERIOR
- \+ RESEARCH + DEVELOPMENT
- \+ STRUCTURE

SITE

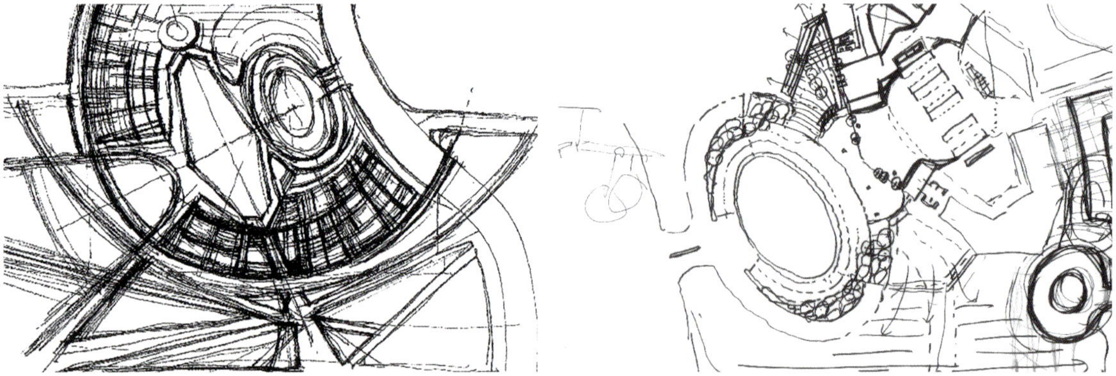

SITE SKETCHES, 2008

Meraas Tower is situated on the northeast edge of the central park in East Park District of the Jumeirah Garden City Master Plan, at the intersection of Northeast Boulevard and Park Road, across from the central park. The tower's active exterior environment defines the main street intersection and provides access to the adjacent park and acknowledges exceptional views of the entire Jumeirah Garden City. With a planned plot size of approximately 45,979 sm, the site's prominent location anchors the east end of the East Park District, is close to amenities, and has convenient transportation links.

Connections to the tower are accessed through a generously landscaped public plaza. This elevated park level provides multiple access points to the tower and the street level. A circular ramp on the north side of building accesses the hotel lobby. Site ramps south of the tower from North Boulevard also connect into the higher park level for direct pedestrian access from the park to the hotel lobby. This entrance point also accommodates a large skylight area and private sunken garden for the hotel ballroom at the concourse level. A pedestrian connection to the Metro Plaza east of tower is also included.

PROGRAM

The main entry is located on Al Hudaiba at the northwest of the building. Direct pedestrian access to the park is available at the lobby level, while service access is located at the east corner of the site. A separate private residential lobby is located west of the tower with its own drop-off. There are two, two-way ramps located at the east of the tower, close to the residential entrance for easy access to the lower level basements.

The hotel is located on Levels LL1, 1, 3, and 5–13 and consists of approximately 300 five-star hotel rooms, with direct access to the grand central atrium. The hotel lobby is located at Level 1 with access and views of the park. An amenity level health center is on Level 3, with a ballroom and conference facilities located at LL1. Serviced apartments are located at level 14–34, consisting of 230 units with central atrium views.

Office Zone 1 is on Level 35 and Levels 38–54, consisting of 18 levels of office space that have shuttle access from the ground-floor lobby, the sky lobby, and the executive office at Level 35. Office Zone 2 is on Levels 55-64, consisting of 10 levels of office space with shuttle access from the ground floor lobby and the sky lobby at Level 35. Office Zone 3 is on Level 65 and Levels 68–80, has 14 levels of office space with shuttle access from the ground-floor lobby, the sky lobby, and the executive office at Level 65. Office Zone 4 is on Levels 81–92, consisting of 12 levels of office space with shuttle access from the ground-floor lobby and the sky lobby at Level 65. Another executive office is located at Level 92.

The Residential Zone is located at Levels 95–109, consisting of 14 levels of residential units that all have shuttle access from the residential lobby. The Restaurant/Club is located at Levels 109–112, consisting of a high-end restaurant and club space, with shuttle access from the ground level lobby.

The below-grade ballroom/conference facility is located on the north side of LL1, with a 1,350 sm ballroom and other meeting room facilities. The prefunction area is naturally lit through a dramatic skylight above. There are two private sunken gardens at the east and west side of the tower that provide natural light and outdoor access.

The service/loading area is located at the northeast of LL1. Hotel back-of-house spaces are located at LL1 and LL2. There are also three full parking levels below LL1 with a total parking capacity of approximately 3,000 cars. The main mechanical floors are located at level 4, 36–37, 66–67, 93–94, and LL1–4.

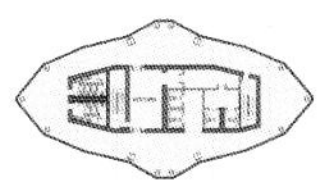

CLUB
LEVEL

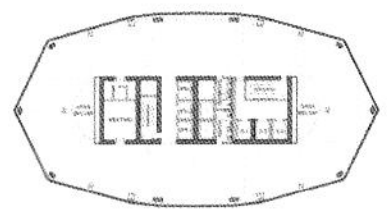

RESIDENTIAL
PLAN

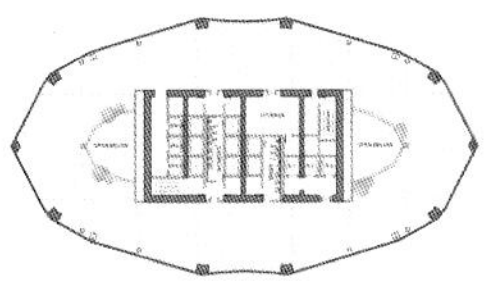

TYPICAL
OFFICE PLAN

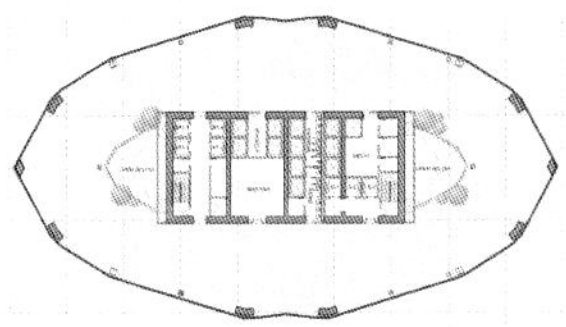

SERVICE
APARTMENT PLAN

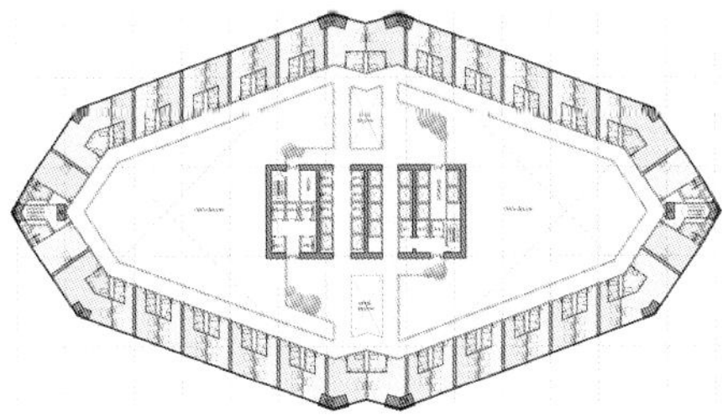

HOTEL
PLAN

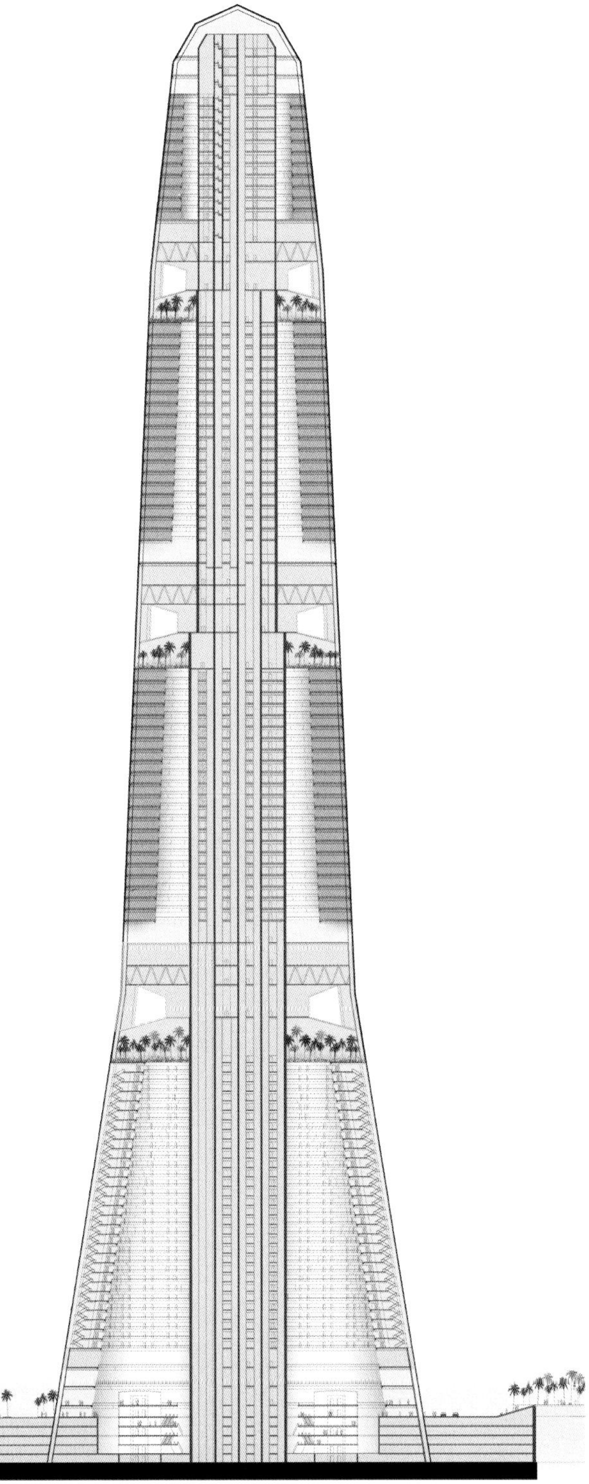

INTERIOR

The geometry of the atria follows the same angular language as the tower, cutting through the hotel and residential floors and ending at the glass skylight toward the top of the building.

Panoramic glass elevators and bridges stretch across the floors, adding focal points at various levels. The landscaped spaces increase the social connectivity of the building, creating community through structure.

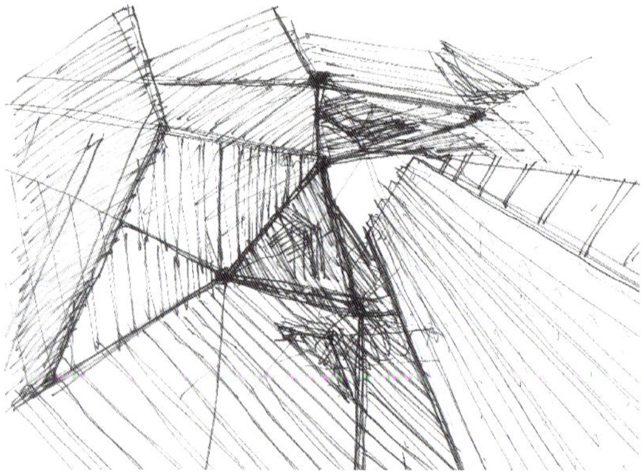

INTERIOR

RESEARCH + DEVELOPMENT

The tower is designed to have optimized solar and wind orientation. The north/south facades capture the natural mid-day light and minimize the solar impact on the east and west facades. The tower also harvests the prevailing wind through the fuselage opening floors facing east/west for energy generation.

WIND-TUNNEL ANALYSIS

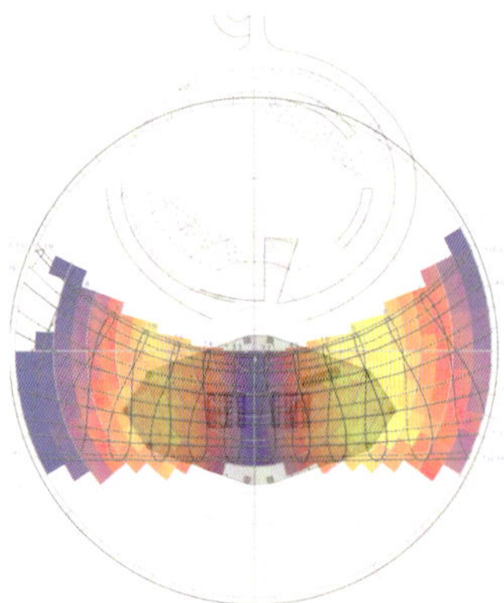

MINIMIZE EAST-WEST EXPOSURE

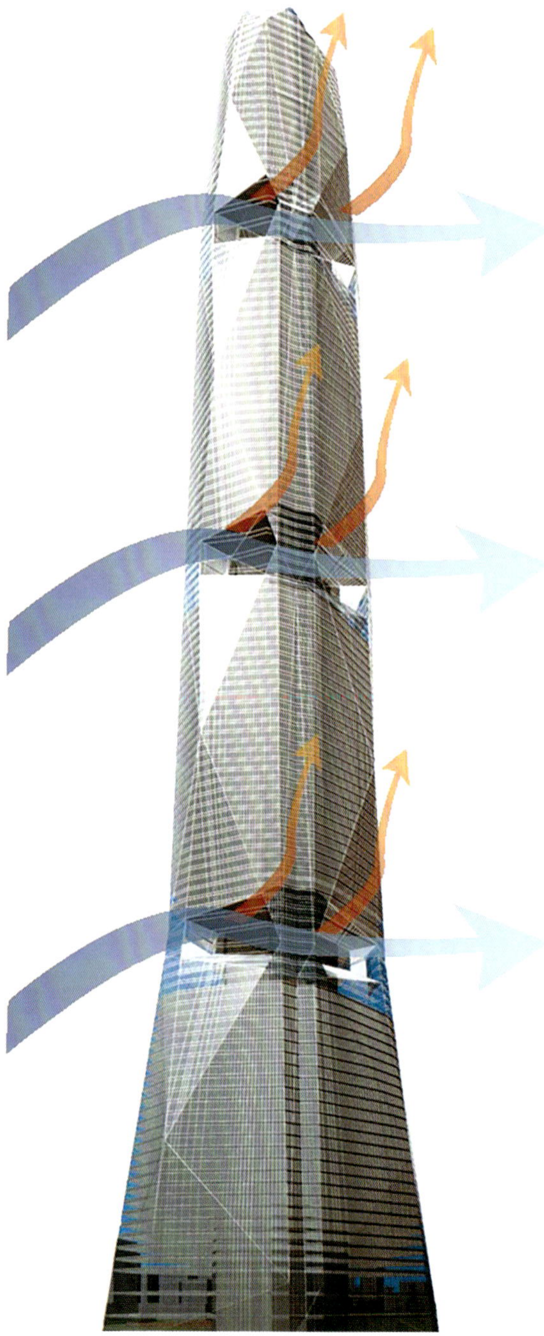

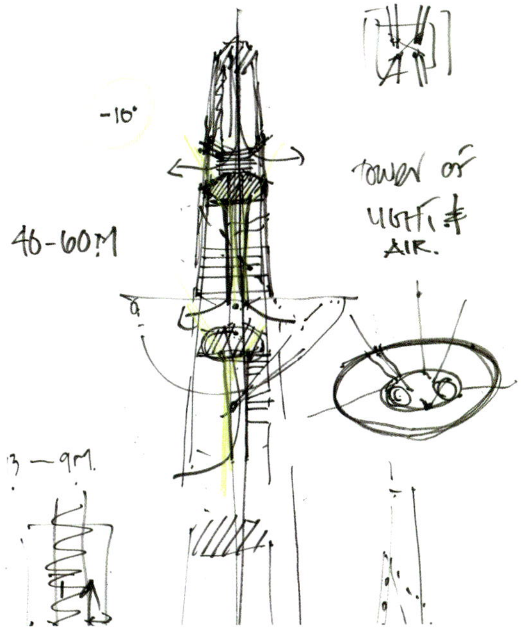

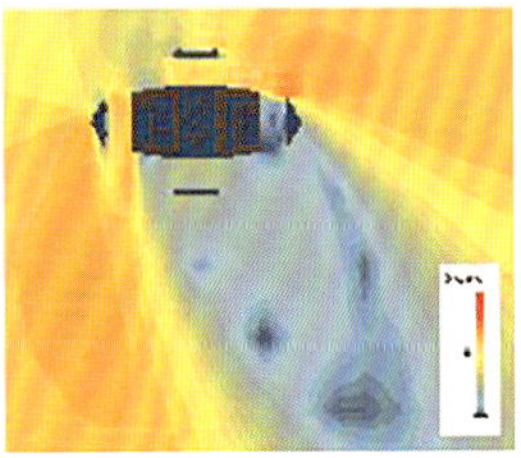

PLAN-A DIRECTION 1

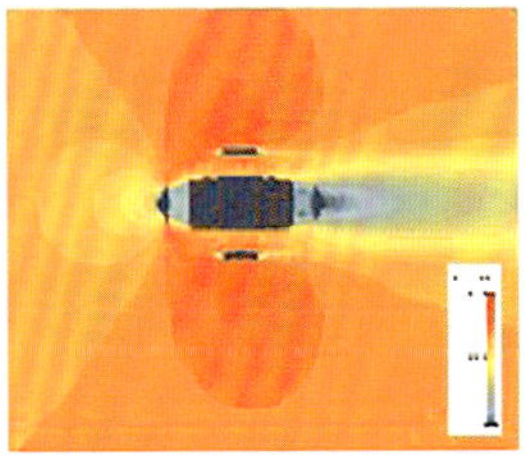

PLAN-A DIRECTION 2

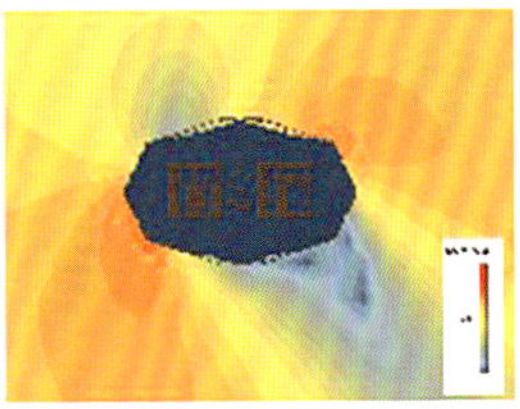

PLAN-B DIRECTION 1

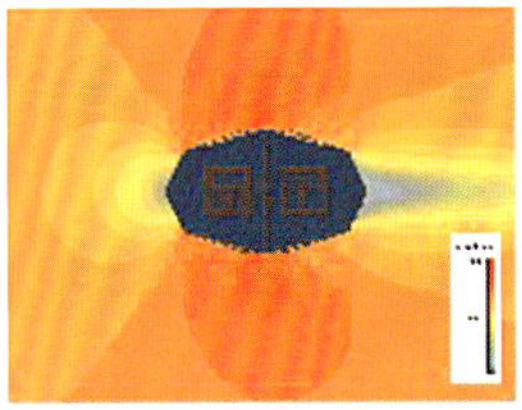

PLAN-B DIRECTION 2

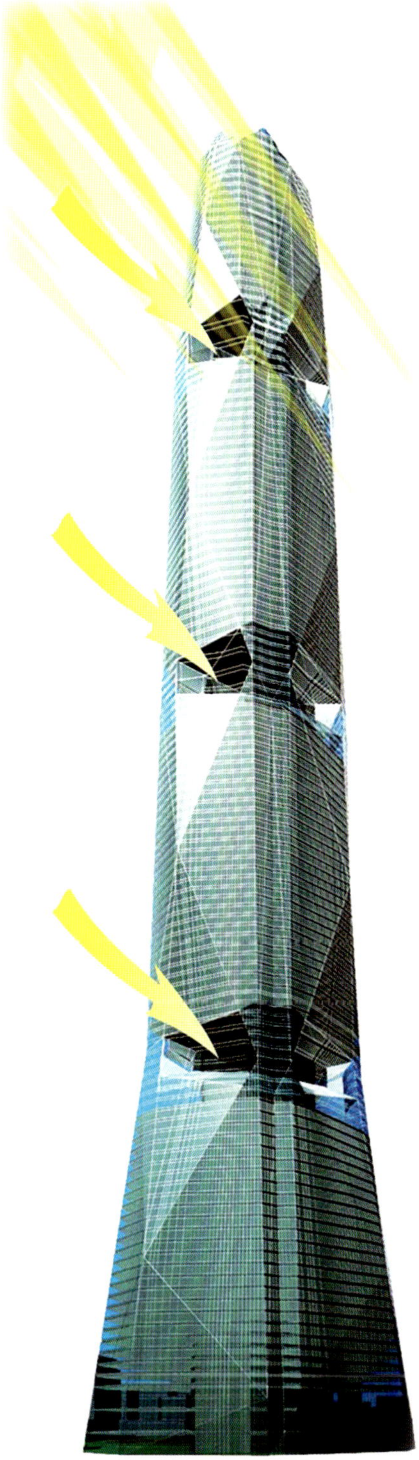

STRUCTURE

THORNTON TOMASETTI, STRUCTURAL ENGINEER

Ten concrete mega-columns extend the full height of the tower, comprised of high-strength concrete with mild steel reinforcements. Two construction options are offered. The first, concrete with embedded steel shapes in the mega-columns connect the exterior braces and aid the erection of steel framing. Compact exterior braces are built from high-strength steel plates in this option. The second option is entirely concrete, with the exterior of the tower structure comprised of closely spaced intermediate columns and spandrel beams to create an efficient concrete tubular shear diaphragm for each vertical building module.

At the three openings throughout the body of the tower, minor intermediate concrete columns along the perimeter are interrupted. A continuous perimeter steel belt truss (mixed option) or concrete belt walls (all concrete option) are provided at each of the mechanical floors to facilitate the intermediate column construction and further stiffen the perimeter structure.

Diaphragm floors are provided at all mega-column kink points over the height of the tower. These floors are comprised of a concrete-encased steel floor truss—mixed option—or a thick reinforced-concrete slab—all concrete option.

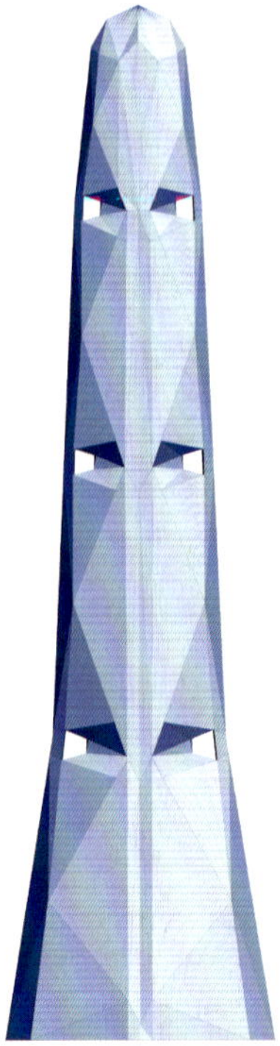

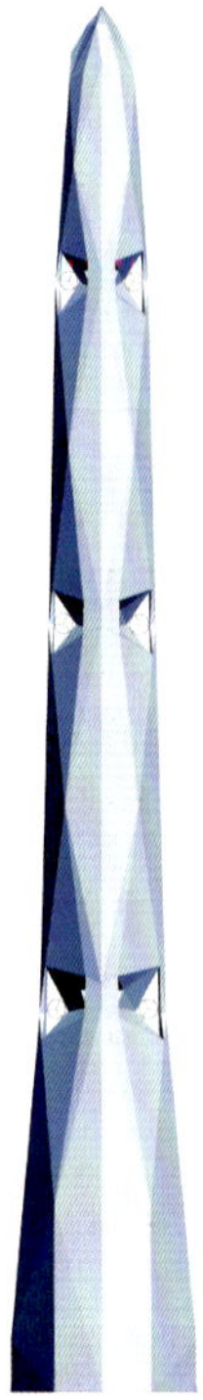

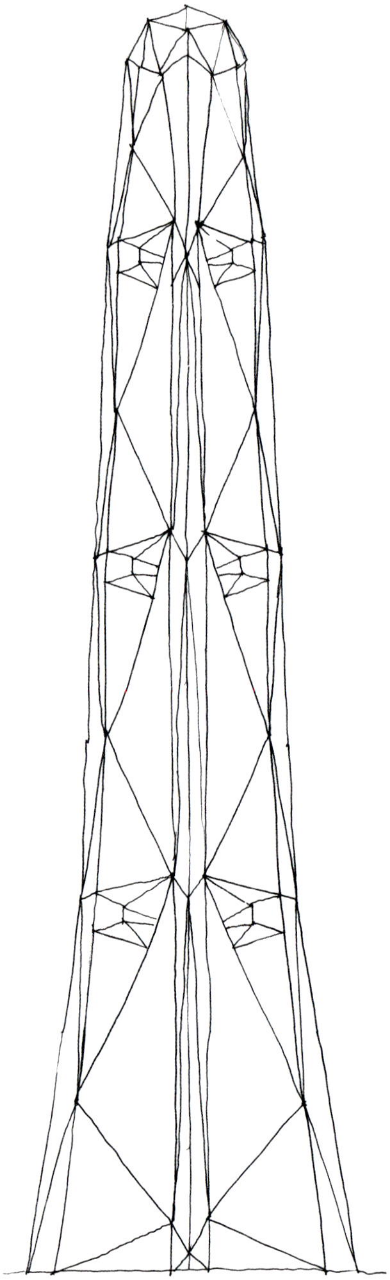

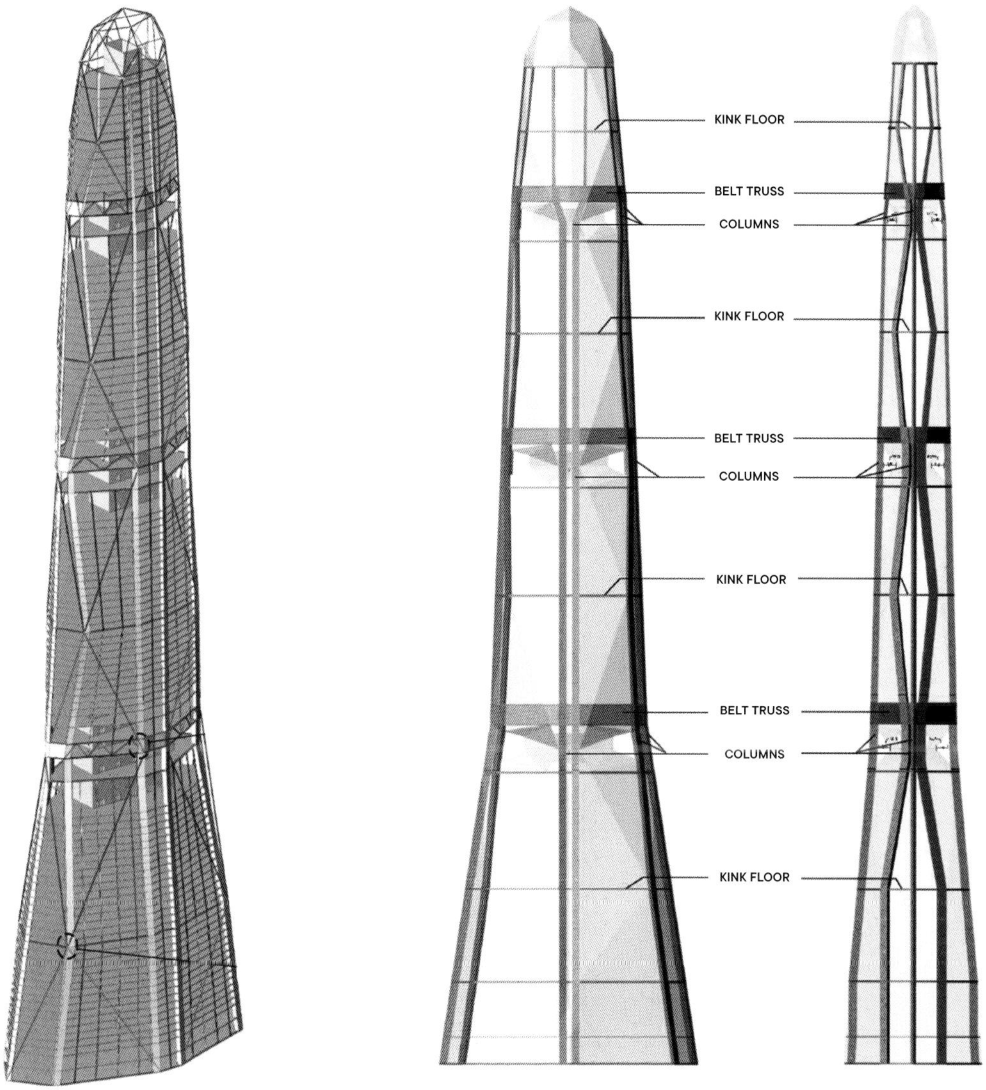
KINK FLOOR
BELT TRUSS
COLUMNS
KINK FLOOR
BELT TRUSS
COLUMNS
KINK FLOOR
BELT TRUSS
COLUMNS
KINK FLOOR

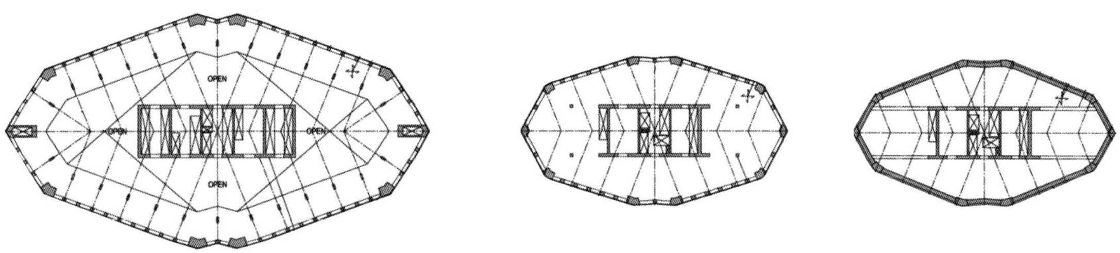
OPEN
OPEN
OPEN
OPEN

STRUCTURE

THORNTON TOMASETTI, STRUCTURAL ENGINEER

The floor framing for the Meraas tower utilizes reinforced-concrete slabs with post-tensioned beams to minimize structural depth. One-way reinforced-concrete slabs spanning between post-tensioned beams, achieve required fire-rating and allow for flexibility for openings to be coordinated. In the upper hotel tiers (Plans C and D) shallower post-tensioned beam framing is utilized as lease spans decrease. To keep floor beam spans down (and to keep constant framing depth) additional columns at the end bays, transferred out at Mechanical zones, are introduced.

The floor functions at mechanical zones are stacked to achieve the architectural design intent of an expressed slot through the building above an amenities atrium roof and to allow for linkage of the building columns to the core to maximize lateral system efficiency. In order to achieve this, isolated transfers are introduced above the building opening zone to transfer out columns that fall outside the exterior wall line at the slot. At the opening level, remaining end bay column transfers occur.

Below the atrium level transferred columns are reintroduced. Finally, at the Mechanical Level) outrigger and belt walls are utilized to equalize stress in the exterior columns and to link the core to the building columns to achieve more lateral stiffness.

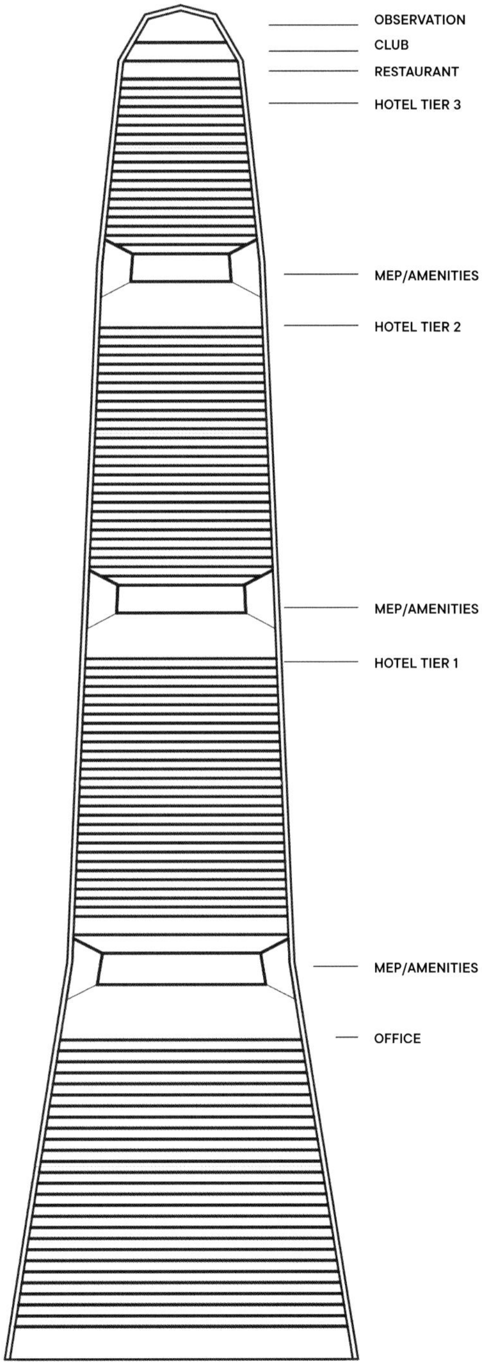

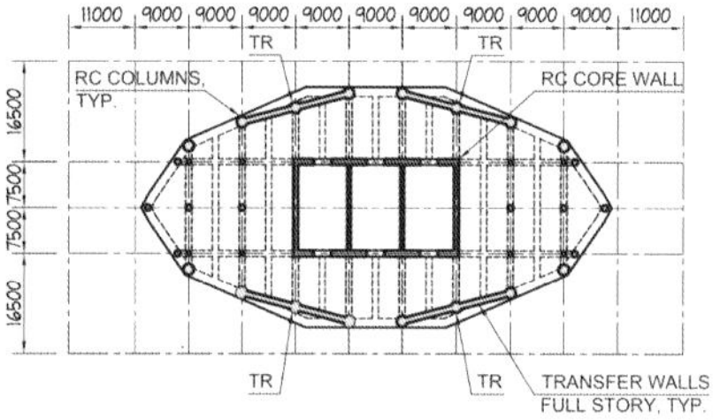

HOTEL FLOOR

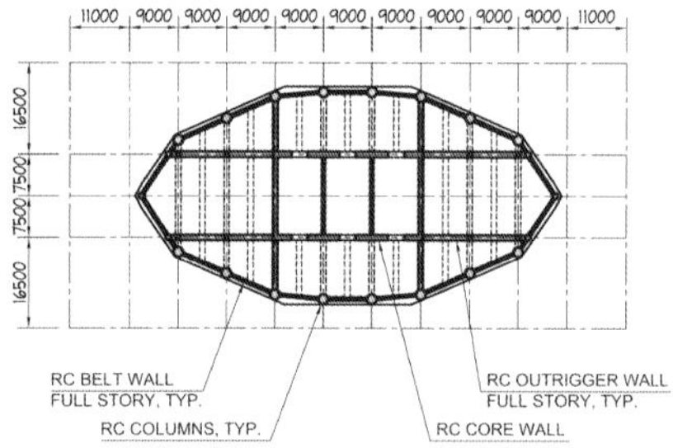

MEP/AMENITIES FLOOR

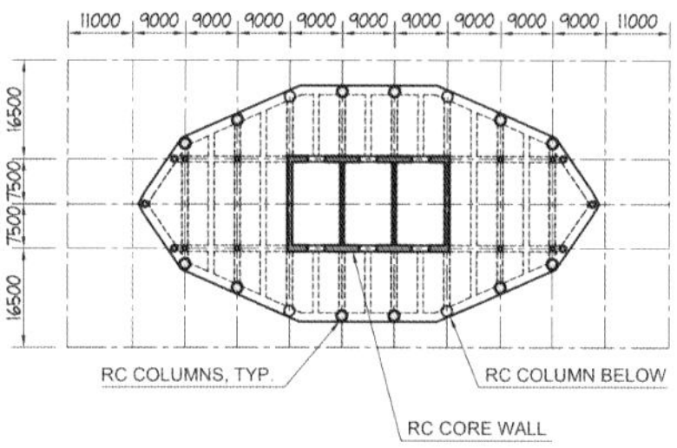

ATRIUM FLOOR

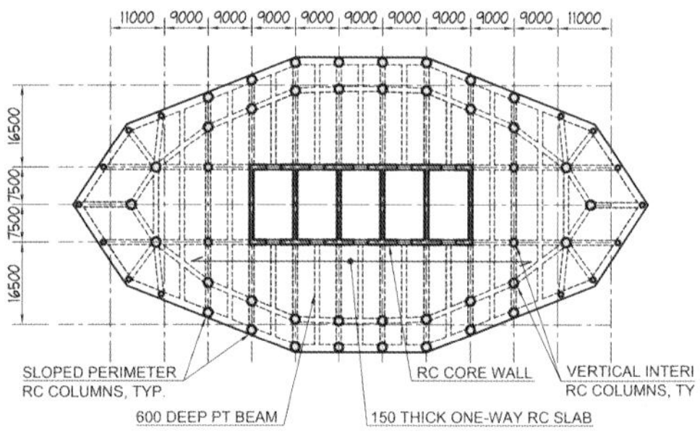

OFFICE FLOOR

The lateral system of the Meraas Tower consists of an interior core wall which runs up the height of the building and provides torsional stiffness to the building. The core wall steps back up the building as elevator banks drop off. An optimum tower design for Meraas Tower is realized when all vertical elements of the structure are fully engaged to resist lateral loads. Linking the core wall to columns on the floor plate and at the perimeter of the building, results in a system that is stiffer than a core-only system.

This linking is achieved through the use of multiple-story outrigger walls and belt walls at each mechanical level. Like a stayed-mast system, the outer columns brace the core and provide a larger, more stable base. Additionally, below the mechanical level in the office tier, a line of columns are introduced to frame out the flared base of the building. Engaging the flared-out columns through the mechanical zone outrigger/belt wall system, results in a stiffer and more optimal lateral-system design.

ANALYSIS MODEL

ANALYSIS MODEL

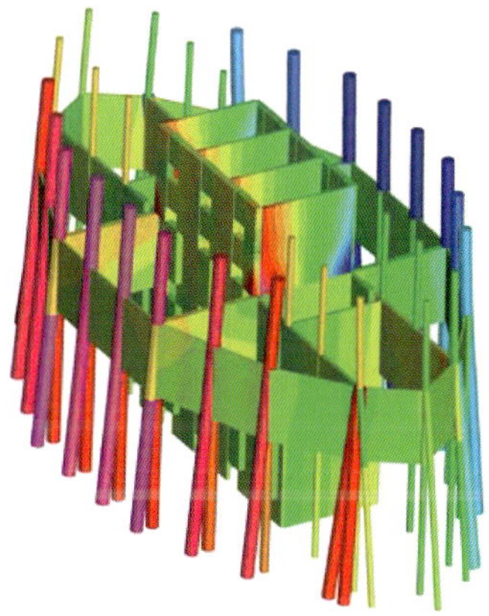

OUTRIGGER AND BELT WALL SYSTEM

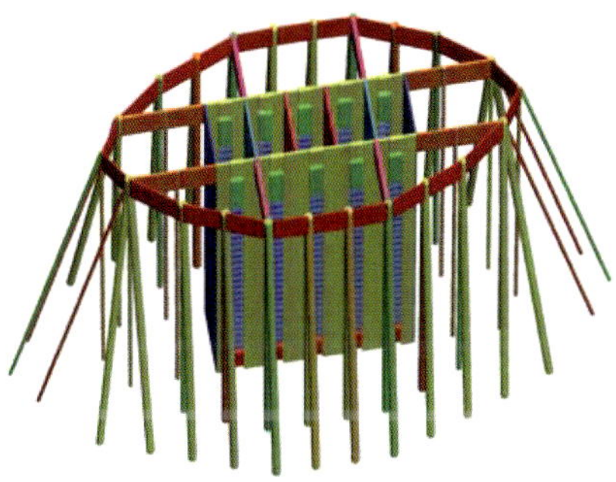

OFFICE TIER COLUMN SPLIT

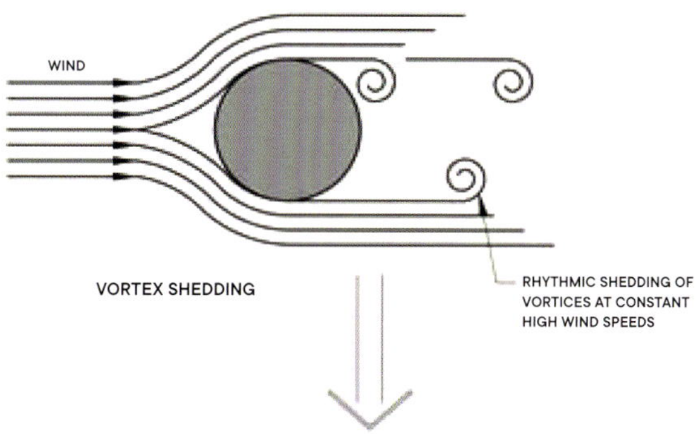

VORTEX SHEDDING

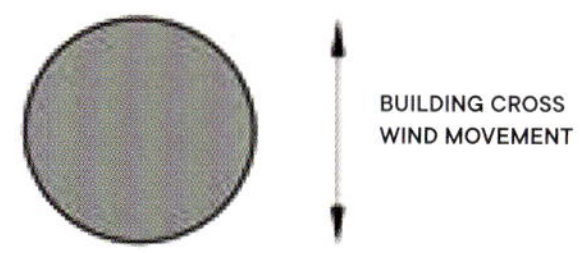

CROSS WIND MOTION

STRUCTURE
THORNTON TOMASETTI, STRUCTURAL ENGINEER

The hotel section of the tower will also contain a secondary stability system to preclude global buckling modes of the mega-column system. This system will take the form of floor-by-floor braces. These floor-by-floor braces will be spaced to match the room widths and partition lines. It is anticipated that the tower's mega columns and core-wall system is supported on a piled-raft foundation. Piles are high capacity, straight shaft, large-diameter bored reinforced-concrete piles or barrette piles.

The wind openings, which coincide with the mechanical and amenity zones, allow the core to come through and the facade is tapered in close to the main core wall. The openings are then visible by the tower occupants, reinforcing the expression of the building to the occupants inside.

WIND NOTCH

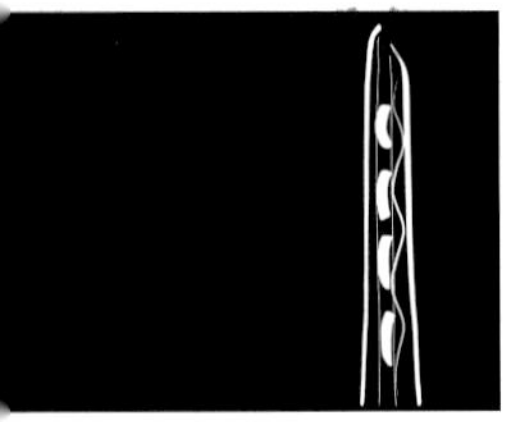

ZA'ABEEL SIGNATURE TOWER I

DUBAI, UAE, 2008

598M

Za'abeel Signature Tower 1 is a conceptual, mixed-use tower that was designed with advanced sustainable features. The project explores the concept of a megatall building: two towers that share a connected program and structure that are integrated as one building and one overall community.

The tower is a self-contained district with residential, amenity, office, and hotel functions. The form, orientation, and sheathing attract airflow, harnessing winds at higher altitudes that are then funneled and accelerated into vertical-axis wind turbines.

Active wind turbines generate power by utilizing wind currents with openings in the tower that allow wind to move through and give "relief" to the wind forces as they hit the broad face of a building. The openings also serve to accelerate the wind, generating more power.

The ladder-like form gives the project structural stability, its "rungs" creating a programmatic connection between the two halves. The structural outrigger system links the two main cores—one in each half of the tower—to the perimeter columns.

- + CONTEXT
- + SITE
- + PROGRAM
- + PERFORMANCE
- + RESEARCH + DEVELOPMENT
- + STRUCTURE

CONTEXT

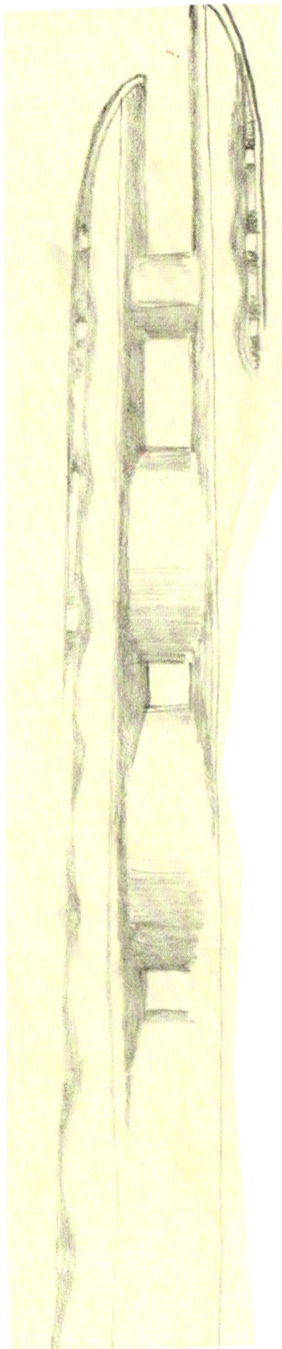

The tower's form is defined by the following design concepts:

Extension: The signature building dwarfs all adjacent towers. It is an iconic form that is supported by a structurally solid base.

Elevation: The ladder-like form increases structural rigidity. The "rungs" of the form create both a conceptual and programmatic connection between the two halves.

Attraction: To harness winds at higher altitudes, the building's form, orientation, and sheathing attracts airflow.

Gateway: The form establishes a distinct focal point. The biaxial arrangement of its composition establishes a hierarchy and its openings evoke a connection through the tower, which acts as a gateway and framing device that recognizes its relationship to the Burj Khalifa, the current world's tallest tower, to the west.

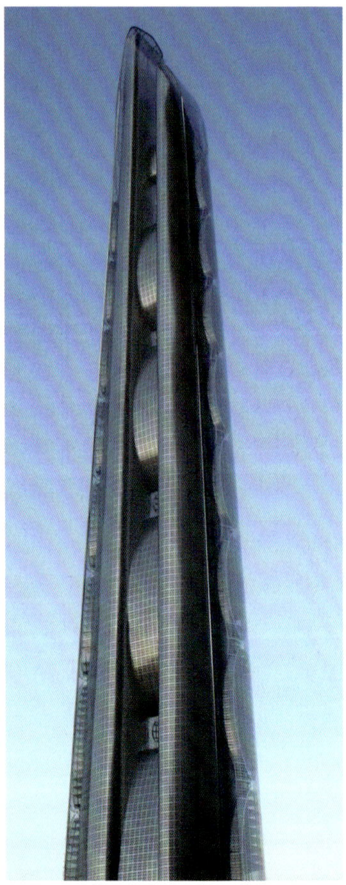

SITE

The project was commissioned when Dubai was growing at an unprecedented rate. Inflation was a significant concern for the client, so the Za'abeel Energy City Master Plan was put on a fast-track design schedule, calling for innovative construction methods. It was less costly to save construction time, even if labor and materials came at a premium.

For example, a two-day difference per floor cycle-time might amount to 270 days over a 135-floor tower, which is almost nine months in additional construction duration. It was proposed to use a self-climbing jump form on the tower core to achieve faster cycle time. Due to a larger perimeter length of the tower, the total number of perimeter columns are to be minimized in order to reduce crane-lifting time.

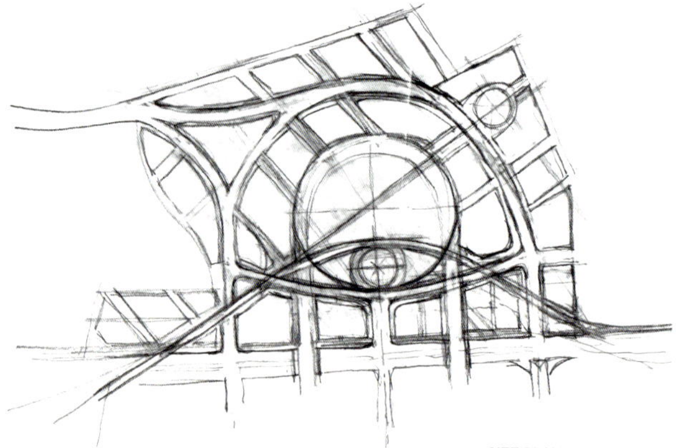

SITE PLAN SKETCH, 2008

SITE PLAN

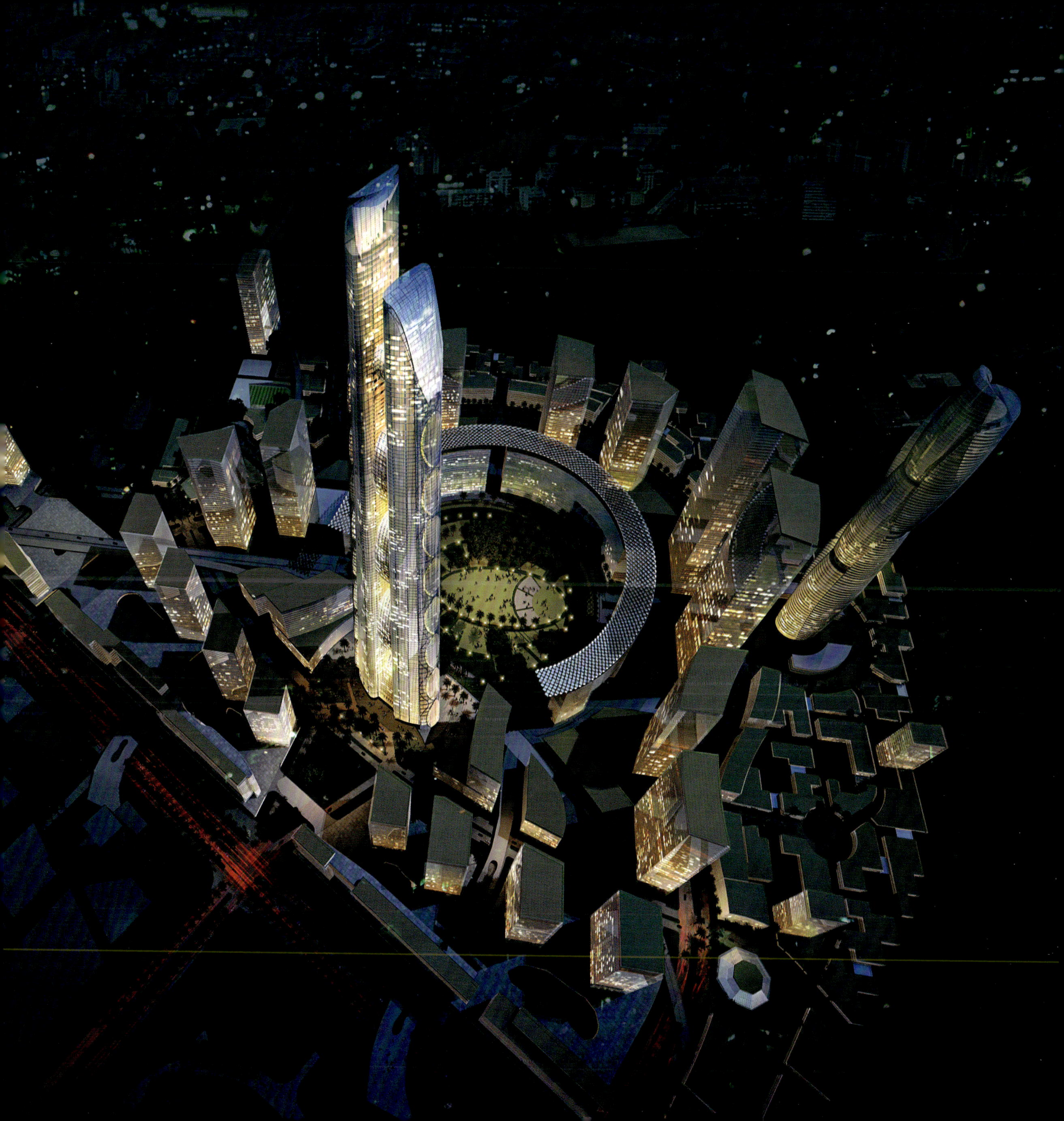

PROGRAM

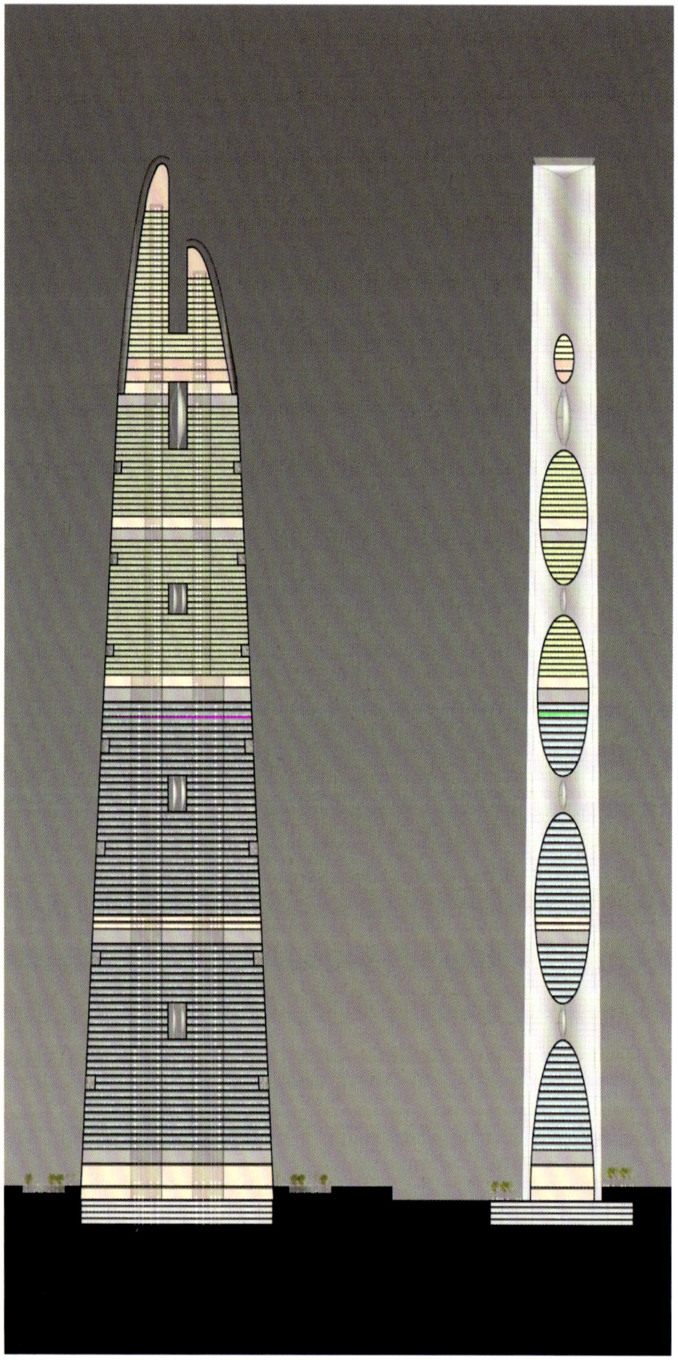

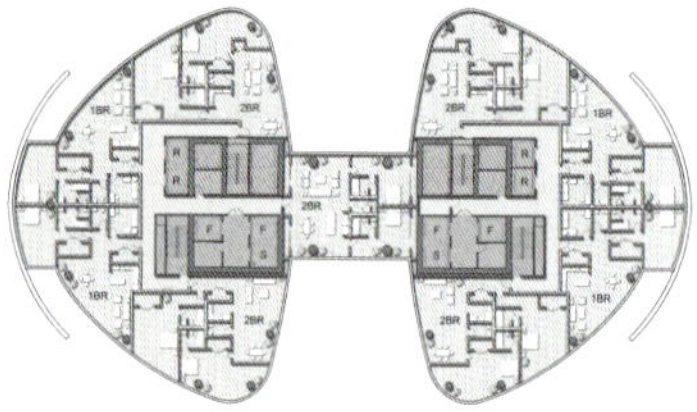

RESIDENTIAL
LEVEL 98

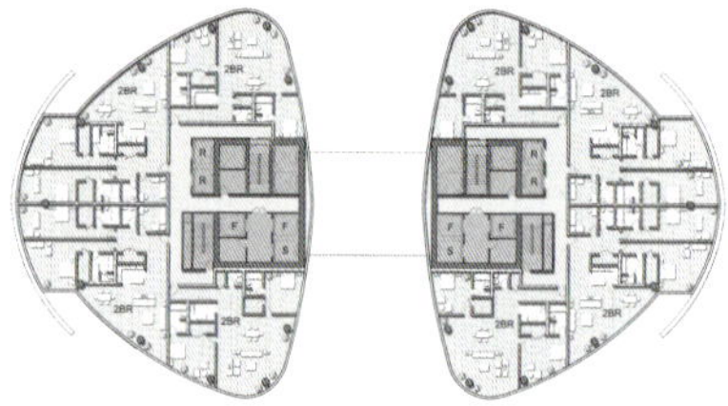

RESIDENTIAL
LEVEL 77

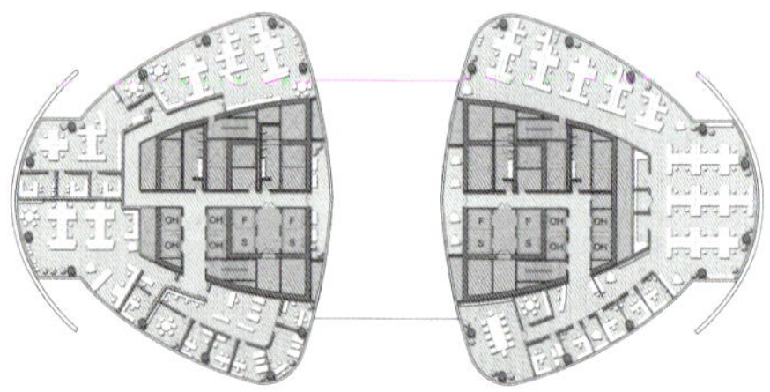

OFFICE
LEVEL 5

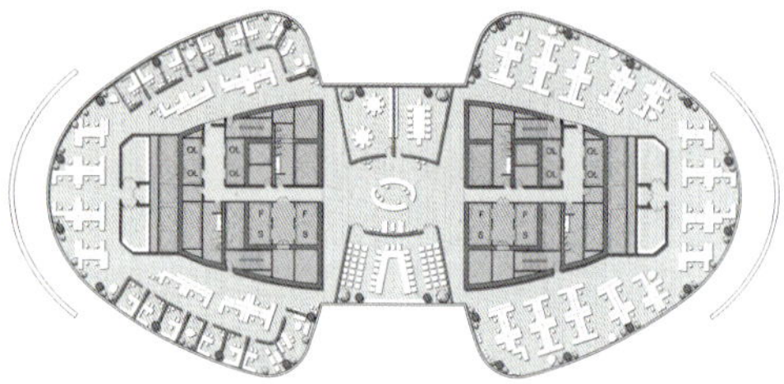

OFFICE
LEVEL 2

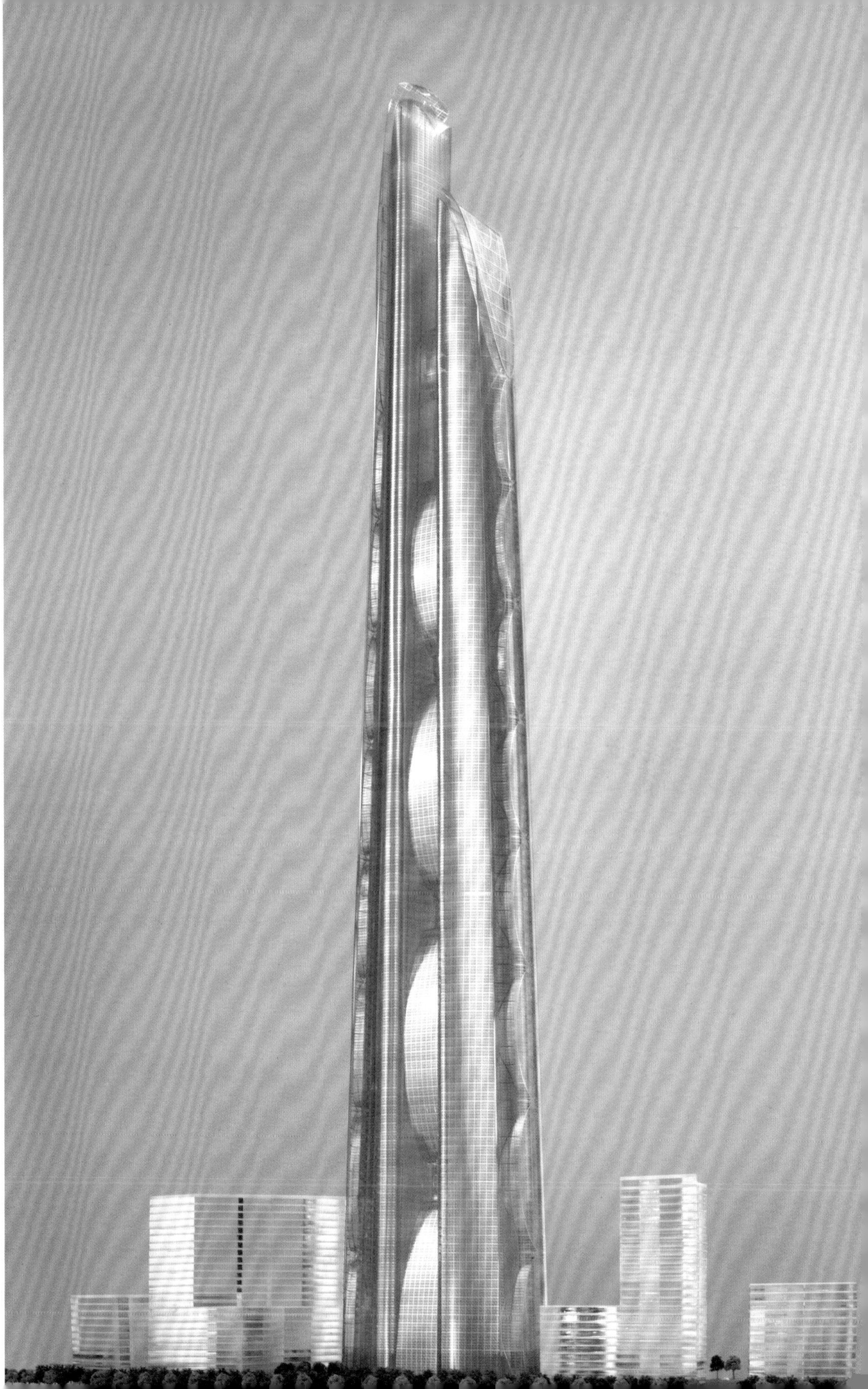

PERFORMANCE

The tower's exterior wall is a simple high-performance, double-glazed continuous glass skin that wraps the length and perimeter of the building. Solar shading is provided by a horizontal frit pattern. A second layer of glass sheaths the north and south offering an additional layer of solar shading. The glass sheathing also helps direct and compress the wind to generate the wind turbines, creating a pressure cavity that attracts airflow and accelerates the wind. Wind energy is produced by the building's orientation with the natural environmental airflow.

WIND TURBINE MODEL DETAIL

WIND TURBINE MODEL DETAIL

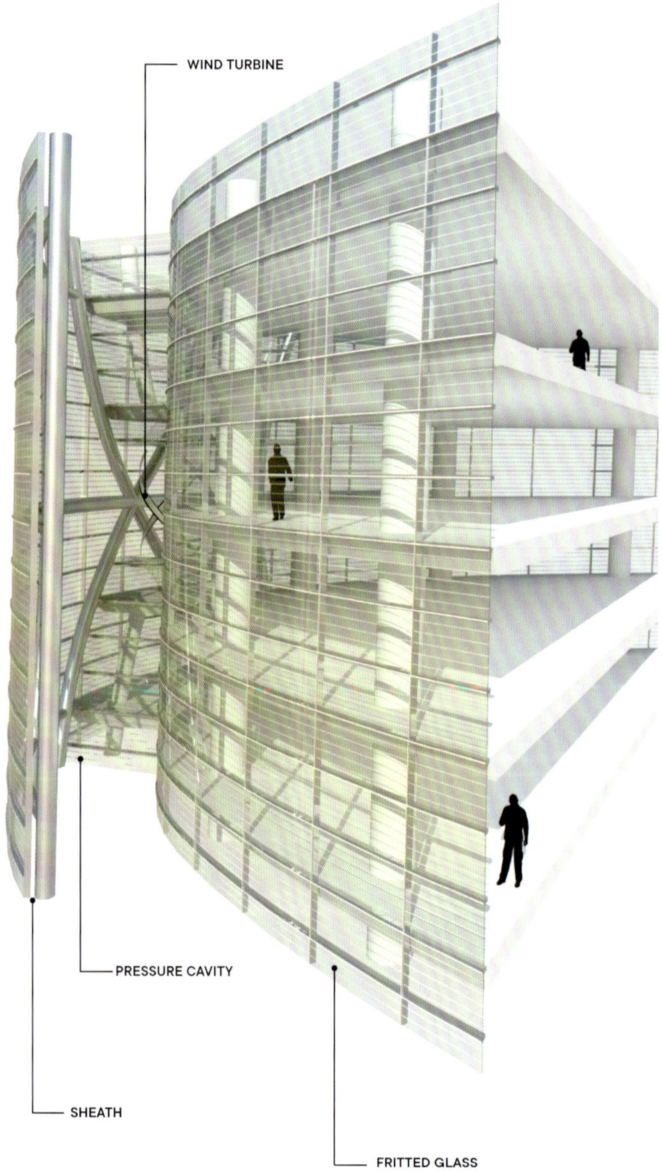

PERFORMANCE

The Persian Gulf is known to have unique wind conditions, including strong Shamal's, a northwesterly wind that has specific directional and velocity profile characteristics.

The tower's openings will bleed wind pressure, reducing overall drag and helping mitigate cross-wind vortex shedding by energizing the building's wake. The vent tunnels can be used to locate the wind turbines.

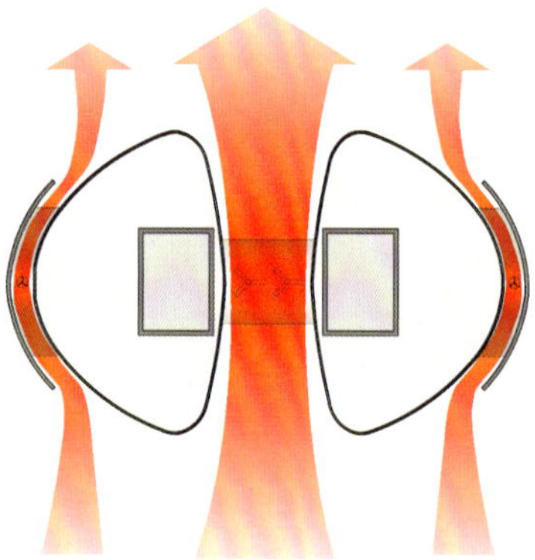

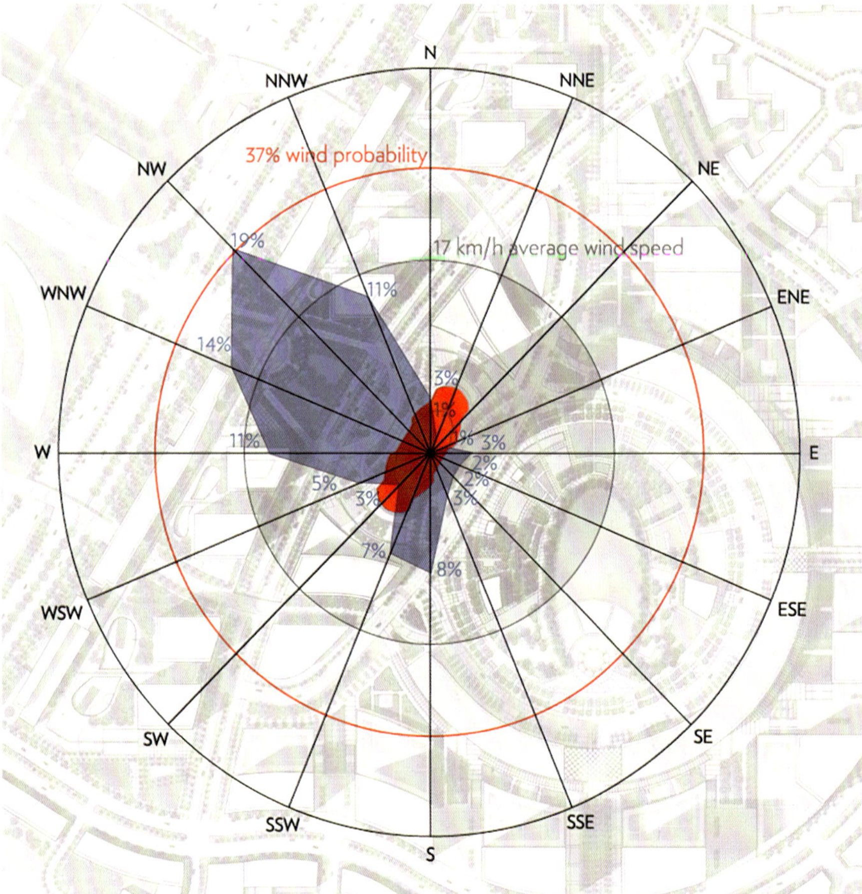

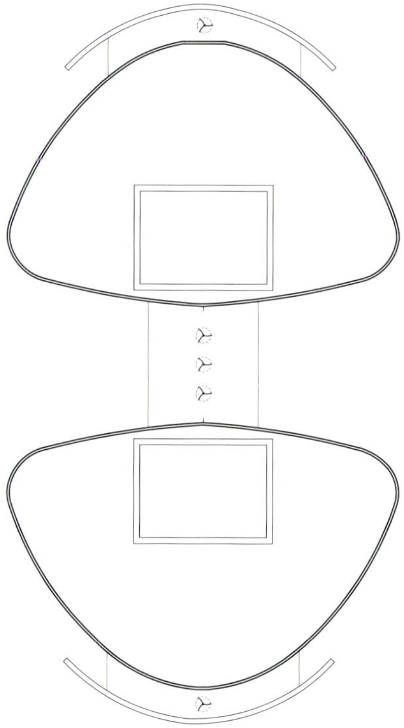

WIND DIAGRAMS

RESEARCH + DEVELOPMENT

Dubai requires fully integrated technology solutions that: make economic sense/account for the local culture and the availability of natural resources/fit seamlessly into the architectural vision for each development

During the project, the design team studied a variety of regionally appropriate energy and embodied-carbon savings strategies and rate them based upon their relative value and cost in order to facilitate decision-making.

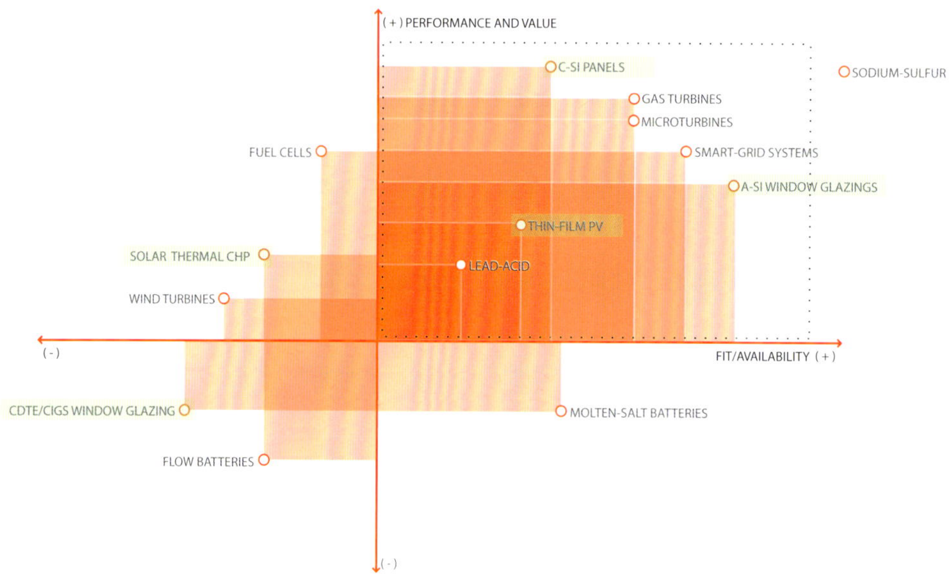

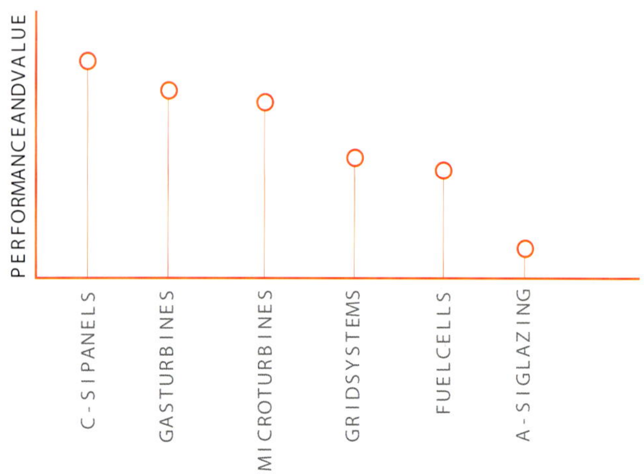

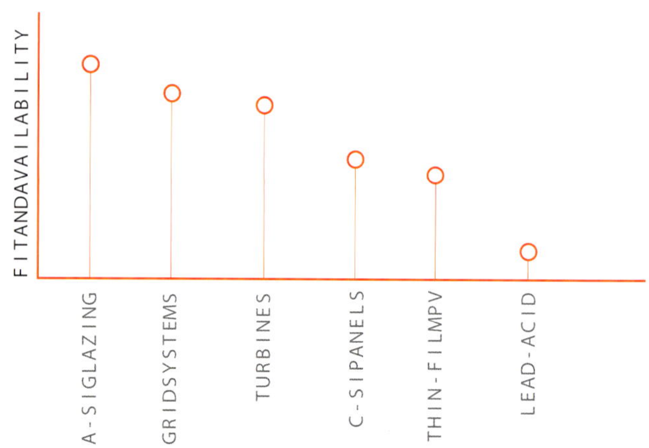

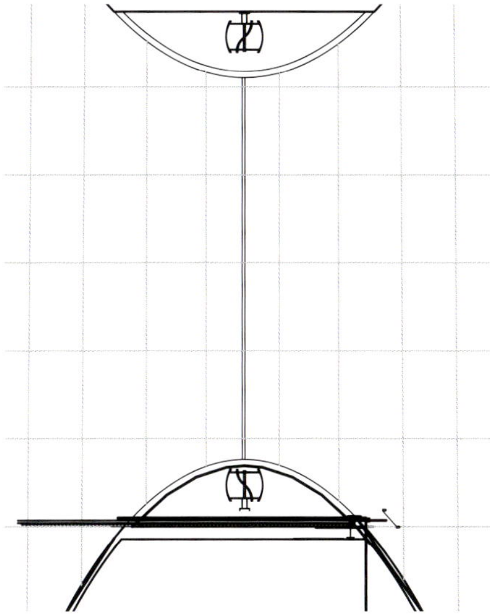

WIND TURBINE DIAGRAMS

STRUCTURE

HYDER, STRUCTURAL ENGINEER

Two slender towers are connected at intervals of approximately 20 floors. By linking the main cores to the perimeter columns through an outrigger system, the columns are engaged as one system and lateral stiffness is increased. Gravity loads flow to the perimeter columns, connecting the outriggers to the perimeter columns and main cores through a belt truss. At each outrigger level, perimeter belt trusses are introduced to resolve other forces from columns above and below the plant rooms, creating a robust system throughout.

On special structural zones, such as MEP areas and where outriggers exist, it is normal to slow down construction time. In this case, structural sections are pre-fabricated rather constructed through traditional formwork and casting. Perimeter columns are concrete-filled steel tubes that allow the steel tubes to be erected 2–3 floor lengths at a time. Another measure used to add speed to the construction time is a non-labor-intensive floor system, such as composite steel pre-cast floor, which can span 12–14 m.

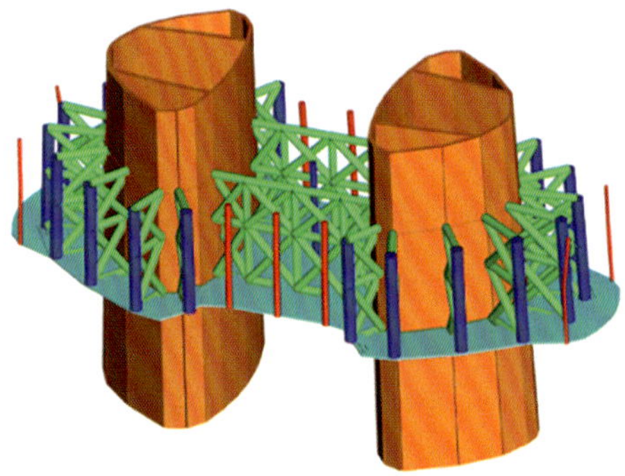

PERIMETER BELT TRUSS

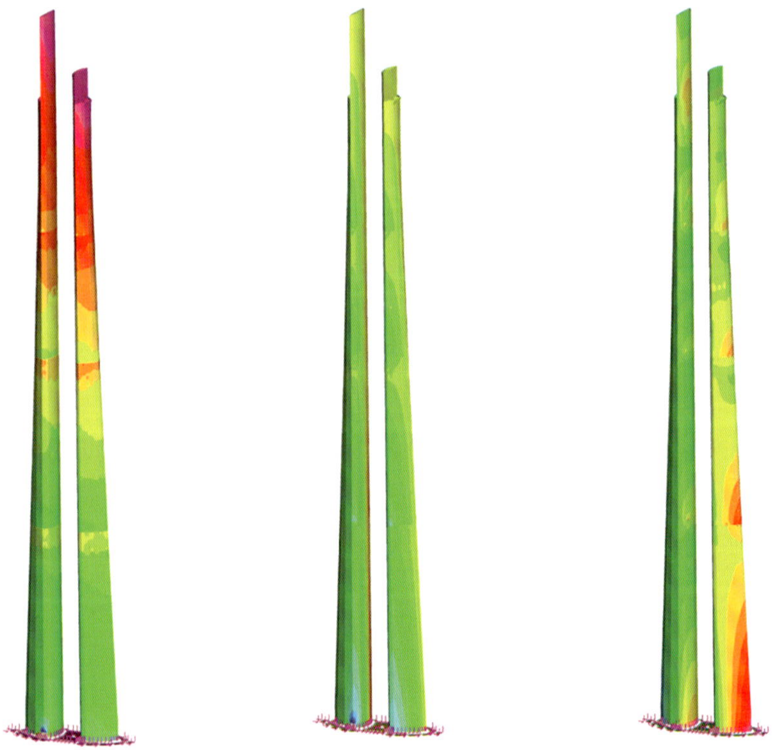

OUTRIGGER DESIGN

The outrigger design has several innovative concepts:

1. Use self-climbing jump form on the tower core to achieve fast cycle time.
2. Minimize the number of perimeter columns to reduce crane lifting time.
3. Use pre-fabricated structural sections rather than the traditional formwork and casting construction strategy.
4. Columns are concrete-filled steel tubes that can be erected 2–3 floor lengths at one time, reducing erection time.
5. Use a non-labor-intensive floor systems, such as composite steel or pre-cast flooring that can span up to 12–14 m to reduce construction time.

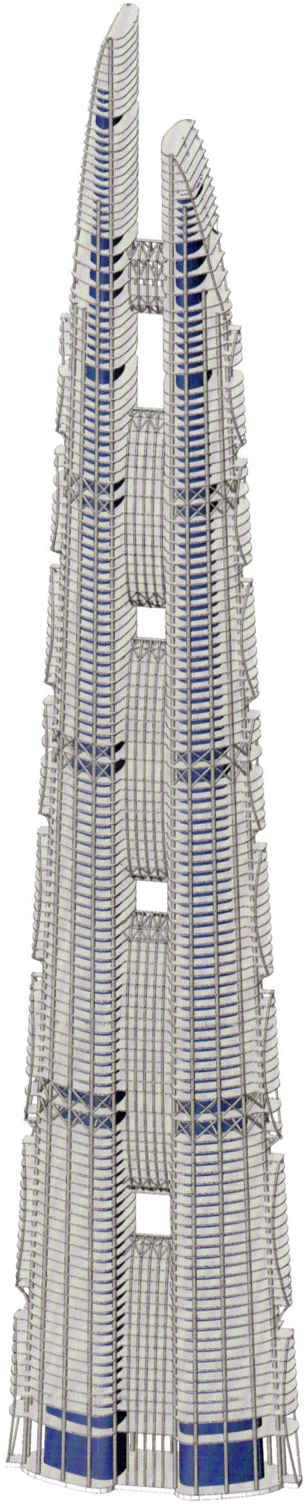

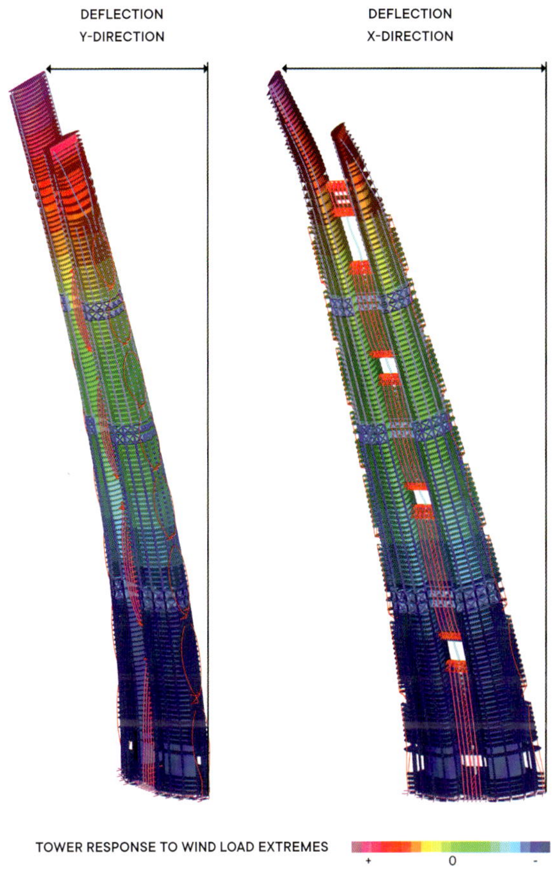

DEFLECTION
Y-DIRECTION
DEFLECTION
X-DIRECTION
TOWER RESPONSE TO WIND LOAD EXTREMES
+
0
-

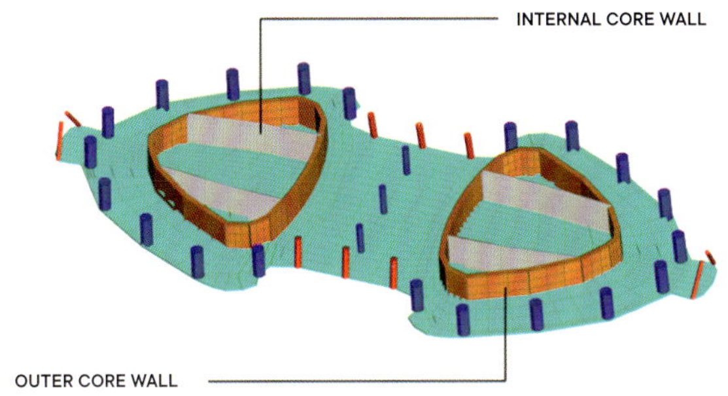

INTERNAL CORE WALL
OUTER CORE WALL

XI'AN GREENLAND TOWER

XI'AN, CHINA, 2017

500M

The Greenland Silk Road International Center is designed to represent the rich cultural heritage of Xian, China. As one of the oldest cities in China—and the oldest of the Four Great Ancient Capitals—Xian symbolizes one of the birth places of Chinese culture. The physical remains of the great empires that once called this city home have become major symbols of Chinese culture.

Xian's rich history is represented by several remaining artifacts including the ornate armors worn by Qin Dynasty warriors, the world-renowned terracotta soldiers, and Xian's great city wall. These protective elements ensured the survival of a great civilization for generations.

The design draws influence from these historical elements to create a unique architectural language, one in which the building's form and its facade were designed as protection from the environment, while creating a connection to the history of Xian.

Borrowing its architectural expression from the city wall, the tower's stone facade creates a sense of mass and impenetrability, while the atrium is light and bright, connecting the building back to the tower. The building's a long rectilinear form has four primary components: the mass, an atrium, the roof pavilions, and a trellis.

- \+ CONTEXT
- \+ SITE
- \+ PROGRAM
- \+ PODIUM
- \+ FACADE
- \+ RESEARCH + DEVELOPMENT
- \+ STRUCTURE

LOUIS VUITTON
H&

CONTEXT

The language of the tower is based on the armor worn by the Qin Dynasty warriors, creating a facade that is highly responsive to its environment. The primary exterior materials are metal and terracotta, chosen to help connect the building to the history of Xian. Metal panels represent the lamellar iron plates further relate to the traditional Chinese warrior's armor.

The building envelope responds to environmental conditions with passive solar controls that create ideal natural lighting levels. Instead of a traditional fully glazed curtain-wall system, a punched window expression changes in density and depth on each surface, depending on its orientation and exposure to the sun. By tuning the facade to protect each side of the building, it dramatically reduces the building's energy consumption, creating a synergy between the look of the building and how it performs. Glazed terracotta tiles frame the windows and sunshades, giving further protection to the glass from the direct sun.

NORTH WEST FACADE

SOUTH EAST FACADE

SITE

The tower is in the core area of the Fengdong New City District, directly west of the city center and this axial relationship is an important part of the overall master plan. The location of the tower is coordinated so that it has a direct axis with the historic bell tower at the center of the Wall City of Xian. On the east-west direction, the tower functions as the primary focal point between itself, the retail mall, and the conference center. The open space has been organized as a series of passages throughout the site, connecting the buildings and re-emphasizing the axial importance of the tower, as well as its role as the anchor for the development. Each building has its own dedicated entrance and identifiable address, with direct access to the site from all directions.

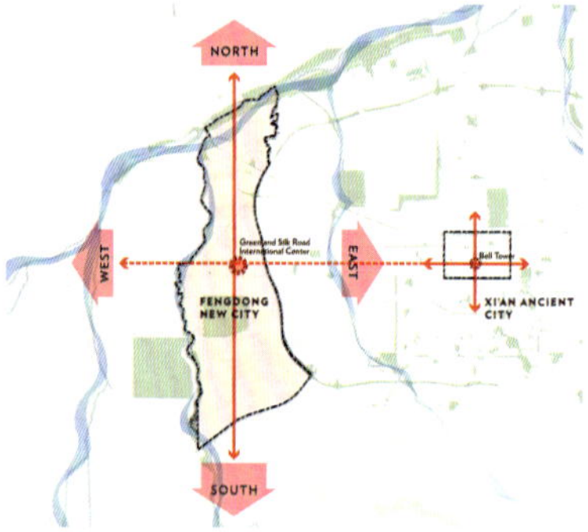

SITE PLAN

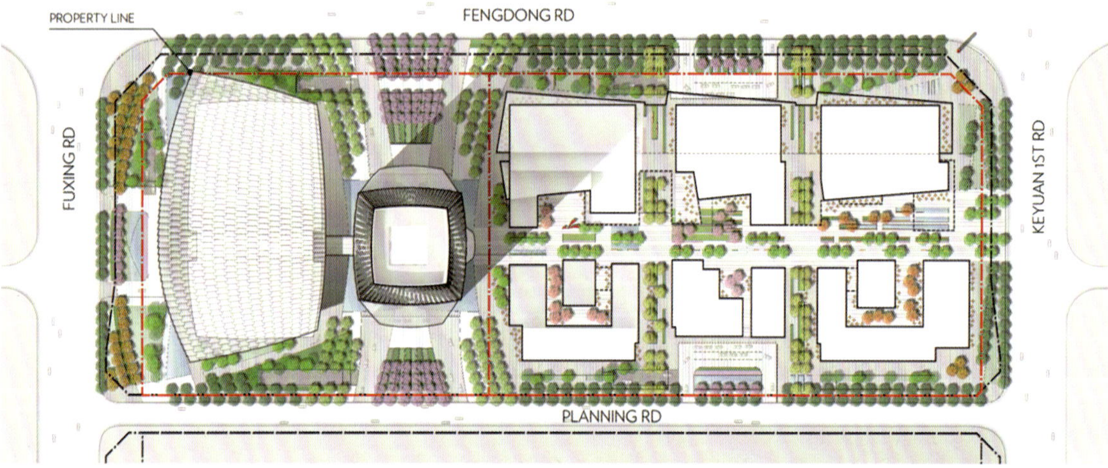

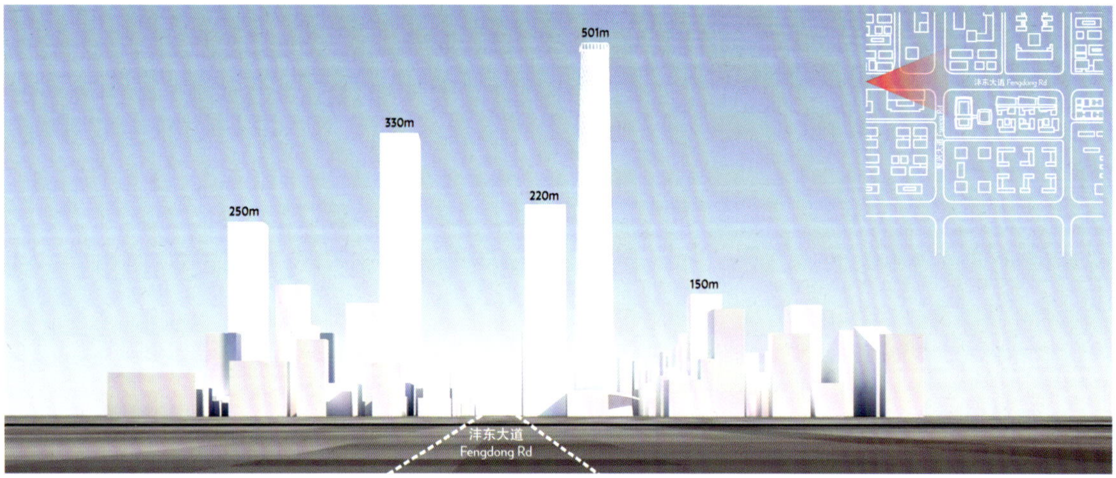

PROGRAM

The mixed-use tower has 101 stories with office space occupying the first 75 floors and hotel on the upper floors. The subtle taper of the tower and the changes to the core as elevators drop off allow an ideal floor plate for uses at their respective locations in the tower.

The office space is divided into eight elevator zones and utilizes two sky lobbies that add efficiency to the core and provide faster travel for occupants. The office elevator groups range from three to six elevators each.

The two sky lobby shuttles are in groups of six, with the hotel zone using three sky lobby shuttles to deliver occupants to Level 78 where they board four local elevators to the hotel floors.

The mechanical and area of refuge floors are located per local requirements and are coordinated with the various zones of office elevators and MEP floors to increase overall efficiency.

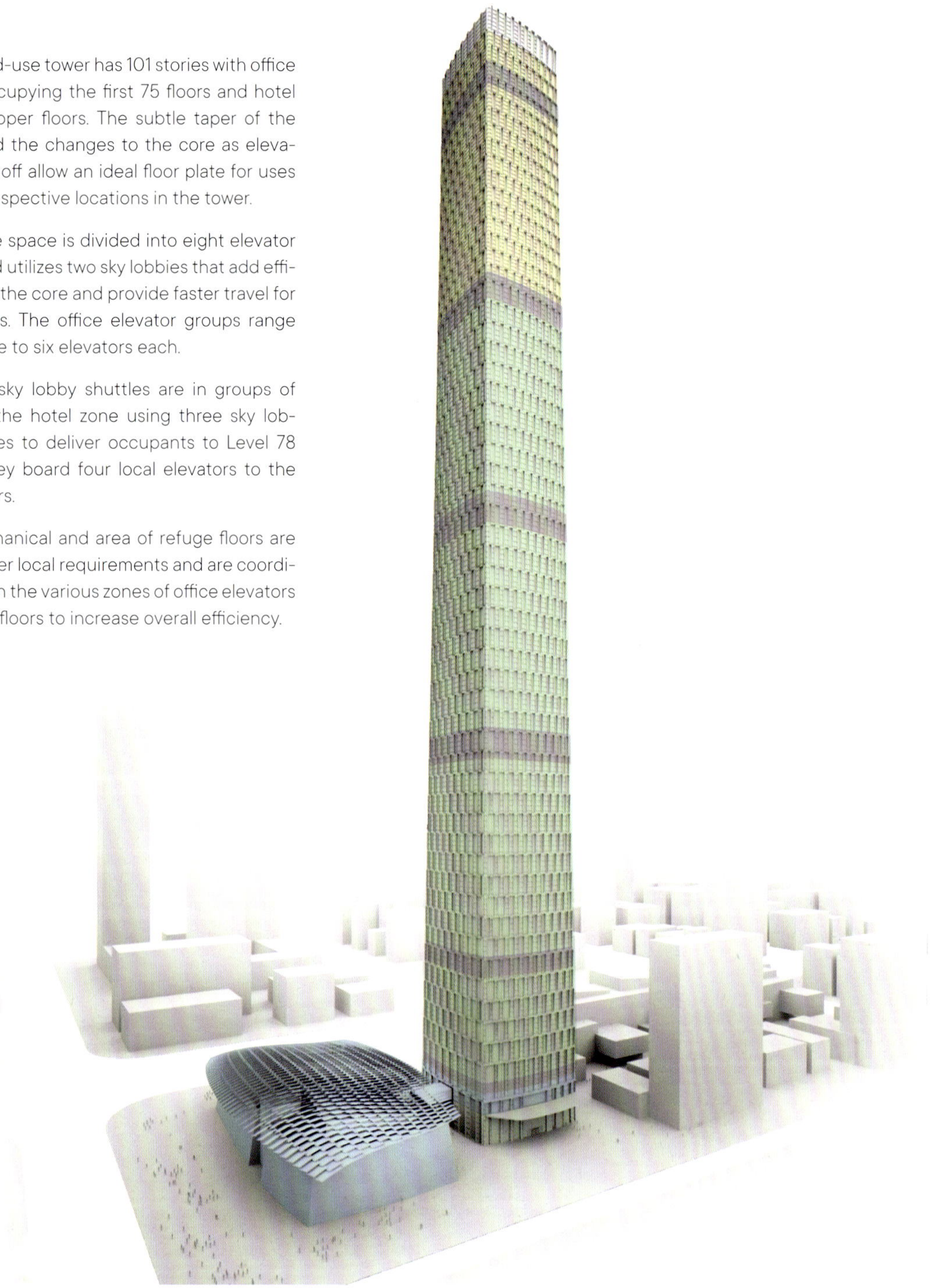

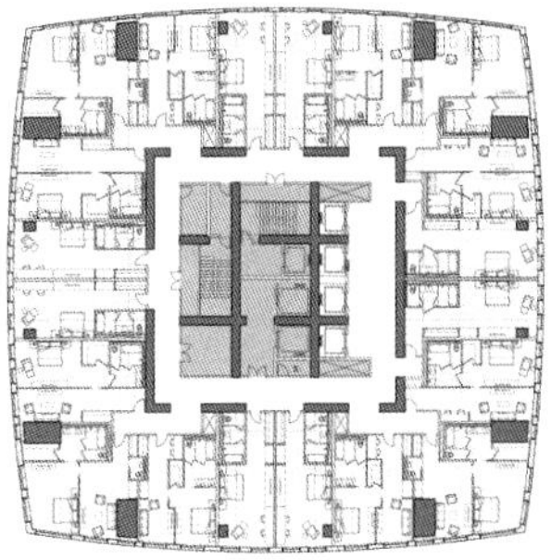

TYPICAL HOTEL

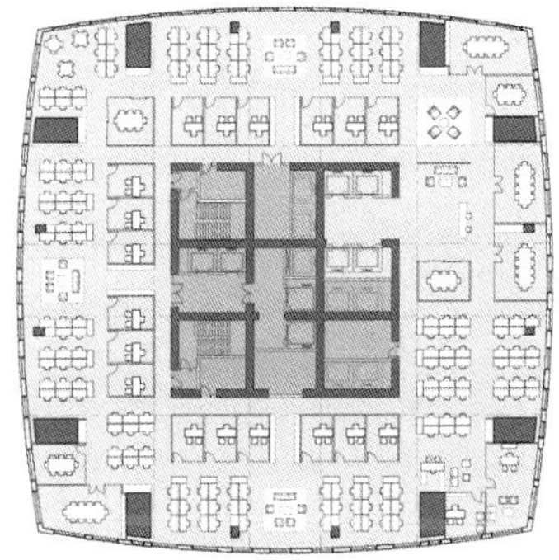

TYPICAL OFFICE
HIGH

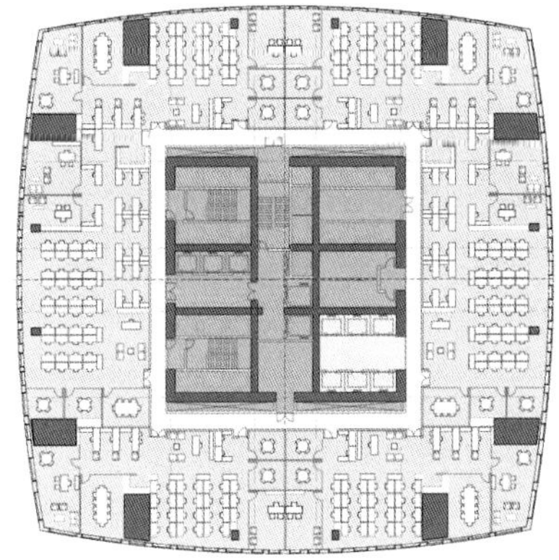

TYPICAL OFFICE
LOW

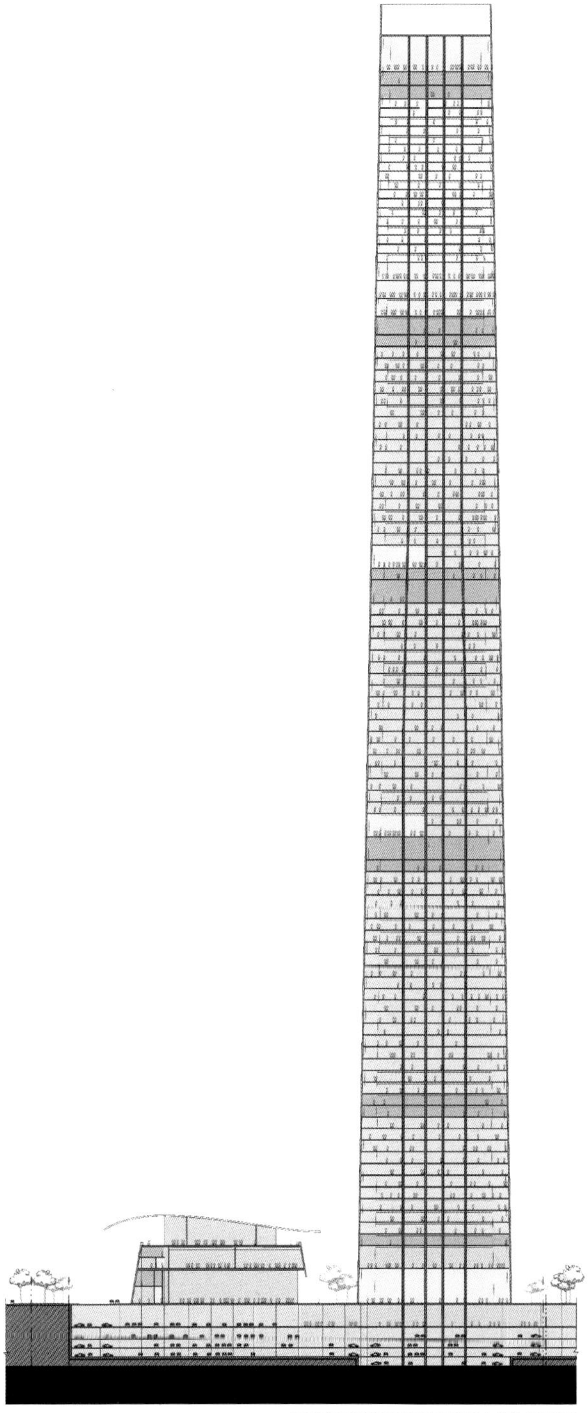

SECTION THROUGH PODIUM AND TOWER

PODIUM

Two pavilions at the top of the podium unify the body of the building to the trellis, the main architectural feature of the building. Its lamellar-like glass fins create a textured surface that defines the architecture of the tower. The trellis also helps create shaded spaces around the building that highlight the entrance and the surrounding outdoor courtyards.

PODIUM SECTION

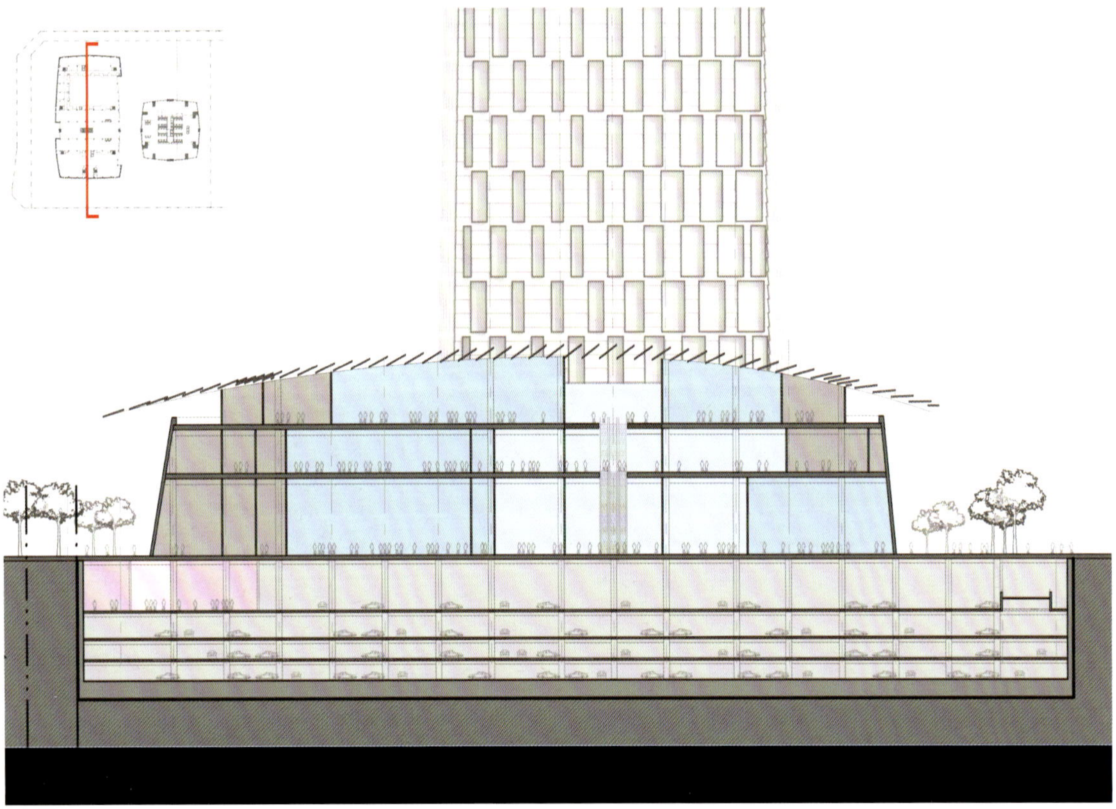

PODIUM ORGANIZATION

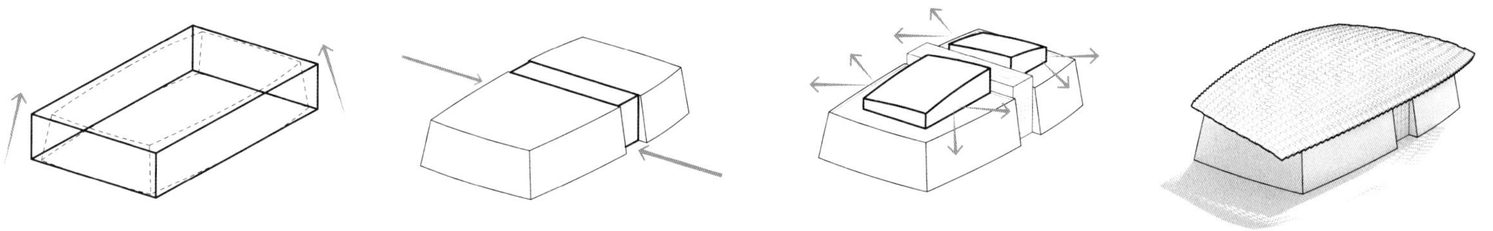

FACADE

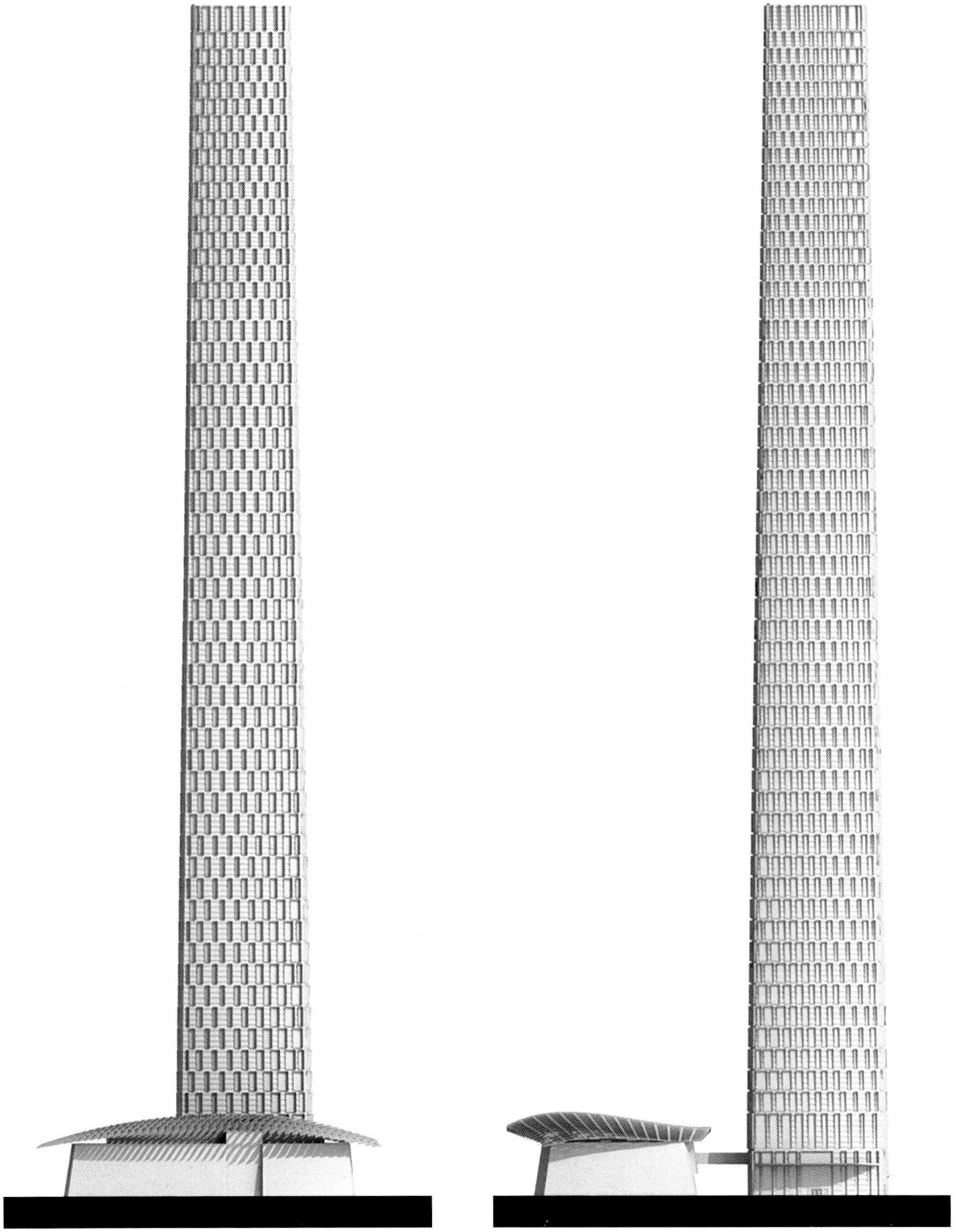

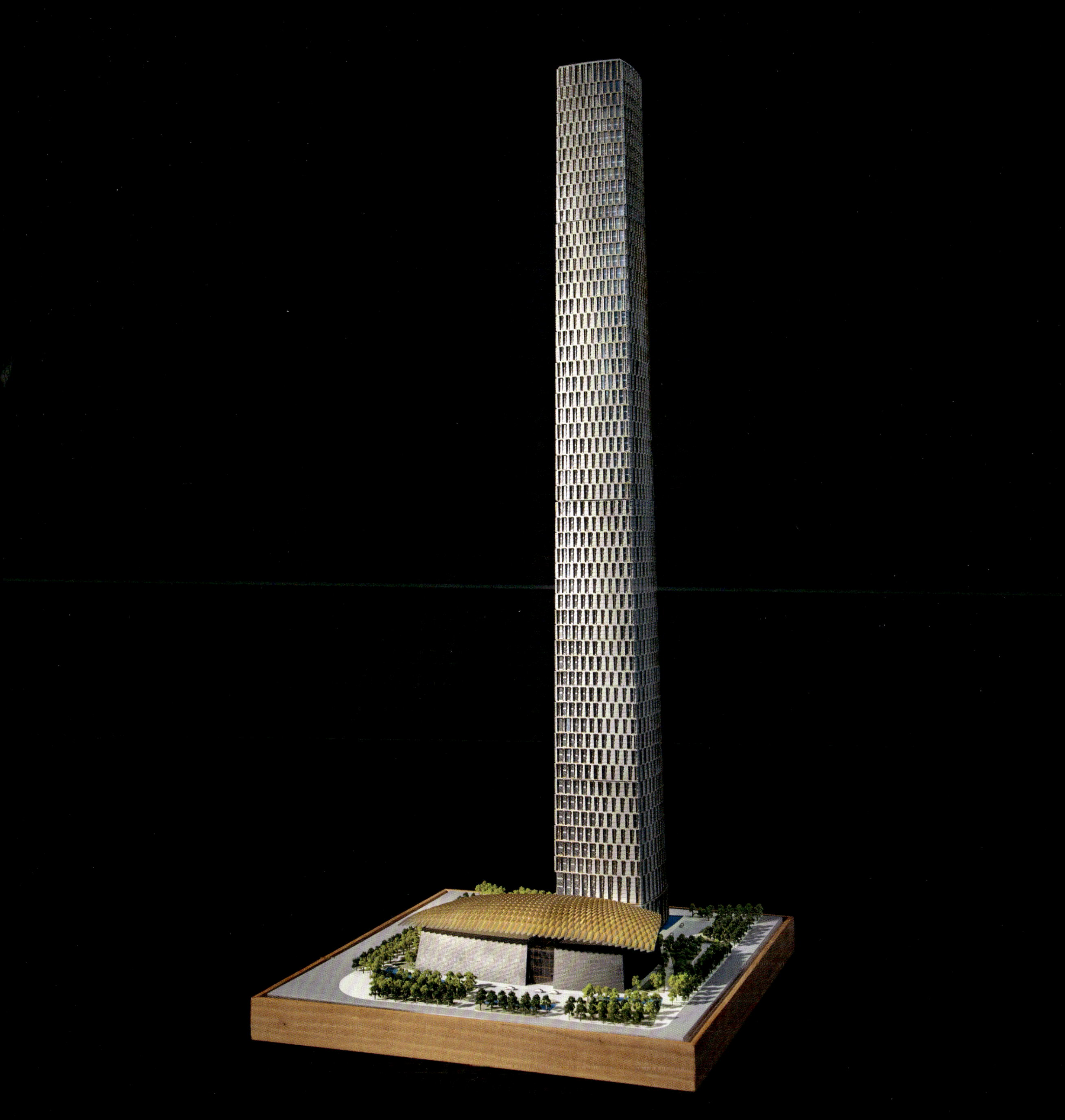

RESEARCH + DEVELOPMENT

Shading elements on the exterior facade provide self-shading, reducing the incident annual solar radiation by 25 percent. With the building's window-to-wall ratio at an average of 60 percent, shading elements are designed to be the deepest on the east and west facades, maximizing protection and self-shading. Conversely, those on the north facade are shallower to maximize diffused daylight. The largest solid panel on this version is 1.5 meters wide.

High-performing glazing and insulated wall assemblies minimize heat transfer through the envelope, reducing the building's cooling and heating demands. Renewable energy technology, such as solar photovoltaics (PV) integrated into the building envelope, can provide 25 percent or more of the building's electrical needs, further reducing the net-energy use of the building. The total energy savings goal versus a baseline building is a 75 percent reduction.

SHAPING DIAGRAMS

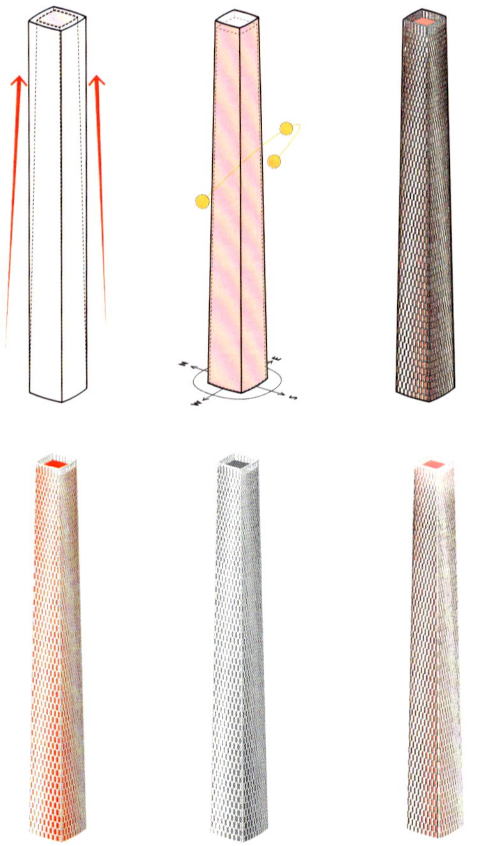

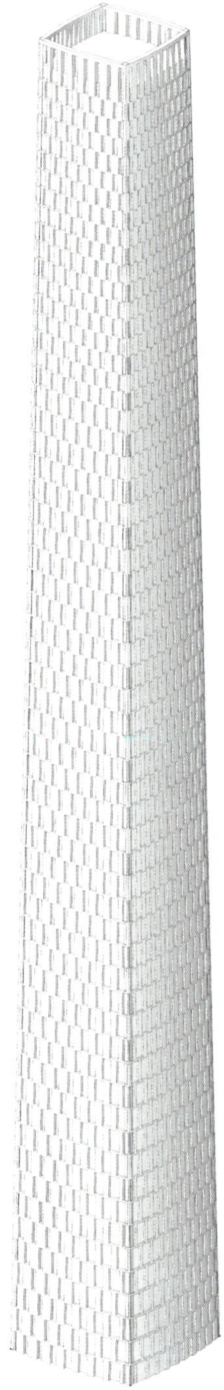

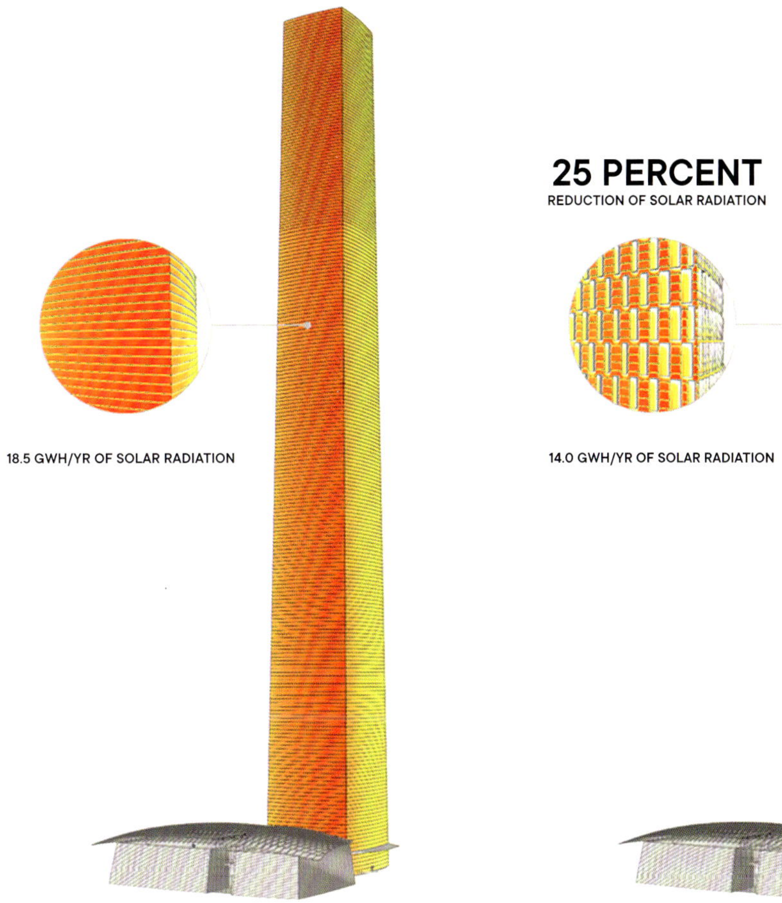

WINDOW OPTIONS

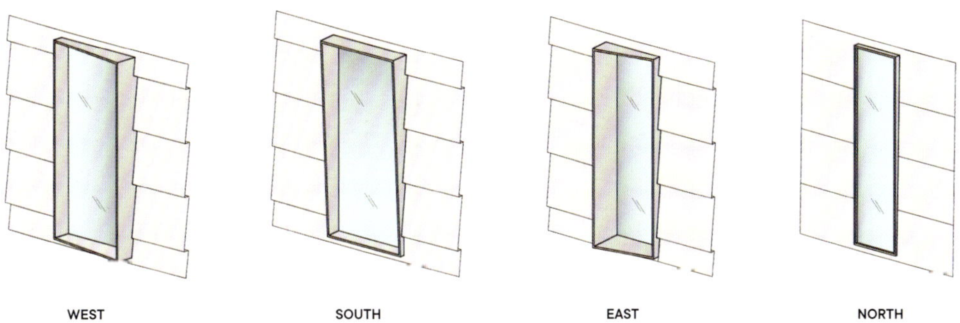

In study option #1, the building's window-to-wall ratio is an average of 60 percent. It has large windows that reduce the amount of solid surface to the exterior facade, with the largest panel at 1.5 meters wide. Study option #2 also has a window-to-wall ratio with an average of 60 percent but introduces a screen for a portion of the window so that the it appears more solid from the outside. Option #2 maintains the same amount of vision glass and does not block interior views.

WINDOW/WALL RATIO
OPTION 1

WINDOW/WALL RATIO
OPTION 2

STRUCTURE

THORNTON TOMASETTI, STRUCTURAL ENGINEER

The tower has a total architecture height of 501 m with a structural height of approximately 475 m. When selecting a lateral system, there are a few architectural constraints and preferences:

1. Plan is close to a square in shape
2. The core is located at the center of building, housing the elevators and MEP spaces
3. Large column spacing is required at the building's perimeter
4. An outrigger truss and belt truss system can be used at limited floors.
5. The tower tapers inward in elevation
6. The proposed lateral system is a Core Wall Outrigger Truss Mega Frame system, which is suitable for a supertall building at or over 300 m. When compared to other systems, this structural system is cost effective and efficient in resisting lateral loads

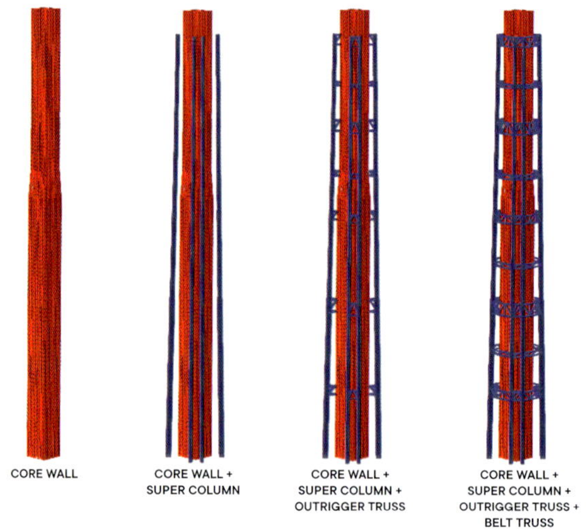

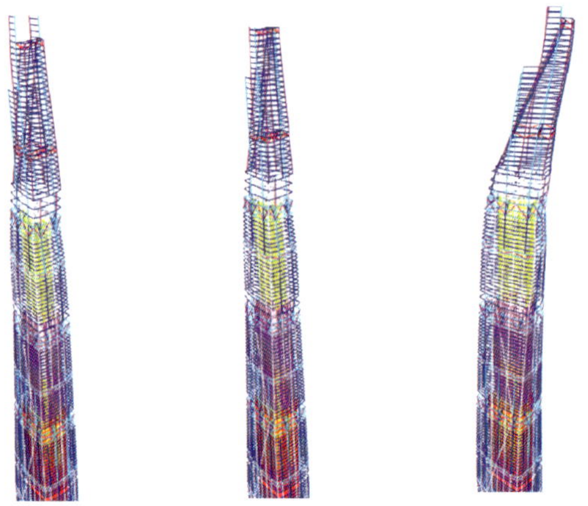

The lateral system contains following components:

1. Reinforced-concrete Core Wall
2. Composite Super Columns
3. Steel Belt Trusses
4. Steel Outrigger Trusses
5. Secondary Steel Perimeter Frame

Elevators are typically at the center core of the building, therefore it is a natural solution to allocate the structural concrete core here. The core is a 26m x 26m square in plan at the bottom and sets back to 22.5m x 22.5m through sloping walls. The flange walls and web walls of the core will decrease in width as the tower ascends.

The tower has eight super columns, with two columns on each side—near the corner—to improve the cost effectiveness of floor cantilever framing and belt trusses at MEP levels. These columns are symmetrical and uniformly spaced, therefore the tributary areas are approximately the same to produce columns of the same sizes, which is aesthetically preferable and results in better occupant space layouts and utilization.

Uniformly spaced columns are also beneficial to the structural performance and can prevent issues like differential settlement between columns and stress concentration. High-strength concrete with high-strength embedded built-up steel columns can be used in the super-column design to reduce the column size and gain more rentable space. The columns will slope inward toward the center of the plan symmetrically.

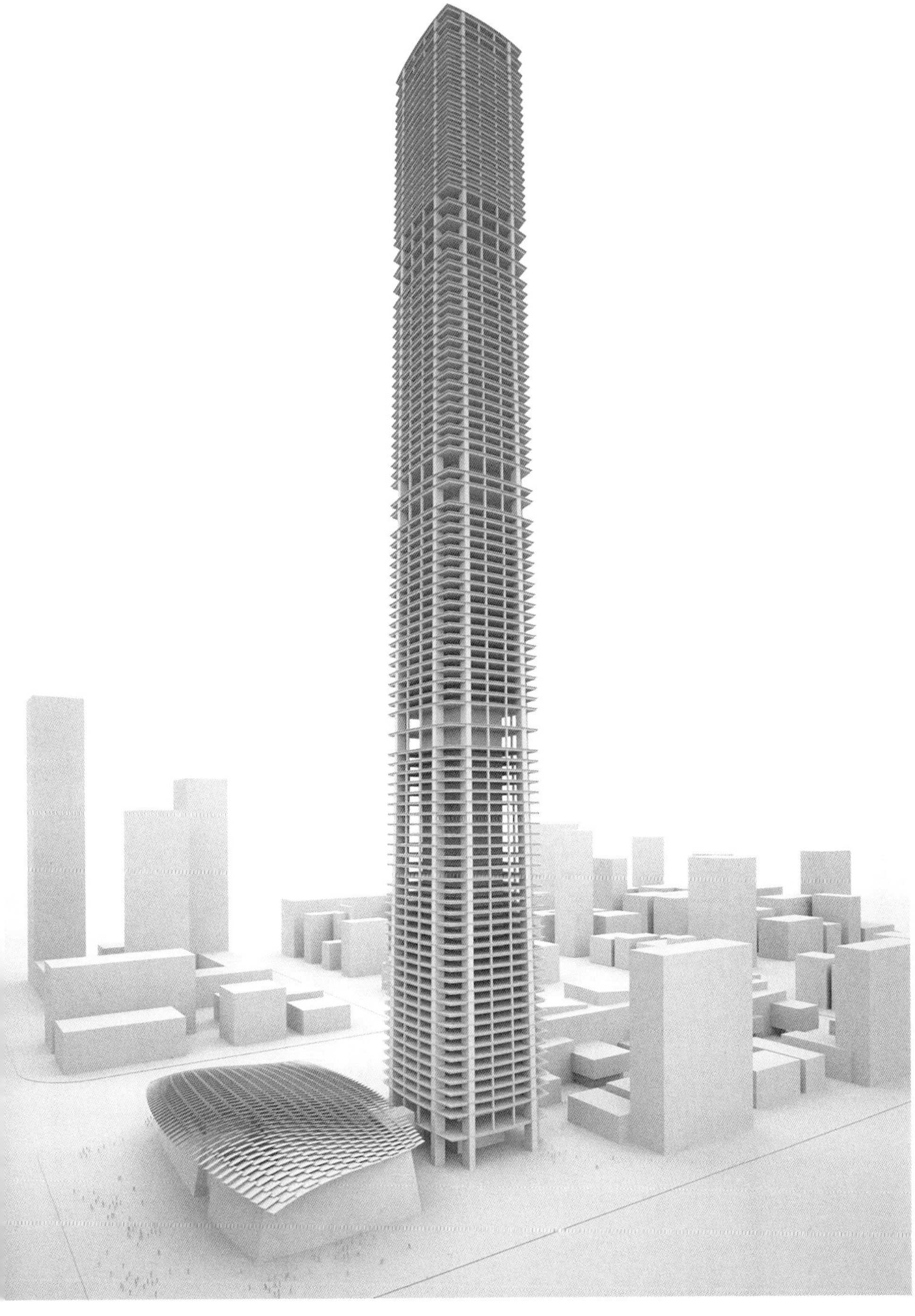

Since the columns slope inward symmetrically, torsion can be avoided. The equivalent size of the super columns will start at approximately 5m x 3m at the bottom and decrease by about 40 percent by the time they reach the top of the building.

Steel belt trusses connecting the super columns are placed around the building perimeter at nine MEP and refuge zone along building height. The belt trusses work with the super columns to serve as the secondary lateral system and to transfer truss to the gravity load from the gravity columns to the super columns. The belt trusses work like hoops to enhance the overall tower's integrity and make stresses in perimeter columns more uniform, while also reducing the unbraced length of the perimeter columns. They also prevent progress collapse due to the local failure of gravity columns and therefore enhance structural safety and redundancy.

The super columns need to connect to the core wall to maximize the overall lateral stiffness of the tower. Outrigger trusses at the MEP floors are widely used in high-rise buildings, which are proved to be cost effective. There are seven outrigger truss zones in the tower, located at the MEP floors: Level 14-16, Level 35-37, Level 56-57, Level 65-66, Level 76-78, Level 86-87, and Level 99-101. The outrigger trusses connect the super columns and the concrete core, extending two bays in the core walls to keep continuous load path. The 1.5 m header truss is also used at the top of this building to reduce the story drifts and keep the integrity of the lateral system. The outrigger trusses are subjected to large tension and compression forces, so high strength steel is used.

The gravity system contains a super column, a core belt truss, and a floor system. The super column, core, belt truss system also serves as a lateral system. The floor system uses a composite slab, composed of metal deck, steel beams, and the concrete slab. The 125 mm thick close-form or 155 mm open-form composite slab is used at the office area, while a 200 mm thick truss slab is used for the mechanical floors. The composite slab has many beneficial features as it is light weight, has a fast construction, a flexible layout, and is renovation friendly, as compared with a normal concrete slab. The composite slab can reduce the size of the foundation and the seismic force and is the preferred floor slabs for supertall buildings. Between each pair of super columns (on each side of the slab) two gravity columns are allocate, with eight gravity columns for the tower.

ZA'ABEEL HOTEL

DUBAI, UAE, 2008
450M

The Za'abeel Hotel Tower was designed as part of the overall Za'abeel Energy City Master Plan, also design by AS+GG, in Dubai, completed in 2008. The project includes the hotel tower, a podium building with a ballroom, and two low-rise office towers.

The hotel's form reaches to the sky, slightly twisting with a program that wraps around a tapering atrium. The exterior wall adds texture to its strong architectural expression. Vertical fins and horizontal shading devices act as a protective curtain, surrounding and protecting the tower. The following design principles formed the concept for the massing:

Connect: The site is at once a connection and transition point. The tower reaches south to connect toward the master plan, rotating to become a pivot-point to address the outer parcels, convention center, Za'abeel Park, and future Dubai developments to the north.

Guide: The top of the tower is shaped like a crescent pointing toward the sky, which will be lit at night to define it as a guiding point within the development and city. The asymmetry of the building sets its orientation so that each vantage point is unique.

Shelter: The tower's east and west faces wrap like a drape, surrounding the pedestrian plazas. These faces feature integrated photovoltaic shading to shelter the atrium from the sun. The podium buildings and the courtyard park are both shaded by the tower's broad shadow.

Dynamic: The tower is designed to be viewed differently from each point in Dubai. The panoramic views from the tower move and change as it ascends, reinforcing its role as a connecting element. The tower is designed to also be viewed from outside and within in dynamic ways, through its tapering and receding geometry.

+ PROGRAM
+ FACADE
+ PERFORMANCE
+ RESEARCH + DEVELOPMENT
+ STRUCTURE

PROGRAM

The mixed-use program has hotel and condominium functions. The hotel is at the lower half of the tower, surrounding the atrium where the building's footprint is broader. A set of hotel elevators has views of the atrium and is accessed via a wrapping corridor with a dramatic lobby that sits at the base of the atrium. The north side of the plan, which is mostly hotel, was designed to have one room drop off every few floors. The plan stays on a consistent structural module so rooms are identical and not tapered.

As the tower ascends, the atrium disappears, and the condominium program begins. The condominium floors have more flexibility in their layout but also keep to the overall structural grid and retain many of the shear walls on the north side. The top of the tower houses a multi-story restaurant and club space that culminates in the pointed tip. The elevator system includes dedicated elevators for the hotel, the hotel services, the condominiums, building services, and the restaurant/observatory.

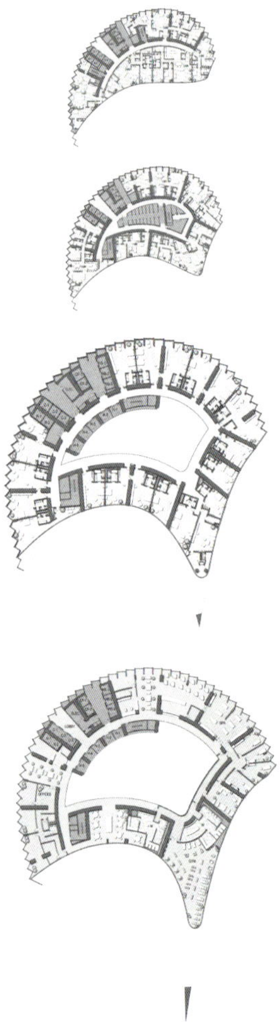

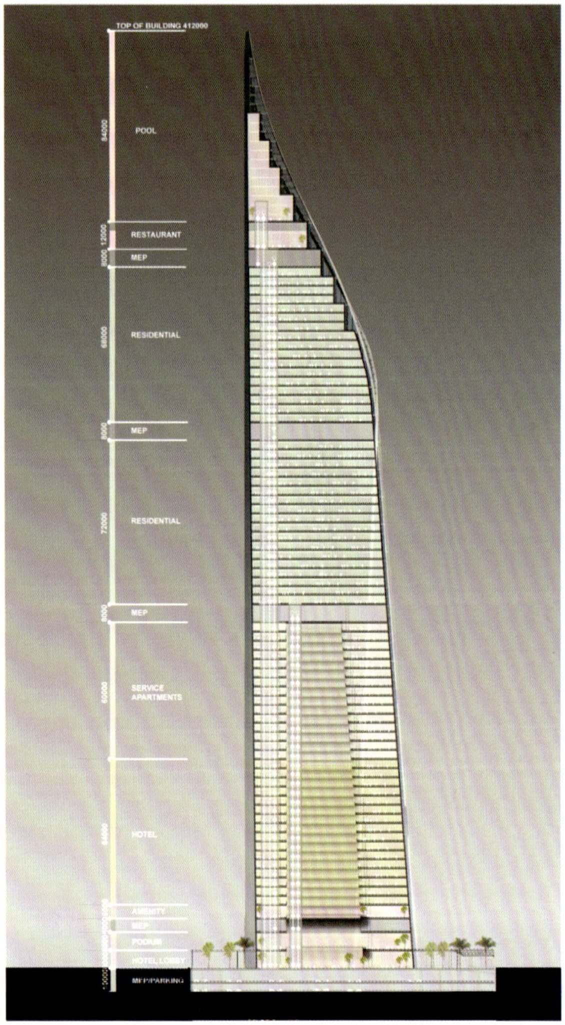

FACADE

The south facade features deep ledges every three floors that shade the glass from direct sunlight and offer the opportunity for the placement of photovoltaic arrays. These ledges form a curved shape, which allows the glass to be flat in tiers of three levels. This is one of the ways that an irregular form was rationalized to make it more constructible.

The triangular east facade is a glass and metal curtain wall behind a large triangular-shaped sun screen that casts its shadow in the morning to reduce glare and protect the south and east facades from the morning sun. This screen also creates the structural support for the building tip against wind loads.

The north facade, which wraps around most of the east and western exposures and is where most of the hotel rooms are located, uses a combination of highly reflective, tinted glass on the east and west to block out solar gain and clear glass facing directly north. This allows maximum views with minimum glare and heat gain.

Other design options included fins that face east and west, made from a solid or stone material, which helps save additional energy.

PERFORMANCE

The east facade culminates in a glass and integrated photovoltaic fin that screens the large balcony at the tip of the building from wind and sun. The balcony is made of a steel structure, which supports the fin against wind loads.

PHOTOVOLTAIC FIN

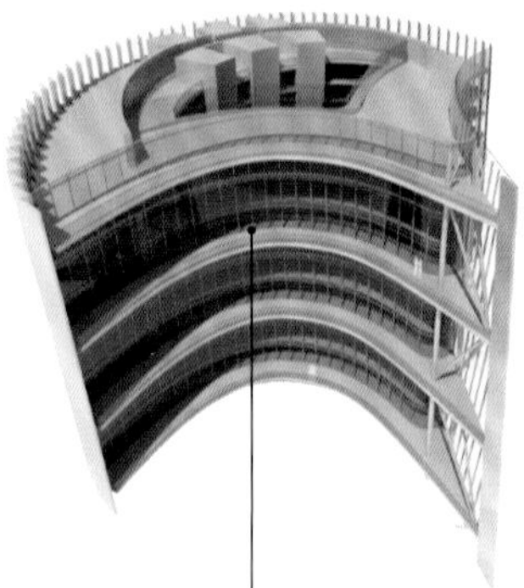

The north facade will use a combination of highly reflective, tinted glass on the east and west side to block out solar gain, and clear glass facing directly north. This will allow maximum vies with minimum glare and heat gain.

Protecting the buildings on the site from solar gain drives the design. By using the hotel tower to shade the rest of the site, human comfort levels are increased, and public areas can be more active spaces.

This solar analysis shows how the hotel's shadow helped the design team optimize the exterior wall designs. The back side of the hotel is highly textured with vertical fins that block the east and west sun.

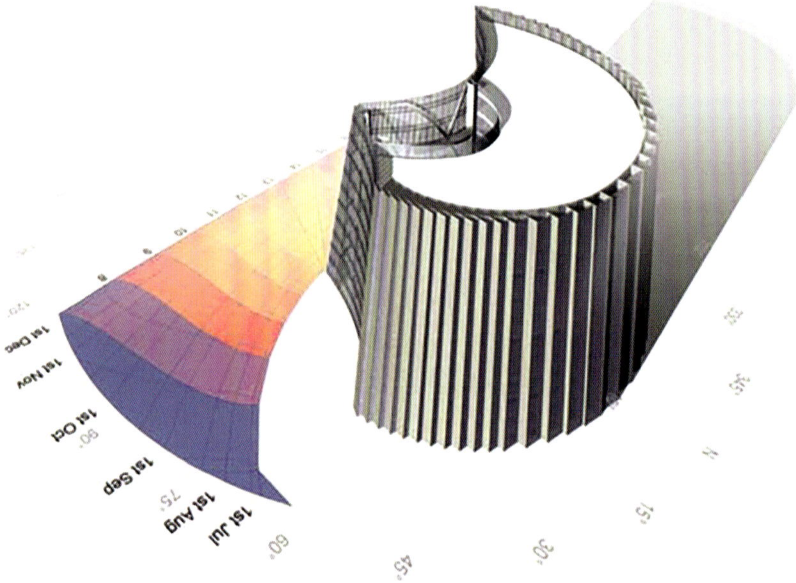

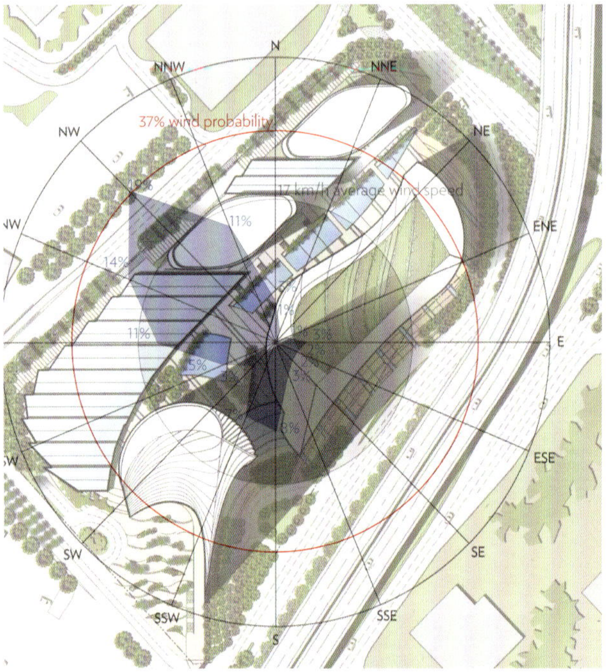

WIND ANALYSIS

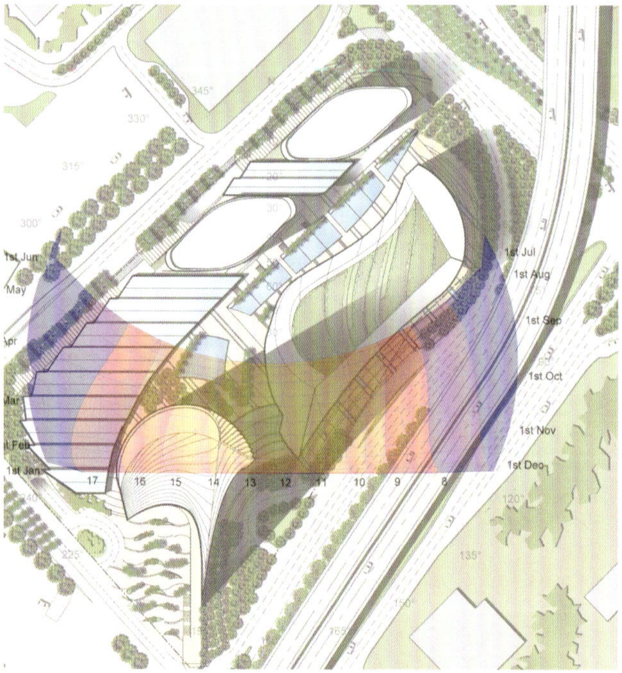

SOLAR ANALYSIS

STRUCTURE

THORNTON TOMASETTI, STRUCTURAL ENGINEER

The structural system uses an integrated arrangement of concrete elements, designed to create superior structural performance required for a supertall tower. The building's unique combination of a centralized core and radiating fin-walls control the response to lateral loading in a manner that increases comfort levels for the building occupants.

The interior atrium's concrete shear walls anchor the lateral-force-resisting system for the hotel tower, while the fin walls, which correlate to the hotel room demising walls, continue above into the residential tier. The centralized shear walls mimic the contour of the corridor, along with the radial concrete walls between the rooms to serve as the primary gravity load supporting system. Between the radial walls, supplementary columns are located at room demising wall locations for additional support of the floor slabs.

Floor framing at the typical hotel and residential levels is comprised of cast-in-place concrete slabs. Elevated balconies that follow the curve of the building atrium are constructed as a continuation of the concrete slabs and are supported as cantilevered regions from the supports below. A single, triangular spine is created using an extension of the concrete floor slabs with diagonal bracing and localized supporting columns near the tip.

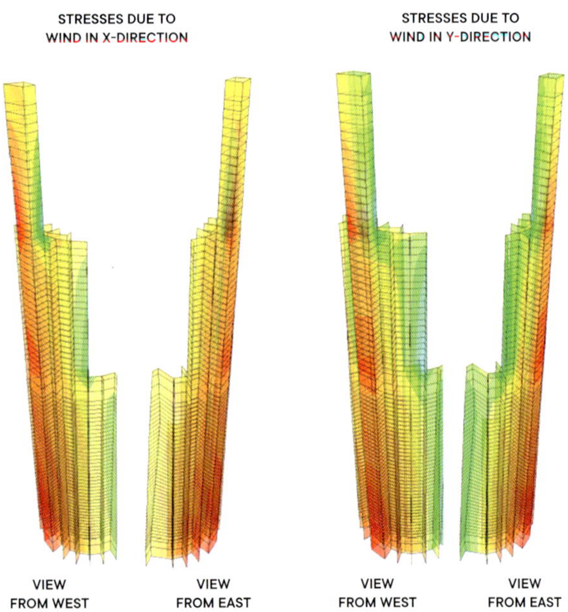

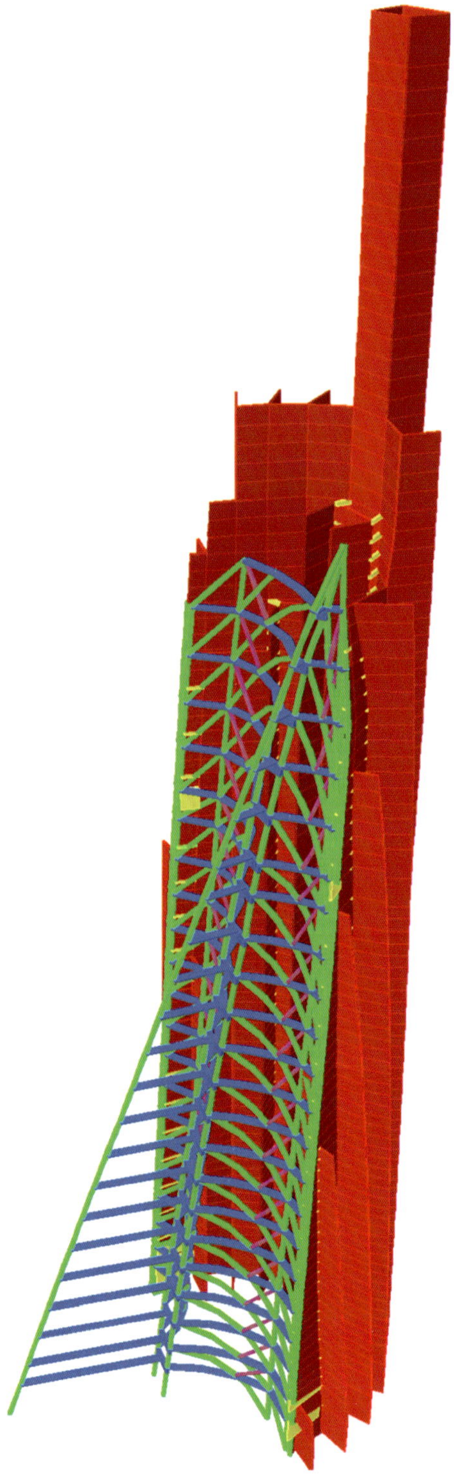

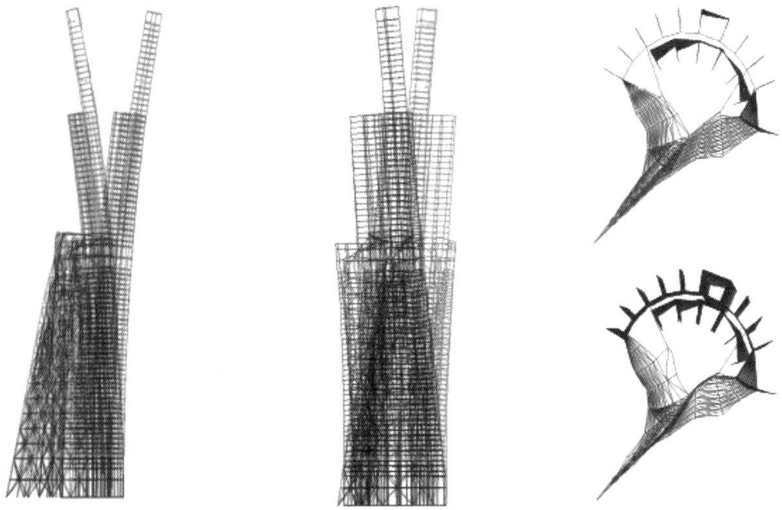

MODE 1
MODE 2
MODE 3

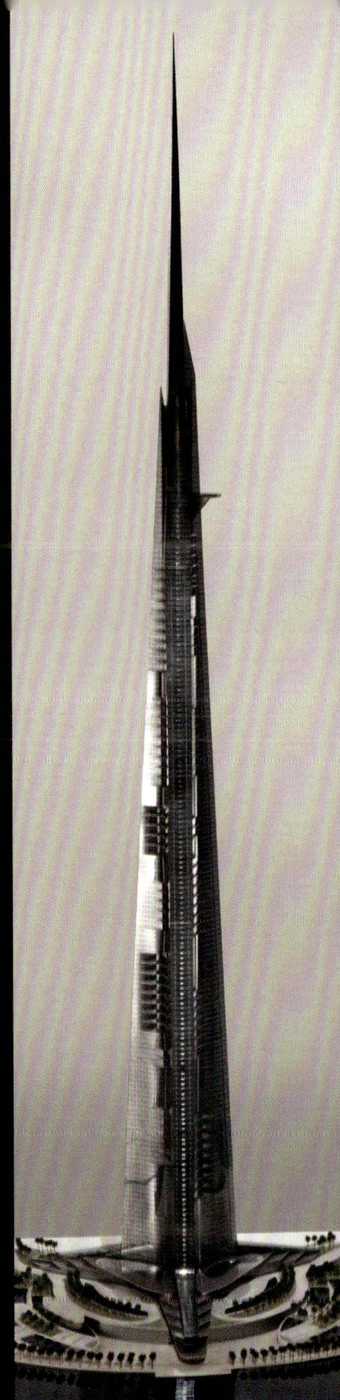

DESIGNING AN ICON: SUPERTALL ICONS AS CATALYSTS FOR DEVELOPMENT

CHAPTER III. DESIGNING AN ICON

SUPERTALL ICONS AS CATALYSTS FOR DEVELOPMENT

From their conception, supertall buildings are understood to be great endeavors. They are undertaken with the ambitious aim of creating a new icon for a city or country. They are designed as an emblem of prestige and an aspirational symbol for the people and communities they serve. The developers of these buildings grasp how critical their presence is and consider them a catalyst for future development.

When designing an icon, the architect must first consider the client and the site. A skyscraper of any caliber will become an important part of the city's skyline; in supertall constructions, it becomes the most identifiable landmark where it is built. The design must be meaningful and specific to the context of its location, while still fulfilling the needs of the client.

Supertall buildings should be constructible, practical, inspiring, and satisfying to the client and users, but it also must be unique to its place. Many of these structures are inherently iconic simply by the virtue of their height, however, they must express the individual character of the place they occupy.

Designing and constructing supertall towers is still a burgeoning field, and we continue to ask many questions about structures of these heights. We recognize that density attracts density, but do the towers benefit from density (New York, Hong Kong) or do they create density (Pudong, Jeddah, Dubai)? Each project has its own parameters for the economic and social drivers so how should architects respond? What makes a supertall tower design truly iconic?

- JEDDAH TOWER
- SHENZHEN HONG KONG INTERNATIONAL CENTER
- CENTRAL PARK TOWER
- AKHMAT TOWER
- HEXI YUZUI TOWER (RUNMAO TOWER)

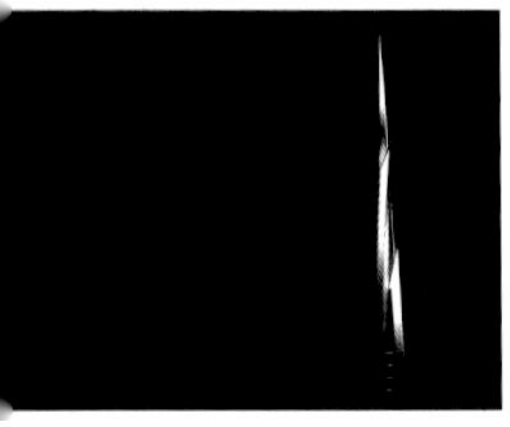

JEDDAH TOWER

JEDDAH, SAUDI ARABIA, 2009

1000+M

At over 1,000 meters (3,280 feet) and a total construction area of 530,000 sm, Jeddah Tower—formerly known as Kingdom Tower—will be the centerpiece and first construction phase of the $20 billion Kingdom City development in Jeddah, Saudi Arabia, near the Red Sea. Expected to cost $1.2 billion to construct, Jeddah Tower will be mixed-use featuring a luxury hotel, office space, serviced apartments, luxury condominiums, and the world's highest observatory.

The design for Jeddah Tower is both highly technical and distinctly organic. With its slender, subtly asymmetrical massing, the tower evokes a bundle of leaves shooting up from the ground—a burst of new life that heralds more growth all around it, symbolizing the tower as a catalyst for increased development.

The sleek, streamlined form can be interpreted as a reference to the folded fronds of young desert plants. The way the fronds sprout upward as a single form, then separate at the top, is an analogy for new growth fused with innovation.

Jeddah Tower's design embraces its architectural pedigree, taking full advantage of the proven design strategies and technological strategies of its lineage, refining and advancing them to achieve new heights. While the design is contextual to Saudi Arabia, it also represents an evolution and a refinement of the architectural continuum of skyscraper design. The three-petal footprint is ideal for residential units and the tapering wings produce an aerodynamic shape that helps reduce structural loading due to wind vortex shedding.

+ CONTEXT
+ SITE
+ PROGRAM
+ FACADE
+ PODIUM
+ INTERIORS
+ OBSERVATION
+ RESEARCH + DEVELOPMENT
+ FIRE + LIFE SAFETY
+ STRUCTURE
+ CONSTRUCTION

CONTEXT

In 2009, Adrian Smith + Gordon Gill Architecture—at the time a relatively new firm—was invited to an architectural design competition led by prince Al-Waleed bin Talal of Kingdom Holdings and Jeddah Economic Company (JEC). Eight of the world's leading architecture firms were invited to compete, including KPF, Pickard Chilton, Pelli Clark Pelli, Foster & Partners, and SOM. At that time, the project was known as "Kingdom Tower."

The criteria for judging included architectural vision and value creation, tower constructability and efficiency, team structure, and work methodology. Each of the four criteria was given a score with the tower's constructability and efficiency valued at half the overall total.

A short list of competitors was determined. AS+GG teamed with structural engineer Thornton Tomasetti and MEP engineering firm Environmental Systems Design. Initial concepts were presented to Prince Waleed in Saudi Arabia using large-scale models and detailed drawings that explained the key aspects of each tower design. The competition process took a year from initial concepts to the final award of the commission, which announced AS+GG the winner on August 2, 2010.

Talal Al Maiman, a board member of JEC said of AS+GG's design, "Prince Alwaleed, Mr. Bakhsh, Mr. Sharbatly, and I were impressed by the boldness and simplicity of the AS+GG design. Jeddah Tower's height is remarkable, obviously, but the building's iconic status will not depend solely on that aspect. Its form is brilliantly sculpted, making it quite simply one of the most beautiful buildings in the world of any height."

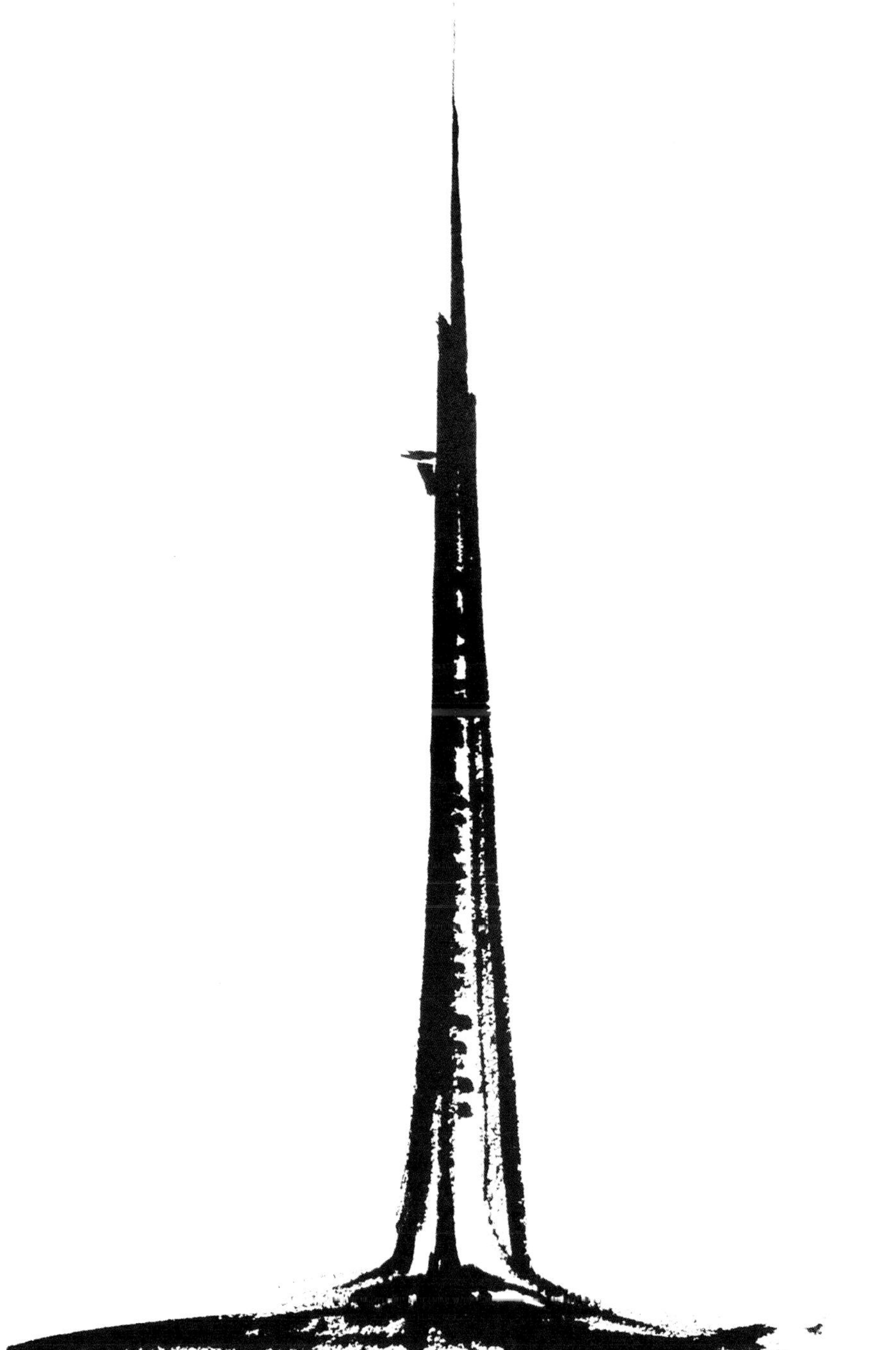

CONTEXT

As part of AS+GG's design process, Global Contextualism, architectural solutions should reflect a specific culture, location, and time. In the case of Jeddah Tower, the solution reflects the desire of JEC, and the leaders of Saudi Arabia, to show the world their vision of the Kingdom as an increasingly important, vital, and thriving member of the international community. The goal was to ensure that the building was simple and cost-effective to build. One of the key elements for addressing the constructability issue is the ability to extend the concrete and climbing form as high and as continuously as possible, with no transfers. Concrete vertical walls rise uninterrupted, with no additional columns at the end of each wing. Different construction companies and component fabricators were consulted early in the process to ensure the assumptions were correct.

GROUND FLOOR PLAN

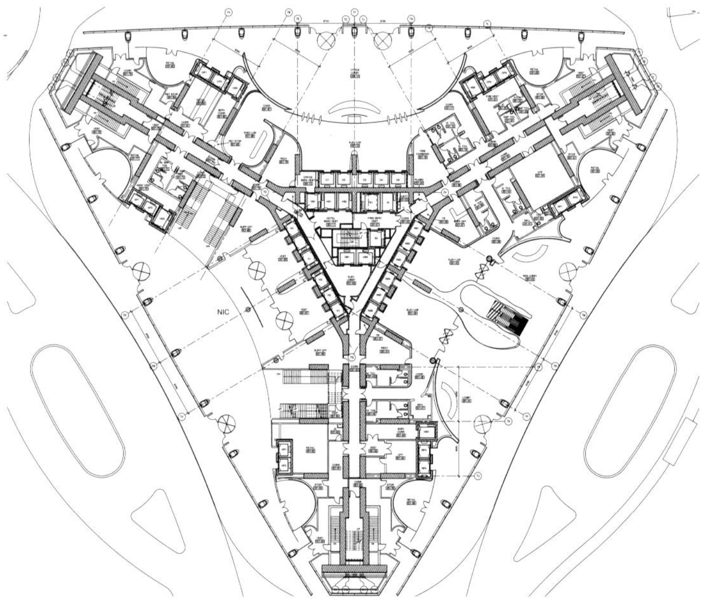

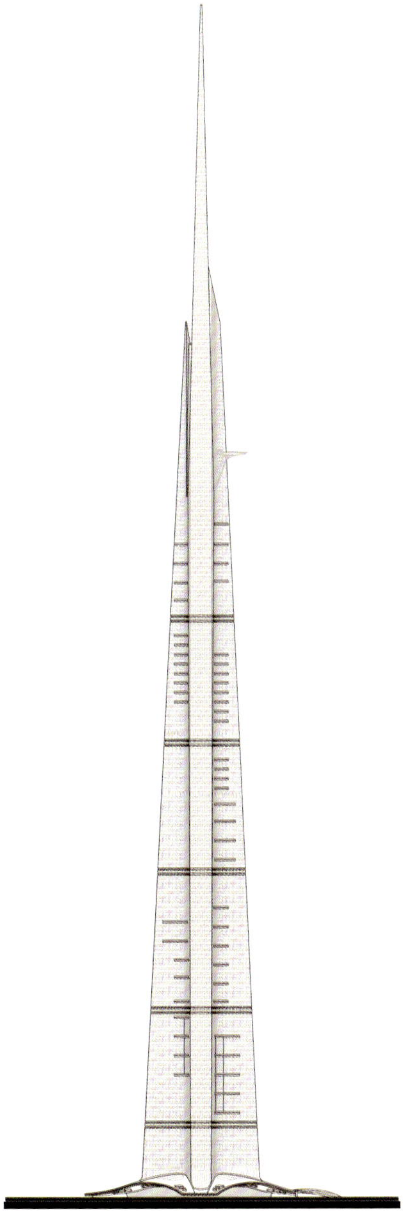

CONTEXT

STEPS TOWARD OPTIMIZATION

1. **Carving The Wings**
   - Removing program area from the wings allows to place it in more valuable areas, at higher levels.
2. **Tapering**
   - Improved structural behavior by reducing vortex shedding.
   - Reach allowable program area at higher levels.
3. **Notching**
   - Relocates program area from lower to higher more valuable floors.
   - Creates valuable terrace spaces.

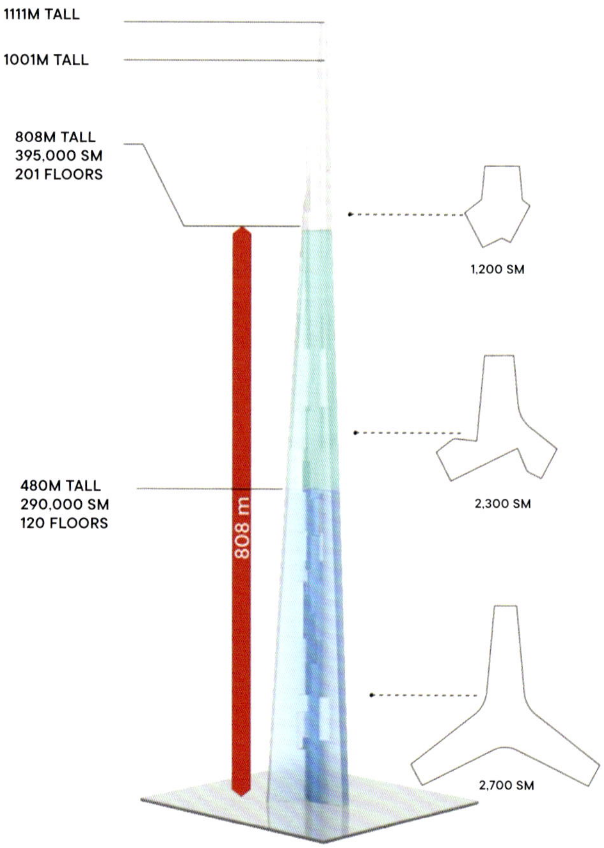

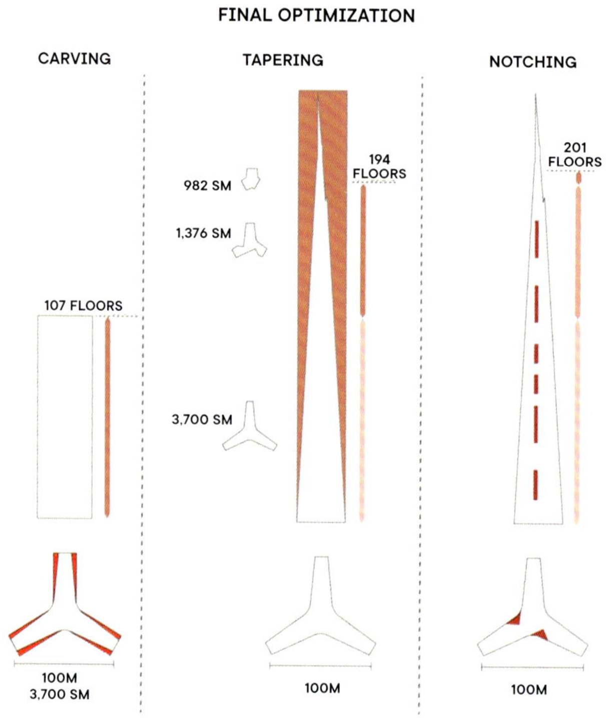

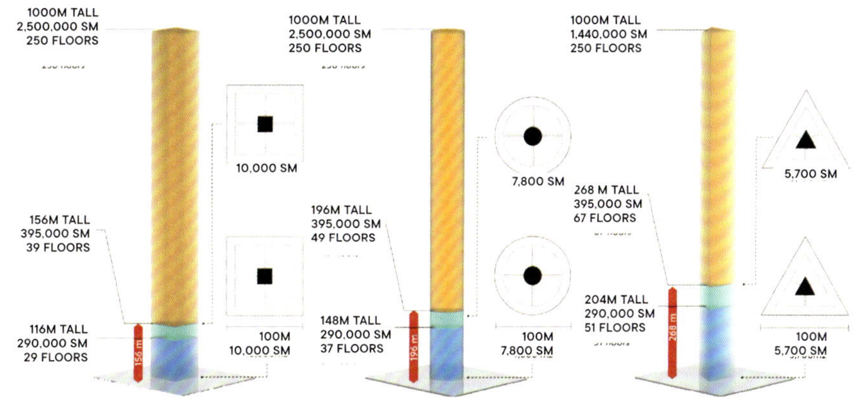

EXTRUDED SHAPES

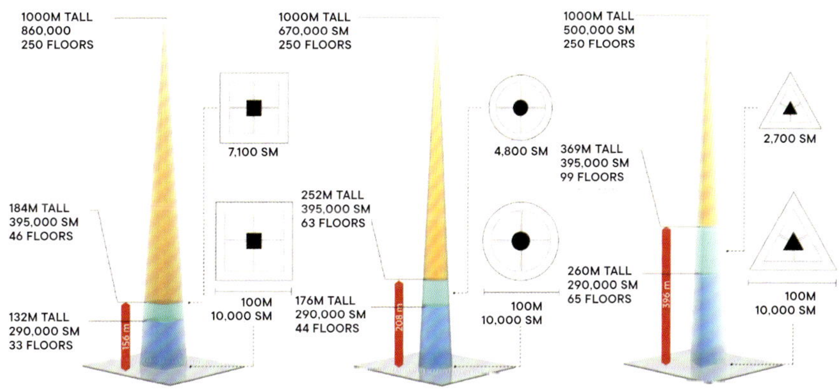

TAPERED MASSING

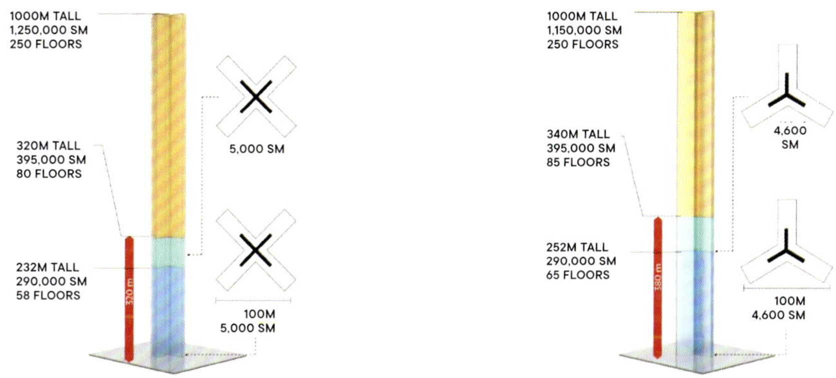

CRUCIFORM + Y-SHAPE

SITE

The project also required the design of a master plan for the area surrounding Jeddah Tower, known as the Kingdom Waterfront District. The 23-hectare Waterfront District provides a cohesive and pedestrian-friendly setting for the tower while creating a pleasant neighborhood experience nestled along the Kingdom City Lakefront.

The district encompasses a high-end shopping mall and additional development parcels that accommodate commercial and high-density residential uses, offices, two luxury hotels, and landscaped open spaces, like the central Tower Plaza. A serene waterfront promenade connects Jeddah Tower to the various development parcels, the open space areas, and the mall. The result is an exciting mixed-use area that offers a concentrated and comprehensive experience for shopping, entertainment, and outdoor activities.

The Waterfront District also provides an array of connections to other areas within Kingdom City's overall master plan. Kingdom City is subdivided into 13 development parcels, the largest of which are the Jeddah Tower parcel at 90,000 sm and the mall parcel at 65,000 sm. Smaller mixed-use parcels that are 5,000–10,000 sm are arranged in two development precincts, North and South, each with its own unifying design language.

The parcel sizes vary depending on the density of each site; the larger sites are farther away from Jeddah Tower, with the smaller sites stepping closer, creating the effect of an architectural amphitheater around the structure, ensuring that the outer buildings also have access to views of Kingdom Tower. Views of Jeddah Tower throughout the District—including the sensitively designed 20–60-story buildings around the tower—are spectacular.

Sun, wind, and view studies, among many other parameters, informed and guided the design process. The tower orientation was adjusted in plan to point one wing toward Mecca, while another points almost directly north. Positioning the tower in this way reduced the overall solar load while simultaneously improving the views of residential units.

The adjustment in orientation also helped mitigate the magnitude of pedestrian-level winds in several of the more critical locations, although it slightly increased the overall load due to design-wind conditions.

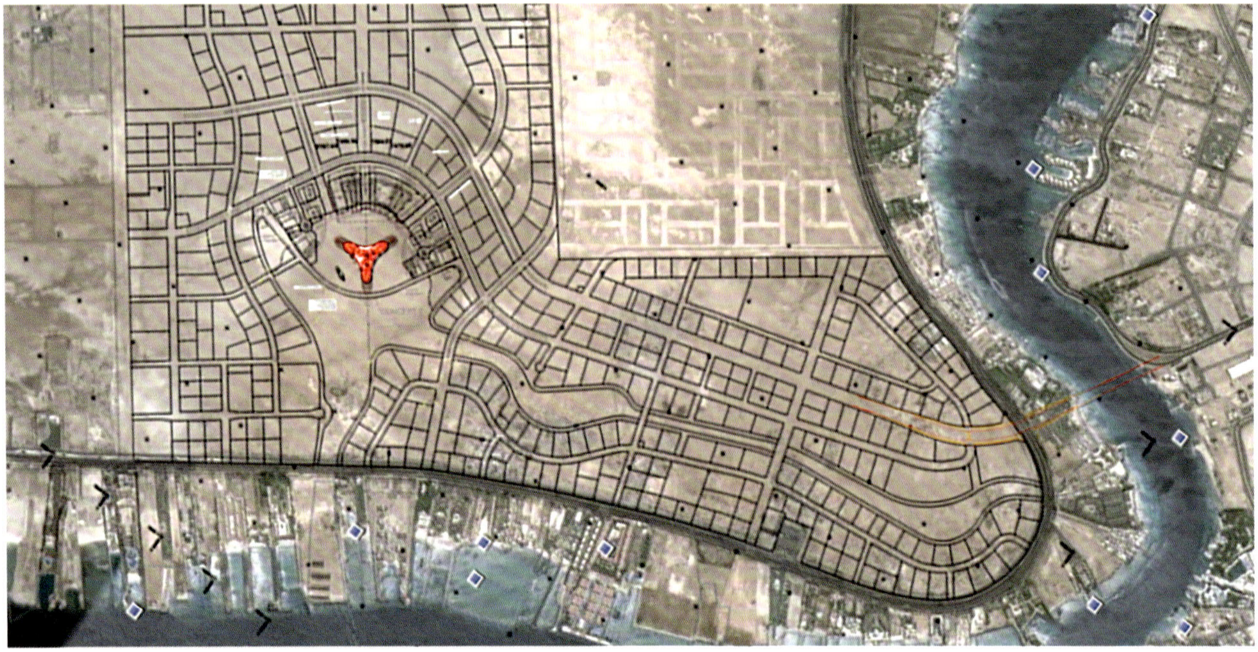

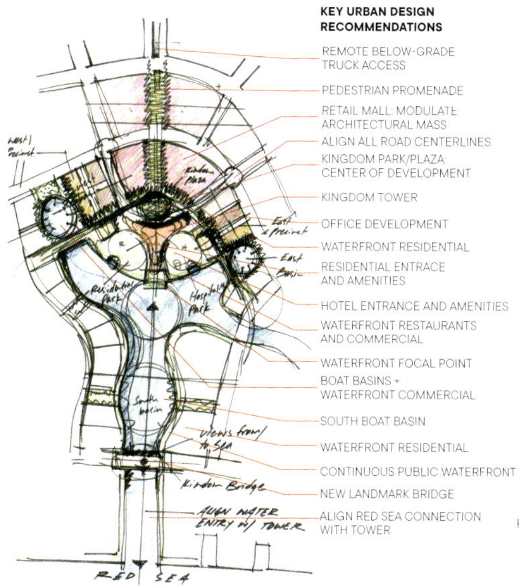

EARLY CONCEPT SKETCH OF BUILDING POSITIONING

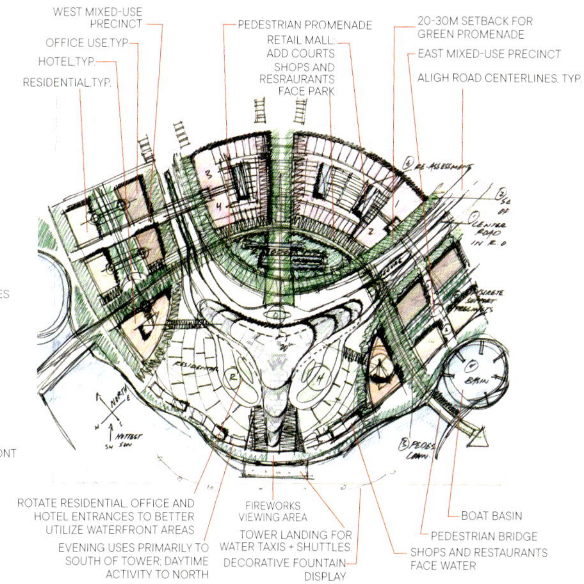

EARLY SKETCH SHOWING STEPS AT THE BASE OF THE LEGS

MASTER PLAN

SITE

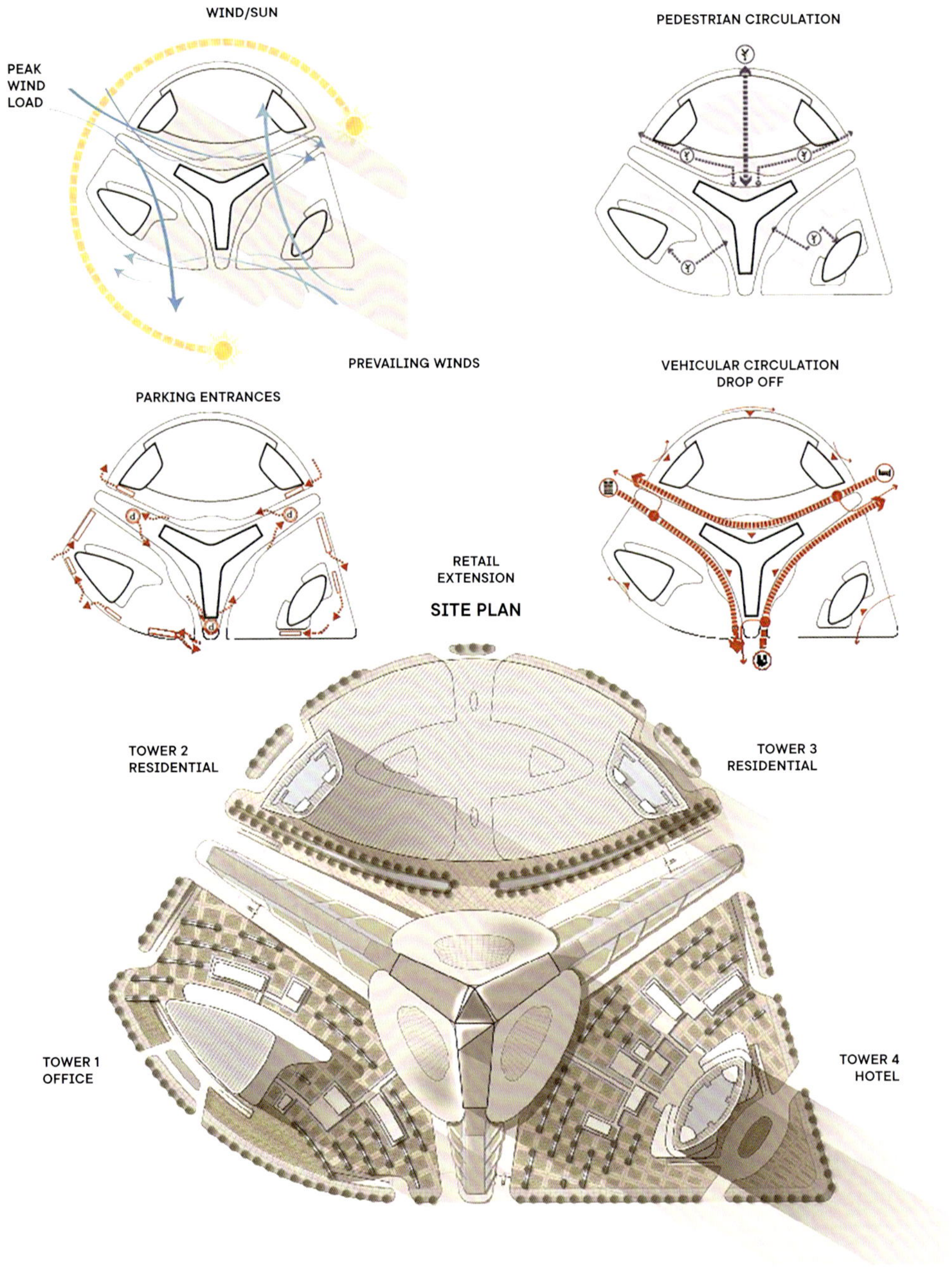
WIND/SUN
PEAK
WIND
LOAD
PREVAILING WINDS
PEDESTRIAN CIRCULATION
PARKING ENTRANCES
VEHICULAR CIRCULATION
DROP OFF
RETAIL
EXTENSION
SITE PLAN
TOWER 2
RESIDENTIAL
TOWER 3
RESIDENTIAL
TOWER 1
OFFICE
TOWER 4
HOTEL

PROGRAM

The competition brief required a 240,000 sm, multi-use tower comprised of a five-star hotel, serviced apartments, office spaces, and residential units. The tapered, Y-shaped plan was an outgrowth of the programmatic requirements needed for narrow lease spans and a relatively low GFA (Gross Floor Area).

These considerations result in a tall and thin structure. For comparison, Taipei 101 has a floor area of 200,000 sm, around half the proposed height of Jeddah Tower. Jeddah Tower's triangular form, in addition to the tapering of the plan from a wide base, to narrower floor plates at the top, enables the tower to achieve the required lease spans and the required overall program area, while reaching the desired height in an efficient way.

The tower stacks the programmatic elements one above the other, starting at the bottom: Office, Hotel, Serviced Apartments, Residential, and Observatory. Multi-story mechanical floors separate the various programmatic uses every 25–30 levels, with refuge floors placed no more than 20 levels apart. Above the uppermost luxury residential penthouses are mechanical spaces and an unoccupied spire, which attains an overall height of over 1,000 meters.

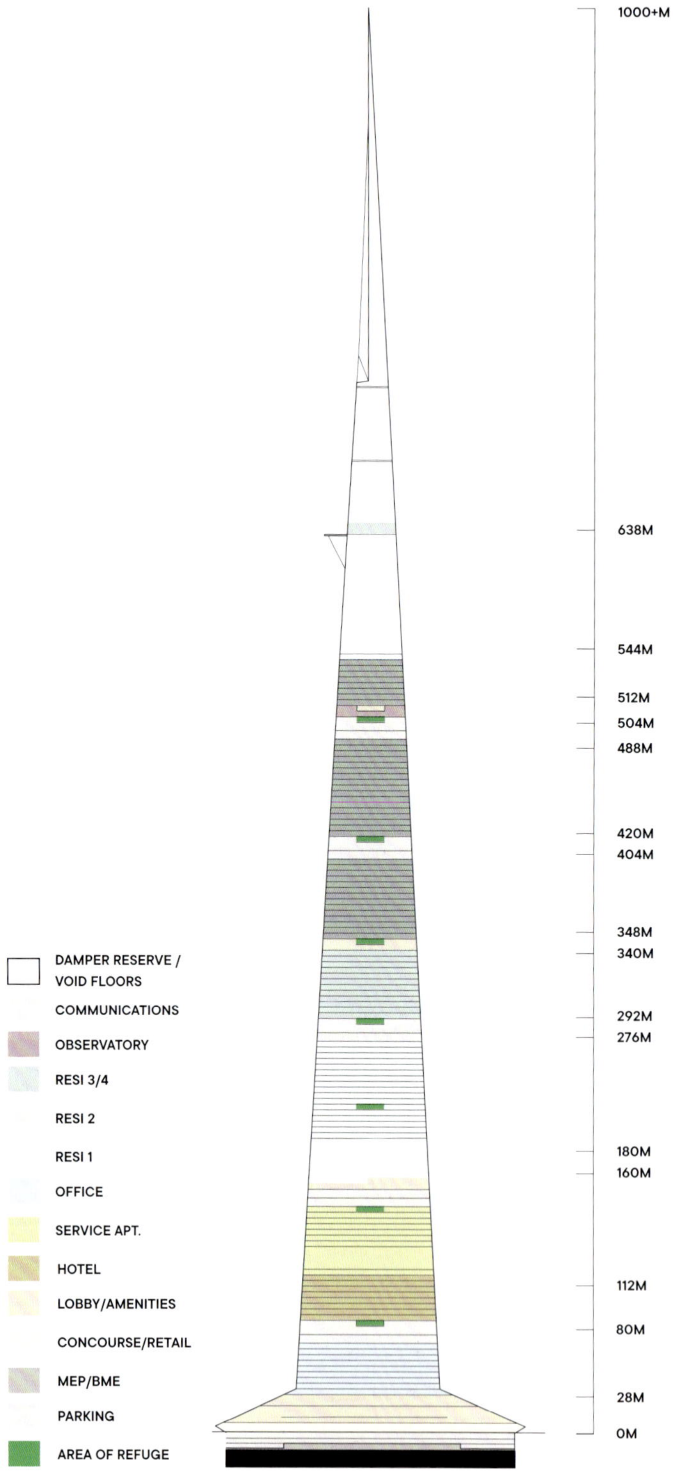

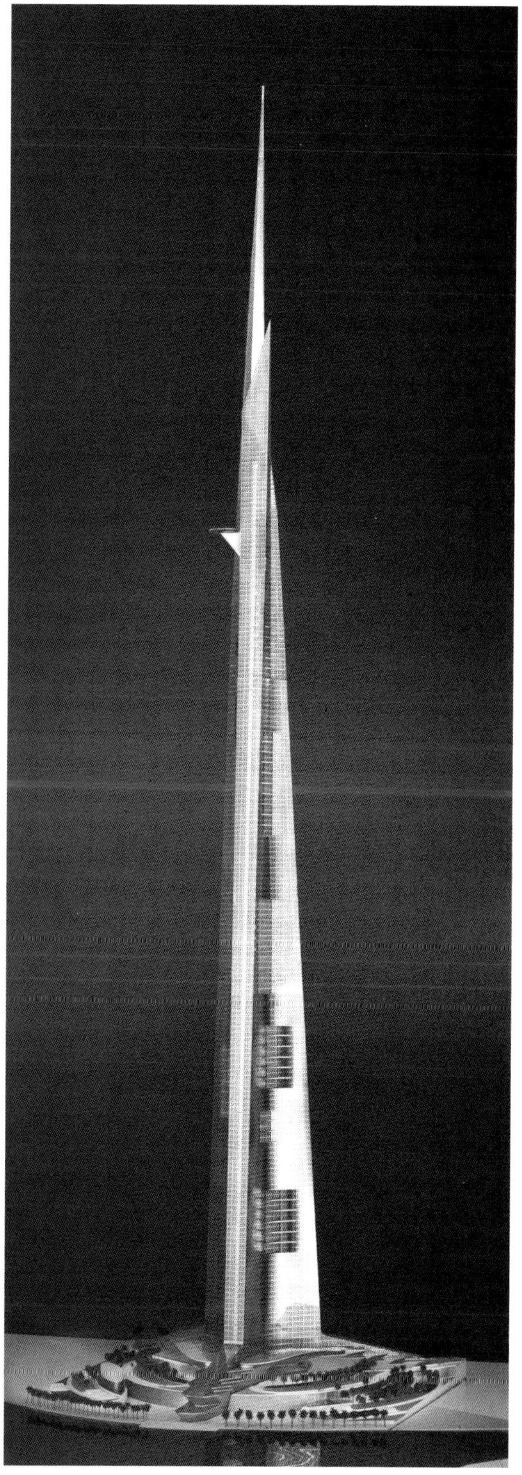

PROGRAM

The podium (Level B3–Level 4) is 191,420 sm with parking for 2,400 cars, loading dock, and central mechanical spaces, as well as lobbies and public areas for the offices, residences, and hotel.

Office floors (Levels 7–13) contain 22,464 sm of commercial office space.

The Hotel (Levels 20– 26) is 20,776 sm with 168 guestrooms for a five-star hotel operated by Four Seasons.

Serviced Apartments (Levels 27–37) are 30,699 sm with 121 units operated by the hotel.

Residential Groups 1–4 (Levels 44–120) has 99,791 sm with 318 luxury residences and two sky lobbies with residential amenity spaces.

Void or Flex Spaces (Levels 126–153) was originally envisioned as flexible space. There are potentially 28 levels with 37,800 sm of space that can be developed as the building is being constructed if sales are strong enough to warrant the expense.

The Observatory/Sky Terrace (Levels 157–159) has multiple levels and an outdoor sky terrace that is over 500 sm in size.

Refuge Floors are at Levels 18, 38, 56, 71, 86, 104, 124 and 154.

Technical Floors are on Levels 15–16, 39–40, 68–69, 95–96, 121–122, 161–169.

The Spire is approximately 300 meters of "aspirational" height and also has potential for future development.

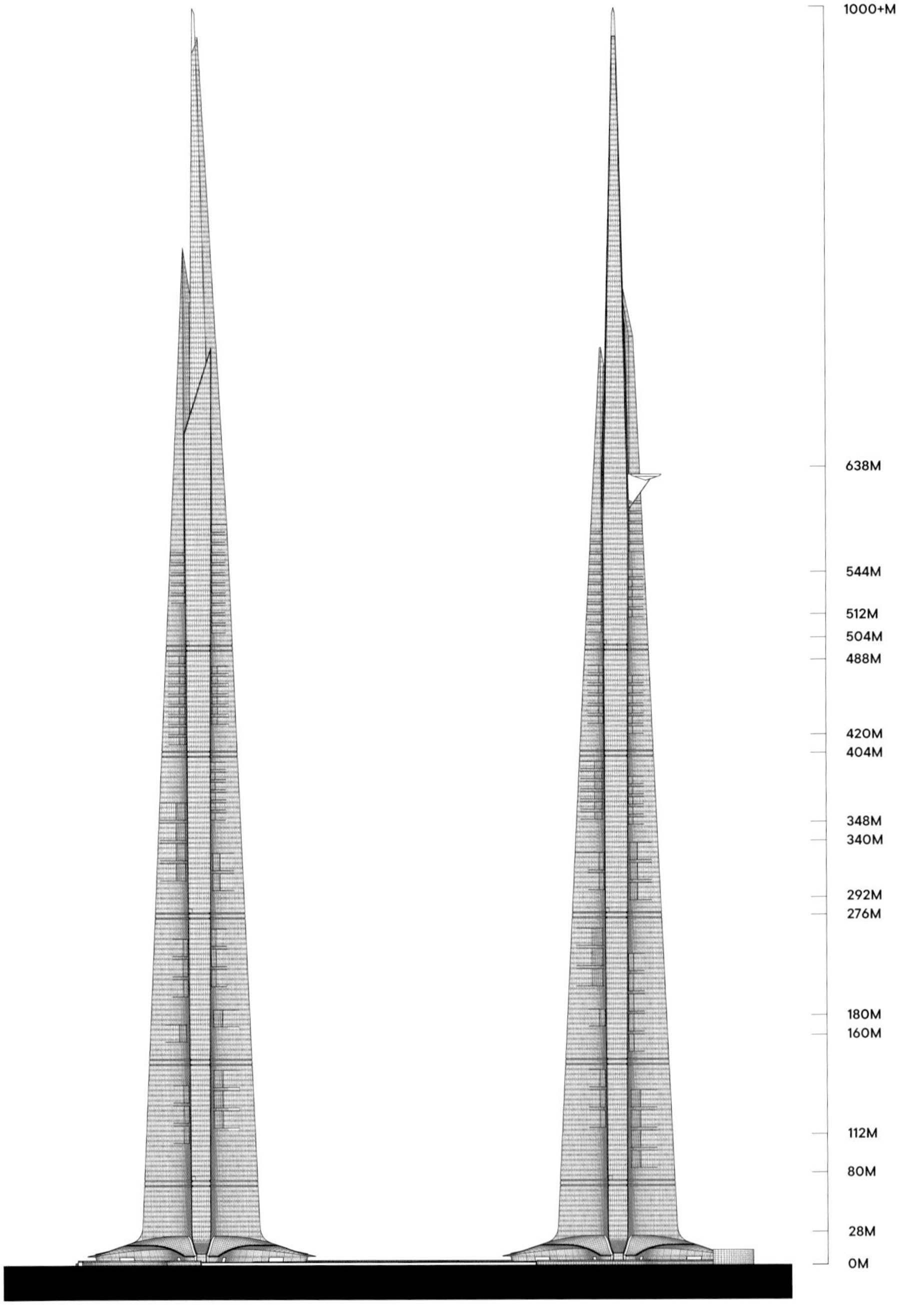

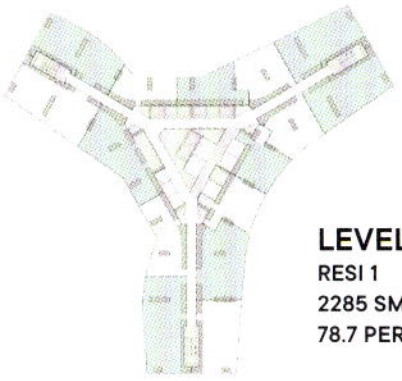

LEVEL 64
RESI 1
2285 SM
78.7 PERCENT EFFICIENCY

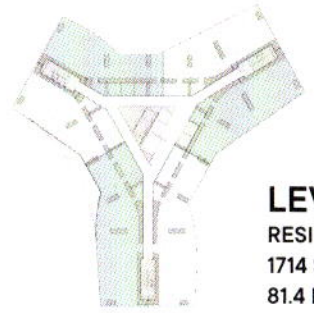

LEVEL 104
RESI 3
1714 SM
81.4 PERCENT EFFICIENCY

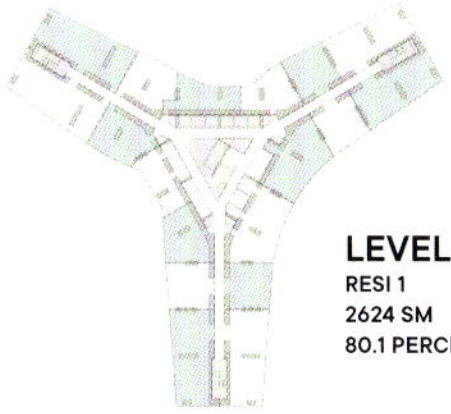

LEVEL 43
RESI 1
2624 SM
80.1 PERCENT EFFICIENCY

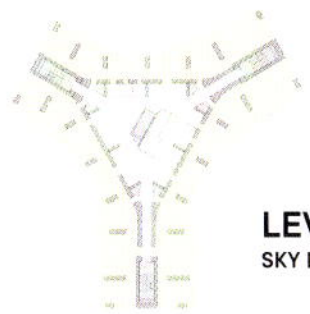

LEVEL 101
SKY LOBBY

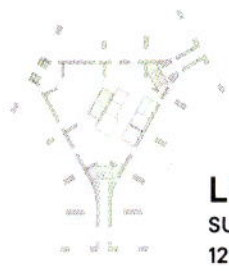

LEVEL 135
SUPER PENTHOUSE
1299 SM
92.2 PERCENT EFFICIENCY

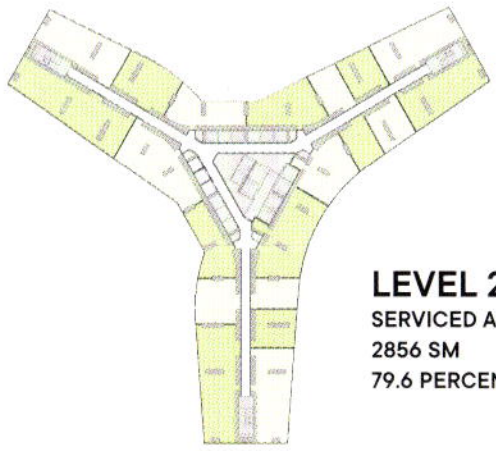

LEVEL 23
SERVICED APARTMENTS
2856 SM
79.6 PERCENT EFFICIENCY

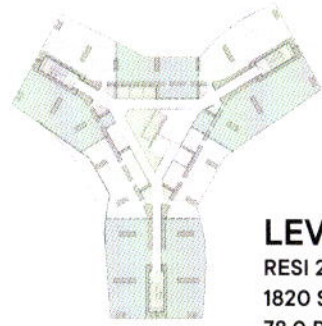

LEVEL 96
RESI 2
1820 SM
78.0 PERCENT EFFICIENCY

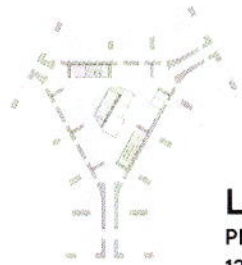

LEVEL 130
PENTHOUSE
1378 SM
93.5 PERCENT EFFICIENCY

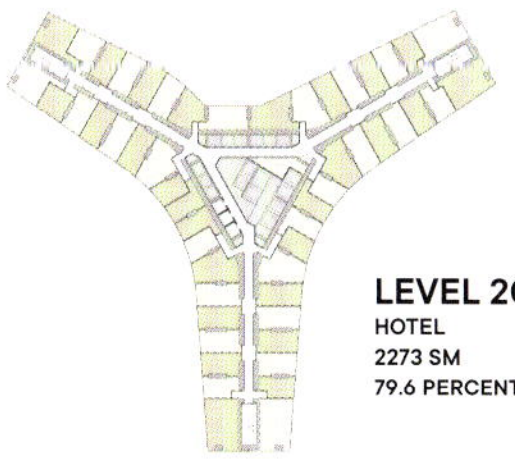

LEVEL 20
HOTEL
2273 SM
79.6 PERCENT EFFICIENCY

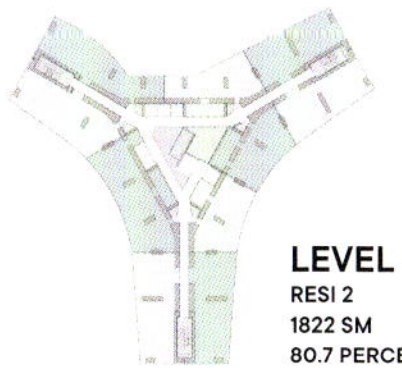

LEVEL 71
RESI 2
1822 SM
80.7 PERCENT EFFICIENCY

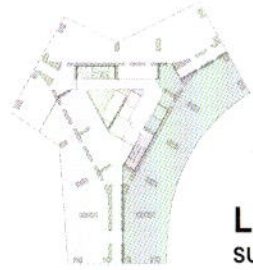

LEVEL 128
SUB-PENTHOUSE
1410 SM
87.4 PERCENT EFFICIENCY

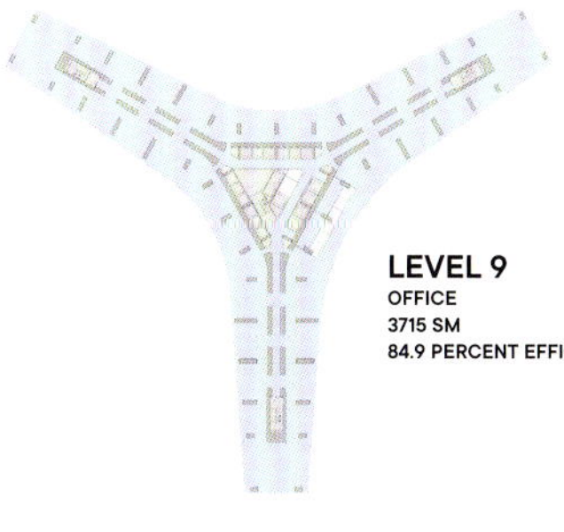

LEVEL 9
OFFICE
3715 SM
84.9 PERCENT EFFICIENCY

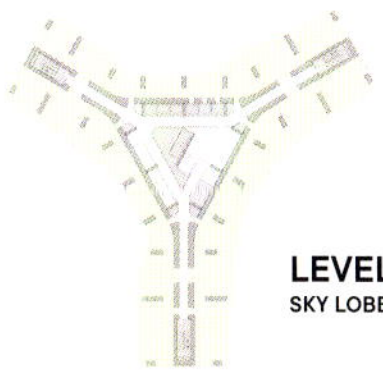

LEVEL 68
SKY LOBBY

LEVEL 125
RESI 3
1417 SM
84.1 PERCENT EFFICIENCY

FACADE

The exterior wall represents a significant portion of the total initial investment on any scale architectural project. In a supertall building like Jeddah Tower, that cost can run upwards of a hundred million dollars. It is understandable that clients are interested in economy, which designers interpret as simplicity, efficiency, and constructability. Therefore, early in the design phase the design team agreed to use one primary, unitized wall type. The final system is made up of flat, rectangular panels to maximize repeatability and minimize the number of panel-type variations.

The inclusion of balconies in this type of building is not very common. However, Jeddah Tower has balconies for a variety of reasons. First, weather conditions in Jeddah are pleasant for a substantial part of the year and balconies are an important amenity in the marketing of a luxury residential unit. At the highest levels of the tower, reduced air temperatures and increased wind speeds make outdoor conditions better than at lower levels.

Second, at a latitude of 21.5 degrees and with the prevailing sunlight intensity, any horizontal projection will create shadows on the tower surface, reducing direct solar radiation.

Third, from the tower massing point of view, the overlapping pattern of the balconies added a layer of intricacy and visual complexity to this mostly vertical structure. The horizon tally overlapping balconies visually tie the tapering wings together and add to the "organic" character of the structure.

The performance-based exterior wall design relies on loading factors in addition to those imposed by wind and gravity. The challenging environment in Jeddah, being both desert and coastal marine, influenced the design criteria and material selection. The curtain wall is designed to accommodate thermal movements due to an ambient temperature range of between 2°C–54°C, as well as a material surface temperature in excess of 82°C.

This is coupled with an extremely humid environment with a dry bulb temperature of 46°C and wet bulb of 29°C. The exterior wall design includes thermally broken aluminum frames, high-performance insulating vision glass and extensive areas of insulated spandrel glazing. Although the tower looks like a fully glazed building, the overall vision glass to spandrel area ratio is 50 percent to 50 percent.

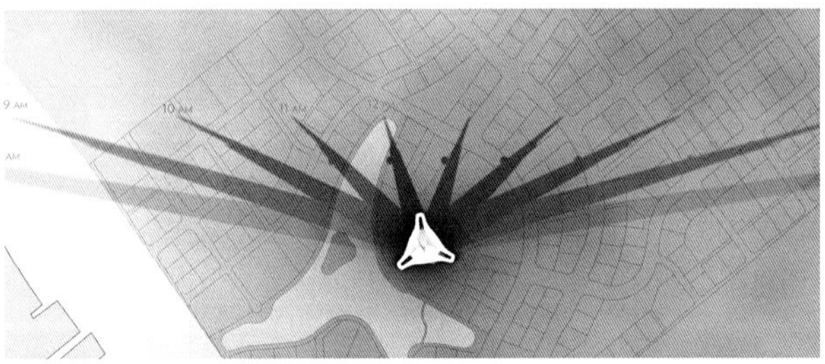

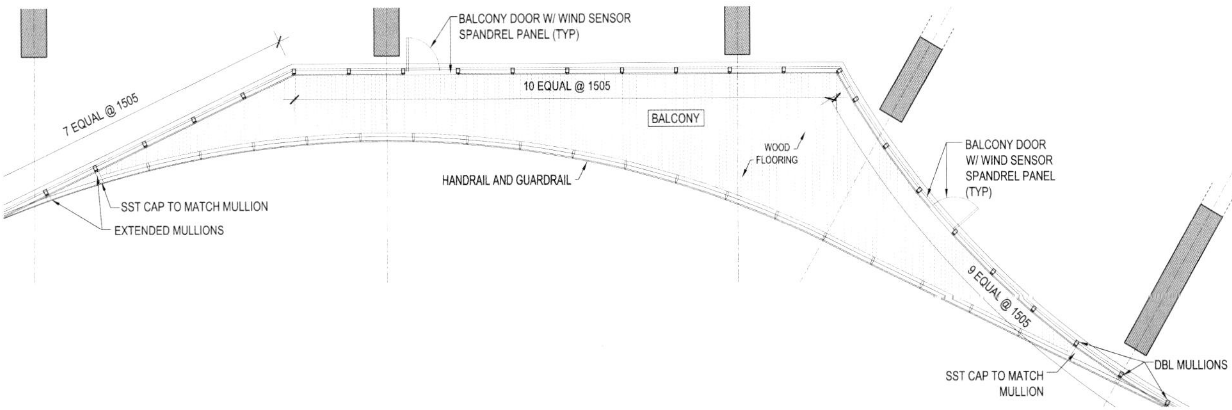
BALCONY DOOR W/ WIND SENSOR
SPANDREL PANEL (TYP)
7 EQUAL @ 1505
10 EQUAL @ 1505
BALCONY
WOOD
FLOORING
BALCONY DOOR
W/ WIND SENSOR
SPANDREL PANEL
(TYP)
HANDRAIL AND GUARDRAIL
SST CAP TO MATCH MULLION
EXTENDED MULLIONS
9 EQUAL @ 1505
DBL MULLIONS
SST CAP TO MATCH
MULLION

FACADE

The simple panel design also allows for early procurement and allows tenders from multiple manufacturers. Establishing a consistent vertical module (4.0 m and horizontal module 1.5 m) allows the repetition of identical panels, which facilitates an assembly line type mass production, thus keeping the costs lower. The ends of each tapered wing are planar and, except for the corners, consist of identical panels over the entire height. The angle of each taper has been designed to relate to the horizontal module, permitting a repetition of the "make-up" unit over the height of the tower. The typical 4.0 m x 1.5 m panel size permits loading into materials hoists and does not require use of tower cranes.

By the introduction of structural beams at the floor line, special double height areas, such as at mechanical floors, sky lobbies, and duplex units, still utilize the typical panel. At double height areas such as duplex, sky lobbies or amenities, reinforced mullions are introduced, and spandrel panels are replaced by vision glass to take maximum advantage of views and special experience. The typical panel is gravity supported (suspended) from its top at the slab edge and laterally supported at Its bottom.

maintenance was also a consideration during the design process. In the Middle East—in particular, cities in Saudi Arabia such as Jeddah—preventing sand-dust collection and the need to clean the facade periodically is an important objective. In response, the goal is to prevent and limit the amount of exterior-wall surfaces at the macro level by reducing the overall amount of exterior wall and, at a micro level, by limiting or eliminating the use of projected elements off the glass surface. The surface will also reduce the materials needed for construction, decreasing embodied carbon.

Regarding facade access, the system utilizes proven, tried-and-tested, state-of-the-art technology. The system is designed to completely wash the windows and clean the exterior wall at least four times a year. Multiple facade access units of various types are required to cover the more than 166,000 sm of cladding. Having multiple units allows for redundancy and enhanced reliability. The system is designed, and machines are sized to permit glass-unit replacement.

MECHANICAL SLOT DETAIL

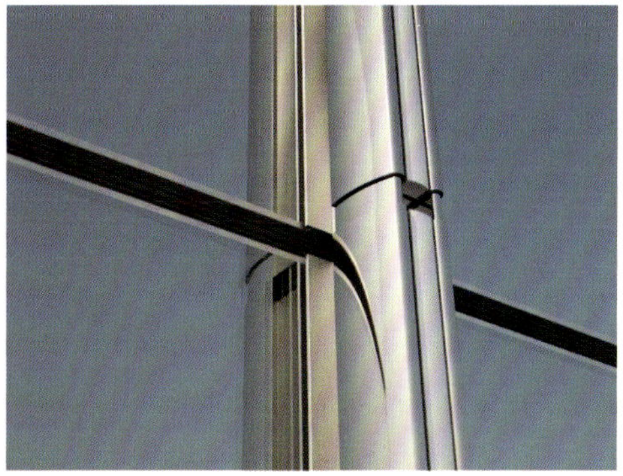

FIN AT STACK JOINT

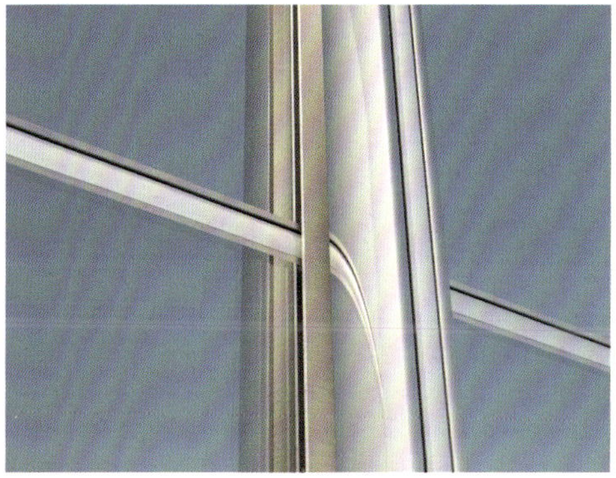

FIN AT TRANSOM

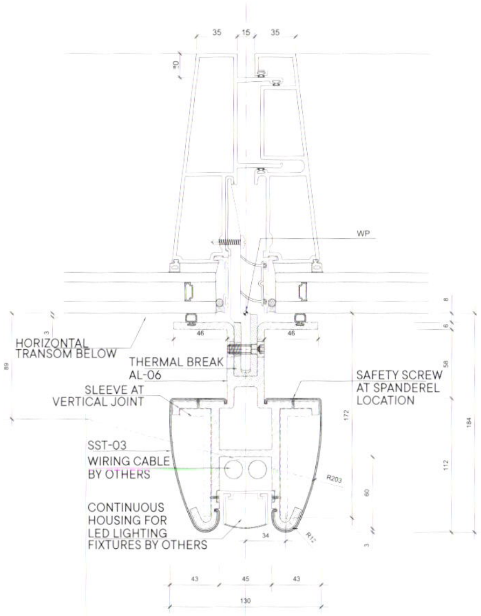

FACADE

After construction documents were completed, JEC asked the design team to re-examine the exterior wall design to incorporate the possibility for festive lighting and fireworks. The new mullion design has a stainless-steel fin that is bisected in the center by a vertical slot where the light fixture is placed. Simulations were done by a lighting consultant to show the various possibilities that are now able to be done in terms of festive lighting for the tower, and this was incorporated in to the design.

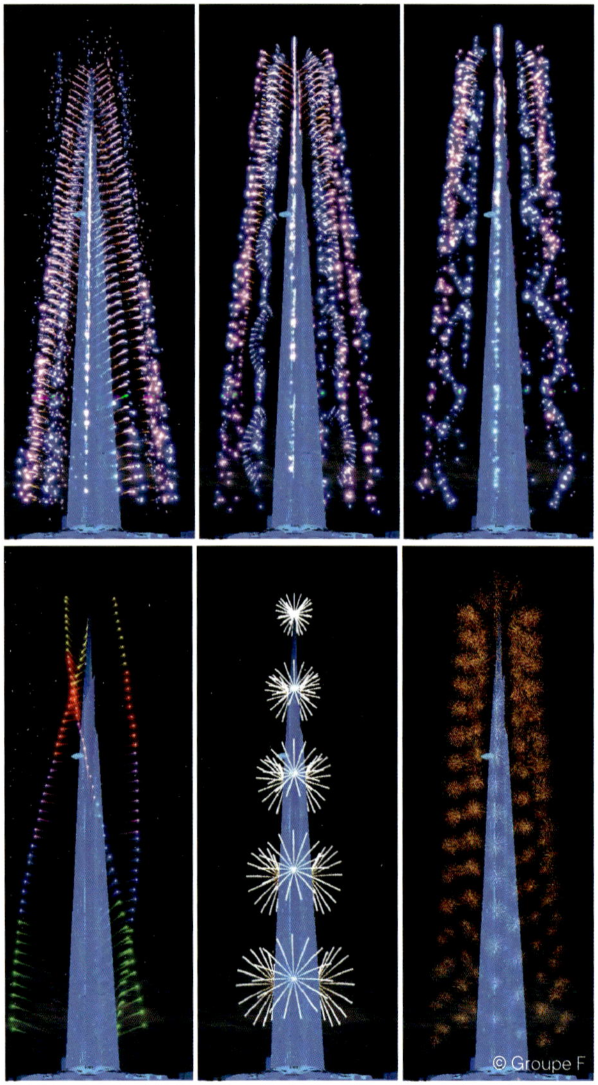

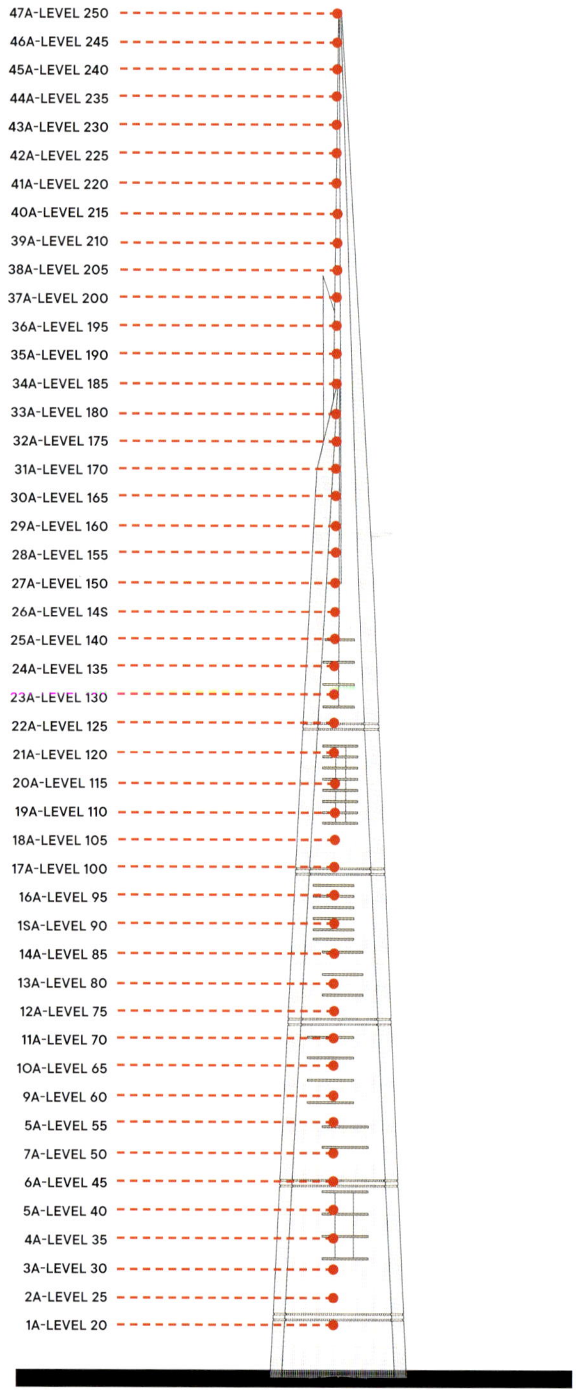

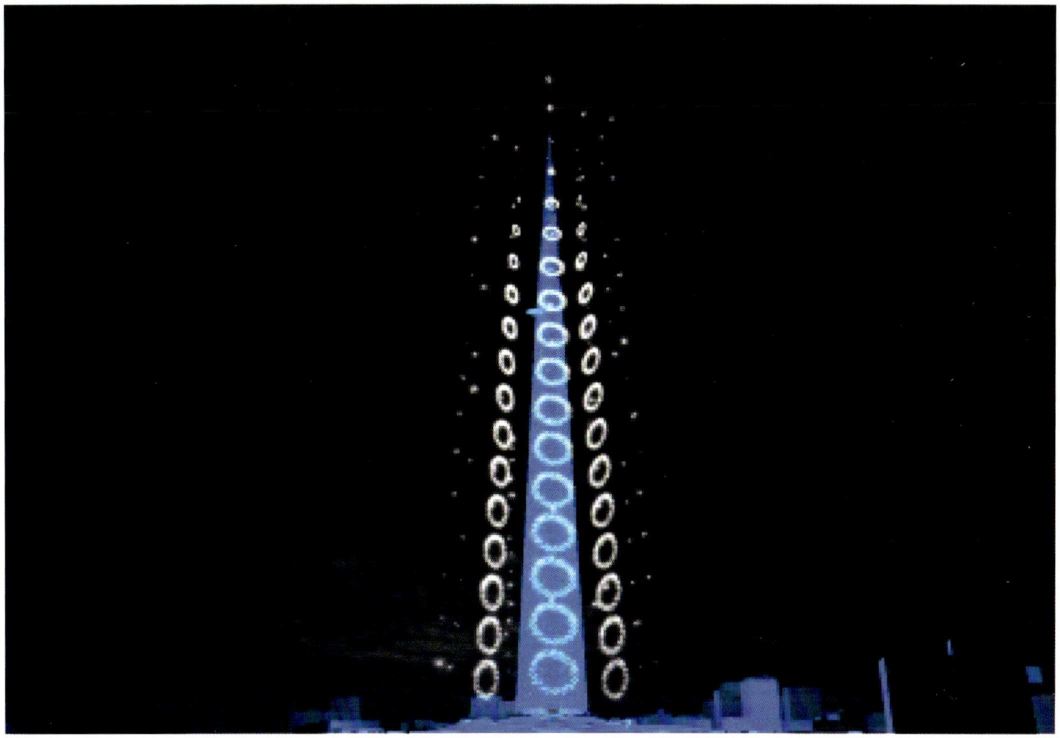

©EC Harris Mace

Drop-off areas were designed as independent entries, separated by the program type. The lobbies are further divided to give exclusivity to each residential group and to allow occupants to access the double-deck elevators when required. There is a private VIP drop off located on the lower level that features luxurious finishes and a ceiling clad in gold tile.

The ground-level drop offs are covered with extensive canopies that were developed from the original competition scheme to schematic design. This is both for solar protection and to give the tower massing a strong base that flows into the landscape design. Softer lines were sculpted and more detailed sun studies were developed to address the required extent of the canopy elements that stop heat gain on the lobbies' clear-glass cable walls. Three extended, softly curved canopies cover the main lobbies and extend horizontally to protect parking ramp entries.

Further development of the canopies' cladding components was considered to address potentially harvesting concentrated sun rays and their use in energy production.

A ballroom pavilion was designed to create a distinct entry to the lower-level hotel assembly spaces. This all-glass building is wrapped with a sun-shade featuring integrated solar shading in the facade. Another significant early design decision was to standardize the floor-to-floor height at four meters for all uses, including office, residential, and hotel. Among other things, this helps elevatoring flexibility and potential change in tower stacking through the different design stages. In agreement with the client, office floors are placed at the bottom to take advantage of larger floor plans and dropping elevator bays.

PODIUM

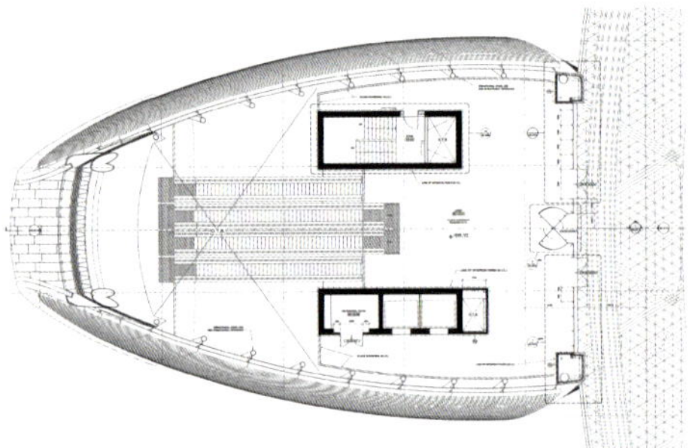

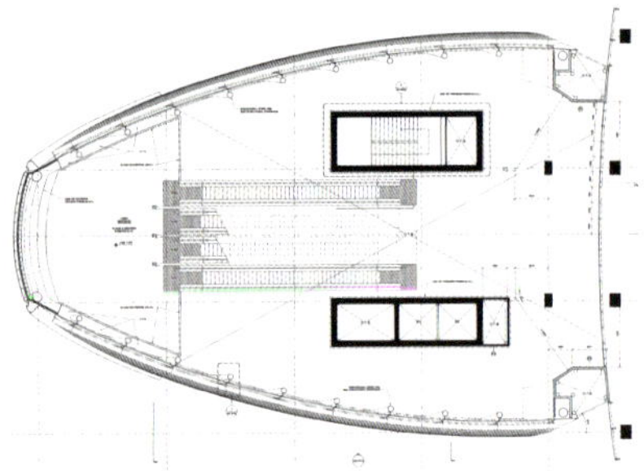

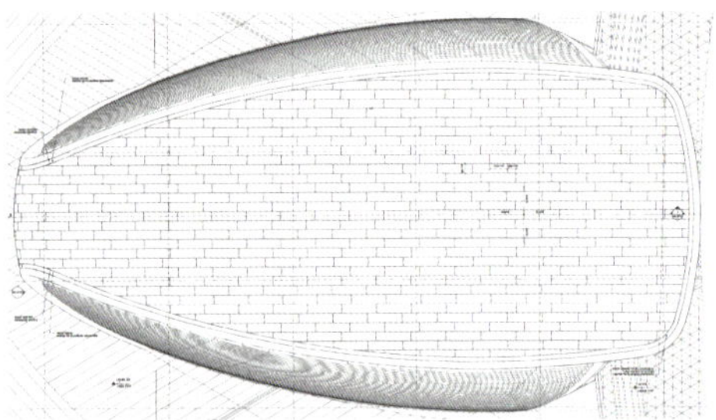

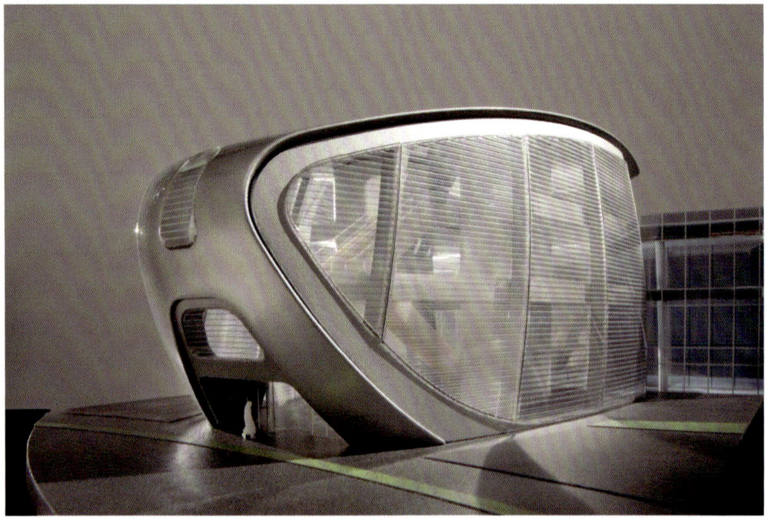

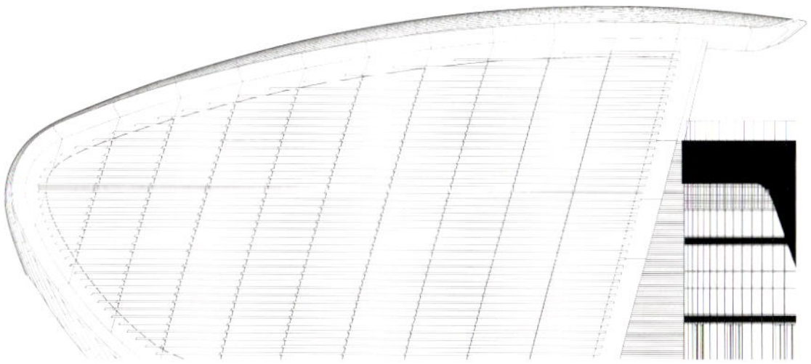

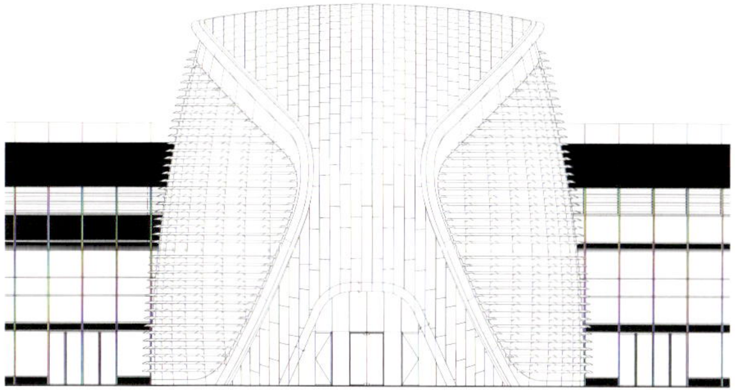

PERFORMANCE

All-glass buildings, depending on the specification of the glazing system and the amount of insulated spandral panels, can reflect significant amounts of incident solar radiation and be a nuisance to adjacent buildings and public areas. While this is a common phenomenon, convex curved geometries present unique challenges in that they can focus reflections onto concentrated locations at given times of the year. This effect can be especially pronounced if the curved facade has a generally southern orientation when located in the northern hemisphere.

Jeddah Tower is fully glazed with three wings that are separated 120 degrees in plan. The straight wings are connected by circular segments, creating a plan that has convex curves on three sides. Originally, the building was oriented so that one wing was directed precisely south.

However, through conducting additional wind-tunnel studies, it was determined that rotating the orientation of the tower 60 degrees o take advantage of the most desirable views, was a better business plan. In doing this, one of the convex surfaces is oriented in a precisely southern direction. Therefore, the final building is oriented so that the convex segments face north-northwest, north-northeast and south.

Realizing that the resulting geometry would likely lead to the concentration of solar energy, a series of investigations were undertaken. First, the team needed to confirm and study the opportunities of the building geometry in this location and orientation. Secondly, the team was to determine where the area of solar convergence would occur, at what climactic conditions, when it would occur, and for how long.

These initial investigations led to further studies and analysis to determine what the cumulative effects of dynamic transitory solar radiation is to anticipate the thermal loading that effects the architecture.

SOLAR CANOPY

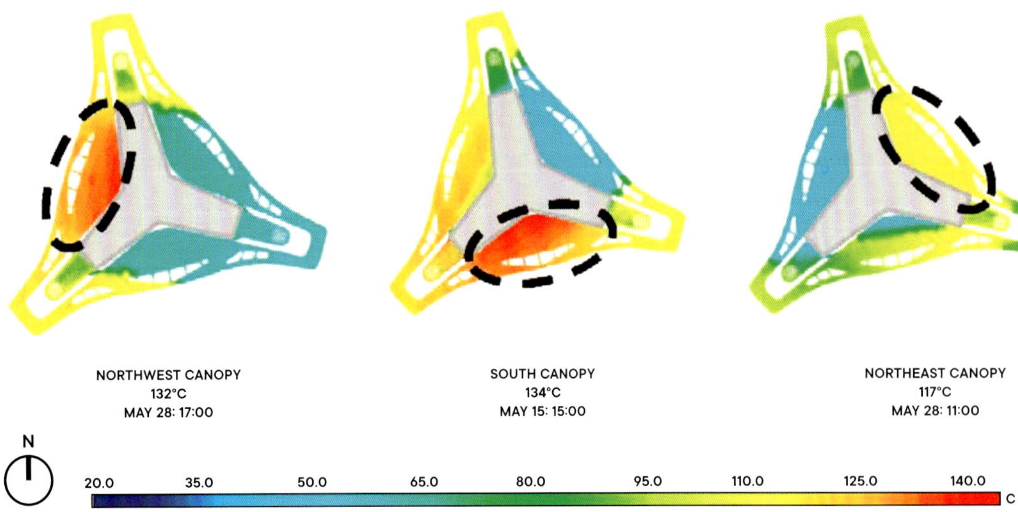

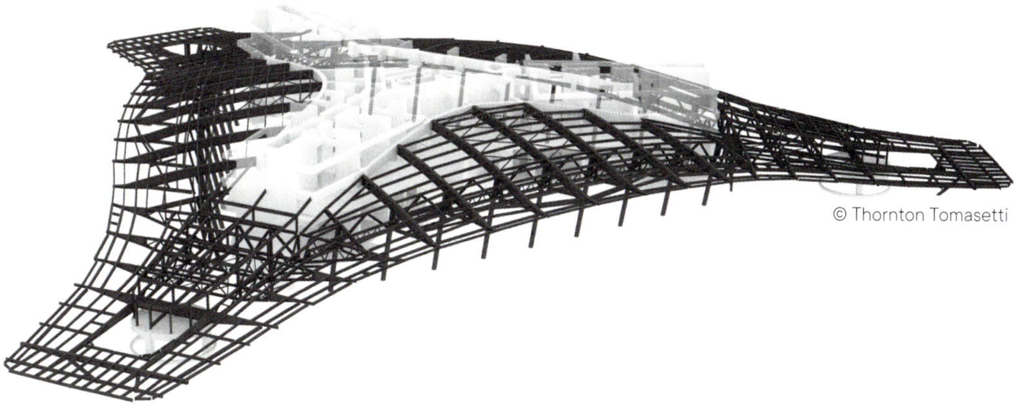

© Thornton Tomasetti

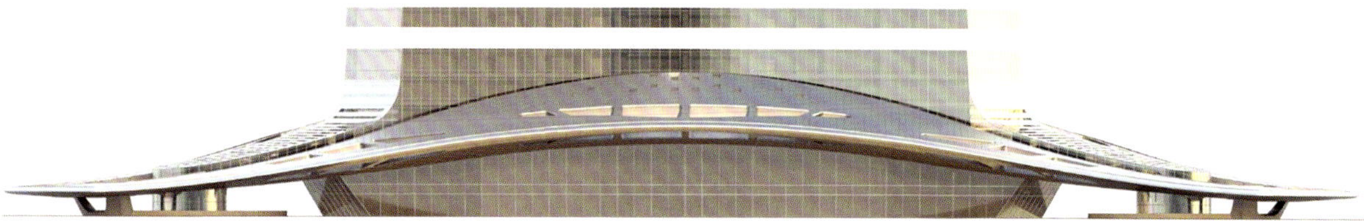

CANOPY RENDERING

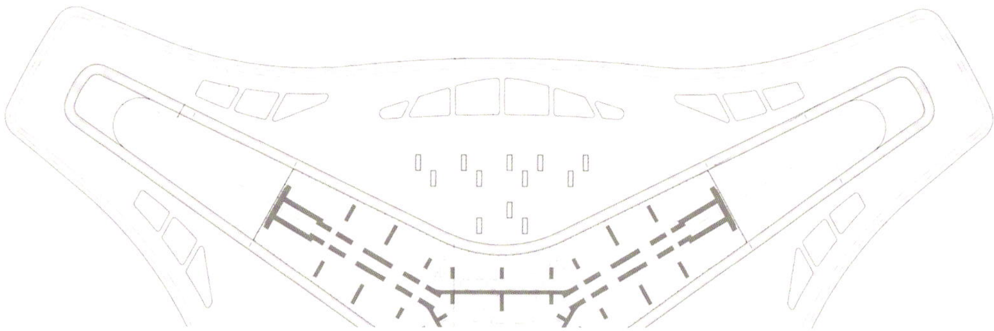

PERFORMANCE

During design of the tower, the team analzyed the impact of reflections from the tower upon the canopies below. The investigation suggested impact on the south canopy at the base of the tower. The team then factored this information into the final detailing of the lower canopies, to protect the temperature-sensitive roofing materials, gaskets, and sealants. Potential solutions to utilize concentrated solar energy utilizing renewable-energy technologies, like solar hot water and solar photovoltaic electricity generation, were also assessed.

A bi-directional scattering function (BDSF) approximation of the actual building's facade system was created using radiance software to quantify the solar load on the canopies over the course of a whole year, as well as each individual month, utilizing real-world weather data to accurately predict cumulative solar exposure on the canopies. A simplified and detailed Revit geometry was prepared for thermal simulations. RadTherm Version 10.3.0 was used to quantify solar and thermal load conditions on the canopies and surrounding areas. These profiles and the System Advisor Model (SAM) tool estimated the thermal energy production potential of solar hot water and power-generation potential of solar-photovoltaic systems. This process greatly informed the final design detailing of the canopy.

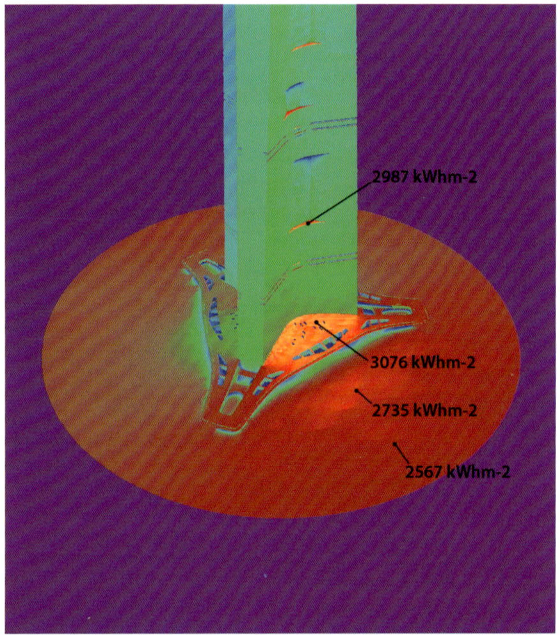

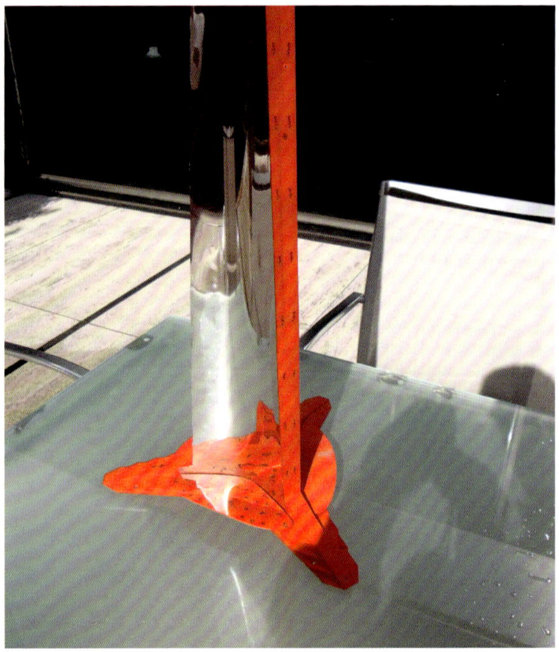

In the modeling, November 15th produced the maximum temperature on the south canopy, and May 28th produced the highest temperatures on the northwest and northeast canopies. The simulations showed that at maximum, the south canopy reaches the highest temperature of 134°C with the northwest and northeast canopies closely following at 132°C and 117°C, respectively.

Based on the simulated results for surface temperatures of 135 degrees celsius or greater on the building's canopy and a better than average yield for various solar-energy strategies, the design team recognized both a potential problem and a potential opportunity. It was documented by manufacturers that excessive heat could reduce efficiency of the panels, but here was also the unknown factor of whether still-developing solar technologies would be able to better handle the increased heat load in the future. Based on the results from the RadTherm study, the team identified the areas on the canopy that have the greatest potential to harvest solar energy, and produced a payback analysis indicated that, even with 15–20 percent efficiency losses, the panels would still have a payback of 8–20 years.

The final canopy detail was a modified open-joint rain-screen system that acts more as sunscreen shading for the roof surface below, from the worst of the increased solar load. The air-space between the open-joint panels and the roof surface below would act as a solar chimney, drawing in more air the hotter the roof panels became. The joints in the open system needed to be sized to deal with the significant thermal expansion the panels might experience without bending and buckling.

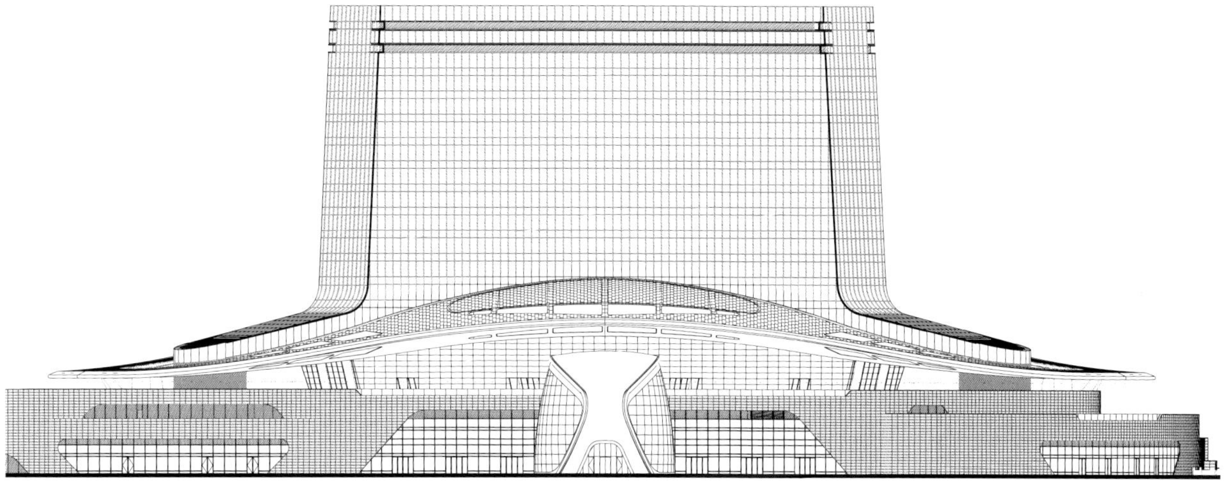

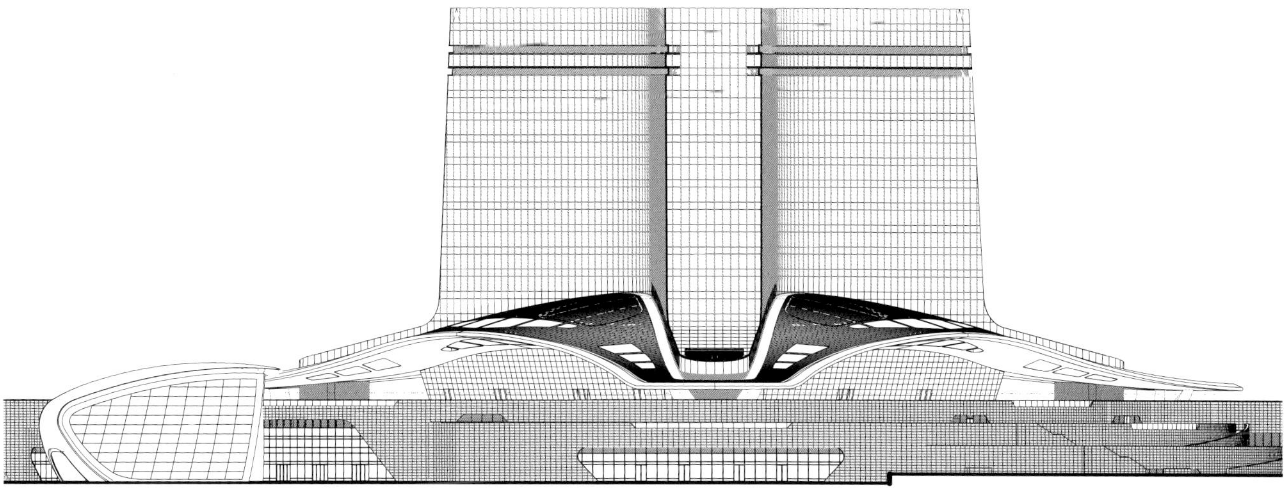

PERFORMANCE

ESD, MEP ENGINEER

There are many ways in which supertall buildings are inherently sustainable. One is land use. Jeddah Tower will occupy a single footprint, and therefore have less environmental impact than 10 towers of 100 meters, which would consume 10 times more land and require significantly more traffic and utilities infrastructure.

Consequently, for people living in supertall buildings, the land footprint per resident is quite low. There are also economies of scale with supertall towers. One roof and one foundation are built rather than the multiple roofs and foundations, which a group of buildings with the same cumulative area would require. Another sustainable aspect of supertall buildings is that they are designed and built to attract development around them. Financial incentives created around these kinds of buildings tend to add density further reducing land use.

Jeddah Tower was designed to be 1,000 meters tall; the final 400 meters is a narrow building-integrated spire with no immediate programmatic use. The spire will house some limited mechanical equipment with a hoist to access and service it, building maintenance units, and a series of stairs and ladders for personnel to reach the top. The strategy for the construction of the spire is to continue the main formwork of the tower and fully enclose it as a concrete tube or silo.

This construction method was the simplest to work with at this height and allows the same means and methods to be used in the spire that are used in the rest of the tower. Where the spire reaches its most narrow, structural steel is used. Intermediate slabs are placed at intervals of 20–30 stories to add stability to the structure and to locate equipment. A sky-raft is placed at the bottom of the spire to link together all the structural walls before the silo begins.

During the early design phases, the team studied ways to use the spire for energy production. One idea was to use the spire for natural stack effect, with wind turbines placed at intervals in the horizontal floor slabs that gather energy from the air cascading up or down the spire, depending on the temperature. It was ultimately found that the energy generated would be minimal and would limit the ability to ventilate the spire, so this approach was not pursued.

A second energy-production strategy that was studied is solar-energy production. Solar radiation can be absorbed through various surfaces on the spire with a large amount of solar energy potentially generated using photovoltaic panels or solar hot-water panels. Although not currently implemented, solar power could be a future addition to offset the carbon emission of the tower.

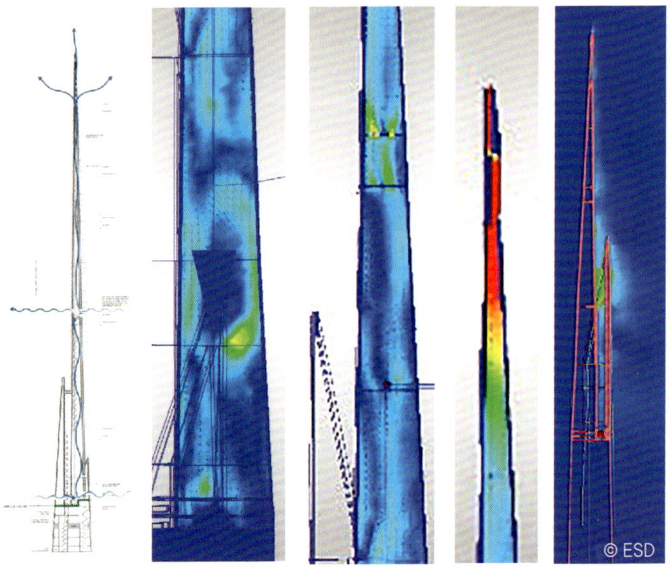

To ensure proper air flow and ventilation, multiple CFD studies were conducted to determine the internal velocity of the air in the interior of the spire.

OPTION 1: SOLAR UPDRAFT POWER SPIRE

This option operates on the principle of convection, utilizing the upward flow of air—a result of hot air rising—to generate power through one or a series of inline wind-turbine generators. Systems such as this one have been tested for many years and have shown to be achievable. Cooler air is drawn into the lower area of the spire, where the greenhouse effect traps of solar energy and thus an increase in temperature. The tapering geometry of the spire leads to an acceleration of the wind velocity, maximizing potential power output.

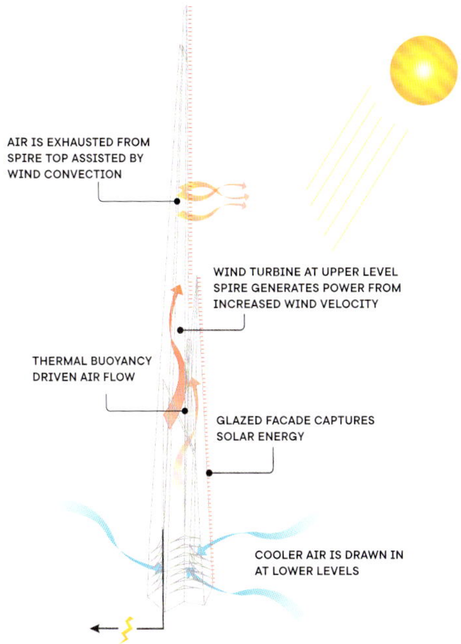

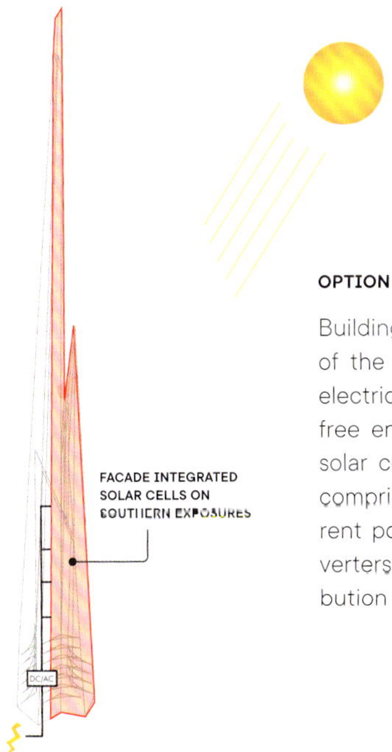

OPTION 2: INTEGRATED PHOTOVOLTAIC SPIRE

Building integrated photovoltaic technology makes use of the physical infrastructure of the curtain wall and electrical distribution system of the tower to generate free energy with minimal investment. Monocrystalline solar cells are integrated within glass modules, which comprise the building envelope that feeds direct-current power to combiner boxes, followed by DC/AC inverters before reaching the building's electrical distribution system.

OPTION 3: SOLAR THERMAL ABSORPTION SPIRE

The solar thermal-absorption system harnesses solar energy thermally with water, oil, or another liquid utilizing parabolic concentrating systems. This thermal energy can then either be transferred to an air-cooled absorption chiller to generate chilled water for the tower or can be used to regenerate a desiccant dehumidification system to reduce the cooling load seen by the outside air-handling units.

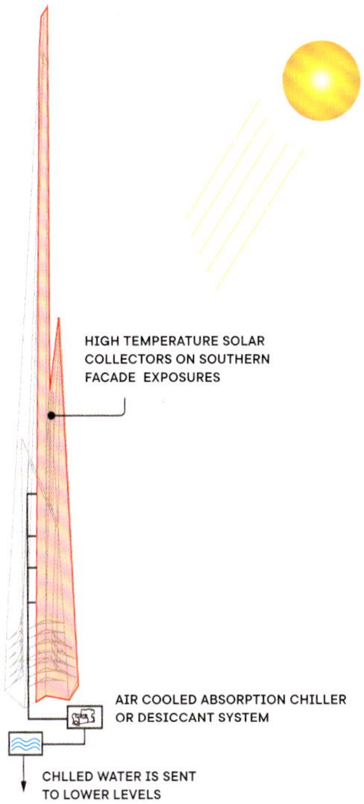

PERFORMANCE

The tower's three sides feature a series of notches that create pockets of shadow, which shield areas of the building from the sun, decreasing solar heat gain in those areas. Excessive solar radiation may also be utilized to produce future energy. In depth radiation studies show a high potential to generate energy from solar harvesting systems such as PVs on the surface of the canopies where tower reflected radiation is concentrated. Ventilation of the spire is important to the energy efficiency of the tower. The mechanical engineers modeled the airflow in the spire using CFD modeling to determine where openings should be placed to provide adequate ventilation for any occupants that may be working in the spire. The structural engineer studied the heat gain on the concrete to ensure it was within an acceptable range.

Water is a critical resource in this kind of environment. To minimize use and maximize re-use and/or water recovery, several systems and design strategies have been incorporated; including condensate recovery, rainwater collection and a gray-water-collection system. Furthermore, the selection of planting materials for landscaping minimizes the irrigation requirements.

The condensate-recovery system collects about 14 Olympic-sized pools of moisture annually and is recycled for irrigation. Specified highly efficient sanitary fittings also help reduce water waste. Water use is generally lower than in similar buildings, as the water supply network has a sophisticated leak-detection system to ensure that the water reaching the building gets used in the building, rather than wasted as non-revenue water.

The embodied carbon is reduced through various means, including designing with less waste produced during construction, specifying that the reinforcing steel used has a high percentage of recycled content, and replacing cement with supplementary materials such as blast-furnace slag, pulverized fly ash, and silica fume. In addition, because Jeddah is a major port city, building materials, particularly those used during fit-out, can be shipped to the construction site by sea instead of using more carbon-intensive road transport. Opportunities for using pre-cast elements are also being implemented where possible.

Solar heat gain through the exterior wall is a key design issue. The design team addressed this by using a high-performance, Low-E reflective glass that reduces heat gain while providing desirable panoramic views. Where glass is not needed for viewing, the design team is specifying an insulated "shadowbox" panel that minimizes heat gain with the same thermal performance as a stone panel.

SPIRE SOLAR RADIATION STUDY

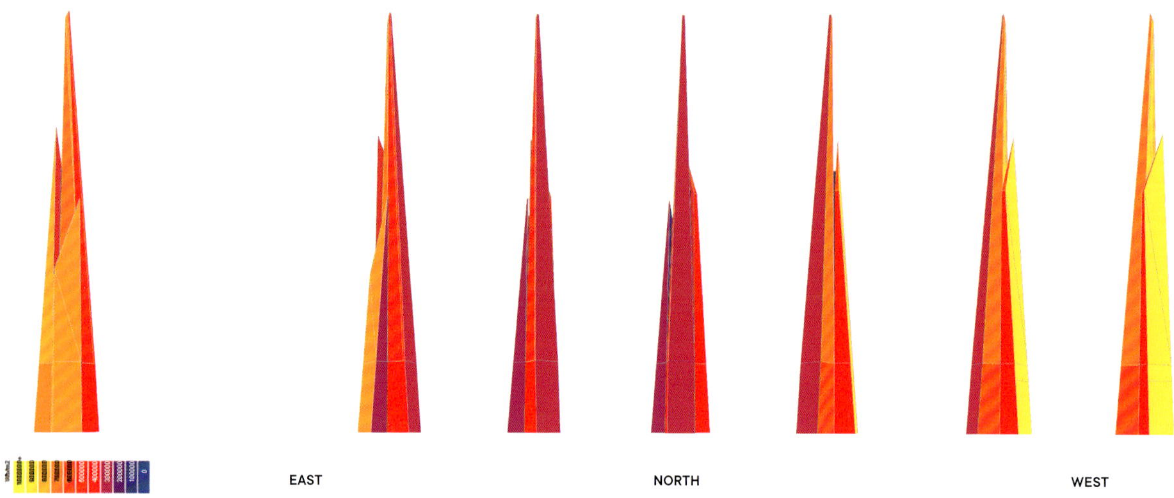

INTERIOR

Jeddah Tower's interior public spaces are distinctly organic with delicate details, echoing the design of the exterior. Spaces are powerfully and intelligently shaped to maximize height between deep structural beams and the double-decker elevator cabs that would otherwise result in low-ceiling spaces.

The feature wall that separates the residential lobbies is a sculptural volume that emits diffused light through a metal mesh veil. Both the residential and office ground-floor lobbies are designed to continue the form of the extensive exterior canopy, blurring the lines between the exterior drop off and the interior lobby. The interior spaces were designed so that they guide users without the need for wayfinding. It was important to not have unnecessary signage and let the ceilings shapes and wall forms create a directional quality.

The organic forms help the spaces feel more open, voluminous, and spacious. As the interior corridors naturally funnel toward the core, the scale of the spaces reduces from grand to human scale.

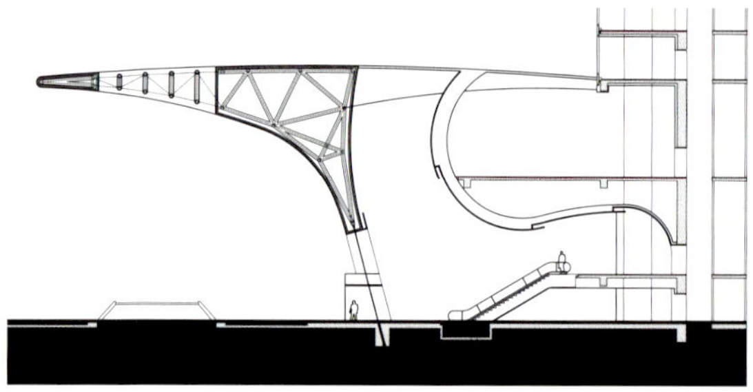

The sculptural ceiling helps transfer natural daylighting deep into the interior spaces. Where artificial lighting is necessary, sources are tucked into coves and troughs to enhance clean uninterrupted planes. These coves and troughs also allow a strategy for placing fire and life safety devices, as well as mechanical grills that are as concealed as the operation allows.

Interior lobby spaces were designed to emulate the high-end residences. Silver-travertine walls and limestone floors are neutral yet classic, transcending trends while coordinating with traditional or modern style sensibilities.

INTERIOR

A sky lobby is positioned on Levels 42, 43 and 83. Residential groups 1 and 2 arrive to Levels 42–43, respectively. The elevator doors open to a grand two-story space that is connected by a grand staircase. Residential group 1 uses the lower double-decker elevator cab and residential group 2 uses the upper-double elevator cab. Residents transfer to local elevators in the core, and at these levels connect to a full range of amenities. On level 83, the sky lobby for residential group 3, the strategy is the same with access to another group of exclusive amenities.

Amenities are segregated between male and female in local culture, including public-function rooms, majlis, media rooms, children's playroom, exercise and locker rooms, prayer and ablution rooms. The spaces are luxurious and emulate the same high-end design sensibility of the other public spaces.

INTERIOR

Residential elevator cabs and corridor interiors take inspiration from aircraft interiors, as well as the shape of the middle eastern Dhow boat. Elevator cabs are clad in wood or leather panels with softly curved walls that distract from the monotony of numerous long corridors, while also concealing mechanical services. Each residential group corridor has a motif that creates a sense of wayfinding to guide residents to and from their units. Each entry unit has custom timber work with custom integrated lighting.

INTERIOR

Unit layouts reflect a true Saudi style. Materials are luxurious, with stone-tile floors and skirting. In kitchens, contemporary high-end cabinetry mixes with either traditional or modern interiors. Cabinetry can be high-gloss lacquer or a highly polished wood with stone counter tops. Layouts allow for staff quarters and service areas.

Public rooms are oriented toward the view and light. Where balconies occur, they are adjacent to public areas. Private rooms are kept together and segregated from the public areas common in the Saudi culture. Private bathrooms are almost always ensuite with the bedroom.

ILLUSTRATIVE RESIDENTIAL PLAN

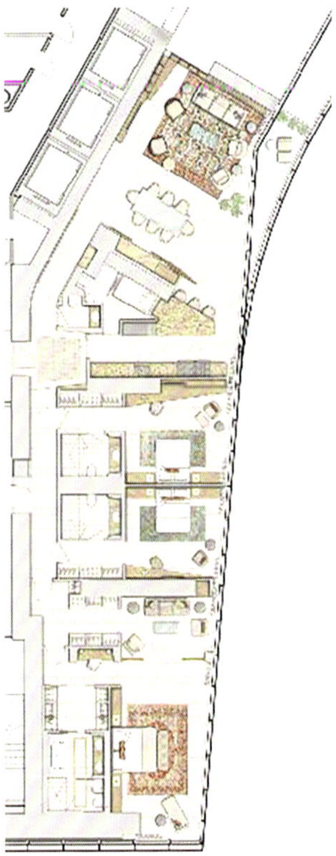

OBSERVATION

A unique feature is the sky terrace, roughly 30 meters (98 feet) in diameter, at Level 157 that will be open to the public. The client initially asked for the inclusion of a helipad for the owner or visitors to the super-penthouse at Level 157.

The original design allowed residents to access or leave the Majlis (lounge) of the penthouse via helicopter. However, further studies and consultation with experienced helicopter pilots and the wind-engineering consultants suggested that the helipad location would make taking off or landing maneuvers extremely dangerous.

However, the platform was already integrated into the overall tower design and it was acknowledged by the contractor that it would be used during construction as a staging area for the spire.

It was then decided that the feature's new use would be as a sky terrace, which would be the highest in the world when completed at an elevation of 630m.

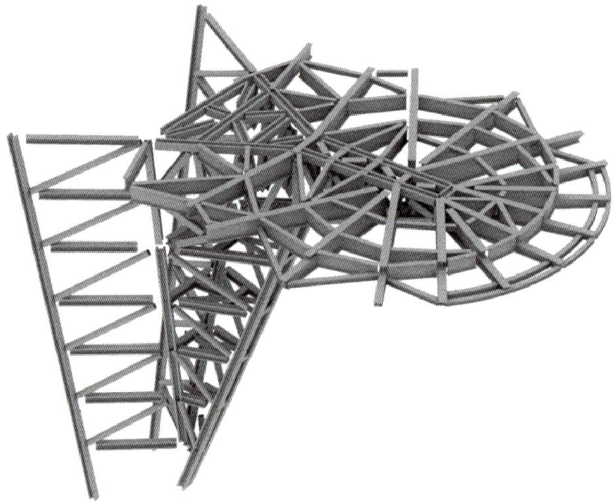

STRUCTURAL DRAWING

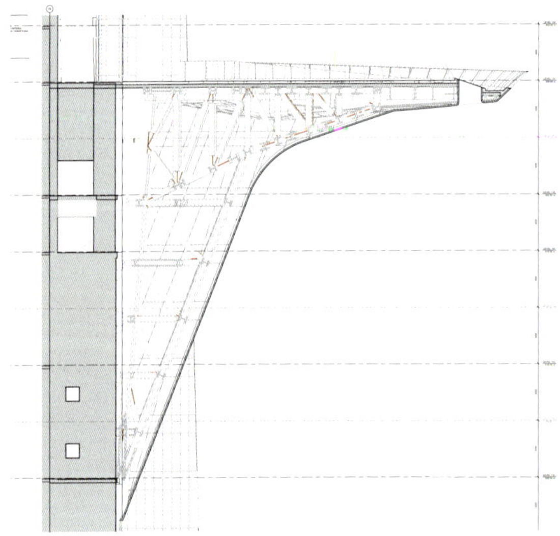

OBSERVATION SECTION

OBSERVATION

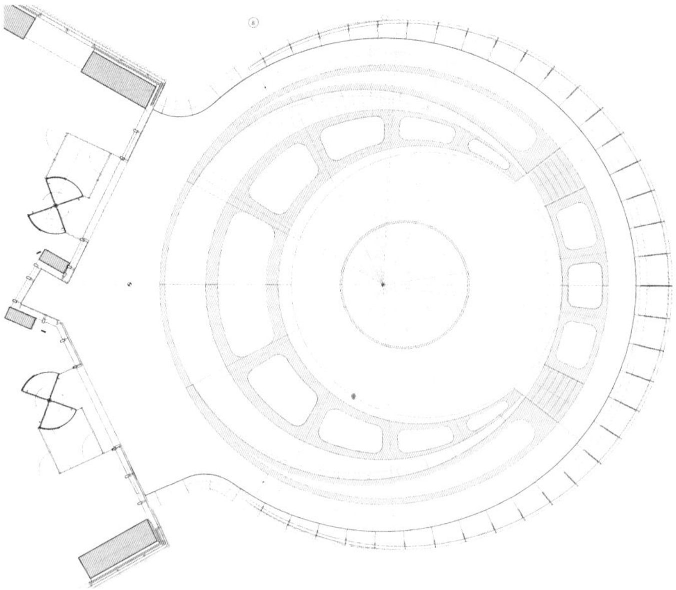

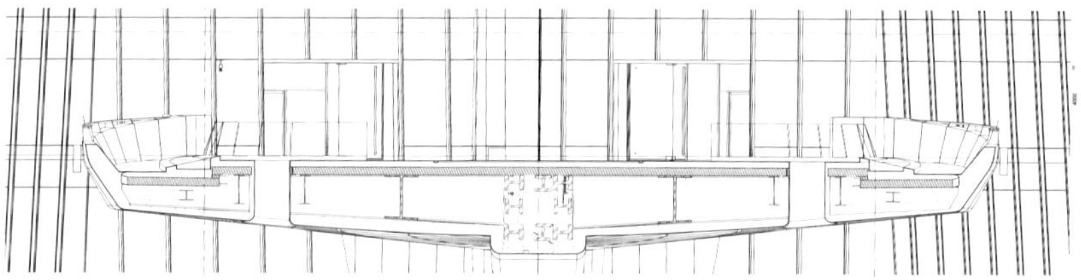

PARTIAL SECTION

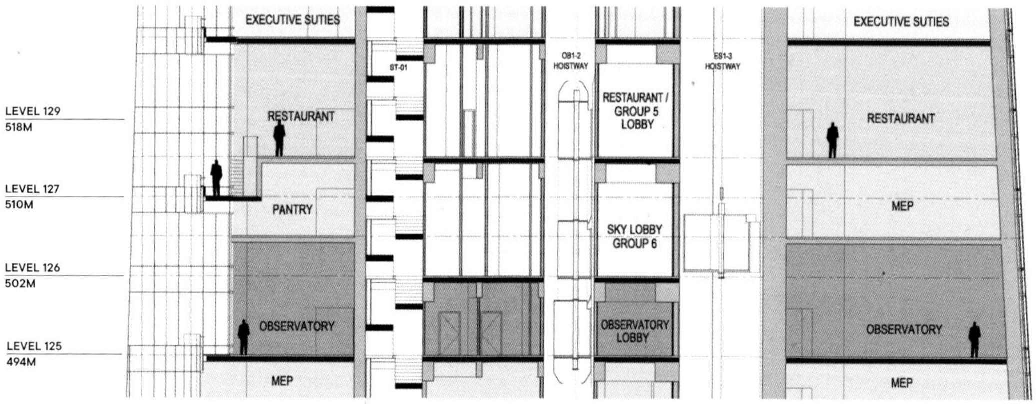

RESEARCH + DEVELOPMENT

THORNTON TOMASETTI + RWDI, ENGINEERS

The key issue in the design of supertall buildings is wind resistance. Wind vortices build up vertically around a building, causing lateral movement in the tower that can be sensed by occupants. To combat this problem, designers look for ways to "confuse the wind" and reduce the buildup of the vortices. Jeddah Tower is sloped, which is slightly more expensive to build because each floor plate is slightly smaller than the one directly below it. But according to wind-tunnel testing consultant Rowan, Williams, Davies & Irwin, Inc. (RWDI), the tower's sloped form is ideal for resisting wind forces, so the cost may be offset by the energy performance of the tower.

Designing for wind loading can have far reaching effects on the economics and structural system performance for any supertall tower.

Located along the Red Sea, Jeddah Tower lies in a moderate wind environment. Based on climatological studies performed by RWDI, the basic wind speed was established as 34.8 m/sec (77.9 mph) 3-second gust at 10 m (33 ft) reference height for a return period of 50 years. The Saudi Building Code (SBC), however, prescribes a basic wind speed of 42.2 m/sec (94.5 mph) and all structural engineering designs for the strength of the tower were conservatively carried out for wind loads derived from this higher wind speed.

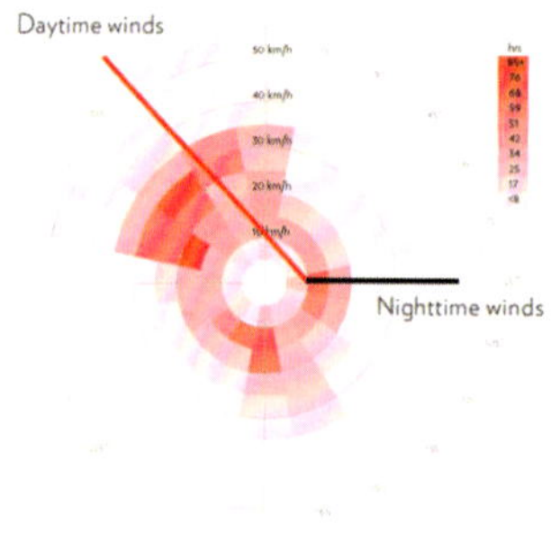

SUMMER

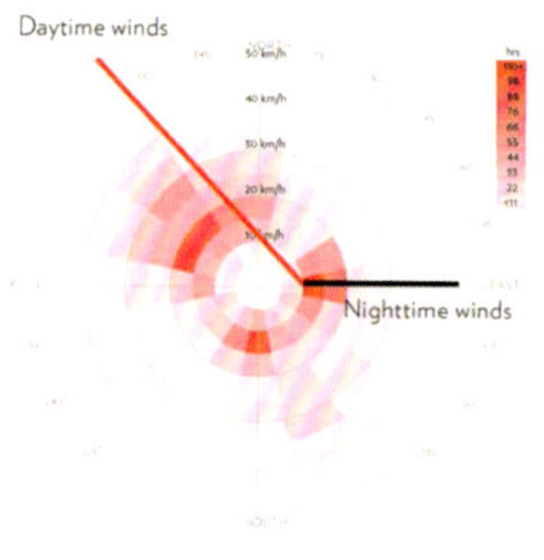

WINTER

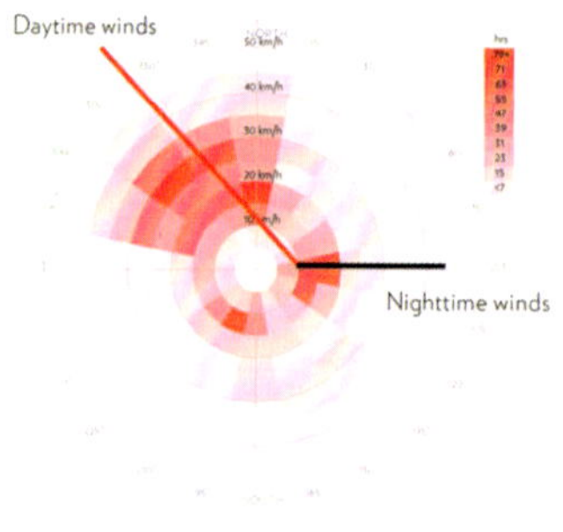

SPRING

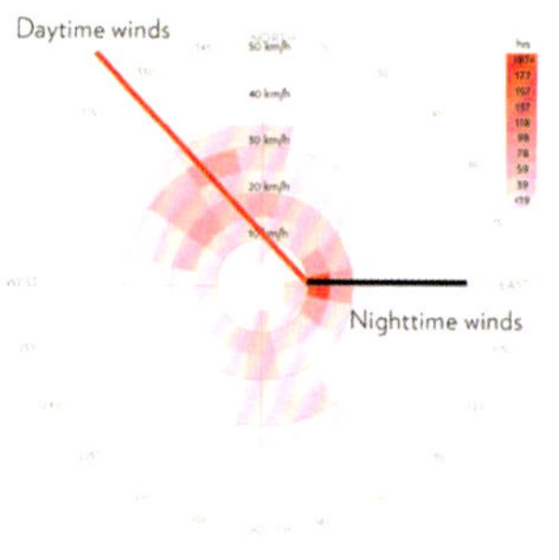

AUTUMN

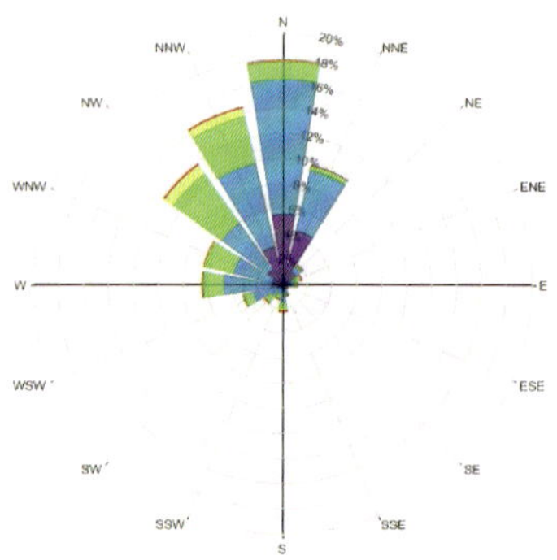

King Abdulaziz IAP

Speed (km/h)	Probability (%) WRF	KAIA
Calm	0	17.5
1	40.3	21.4
2	45.9	40.5
3	12.6	17.5
4	1.3	2.6
5	0	0.4

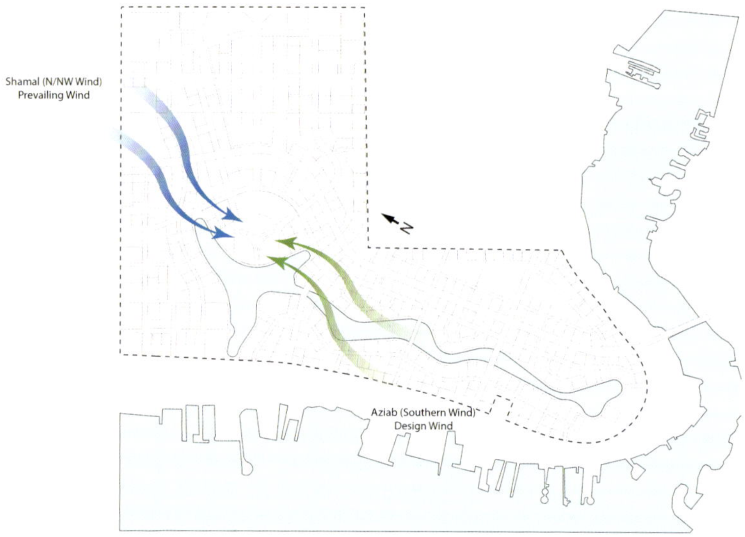

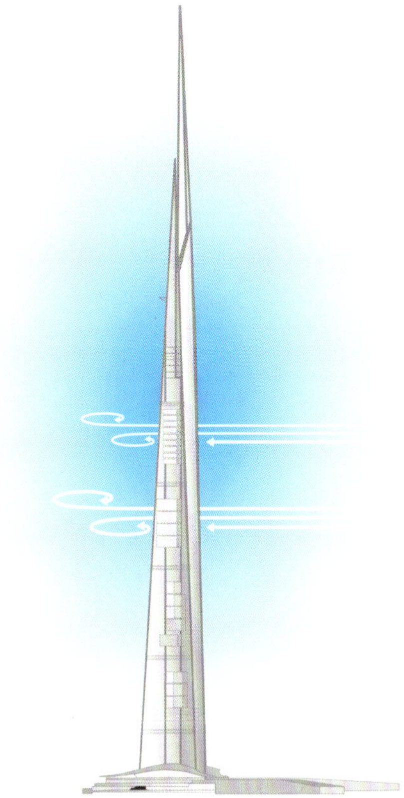

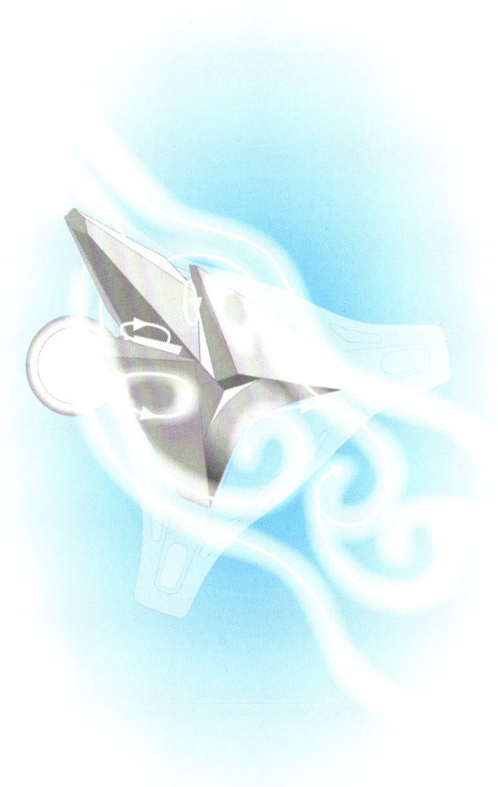

AERODYNAMIC STRATEGIES

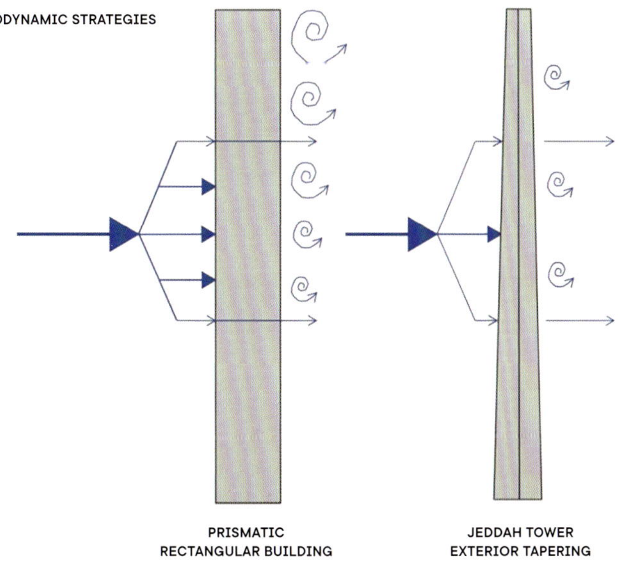

As wind loads generally are proportional to a square of the wind speed, a significant increase in wind loads was required to meet the intent of the local building code. All structural designs for strength of the tower were conservatively carried out for wind loads derived from a higher wind speed.

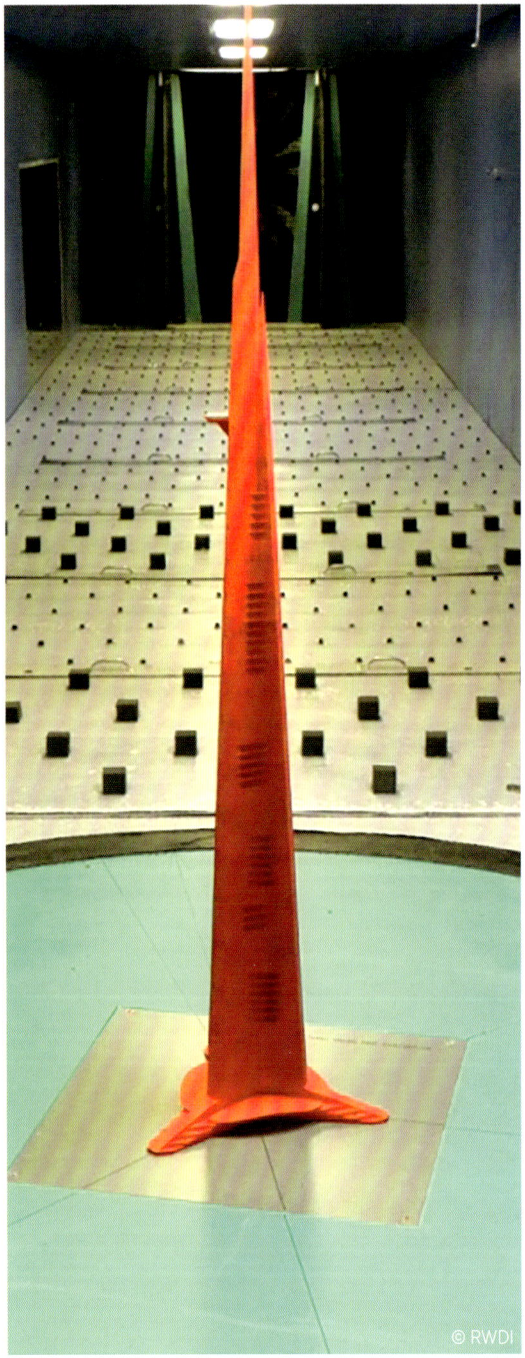
© RWDI

© RWDI

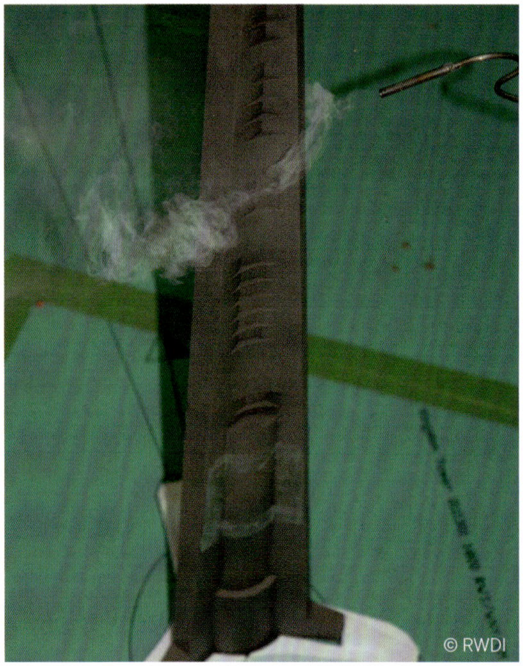
© RWDI

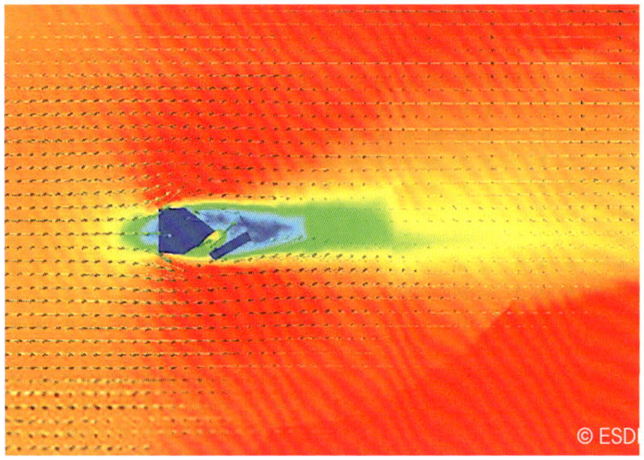

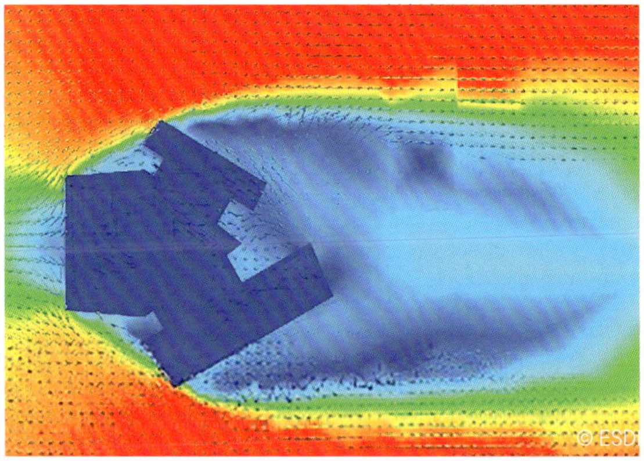

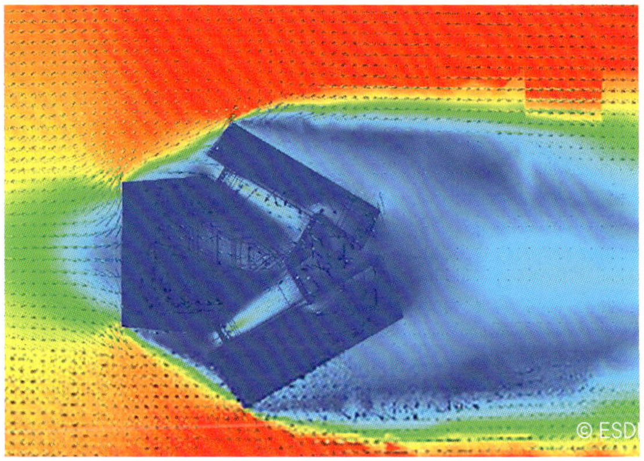

While the design of the tower for strength due to overturning effects from wind can be conservatively estimated, the profile of wind speed at the extreme heights of the tower require special consideration.

Several wind-tunnel tests of increasing scale and complexity were conducted during the design process.

Beginning with smaller scale (1:800) fixed-base High Frequency Force Balance (HFFB) model tests through High Frequency Pressure Integration (HPPI) and finally Aeroelastic model tests at 1:600 scale was utilized.

As the amount of instrumentation for the spire at the larger scales was difficult, a separate 1:400 scale model test of the spire alone was also included in the testing regime. A parallel test for comparison purposes was also conducted at the Boundary Layer Wind-tunnel Laboratory at the University of Western Ontario yielding results consistent with the RWDI testing. The natural periods of vibration for the tower are 12 and 11 seconds respectively in the two translational directions and six seconds in the third mode, which is primarily torsional. The predicted natural periods are indicative of a very stiff structure for a tower of this extreme height, particularly as the tower is quite massive in comparison to other supertall towers.

The results of the wind-tunnel testing proved that the tower structure is very robust in terms of the resistance to adverse wind effects. The system is likewise insensitive to modest changes in structural properties of the tower as a complete sensitivity study of the tower to variations in period, mass, stiffness, and damping was performed. In terms of estimated building motions under wind as perceived by the building occupants, the tower is predicted to be comfortable without the need of auxiliary damping. Although the spire is uninhabited and thus not susceptible to objectionable complaints about motion, the movements under wind require consideration.

The predicted accelerations along the height of the tower generally follow the non-linearity of the fundamental mode shape and as such tend to increase dramatically within the upper reaches of the spire and spire pinnacle. An auxiliary two-staged damper has been specified to limit the movements in the spire only. The design for the spire damper calls for reduction in the motions in the spire of approximately 30 percent.

Jeddah Tower can be likened to a small city that is arranged vertically; this great height necessitates one of the most sophisticated elevator systems in the world. The building has 59 elevators, including 54 single-deck and five double-deck elevators, along with 12 escalators. Elevators serving the observatory travel at a rate of 10 meters per second in both directions. Because of the scale, the arrangement of the various functions must be rationalization with the means and methods of transportation of the occupants, emergency responders, services, goods, and materials both into and out of the tower.

The efficient design of the vertical transportation system is essential to the functioning, safety, and economic success of the project.

In the initial stages of the design process, alternates for the programed use of the upper portions of the tower were investigated. Not only would there be an observatory higher than 600 meters tall, consisting of multiple floors, but there was initially a desire to locate luxurious "royal" residences above the observatory. Given the mixed-use aspect and the client's desire to maximize the number of tourists that could use the observatory, AS+GG undertook several studies that compared conventional shuttle elevator arrangements with double- and triple-deck arrangements.

The first challenge was height. At over 600 meters in height, the shuttle elevators are 100 meters taller than the tallest single-shuttle elevator constructed to date. Furthermore, considering double or triple decks made the technical challenge significantly more daunting. As part of the studies, four of the major elevator manufacturers met in Chicago to present their capabilities and future R+D efforts. At those meetings it was confirmed that the manufacturers were anticipating the challenge and were prepared to take various approaches, including the development of innovative materials to produce lighter weight, stronger cables. Other manufacturers applied advanced technology to increase the capacity of their hoisting machines and controls. Because of these technologies, the height of the elevator travel was no longer a concern.

The second challenge was the elevator's speed and the speed at which they can be loaded and unloaded to optimize turn-over on the observatory floors. Bringing as many occupants to the observation was key, as was enabling them to leave as quickly as possible. At one time, a speed of 20 m/s [up] and 10 m/s [down] was proposed. The down speed is slower due to the limited ability of the human inner ear to adjust quickly enough to the increase in air pressure. However, with increased speed came concerns of occupant comfort and the pit depth of the elevator that would have to penetrate below the bottom of the structural raft of the building.

The third challenge was the multi-use program. In addition to the tourists visiting the observatory, the initial design called for luxurious residences above the observatory.

The owner wanted to separate VIP visitors and the VVIP occupant, therefore the idea of a third deck was studied. Under this proposal, the lower deck of the triple deck would be the VIP and VVIP elevator cab and the two upper decks would be used by the visiting public. By having three decks loading at once, the number of visitors can be increased, and the VIP/VVIP lower deck can have higher-quality finishes with a separate lobby. However, this approach added complications to the plan, which included the need to carve out more space for queuing and loading at three different levels near the ground and added complexity to the observation floors above.

After several months of study, the client decided to remove the residences above the observatory, thereby designating the observatory as public use, making it the highest occupied floors of the tower. It was also agreed that if a VIP visitor wanted to go up to the observatory, they can take an empty elevator that is managed and escorted by designated staff. Given the simplification, although technically feasible, it was decided that the added cost and complexity of the third deck was not required and that two decks were sufficient. It was also decided to retain the still relatively fast speed of 10 m/s in both directions, but in order to increase capacity of the observatory and optimize turn-over, the observatory was configured with multiple levels.

The project proceeded through construction documents with two double-deck elevators. Elevator manufacturer, Kone, won the elevator contract and is employing new lightweight-cable technology for the shuttles. Had the triple deck elevator proceeded, they may have been the fastest multi-deck elevator in the world and the only triple-deck elevators in the world. When completed, the double-deck elevator will boast the longest travel achieved by a multi-deck elevator in the world.

Although Jeddah Tower requires 57 elevators, the core only has space for 18. Therefore, efficiency in the design of the core resides in stacking elevators in the same order that the program of the

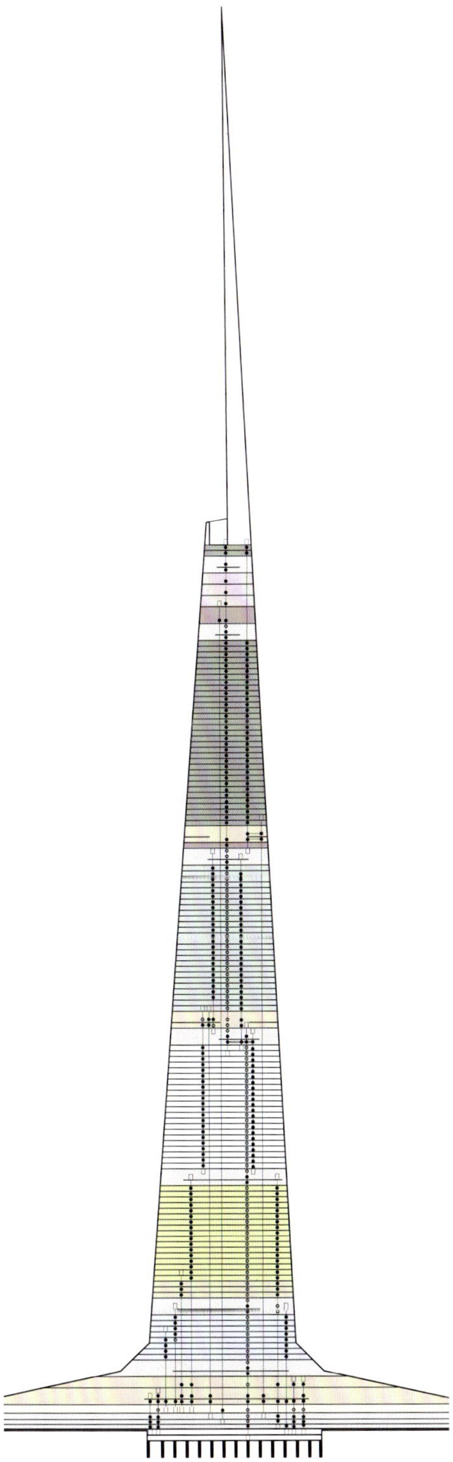

building is stacked. Groups of high-speed shuttle elevators originating at the bottom of the tower serve the residential sky lobbies for passengers to transfer into groups of local elevators that serve each residential floor. The local elevators in the upper zones are in the same position as the local elevators in the lower zones because there are multi-story technical floors below each sky lobby. The height of the technical floors allows for the pit of the upper locals to be positioned directly over the machine room serving the lower locals. In this way, the shaft space is recaptured as the tower rises, allowing 50+ elevators to be in the 18 shaft spaces in the core.

Travel distance, which in the case of Jeddah Tower's observatory shuttles is over 640 meters, is also an important consideration. At a speed of 9 mps, it will still take more than a minute and a half to get from the mezzanine lobby to the observatory. Manufacturers have been developing technologies that allow for faster and higher elevator service and with the development of UltraRope—a cable with a carbon-fiber core—Finnish manufacturer Kone has cut the weight of the cables to a fraction of what is required for steel, opening the possibility of elevator travel distance of one kilometer and beyond.

Windage is concerned with the issue of ride quality for passengers in an elevator cab that is traveling at a high speed within an enclosed shaft. The cab itself acts like a piston in an automobile engine cylinder, creating high pressure in the direction of travel and low pressure behind. As the air rushes past the cab going from high to low, buffeting and noise can make the passengers uncomfortable. Therefore, the aerodynamics of the high-speed cabs, as well as designing ways to ease the movement of air and generally reduce the amount of noise within the cab, was important.

Mitigation measures include the proper sizing of the shaft, aerodynamic cab shrouding, cladding the inside surface of the shaft, specifying active roller guides, and providing pressure relief between shafts. Building sway is another issue that must be addressed at an early stage in the design. All buildings move when lateral loads: wind and seismic events - are applied. Seismic events, being rare occurrences, are responded to by temporarily shutting down the elevators to prevent damage to the equipment.

Wind, being a daily occurrence and high winds, especially at the extreme heights of supertall buildings, must be dealt with in the fundamental design of the system. We start by analyzing the building's behavior under wind using computational models and wind-tunnel testing.

A building Sway Report, describing the fundamental modes of movement, including both amplitude and period, is issued along with the contract documents to the elevator manufacturer.

An elevator system is essentially a pendulum with the cab's weight hung on a cable from a fixed point. Given the advanced knowledge of building sway, the manufacturer analyzes the design to prevent it from reaching resonant frequency.

That is to say, the cab and cables were excited to the point, and their movements is amplified to the point that they slam into the walls of the hoistway, guide rails, etc. Even with the best design and mitigation measures, we will still install accelerometers in certain locations up the tower to monitor lateral movements. If the building movements approach that equipment resonance or exceed a certain amplitude, the elevators will be slowed down or temporarily stopped to prevent damage.

FIRE + LIFE SAFETY

RJA, FIRE + LIFE SAFETY

Due to the significance of Jeddah Tower, and the lack of clearly identified national and local codes and defined authority review and approval processes, the design team initially applied recognized international codes and standards. Those included, not limited to, the codes and standards applied on other supertall buildings like the Burj Khalifa such as the International Building Code (IBC), National Fire Protection Association Life Safety Code (NFPA 101), and related referenced Standards. As the design of Jeddah Tower proceeded and various stakeholders expressed their opinions, the design team adopted a more comprehensive set of regulations, including portions of relevant local, Saudi, and Gulf Cooperation Council (GCC) codes and standards.

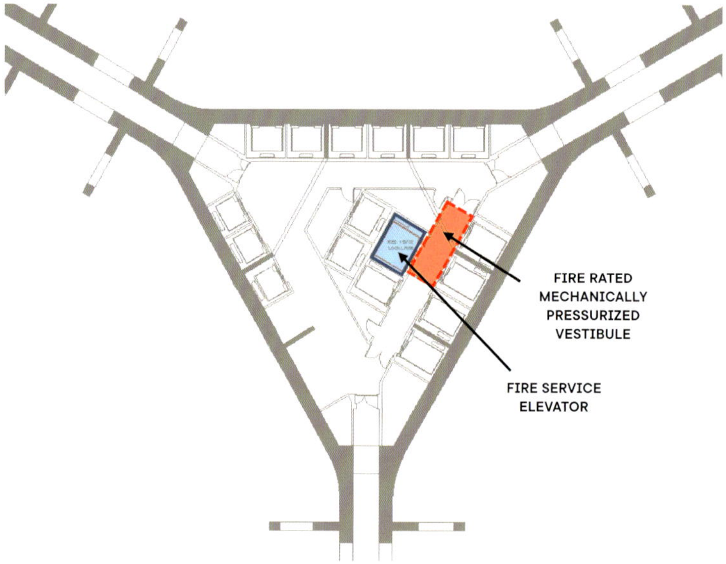

The use of US-based design codes and standards is common in the Middle East and were adopted for the structural engineering design of the tower. American Concrete Institute code ACI-318(08) was used for the design of all reinforced-concrete elements of the tower structure. AISC, ASTM, and other ACI and PCA standards and references were written into the technical specifications for the project. Where specific provisions of the Saudi Building Code (SBC) exceeded the provisions of the IBC 2009 or ACI-318, the design met the more stringent provisions of the SBC.

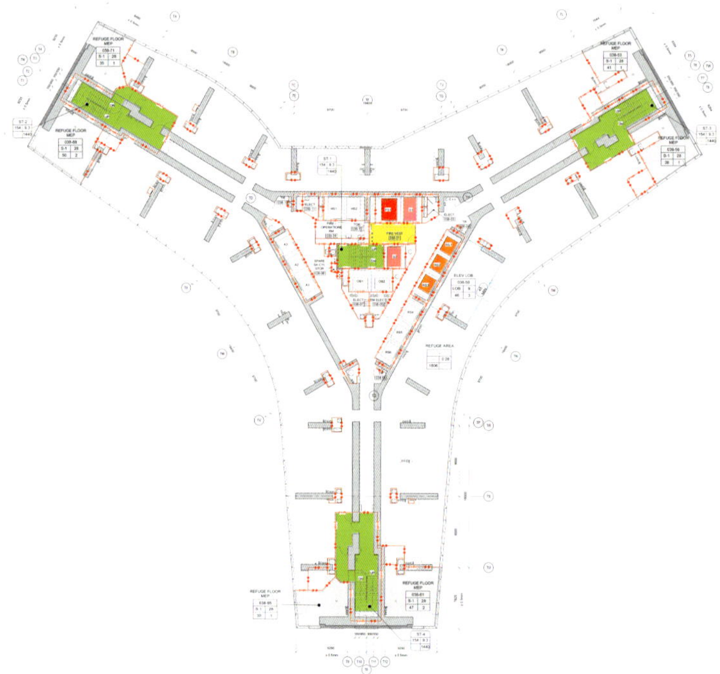

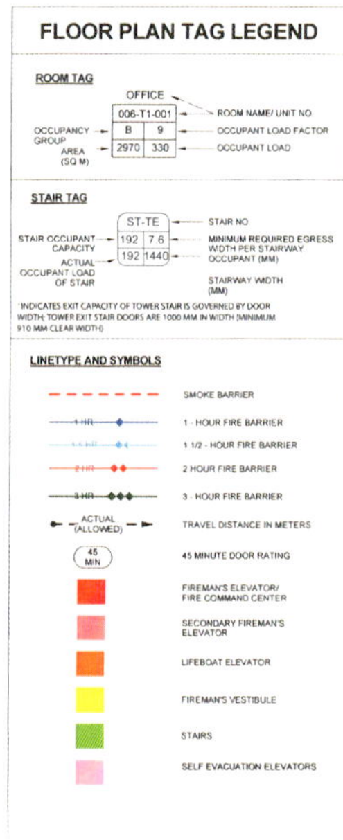

Since the World Trade Center tragedy of September 11, 2001, there has been much discussion about speeding up the process of full building emergency evacuation. Specifically, the use of elevators to supplement the exit stairs, under certain circumstances, has been perceived as a no - or low-cost enhancement. As it stands now, both US Model Codes (IBC and NFPA) recognize the use of elevators, if properly designed and protected from fire and smoke, for supplemental building occupant evacuation.

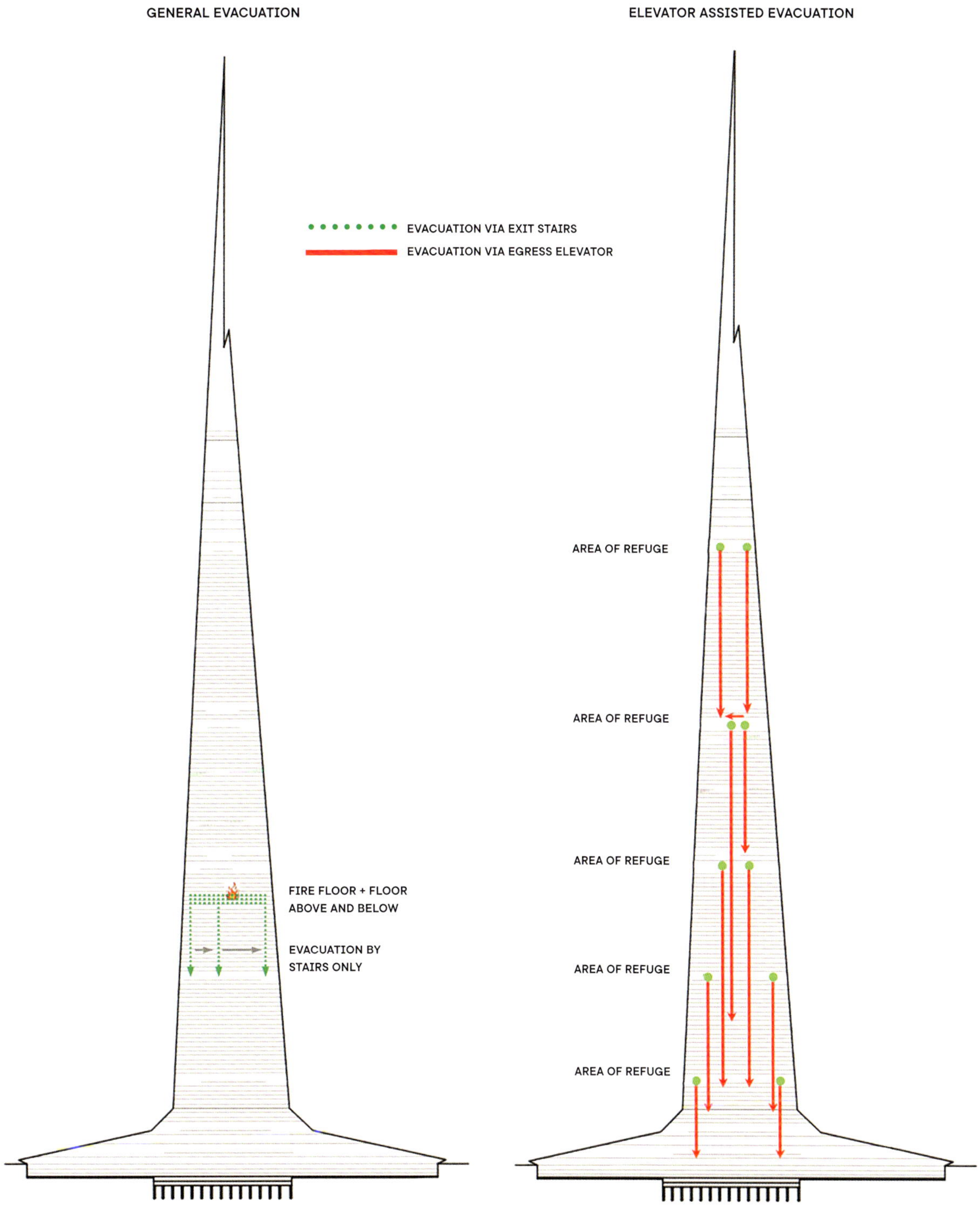
GENERAL EVACUATION
ELEVATOR ASSISTED EVACUATION
EVACUATION VIA EXIT STAIRS
EVACUATION VIA EGRESS ELEVATOR
FIRE FLOOR + FLOOR ABOVE AND BELOW
EVACUATION BY STAIRS ONLY
AREA OF REFUGE
AREA OF REFUGE
AREA OF REFUGE
AREA OF REFUGE
AREA OF REFUGE

FIRE + LIFE SAFETY

RJA, FIRE + LIFE SAFETY

In the case of Jeddah Tower, the local applicable codes do not recognize the use of elevators as a means of escape. However, due to the great height of the building, the use of elevators to augment evacuation, primarily for extraordinary events, has been a fundamental aspect of the fire and life safety enhancements incorporated into the design. Partial or phased evacuation due to a "normal" emergency event, such as a fire in the building, would be handled in a normal manner via the exit stairs, without the use of elevators.

In the case of extraordinary events, which includes, but are not limited to, district power outages, seismic events, and general or specific security threats to the development, a tenant or to the building itself, would call into operation "Lifeboat" Evacuation. The intent is to reduce the time it would take for Full Building Evacuation.

The Design Approach for Jeddah Tower is to employ shuttle elevators with protection features to ensure operation. The key features of the life-boat evacuation elevators include resistance to water infiltration, access to emergency power, individually operated cabs, video inspection of the hoistway shaft, limited stops within the lobby to refuge floor range, cabs operated by trained staff, a fully realized emergency management plan, full building evacuation possible in less than two hours, and fire service elevators remaining dedicated for firefighting and disabled rescue assistance.

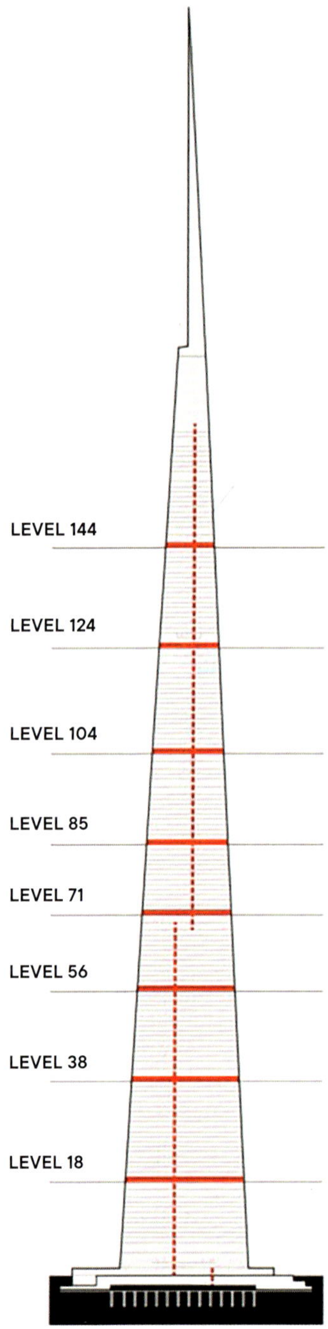

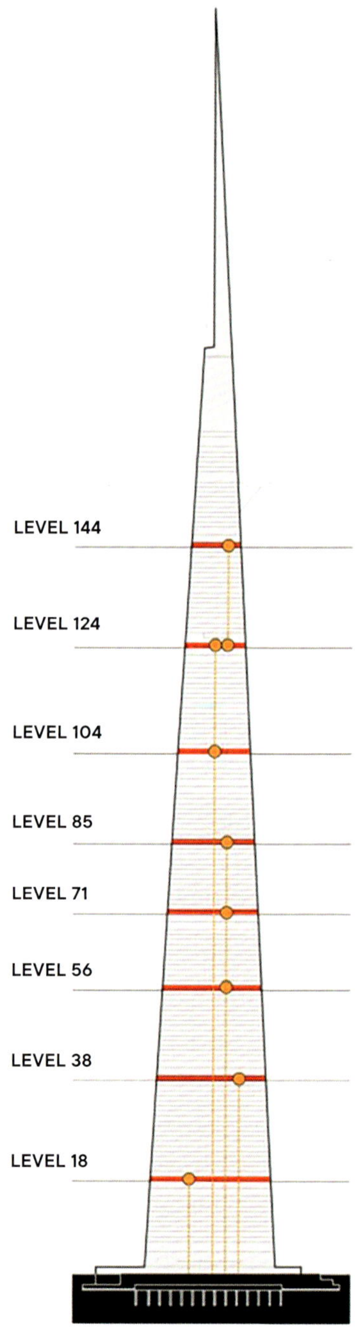

FULL FLOOR AREAS OF REFUGE

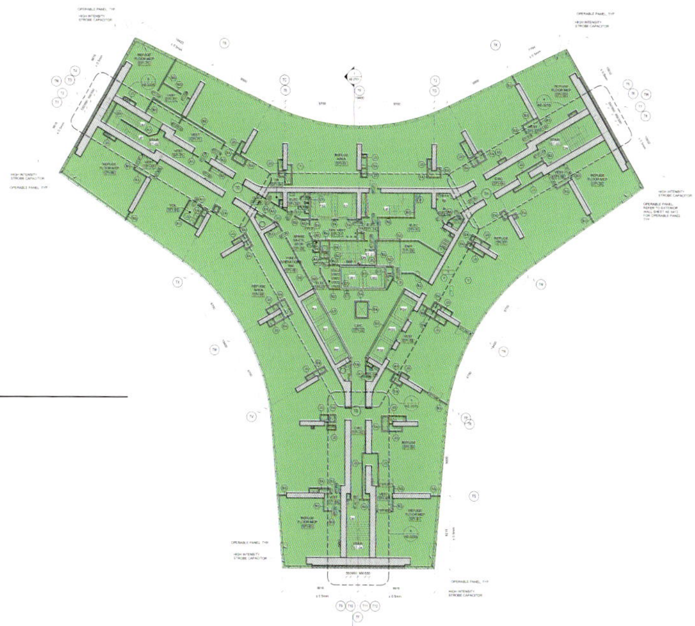

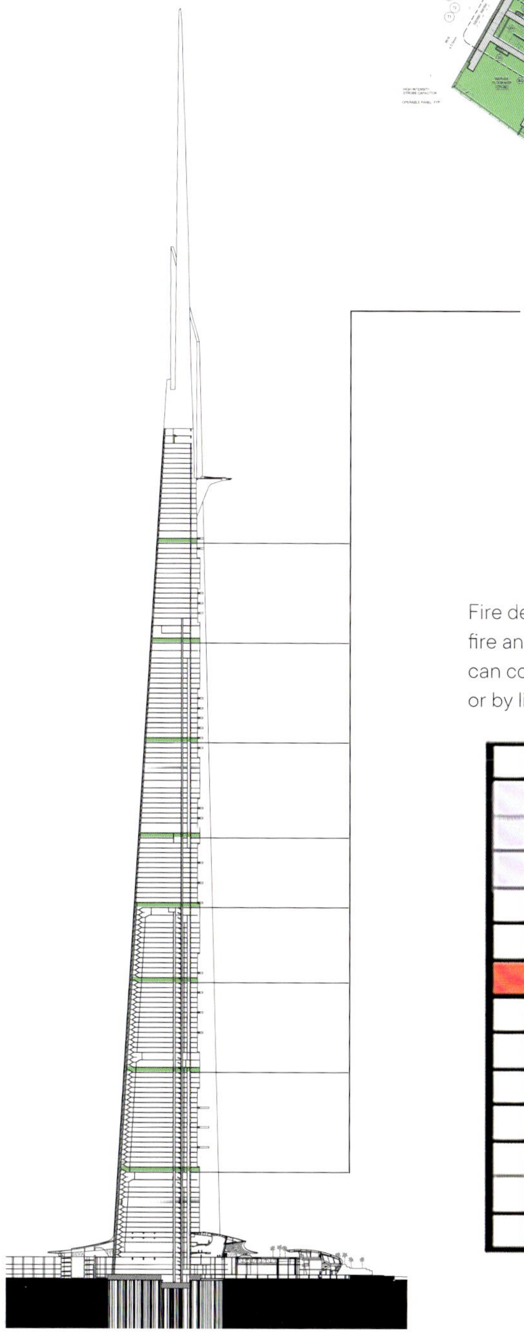

Fire department is dispatched to fire and refuel floor, and occupants can continue evacuation by stairs or by lifeboat elevator.

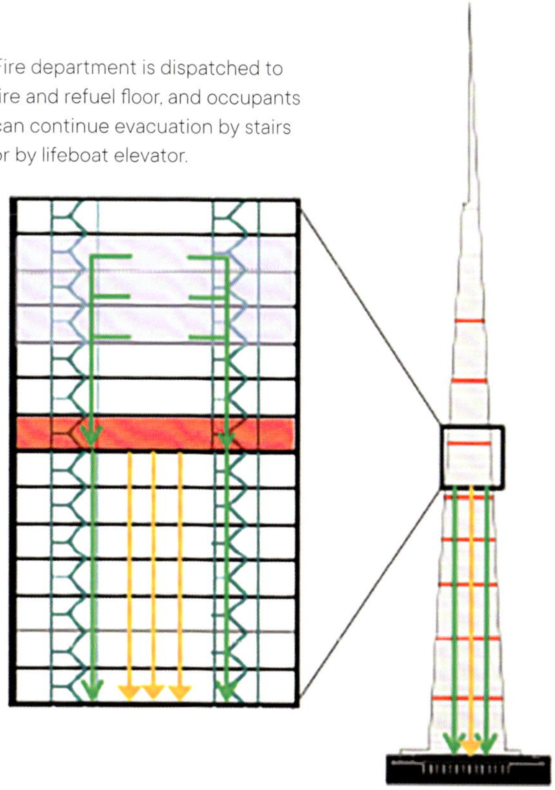

STRUCTURE

THORNTON TOMASETTI, STRUCTURAL ENGINEER

There is a relatively small menu of structural systems to choose from in selecting an appropriate solution for a supertall building—and an even smaller set for a 200,000 sm, one-kilometer-tall tower. Another limiting factor was the expertise of available contractors, and the predominance of local systems and construction materials, which further limited the system choices. The architectural constraints like the building program and use, are primary drivers for the structural system selection.

During the early stages of the competition phase, it was clear that as a matter of risk-management for this first-of-its-kind tower, the structural system should fundamentally build upon the success of the recently completed Burj Khalifa, designed by Adrian Smith while he was at SOM Chicago. Jeddah Tower refines and improves on the elements of the system that proved to be problematical during the construction and realization of the Dubai tower.

In the most basic engineering terms, the structure for Jeddah Tower utilizes a cast-in-place reinforced-concrete bearing-wall system. While the scale of the structure is without precedent, the concept and antecedents for the system can be traced as far back as the CN Tower in Toronto, Canada completed in 1976, among others, that are three-legged structures. The entire tower form is populated with a series of intersecting walls radiating from a central closed prismatic tube. The wall elements form a series of closed cells that extend to the extremities of the tower, creating the requisite gravity, lateral, and torsional load resistance and stiffness.

The system is uniquely suited for residential functions, including hotel, condominium, apartment because the plan naturally has a distinct set of discrete spaces bounded by structural walls without particularly long floor spans. Given the overwhelming preference for reinforced-concrete construction in Saudi Arabia, the bearing-wall system of reinforced-concrete was quickly selected and then refined by the design team.

The fundamentals of the system remained consistent from the earliest days of the competition to the completion of design documents. Other walls are vertical and reduce along the tower's height, as the end walls move closer to the central core triangle. A pair of walls in each wing defines the extent of the public corridors that lead from the central service core to the office and residential units. "Fin" walls placed 9 m (30 feet) on center and perpendicular to the corridor walls provide stiffening and stability to the system.

The central triangular core wall arrangement provides significant torsional strength and stiffness to the overall structural system while housing the elevator shafts from the foundation to the uppermost occupied levels of the tower.

Unlike other supertall towers, Jeddah Tower's structure has no outrigger walls or trusses, no column transfer girders, and no "gravity columns" disengaged from the lateral load resisting system.

Walls are structurally connected and participant in resisting lateral wind and seismic loads. Coupling beams are typically 1.5 m or 1.6 m deep allowing doors into the residential and office units. Wall thicknesses range from 1200 mm for the end walls at the base to 600 mm in the spire. The tower's vertical structure requires high-strength concrete at strengths commonly supplied to tall building projects previously in the Middle East. The lower part of the building uses 85 MPa concrete and the upper floors and spire reduce to 75 and 65 MPa, respectively. The high-strength concrete mix includes multiple cementitious materials, like Portland cement, fly ash, and micosilica, next generation Superplasticizers, and ice to control heat gain during concrete hydration in the thick mass concrete elements.

Reinforcing bars are conventional 60 and 75 ksi (415 and 520 MPa) yield strength material with diameters up to 40 mm (1.6"). At approximately elevation 675 m, the massing narrows and the programed space ends. The upper 325 m (1070') of as the tower ascends to its top. The tower's spire is structured in a closed-concrete "silo" of walls without openings to the exterior. This silo structure rests on a 4 m thick concrete "sky-raft" that forms the transition between the closed spire wall system and the system of wall/coupling beams of the inhabited tower proper. The end walls defining the extremity of the structural system continue uninterrupted from the lower portion of the residential tower to the sky-raft and upward into the spire forming three faces of the spire wall system.

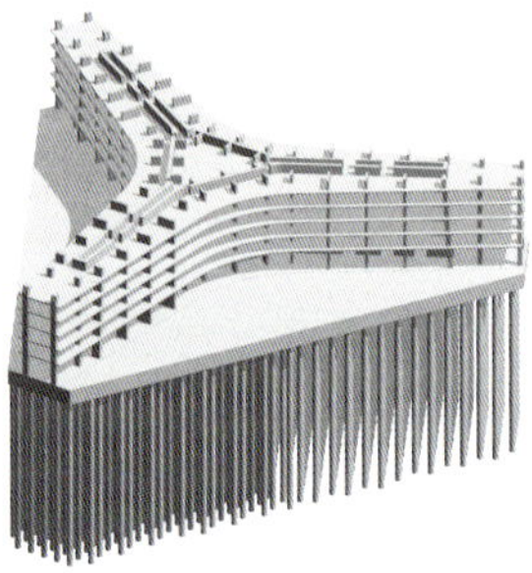

It is anticipated that the concrete for the upper 300 m will require staged pumping, where concrete is initially pumped to a height of 700 m with a second stage that pump lifts it to the required elevation in the spire structure.

FOUNDATION FOR TOWER CORE

STRUCTURE

THORNTON TOMASETTI, STRUCTURAL ENGINEER

The tower floor system has been configured to allow for the utmost speed and repetition in the construction of the structure. Floors are typically framed with 250 mm thick flat plate reinforced-concrete two-way spanning slabs between the walls spaced 9m on center, without floor beams. At some floor locations at the ends of the three wings, based on where the fin walls drop off in elevation, the span between walls is significantly greater than 9 m requiring thicker slabs to control floor deflections. At the edges of the end walls in the corners of the three wings, cantilevered concrete beams are used to limit movements of the floor system.

At the center of the building, an arrangement of exterior cantilevered balconies on alternate floors are structured with cantilevered beams and a variety of slab edge geometries. The supporting walls in these areas are vertical and continuous, however, simplifying the construction. The general contractor for the tower plans to advance the wall construction several levels above the floor construction to maintain simplicity in the jump form system. The slabs will be connected to the walls through a system of keyways and dowel couplers at the slab/wall interface.

The subgrade conditions adjacent to the Red Sea are challenging for supporting the tower. There is no solid bedrock near the ground surface. The top 50 meters of subgrade is composed of limestone formed from the remains of ancient coral reefs, called coralline limestone. Below the limestone are thin layers of siltstone and gravel. Finally, poor-to-strong sandstone layers complete the soil stratigraphy at the site.

Pre-construction exploratory boreholes were drilled to a depth of up to 200 m within the tower footprint. Both down-hole and laboratory testing of soil samples were performed. The foundation system for the tower is a combined piled raft that is comprised of 270 1.5 m and 1.8 m diameter straight shaft. Augured reinforced-concrete piles are arranged in a matrix over the footprint of the tower. The piles are bored to a depth of 105 m in the center of the tower varying to 50 m deep, below the ends of the three wings. The entire pile system is connected by a reinforced-concrete raft slab varying in thickness from 5.0 m (16.4 ft) at the ends of the wings to 4.5 m (14.8 ft) in the center of the tower. The piles are constructed under polymer slurry and deliver load to the ground primarily through friction along the pile shafts.

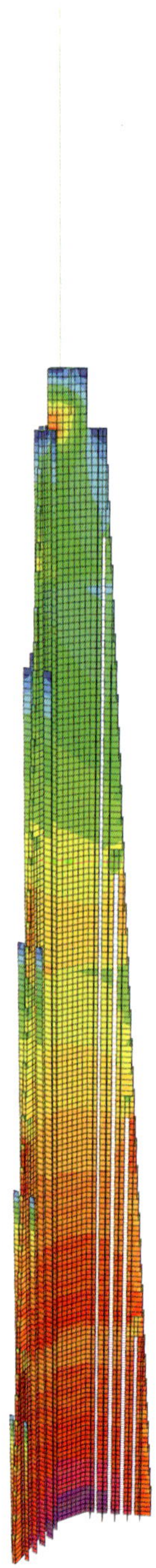

DEAD LOAD STRESSES

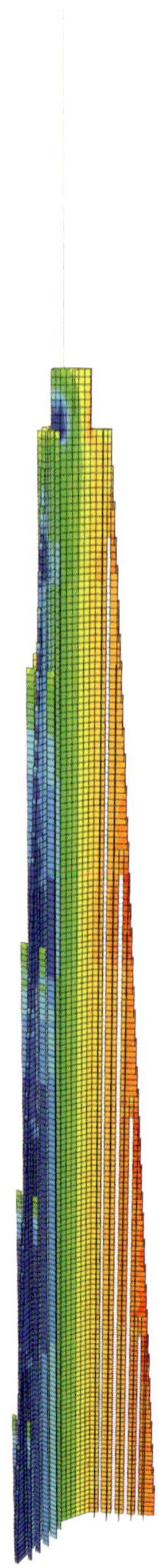

WIND LOAD STRESSES

QUANTITY OF CONCRETE VOLUME	
CONCRETE SLABS (APPLY TO TOWER AND PODIUM TCA)	0.25 m^3 / m^2
CONCRETE WALLS AND COUPLING BEAMS (APPLY TO TOWER TCA)	0.55 m^3 / m^2
CONCRETE WALLS AND COUPLING BEAMS (APPLY TO PODIUM TCA)	0.10 m^3 / m^2
TRANSFER (SKY) RAFTS	2000 m^3
SPIRES CONCRETE SHELL	8000 m^3
Mat Foundation (THICKNESS = 4m)	19,555 m^3
1.5m DIA BORED PILES (50m DEPTH)	276 TOTAL PILES
TOTAL CONSTRUCTED AREA (TCA)	
TOWER TCA	317,591 m^2
PODIUM TCA	149,059 m^2

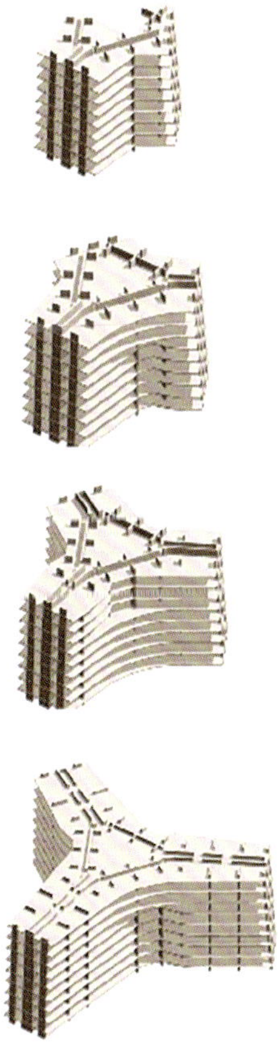

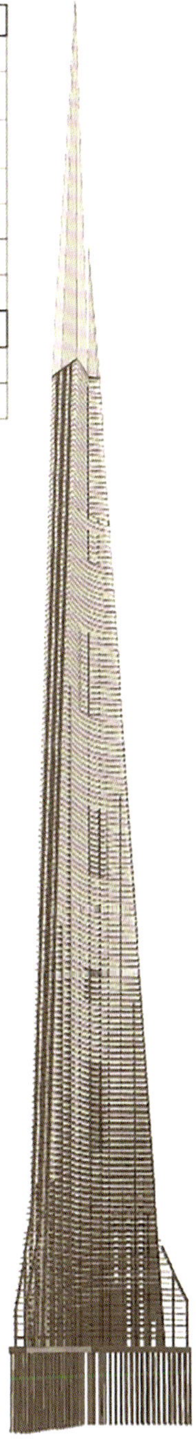

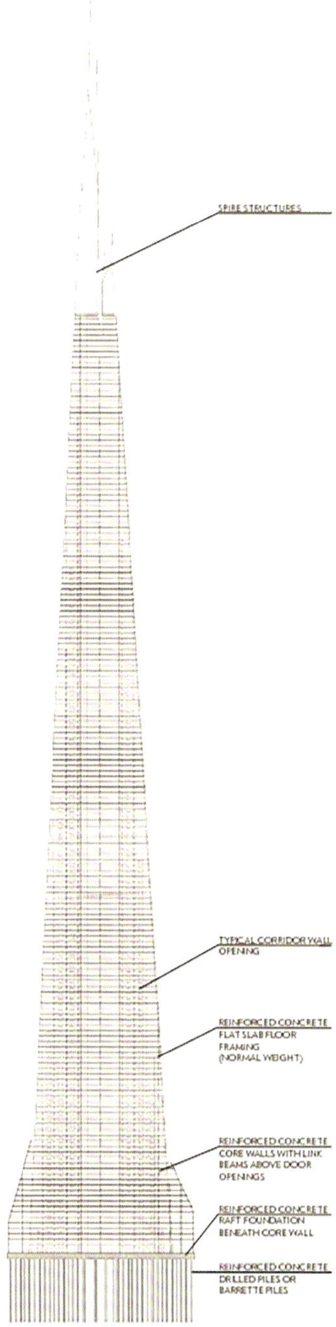

3D REVIT (BIM) MODEL **3D ISOMETRIC SECTIONS** **3D PERSPECTIVE VIEW** **UNWRAPPED SECTION / ELEVATION VIEW**

© Thornton Tomasetti

STRUCTURE

THORNTON TOMASETTI, STRUCTURAL ENGINEER

A portion of the weight of the tower is transferred directly to the ground below the underside of the raft slab. A comprehensive battery of preconstruction full scale pile load testing was completed to estimate the load-carrying and settlement characteristics of the system design.

It was important to have not only a strong foundation system but particularly a stiff one as the tower superstructure load distribution is sensitive to the foundation characteristics. It is anticipated that the overall long-term settlement of the tower will be on the order of 100 mm with differential settlements between the center and wing ends less than 20 mm.

The "sky terrace" outdoor platform, which is at an elevation above 600 m is a particularly challenging steel structure specifically planned as a public amenity for the observation experience. A central steel box-truss is cantilevered from and encased within the main body of the tower wall structure. From this central spine support, transverse girders are doubly cantilevered and organized around various apertures allowing viewing to below.

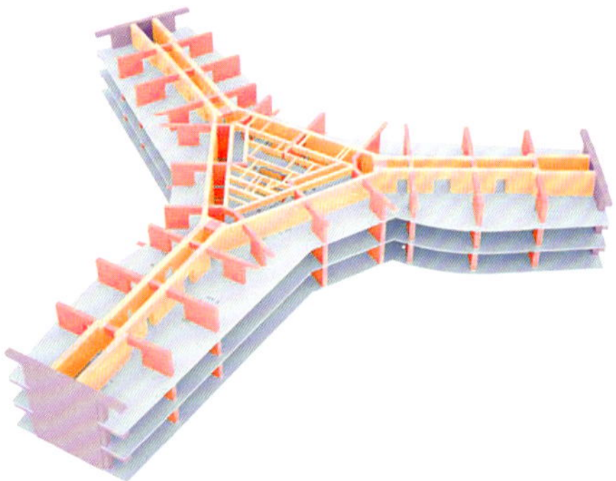

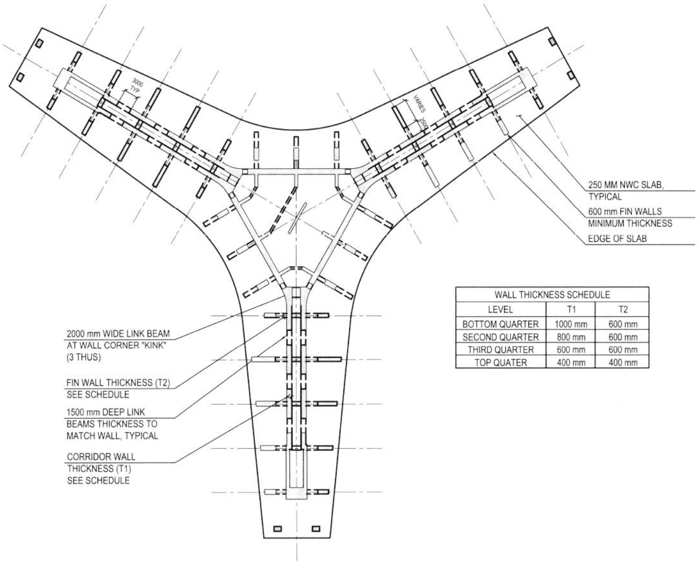

WALL THICKNESS SCHEDULE		
LEVEL	T1	T2
BOTTOM QUARTER	1000 mm	600 mm
SECOND QUARTER	800 mm	600 mm
THIRD QUARTER	600 mm	600 mm
TOP QUATER	400 mm	400 mm

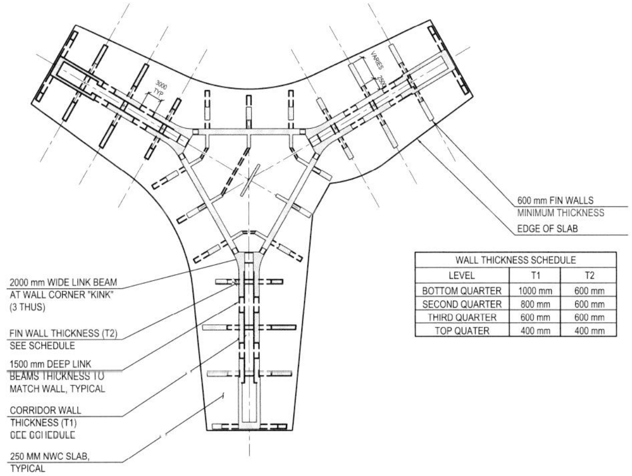

WALL THICKNESS SCHEDULE		
LEVEL	T1	T2
BOTTOM QUARTER	1000 mm	600 mm
SECOND QUARTER	800 mm	600 mm
THIRD QUARTER	600 mm	600 mm
TOP QUATER	400 mm	400 mm

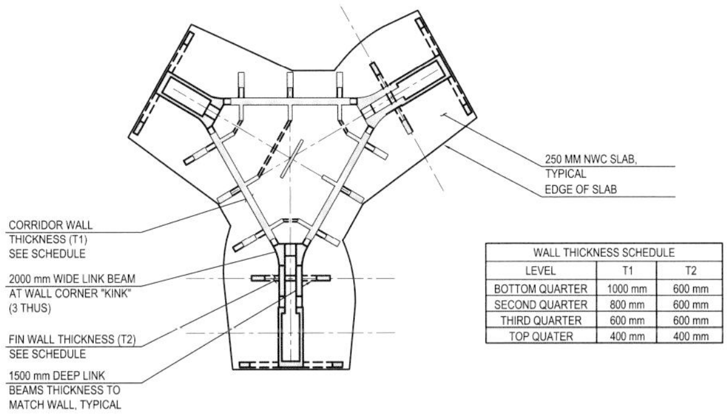

WALL THICKNESS SCHEDULE		
LEVEL	T1	T2
BOTTOM QUARTER	1000 mm	600 mm
SECOND QUARTER	800 mm	600 mm
THIRD QUARTER	600 mm	600 mm
TOP QUATER	400 mm	400 mm

CONSTRUCTION

Construction began on April 1, 2013 and piling was completed in December of that same year. As of the year 2020, over 58 floors have been completed, although construction has been delayed from the original goal of completion within five years.

©Thornton Tomasetti

©Thornton Tomasetti

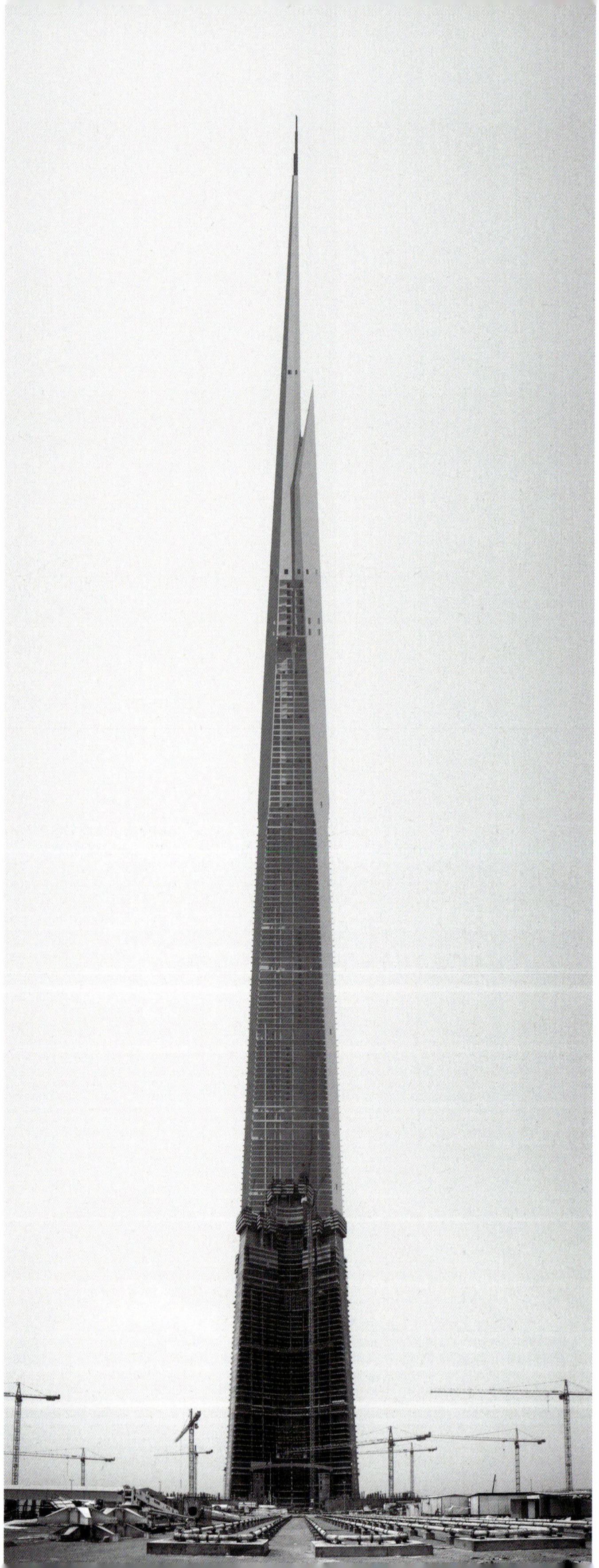

©EC Harris Mace

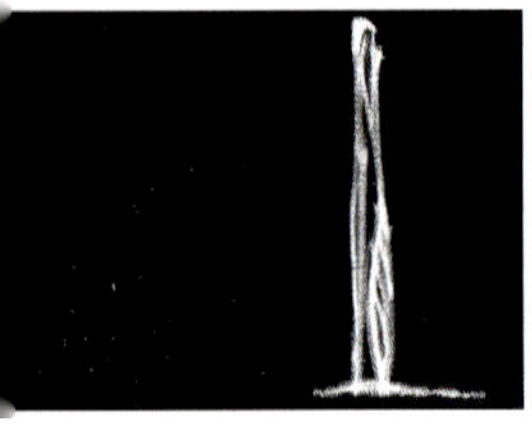

SHENZHEN HONG KONG INTERNATIONAL CENTER

SHENZHEN, CHINA, 2019
668M

The design for Shenzhen Hong Kong International Center is an ambitious tower for one of China's fastest growing cities. Set between the foothills of Longcheng Park and the Dayun National Park, Shenzhen Hong Kong International Center is adjacent to several major sporting venues.

The muscular form references anthropomorphic characteristics, offering a new sculptural icon for northwest Shenzhen's skyline.

The new tower is located at the center of the Shimao Shenzhen Longgang Master Plan and is the main focal point for every office and apartment building within the development. It is envisioned as one of the tallest towers in the world, at approximately 700 meters. In the evenings, the tower will transform into a visual, sound, and light show, reinforcing the district's athletic and entertainment purposes.

The tower's top will have one of the world's highest observation experiences and additional club facilities that include a restaurant, a night club, spa services, and a grand swimming pool, all with views of Shenzhen and beyond.

+ CONTEXT
+ SITE
+ PROGRAM
+ PERFORMANCE
+ EXPERIENCE
+ STRUCTURE

CONTEXT

In an abstract way, the tower is anthropomorphic in its character, representing and honoring the athletes that train—and struggle—to have the opportunity to perform in the world-class stadiums, arenas, and natatorium directly adjacent to and integrated into the overall Shimao Shenzhen Longgang Master Plan. In this way, it adds a subtle layer of contextualism to the activities that these performance spaces contain.

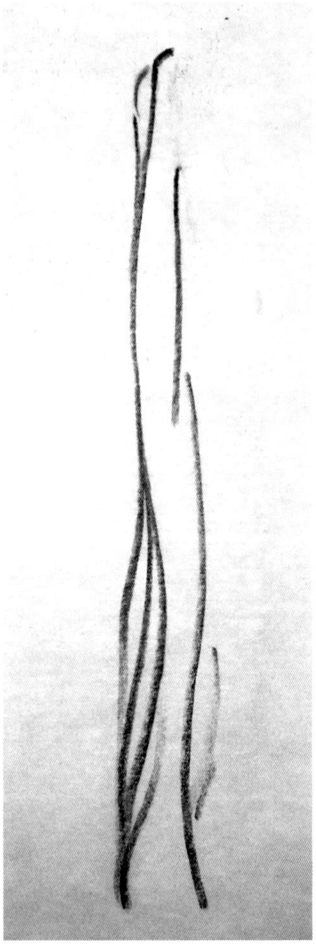

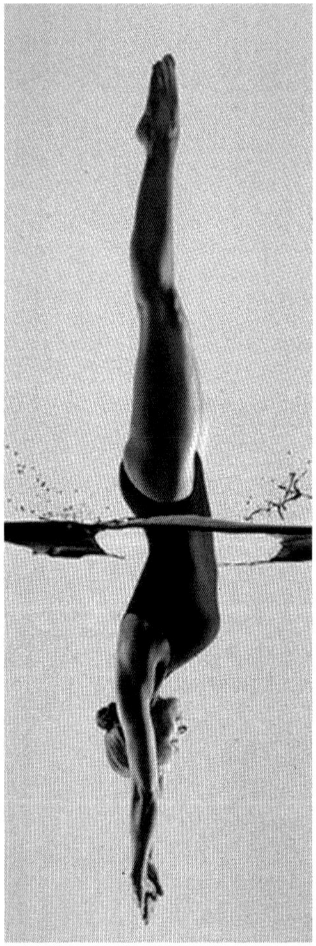

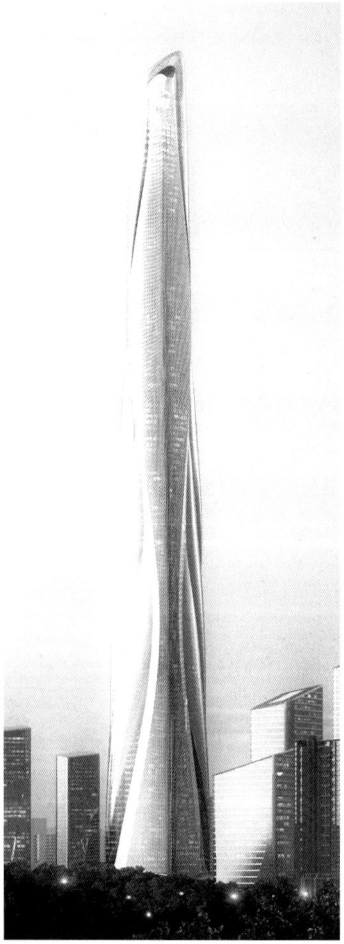

SITE

The mixed-use district that surrounds and connects with the tower contains a five-star hotel, offices, and conference facilities. A major retail facility defines the northeast corner of the site, while a community of apartment towers occupies the northwest section.

The master plan integrates a dynamic new public realm that combines cultural and retail programs anchored by a cultural center and a main library. Programed venues have open and enclosed spaces for recreation, leisure, tourism, art, dining, and social gatherings.

Shenzhen is known for heavy rains and flooding during the summer months, so it was crucial that the site can manage 100 percent of a 100-year storm event.

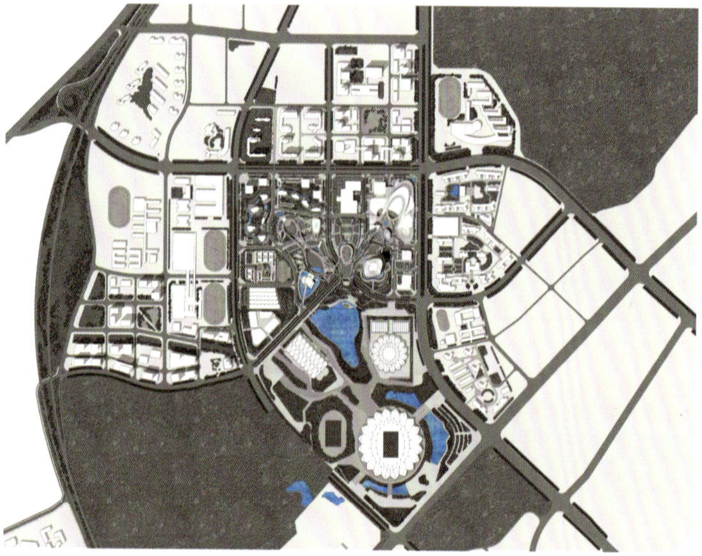

SITE PLAN

SITE

Beautifully landscaped promenades connect patrons and visitors to every aspect of activity. Gardens and open spaces are designed to accommodate memorable and unique experiences. Through an optimized configuration of the buildings and the inclusion of water features, a successful microclimate improves outdoor comfort throughout the year.

PROGRAM

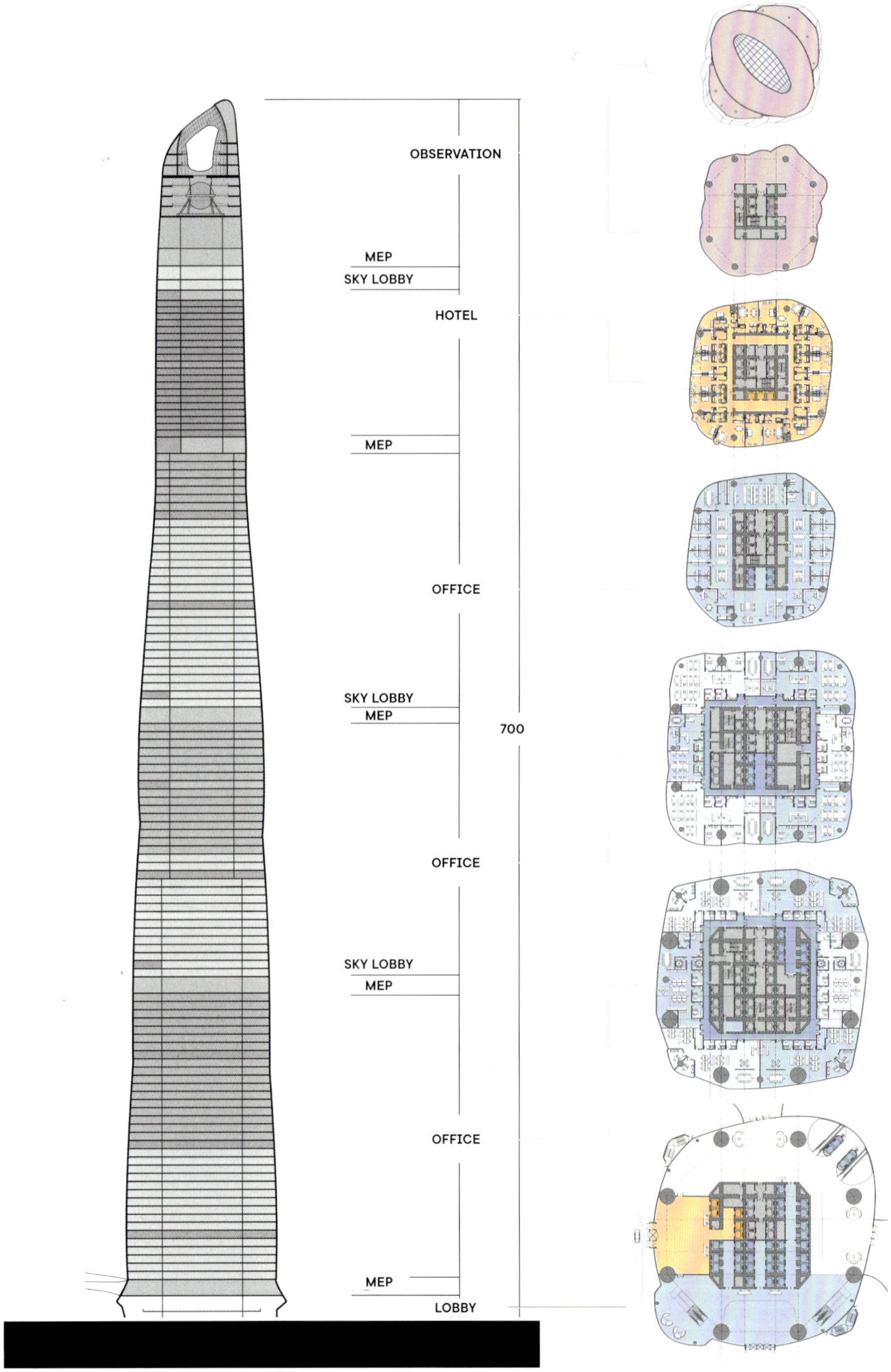

OBSERVATION
MEP
SKY LOBBY
HOTEL
MEP
OFFICE
SKY LOBBY
MEP
700
OFFICE
SKY LOBBY
MEP
OFFICE
MEP
LOBBY

PERFORMANCE

Shenzhen's wind climate presents a significant design and engineering challenge for the Shenzhen-Hong Kong International Center. Due to the high typhoon-driven wind speeds of the region, a tower of this height is subjected to extremely high wind forces and demands a process of architectural and structural design that maximizes efficiency and occupant comfort, while minimizing construction costs.

Tapering: Design optimization begins with a primary tapering of the form to reduce the "sail area" as the tower increases in height.

Smooth Geometry: Optimization for aerodynamics includes refinement of the tower's geometry to further smooth and allow better wind movement off the faces and around the corners to reduce interactions with the wind.

Surface Sculpting: The tower's form is further sculpted to present varied and articulated surfaces that work with the tapered form to "confuse" the wind by varying the vortex shedding action and reducing the dynamic effect on the tower. The form's slight asymmetry balances the wind forces around the tower, limiting harmonic interactions and reducing the peak lateral/cross wind forces on the tower.

Orientation and Tuned Mass Damper: The tower's orientation is based on initial understandings of the local wind condition and further fine-tuning during wind-tunnel testing. Ongoing design refinement will further optimize the wind performance to control accelerations for improved human comfort. A TMD (Tuned Mass Damper) will be provided at the top of the building to control tower movement, if necessary.

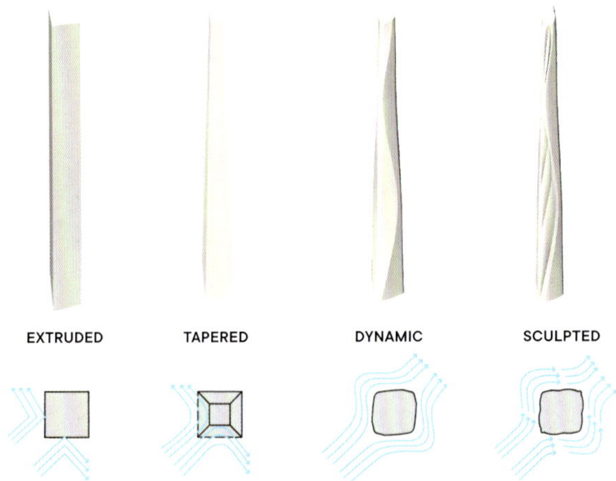

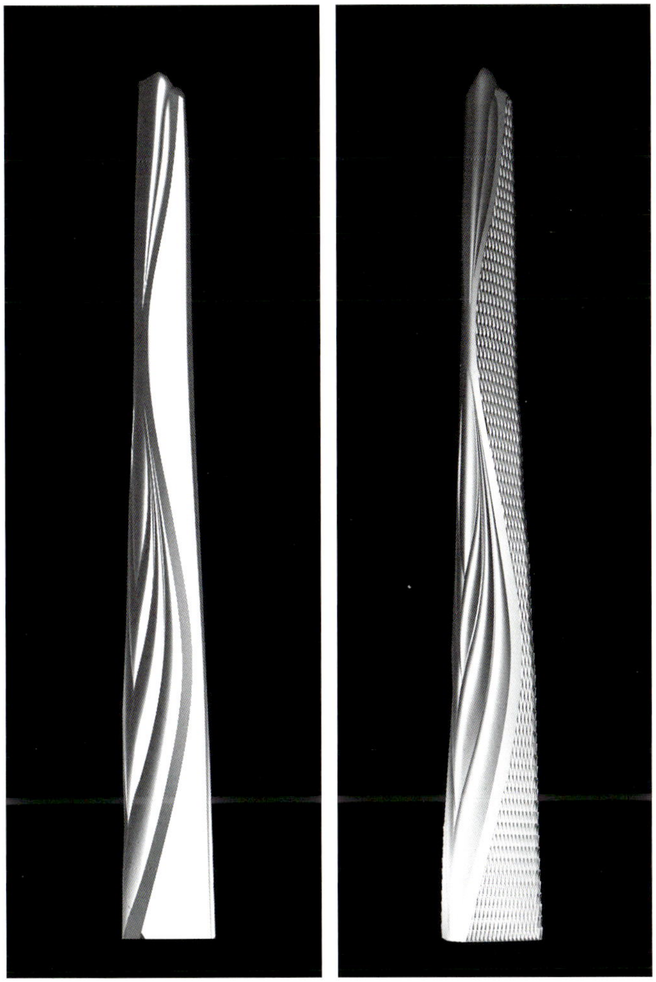

In the elevation, the tower gradually curves all the way to the top of the building, creating a dynamic architectural effect.

This streamlined edge creates visual interest but also helps to avoid vortex shedding, reducing the cross-wind agitation of the tower.

The overall shape of the floors decreases gradually from the bottom to the top. Although the tower's structure is close-to symmetrical in plan, providing the same structural behavior in the two principle directions, it also minimizes the torsional behavior in the tower, making the structure more stable.

Due to high wind load in Shenzhen, the design of the top of the tower plays an important role in the wind engineering. When an opening is introduced at the tower's crown, both the wind sail area and the shape factor are reduced, thereby minimizing the wind's impact.

EXPERIENCE

For supertall buildings to remain cutting edge, we have created an architectural feature that carves out "special" event or gathering spaces at the top of the tower. These spaces take advantage of the prime location, offering spectacular views and provide experiences that are unforgettable. Typical experiences include spectacular viewing areas, exhilarating rides, and fine dining.

The tower's top has additional club facilities that include a restaurant, a night club, spa services, and a grand swimming pool, all with views of Shenzhen and beyond. We envision a multi-dimensional venue where the visitor will be submerged in the experience through state-of-the-art virtual reality, immersive holographic concerts. The space will also offer visitors a world-class sky garden and live shows. The tower top will also be visually identifiable from the exterior.

We believe that we should expand the role of supertall buildings within a community. Shenzhen Hong Kong International Center, once completed, will be a majestic structure for the city of Shenzhen, one that generates wonder and contributes to the human experience by pushing beyond known technological boundaries.

PINNACLE EXPERIENCE

STRUCTURE

THORNTON TOMASETTI, STRUCTURAL ENGINEER

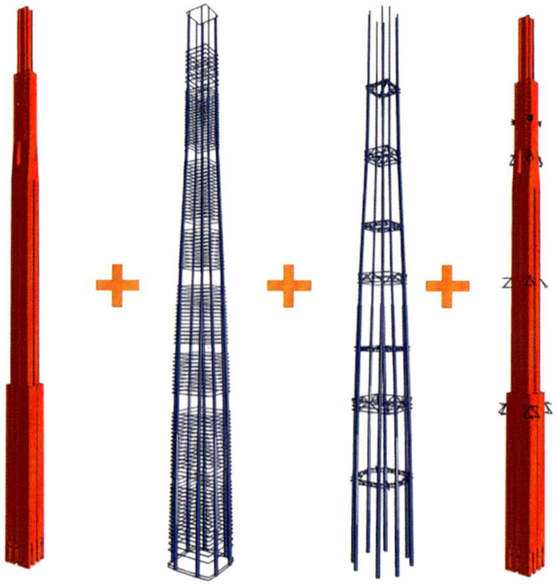

The lateral system is a Core Wall Outrigger Truss Mega Frame system, which is suitable for a supertall building at or over 300 m tall. The lateral system contains a reinforced-concrete core wall, composite super columns, and steel outrigger trusses.

Reinforced-concrete Core: Elevators are at the center core of the building; therefore the structural concrete core is allocated to the center of the building. The core is a 32m x 32m square, with minor chamfers at the base of the tower up to Level 39. From Level 40, the core is 25 m x 25 m square by dropping the outermost layer of the flange wall. Then from Level 93–104, the core reduces gradually to a 17 m x 25 m rectangle by sloping the east and west flange walls inward. The core reduces to a cruciform by dropping the corners at Level 126.

The flange walls are approximately 1200 mm thick at the bottom and gradually decrease to 600 mm. The web walls are approximately 800 mm thick at the bottom and gradually decrease to 300 mm thick at the top. Through these efficient, elegant, and subtle transitions, the size of the core is minimized, the rentable space is maximized, and the leasing span is kept in a reasonable range.

Super Columns: The tower has eight circular super columns—two on each side—that introduce open spaces between the columns that are uniformly spaced in plan, causing the tributary areas of the columns to be the same, which allows aesthetically preferable columns of the same sizes. Uniformly spaced columns can also prevent issues like differential settlement between columns and stress concentration. The columns slope inward orthogonally toward the center of the plan. The diameter is approximately 5000 mm at the bottom and gradually decreases to 2000 mm at the top.

Outrigger Trusses And Belt Trusses: Four sets of outrigger trusses sit between the core wall and the super columns. The outrigger trusses can increase the tower's lateral stiffness, reducing the drifts and acceleration under lateral loads while improving comfort levels. It is common in supertalls building design to use the MEP floors to accommodate the outrigger trusses to connect the perimeter column and core wall together and has proved an economical solution in this design. Steel belt trusses connecting the super columns are placed around the building perimeter at Level 7 MEP and the refuge zones along building's height.

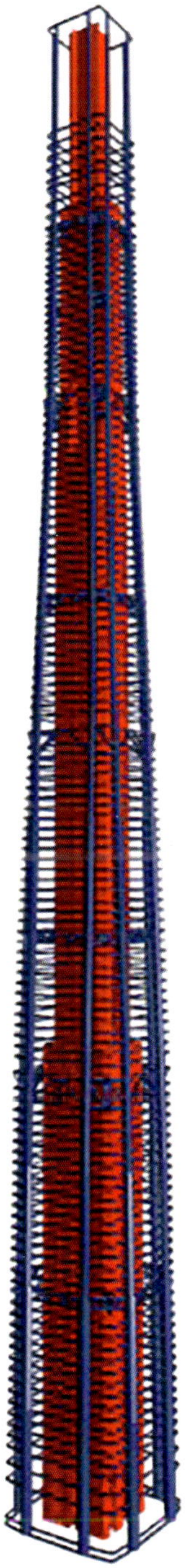

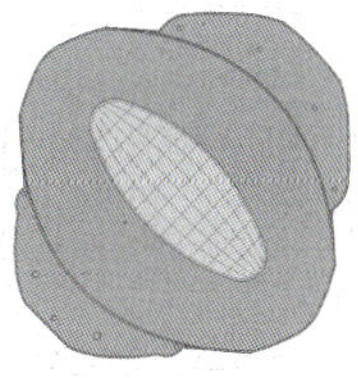

OBSERVATION

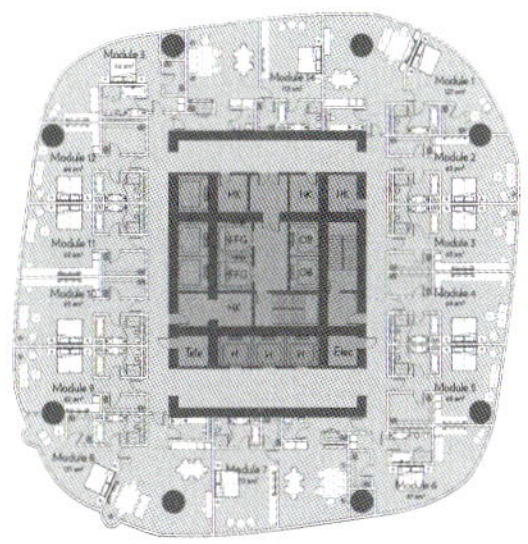

HOTEL

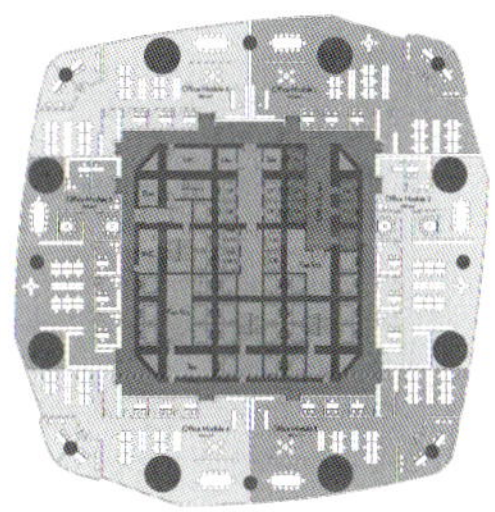

OFFICE

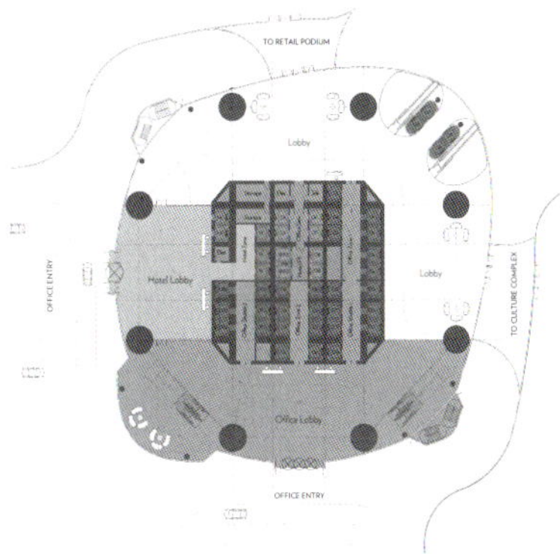

GROUND FLOOR

BELT TRUSSES FUNCTIONS

1. Work with the super columns to serve as the secondary lateral system.
2. Work as transfer truss to transfer the gravity load from the gravity columns to the super columns.
3. Enhance the overall tower integrity and make stresses in perimeter columns more uniform.
4. Reduce the unbraced length of the perimeter columns.
5. Work like hoops to increase tower integrity and stability.
6. Prevent progress collapse due to the local failure of gravity column and thus enhance structural safety and redundancy.
7. The core wall takes most of the base shear. And the core will work with the mega frame and outrigger trusses to take most of the overturning moment.

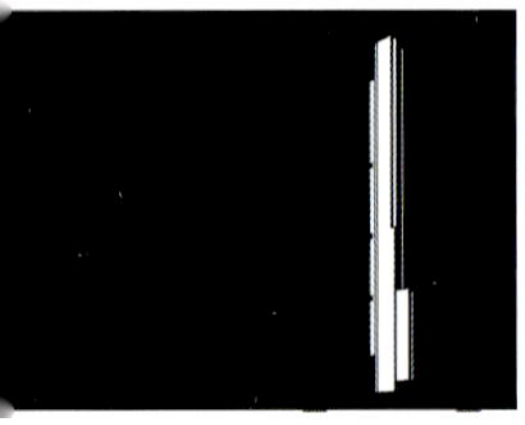

CENTRAL PARK TOWER

NEW YORK, USA, 2020

472M

A beacon of glass and steel rising from the famed Billionaire's Row in New York City, Central Park Tower is one of the most prestigious addresses in the world and will be the world's tallest residential tower once completed in late 2020.

Offering endless views, exquisite architecture, gracious layouts, and an unprecedented level of service, Central Park Tower will be the definitive New York skyscraper.

Located on West 57th Street, New York City's most prestigious corridor, each Central Park Tower residence will have grand living and entertaining spaces that maximize multiple panoramas and citywide views. Structural elements are discreetly located between the residential units, resulting in floor-to-ceiling windows, unencumbered views, and gracious layouts.

The base of the tower features a 300,000 sf, seven-story Nordstrom department store. After a 30-year search for the optimum site, the Seattle-based fashion retailer selected Central Park Tower as the location for its premier flagship story in New York City, the first in its over 100-year history.

AS+GG, recommended by Nordstrom, Inc., succeeded over several contenders for the design including Herzog & de Meuron, SHoP Architects, Jean Nouvel, Foster + Partners, and Rogers Stirk Harbour + Partners.

- + CONTEXT
- + PROGRAM
- + PERFORMANCE
- + RESEARCH + DEVELOPMENT

NOVOTEL
DUANEreade
BROADWAY

CONTEXT

ORIGINAL CONCEPT

The project originated as a design competition for a mixed-use residential tower to be located on a tight site along 57th street in downtown Manhattan. The area of the site was 40,705 sf with street exposure on West 58th Street, West 57th Street, and Broadway. Primary residential and retail entrances to the site were allotted on 57th Street. The site provided additional retail entrances on 58th Street, as well as from the landmarked 1780 Broadway Building. Other specifics of the design brief included loading docks at grade level and employee entrances on 58th Street.

A through-block pedestrian arcade, connecting 57th and 58th Streets, was also required along the eastern edge of the site.

After the initial concept was presented, the client asked for additional high-end residential units—condominium units with views to Central Park—to be located on higher floors. The client also wanted to increase their space through accessing air rights that would enable them to cantilever the tower over an adjacent site, the Art Students League of New York, to further improve the views. In this market these views are worth the structural premiums involved.

The originally proposed scheme was symmetrical about its north-south axis and tapered from the north to the south, providing smaller floors towards the top of the tower with a wider base. The taper of the tower offered an elegant massing solution that would have been quite different from other towers on the New York skyline.

ORIGINALLY PROPOSED SCHEME

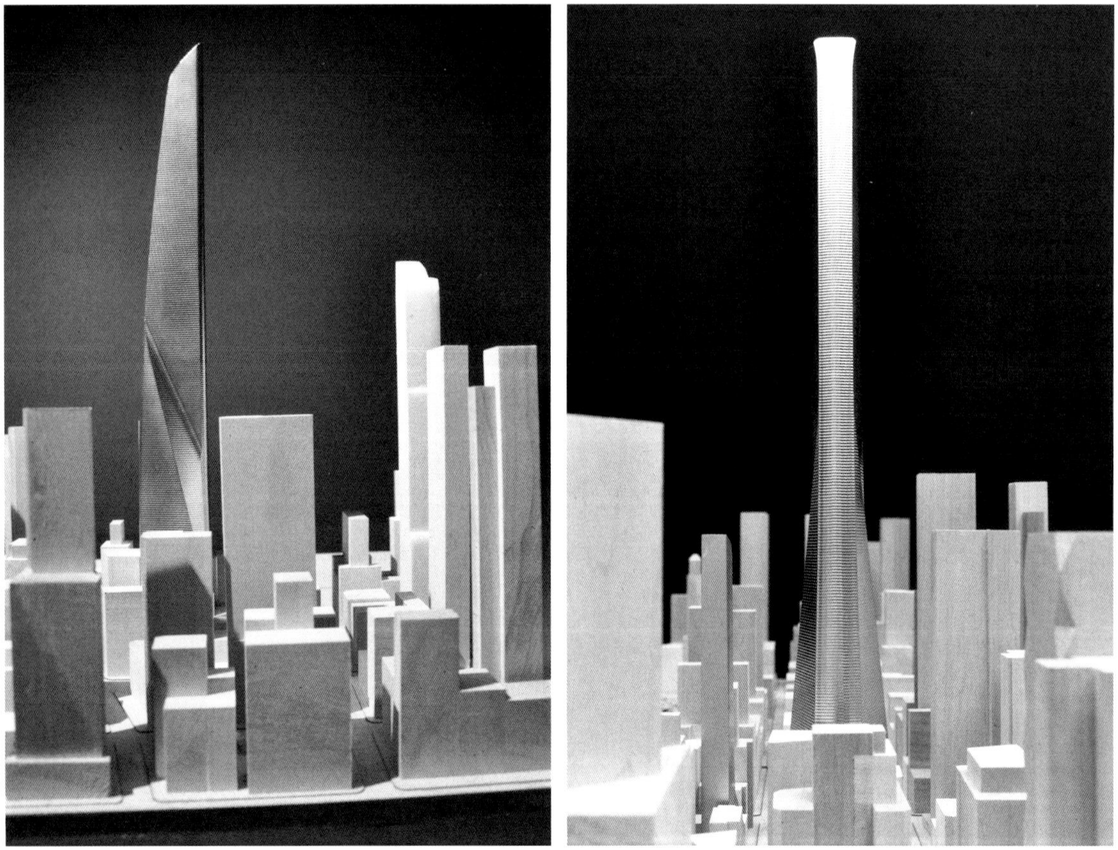

CONTEXT
ORIGINAL CONCEPT

PROGRAM

The final scheme for Central Park Tower is a more orthogonal design, utilizing a large cantilever to take advantage of the site and views. The residential program begins at 300 feet above the ground with 179 ultra-luxury residences ranging from one to four bedrooms, and studio suites, full floor, duplex and triplex homes. The program is organized vertically into a series of tiers, or tranches, that are separated and distinguished by the major mechanical floors distributed through the tower.

Tranche 1 and Tranche 2 have floor-to-floor heights of 11 feet 10 inches and are composed mainly of to three-bedroom units with two to six units per floor. Tranches 3 and 4, higher up in the tower, have a floor-to-floor height of 12 feet and 10 inches and have four and five-bedroom units.

Tranche 3 has 2 units per floor, and Tranche 4—the most well-appointed—has one unit per floor.

The tower also features a private club, dubbed "Central Park Club," which has approximately 50,000 sf of curated luxury amenities across three floors, each providing a unique experience complemented by five-star service. The first club level, located on the 14th floor, has a residents' lounge with billiards, screening, and function rooms.

The centerpiece of the floor is a 15,000 sf outdoor terrace with a 60-foot swimming pool, along with cabanas, a bar, a screening wall, food and beverage service, and an outdoor children's playground.

FINAL SCHEME RENDERINGS

TRANCHE 4 PENTHOUSE

TYPICAL TRANCHE 1-3

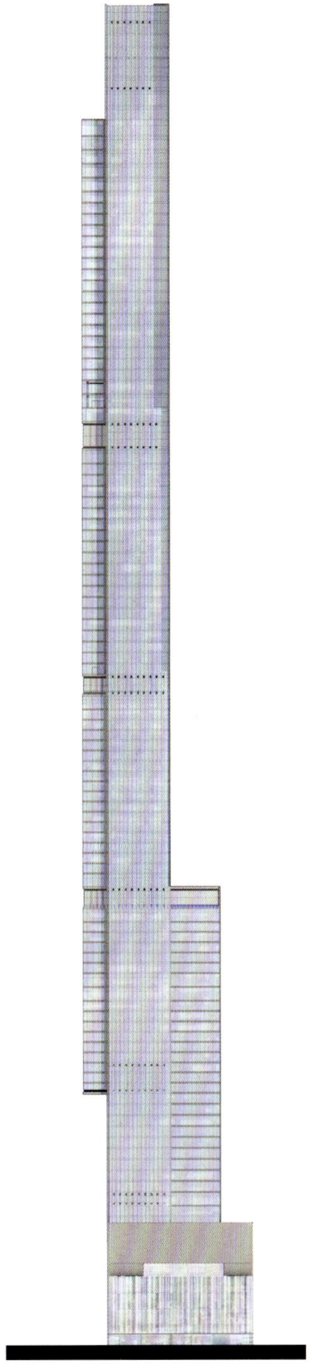

Nordstrom announced their intent to deliver their first store in New York City with a 225,000 sf space in the podium of Central Park Tower. The new retail store has seven retail sales floors: two floors below grade and five floors above grade, including the ground floor. Also included is an upper-level mechanical floor and a below-grade retail back-of house floor.

The podium features an undulating curved glass wall that brings prominence to the flagship store. The design of the facade needed to be articulated to respond to the scale of the streetscape and establish relationships with the horizontal lines of the adjacent buildings on 57th and 58th Streets.

The store will occupy portions of the adjacent 1790 Broadway and 1776 Broadway buildings and will occupy the entire building at 1780 Broadway. It will have entrances at both 1780 and 1790 Broadway, as well as at West 57th and West 58th Streets.

The project also has several historic requirements that relate to the existing building on the site. The facade at 1780 Broadway is being restored to its original condition, while the interior is being fully renovated to represent Nordstrom's branding.

Above the retail store are two levels of residential amenities. Level 8 has space for functions such as daycare, lounges, and entertaining, as well as large areas of outdoor landscaped terrace space. Level 9 has an indoor swimming pool with exercise and spa areas. Additional amenities such as storage lockers, dry cleaning, bike storage and other support spaces will be located on Sub Cellar 3.

© Paul Clemence

© Evan Joseph

The design integrates passive sustainable elements that can promote the tower's prestige once fully implemented, including water-use strategies that reduce the use of water by 25–30 percent. If achieved, the project will receive a fee reduction through the Comprehensive Water Reuse Program, which is awarded to buildings that use a water-reuse system that achieves a minimum reduction of water consumption of at least 25 percent. Other incorporated sustainable systems included gray-water recycling, condensate collection, passive cooling through natural ventilation, radiant heating, and smart meters.

As the tower climbs vertically, the corners set back and notch, helping counteract wind loads. This provides the ability for the floor area on each level to reduce and better achieve the desirable unit size and layouts of the upper two tranches, while simultaneously accommodating private terraces for special residential units. After the cantilever cones to its vertical terminus, the central tower shaft and the blade wall extend upward to an elevation of 1478 feet and 10 inches.

As blade wall ascends toward its peak, 2-foot deep recessed windows within the blade wall begin a rhythm that continues upward, extending above the roof parapet in the form of a three-pronged spire. At an early stage a spire was studied and introduced to give the building more height. This was later eliminated in deference to 1 World Trade Center. The northern edge of the blade wall that would have run along the eastern property line would spring up as a continuation of the steel knife edge to become the highest point of the spire, reaching a top elevation of 1,773 feet.

At the tower's crown, the central shaft is articulated by vertical metal screen slits, reminiscent of the mechanical slots below, providing a strong articulation and completion to the glass shaft arising from the podium.

Studies for a large antenna on top of the tower were done, although ultimately the client decided it was not a worthwhile investment. The antenna would have added an extra flourish to the pinnacle of the tower.

© Michael Young

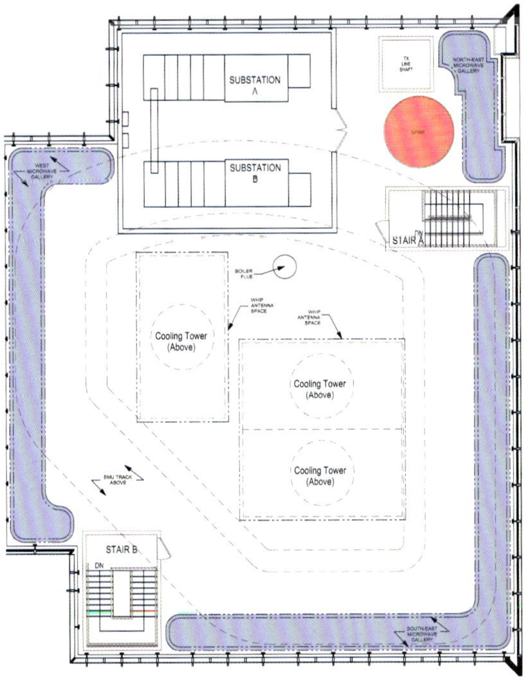

MICROWAVE GALLERY COMPONENTS

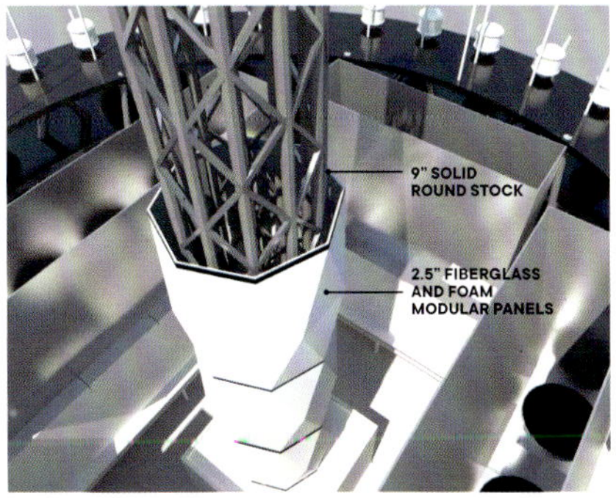

RADOME STRUCTURE

RESEARCH + DEVELOPMENT

RWDI, CONSULTING ENGINEER

The building's form responds to the conditions and opportunities presented by the site's context and the project's functional program. At the base of the tower, the form respects both the human scale and the scale of the adjacent structures. The base volume is mainly comprised of retail with two 21-foot-tall mechanical floors sitting above. The 57th Street massing holds this volume as a single expression.

The 58th Street volume steps back by 20 feet on Level 5 to adhere to the zoning guidelines, and although not adherent to the same zoning, to maintain symmetry, the expression at 57th Street is similar. The building base is framed by a steel blade wall articulation on the east and west sides, which extends upward through the tower. This articulation ties the language of the Nordstrom facade with that of the tower.

Above Level 8, the tower emerges; set back from the base a landscaped outdoor space is exposed. Above the extrusion, the tower rises in a series of articulated extruded volumes. The residential units are separated from the amenity program by an extended unoccupied volume that boosts the residential units and related views to a higher, more prominent location.

The main tower shaft incorporates a vertical expression with flat, high-performance insulated glazing on a five-foot module used to catch the sun's light at varying angles. Additionally, these super-mullions will provide a clean, outboard means of engagement for the use of facade access. Integrated operable glazing panels are stacked vertically on the facade providing a clean secondary vertical expression.

At the mechanical floors, recessed angled louvers provide the required ventilation without subtracting from the vertical expression of the shaft. Adjacent to the central vertical shaft, two volumes rise, distinguishing themselves from the main shaft as a horizontal expression. Each floor module is distinguishable through the introduction of a three-dimensional frame, which at the spandrel and edges, sets back by 5.5 inches to provide depth and separation from the high-performance insulated glazing plane.

These two volumes rise to different elevations, allowing for a play in the composition. Atop each volume reside large private residential terraces supporting stunning views of the park and city skyline.

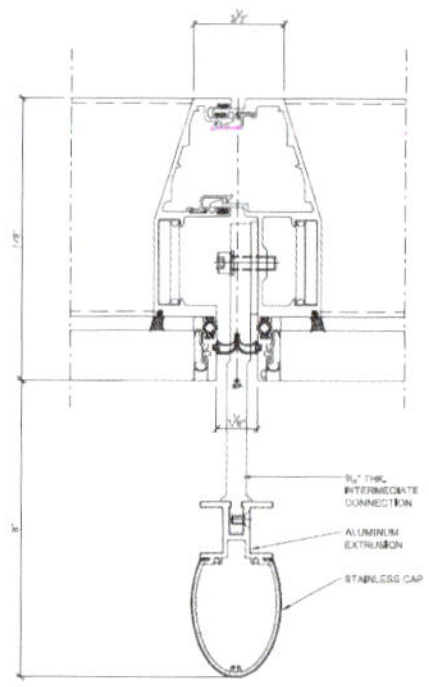

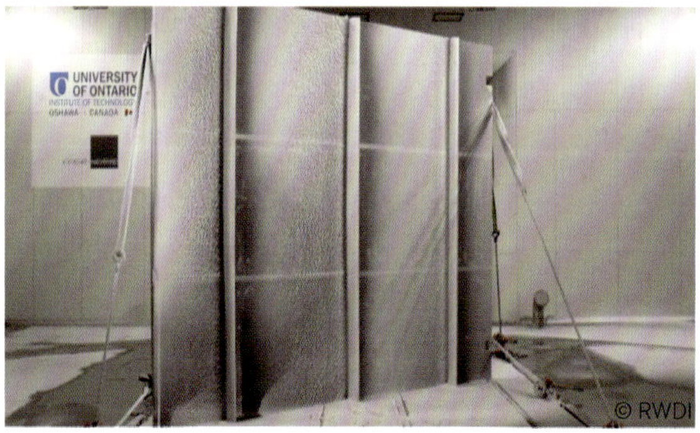

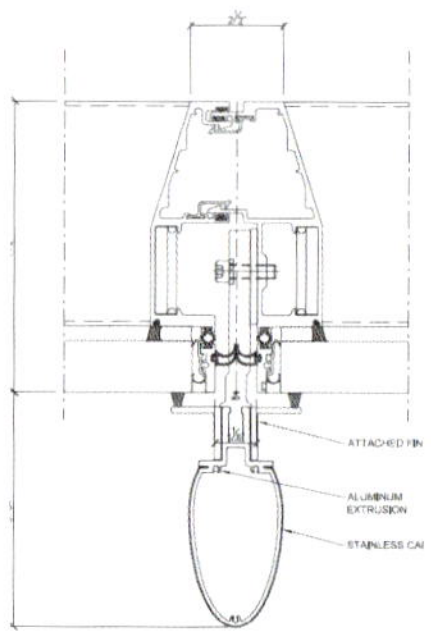

Snow and ice studies were performed to determine the best design for the super mullions. Snow build up in the winter was a major concern for this tall structure with regards to the protruding stainless-steel mullion fins and many shapes and sizes were explored to develop the best solution for minimum snow build up.

RWDI was engaged to do simulations in which the conditions of the site were simulated on a piece of the facade. This informed the design of the mullions, changing them from the original elongated oval to the ultimate design which was a rotated oval that was better able to shed ice and snow.

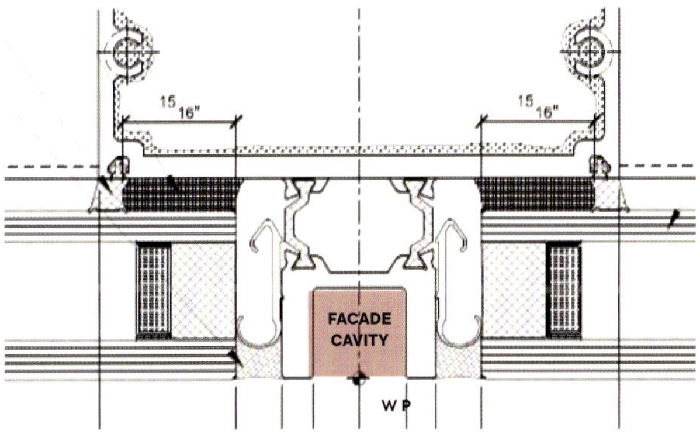

VERTICAL MULLION AT SPANDREL

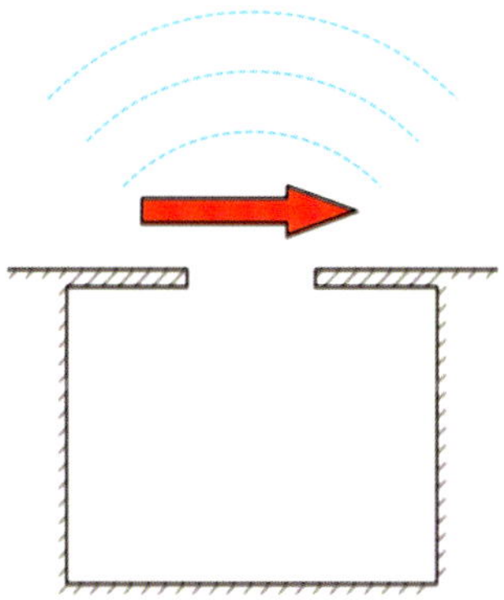

CAVITY RESONANCE DUE TO GRAZING FLOW

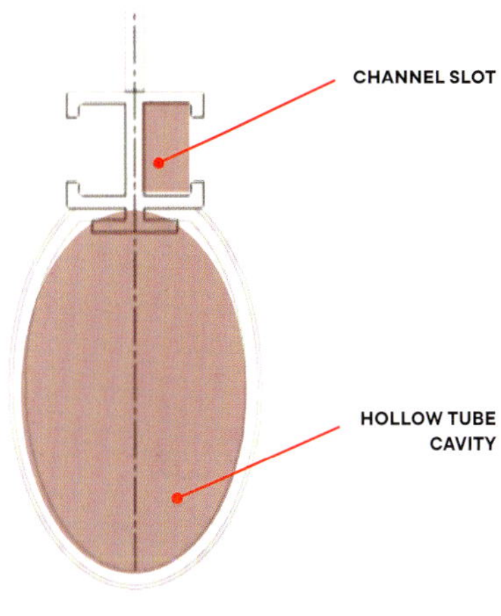

POTENTIAL CAVITIES IN SUPER MULLION

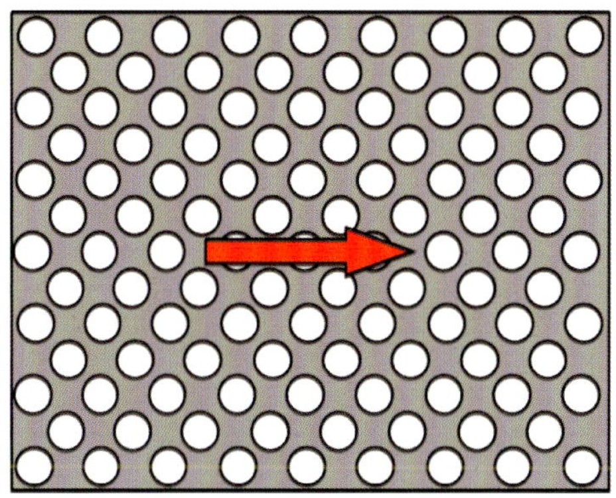

PERFORATED PLATE

RESEARCH + DEVELOPMENT

RWDI, CONSULTING ENGINEER

During the design process there was a concern that the east facade of the building would cast unwanted reflections and daylighting onto the adjacent building. Studies determined the extent of the extra reflections depending on the material chosen.

A zinc facade was chosen because of its lesser reflectivity and it is also a durable facade material, which has a natural finish that slightly weathers over time.

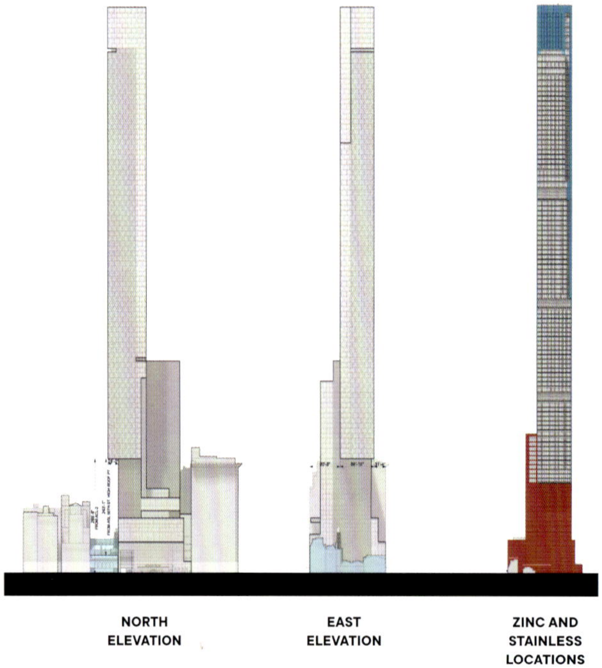

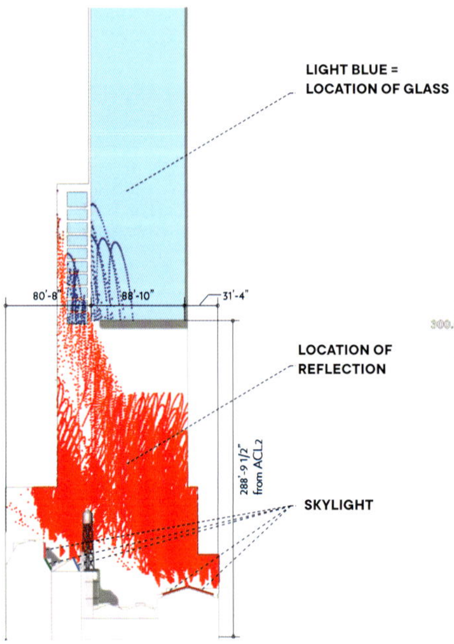

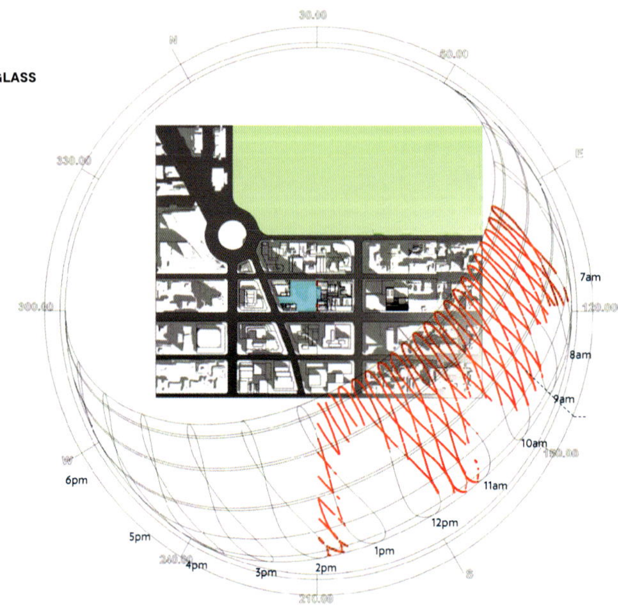

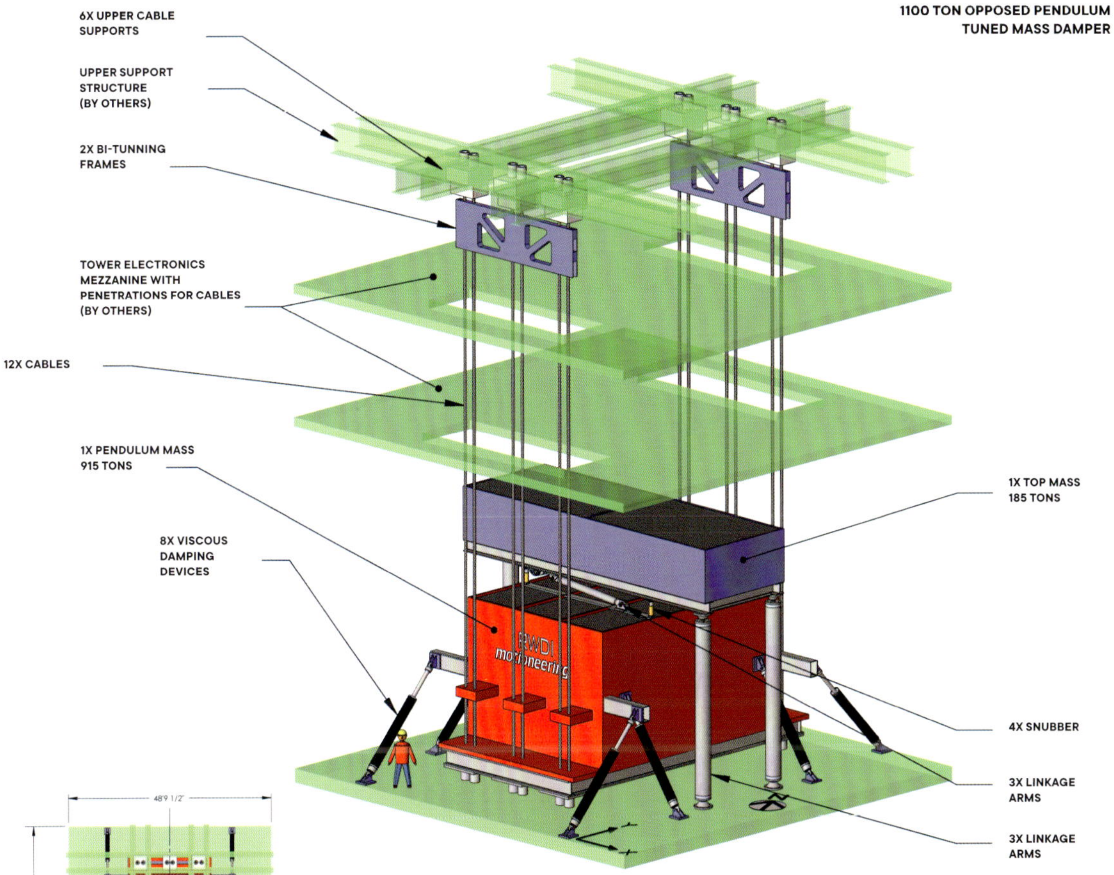

© RWDI

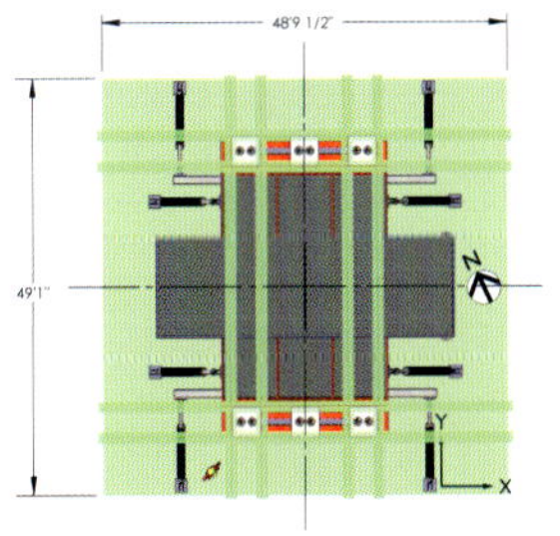

PLAN VIEW

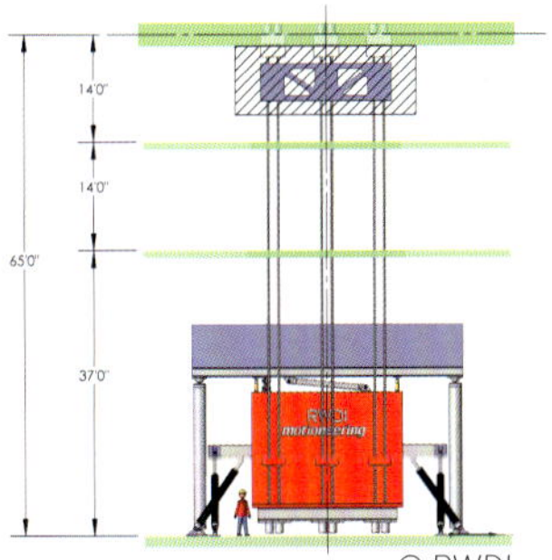

© RWDI

ELEVATION VIEW LOOKING NORTH

The building requires a tuned mass damper. Studies were done to find the ideal configuration and the damper was ultimately placed in the center of the building. A Tuned Mass Damper [TMD] with a mass of approximately 1,100 tons was recommended to improve the acceleration performance of the building and was incorporated into the tower design at the 94th floor.

To accommodate equipment, two mezzanines with approximately 37 feet and 51 feet were needed above the TMD chamber floor. Slots within the mezzanine floors enable the TMD support cables that penetrate the floor to benefit from the full 65-foot height.

The TMD is an "opposed-pendulum" type, which enables a TMD to be tuned to a long period building without requiring impractical cable lengths and room heights. To minimize material costs, it is estimated that there is adequate volume available to employ 600 tons of concrete, while the remainder will be steel.

At 291 feet above the adjacent Art Students League, the tower protrudes eastward with an 88-foot, 10-inch by 28-foot cantilever. The added space improves the residential program's unit layouts, views, and structural depths.

The cantilever takes on the horizontal expression of the extruded southern and western wings with each mechanical floor in the cantilevered zone set back to allow for rhythmic separation of each tranche and to fully express the cantilever of the floors. The corresponding residential floors within the cantilever directly above and below these expressed mechanical zones walk the columns inward one foot, allowing for a visual distinction and a building silhouette expressive of the division into distinct residential unit layouts and an appropriate modulation of scale.

This language is also adopted atop the western wing extrusion for consistency and balance. The top of the cantilever coincides with the Level 92 EMR floor, reaching a height of 1,413-foot, 2 inches and houses an opportunity for future development of an expansive penthouse roof terrace.

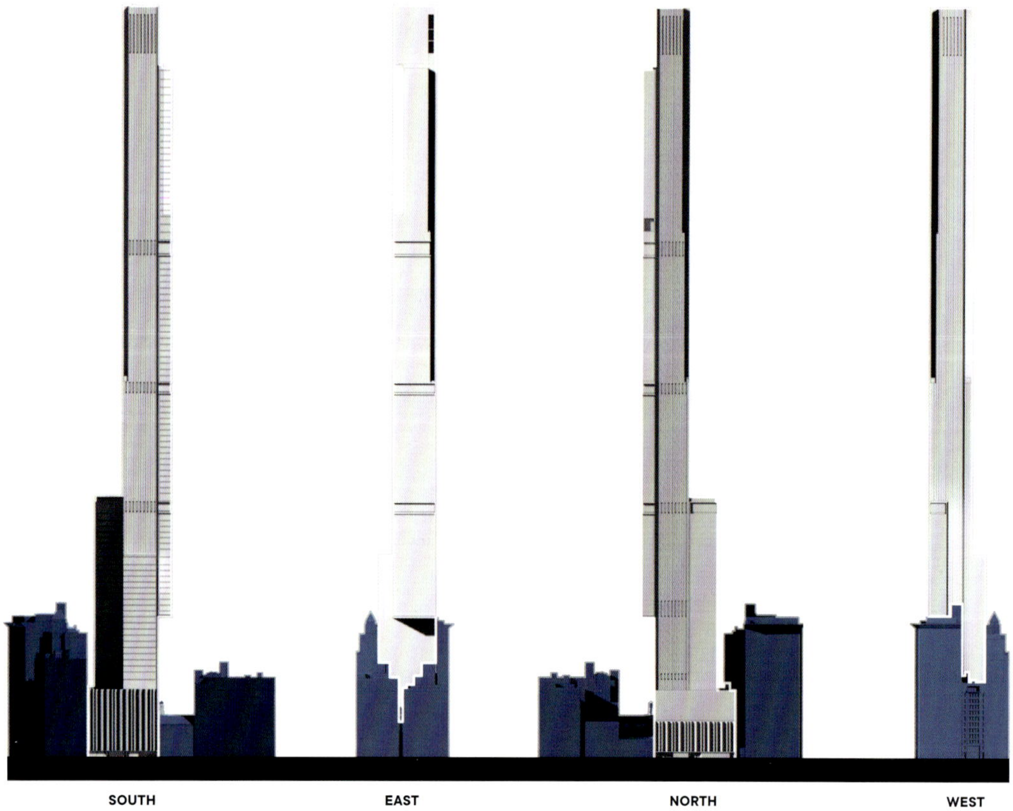

© Paul Clemence

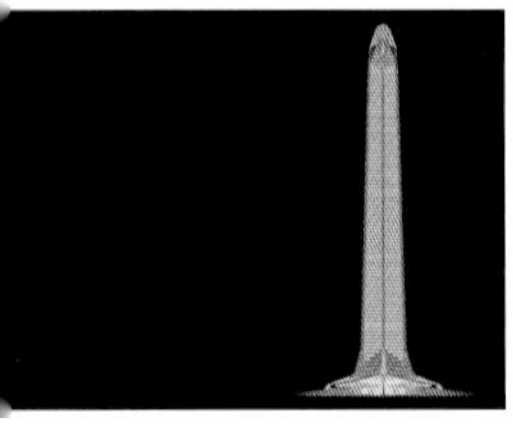

AKHMAT TOWER

GROZNY, CHECHEN REPUBLIC, 2014

435M

Akhmat Tower is a 435-meter supertall building that is currently under construction in Grozny in the Chechen Republic, in the North Caucasus region of Russia. The design of the tower was a collaborative process by a multi-disciplinary architectural and engineering team, based primarily in the United States and Russia.

Named after the first President of Chechnya, Akhmat Haji Kadyrov, the crystalline-shaped tower is both an aesthetic statement and a performative architectural solution that will be a new landmark for the region.

The design team worked closely with the client through a series of workshops. During the early concept design phase, three independent massings with a tapering pyramidal tower form with a complex geometry of the tower base and tower crown, as its primary features were proposed.

The selected scheme is a simple, pyramidal form with a crystalline geometric base, and sculpted top which contain special program spaces. The geometry in plan, the texture, and the overall shape have strong local cultural references.

- CONTEXT
- SITE
- PROGRAM
- PODIUM
- CROWN
- PERFORMANCE
- RESEARCH + DEVELOPMENT
- STRUCTURE

CONTEXT

The tower is influenced by traditional Nakh watchtowers, the most recognizable symbol of historical Chechen architecture.

The towers were typically constructed on a hill or mountain top and were also used as beacons for communication from one village to another. Nakh watchtowers are a prime example of the advanced building techniques found in medieval Chechnya, featuring a square plan with the pinnacle either flat or a slightly pyramidal shape with a capstone.

The design vision shares a strong geometric relationship with this architectural proportion, in the use of a four-sided shape, and pyramidal monumental top. The use of the square plan, and the symbolism of the geometry formed by two intersecting squares, is an important historical reference to Chechen architecture, which used square plans in most of the historical buildings.

The shape formed by two intersecting squares, one rotated at 45 degrees to the other, is also seen in traditional Islamic patterns. The idea of the square, diamond, or rotated square geometry is repeated throughout different elements of the tower and in the exterior wall panels.

The tower base design incorporates flared geometry and earth berms, both references to the traditional Nakh towers. The division of the tower form into a distinctive upper, middle, and lower zone also parallels the watchtower design, which consist of the same three parts. During the design, the prominence and size of the pinnacle was carefully considered to reinforce the relationship to the traditional tower. The crystalline shape of the pinnacle has a specific indented center to its geometry whose location relates to the location of the window opening that is typically present in Nakh watchtowers.

MODEL, 2014

VAINAKH TOWER ARCHITECTURE (NAKH WATCHTOWERS)

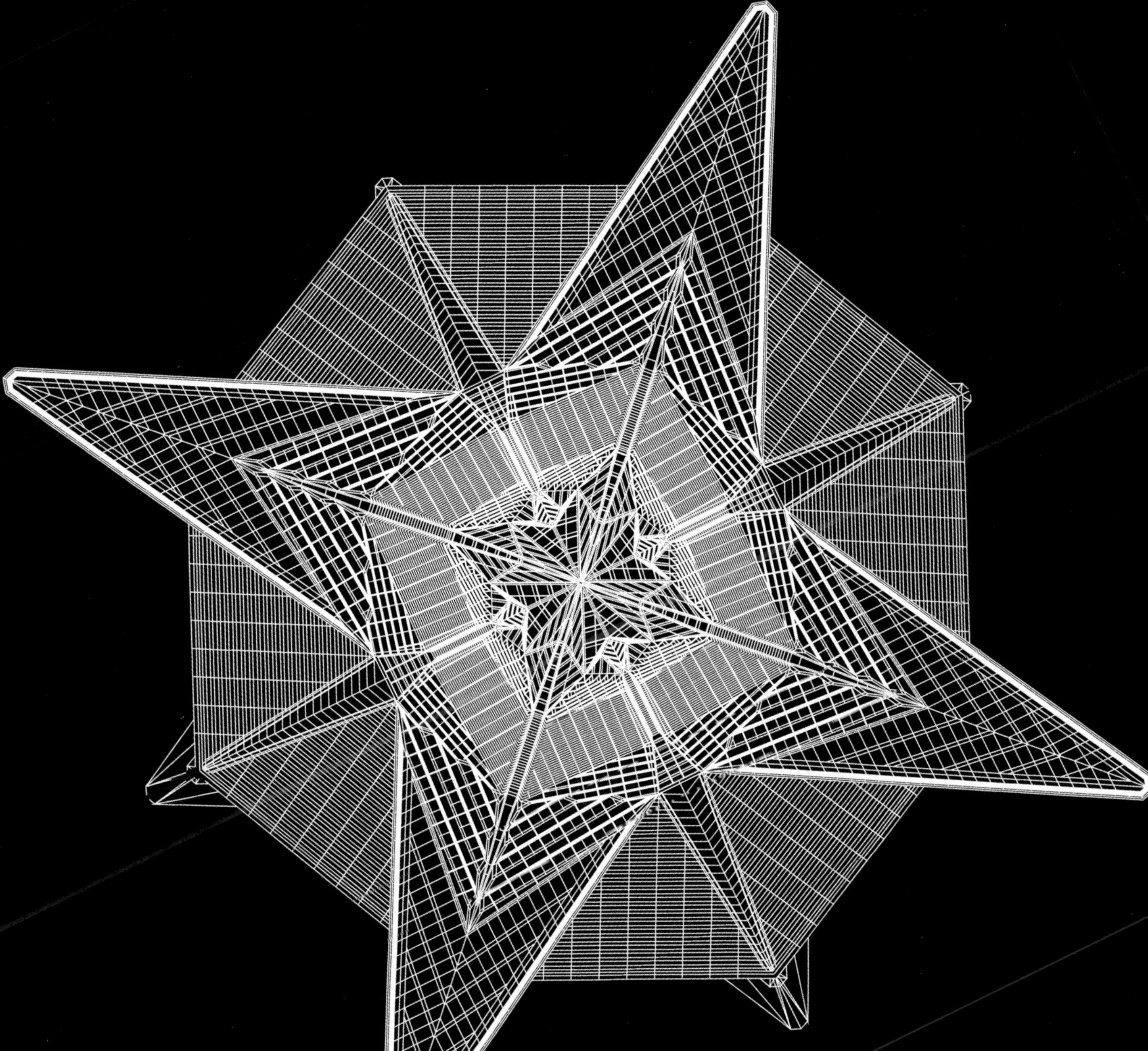

SITE

Similar to the setting of Nakh watchtowers, Akhmat Tower's landscape design situates the building and its multi-level lobbies on a hill. Drop-off zones for different uses of the tower are reached through roads at various levels, accessing the different sides of the tower with elegant earth berms that negotiate the elevational differences.

The free-flowing berms contrast with the sharp geometry of the tower's design in the same way the historical towers were juxtaposed against the green hills of the North Caucasus region. Native plantings and trees are used throughout the design. Water features welcome visitors in the drop-off areas of the tower, recalling the rivers found in the region.

The tower features three separate drop-off zones: The hotel lobby is located on Level 3 and is accessed from the east. The observatory visitors, including any tour buses and large vehicles, enter through a separate road on the north and are dropped off in front of a retail area that leads directly to the observation area. The small office drop-off is located on Level 1, to the south. The residential office is the most discreet and is located to the west.

The texture and tilt of the exterior wall is continuous from the tower's pinnacle to the canopies at Level 2. The wall flares dramatically at the base, forming the eight-story atria that frame each lobby of the building. The atria create a double-skinned wall—a monumental volumetric space that can be viewed from the lobbies below and from the lower office floors.

The atrium base extends out to form glass wings that act as sky-lit spaces, which frame the entries to the lobbies. Triangular, shingled canopies extend dramatically over each drop-off.

SITE PLAN

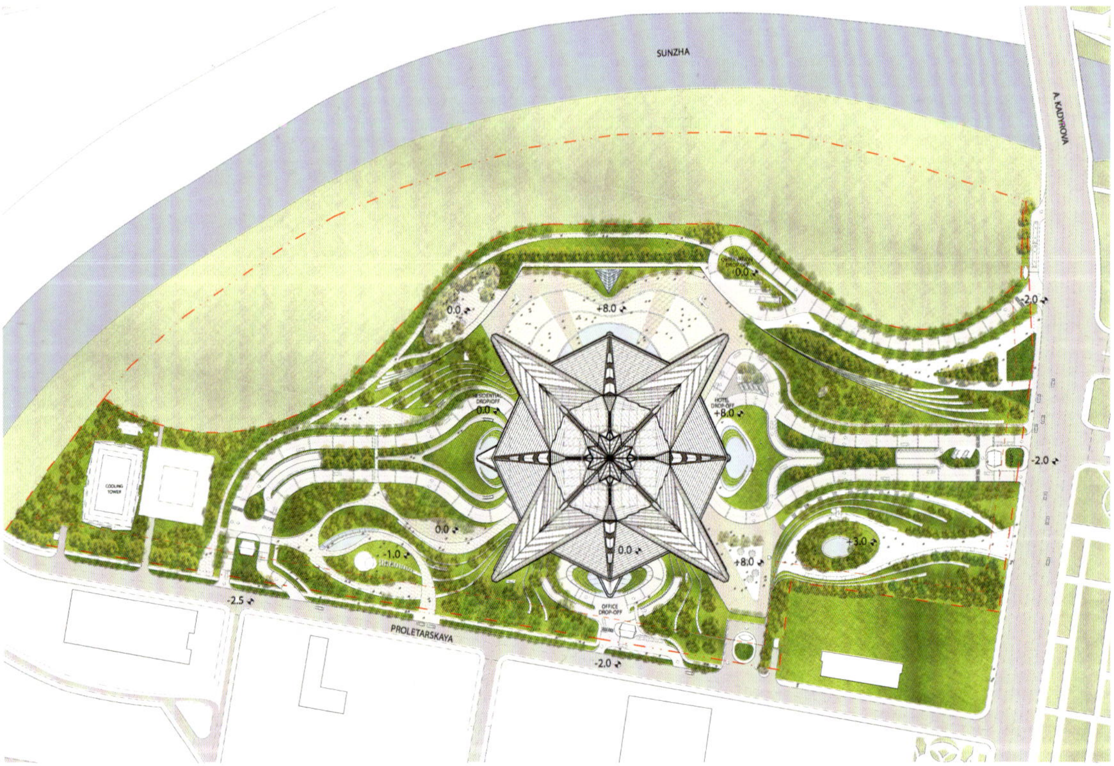

PROGRAM

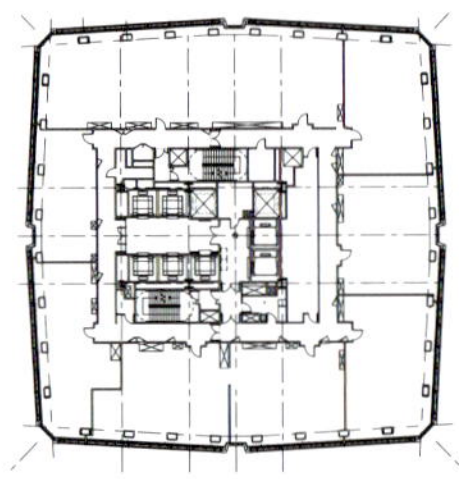

RESIDENTIAL

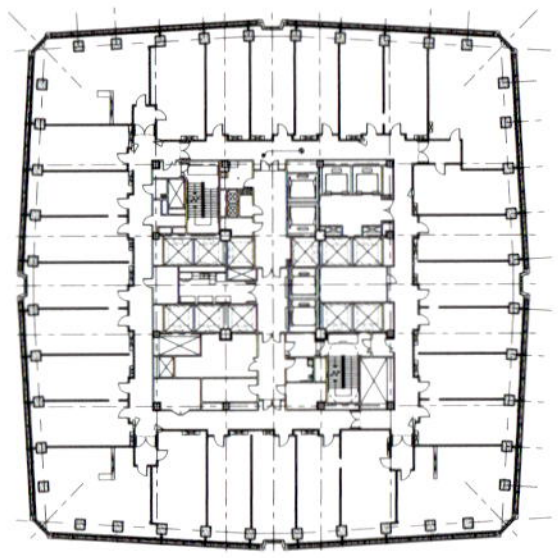

HOTEL

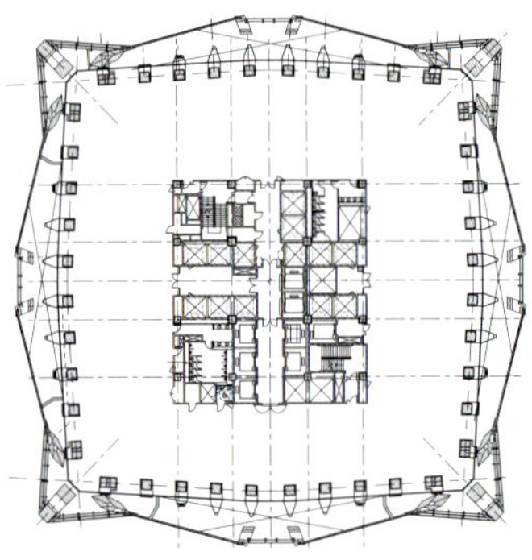

OFFICE

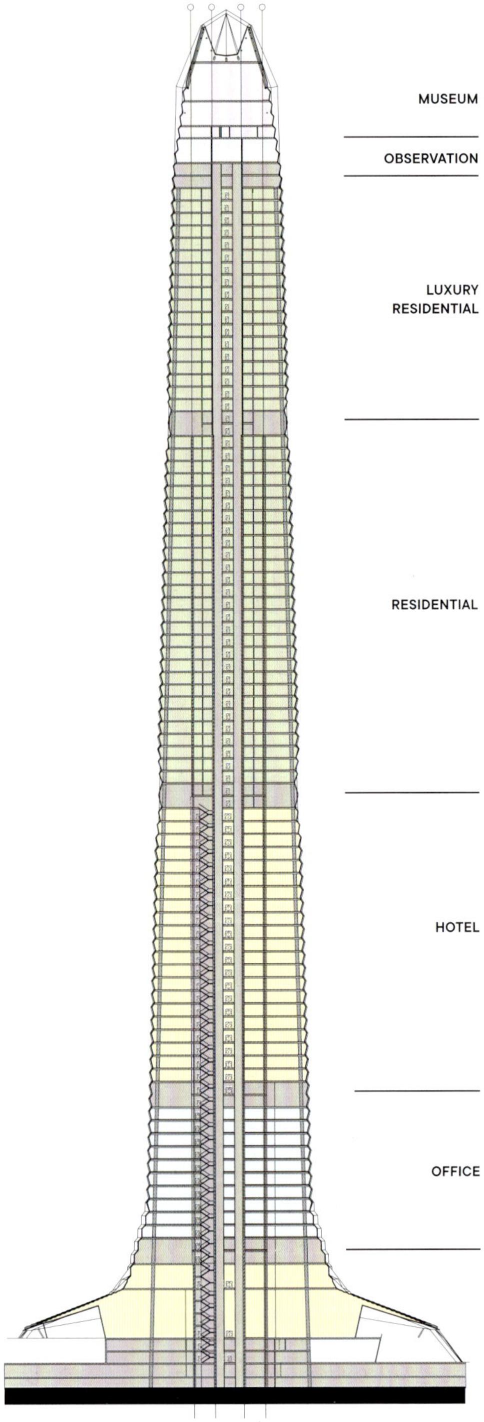

PODIUM

The tower podium's atrium exterior wall system features operable metal louvers that are linked to the smoke evacuation system, using the tapering shape of the atrium to help draw air up and out. Exaggerated column enclosures allow passive air to circulate by way of a series of integrated grilles and ducts that move the air though natural convection.

The shape of the base informs the unique spatial opportunities of the interior design of the office, apartment, and hotel lobbies and is a primary influencer of the design. The office and apartment drop-off elevations are situated below the hotel lobby on Level 1, allowing for a continuous space for the hotel program above with an almost totally circular flow for occupants around the core at Level 3.

Both upper and lower lobbies take advantage of the soaring, naturally lit, sculptural spaces created by the base form outside of the tower columns. The structure creates a division for the office and apartments' inner lobbies, respectively, forming more intimate spaces. The form also creates a virtually column-free space for a 700 sm ballroom that has column-free and sunlit pre-function area.

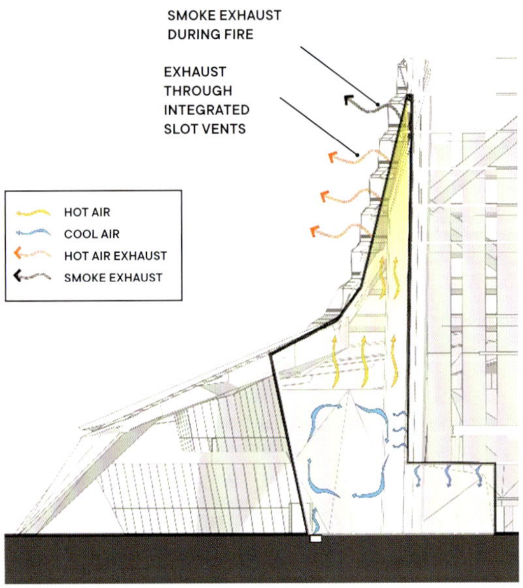

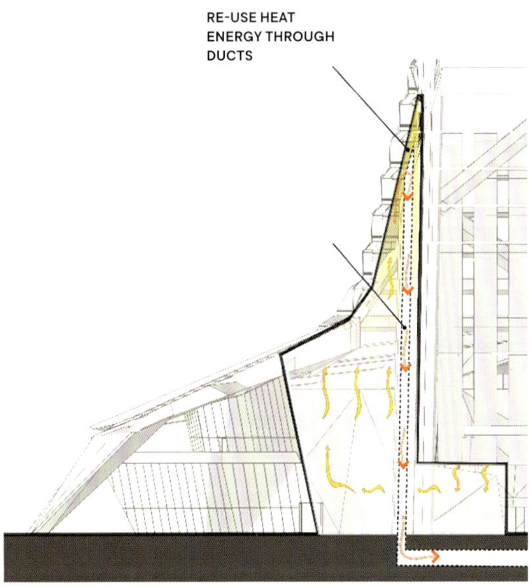

CROWN

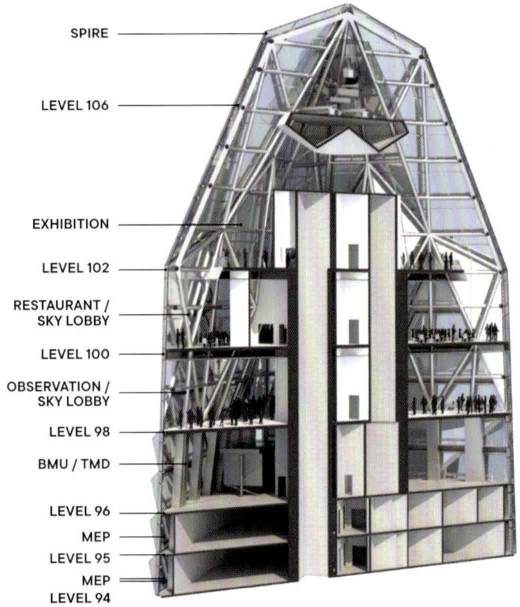

SPIRE
LEVEL 106
EXHIBITION
LEVEL 102
RESTAURANT / SKY LOBBY
LEVEL 100
OBSERVATION / SKY LOBBY
LEVEL 98
BMU / TMD
LEVEL 96
MEP
LEVEL 95
MEP
LEVEL 94

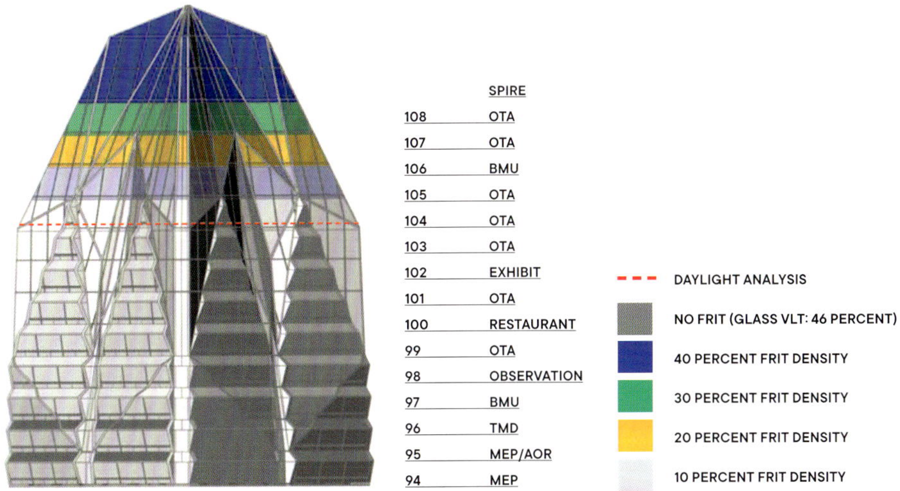

FRIT DENSITY

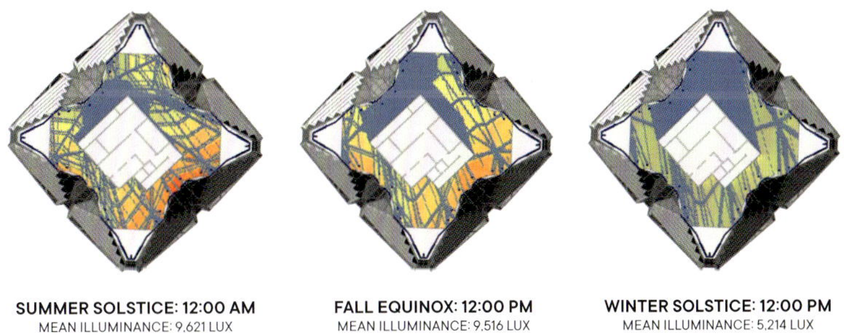

AKHMAT TOWER CROWN DAYLIGHT ANALYSIS

The crystalline geometry of the tower pinnacle is a special feature in the exterior wall design. The many facets catch the light as it hits the building at different angles. The volumetric spaces inside the pinnacle include the two-story tuned mass damper, which was designed as part of the public observation area, as well as a multi-story volume at the top that forms the museum and restaurant.

The steel tube structure is minimally clad, in order to expose the complex geometry; glass with a frit pattern are used to control glare. Studies were done to determine the appropriate amount of frit that would be required for optimal comfort. The ideal density used the strongest frit at the top of the space, where views were not as important, and got increasingly less dense as it reached the bottom.

PERFORMANCE

The overall form of the building was influenced by wind performance studies, and enhanced for the user experience and the aesthetic of the tower. A square-shaped plan with a flat top and sharp, square corners is not the ideal wind performance profile for a supertall tower, therefore design refinements were done, with improved performance and comfort in mind.

Early in the design phase, it was determined that the overall tapering pyramidal shape was intrinsic to the contextual design concept and building function.

An initial force-balance test of early conceptual designs, which included a version with a flat top with square corners, yielded a wind-load response that was estimated to be up to 15 percent greater than the final design, which featured the 2 meter chamfered corners and a 45 meter-tall, sculpted, crystalline top. The design process for the pinnacle was therefore influenced by the wind-tunnel results and the aesthetic desire for a more crystalline form, which worked together in influencing the final design.

The shaping of the bottom of the building also showed a measurable benefit in pedestrian wind comfort versus an extruded building base, as it was found that pedestrian wind comfort in the spring, summer, and fall would generally be in an acceptable range without mitigation. Measures to improve wind comfort in the winter—such as with strategic landscape design—were only necessary on a few areas around the building.

Stone wall patterns of traditional architecture of Chechnya are reinterpreted in the design, represented with a three-dimensional glass, aluminum, and stainless-steel wall. The unitized curtain wall protrudes at each floor and slopes back toward the main volume.

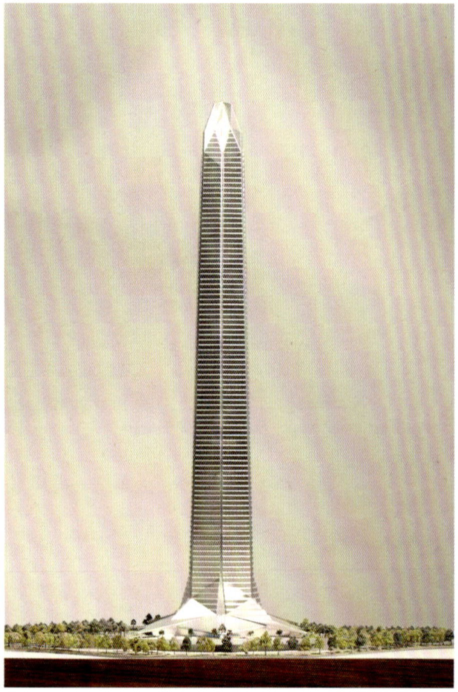

MODELS

VENTILATED MULLION DE TAIL

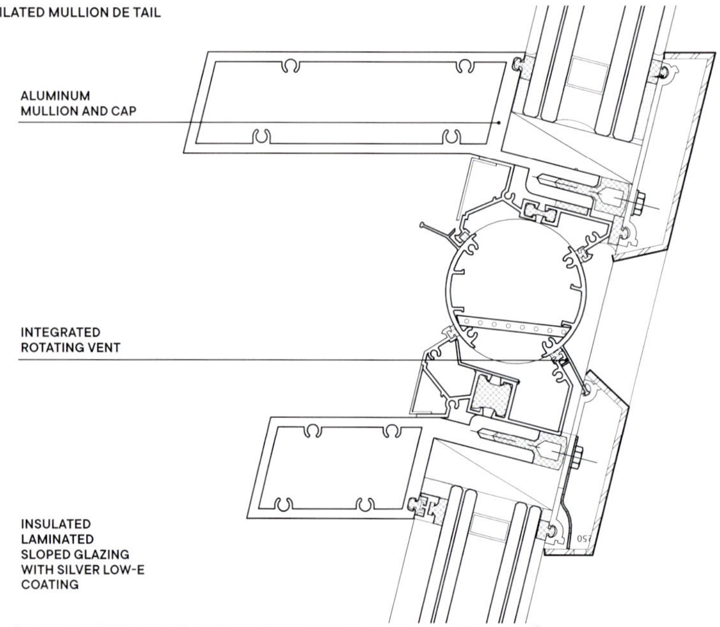

The slope of the wall creates a horizontal sunshade that reduces glare and solar heat gain to the overall facade. The shingled wall has a curved corner that forms a stainless-steel accent piece that catches the sunlight.

Operable mullions are fully integrated into the wall design—hidden within the profile of the facade mullions within each curtain wall unit—enabling the facade to have a strong consistency. Purposefully designed picture windows at the corners offer enhanced views while also helping wind performance.

The typical wall has a 14-degree downward tilt that was demonstrated by solar radiation analysis to have the most effect for reduced solar gain. The incorporation of the 80-millimeter-tall rotating ventilated mullions provide for natural ventilation for all the residential, hotel, and office uses. The operable mullion provides controlled natural ventilation by utilizing a button to open and close the device. This encourages natural ventilation to be used during more times of the year and alleviates some of the perceived safety concerns associated with open windows at such heights.

FACADE PERFORMANCE ANALYSIS: ANNUAL THERMAL LOADS

BASELINE
WWR: 67 PERCENT
U-VALUE (W/M2K)/SHGC/VLT: 1.1/0.4/0.4

NEW SCHEME (CURRENT)
WWR: 57 PERCENT
U-VALUE (W/M2K)/SHGC/VLT: 1.1/0.4/0.4

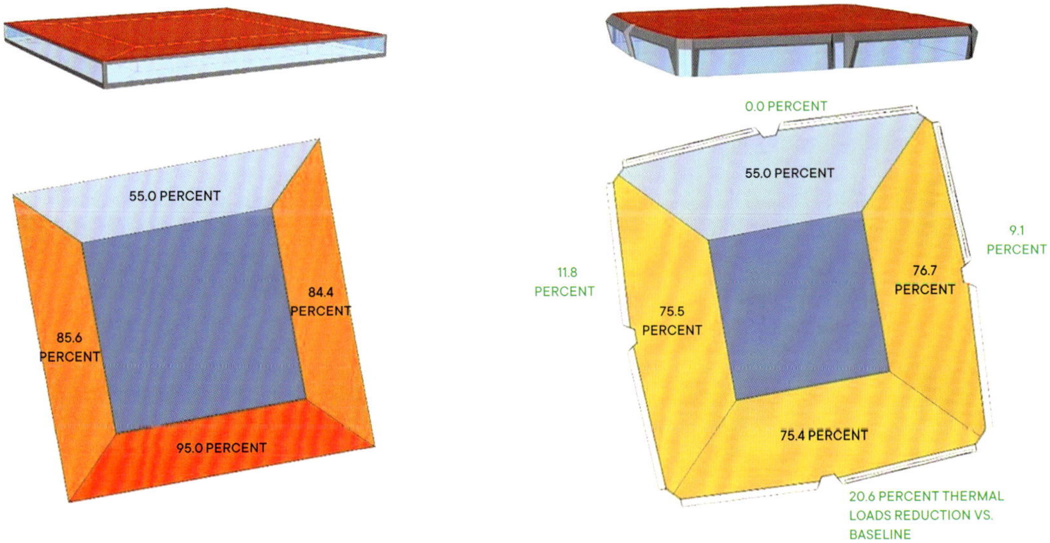

OVERALL ANNUAL THERMAL ENERGY: 320.0 KWH

OVERALL ANNUAL THERMAL ENERGY: 282.0 KWH
(11.6 PERCENT REDUCTION)

ANALYSIS PERIOD: JAN 01 1:00 - DEC 31 24:00
IN BLACK: TOTAL THERMAL ENERGY FOR EACH ZONE IN KWH/YEAR (HEATING + COOLING LOADS)
IN GREEN: PERCENT THERMAL ENERGY REDUCTION COMPARED TO THE BASELINE CASE

MODEL ASSUMPTIONS:

APARTMENT OCCUPANCY SCHEDULE
INTERNAL LOADS (PEOPLE, LIGHTING, EQUIPMENT)
EXTERNAL LOADS (SOLAR GAINS, INFILTRATION, HEAT CONDUCTION THROUGH BUILDING ENVELOPE)

GLASS U-VALUE (W/M2K)/SHGC/VLT: 1.1/0.4/0.4
METAL PANEL U-VALUE (W/M2K):0.15
ROOF: ADIABATIC BOUNDARY CONDITION
FLOOR: ADIABATIC BOUNDARY CONDITION

RESEARCH + DEVELOPMENT

THORNTON TOMASETTI + RWDI

One of the biggest challenges of achieving this design was to properly integrate the architectural and structural geometries. The two teams worked closely together to develop framing that was seamless and became part of the geometry of the large skylit areas of the podium wings and canopy.

Two tuned-mass dampers (TMDs) are required to ensure occupant comfort, rather than for structural strength. The steel structure is designed to withstand more movement than a concrete structure, which is one of the reasons it performs so well in an earthquake. The damping is required so upper floors are comfortable for occupants when the building shifts during a frequent seismic event.

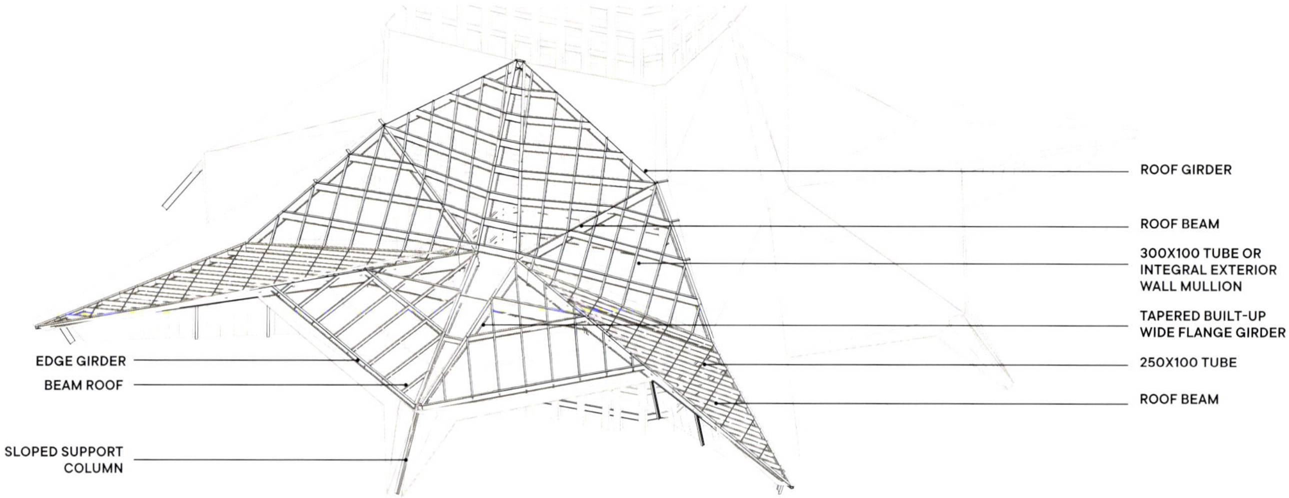

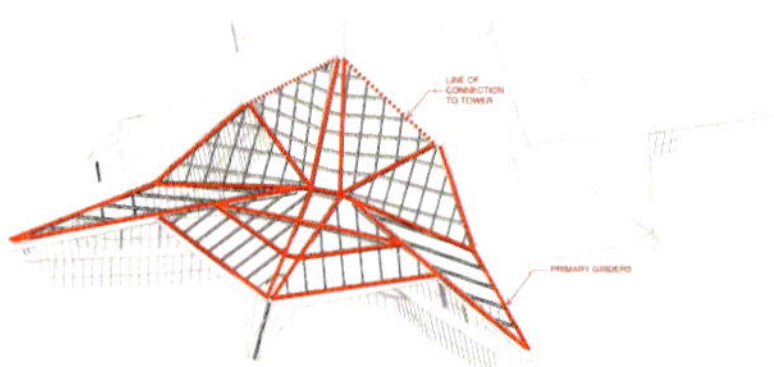

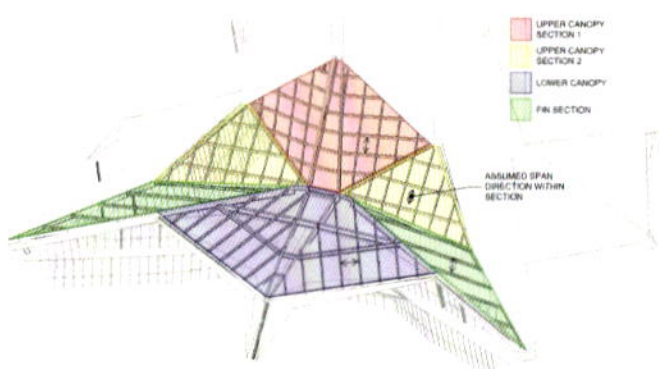

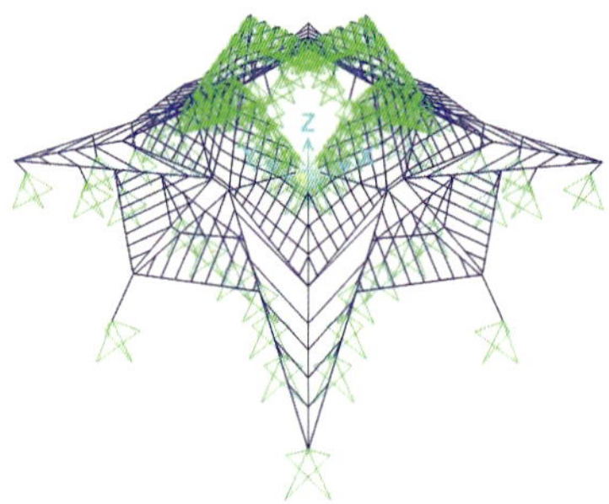

To achieve the TMD in plan, the cables extend up through Level 98, into the observation deck. Glass handrails are built around the cables and a glass floor allows visitors to see the TMDs, creating an architectural feature and an educational exhibit on how dampers are used in supertall buildings.

The TMD also shares space with the building's maintenance units at Level 96. The 1400-ton system mass required was split evenly between two 700-ton opposed pendulum TMDs to the north and south of the tower's core. To achieve the required supplemental damping target of 5 percent, an approximate 2 m of swing distance is required in either direction. The supporting cables of the TMD's main pendulum extend through the observation sky lobby space at Level 98 and are anchored at the floor framing of Level 99. This cable extension allows for the required 12 m swing height that corresponds to the required 2 m swing distance in either direction.

Viscous damping devices (VDDs) are utilized to dissipate the inertial energy generated by the opposed pendulum system and are attached to the tower structure on Levels 96 and 98.

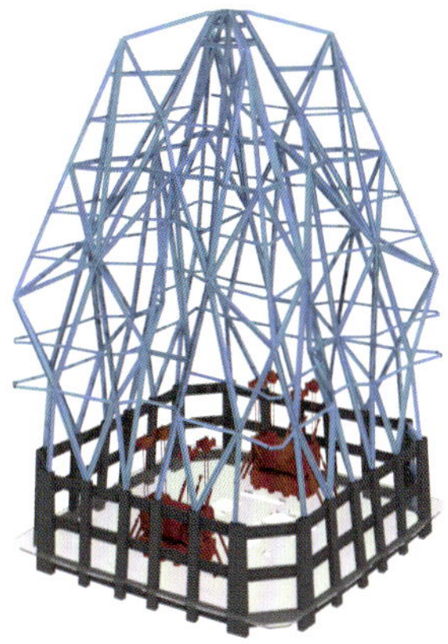

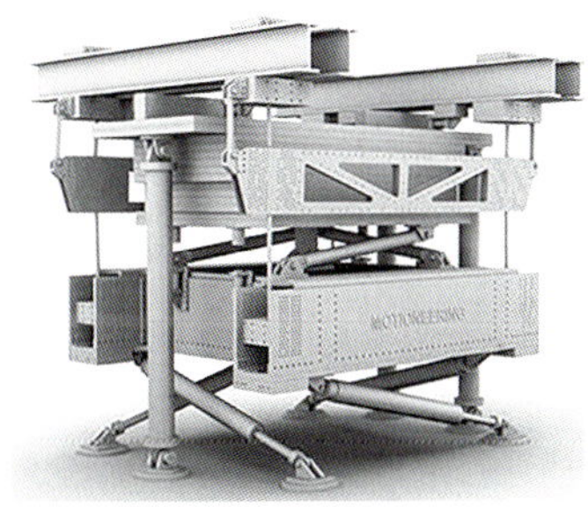

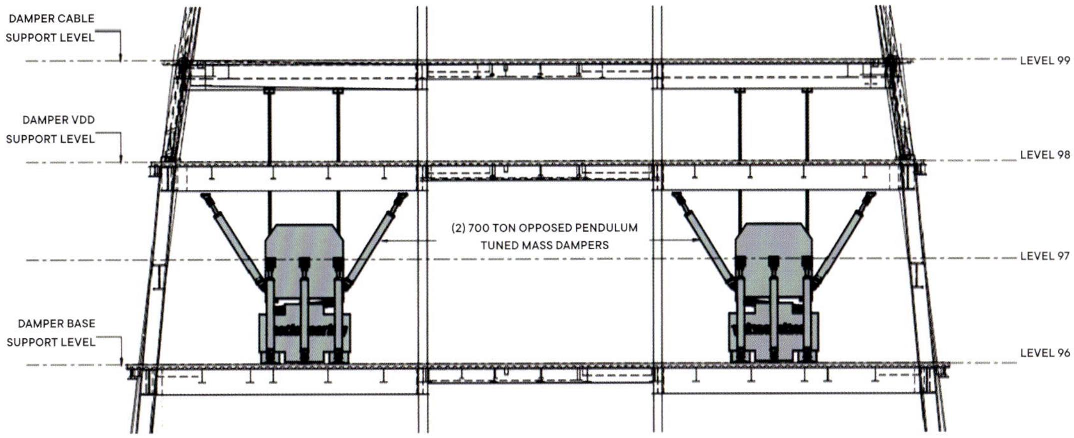

STRUCTURE

THORNTON TOMASETTI, STRUCTURAL ENGINEER

The seismicity of Grozny is one of the highest in the world, exceeding San Francisco by 50 percent. A building that behaves well in a highly seismic area needs to be sufficiently ductile and should have a uniformity to the structural design to minimize any areas where loads could be concentrated during an earthquake event.

Therefore, a customized, evolved version of the steel "perimeter tube" system was developed. The system requires a closely spaced set of columns at the perimeter of the building. The perimeter columns and coupling beams create the world's tallest "special moment frame" seismic resisting system once realized. The perimeter columns, spaced at 4.5 m on center, are sufficiently small as to minimize their impact on the usable interior spaces—the columns are approximately 1 m in size that is an advantage over a Mega Column system where they are typically as much as 2 m.

The column layout is designed so that there is no corner column, allowing the corners to be chamfered and include windows that offer views out diagonally. The use of a special moment frame structure meant that the technical floors could be designed without large outrigger trusses, making them faster and simpler to construct, and easing the layout in terms of fitting the mechanical equipment on those floors.

Because of the high seismicity and a tube system that offers the most efficient design, certain architectural constrains occur. For example, columns cannot be eliminated to open large spans in the lobbies. However, because the tower base flares beyond the main super structure, this was a very manageable part of the design and the lobbies are still able to be virtually free of columns. When one enters the core area of the building, they pass through the columns at 4.5 m on center, which act as a gateway into the interior core.

The 58 m tall entrance structure is designed as a flowing structural steel frame, integral with the tower structure, to provide a dramatic point of entry into the building. Tapered steel plate girders and structural steel shapes are customized to fit within the architectural massing to provide a structure that is both efficient and open to allow for the architecturally desired open lobby expression.

Custom-built structural steel columns provide support along the perimeter of the podium facade and are coordinated closely with architectural requirements. Steel columns transfer at their base to not interfere with the structural grid requirements of the parking levels below. The entrance structure ties into the main tower structural system to avoid the requirement of architecturally problematic seismic expansion joints between the tower and exterior wall.

Therefore, the lateral loads applied to the basement structure are anchored by the tower's main perimeter special moment frame, which finally transfers the signature entrance structural loads to the ground at the tower raft. The structural system is divided into four main sections separated by primary girders. These primary girders follow the ridges of the architectural massing. Each of these four main sections operates as a one-way system.

In the upper sections, vertical members were added to help control deflections of the longer spans. In the upper and lower sections, the main "beam" members are built-up tubes while in the fin section the main "beam" members are built-up wide flanges. The canopy is essentially symmetrical about both axes of the tower. The canopy is connected to the tower at Levels 10–14 in addition to the base of the canopy.

The south and west sides of the canopy feature double-height curtain walls that begin from Level 1 and span up to the canopy while the north and east sides have curtain walls which span from Level 3 to the canopy.

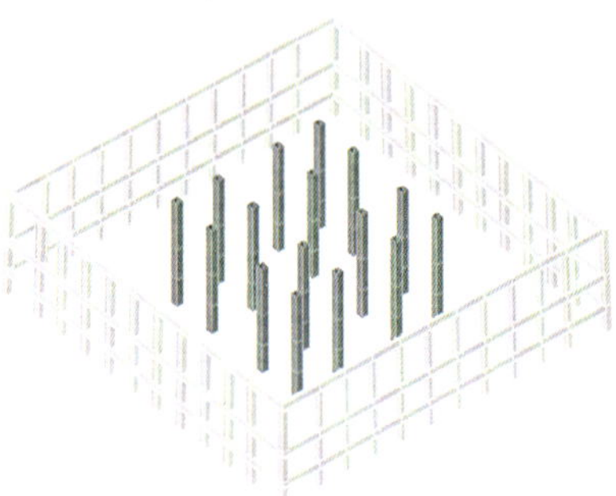

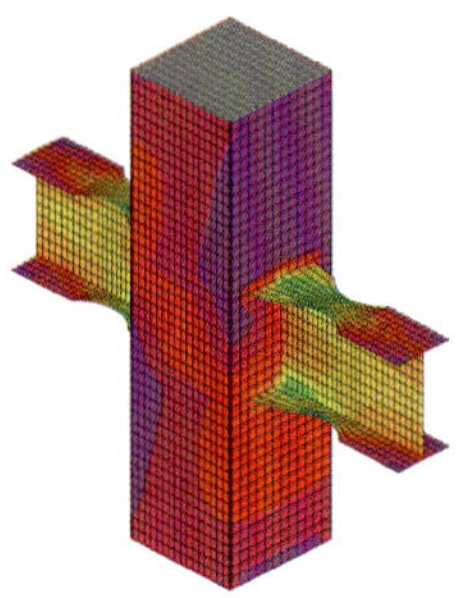

SPECIAL CONCENTRIC
BRACED FRAME
SPECIAL CONCENTRIC
BRACED FRAME
TOWER BASE

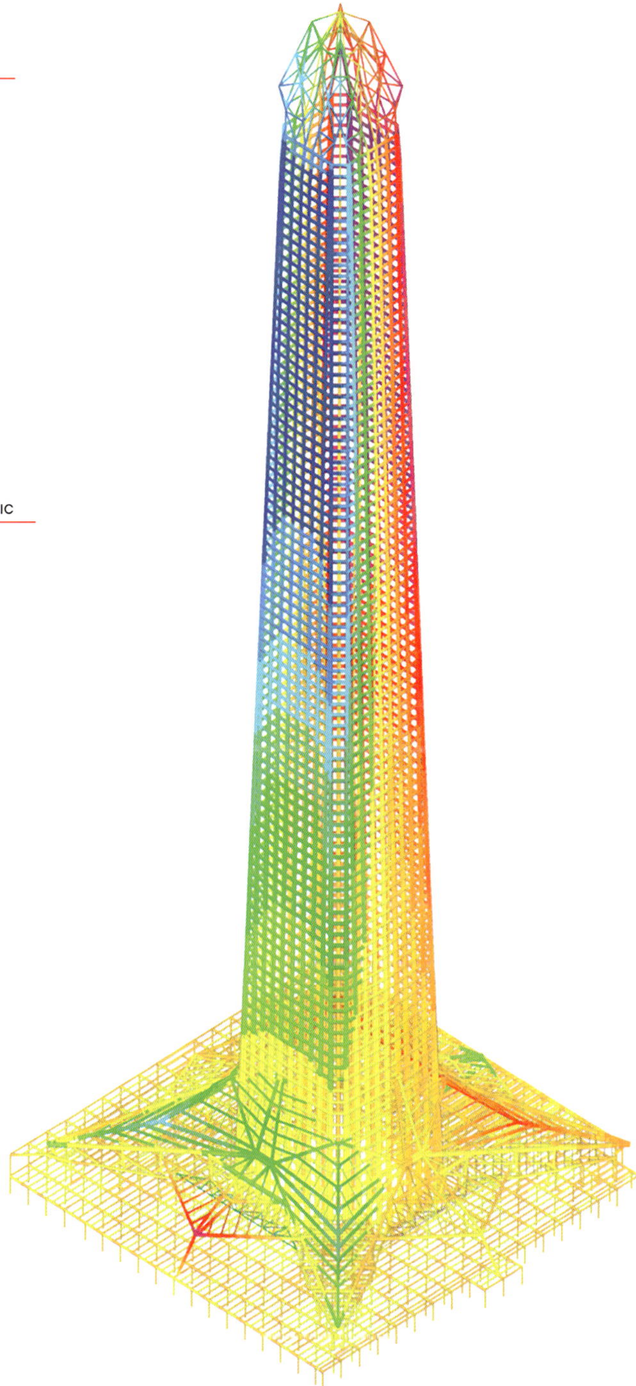

HEXI YUZUI TOWER (RUNMAO TOWER)

NANJING, CHINA, 2017

500M

Runmao Tower, locally known as South HeXi Yuzui Financial Tower, is a mixed-use, 500-meter building at the heart of Nanjing's newest central business district. The tower's design is inspired by the Yangtze River and the colorful, smooth stones found along its banks.

Like the river, the tower's facade reflects light, casting textures and dimensions.

Once completed, Runmao Tower will anchor the Central Business District in Nanjing with networks to access the riverfront, public transit, and many new cultural, natural, and technological opportunities. The district invites the user to experience the district either as a live-work environment or as a visitor to one of the many public parks and art centers.

The architectural scheme is hexagonal in form, gradually curving the length of the elevation, creating a dynamic architectural effect. The overall shape of the floors gradually decreases toward the top. This tapering geometry helps mitigate wind vortices by reducing wind loads and seismic loads. The form also helps optimize views and enhances both the structure and the program.

In addition to the main tower, the master plan includes 100-meter, 155-meter, 220-meter and 350-meter office towers and an 86-meter-tall residential tower.

+ CONTEXT
+ SITE
+ PROGRAM
+ PODIUM
+ CROWN
+ EXPERIENCE
+ PERFORMANCE
+ STRUCTURE

CONTEXT

The tower site is located at the west end of the new Hexi New Business District, facing the broad Yangtze River to the west and Jinling, the ancient capital of six dynasties, to the east. The main tower connects with the end of the canal axis.

Drop-off areas for the office and executive office programs are located on the north and south sides of the tower. The tower is connected with the metro station and Yuzui Park at the west sunken garden, open to the tower.

It was important for the tower to be directly connected to the rest of Nanjing because supertall towers draw business, tourism, and retail in both the national and international tourist markets. It was also important for the design to feel contextual to the new riverside district, increasing its individual identity, separate from Nanjing.

Design inspiration was taken from the dynamic qualities of the Yangtze River and rain flower stones, also known as Yuhua stones, found only in Nanjing.

The tower, and new district, will become a point of local pride, creating an effective focal point to the district and adding value to the surrounding sites.

YUHUA STONE

SITE

The master plan features a variety of community outdoor spaces ranging from a large public park, to smaller district parks, boulevards, and linear greenways. The strategic location of the project in this context, and the way it is developed, will have an impact on the success of the district.

Connectivity and the flow of people are key aspects that were addressed, as they are crucial for the integration of the project to the fabric of the city. The design uses an elevated spine as the main urban axis for a quick and safe pedestrian path. District users can safely navigate from the access at the canal system to the main park.

The public realm design promotes pedestrian at-grade walk-ability and inter-parcel connection by providing landscaped and accessible sidewalks and alternative pedestrian routes. It includes a circuit-like system below grade, which interconnects the district parcels among themselves, as well as with adjacent parcels, the subway, and the main park. This system also connects to a series of sunken gardens and atria that line the lower level to grade and Level 2.

Multiple green spaces also enhance the tower site. These spaces allow users to experience the tactile sensations of the landscaping elements that are shown to promote a sense of well-being, as well as improve the air quality and the local micro-climate. The tower is also positioned to take advantage of the winds, the sun, and the rain in Nanjing.

Through integrating rainwater harvesting on the sky gardens, the building is targeting on-site management of greater than 100 percent of rainfall. Rainwater will be collected using sponge city concepts such as sub-soil collection, permeable paving and recessed green space. Collected rainwater will be drained to tanks in the basement where it will be treated and stored for reuse. A 55 percent reduction in total indoor water use is predicted.

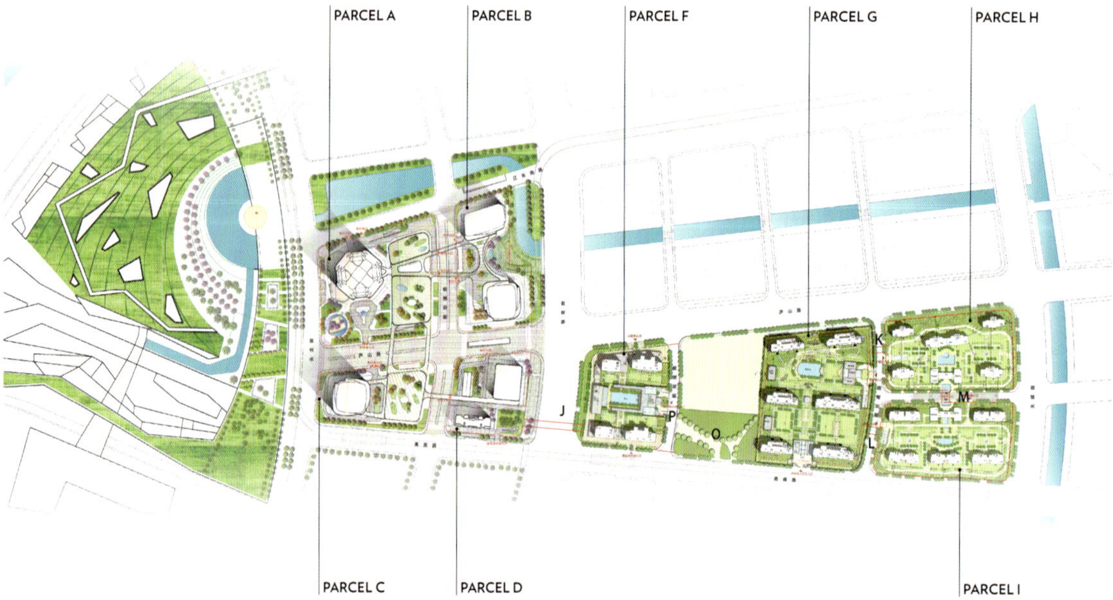

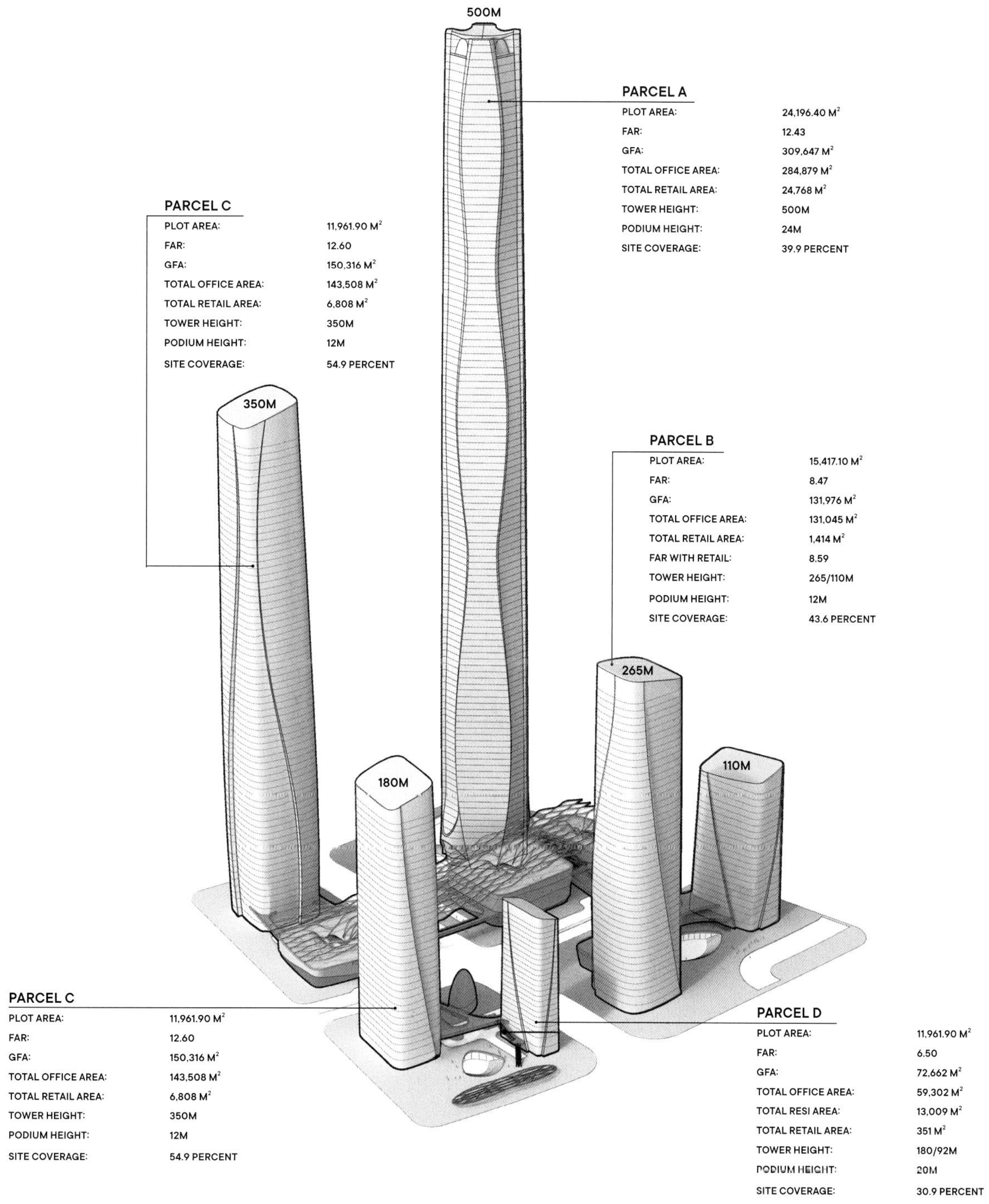
500M
PARCEL A
PLOT AREA: 24,196.40 M²
FAR: 12.43
GFA: 309,647 M²
TOTAL OFFICE AREA: 284,879 M²
TOTAL RETAIL AREA: 24,768 M²
TOWER HEIGHT: 500M
PODIUM HEIGHT: 24M
SITE COVERAGE: 39.9 PERCENT
PARCEL C
PLOT AREA: 11,961.90 M²
FAR: 12.60
GFA: 150,316 M²
TOTAL OFFICE AREA: 143,508 M²
TOTAL RETAIL AREA: 6,808 M²
TOWER HEIGHT: 350M
PODIUM HEIGHT: 12M
SITE COVERAGE: 54.9 PERCENT
350M
PARCEL B
PLOT AREA: 15,417.10 M²
FAR: 8.47
GFA: 131,976 M²
TOTAL OFFICE AREA: 131,045 M²
TOTAL RETAIL AREA: 1,414 M²
FAR WITH RETAIL: 8.59
TOWER HEIGHT: 265/110M
PODIUM HEIGHT: 12M
SITE COVERAGE: 43.6 PERCENT
265M
180M
110M
PARCEL C
PLOT AREA: 11,961.90 M²
FAR: 12.60
GFA: 150,316 M²
TOTAL OFFICE AREA: 143,508 M²
TOTAL RETAIL AREA: 6,808 M²
TOWER HEIGHT: 350M
PODIUM HEIGHT: 12M
SITE COVERAGE: 54.9 PERCENT
PARCEL D
PLOT AREA: 11,961.90 M²
FAR: 6.50
GFA: 72,662 M²
TOTAL OFFICE AREA: 59,302 M²
TOTAL RESI AREA: 13,009 M²
TOTAL RETAIL AREA: 351 M²
TOWER HEIGHT: 180/92M
PODIUM HEIGHT: 20M
SITE COVERAGE: 30.9 PERCENT

PROGRAM

The tower is tapered symmetrically to produce a rational structure that provides multiple, dynamic viewing surfaces, improves wind dynamics, and creates a distinctive landmark icon. Composed of seven typical office zones including one sky lobby, a special trading floor, and two executive office zones. The office program is capped by a unique observatory amenity with a special roof courtyard and viewing platform. Refuge floors are provided as needed for code requirements.

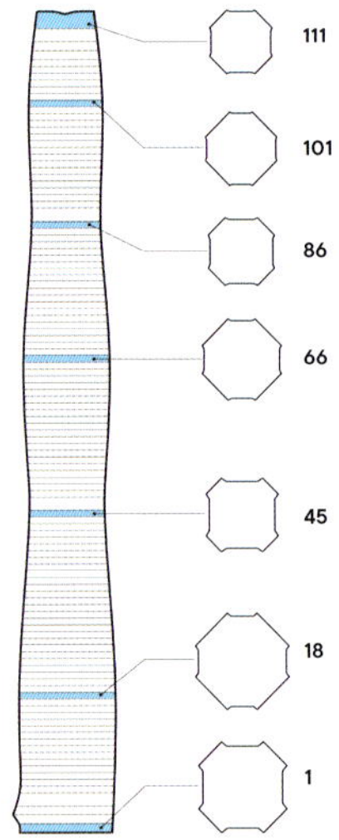

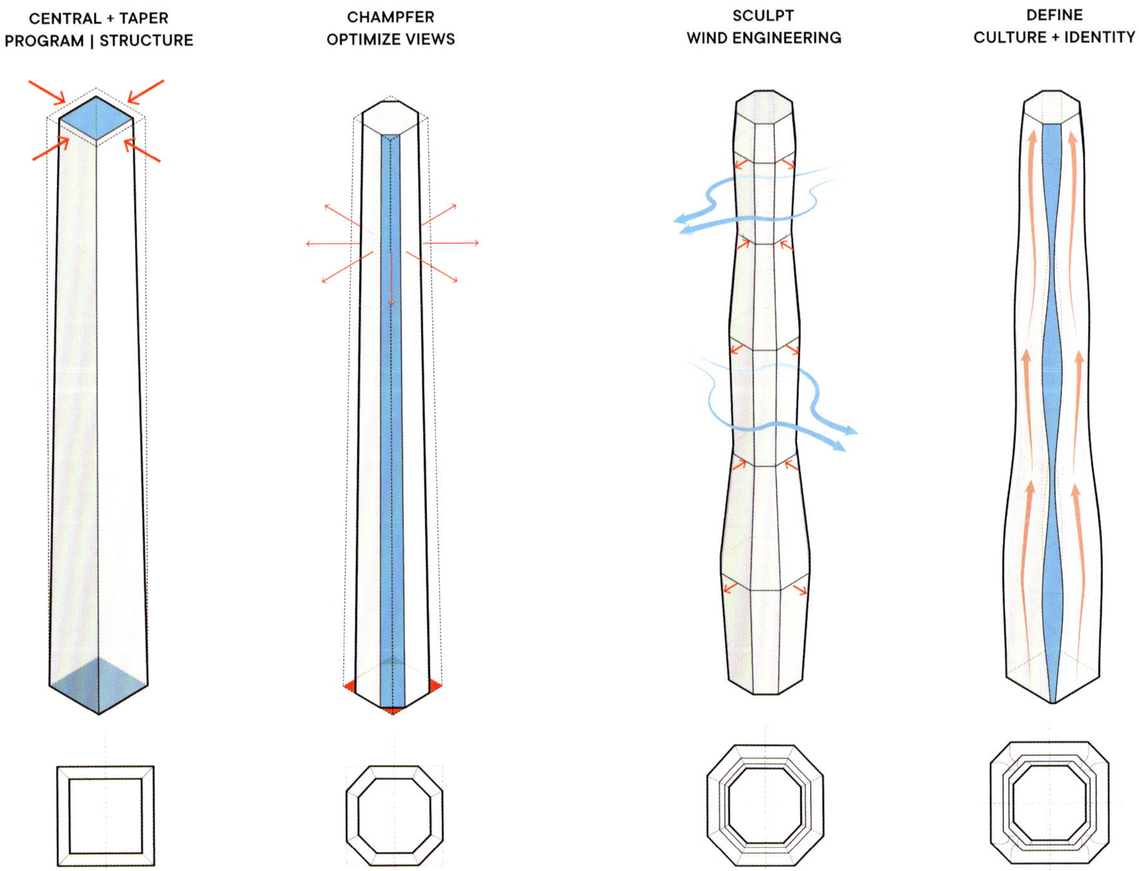

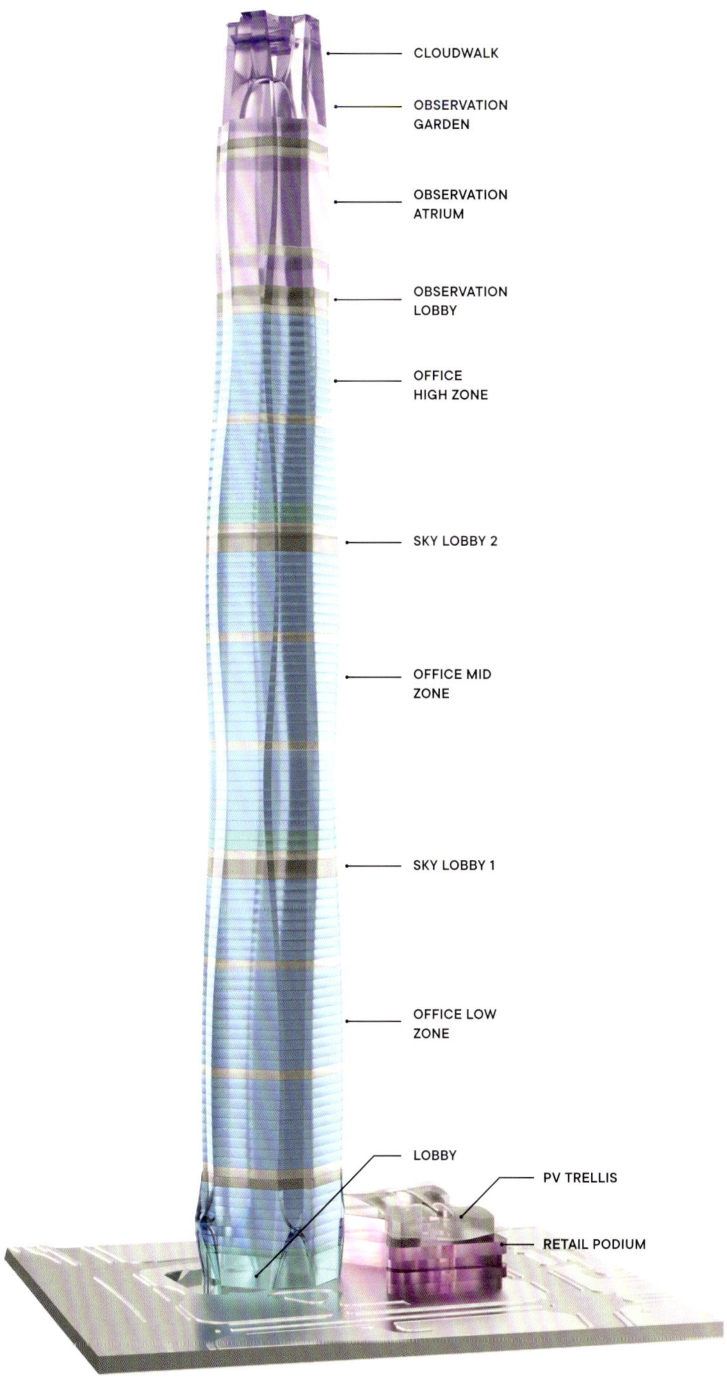
CLOUDWALK
OBSERVATION GARDEN
OBSERVATION ATRIUM
OBSERVATION LOBBY
OFFICE HIGH ZONE
SKY LOBBY 2
OFFICE MID ZONE
SKY LOBBY 1
OFFICE LOW ZONE
LOBBY
PV TRELLIS
RETAIL PODIUM

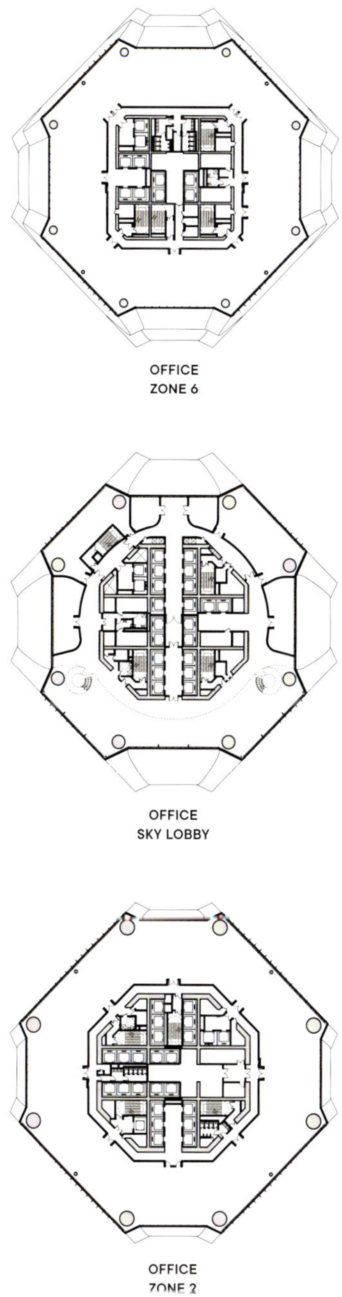
OFFICE ZONE 6
OFFICE SKY LOBBY
OFFICE ZONE 2

PODIUM

One of the principles of the development is to create the memorable and recognizable experience through multiple dimensions including material, texture, scale, and light. The tower entry was envisioned as the important urban scale reference in the pedestrian level. Four, twenty-four-meter tall archways, matching the height of podium buildings of the master plan, anchor the tower's two vehicular drop-off and two pedestrian entries including one that connects down to the sunken garden, giving tower the appropriate scale and unique expression to ground.

A "oculus" was created at the top of each the archway to reveal the memorable experience to look up at the tower above when people are entering the tower. The elliptical light through the oculus casting on the lobby floor moves when the sun moves to indicate the movement of the time. Pedestrain scale canopies are placed in front of the entrance doors as the standing scupltural art pieces.

MODEL OF THE TOWER ENTRY

CROWN

The tower will be visually stunning from the exterior. A cloud-like pod that forms the pinnacle event space will be visible through the exterior wall at the top of the tower, adding interest and intrigue, further encouraging visitors to visit the experience.

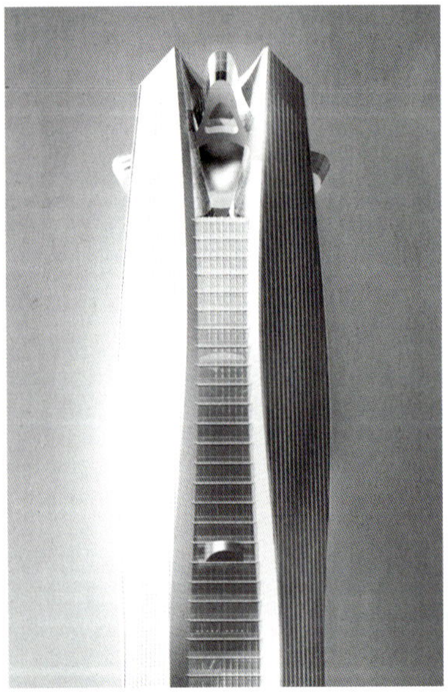

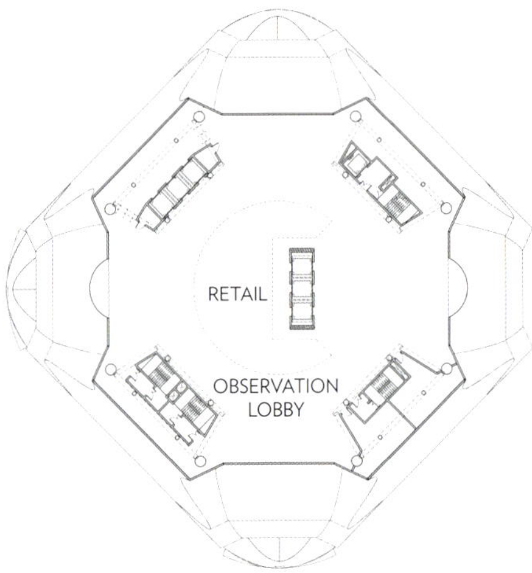

LEVEL 95
OBSERVATION TERRACE

CROWN

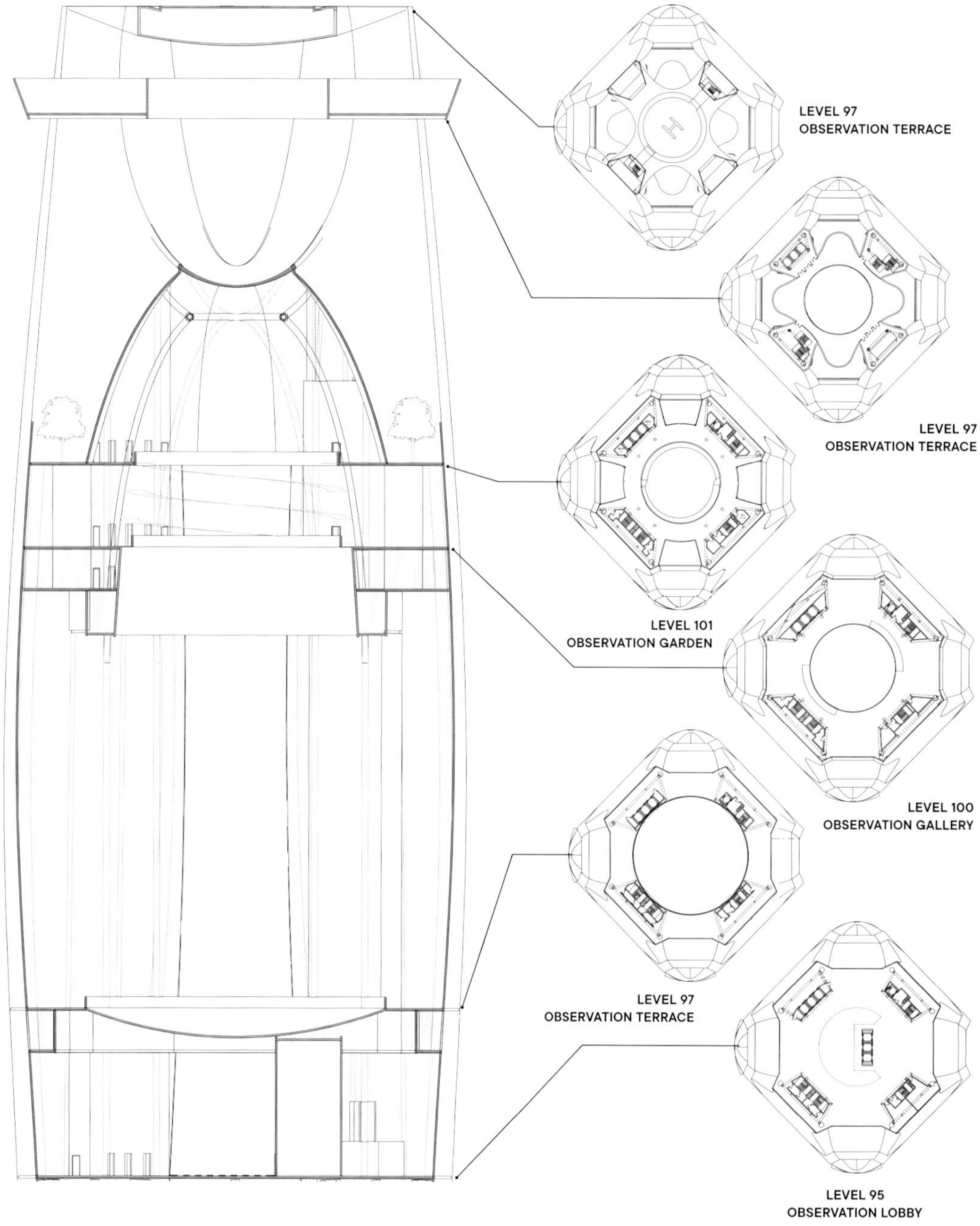

LEVEL 97
OBSERVATION TERRACE
LEVEL 97
OBSERVATION TERRACE
LEVEL 101
OBSERVATION GARDEN
LEVEL 100
OBSERVATION GALLERY
LEVEL 97
OBSERVATION TERRACE
LEVEL 95
OBSERVATION LOBBY

EXPERIENCE

Throughout human history the height of man-made structures has been an indicator of social development, wealth, and status. Humankind is fascinated by constructing taller and taller buildings, reaching higher to create land value, establish a focal point, or demonstrate community strength. In the past 25 years, there have been more supertall buildings built than in all previously recorded history.

Building tall is no longer a challenge but instead, an expectation. Today, height is no longer the sole factor that makes a building unique, attractive, or interesting.

The current global trend is to carve "special" event or gathering spaces out of the top of the tower. These spaces take advantage of the prime location, offering spectacular views and generating revenue by providing experiences that are unforgettable. Typical experiences include observation decks, stimulating rides, or fine dining.

Simultaneously, another global architectural trend is to add cultural and entertainment spaces to supertall buildings, spaces that address the culture and art of a region.

HeXi Yuzui Tower takes these two trends and blends them into one space; a space that is both innovative and unique. The design team envisioned the tower as a first of its kind, a supertall building with a stunning observation area that also offers an interactive cultural program. A multi-dimensional venue where the visitors are submerged with state-of-the-art virtual reality, immersive holographic concerts, and interactive 7D rides. The space will also offer fine dining, a world-class sky garden, and live shows.

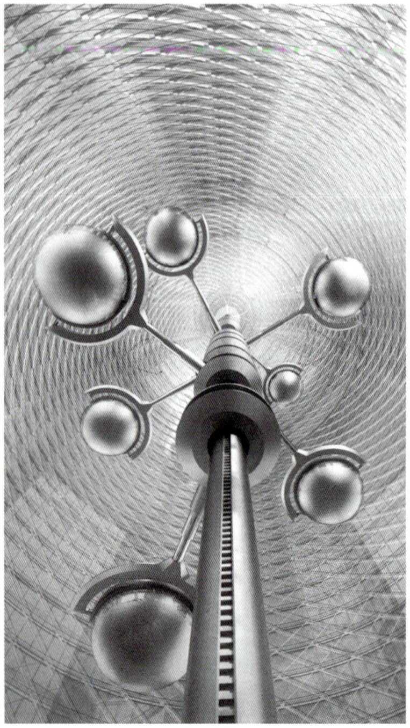

PERFORMANCE

The building's performance is the catalyst for the design of its form, expression, and functionality. Shaped through several studies and models, the tower will reach LEED Gold certification through a variety of means. The tower seeks a 10 percent overall energy reduction with a combination of energy strategies that include reducing the cooling load, a high-performance facade, reducing heating loads, reducing lighting loads, and reducing plug loads.

Renewable energy will be captured through podium roof garden shading trellis with PV panels. A comprehensive system of sponge city strategies is designed through landscape and building to manage store water.

A high-performance, Low-E insulated curtain-wall system with unique, carefully designed fins that works with the building geometry in four diagonal facades with undulating profile and east/west orientation to efficiently reduce 19% solar heat gain and provide the effective protection to indoor environment, while maintaining access to daylighting and controlling glare.

The fins are further elevated as the visual elements to sculpt the facade texture to simulate water waves, accentuating the light movement on the facade.

Five depths of the fins were designed with curve profile as the result of the rationalization to balance the cost, performance and visual effect. The brushed stainless steel would catch and reflect the light. The articulated tower form, compared to the traditional square plan baseline building, has 7 percent less surface area to construct. This equates to 15 percent less annual solar heat gain to cool down, and 40 percent less of wind load to resist with the opening through the crown.

The exterior lighting is choreographed to emphasize and articulate the building's fluid facade gestures. A complementing lighting scheme at the top of the tower includes an illuminated Cloud Walk that generates a visual peak into the Nanjing skyline. The research of light projection on glass and drone lighting are investigated for next generation innovations.

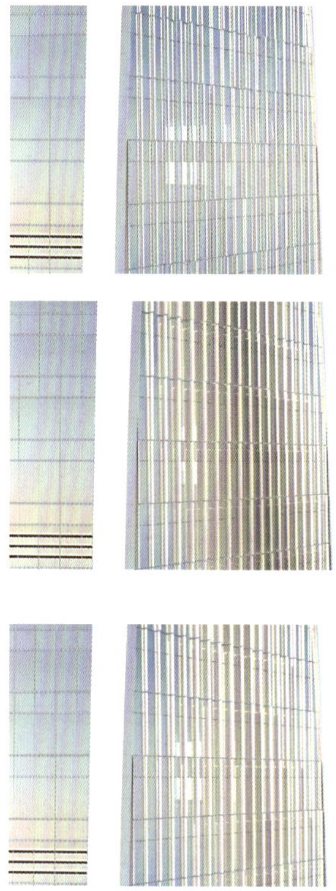

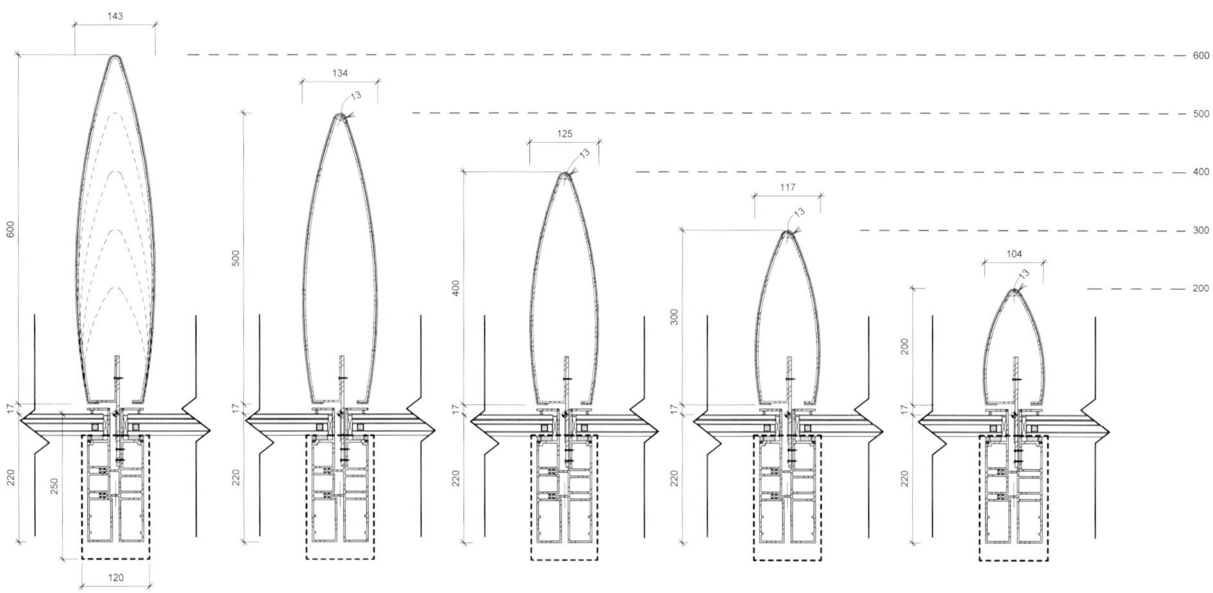

PERFORMANCE

AVERAGE FIN DEPTH
425 MM

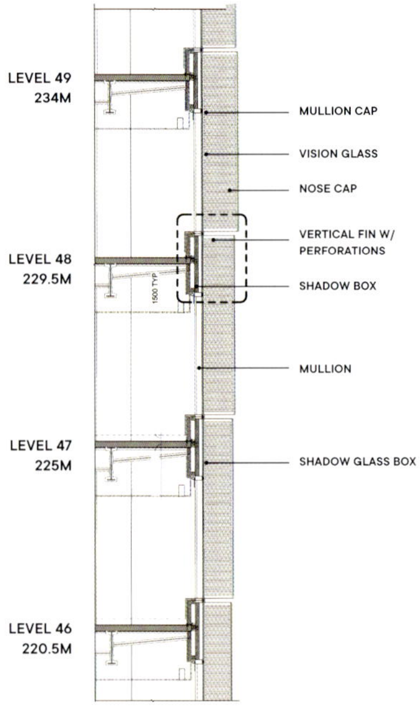

HORIZONTAL SHADE STUDY -SECTION

DOUBLE
HORIZONTAL SHADE

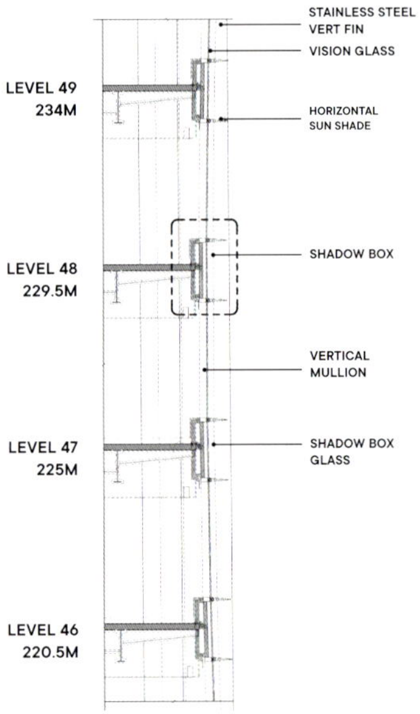

SINGLE
HORIZONTAL SHADE

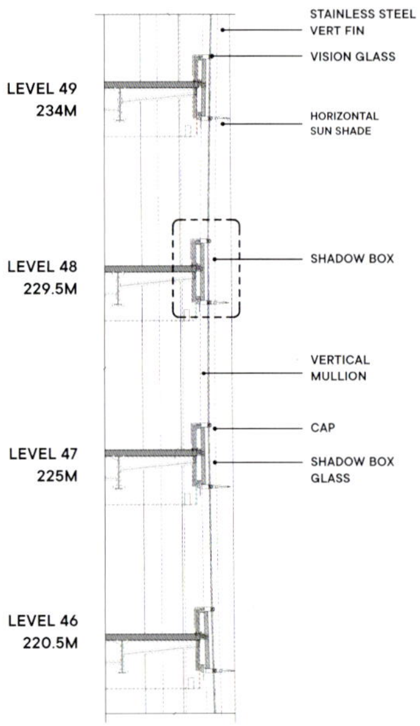

DOUBLE
HORIZONTAL CAP

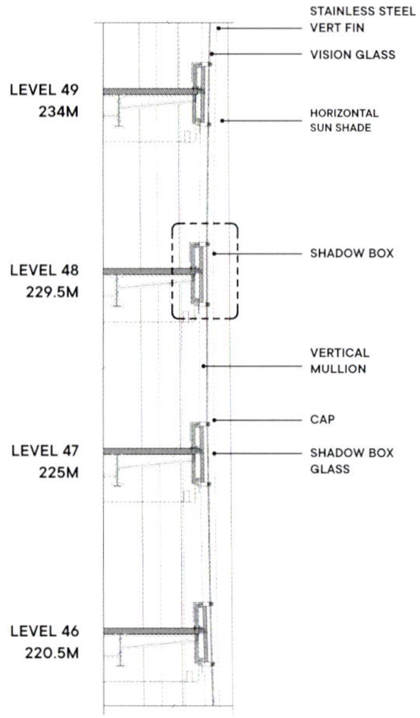

DOUBLE
HORIZONTAL SHADE

SINGLE
HORIZONTAL SHADE

DOUBLE
HORIZONTAL CAP

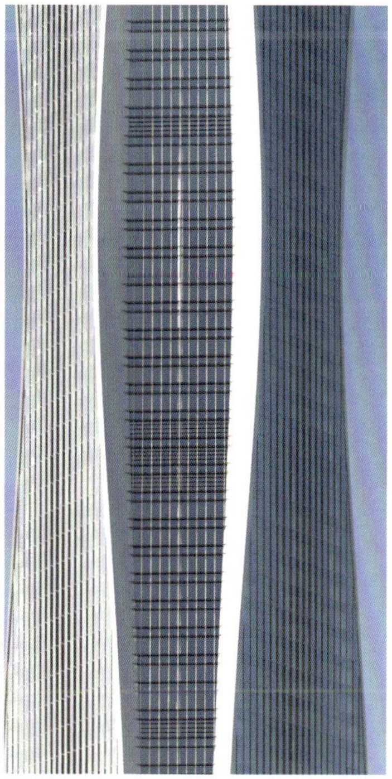

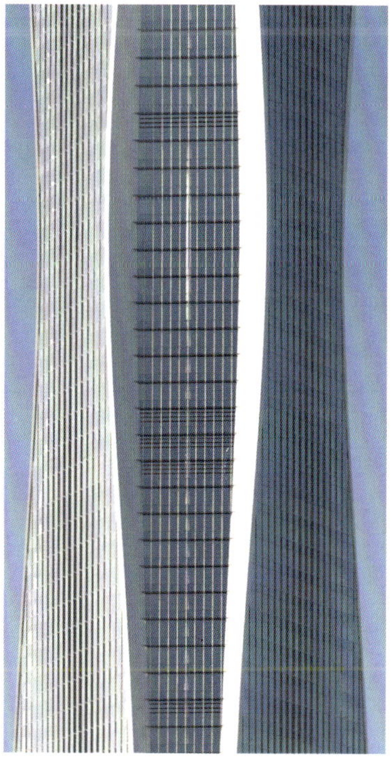

STRUCTURE

THORNTON TOMASETTI, STRUCTURAL ENGINEER

The structure is symmetrical in plan, providing the same structural behavior at the north and south. The symmetry also minimizes any torsional behavior in the tower, making the structure more stable.

The total height is 500 m. The lateral system is A Core Wall- Outrigger Truss-Mega Frame system, which is suitable for a supertall building at or over 300 m. The lateral system in comprised of a reinforced-concrete core wall, composite super columns, and steel outrigger trusses.

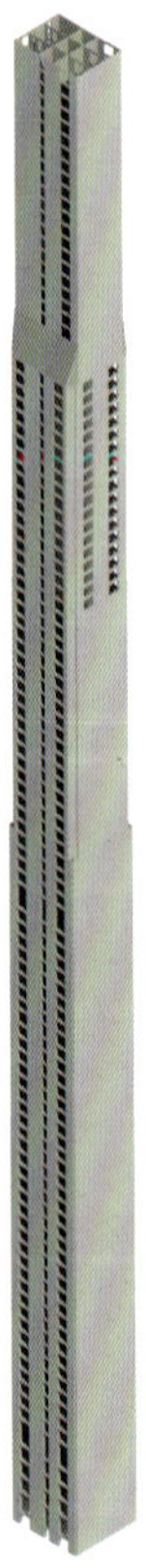

CORE

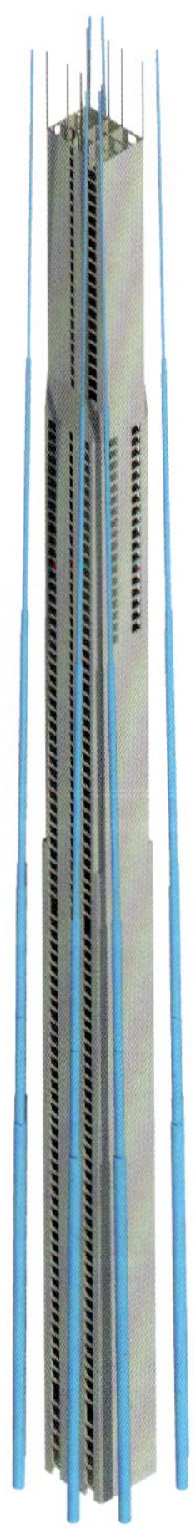

PERIMETER COLUMNS

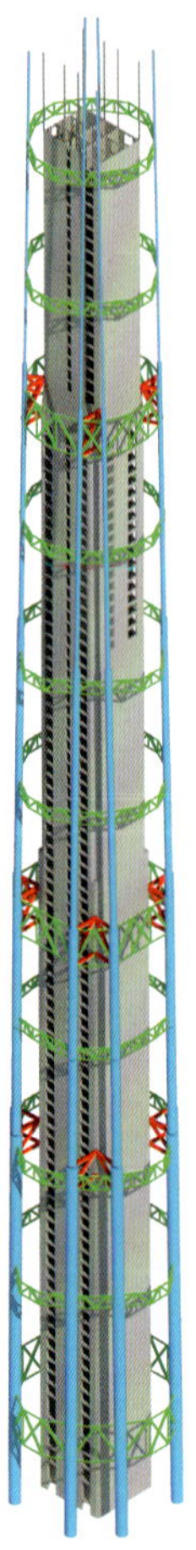

BELT TRUSSES AND OUTRIGGERS

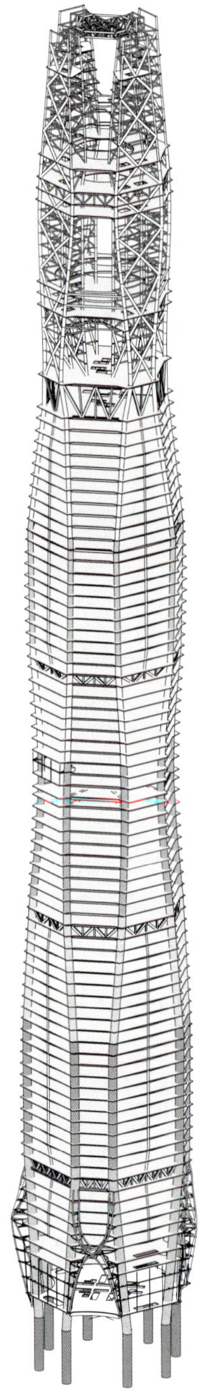

OVERALL STRUCTURAL SYSTEM

CHAPTER IV. EXTENDING ECOLOGIES

INTEGRATED SKY GARDENS + LANDSCAPES

Supertall towers often have unique landscaped spaces at their pinnacle that are open to visitors and tenants. By allowing green landscaping to be integrated into the design and structure, the occupant experience is enhanced with areas dedicated to community interaction. Sky terraces can act as parks within the tower, providing opportunities for extraordinary views, access to fresh air, and communal gardening.

Outdoor green spaces have a multitude of positive affects on the building. Studies have show that incorporating green elements can help offset carbon emissions from the building. Green spaces also help reduce the heat island effect through shading and by creating a lush microclimate. Green spaces also can improve air quality and ventilation within the building. Recent research has also determined that sky gardens can increase productivity and foster a sense of well-being among tenants.

Structurally, green spaces provide spans in the building that offers relief to wind forces. Sky terraces also help temper the experience of extreme heights, which can be thought of as isolating, by bringing natural elements from the earth.

+ ELPHINSTONE MILLS
+ BIOPHILIC TOWER
+ KLIFD TOWER
+ DOHA TOWER
+ IMPERIAL TOWER

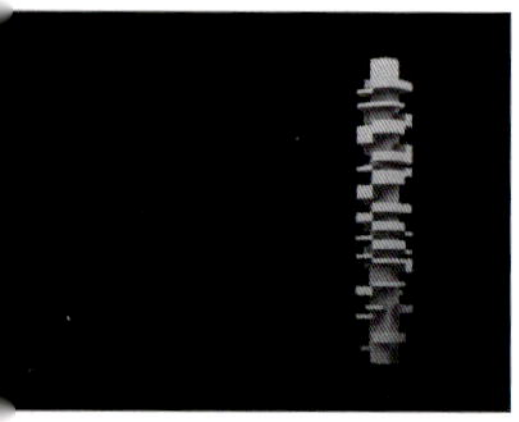

ELPHINSTONE MILLS

MUMBAI, INDIA, 2007

300M

In 2007, Adrian Smith + Gordon Gill Architecture was engaged to design a tower that incorporated gardens in every unit for a site in Mumbai, India. We explored the concept of dispersing the residential program over a height that allowed for open outdoor spaces and landscaped terraces.

While the overall construction area increased, the height increase created unique residential units with generous access to private outdoor amenity areas that span the size of the residential unit below. These green spaces become the overall expression of the tower's form.

The 300 m tower has 75 floors, with programed space occupying 38 floors. In high-rise buildings, upper-level units traditionally have more value than lower-level units. Therefore AS+GG's scheme shifts the occupied floors to the highest floors, where the units benefit from more expansive views of the city and the developer can make more profitable returns on their investment.

The additional cost a developer may incur to build higher can traditionally be offset by higher investment returns.

- FORM
- PERFORMANCE
- RESEARCH + DEVELOPMENT

FORM

Elphinstone Mills explores a new way to look at—and think about—tall buildings, not as just a mechanism to contain a program but as vertical gardens that can make a significant mark on the skylines, while offsetting their carbon use with vertical landscapes. The design also considers whether the core of the building can act as an atrium that draws cool air downward in the evening and warm air upward during the day, creating natural air flow and ventilation. There is also generous air flow between the massings, treating each unit as an individual residence.

Each of AS+GG's designs is developed to meet the needs of specific clients and is shaped according to its site and climate. If we had moved past concept design, this building may have evolved as the design was further studied.

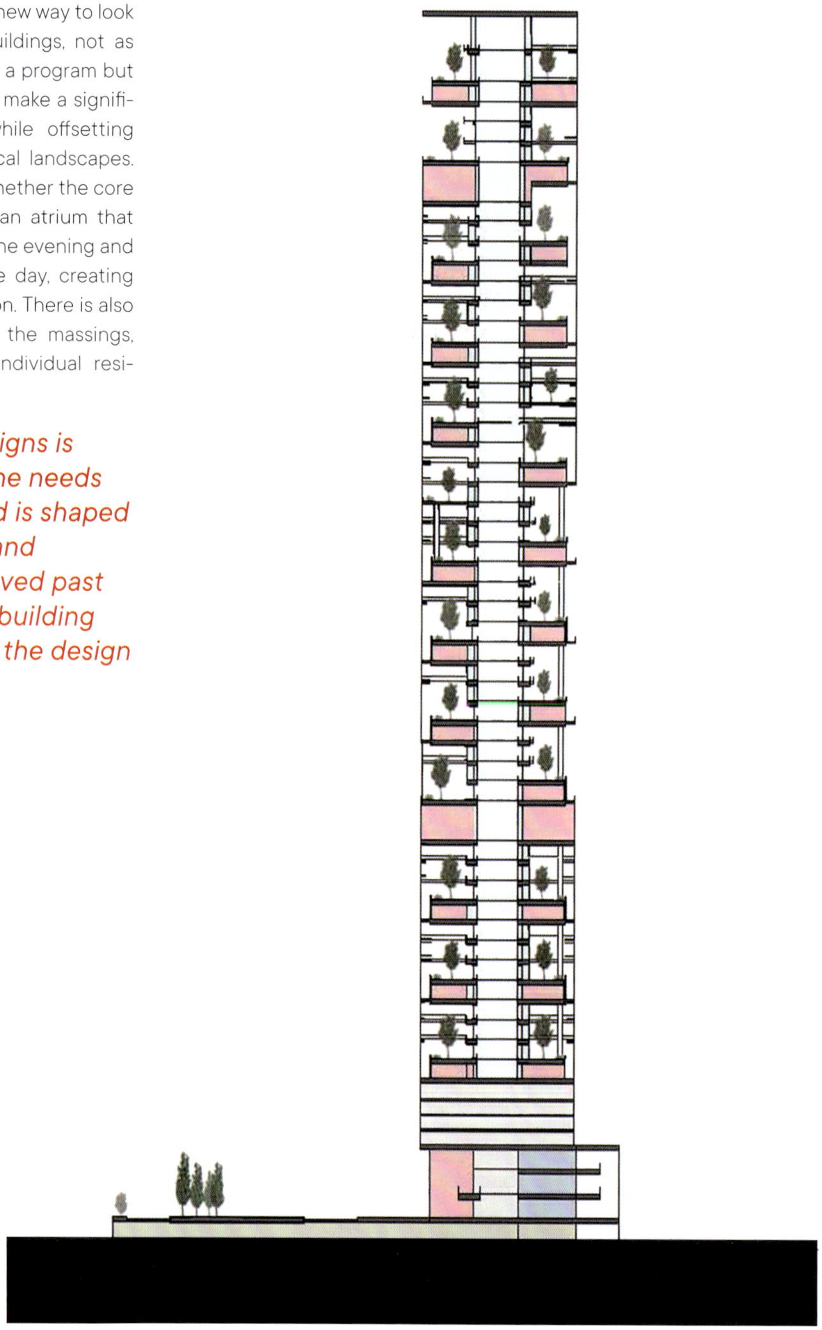

TEMPERATURE AND STACK EFFECT HYPOTHESIS

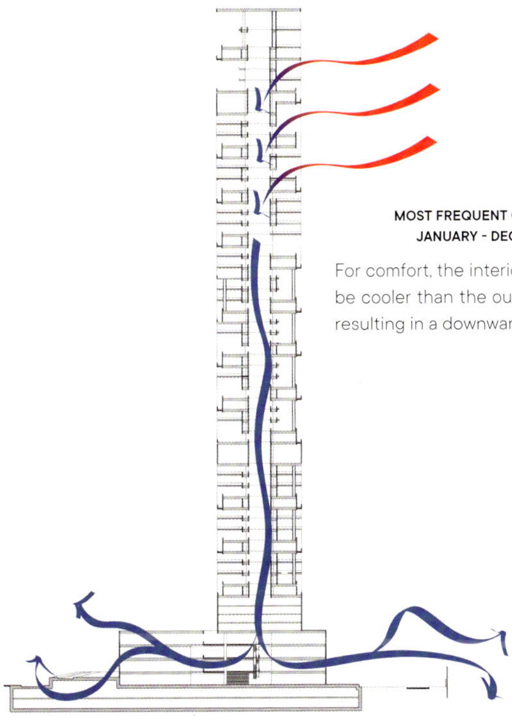

MOST FREQUENT CONDITION
JANUARY - DECEMBER

For comfort, the interior environment will be cooler than the outside environment, resulting in a downward stack effect.

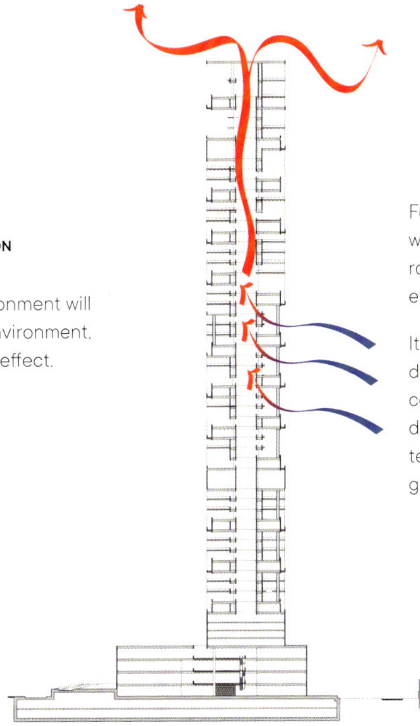

FRINGE CONDITION
NOVEMBER - MARCH

For comfort, the interior environment will be warmer than the outside environment, resulting in an upward stack effect.

It is possible that a flipflop from the downward condition to the upward condition could occur on the cooler days or between day and night when temperatures drop to or below 20 degrees celsius.

NATURAL VENTILATION

Air flow from the terraces and balconies facilitates natural ventilation through the building via the atrium.

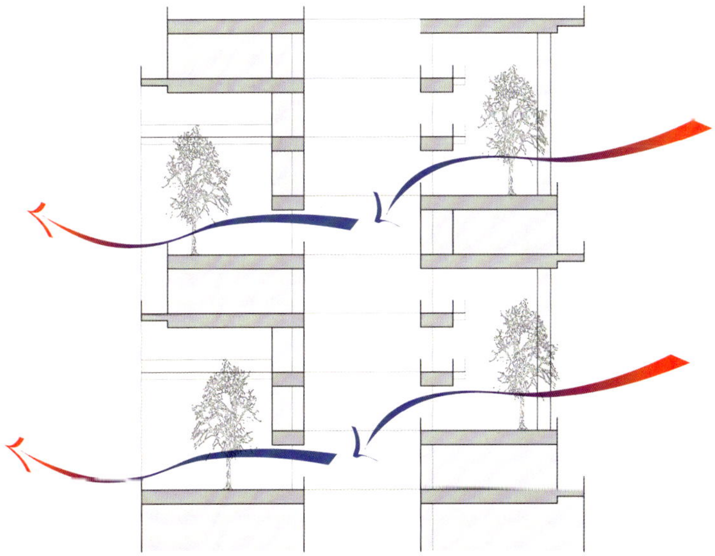

PERFORMANCE

In order to allow the apartment units to start and stop in the massing, the structure of the tower floors is cantilevered off a central core that holds the elevators, service areas, and exit stairs. This allows for a column-free exterior facade that adds luxury to the residential units. The tower's shaft, or core, is expressed when the units are absent.

The voids left help the improve the wind performance of the tower with areas that the wind travels through. The placement of trees at the terraces improves occupant comfort and protects the outdoor spaces from the wind, particularly on the upper floors.

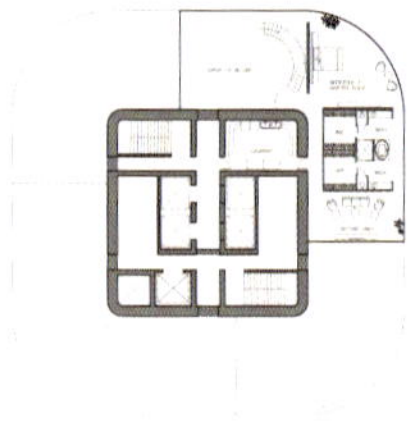

UPPER UNIT
3 BEDROOM DUPLEX

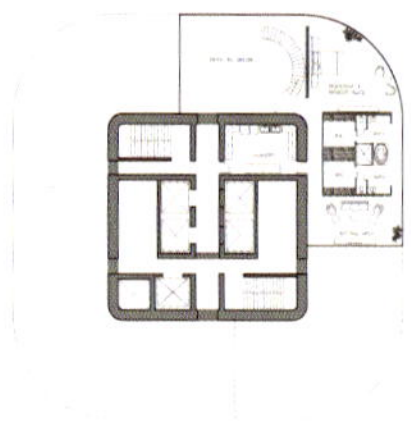

UPPER UNIT
LUXURY 4 BEDROOM DUPLEX

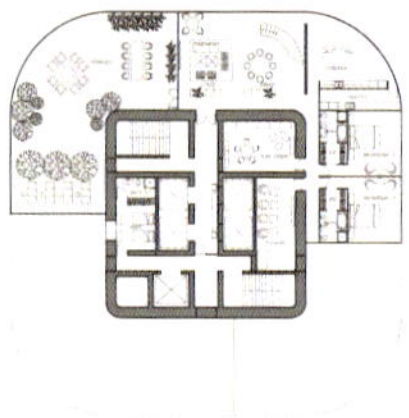

LOWER UNIT
3 BEDROOM DUPLEX

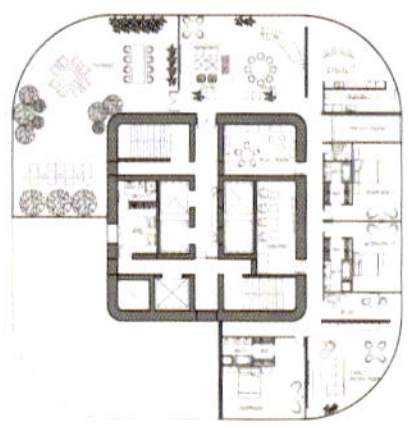

LOWER UNIT
LUXURY 4 BEDROOM DUPLEX

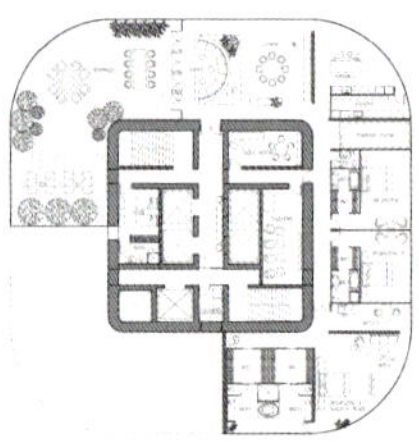

LUXURY 3 BEDROOM

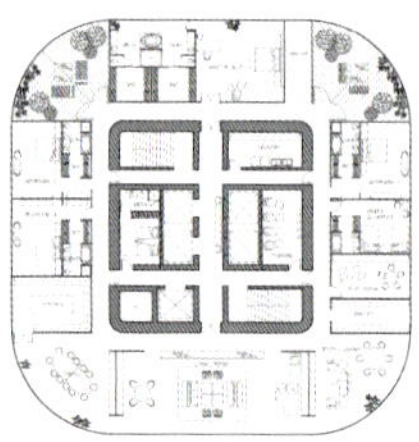

LUXURY 4 BEDROOM

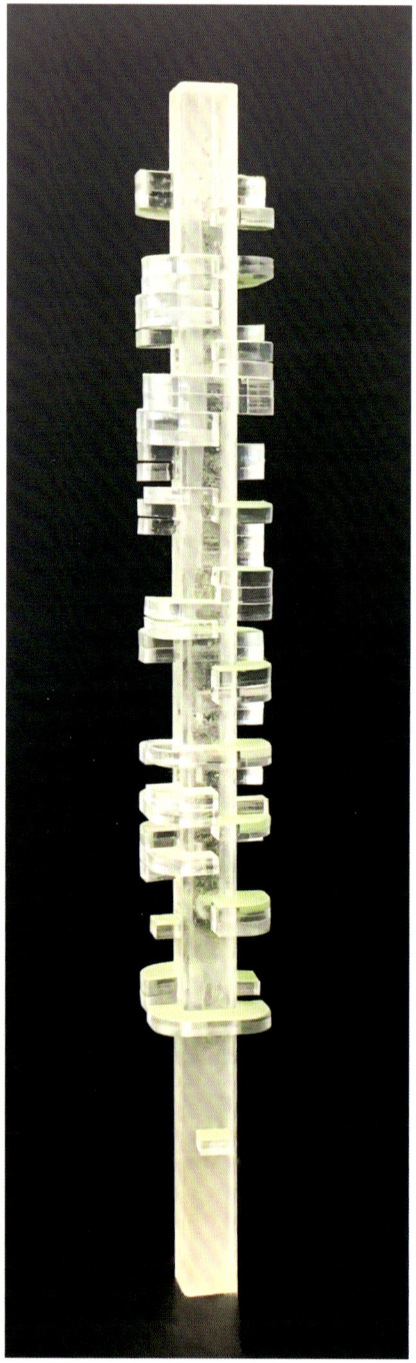

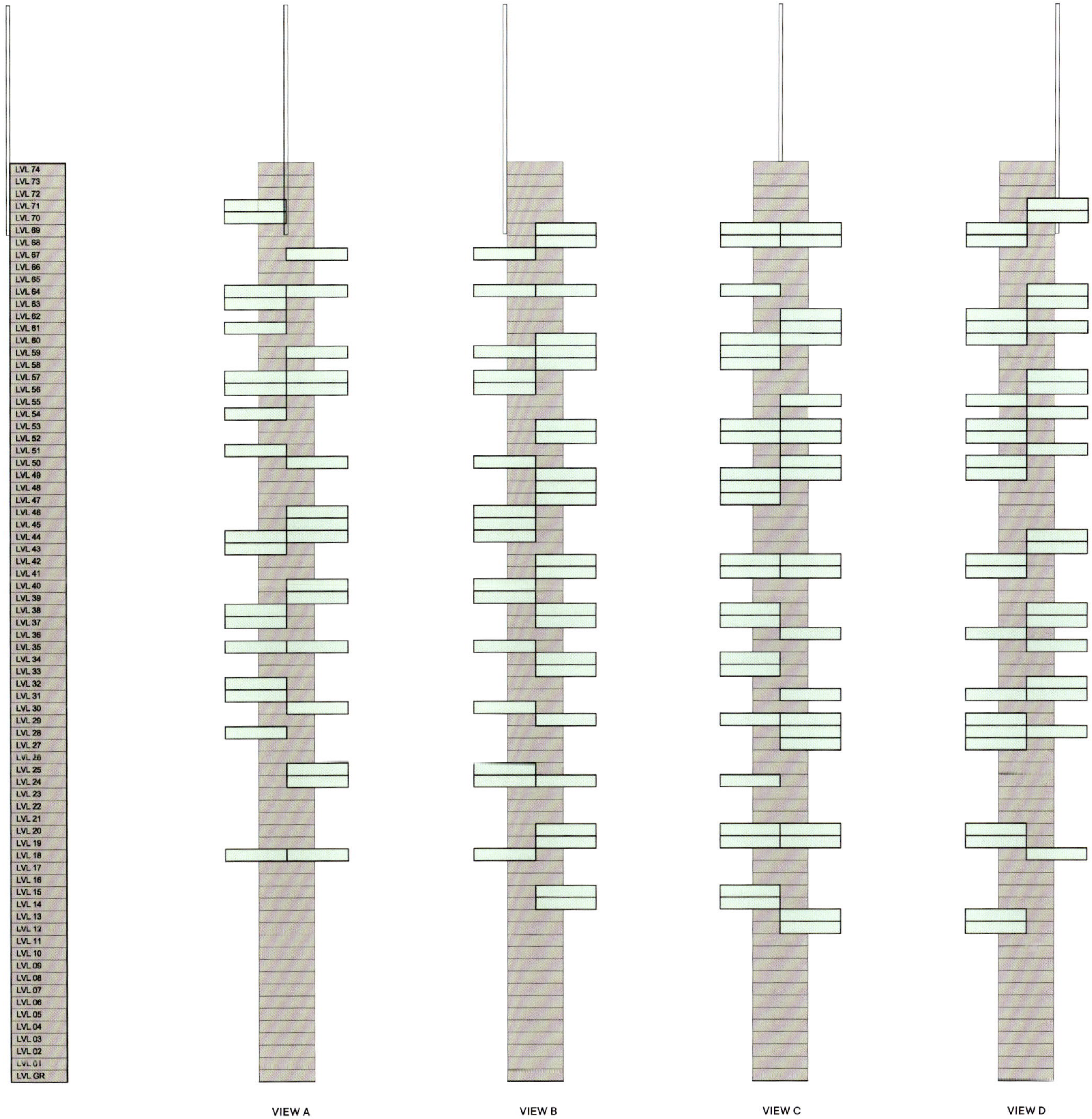
LVL 74
LVL 73
LVL 72
LVL 71
LVL 70
LVL 69
LVL 68
LVL 67
LVL 66
LVL 65
LVL 64
LVL 63
LVL 62
LVL 61
LVL 60
LVL 59
LVL 58
LVL 57
LVL 56
LVL 55
LVL 54
LVL 53
LVL 52
LVL 51
LVL 50
LVL 49
LVL 48
LVL 47
LVL 46
LVL 45
LVL 44
LVL 43
LVL 42
LVL 41
LVL 40
LVL 39
LVL 38
LVL 37
LVL 36
LVL 35
LVL 34
LVL 33
LVL 32
LVL 31
LVL 30
LVL 29
LVL 28
LVL 27
LVL 26
LVL 25
LVL 24
LVL 23
LVL 22
LVL 21
LVL 20
LVL 19
LVL 18
LVL 17
LVL 16
LVL 15
LVL 14
LVL 13
LVL 12
LVL 11
LVL 10
LVL 09
LVL 08
LVL 07
LVL 06
LVL 05
LVL 04
LVL 03
LVL 02
LVL 01
LVL GR
VIEW A
VIEW B
VIEW C
VIEW D

A prototype was developed through concept design and influenced future design explorations. Issues that warranted further study included:

- How would mechanical, electrical, and plumbing services and shafts be routed to the units given the gaps in the massing of the building, where these services would have to transfer in, and out, of the core?
- What structure would be necessary to support the trees, and would it then inform their placement?
- Would deflections be a concern?
- What effect would the increased building envelope have on overall performance? Noting that this building is in Mumbai, where winter heating loads are not a significant concern.
- How would the public react to these unique residential units? Would the value add be worthwhile given the additional cost to build higher?
- How would zoning treat the overall "area" of the building? i.e. would the express zone of the core be allowed to be completely discounted
- What would be the proper balance between the "voids" in the building and the occupied floors?
- What would the wind-tunnel results have shown and how would that inform the design?

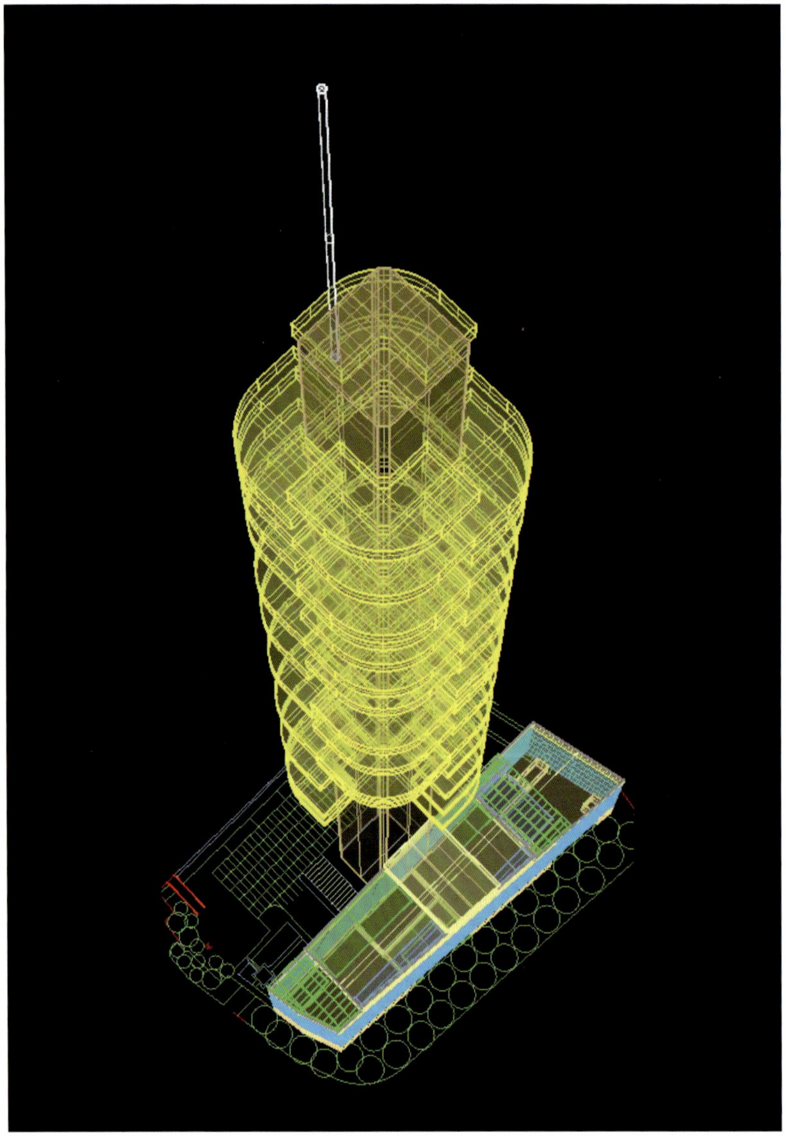

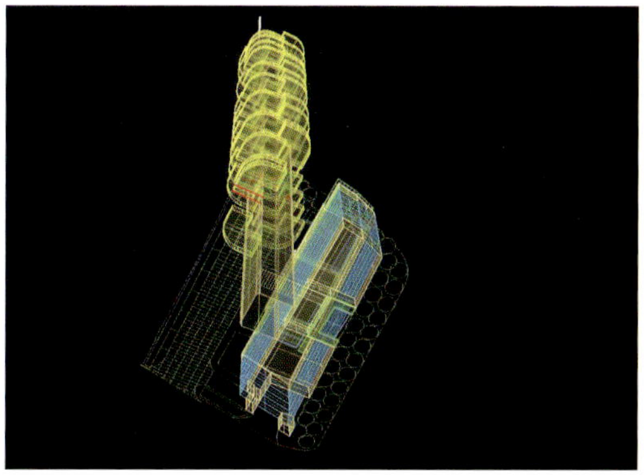

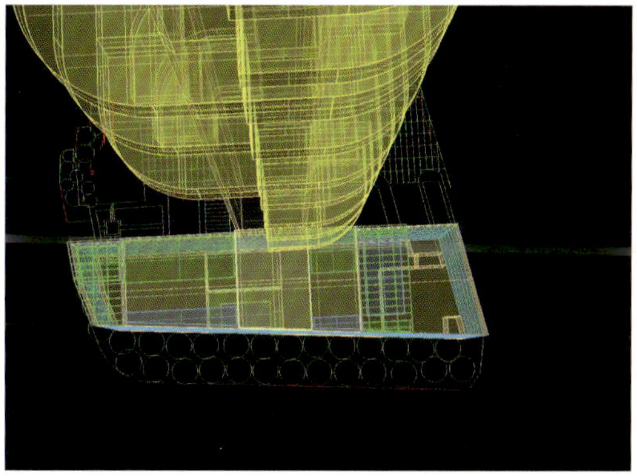

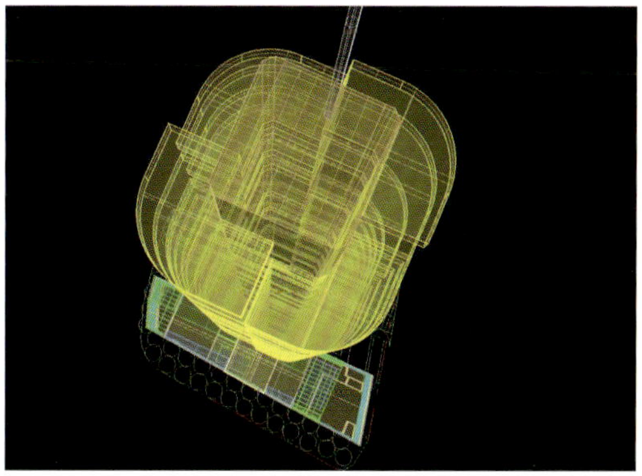

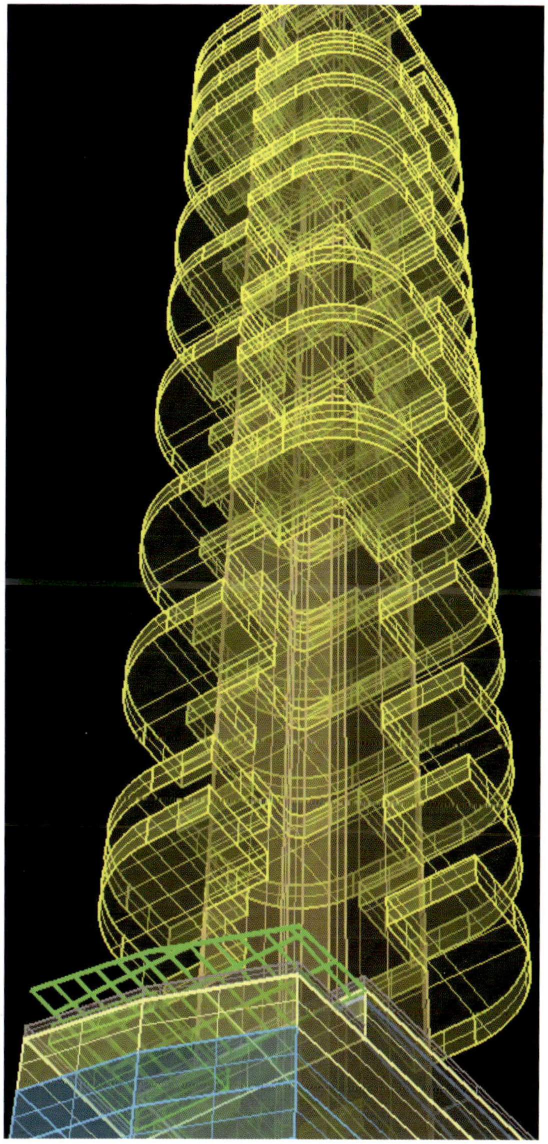

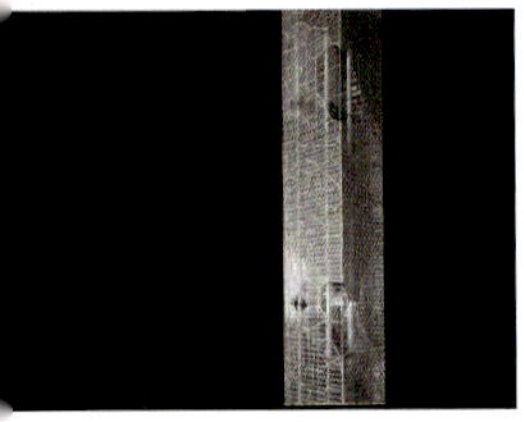

BIOPHILIC TOWER

SUZHOU, CHINA, 2012

668M

The Biophilic Tower design represents the next generation in skyscrapers: A self-sustaining, intelligent structure that combines optimal performance with aesthetic beauty; a tower that focuses on a human being's innate, emotional attraction to nature.

One of the tower's main features is a continuous vertical garden environment that wraps around the building from ground level to the top. Each of the 119 floors have access to this lush atrium space, giving occupants a multi-sensory connection to nature.

The tower is shaped to take advantage of the natural light available to the site. By carving the atrium space deep into the massing of the building, natural light enters the building beyond the perimeter envelope and extends into the floor plates.

Fractal patterns, which have shown to positively affect human neural activity by increasing work productivity and physical and mental health, were used as design inspiration. A common fractal pattern, the Voronoi diagram, was used to add another natural layer to the tower's indoor/outdoor environment.

The tower also offers stunning views, east to Jinji Lake and west to the Old City.

- CONTEXT
- SITE
- PROGRAM
- PERFORMANCE
- RESEARCH + DEVELOPMENT

CONTEXT

The Biophilic Tower was designed with three key concepts in mind:

Nature in Space: Integrate water elements, courtyard gardens, and views of nature from inside the tower.

Nature of Space: Adapt human psychological and physiological responses to different spatial configurations that improve concentration, connectivity, and productivity.

Natural Analogues: Use materials and patterns that evoke nature, including building elements that mimic shells and leaves, furniture with organic rather than geometric shapes, and visible wood grains.

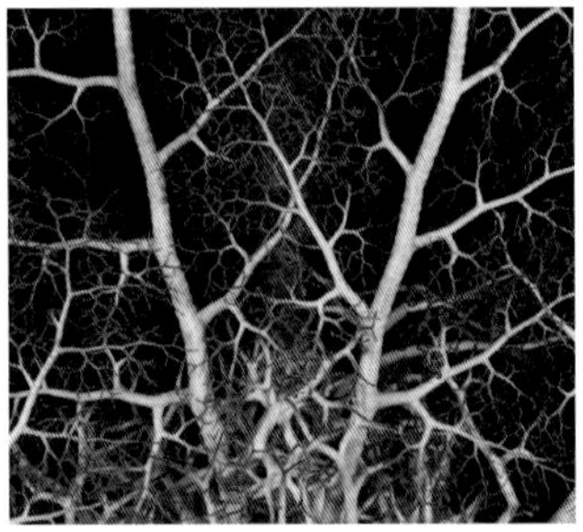

CONTEXT

The spiral pattern is not just found in nature. It is one of the earliest examples of human creative expression, appearing in nearly every society in the ancient world. The spiral has universal appeal and a mysterious resonance with the human spirit; it is complex yet simple, intriguing, and beautiful.

In nature, the spiral is often used as a structural or organizational tool. Biophilic Tower's design uses the spiral to organize the continuous garden space that wraps up and around the tower.

As the space spirals around the building, occupants have views of the atrium rotating. This creates a visual connection that links one space to another along the entire height of the tower.

The design also features fractal patterns, which appear the same from near as from far, and which can positively affect human neural activity, increasing work productivity and physical and mental health.

The Voronoi diagram is incorporated into the curtain wall design, primarily as a solar shading strategy that helps reduce heat gain in the internal occupied spaces, as well as in the naturally ventilated gardens.

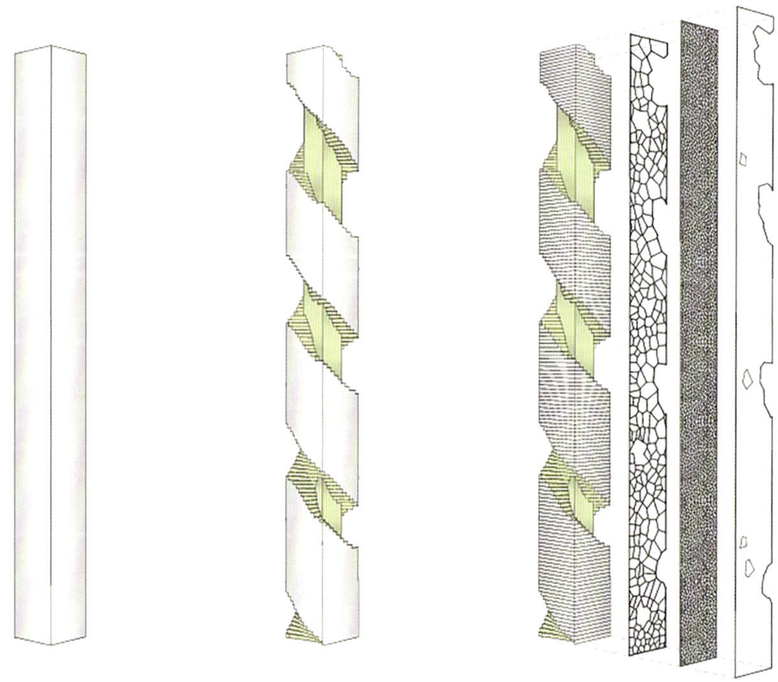

BEGIN WITH A SIMPLE, SHAPE

CARVE ATRIA THROUGHOUT THE TOWER

APPLY LAYERS TO CREATE A CULTURALLY CONNECTED FACADE

SITE

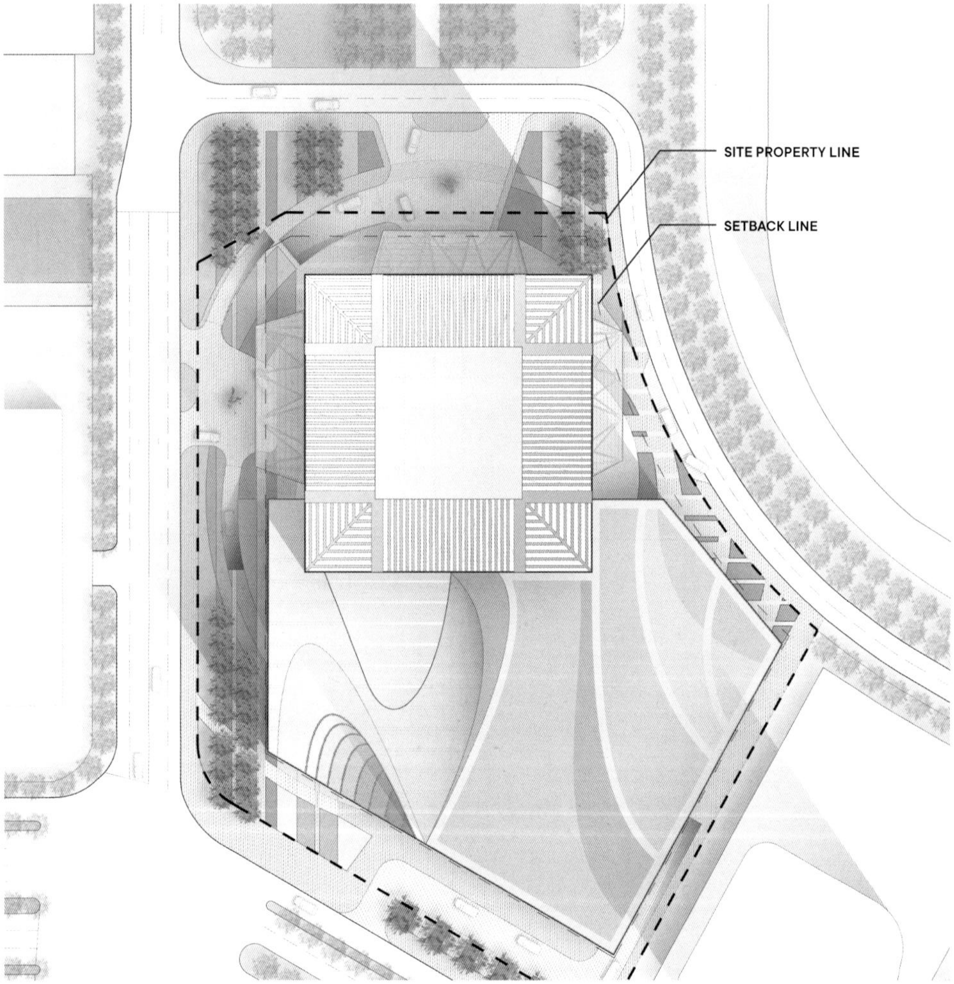

Looking east to Jinji Lake and west to the Old City, the Biophilic Tower has some of the most powerful and significant views of Suzhou. As the outdoor atrium spirals up the building, floor plates are incrementally cut back to create spaces with a greater range of views. In addition, tenants have close-range views of indoor and outdoor gardens in the atrium spaces.

PROGRAM

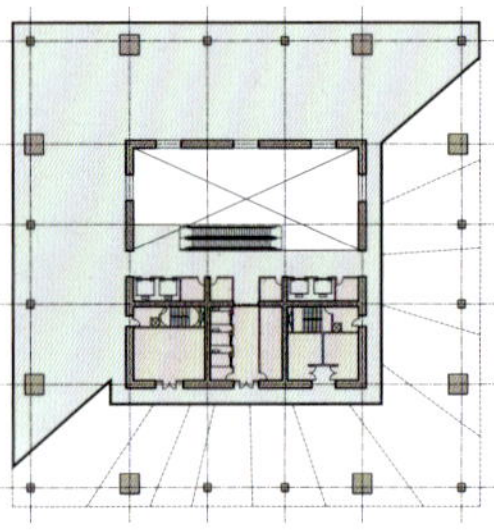

LEVEL 118

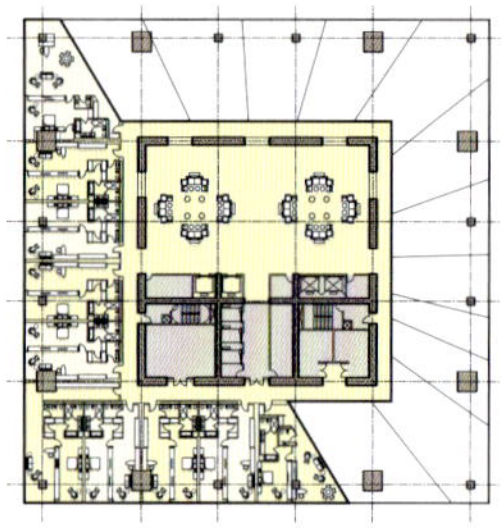

LEVEL 112

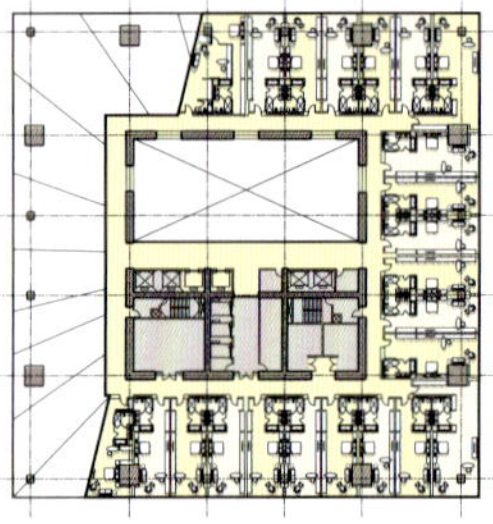

LEVEL 98

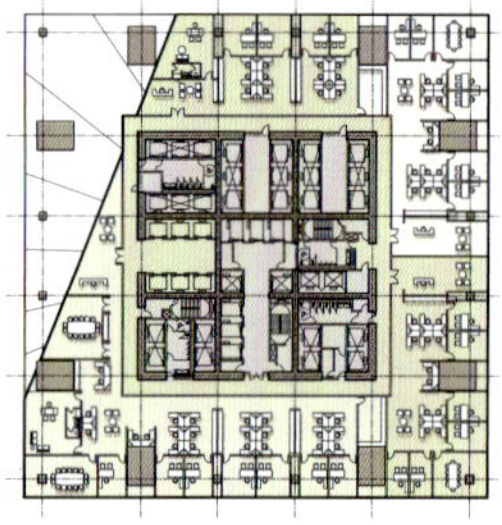

LEVEL 62

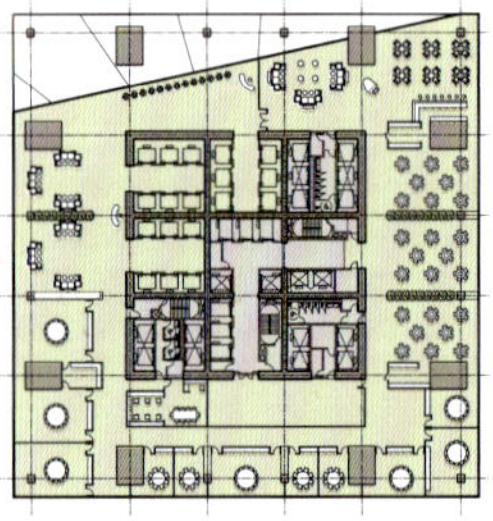

LEVEL 22

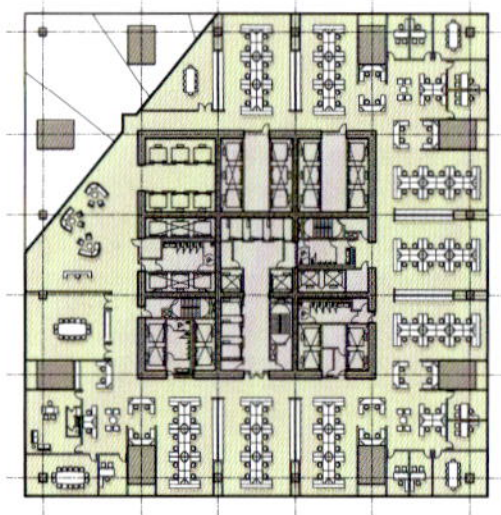

LEVEL 8

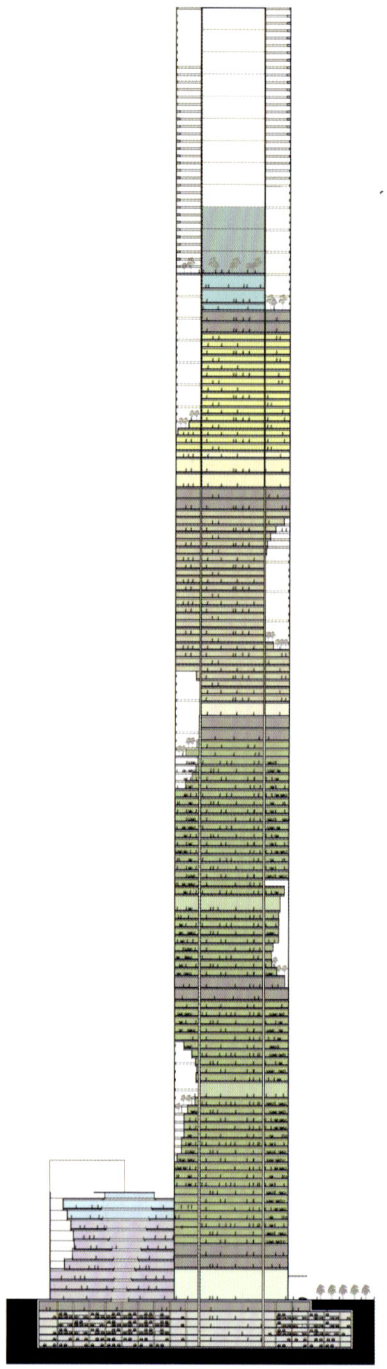

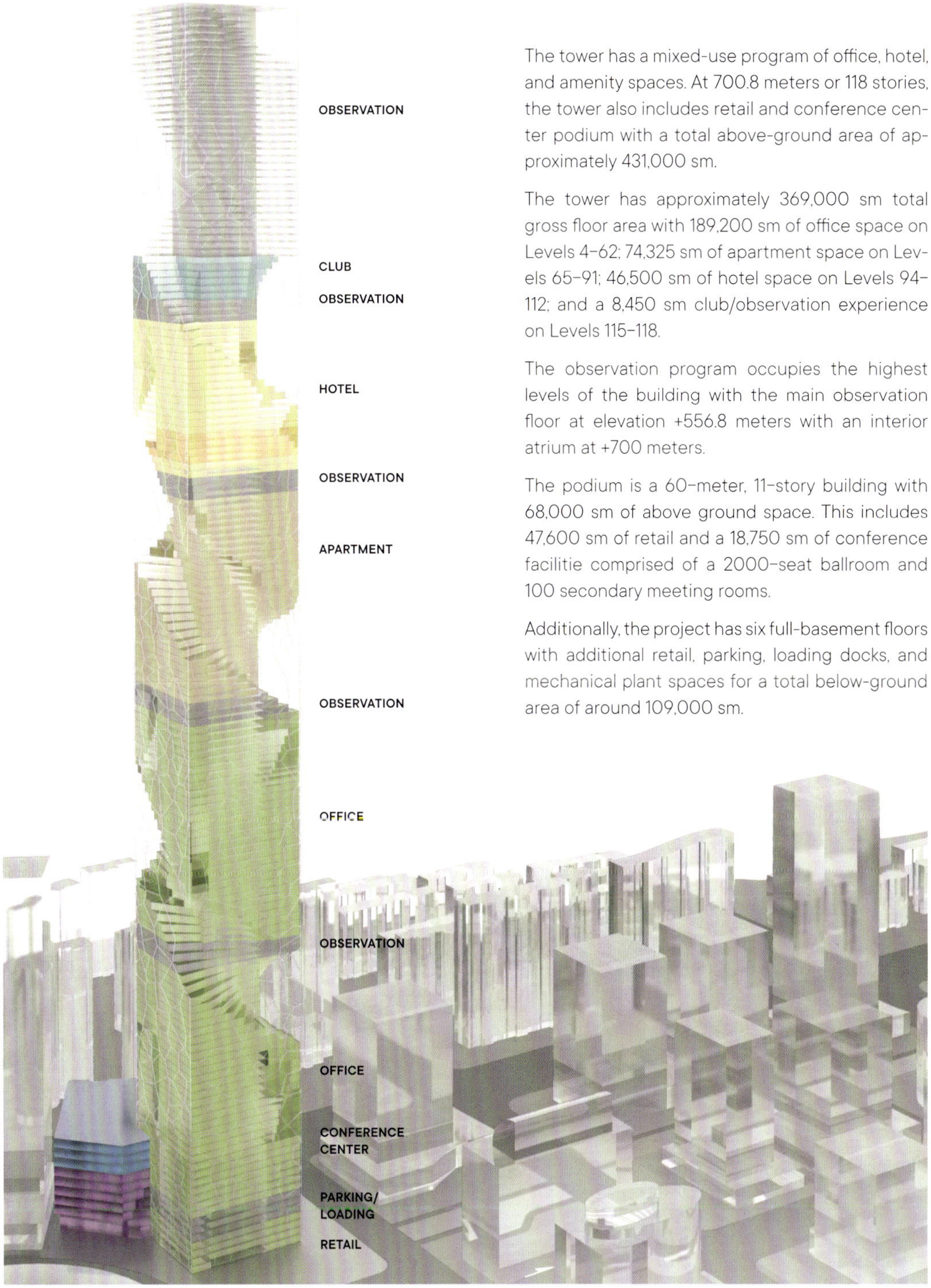

The tower has a mixed-use program of office, hotel, and amenity spaces. At 700.8 meters or 118 stories, the tower also includes retail and conference center podium with a total above-ground area of approximately 431,000 sm.

The tower has approximately 369,000 sm total gross floor area with 189,200 sm of office space on Levels 4–62; 74,325 sm of apartment space on Levels 65–91; 46,500 sm of hotel space on Levels 94–112; and a 8,450 sm club/observation experience on Levels 115–118.

The observation program occupies the highest levels of the building with the main observation floor at elevation +556.8 meters with an interior atrium at +700 meters.

The podium is a 60-meter, 11-story building with 68,000 sm of above ground space. This includes 47,600 sm of retail and a 18,750 sm of conference facilitie comprised of a 2000-seat ballroom and 100 secondary meeting rooms.

Additionally, the project has six full-basement floors with additional retail, parking, loading docks, and mechanical plant spaces for a total below-ground area of around 109,000 sm.

PERFORMANCE

In supertall buildings, wind forces and acceleration is heavily influenced by the building's form. Therefore, it is critical for the performance of the building that the form is developed with wind engineering in mind.

Compared to a tapering smooth tower, the Biophilic Tower's design maintains a simple extruded profile with strategic openings that permit air to flow through the building. The shape helps reduce the wind sail effect and allows the building to perform very similarly to a tapering tower.

The building is shaped to take advantage of the natural light available, which lowers energy consumption and costs. By carving the atrium spaces into the massing of the building, natural light can enter beyond the perimeter envelope and penetrate the floor plates.

Reducing energy consumption while maximizing visual comfort is important for all high-performing buildings.

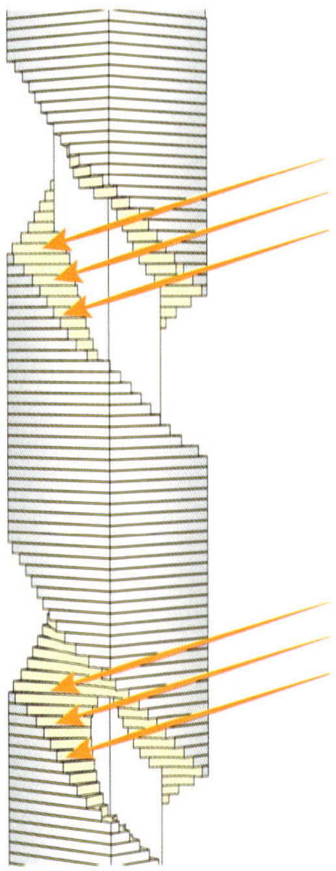

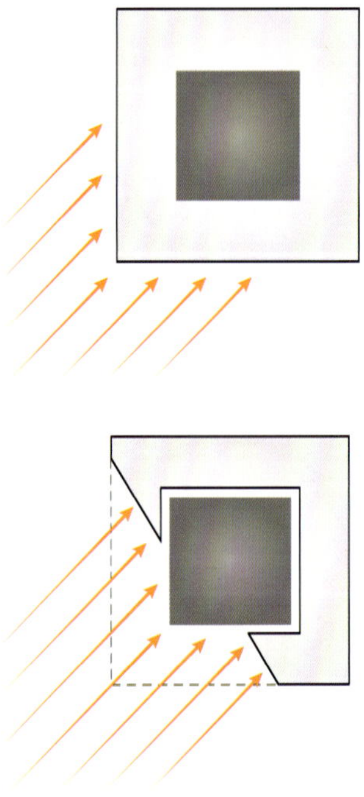

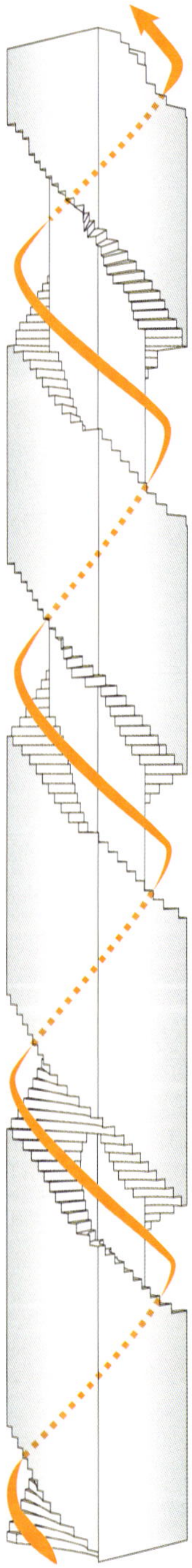

The garden is a uniquely, and naturally, ventilated space that is a vertical representation of traditional Suzhou gardens. Each function in the building has views of the atrium, which creates communal spaces that tenants can share, increasing user interactions.

The hotel floors feature an interior atrium in the center of the floor, creating bridges with unique viewing opportunities of both the outside and the inside of the building.

KLIFD TOWER

KUALA LUMPUR, MALAYSIA, 2010

380M

The conceptual centerpiece tower for the Kuala Lumpur International Financial District (KLIFD) was designed to be the new iconic symbol of Kuala Lumpur. Covering over 75 acres of downtown Kuala Lumpur, KLIFD has over 23-million square feet of accommodation, consisting of Class-A office towers, high-end residential towers, serviced apartments, a business school, a five-star boutique hotel, prominent retail featuring high-end boutiques, museum, athletic facilities, and a transit hub.

KLIFD Tower provides exceptional access and roadway networks, first-class architecture, and a comprehensive open space plan that unifies the site. The layout of the site creates an organic pattern that is uniquely Malaysian yet retains an order and hierarchy suitable for a business and retail environment.

KLIFD Tower is shaped by the physical and environmental systems present on the site, its plan is oriented to minimize the impact of the strong lower sun radiation. Its dynamic, folded form serves dual purposes: the downward slope of the glass minimizes solar heat gain and glare while permitting daylight and the upper fold faces toward the sun to create energy through building integrated photovoltaics (BIPV).

The cultural context has also impacted the form of the tower. Toward the north west, a park and views to Petronas and Kuala Lumpur Towers have informed the massing. An incision on the north west wall allows directed and protected views, as do the outdoor spaces that face the park and the surrounding important architecture. As a response to the adjacent park, the west side of the tower has landscaping that flows through the tower from the lobby level to the club/observation level at the top.

The form maximizes the conditions of the site. It is vernacular through its relationship to place and time and yet, futuristic as it looks to utilizing the highest-end materials, technologies and minimizing its resources requirements.

+ SITE
+ PROGRAM
+ PERFORMANCE
+ OBSERVATION
+ RESEARCH + DEVELOPMENT

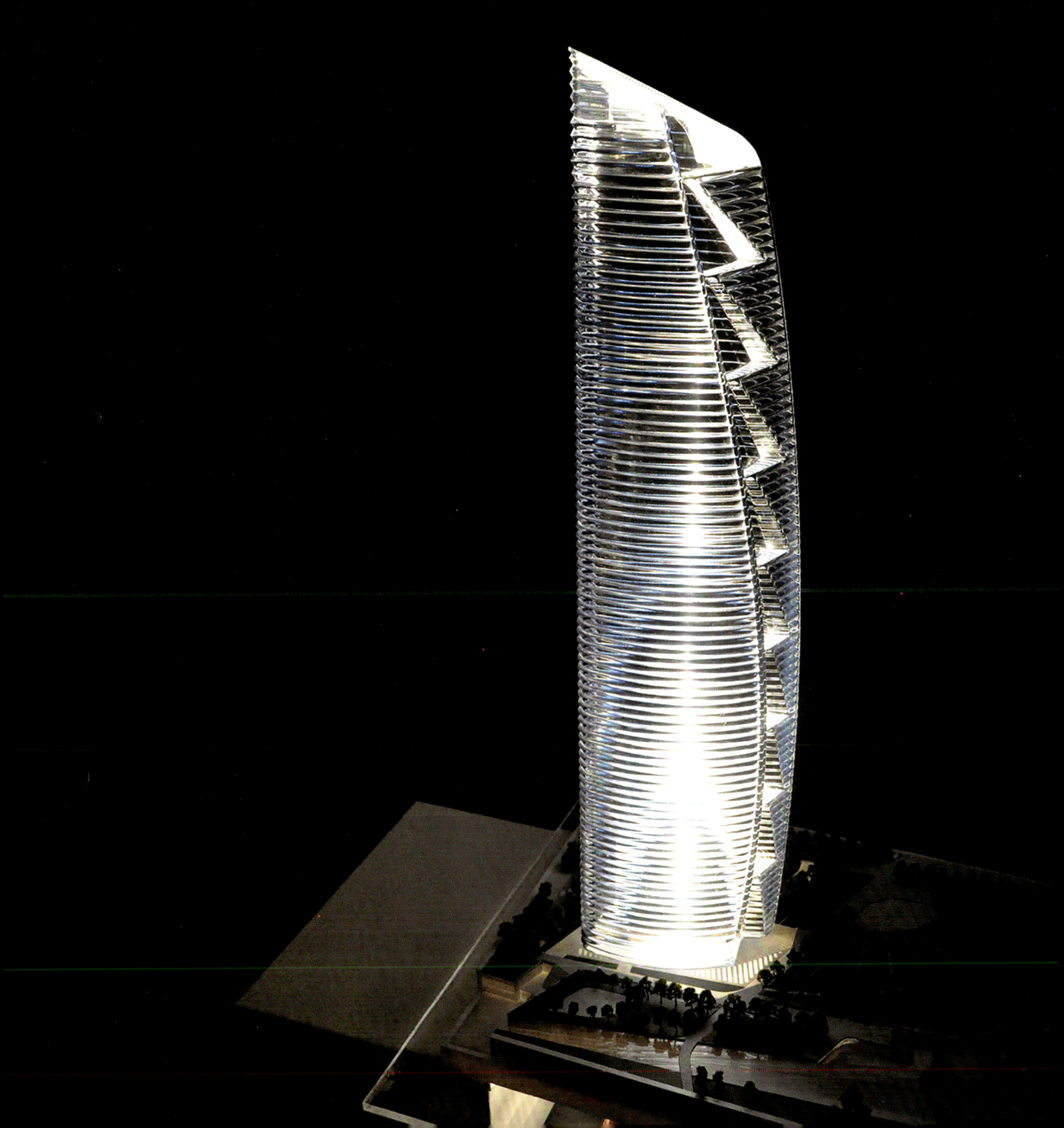

SITE

The signature tower will anchor the district in three significant ways. First, it serves as the primary physical marker of the district on a city scale and will become an important addition to the Kuala Lumpur skyline, both through its height and its high level of architectural design. Second, as a result of the tower's siting, it is framed dramatically by flanking buildings, creating a powerful and elegant composition for users of the site and passengers of vehicles arriving from the MEX and MRR2. Third, the tower will terminate the major pedestrian access to KLIFD from the Bukit Bintang area.

The tower will be a dramatic backstop for KLIFD at both the pedestrian and city scale. The site has several opportunities to share a variety of spaces, materials, and textures. Automobile circulation is in the front of the building, with the least possible impact on the site. Access to parking is provided from the central Palm Court in a simple double-helix ramp configuration.

SITE PLAN

It was important that pedestrian circulation dominated the site, providing safe, convenient, and comfortable connections to all adjacent parcels and throughout the signature tower site. At grade, the tower connects directly to a ravine through the mall concourse, stores, and restaurants, enhancing the site user's movement between the tower and the ravine.

A signature landscaping element is the raised light-wells ground plane. These lights provide illumination for the below-ground retail spaces, and their soft, hill-like appearance doubles as seating for performances in the adjacent stage. Office workers, picnickers, and theater-goers alike can use these unique mounds to relax, watch a play, or listen to a concert.

CIRCULATION PLAN

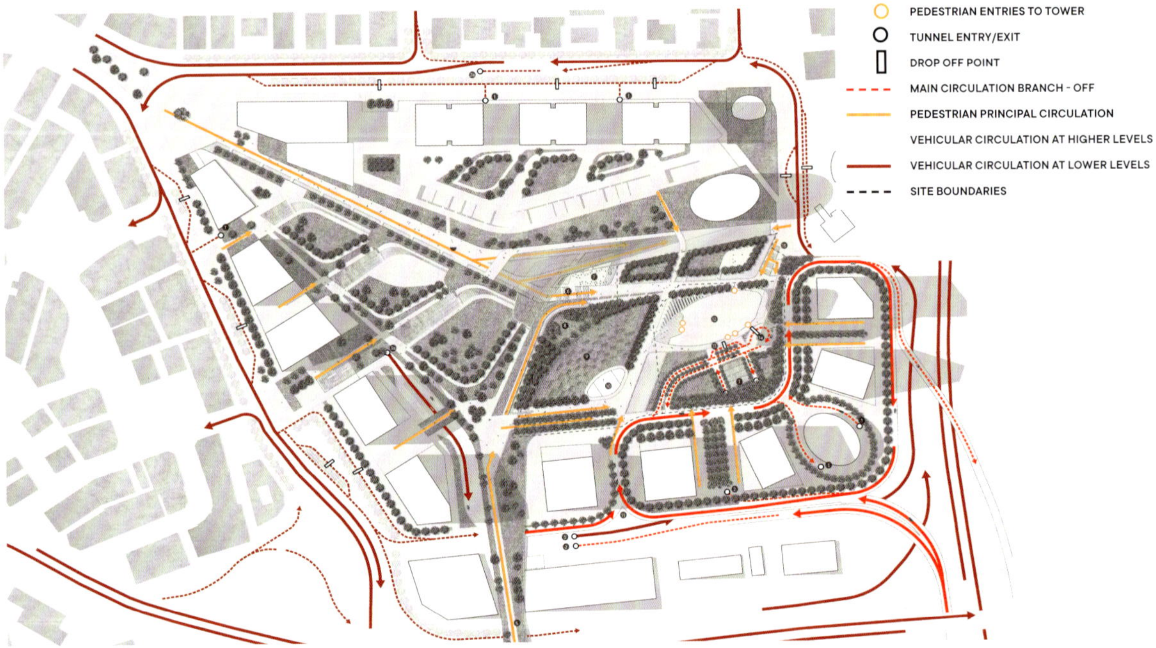

PROGRAM

Visitors and employees enter a spacious, naturally-lit, triple-height lobby through the drop-off area at the south, from the park through the west entrance, or from the mall levels by elevator, escalator, or stairs. The lobby features informal meeting spaces grounded by a coffee bar.

The lobby features a visually compelling media wall that displays dashboard-style information about the building's environmental performance, including daily and cumulative CO2 emissions, and building energy and water consumption. The board also highlights energy savings against an established baseline that results from the high performance of the building and the conservation measures employed.

The media wall also includes useful information such as train and bus schedules and general information such as directions or environmental information of interest.

Entering through the security gates from the lobby or the office reception areas at the lower levels, tenants and visitors are assigned an elevator via a destination dispatch system, with double-decker express elevators on the outside and double-deck local elevators toward the center of the core.

A RFID system reduces congestion at the entry points to the office levels. Executives with private offices automatically register on the building roster, triggering the BMS to adjust the temperature controller in their office to the user's preferred setting, from its default energy saving temperature setting.

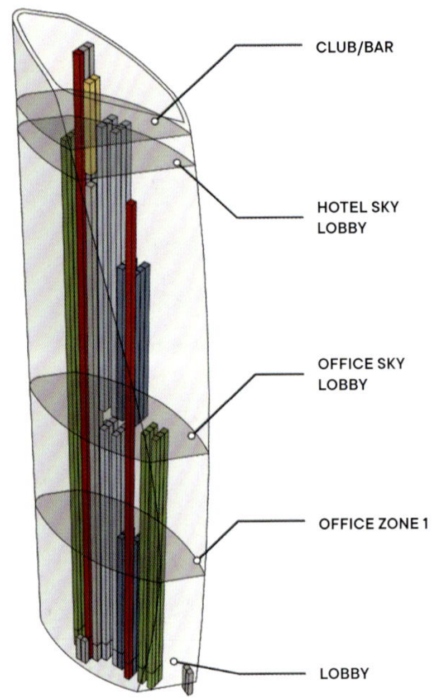

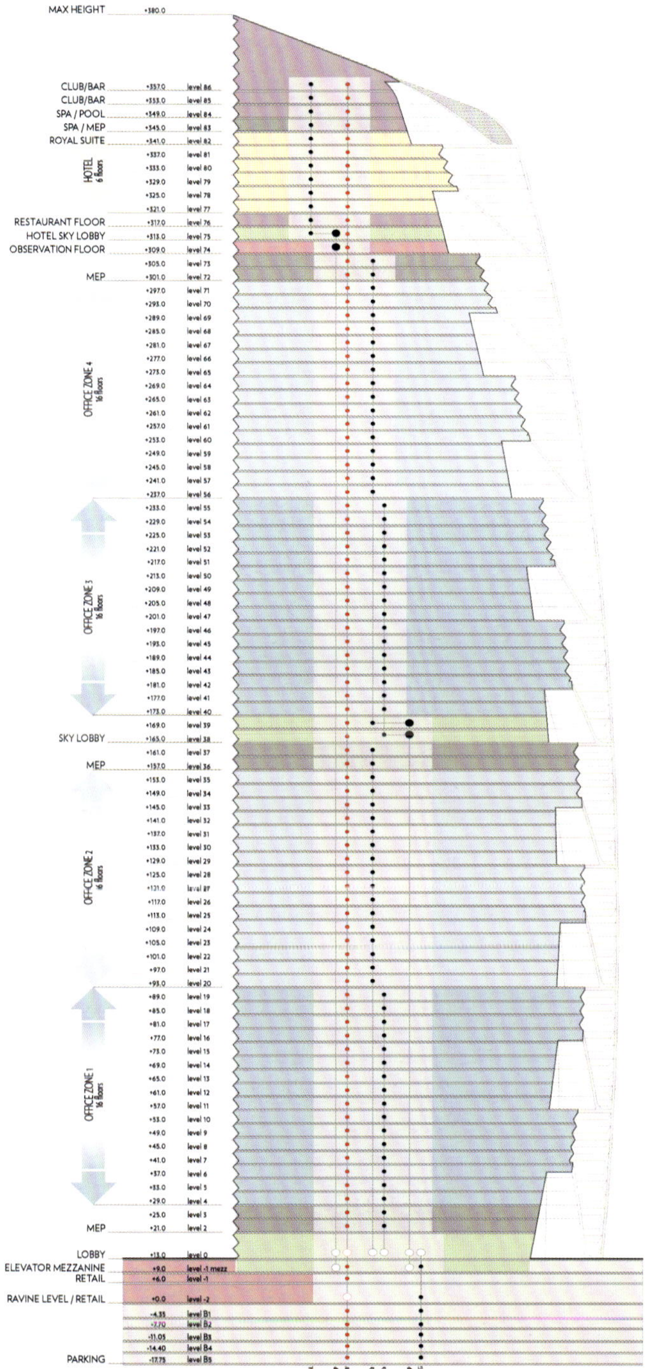

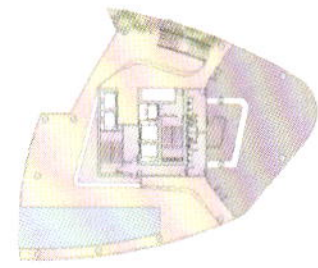

CLUB/BAR

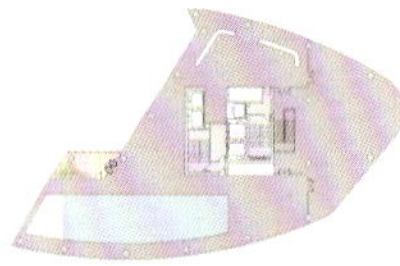

SPA/INDOOR POOL

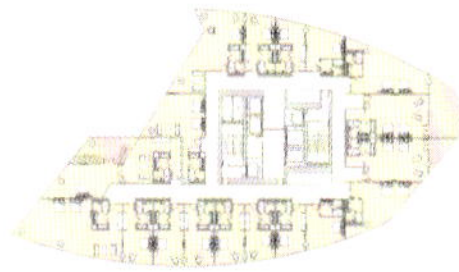

TYPICAL HOTEL

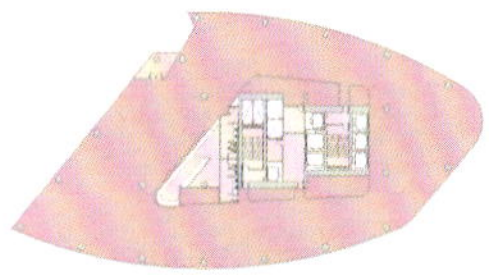

OBSERVATION

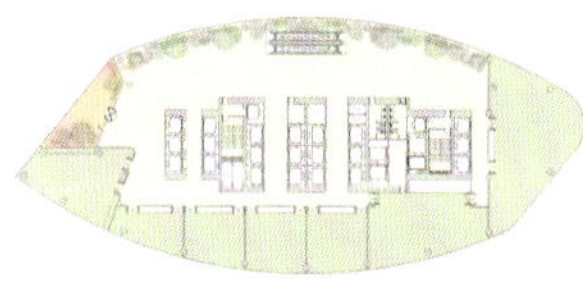

OFFICE SKY LOBBY

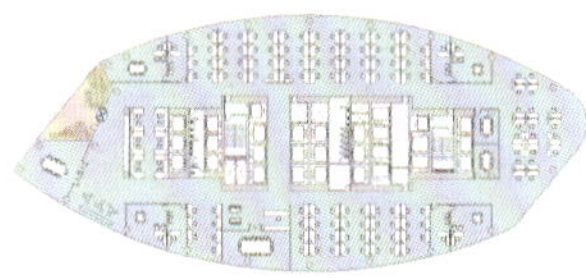

OFFICE ZONE 1

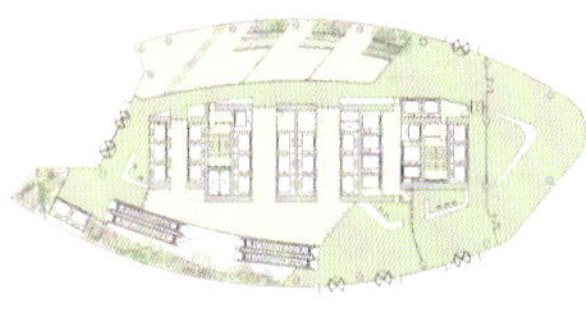

GROUND FLOOR LOBBY

PERFORMANCE

Several atria and sky gardens occur at various places in the building. Each space is landscaped with native plantings that create a cooler microclimate through transpiration, producing an ecosystem where the vegetation is a functional part of the building rather than just a landscape feature.

The gardens harvest rainwater that is stored in tanks on the mechanical floors and will be used for landscape irrigation and other non-potable water applications.

A roof-top club on Level 85 includes a bar and an infinity pool within a lush green indoor landscape that produces a dynamic shaded retreat that responds to the natural ventilation and sunlight patterns that permeate the roof environment.

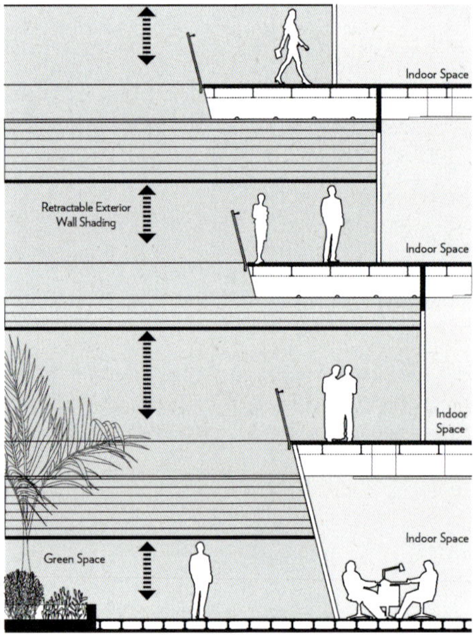

OBSERVATION

A split-level bar is located on Levels 85–86, on the east side of the tower. During the day, it acts as a panoramic dining and observation area. At night it transforms into an exclusive nightclub for members and hotel guests, providing one of the most unique amenity experience in Kuala Lumpur. The club includes an indoor, landscaped infinity pool.

The natural modulation of microclimate by vegetation within the space provides a unique atmosphere and experience for people to dine, meet, or relax. Native plants, irrigated using recycled water or treated graywater from the hotel floors, provides a sense of connection with the natural environment that serves to enhance the well-being of the people using the space. Tenants will feel comfortable bringing guests, as the views will be a key attractant and revenue generator for the building operator.

Floor plates for the tower were designed to consider views and maximize flexibility. The office floor plates have raised access floors for cabling, so the layouts can accommodate partitioned cellular offices or open office seating. Shallow floor plates maximize natural daylighting and provide views of the city and the tower's green space.

The north and south facades respond to the environmental conditions through a unitized self-shading design. The vision glass slopes inwards at an angle of 15 degrees. This angle was selected for its high solar performance while not requiring specialist, expensive glazing protection treatment. BIPV panels form spandrel panels angled optimally at 30 degrees the north and at 40 degrees on the south.

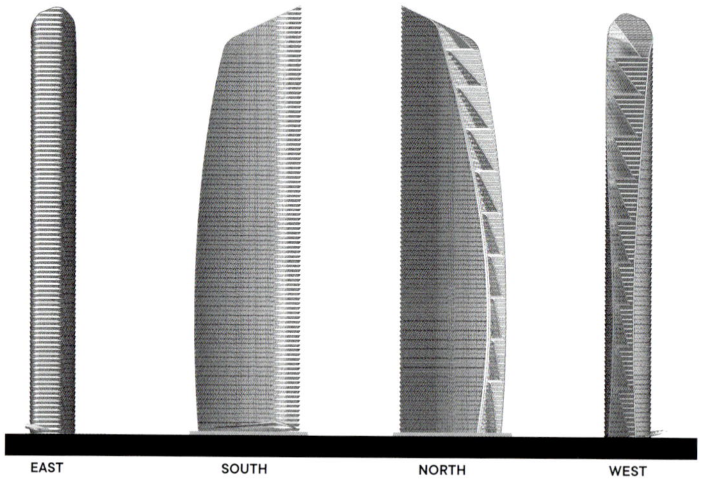

As the facade curves toward the east, the slope of the vision glass transitions from 15 to 30 degrees to manage the increased solar exposure on the surface. Concurrently, the slope of the PV becomes shallower, although the power generation potential remains largely the same due to increased surface area.

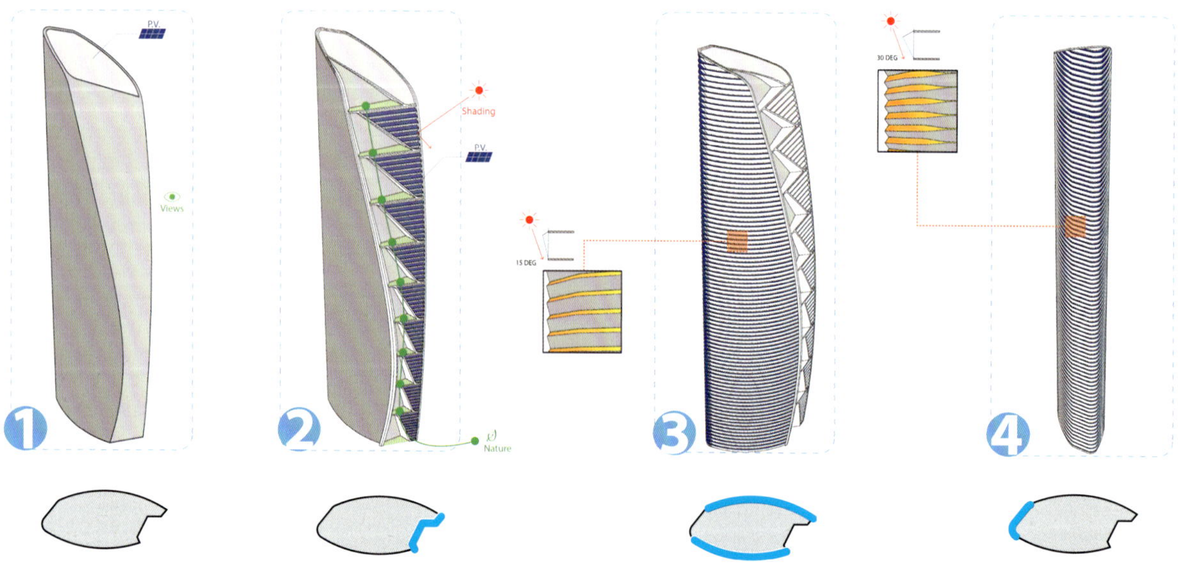

Given the specifics of the site, the west facade serves multiple purposes. It serves as the primary means of minimizing solar heat gain so to meet these requirements the walls are designed in three different ways. The first type is a recess wall that protects the interior spaces with a retractable shading system. The second type effects the outermost portion of the wall with a folding, inward-sloping vision glass and outward-sloping PVs. The third type of exterior wall is oriented directly north and downward. The west facade also has view-oriented balconies with outdoor spaces that feature magnificent views of the Kuala Lumpur skyline.

The roof is designed as a multi-functional envelope that encourages the wind to create a naturally ventilated semi-conditioned space. Louvers operated by the BMS are integrated with semi-transparent film photovoltaics to provide shade and rain protection when in the closed position. These louvers simultaneously allow ventilation and solar-energy harvesting while providing shade. Rather than a shingled roof, the louvers have clear glass vertical glazing elements that let indirect natural lighting into the space, creating a well-lit environment that significantly reduces heat gain and glare.

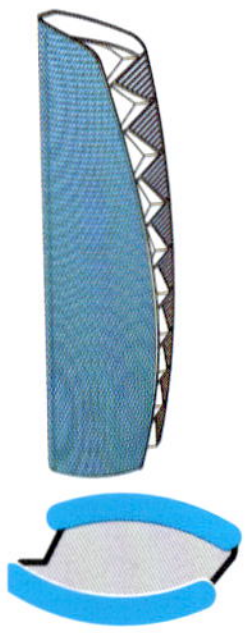

NORTH AND SOUTH FACADE

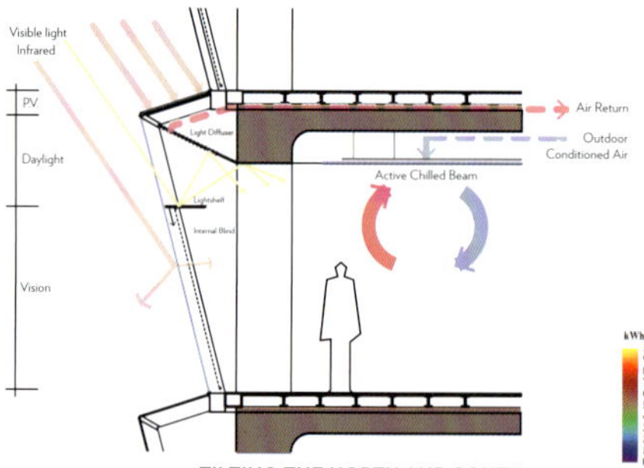

TILTING THE NORTH AND SOUTH WALLS BY 15° REDUCES THE AMOUNT OF INCIDENT SOLAR RADIATION BY 35 PERCENT.

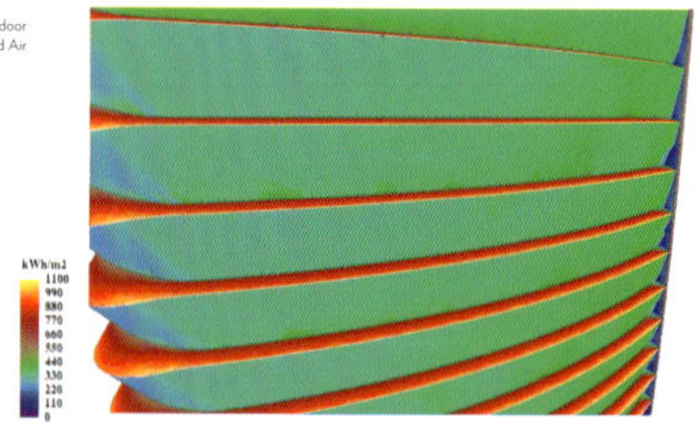

35 PERCENT LESS RADIATION ON THE GLAZING IN COMPARISON TO TYPICAL CURTAIN WALL.

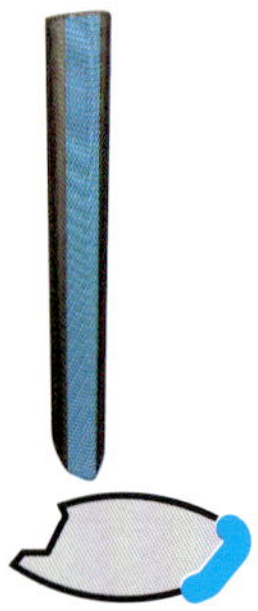

EAST FACADE

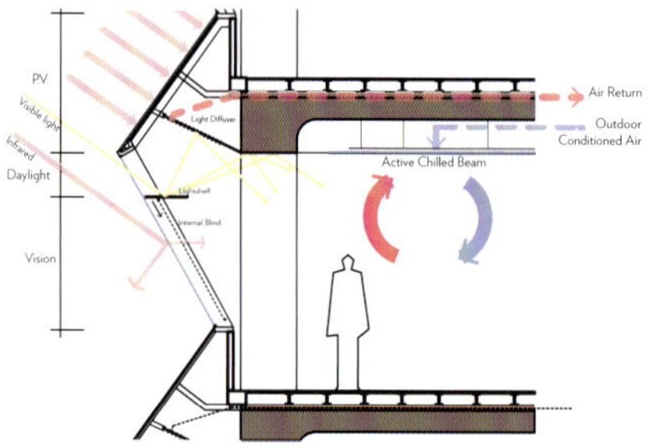

TILTING THE EAST WALL BY 30° REDUCES THE AMOUNT OF INCIDENT SOLAR RADIATION BY 58 PERCENT.

58 PERCENT LESS RADIATION ON THE GLAZING IN COMPARISON TO TYPICAL CURTAIN WALL.

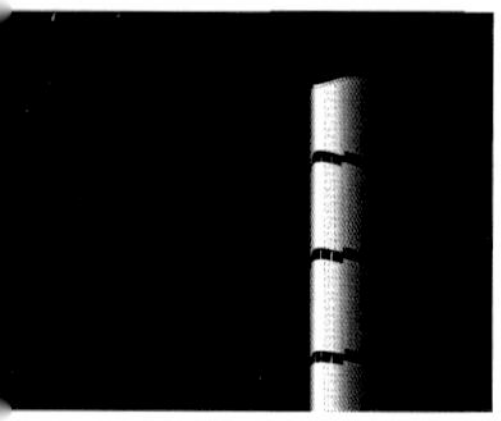

DOHA TOWER

DOHA, QATAR, 2010

470M

Flanked by two supertall developments in Doha, Qatar, the elegant 470-meter tower design features a network of interior urban oases in the form of sky terraces and naturally illuminated gardens. Horizontal and vertical sky gardens are cut into the tower's curving form, creating a series of playful and highly functional outdoor spaces.

The mixed-use tower includes office, residential, and hotel functions and each floor has access to the landscaped terraces and gardens. An atrium at the hotel level receives light filtered through a textured sky garden roof and vertical slots carved out of the exterior skin. An atrium at the residential level receives morning and afternoon light through the exterior sky gardens.

The tower is highly sustainable. Its facade design minimizes energy loss and heat gain, while photovoltaic cells, integrated wind turbines, and solar hot water panels reduce energy consumption. The building is also oriented for maximum views of the Persian Gulf and the adjacent corniche park.

+ PROGRAM
+ PERFORMANCE
+ RESEARCH + DEVELOPMENT

PROGRAM

At the tower's base, three lobbies connect pedestrian and vehicular circulation with the four programmatic zones.

As the building ascends, the four programmatic zones include 35 levels of office space, with plans for single or double tenancy that are serviced by two zones of dedicated elevators; 35 levels of residential space, which is a mixture of studios, one bedroom, two bedroom, three bedroom, and four bedroom units; seven levels of service apartments include studio, one-bedroom, two-bedroom, and four-bedroom unit options; and eight floors for a boutique hotel near the tower's top that is accessible through a sky lobby.

Special features include double height observation rooms at the northeast corner, duplex floors with surrounding gardens, and sky gardens for private and communal use. The sky lobby includes restaurants and retail amenities. The hotel amenities, located near the top of the building, are part of their own dedicated multi-story atrium space with view to the roof skylight.

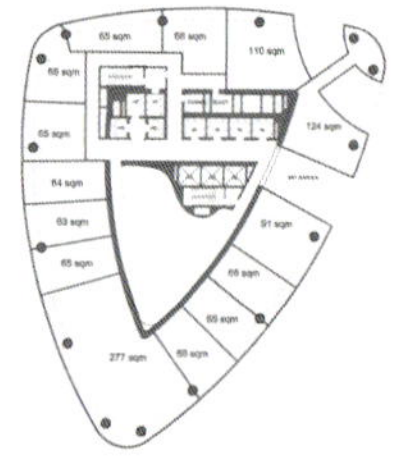

LEVEL 97-98
BOUTIQUE HOTEL

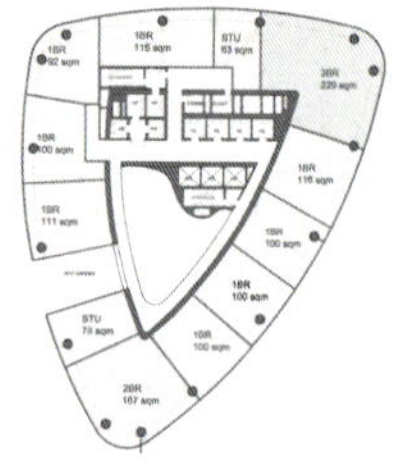

LEVEL 92-95
SERVICE APARTMENT

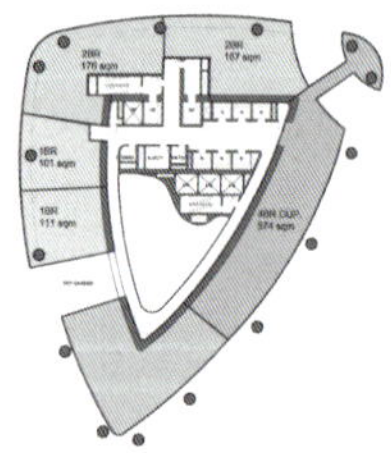

LEVEL 55
RESIDENTIAL

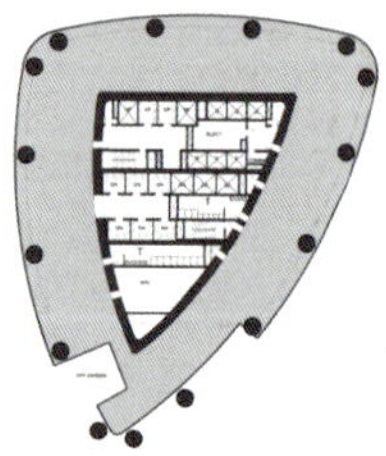

LEVEL 38
OFFICE

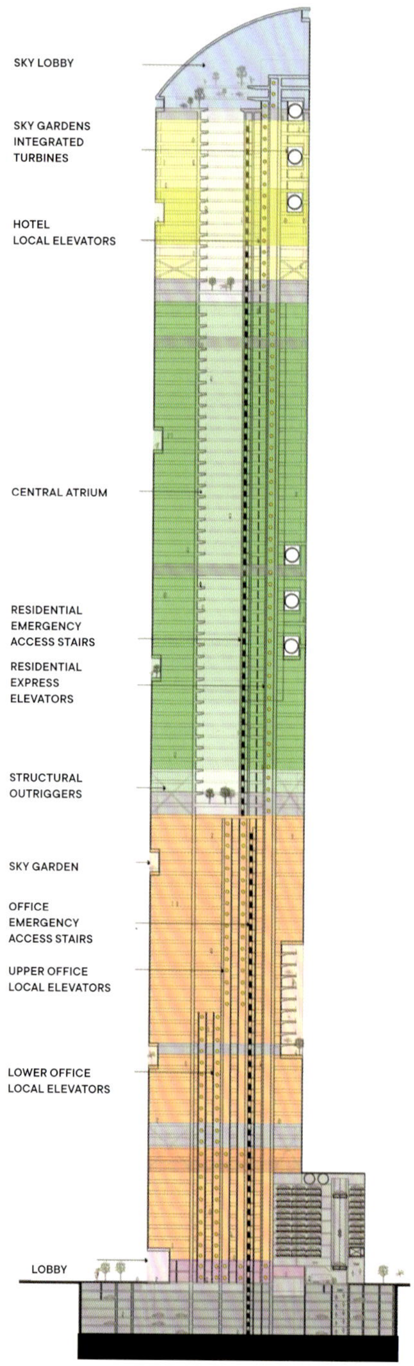

PERFORMANCE

The climate in Doha is low-latitude sub-tropical desert. In the summer it is hot and humid; in the winter, it is arid and mild. The winds can drive up to 20m/s, with a consistent wind out of the northwest during most parts of the year. The design team used these environmental constraints as opportunities to design a high-performance tower that functions in symbiosis with the natural environment.

The building takes advantage of the wind by using wind turbines to generate electrical energy with the prevailing wind currents as they increase in speed around the building. The performance of the wind turbines is increased by locating the mechanisms toward the corners of the building where wind speeds are stronger.

Gardens located throughout the building provide natural cooling through evapotranspiration. Connections to the natural environment have been shown to increase inhabitant comfort, well-being, and productivity. Plants create a calming, less stressful environment and can improve inhabitant's productivity.

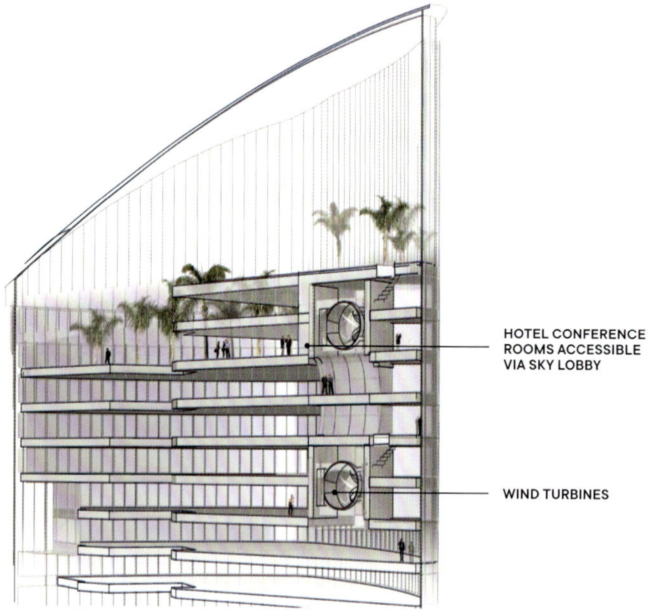

HOTEL + SKY LOBBY TERRACE CONDITION

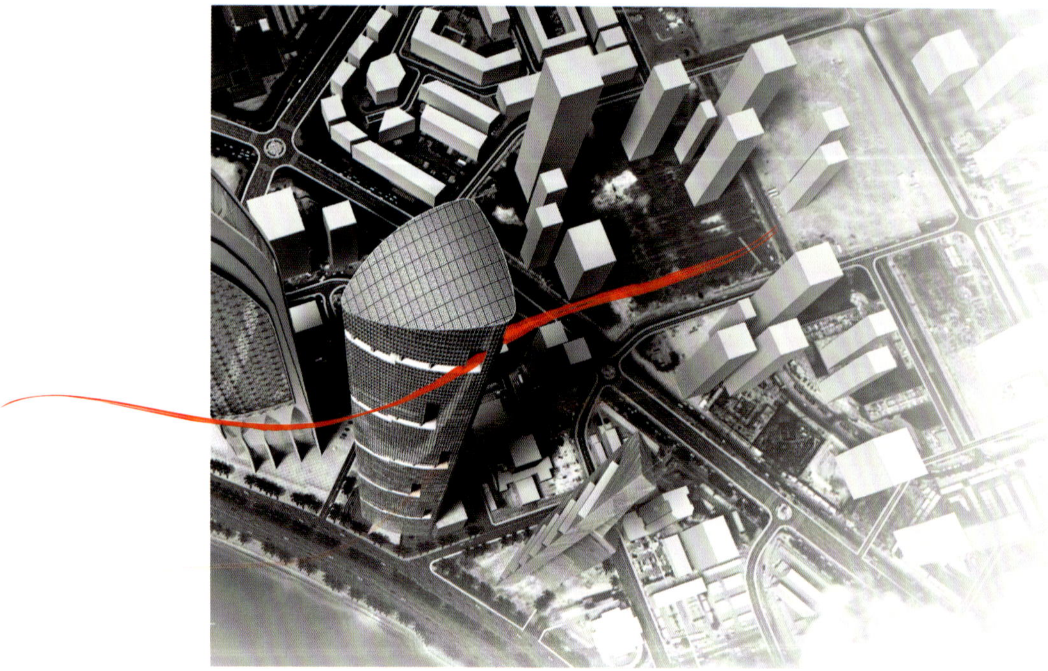

PERFORMANCE

With over 2,000 kwh/sqm/yr of solar energy available in Qatar, solar thermal collection is the most efficient means of harnessing energy that can heat water or drive a cooling/dehumidification process for ventilation air by way of desiccants or absorption cooling. To maximize the solar energy potential, the exterior wall is tilted in both the vertical and horizontal directions.

Tilting the exterior panels reduces as much solar gain as possible, while preserving the views. The tilt also allows solar panels to be installed on the solid portions that face toward the highest solar exposure. The tilt of the panels vary as they traverse around the building, their position situated to be the most efficient. The north side of the building is smooth where it is unnecessary to block solar gain.

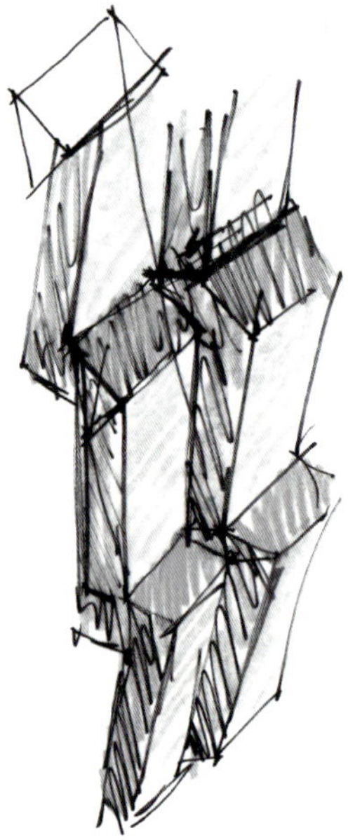

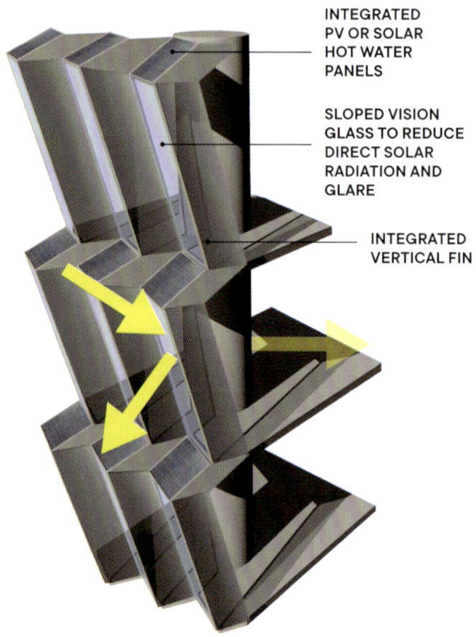

RESEARCH + DEVELOPMENT

Light is the defining element in the tower's design and was studied at length. Naturally lit atria are found throughout the tower, allowing for bright, lively interior environments.

An atrium at the hotel level receives light filtered through a textured sky garden roof and vertical slots carved out of the exterior skin. An atrium at the residential level receives morning and afternoon sunlight through gardens carved out of the exterior tower skin.

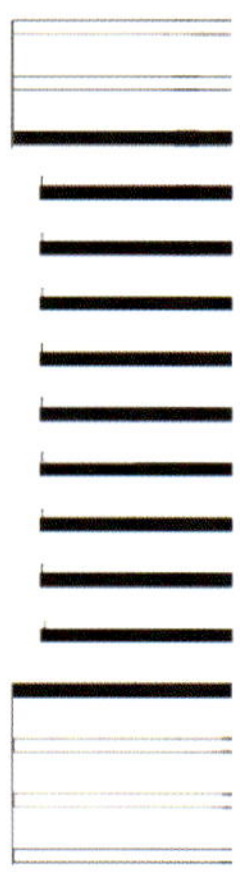

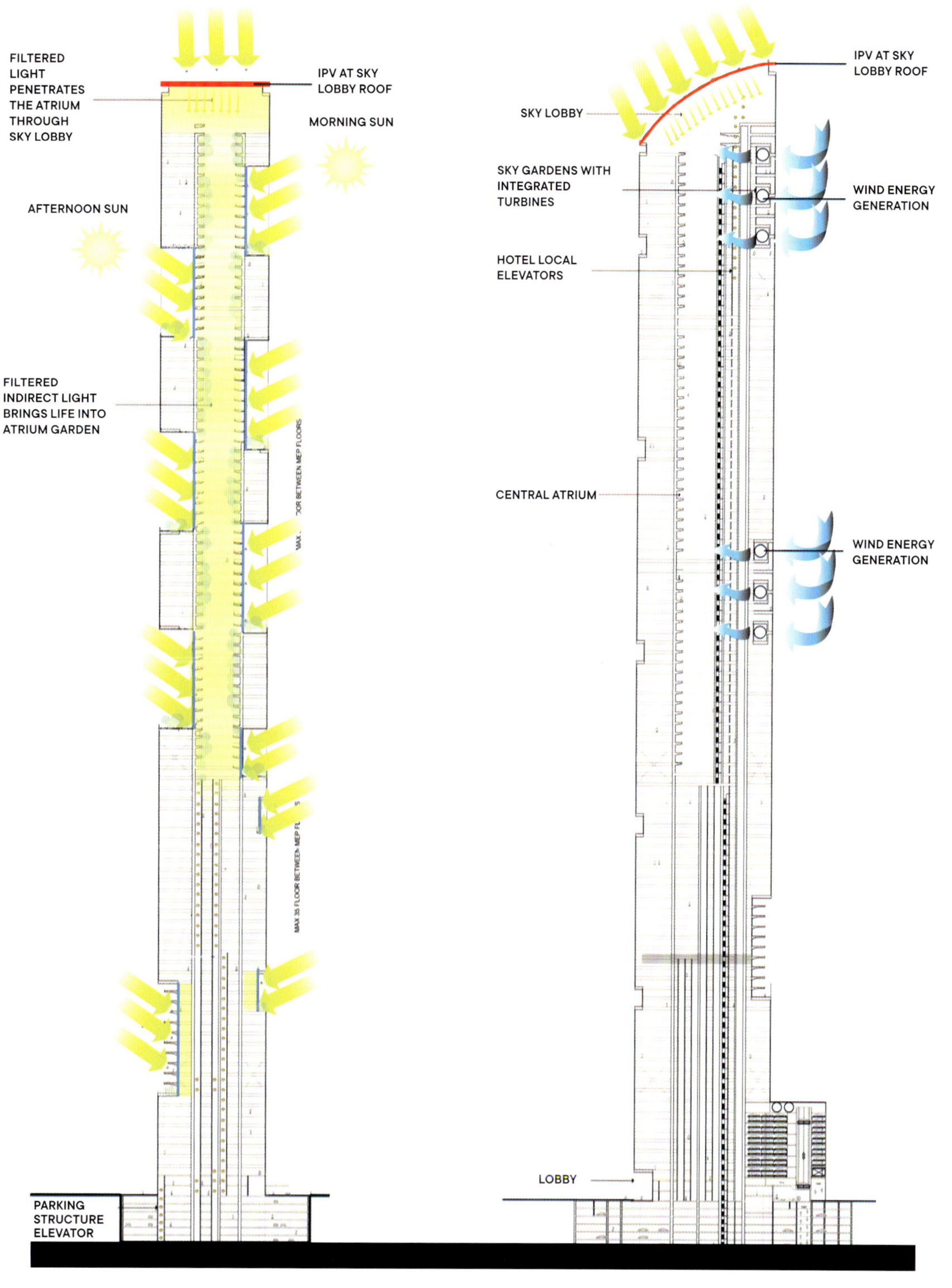

FILTERED LIGHT PENETRATES THE ATRIUM THROUGH SKY LOBBY
IPV AT SKY LOBBY ROOF
MORNING SUN
AFTERNOON SUN
FILTERED INDIRECT LIGHT BRINGS LIFE INTO ATRIUM GARDEN
PARKING STRUCTURE ELEVATOR
IPV AT SKY LOBBY ROOF
SKY LOBBY
SKY GARDENS WITH INTEGRATED TURBINES
WIND ENERGY GENERATION
HOTEL LOCAL ELEVATORS
CENTRAL ATRIUM
WIND ENERGY GENERATION
LOBBY

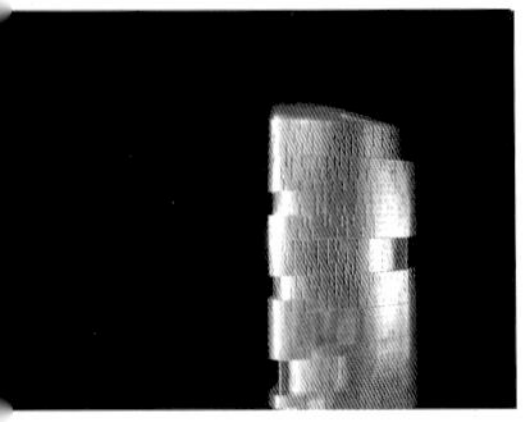

IMPERIAL TOWER

MUMBAI, INDIA, 2010

400M

At 400-meter-tall, Imperial Tower was designed to be the tallest building in Mumbai, India, as well as a prototype for the densely developed but mostly low-rise metropolis whose urban future revolves around tall residential towers. The soft curvilinear form of the elegantly slender tower is aerodynamically shaped to confuse the wind, minimizing the negative effects of wind action on the tower. Wind vortex shedding is also mitigated by the north- and south-facing sky gardens, which break up wind currents around the tower.

Imperial Tower offers the most spacious and luxurious residences in Mumbai, with the upper-story condominiums offering breathtaking views of the Arabian Sea. Sky gardens provide unprecedented access to light, views, and connections to the natural world that is unprecedented in Mumbai.

The exterior wall has a strong visual contrast with the heavy masonry cladding of the surrounding buildings. The exterior wall is highly sustainable, blocking heat gain and diffusing direct sunlight in the hot and humid climate. Sustainability is also evident in the treatment of water, one of the area's most precious resources. Water from the MEP systems is collected and treated as gray water; rainfall is also collected for re-use.

High-efficiency mechanical systems, a green-wall podium and the use of native plants in the landscaping and sky gardens adds to the project's sustainable performance. Utilizing systems to offset the urban demands and growth in Mumbai, the tower strives to be a benchmark to which all others are measured regarding sustainable building orientation, water collection, and waste management.

+ SITE
+ PROGRAM
+ SKY GARDEN
+ STRUCTURE

SITE

SITE PLAN

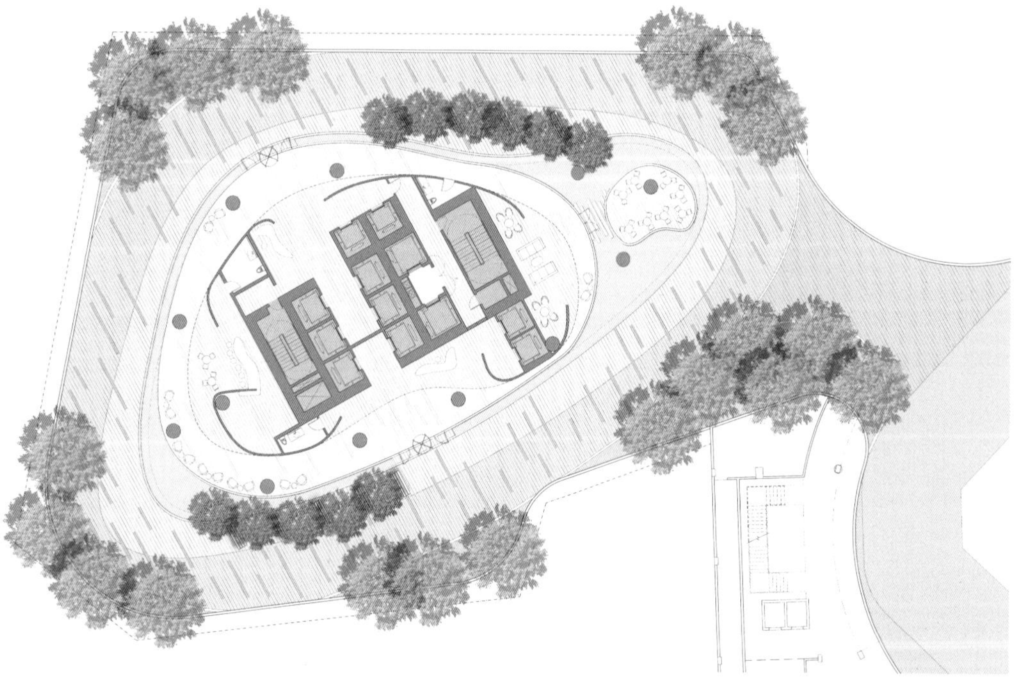

PROGRAM

At 116 stories, Imperial Tower would be India's tallest tower. Two zones of dedicated residential units have 129 units that contain three-, four-, five-, and six bedroom, single, duplex, and penthouse units. An additional 100 service apartments are located on Levels 16–35.

A double-height amenity level at the top of the podium serves the tower residents. A triple-height entry level at the top of the podium has separate entry lobbies for the service apartments and residences. Nine above-grade podium levels of parking for 600 automobiles are served by separately dedicated serviced apartment and residential parking shuttle elevators.

The residential and service apartment occupants access the parking levels by parking shuttles that take them to the lobby. The design separates each type of traffic by zone and function, so that the various tenants, visitors, employees, and service requirements are separated with private building entrance and exit points.

Elevators incorporate state-of-the-art technologies such as emergency evacuations routes, destination dispatching with integrated building security lobby turnstiles, and green power regenerative technologies. The service apartments, low-rise residential, and high-rise residential have sets of two elevators each to service their floors.

There will be two service elevators, one primarily for the serviced apartments and one servicing the balance of the tower, as well as the required fire-fighting use.

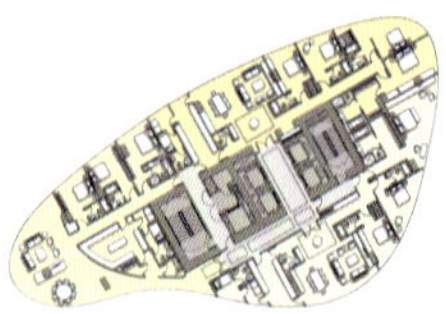

RESIDENTIAL
LOW

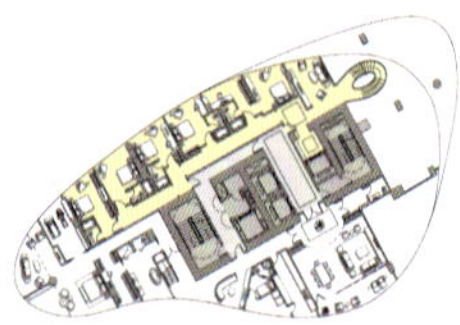

RESIDENTIAL
MID

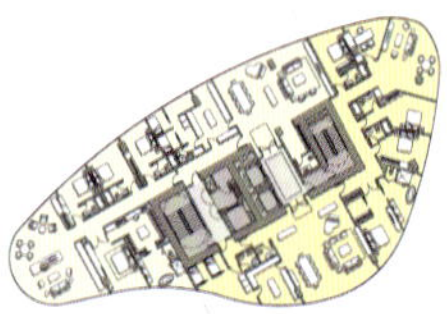

RESIDENTIAL
HIGH

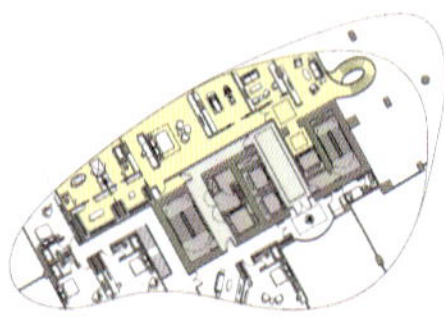

TRIPLEX
UPPER

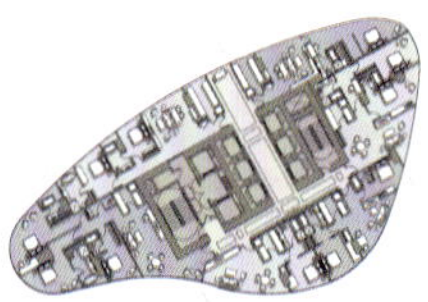

SERVICE
APARTMENT

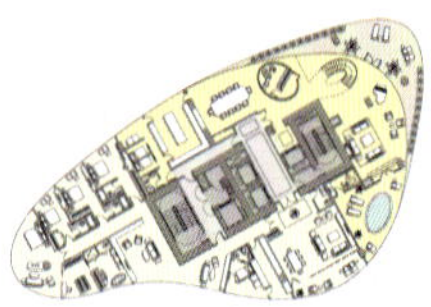

DUPLEX
LOWER

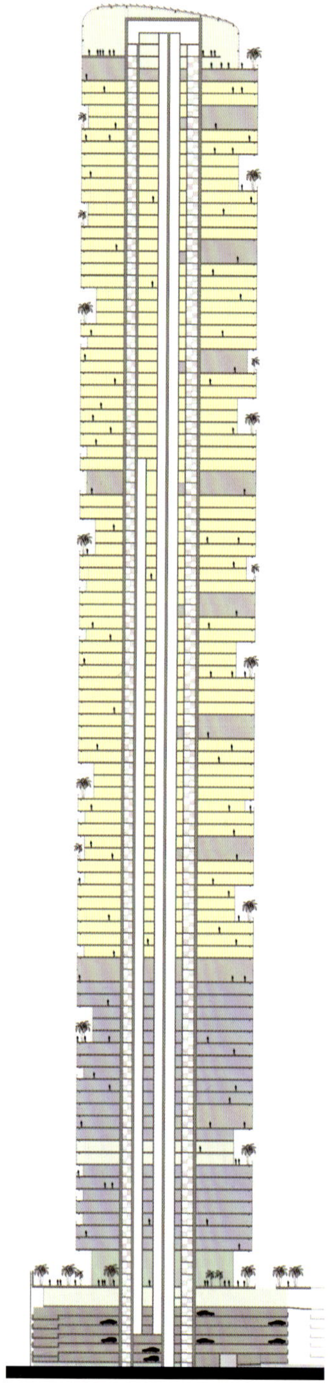

SKY GARDEN

The tower's distinctive terraces are carved out of the massing's curved-linear form. The spaces are multi-story and sized in consideration of the climate in Mumbai, which makes outdoor space usable during many parts of the year.

The incorporation of trees is important in slowing the wind and making the balconies comfortable, as well as giving the building the expression of a vertical landscape at various levels and vantage points around the tower.

At night, the soffits of the carved balconies are softly lit, further adding to the building's expression on the skyline. The amenity floors also feature generously landscaped decks above the parking podium.

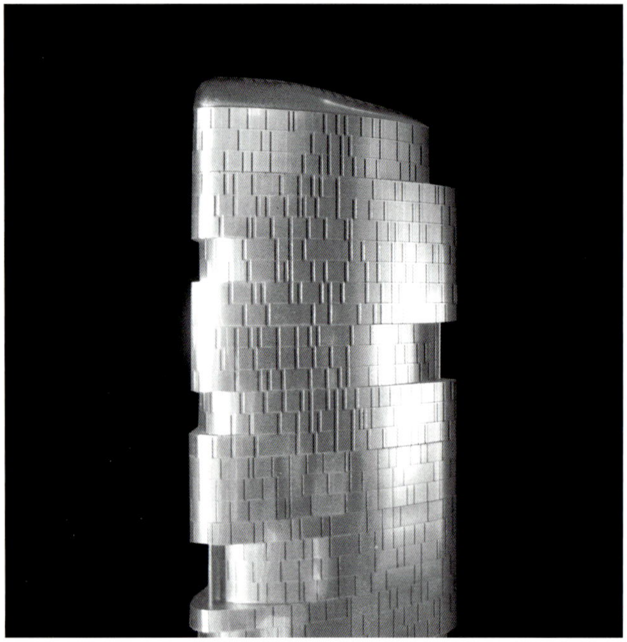

SKY GARDEN

UPPER
SKY GARDEN

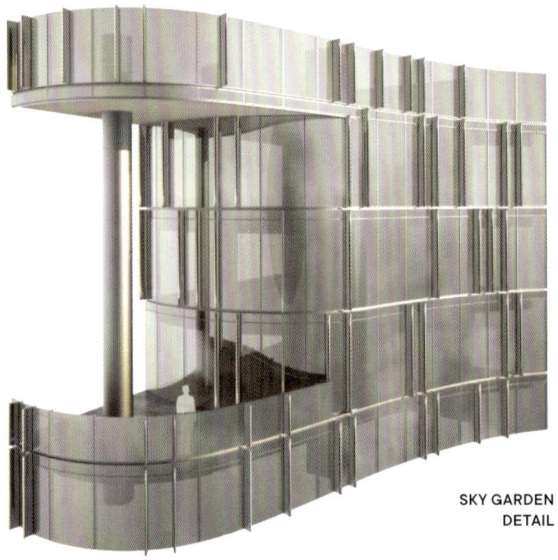

SKY GARDEN
DETAIL

MIDDLE
SKY GARDEN

TERRACE
AMENITY

LOWER
SKY GARDEN

STRUCTURE

The primary lateral system for the tower is reinforced-concrete core shear walls with link beams, which are linked to exterior columns via deep outrigger walls at the mechanical levels. The central core reduces in size as it ascends through the high-rise residential floors and the low-rise elevators drop off. The tower's lateral system was studied using wind and seismic code requirements for drift and strength.

The gravity system of the tower on the apartment floors is reinforced-concrete two-way flat plate. This structural system is the most cost-effective for apartment floors to maximize height and provide efficiency and speed in construction. To control slab deflections along the exterior wall and at the cantilever balconies, a concrete drop beam has been introduced around the entire perimeter.

Depths of reinforced-concrete framing vary depending on spans and cantilever lengths, with a beam depth range of 650–750 mm and a slab depth of 250–275 mm. The amount of post-tensioning utilized is minimized but to reduce apartment slab thicknesses, it may be possible to pursue a fully post-tensioned scheme. A reinforced-concrete raft foundation shall be cast in situ on unweathered basalt rock sub grade.

CHAPTER V. ACHIEVING MEGATALL

MULTIPLE TOWERS LINKED TOGETHER

There are many practical reasons for building to extreme heights, including maximizing density because of land costs, perceived value of occupying high spaces in buildings, and harnessing unmatchable views.

A major benefit is that supertall towers bring economic value to their city through new tourism revenue. A world's tallest building title creates global attention and publicity. The title is a valuable marketing tool for the countries, states, and cities in which they are built, and for the architects, contractors, and owners. Throughout human history there have been less than two dozen buildings that can claim this title.

Supertalls also represent a meaningful step forward as a symbol of progress and optimism for the future. If cities fail to improve their conditions, they run the risk of becoming obsolete. A supertall tower, and its surrounding district, can increase a city's chance for a productive future. However, there is a height at which buildings are no longer efficient, or usable, as a single conventional tower that is unbroken by large central atria, wind tunnels, or manipulated forms.

We understand that height is limited by material strength, flexibility, vertical transportation systems, site soil, wind and seismic conditions, economics, and human comfort. There are other physical parameters to consider. For example, to occupy spaces in excess of 600 m it is necessary to augment the space with oxygen. Gardens and plant life may be helpful but due to the thin air at these heights, supplemental means of oxygen delivery will need to be explored.

As designers, we explore what the next steps are in the evolution of mega-tall structures as the building owners strive to reach new heights, and scales. The buildings in this chapter explore the idea of whether the mega-tall tower becomes the "mega building"—multiple towers linked together, forming a symbiotic relationship with one another.

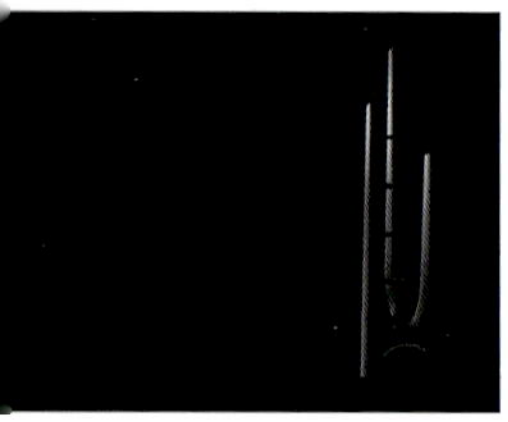

1 DUBAI ATRIUM CITY

DUBAI, UAE, 2008

1000+M

One Dubai combines simple geometric principles and new and emerging technologies with the highest environmental and performance standards to create three of the world's tallest buildings. The conjoined towers rise above a canal, forming an oasis at the center of its tripodal base.

Between the towers an atrium-like space transforms into one of the world's most unique event and performance spaces. On special occasions, the space becomes a spectacular venue with a floating stage surrounded by barges that double as seating banks.

A state-of-the-art sound and light show will feature projected holograms in the air and on the building's mosaic-like glass and aluminum skin.

At night, a virtual fourth tower, in the form of a colossal beam of light, pierces the atrium, creating a shining beacon.

Above, a series of three-story sky bridges connect the towers as they taper upward. The sky bridges have stunning views of the Gulf and Dubai and stabilize the towers structurally and facilitate interfloor circulation.

+ CONTEXT
+ SITE
+ PROGRAM
+ PODIUM
+ SKY BRIDGE
+ EXPERIENCE
+ PERFORMANCE
+ RESEARCH + DEVELOPMENT
+ STRUCTURE

CONTEXT

The client's original vision was a two-tower complex that framed views of the adjacent Burj Khalifa, the current world's tallest building, designed by AS+GG's Adrian Smith, while Design Partner at Skidmore, Owings & Merrill. AS+GG developed a scheme with three towers joined near the base with a saddle-like structure and above by a series of sky bridges. The t-shaped site is intersected with waterway canals, creating an ideal condition for a three tower base, situating one leg on each corner. The final design was not what the client had envisioned but the scheme won the design competition against four other top firms.

SITE

One Dubai is situated at the center of AS+GG's Jumeirah Gardens Master Plan, adjacent to Sheikh Zayed Road and near several public transportation options. The tower connects to the planned central park and provides an impressive focal point for the new district.

The is site will also be accessible by boat, directly from the canal. The canal is a vital link to the entire development, acting as the central organizing open space element for the district, and was designed as an active, continuous system of parks, plazas, and pathways.

At the canal's edge, a promenade carries pedestrian and bicycle traffic with meandering paths at the north and south of the development through a series of experiential elements. The district is marked by shaded arcades, landscaped parkways, and bike lanes to encourage pedestrian interaction with the environment.

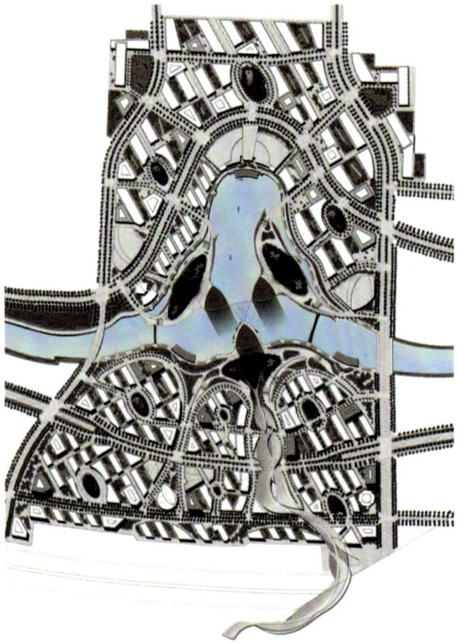

SITE PLAN

LAND USE PLAN

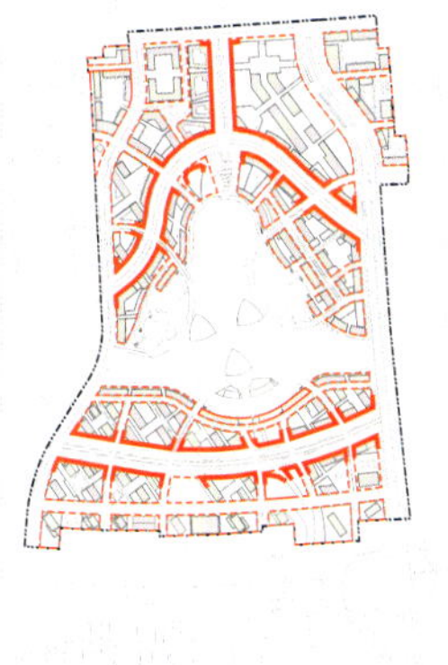

LOT LINE RELATIONSHIP

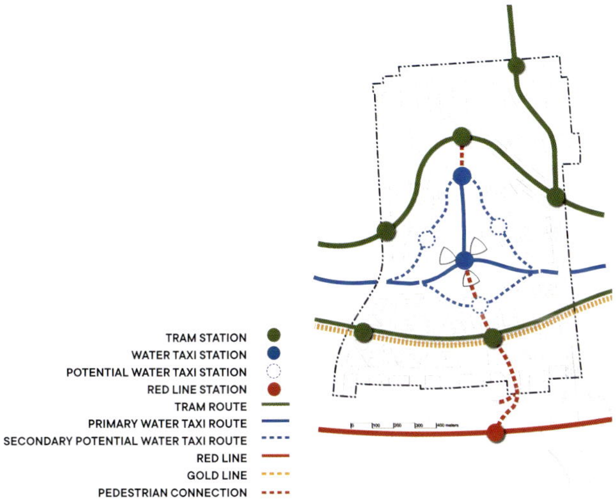

TRANSIT SYSTEMS

GROUND USE

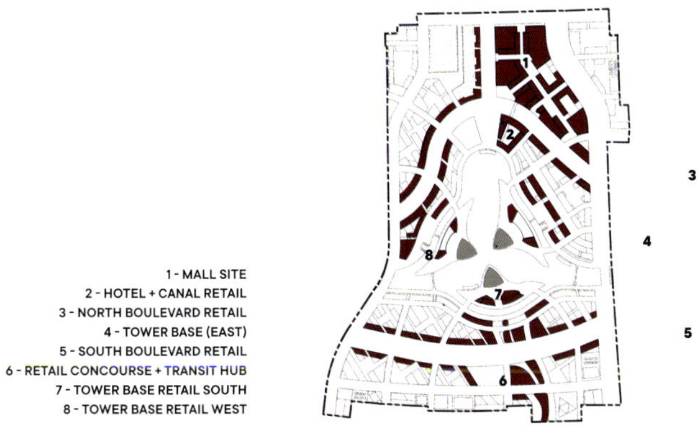

RETAIL STRATEGY

OPEN SPACE STRATEGY

PROGRAM

The program is tied to the form with 1.3 million sm of above-grade space with an additional 600,000 sm of parking and mechanical areas below grade. The proposed program mix, not including the mechanical and parking floors, is 28 percent Office, 50 percent residential, 14 percent Hotel, and 8 percent Amenity.

The towers were designed to offer some of the most spectacular views in the world. Residential corner units culminate with mini-observatories that have 180-degree views of the natural and architectural wonders of the city, including the Burj Khalifa. Balconies are protected by 1 Dubai's outer wall wrap around the corner units on either side, have excellent access to views.

The saddle floors form the podium of the building with 10 floors. One of the three saddle connectors contain the hotel amenities, ballroom, and spa. The other two are programed with office space and a potential university. The top floor of the saddle is a multi-story space that has opportunities for a solarium and indoor landscape.

Other facilities and amenities include two trading floors with 8.4-meter floor-to-ceiling heights; ballrooms; conference facilities; and a spa with full-size basketball courts, volleyball courts, and an Olympic-sized swimming pool. Tower 1 will also feature one of the world's highest exclusive club/observation halls.

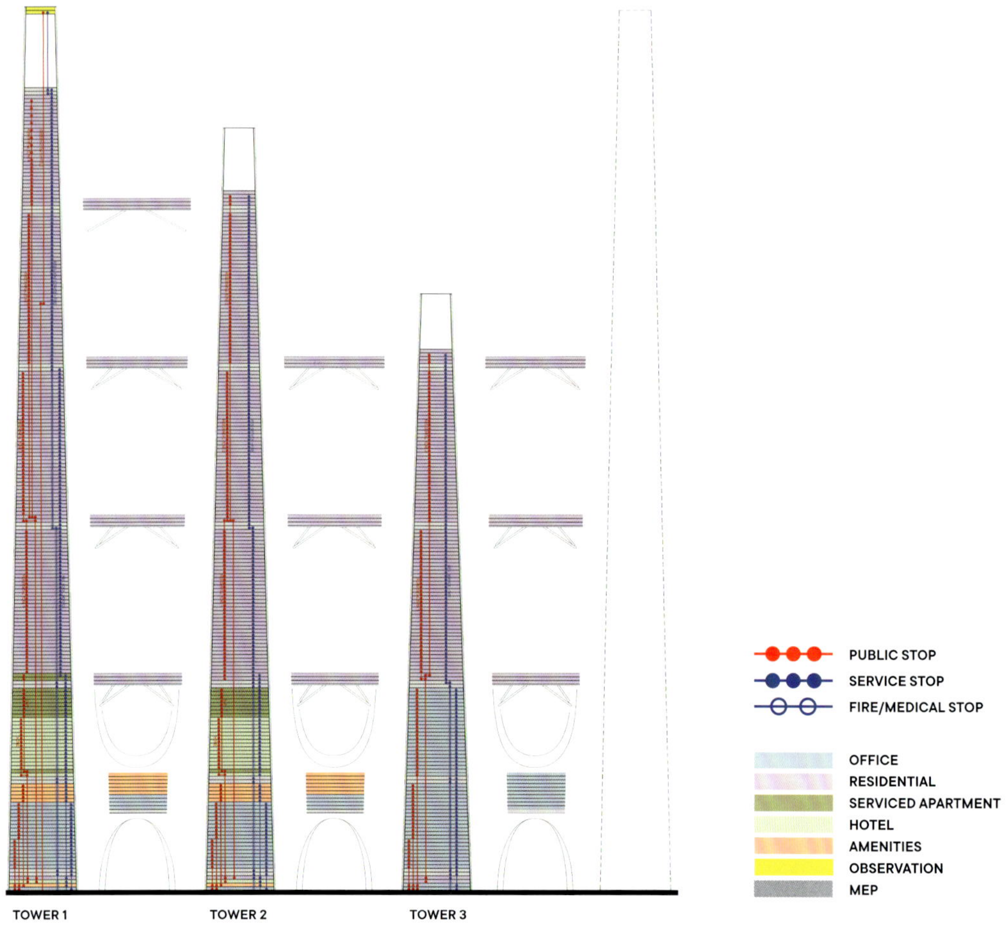

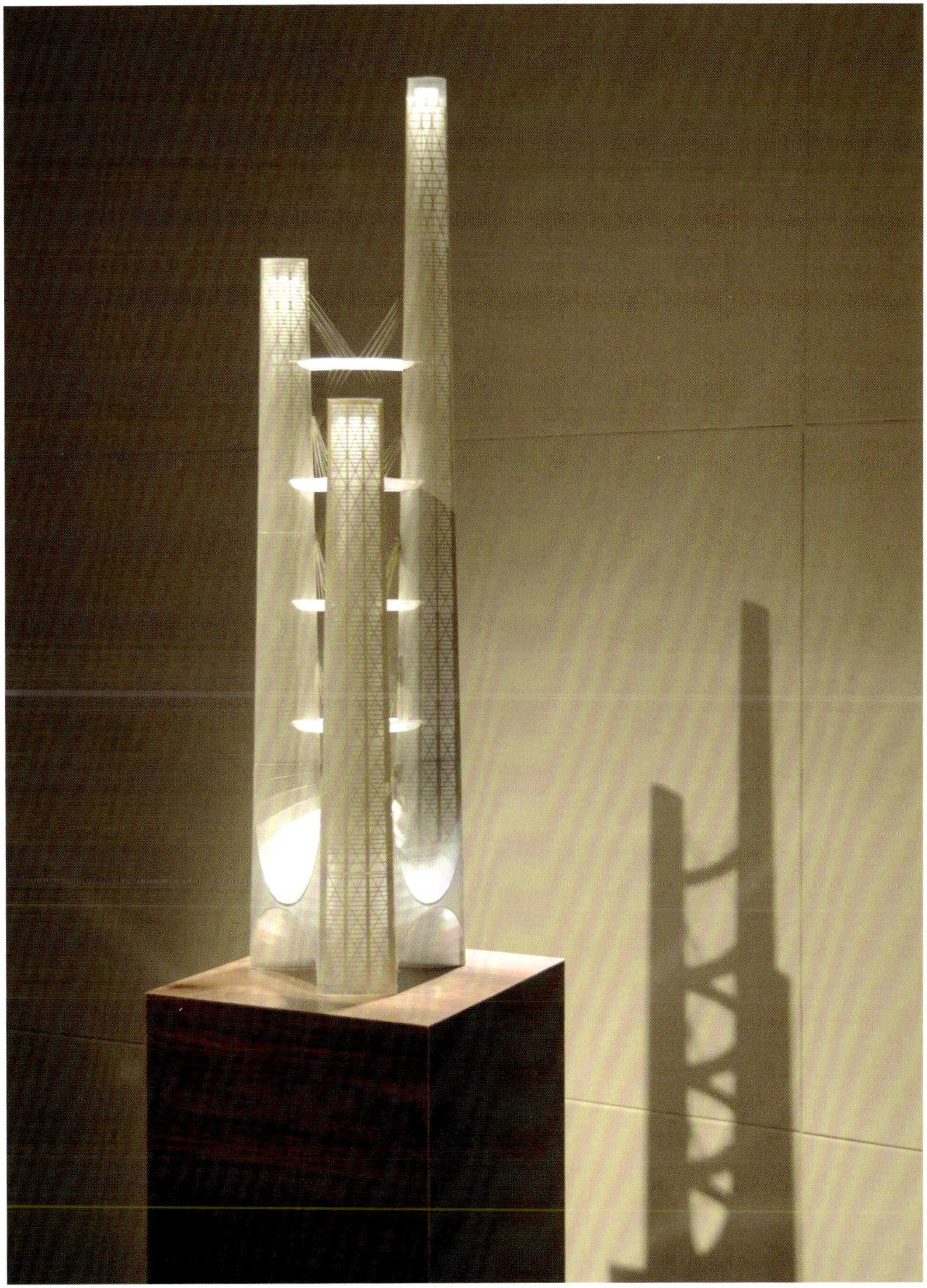

PROGRAM

The tallest tower, T1, has 229 stories and tops out at 1,000 m.

T1 has a program of office (at the base), hotel, and residential. The above grade GCA is 501,162 sm and includes:

- Office (177,856 sm): Level 3–12, 14–20, 26–27, 29–59
- Hotel, Six-Star (84,934 sm): Level 61–94
- Residential (175,973 sm): Levels 97–129, 131–164, 166–195, and 197–226 (duplexed)
- MEP: Levels B1, 13, 28, 60, 95, 130, 165, 196, and 227

The middle tower, T2, has 182 stories and has a height of 800 m. T2 has a similar stacking as T1, with office at the base, hotel, service apartments, and four tiers of residential units. The tower has 410,964 sm, which includes:

- Office (108,629 sm): Levels 3–12, 14–20, 26–27, and saddle Levels 20–28
- Hotel, Five-Star (92,853 sm): Level 29–59, 61–63
- Residential (168,520 sm): Levels 64–94, 96–98 (sky bridge), 99–129, 131–133 (sky bridge), 134–164, and 166–181 (duplexed)
- MEP: Levels B1, 13, 28, 60, 95, 130, 165, and 182

The shortest tower, T3, has 149 stories and is 650 m in height. T3 has an above-grade GCA of 344,933 sm and includes:

- Office (196,782 sm): Levels 3–19, 20–28, and 30–59
- Hotel, Six-Star (9,147 sm): Levels 61–63 (sky bridge)
- Residential (113,761 sm): Levels 64–94, 96–98 (sk bridge), 99–129, 131–133 (sky bridge), 134–149
- MEP: Levels B1, 13, 28, 60, 95, 130, and 150

Mechanical floors are located at the base of each bridge in the tower stacking. This allows the floors underneath the bridges, which have less natural light, to use their space more efficiently, and for stacking changes and sky lobbies at the locations of the bridges.

1 Dubai has four basement levels and over 10,000 parking spaces, as well as 36 loading spaces for trucks. Below the lowest basement is a shuttle train. Each tower has its own drop-off area and ramping system to access the three portions of the parking garage, which are planned separately for each tower on Levels B2–B3 and connected on Levels B4 and B5.

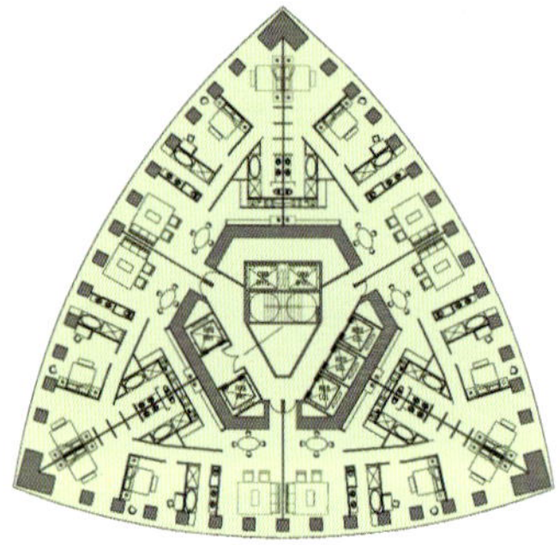

HOTEL PLAN
LEVEL 120

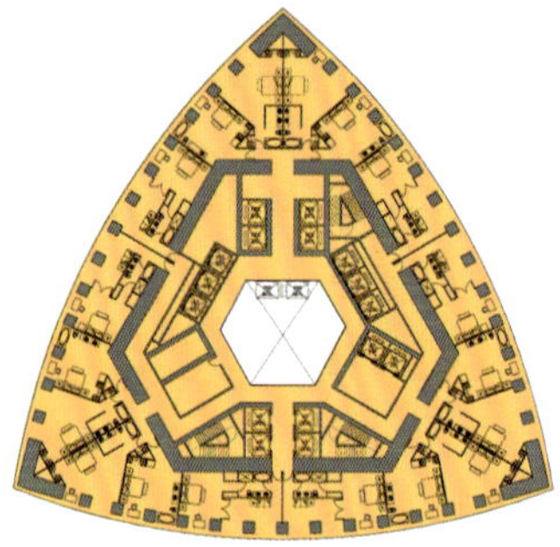

AMENITIES PLAN
LEVEL 44

OFFICE PLAN
LEVEL 14

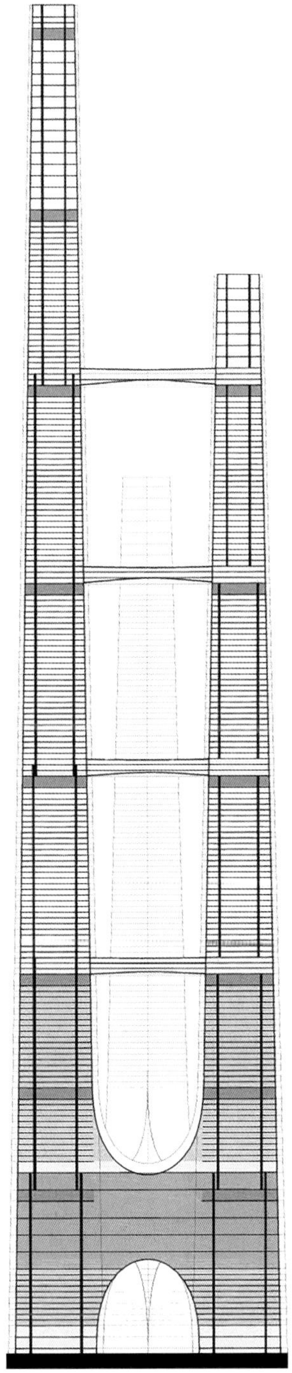

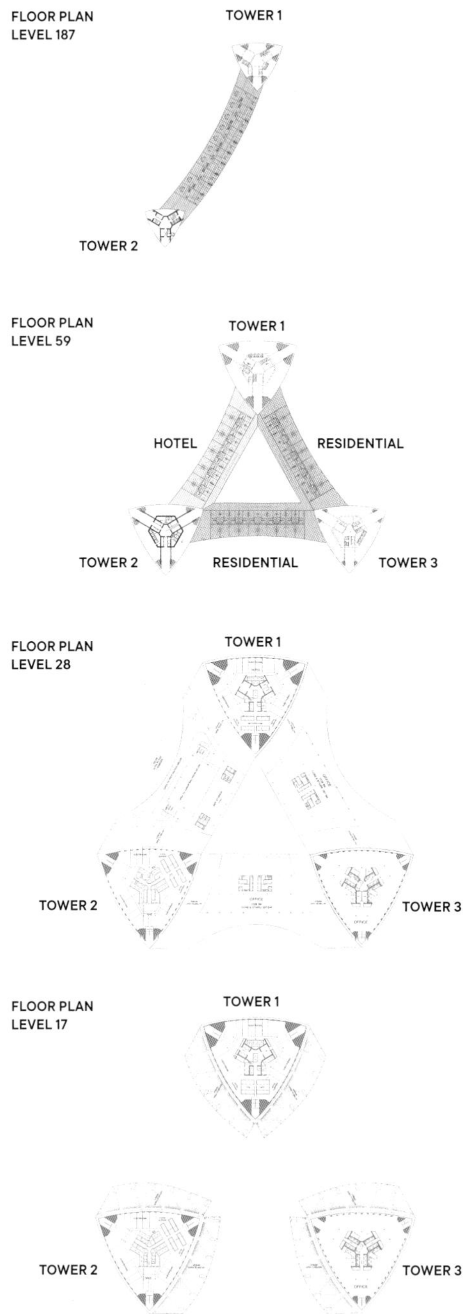
FLOOR PLAN
LEVEL 187
TOWER 1
TOWER 2
FLOOR PLAN
LEVEL 59
TOWER 1
HOTEL
RESIDENTIAL
TOWER 2
RESIDENTIAL
TOWER 3
FLOOR PLAN
LEVEL 28
TOWER 1
TOWER 2
TOWER 3
FLOOR PLAN
LEVEL 17
TOWER 1
TOWER 2
TOWER 3

PROGRAM

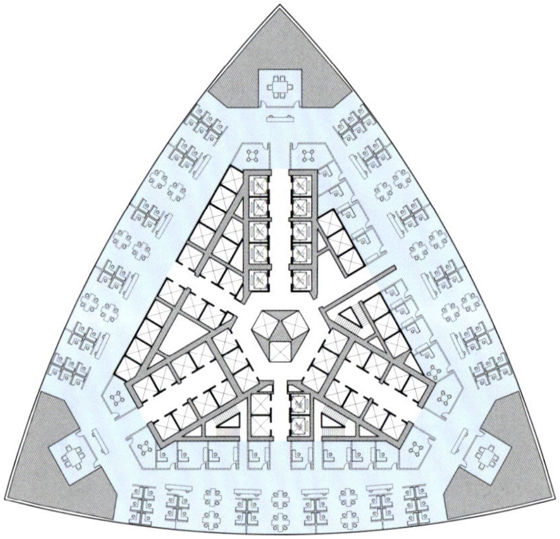

OFFICE
LEVEL 12

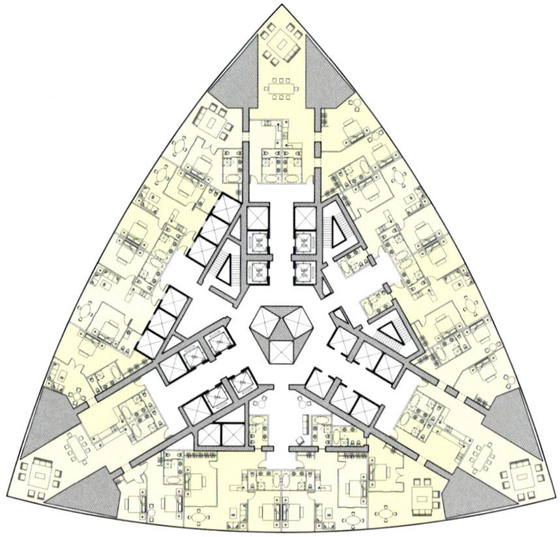

SERVICE APARTMENT
LEVEL 54

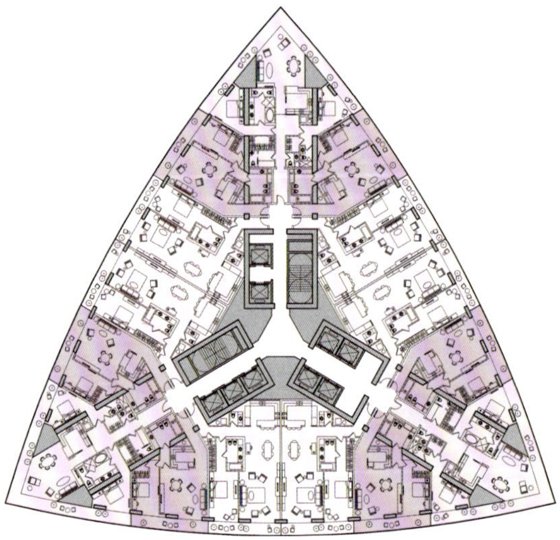

RESIDENTIAL
LEVEL 60

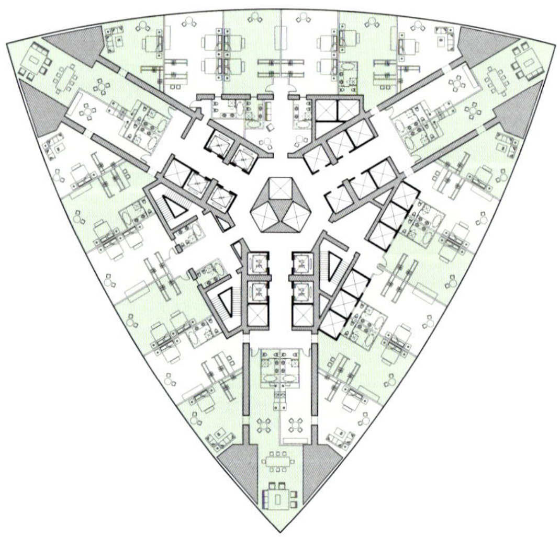

HOTEL
LEVEL 37

PODIUM

A mega building as vast as 1 Dubai must have an arrival sequence that is of a human scale.

The drop-off areas at the base of the towers were designed with canopies and accesses to the multiple programs. Vehicular accesses are located on the edges of the towers, leaving generously landscape pedestrian areas to create a walkable park-like atmosphere between the towers.

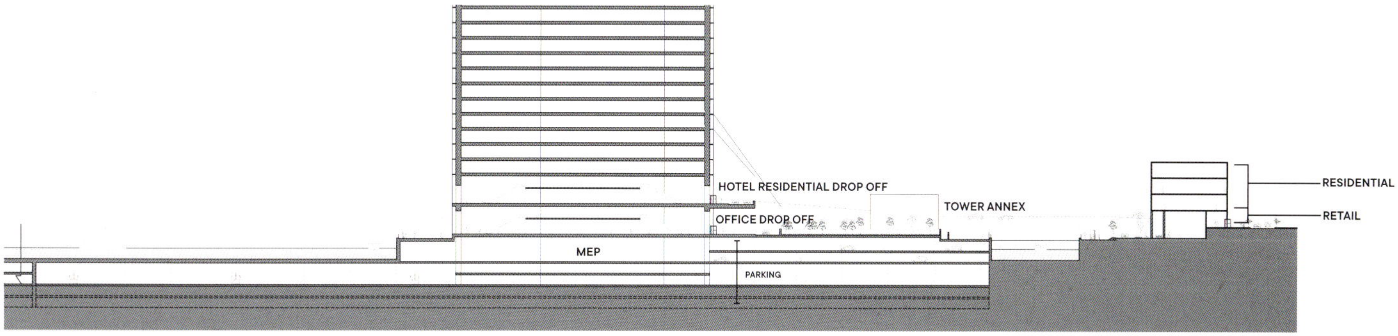
HOTEL RESIDENTIAL DROP OFF
TOWER ANNEX
OFFICE DROP OFF
MEP
PARKING
RESIDENTIAL
RETAIL

PODIUM

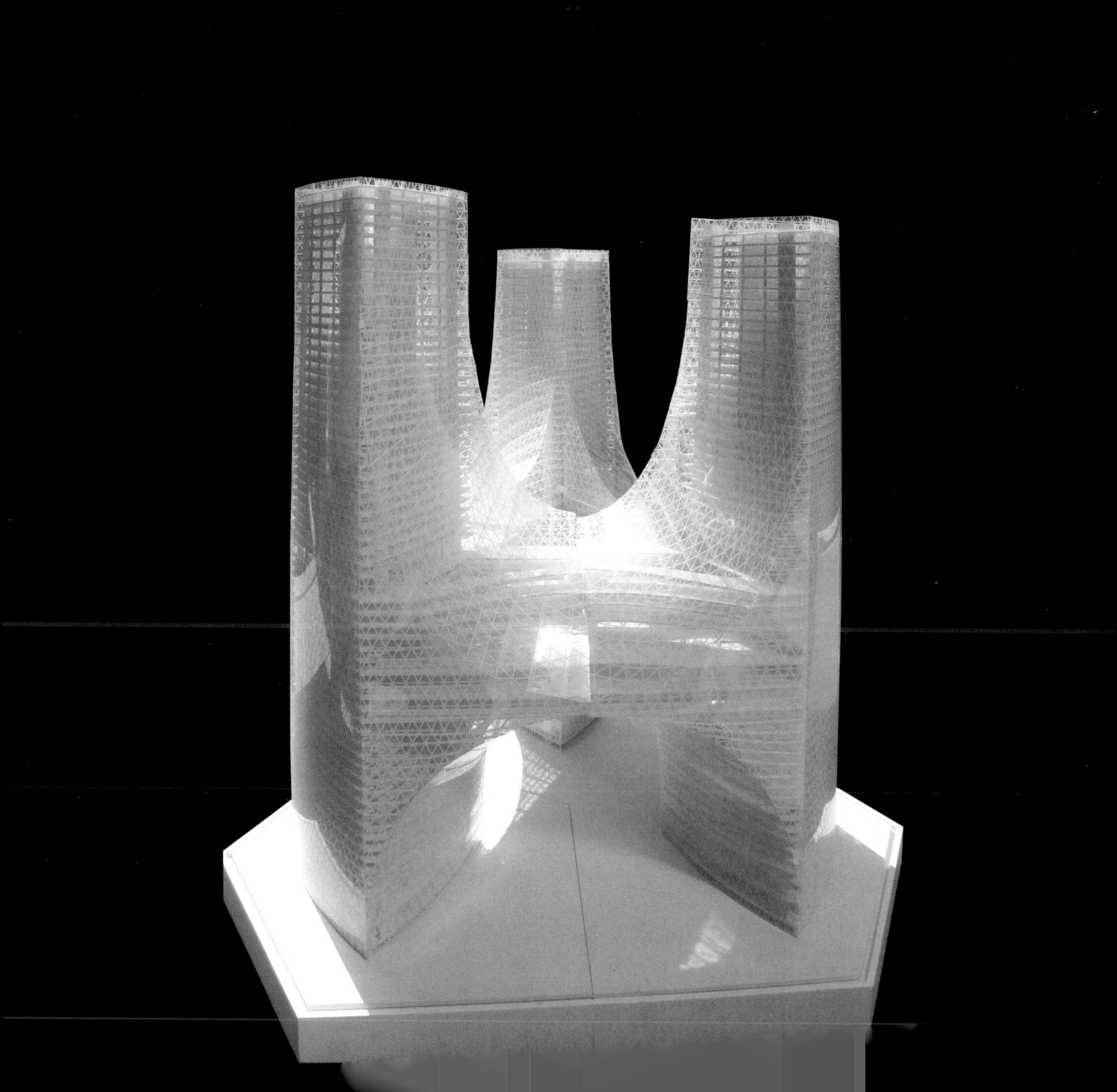

SKY BRIDGE

The sky bridges are one of the most distinctive features of 1 Dubai. They connect the towers structurally and form important programmatic and social connections necessary in the mega-building typology. Sky bridge floors have opportunities for retail, amenities, and outdoor spaces shared building occupants, and are suitable for local elevator transfers. The bridges are stabilized by cables, which are also dynamic elements in the design. The sky bridges are located on several floors:

- Sky Bridge 1 (27,407 sm): Levels 61–63
- Sky Bridge 2 (26,869 sm): Levels 96–98
- Sky Bridge 3 (26,020 sm): Levels 131–133
- Sky Bridge 4 (9,097 sm): Levels 166–168

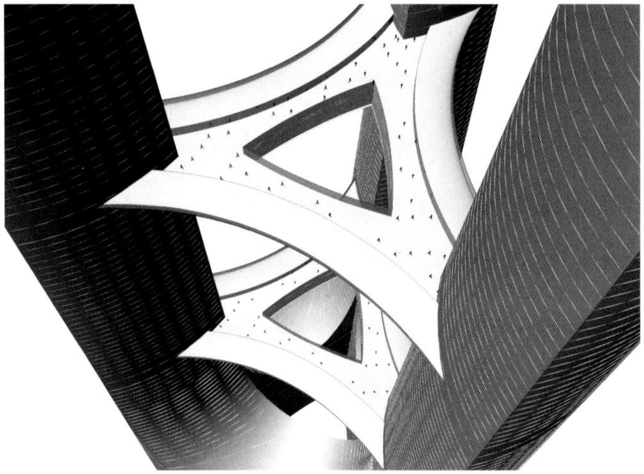

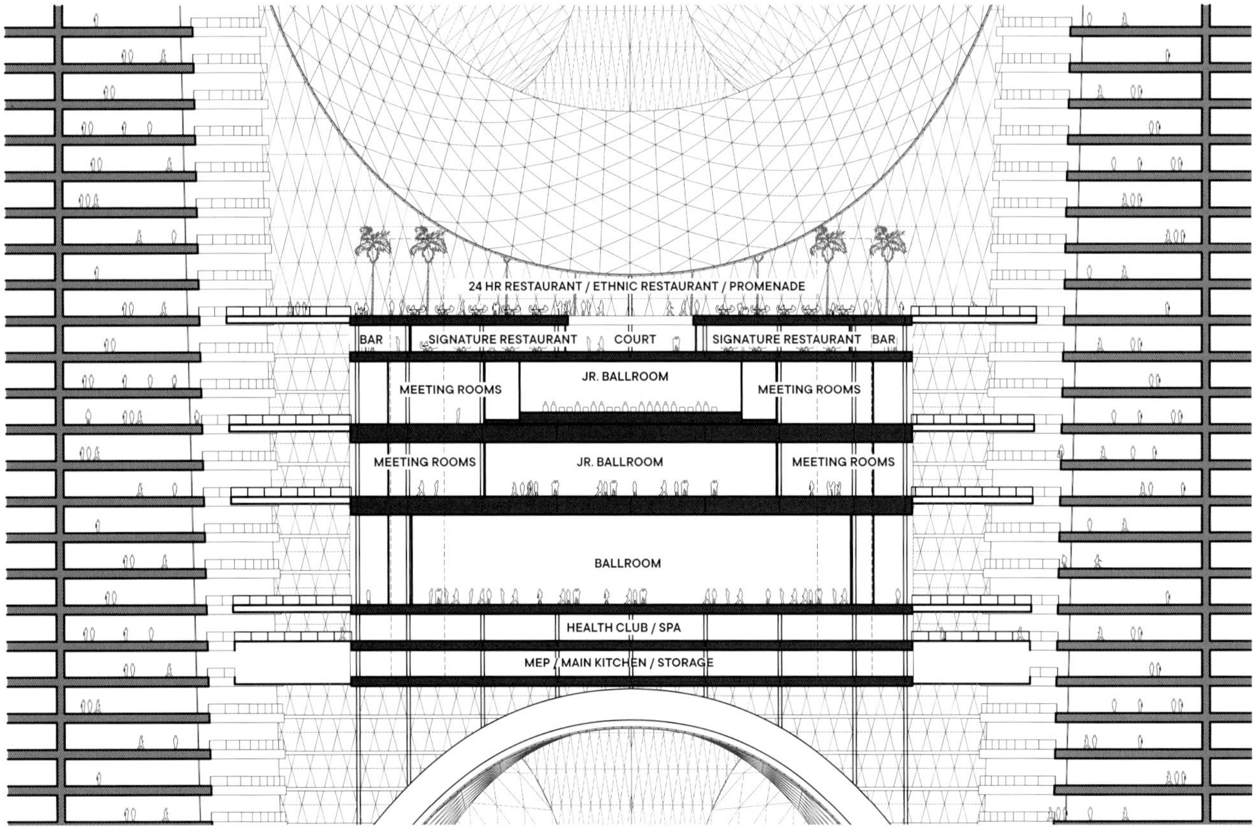

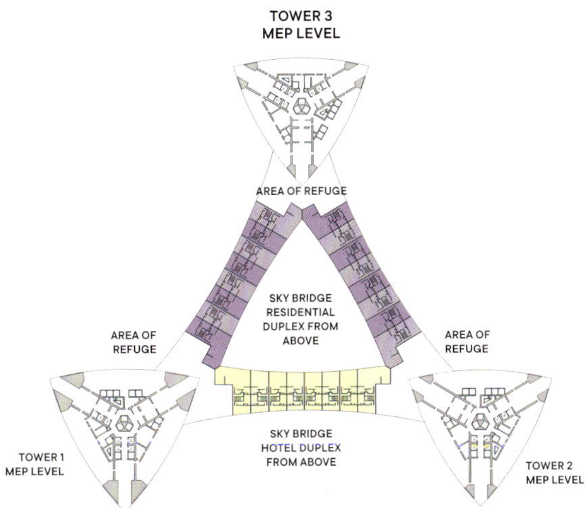
TOWER 3
MEP LEVEL
AREA OF REFUGE
SKY BRIDGE
RESIDENTIAL
DUPLEX FROM
ABOVE
AREA OF
REFUGE
AREA OF
REFUGE
TOWER 1
MEP LEVEL
SKY BRIDGE
HOTEL DUPLEX
FROM ABOVE
TOWER 2
MEP LEVEL

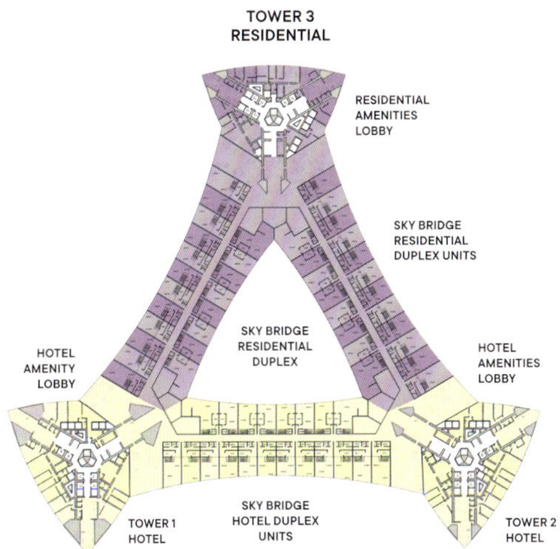
TOWER 3
RESIDENTIAL
RESIDENTIAL
AMENITIES
LOBBY
SKY BRIDGE
RESIDENTIAL
DUPLEX UNITS
SKY BRIDGE
RESIDENTIAL
DUPLEX
HOTEL
AMENITY
LOBBY
HOTEL
AMENITIES
LOBBY
TOWER 1
HOTEL
SKY BRIDGE
HOTEL DUPLEX
UNITS
TOWER 2
HOTEL

SKY BRIDGE

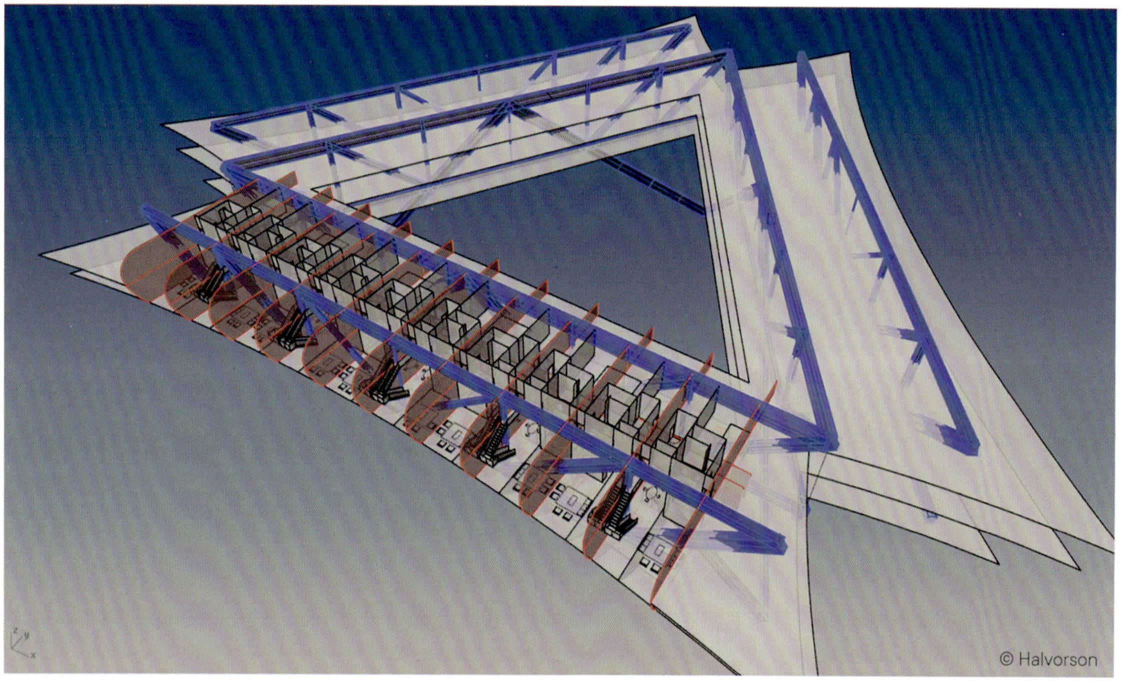

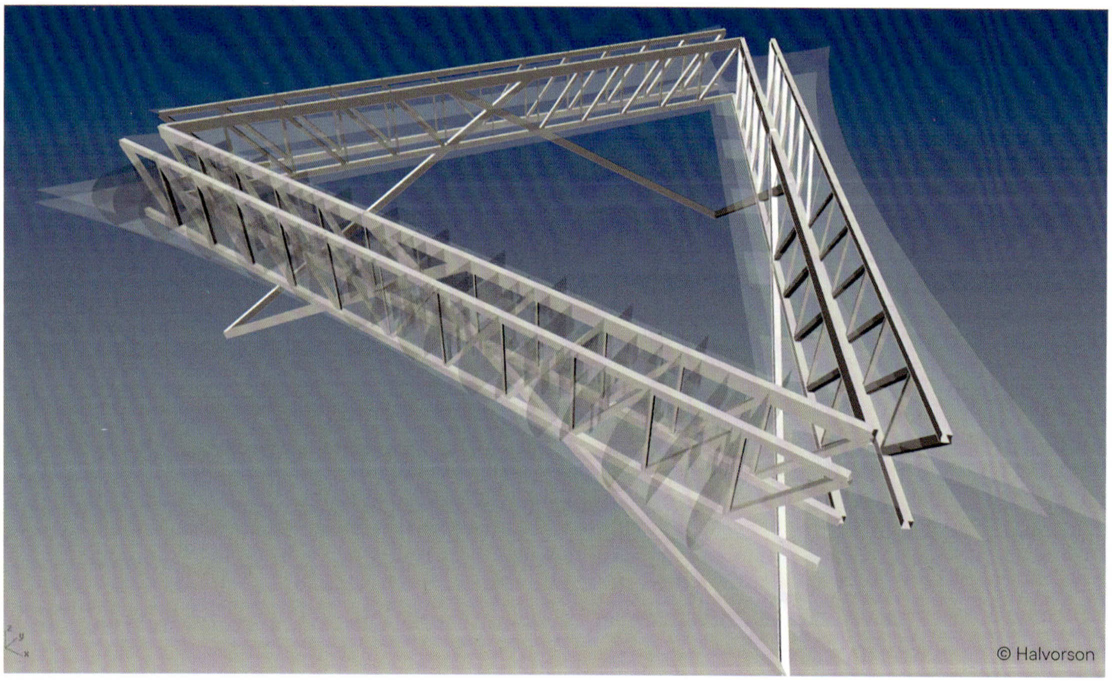

TOWER ORIGIN DIAGRAM
PROPOSED TOWER ORIGIN DIMENSIONS

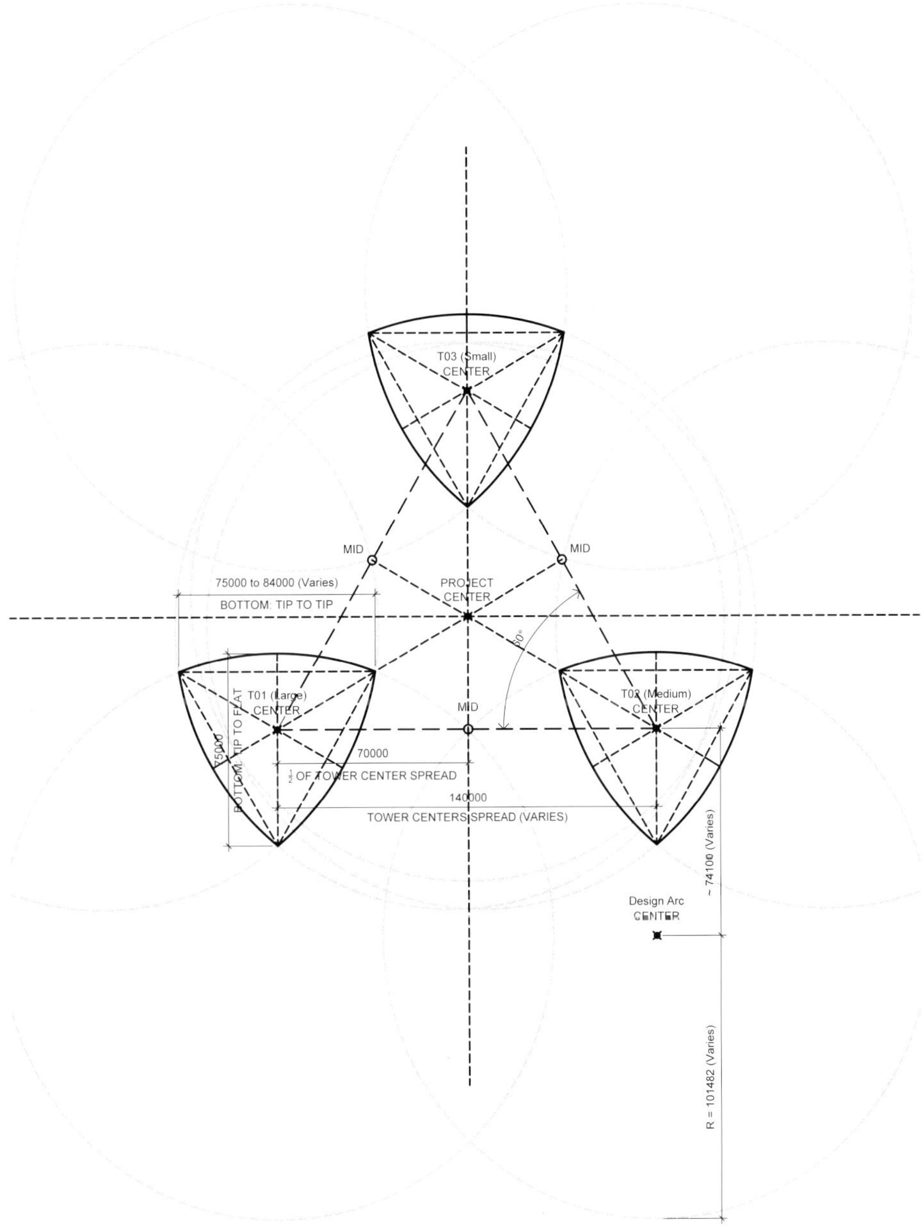

SKY BRIDGE

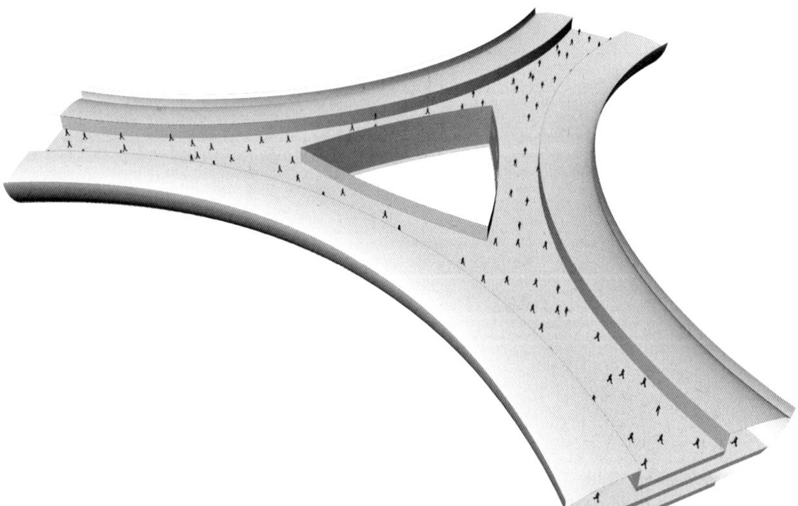

08·30·08

SCÉNO PLUS SKETCH, 2008

To fully represent the light show experience, Montreal-based firm Scéno Plus, known internationally for its arts and entertainment venue designs, created the vision for the sound and light shows for the space.

At the base of the tower within the canal, it was important to include a special and unique entertainment feature for the public to enjoy. The podium creates a very special space where the 3 towers are interlinked and it is possible to look up through the bridges. In this space it was envisioned that there would be floating seating in the water, surrounding an area where a 3-dimensional light show could be projected between the buildings. This light show would be able to tell a story using dramatic effects within the special area formed by the negative space of the building mass.

SCÉNO PLUS SKETCH, 2008

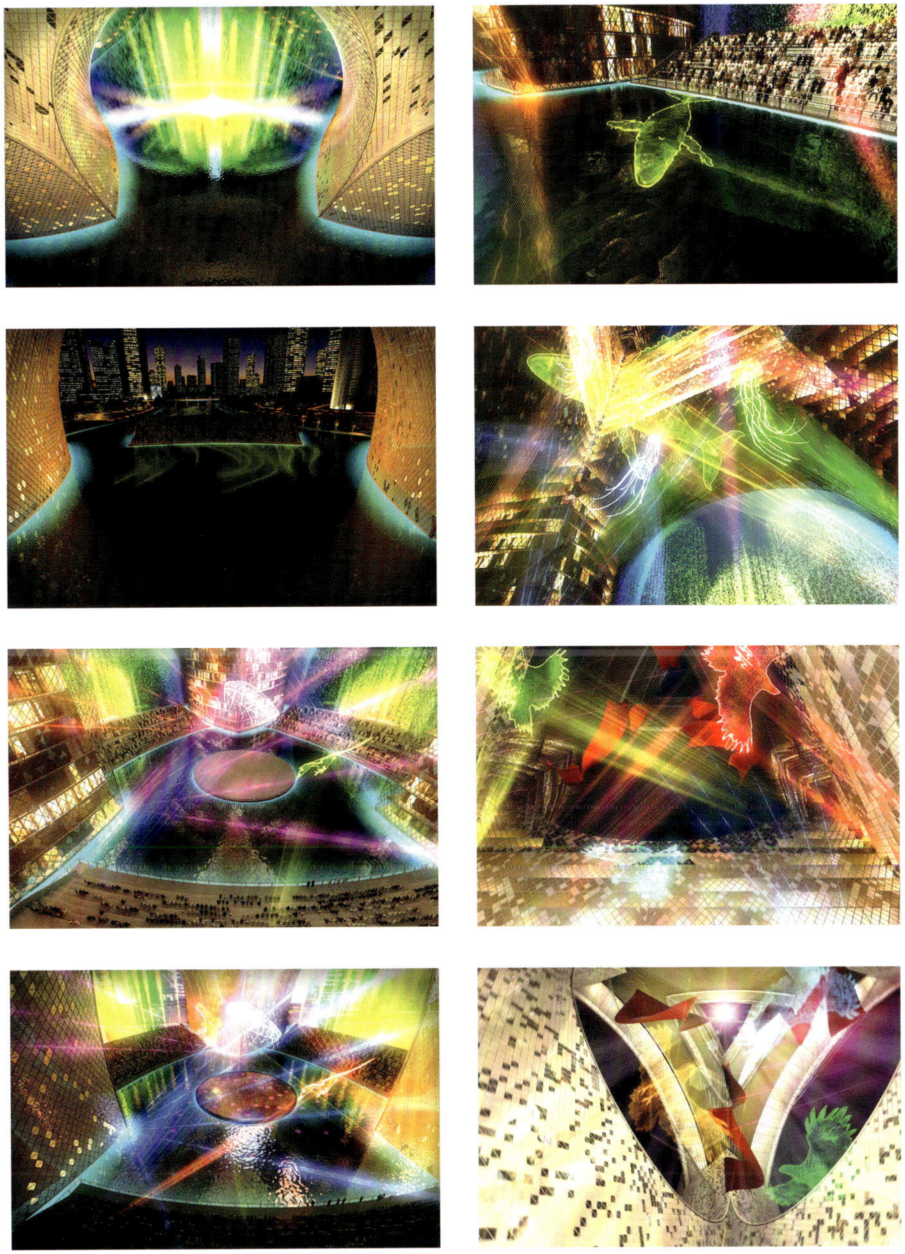

© Orphanage Animation Studios

PERFORMANCE

HALVORSON & PARTNERS, STRUCTURAL ENGINEER

Typical floor framing in the Office, Residential, and Hotel floors consists of 85 mm lightweight topping slab over 80 mm 1.2 mm composite deck supporting wide flange composite beams. The composite beams span between the diagrid system on the exterior wall and the reinforced-concrete core wall.

The tower foundations consist of reinforced-concrete mats supported by reinforced-concrete bored piles, which minimize shears in the mat and allow the loads of each tower to be transferred as directly as possible from the tower walls/columns to the reinforced-concrete bored piles. The preliminary tower pile design indicates that a grid of 2000 mm diameter bored piles of C70 concrete is required to support the towers and may vary between 4–6 m depending on final tower loading.

Parking levels use a reinforced-concrete two-way flat slab system (200 mm slab with 150 mm drops). A structural column grid, established on an 8.5 m grid, is used for standard parking layouts. Reinforced-concrete walls distributed throughout the space resist the lateral loads from the perimeter basement walls and allow the basement to be divided for phased construction.

Wind-tunnel testing ensured the bridges were designed for the relative pattern loading that could occur from the three towers. The wind-tunnel also reviewed whether additional damping devices are required in the bridge structures.

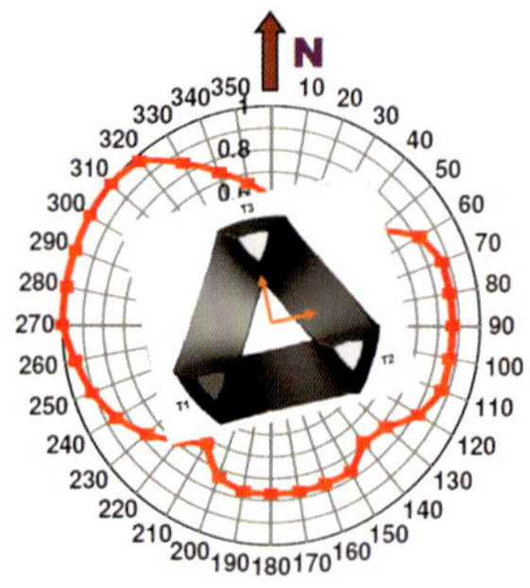

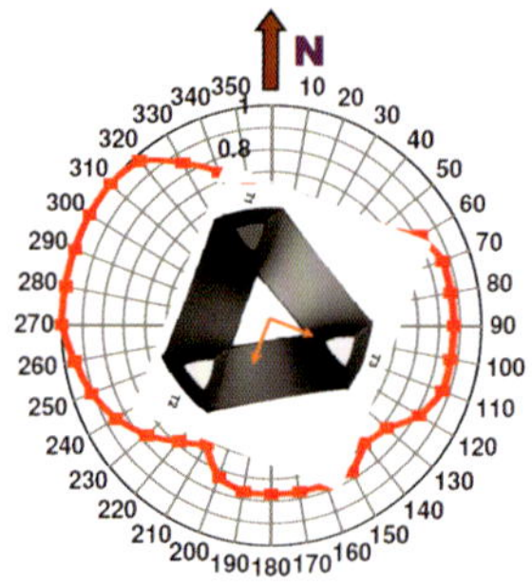

© RWDI

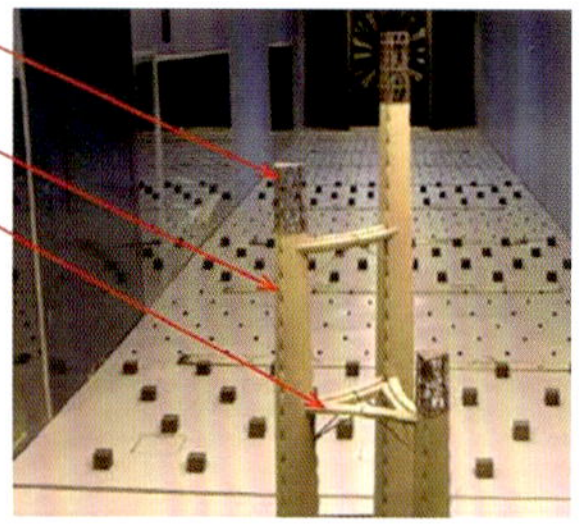

PERFORMANCE

The towers are designed to have optimized solar orientation so that the taller tower shades the shorter towers beside. Solar studies were performed to optimize the amount of solid area versus glazed area on each facade. Various patterns in the diagonal panels were studied based on their solar gain. Some openings were left unglazed for ventilation and fitted with stainless-steel mesh for security and protection for bird collisions. The interior wall, or concrete tube, has punched window openings. It is clad with metal panel and the window openings are infilled with insulated glazing units which are operable in aluminum frames.

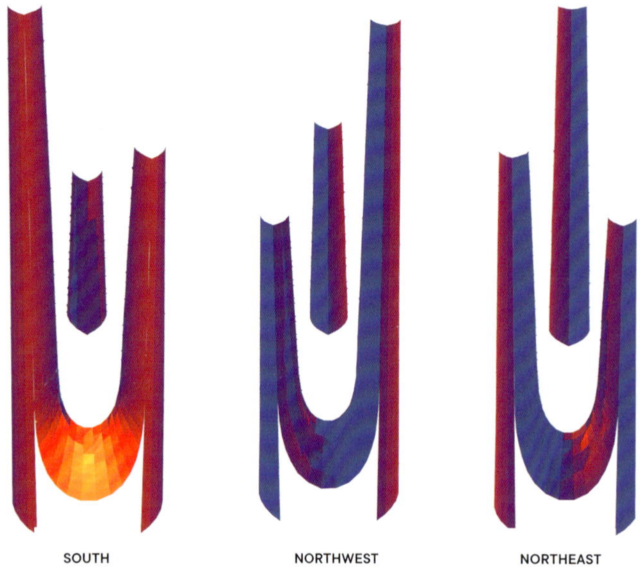

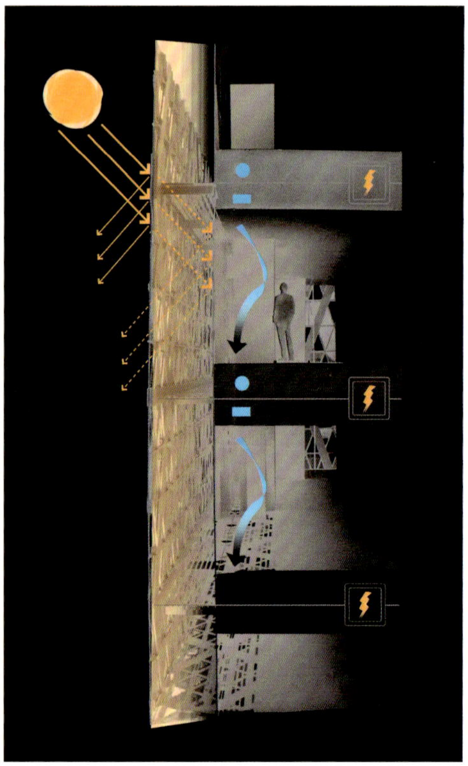

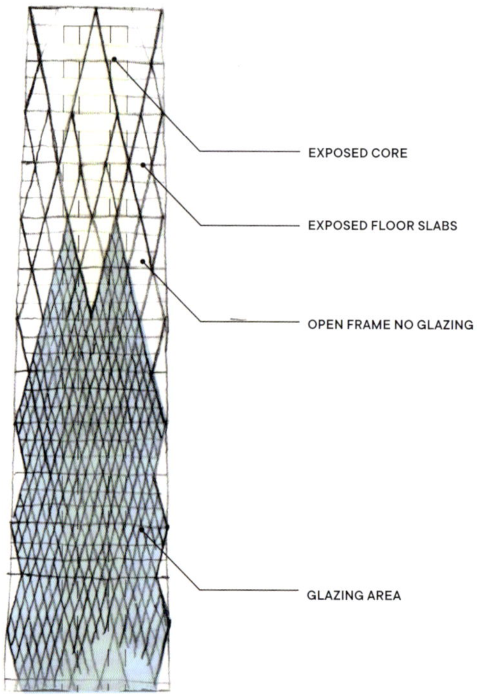

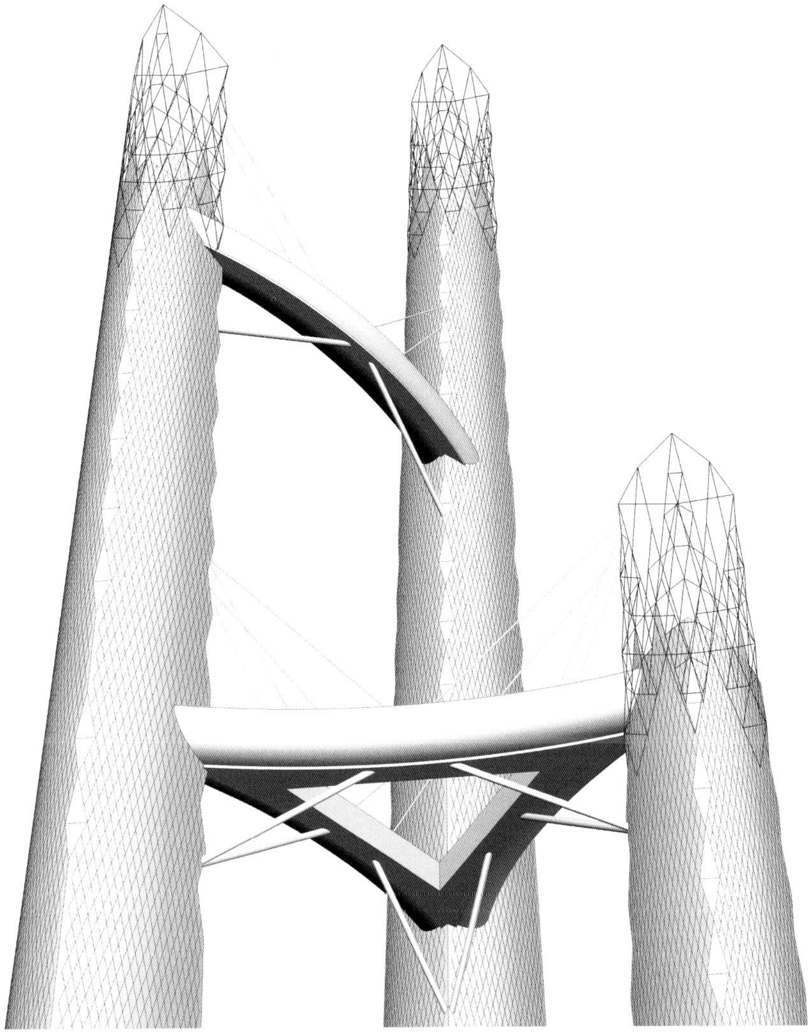

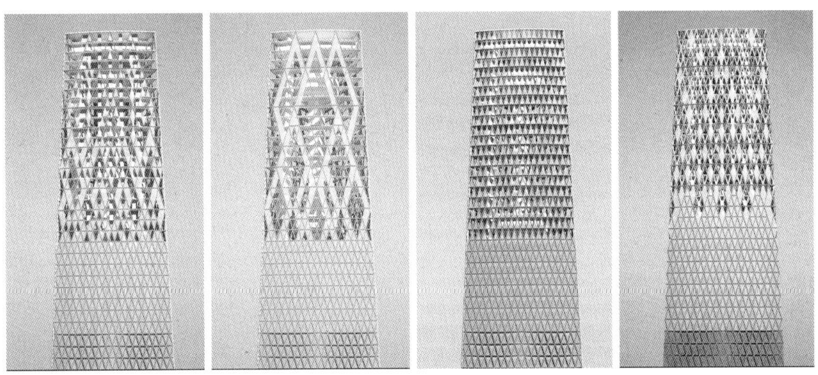

TOP STUDIES FOR WIND-TUNNEL TESTING

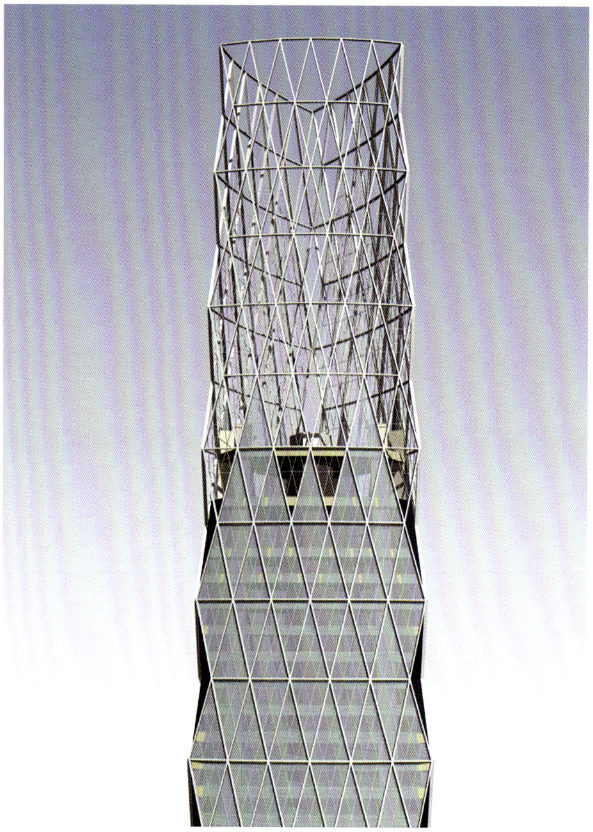

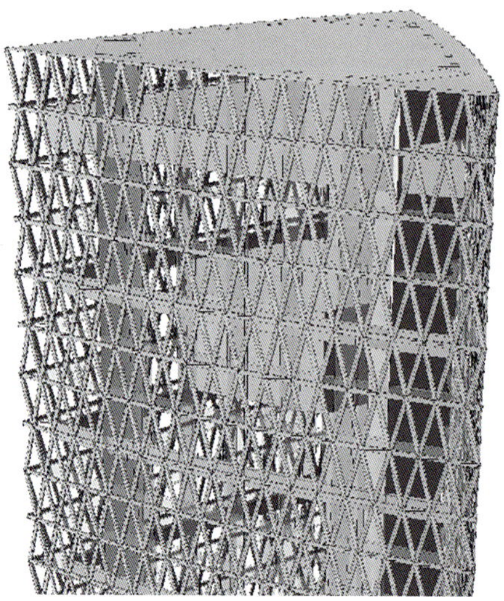

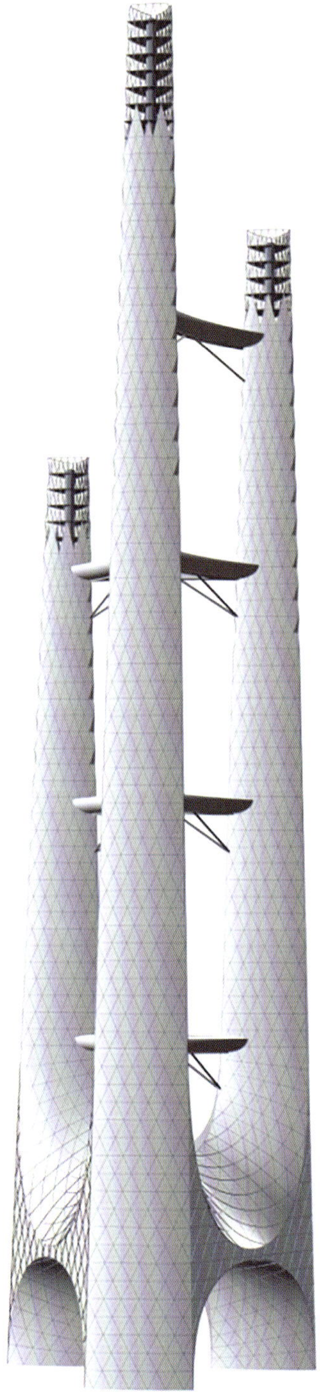

Two exterior wall system options were explored during schematic design phase. Option 1 investigated a version of a diagrid system, designed to efficiently deal with the tapering geometry of the towers. Option 2 explored wall systems comprised of glass panels and vertical glass fins.

Both options are layered facades, featuring a 1.5 m zone of solarium or accessible balcony space around the perimeter that controls heat gain and allows for controlled natural ventilation. The structure of the tower, which is located at the back of the 1.5 m zone, is a concrete tube with punched window openings.

In Option 1, several different module configurations of the diagrid were studied. The number of solid panels versus glazing was optimized based upon the orientation of each wall to let in the appropriate amount of natural light and to control heat gain. The panels are made up of extruded aluminum with a high-performance paint finish and are designed to be flat, but to be erected in a faceted manner in order to conform to the building's bowed and sloped shape.

The proposed triangular panels range from approximately 4 m on each side at ground level, to 4 m x 4 m x 1.8 m near the top of the tower. Within that panel, the glazing is broken up into 9–16 smaller triangles that can be infilled with glass or with shading devices and other solid materials. To avoid the use of triangular glass, the monolithic pieces of glass are panelized into trapezoids and the divisions are made by metal screen pieces on top of the glass.

Option 2 is made up of unitized quadrilateral window wall panels, .75 m x 4 m. The panels are flat but erected in a faceted manner to conform to the tower shape. Shading fins are 450 mm deep and consist of tinted or clear-laminated glass with a variety of colored inter layers. The solarium is designed in the same way as Option 1.

OPTION 1

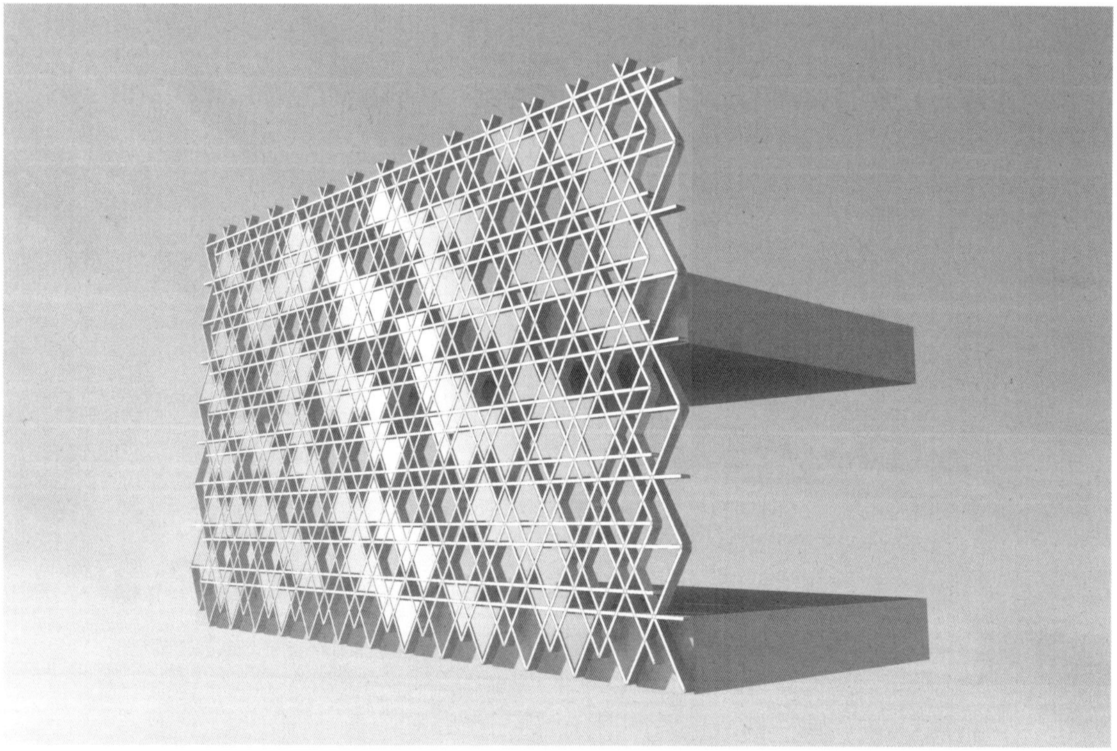

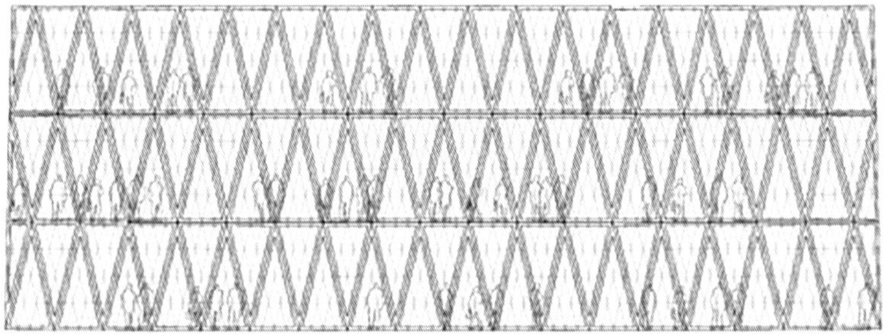

L-200

L-199

L-198

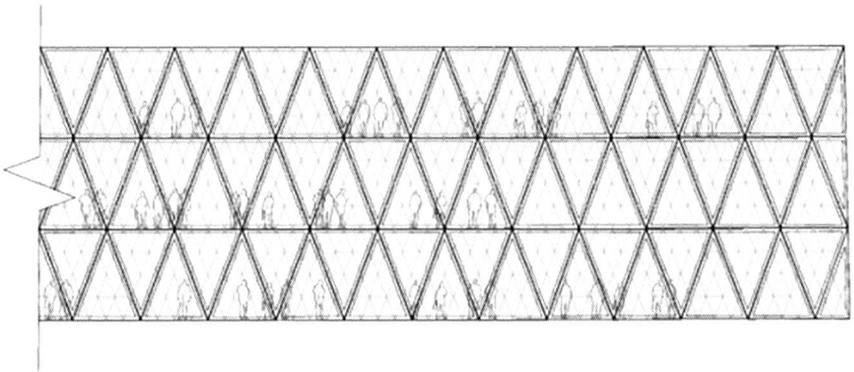

L-102

L-101

L-100

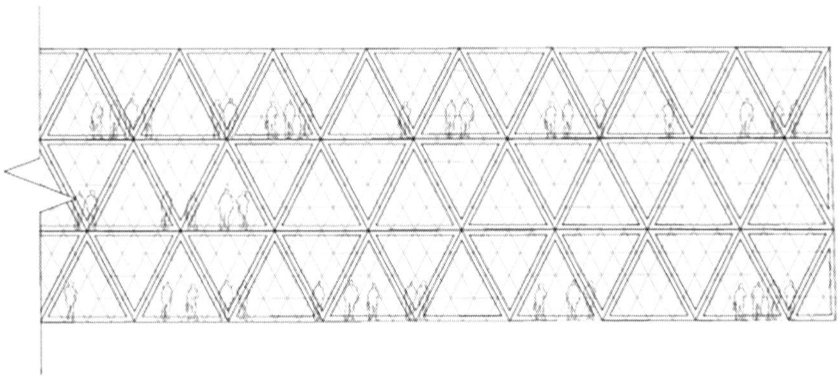

L-003

L-002

L-001

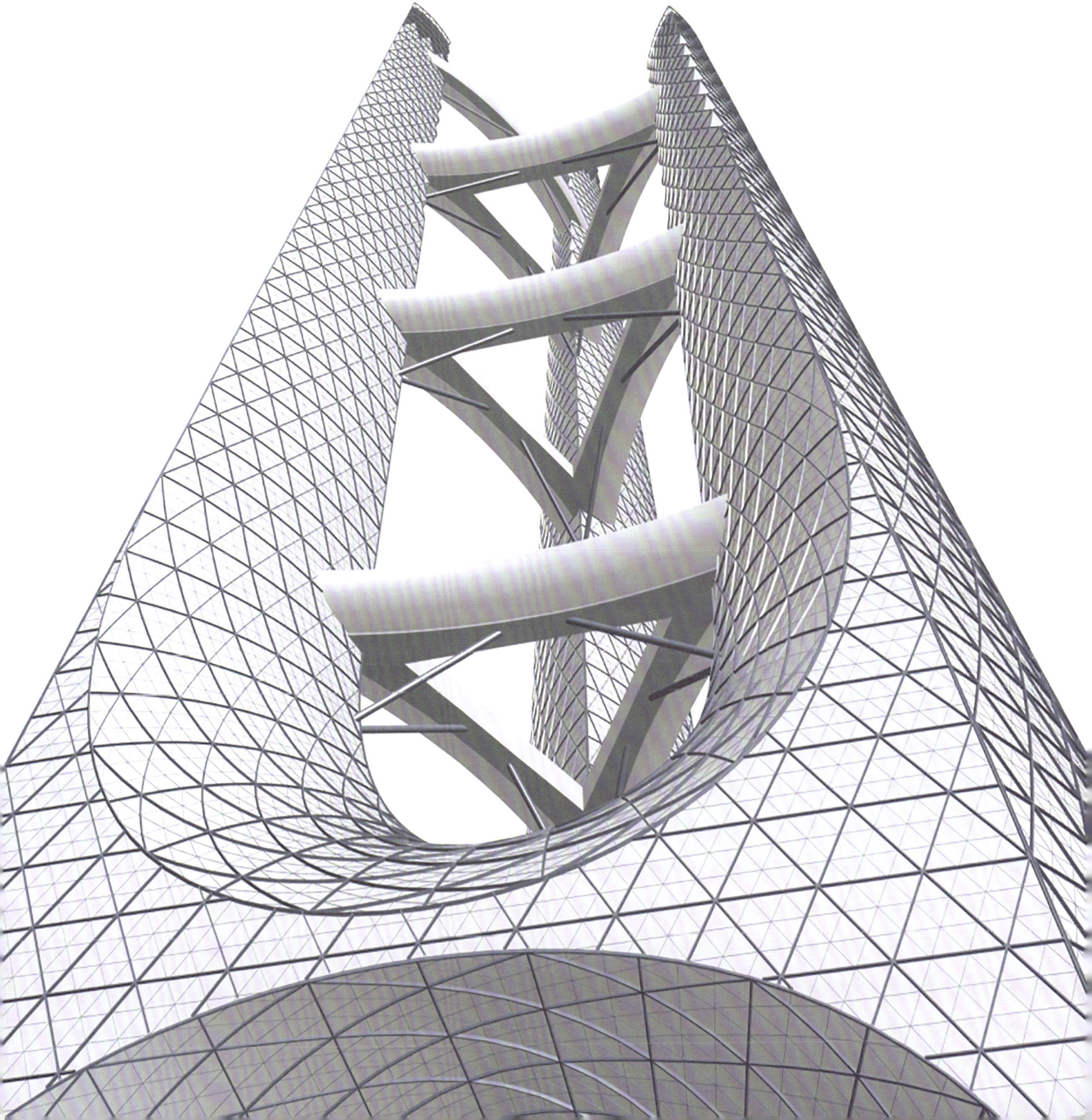

RESEARCH + DEVELOPMENT

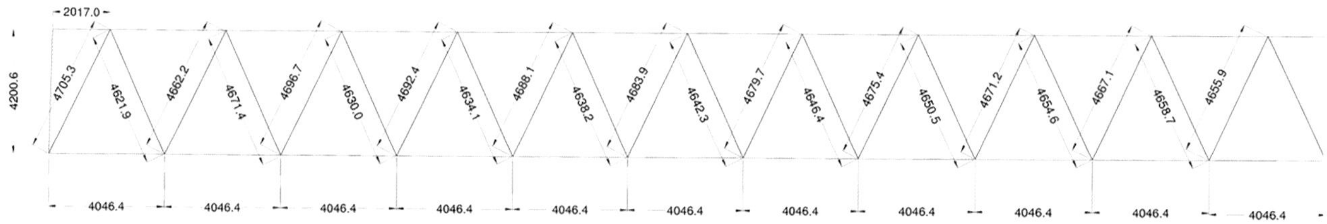

PANEL DEVIATIONS

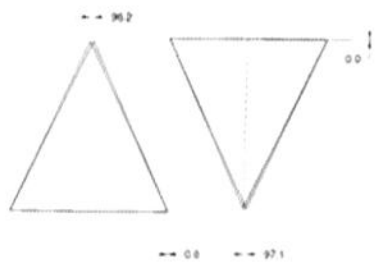

PANEL OVERLAY

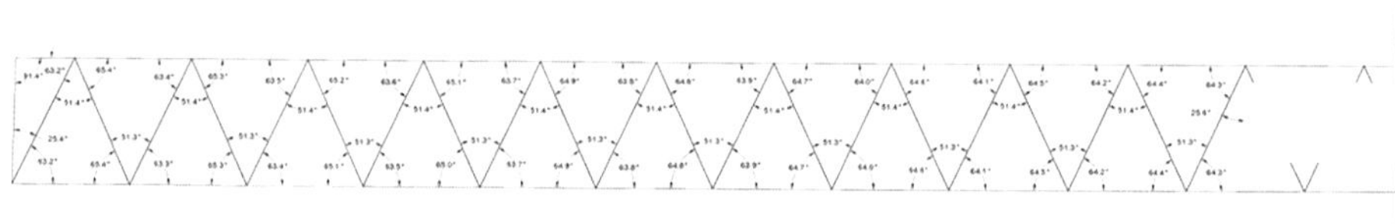

ANGLE VARIATIONS

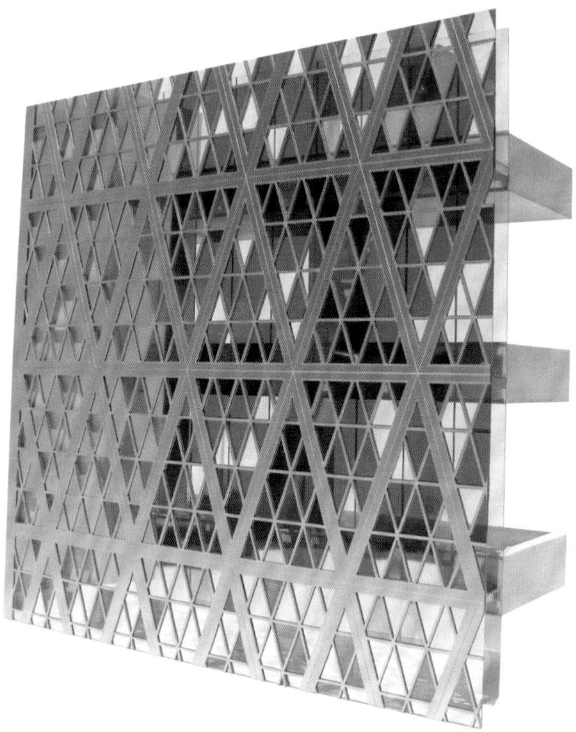

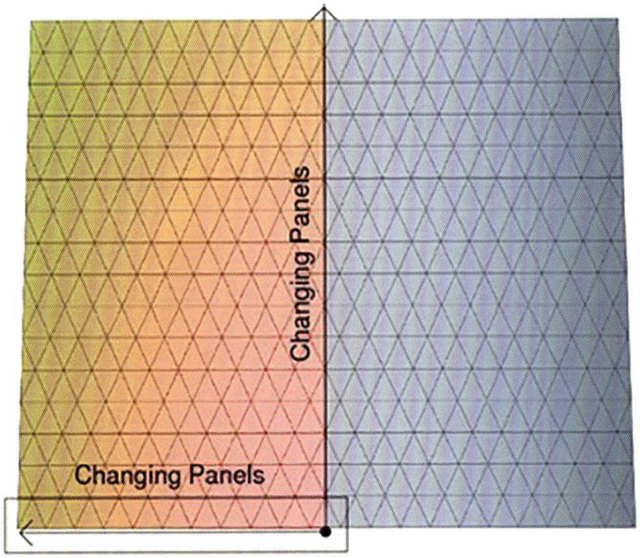

UNIQUE PANELS AT ROW 1

MIRRORED PANELS AT ROW 1

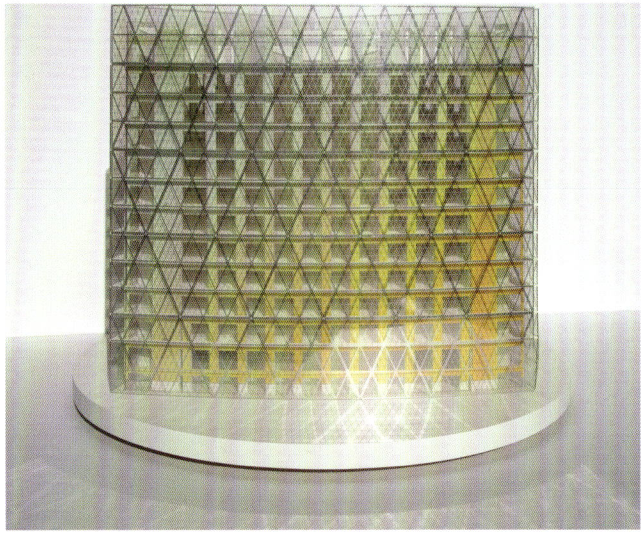

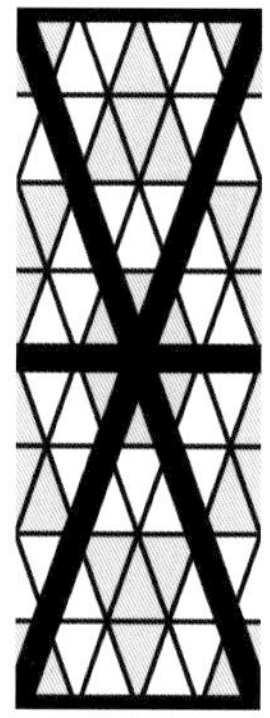
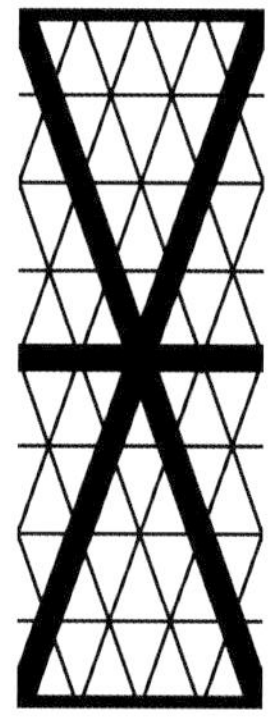
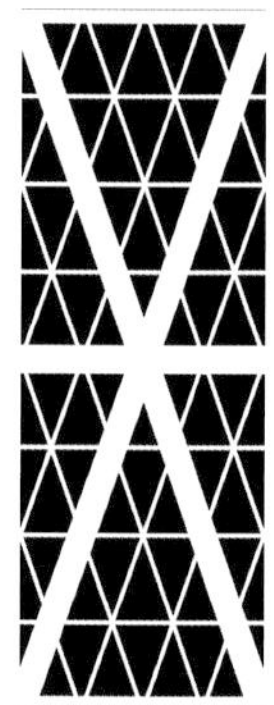
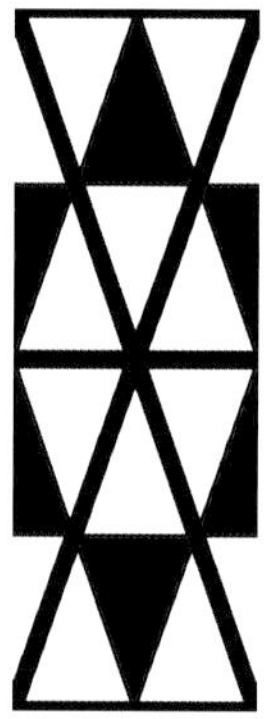
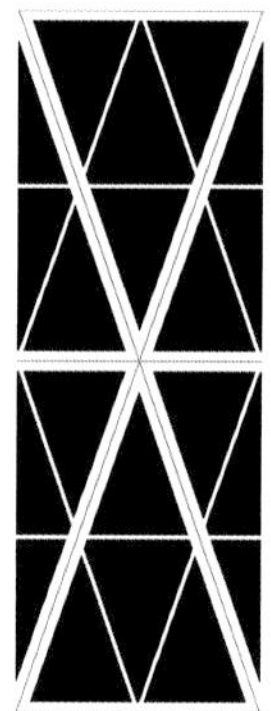
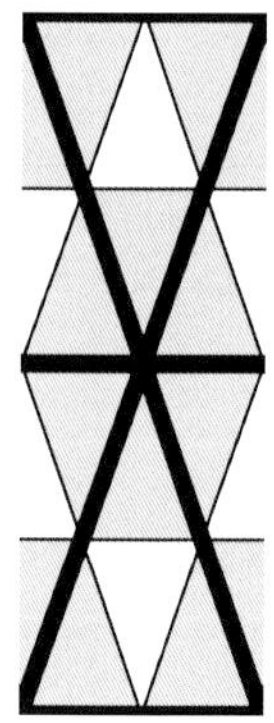

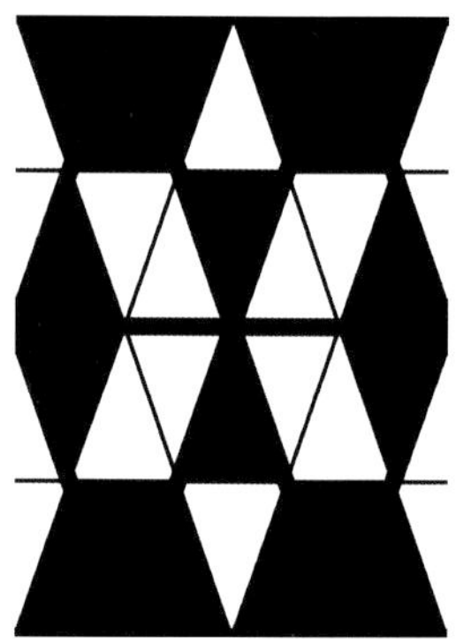

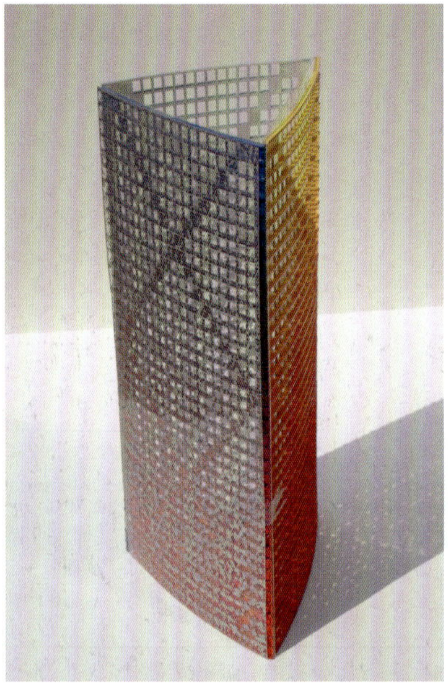

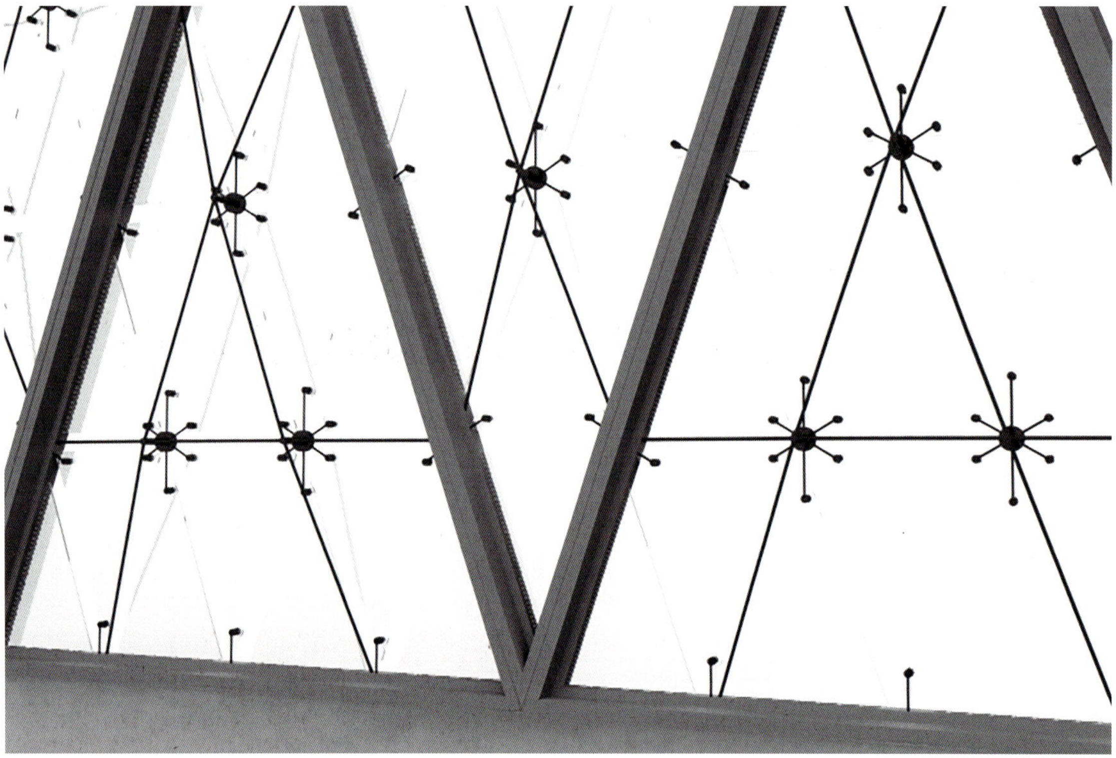

OPTION 2

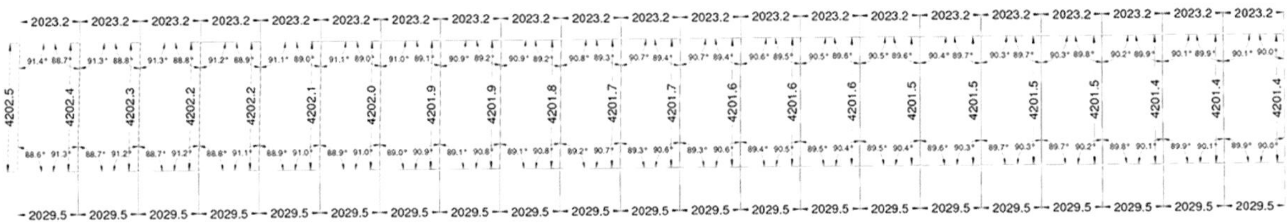

ANGLE VARIATIONS

PANEL DEVIATIONS

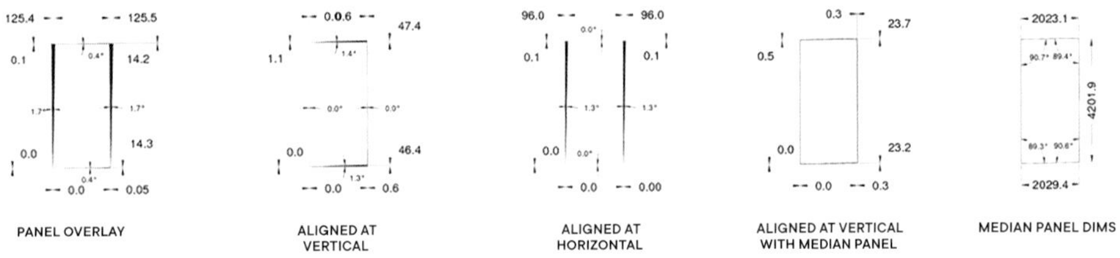

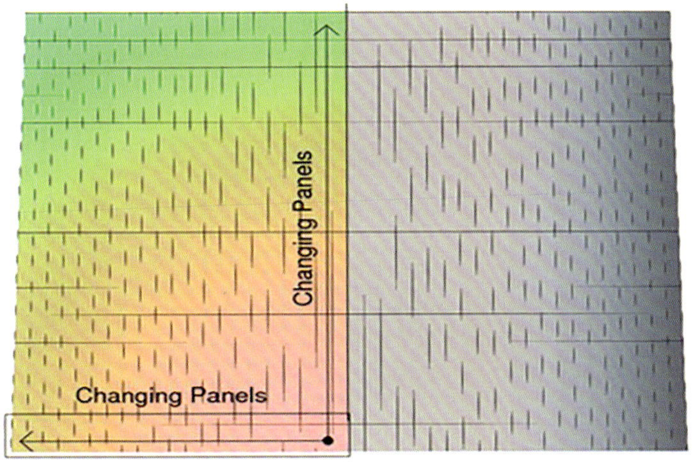

UNIQUE PANELS AT ROW 1 MIRRORED PANELS AT ROW 1

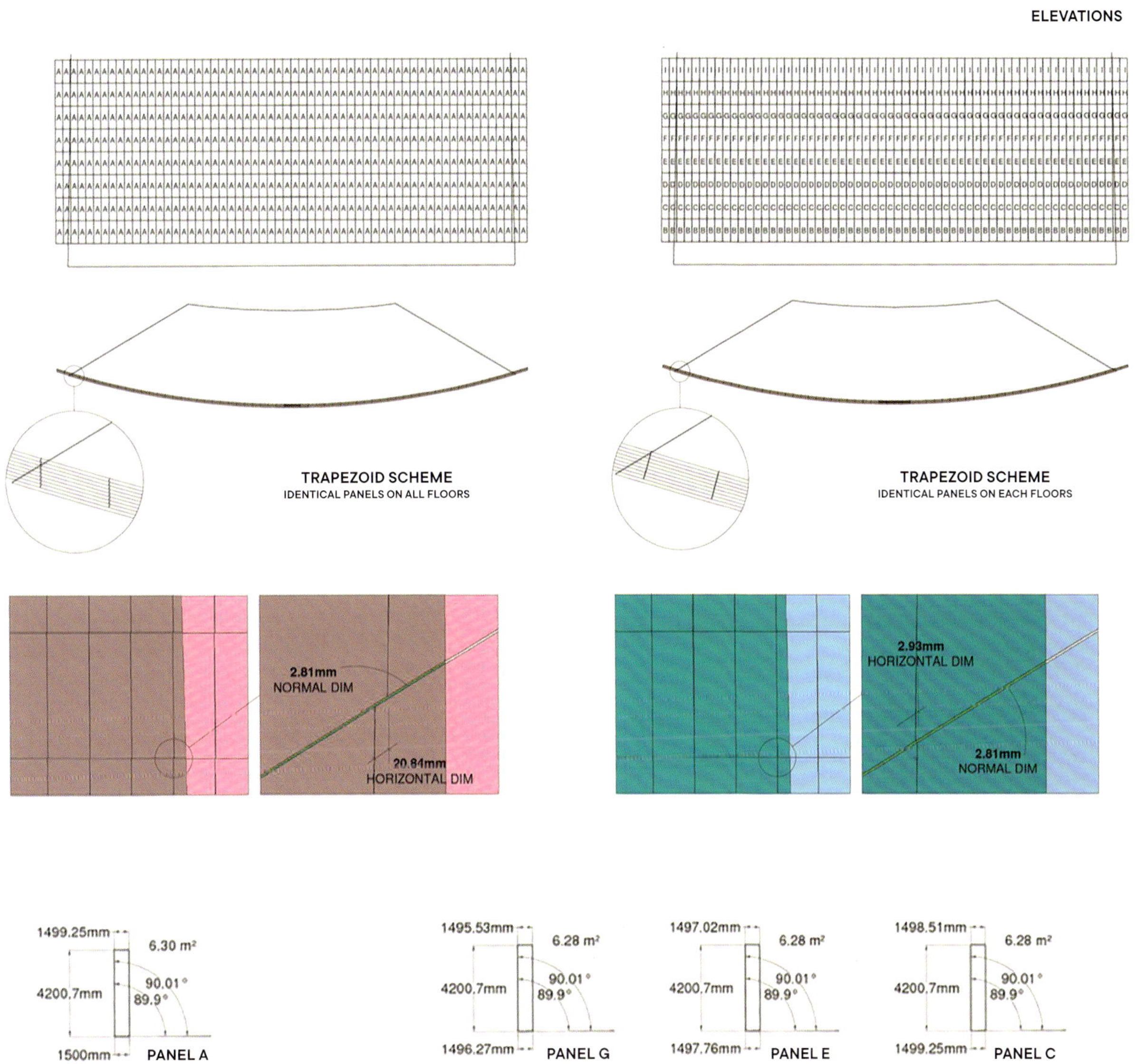
ELEVATIONS
TRAPEZOID SCHEME
IDENTICAL PANELS ON ALL FLOORS
TRAPEZOID SCHEME
IDENTICAL PANELS ON EACH FLOORS
2.81mm
NORMAL DIM
20.84mm
HORIZONTAL DIM
2.93mm
HORIZONTAL DIM
2.81mm
NORMAL DIM
1499.25mm
6.30 m²
4200.7mm
90.01°
89.9°
1500mm
PANEL A
1495.53mm
6.28 m²
4200.7mm
90.01°
89.9°
1496.27mm
PANEL G
1497.02mm
6.28 m²
4200.7mm
90.01°
89.9°
1497.76mm
PANEL E
1498.51mm
6.28 m²
4200.7mm
90.01°
89.9°
1499.25mm
PANEL C

STRUCTURE

HALVORSON & PARTNERS, STRUCTURAL ENGINEER

The tower structures are comprised of a composite system that resists lateral loads and transfers gravity loading to the foundations. Each tower system will consist of a reinforced-concrete core linked to reinforced-concrete corner mega-columns at the exterior to resist gravity and lateral wind and seismic loading.

This linking will be achieved using reinforced-concrete walls at the residential and hotel levels, by outriggers at the mechanical levels, and by a steel diagrid system between corner mega-columns on the exterior of the building. A silo wall, approximately 120-meters high, will be utilized at the exterior line through the amenity floors to stiffen the base of each tower.

In addition to the independent tower system proportioning, the bridge links between the three towers, will be engaged to meet serviceability limits for the buildings, including drift and motion perception. The bridge links occur at three locations and at one location between T1 and T2. The bridges incorporate three-story deep steel trusses to span between the towers. The links also transfer shear forces between the towers through steel diaphragm bracing in the floors at three levels of each bridge.

The amount of shear force transferred is based on stiffness of the bridges, relative stiffness of the towers, tower cumulative shears at the bridge levels, and dynamic behavior of the towers relative to the wind loading considered.

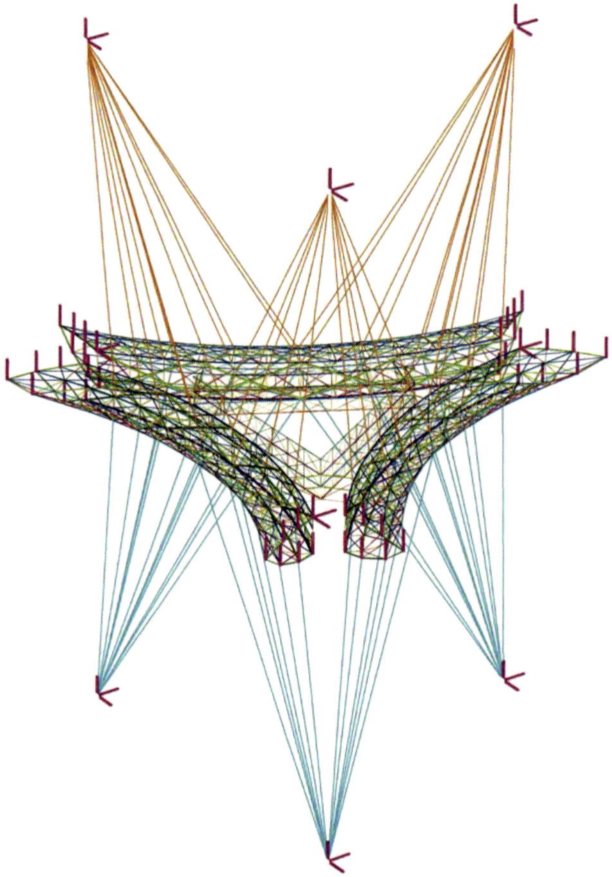

BRIDGE MODEL

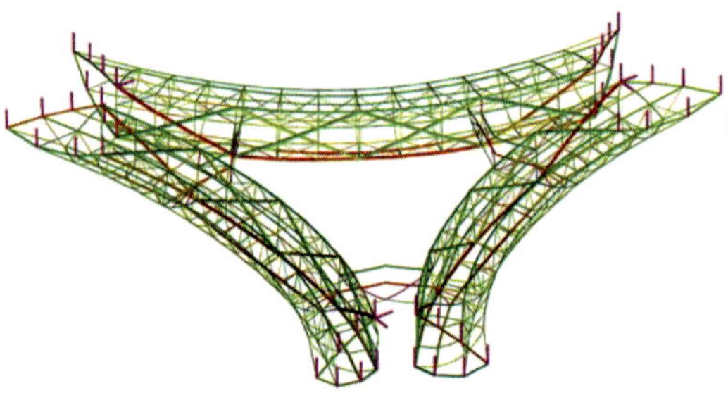

AXIAL STRESS

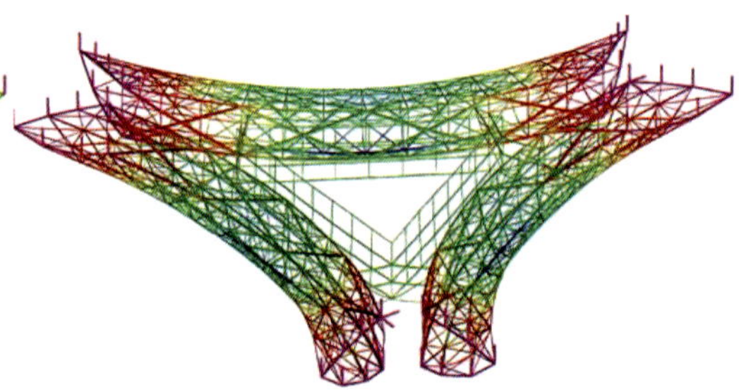

DEFLECTIONS

LINKED TOWERS
STRUCTURAL MODEL

LINKED TOWERS
LATERAL ANALYSIS

WIND DISPLACEMENTS
-15 PERCENT STIFFER

WIND AXIAL STRESS

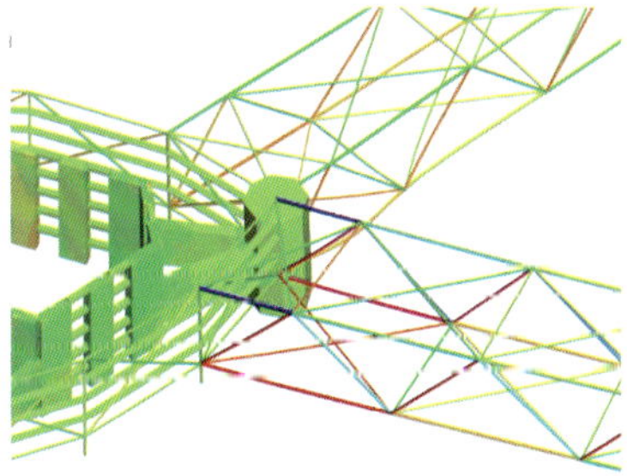

BRIDGE AXIAL STRESS

LINKED TOWERS
DYNAMIC ANALYSIS

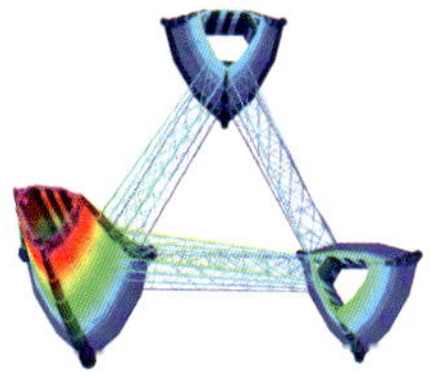

MODE 1
T = 12.5 SECS

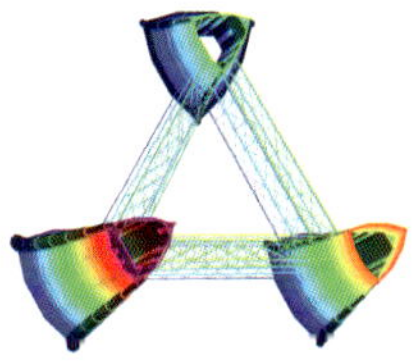

MODE 2
T = 11.5 SECS

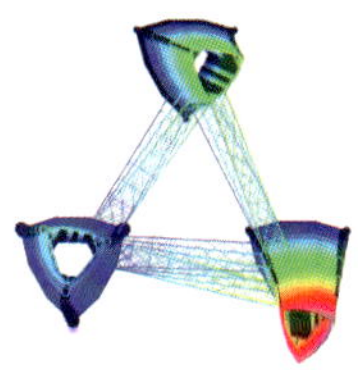

MODE 3
T = 8.1 SECS

STRUCTURE

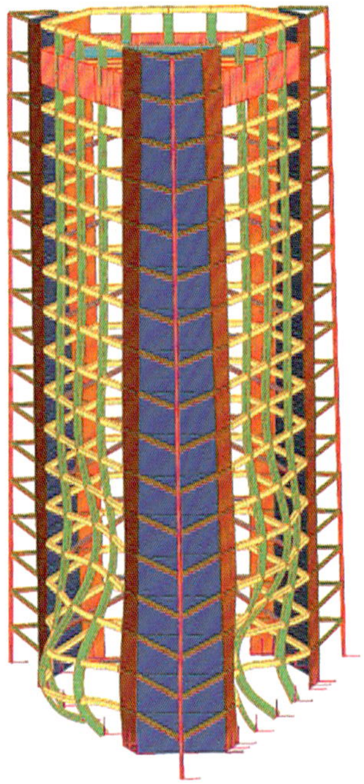

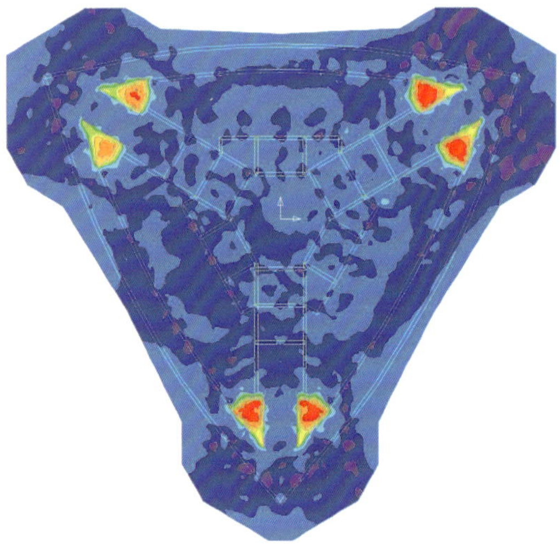

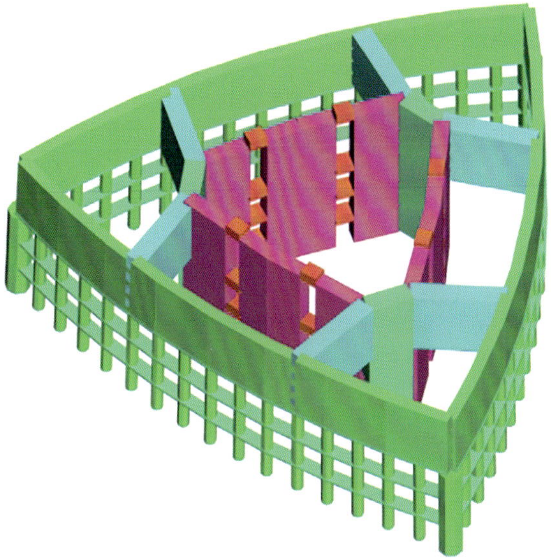

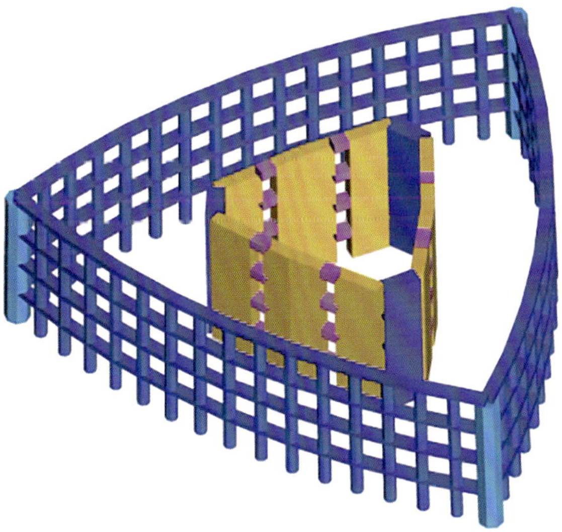

STRUCTURE

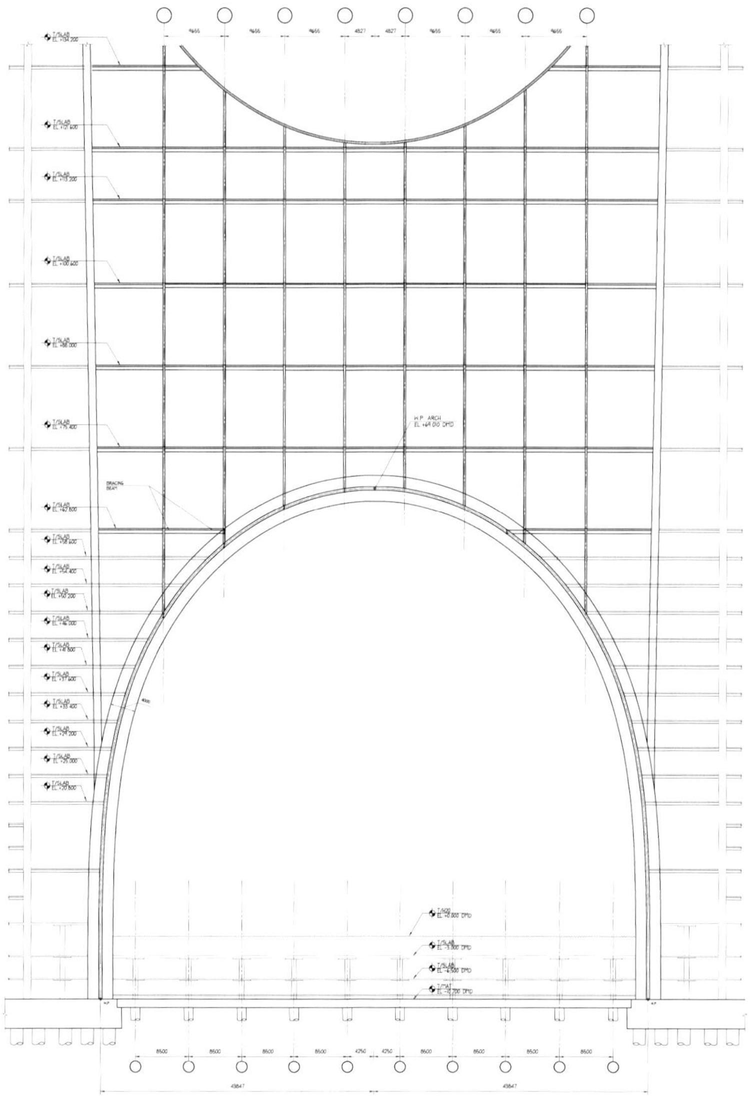

© Halvorson & Partners

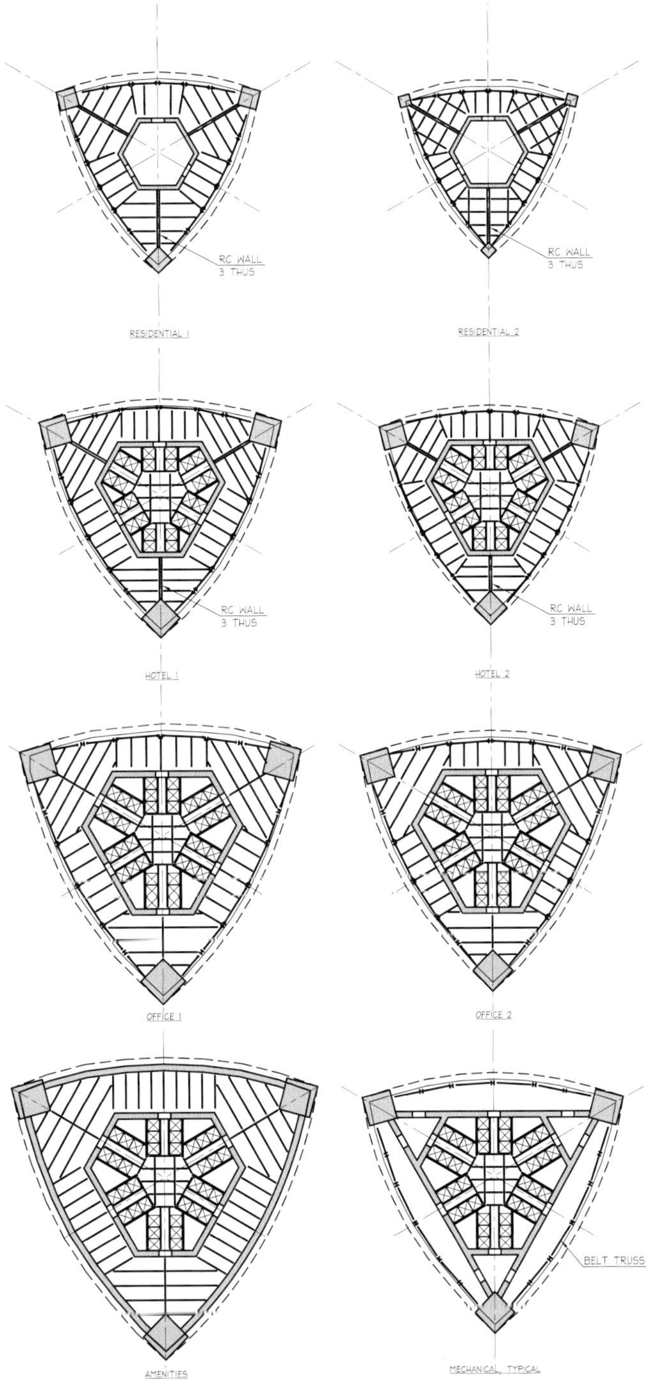

TOWER 1 PLANS
SCALE = 1:300

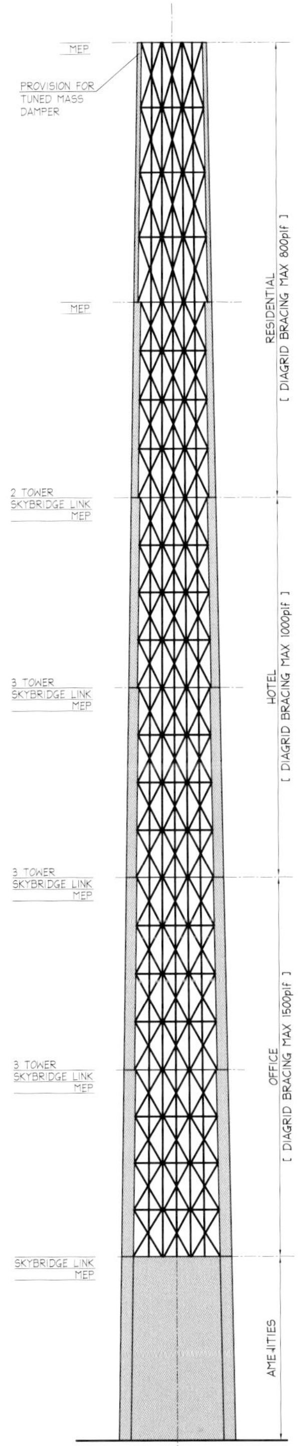

TOWER 1 ELEVATION
SCALE = 1:800

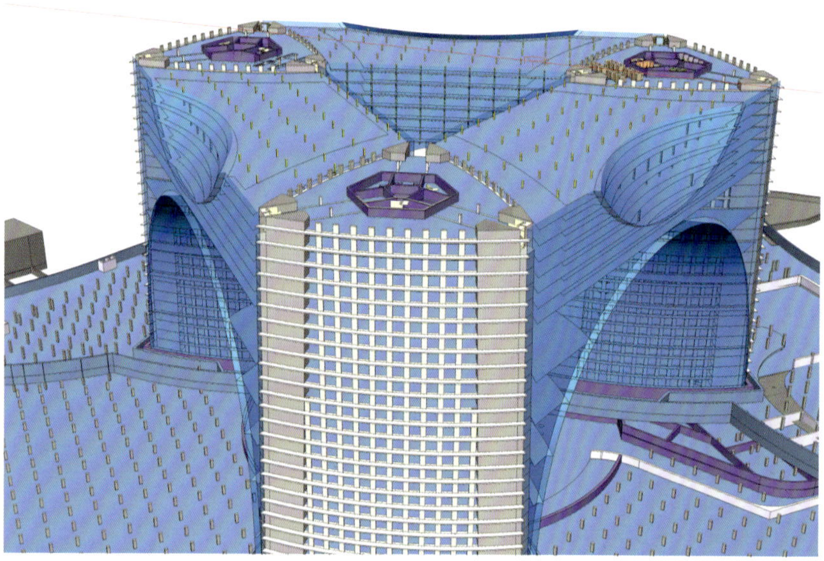

© Halvorson & Partners

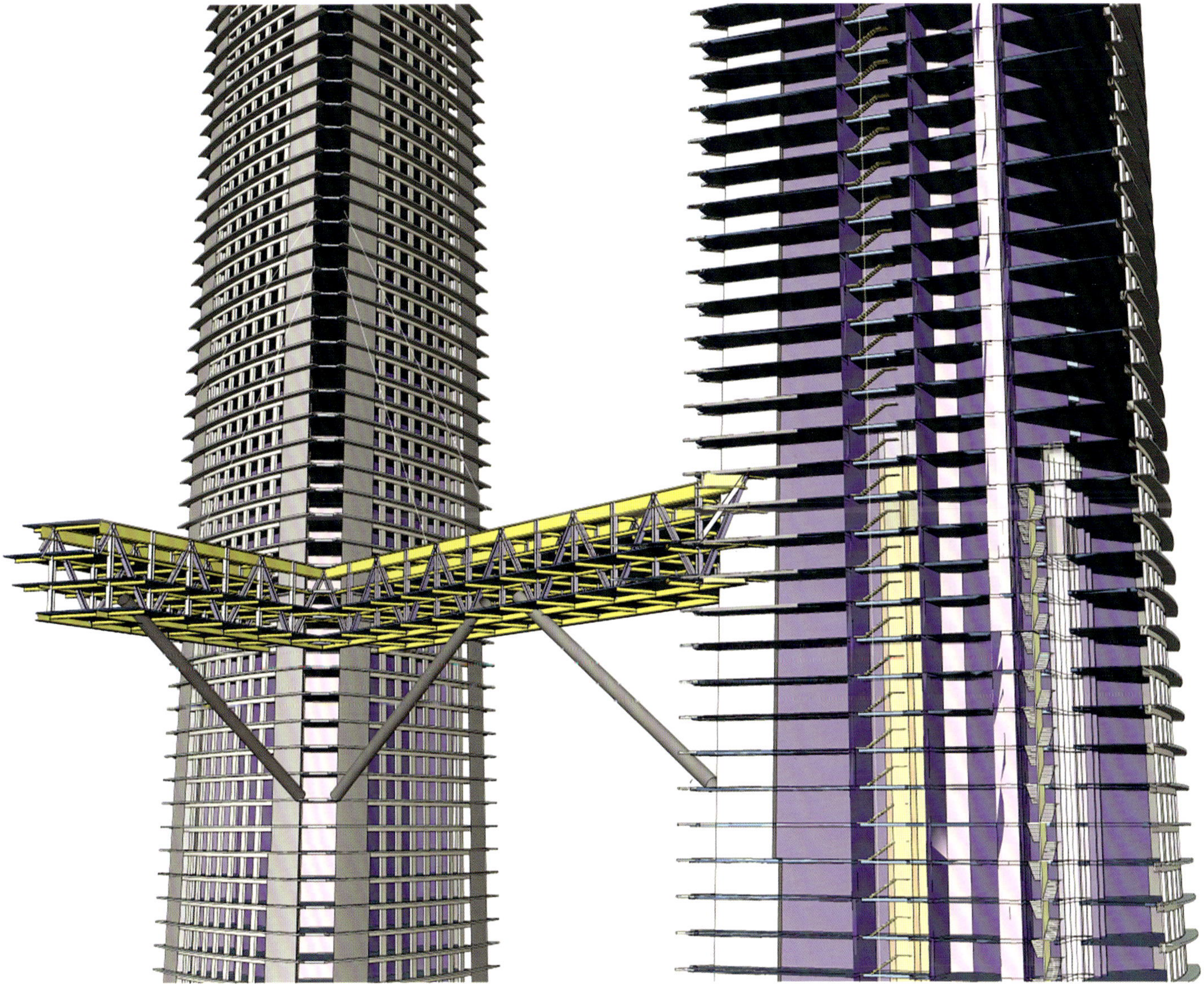

© Halvorson & Partners

STRUCTURE

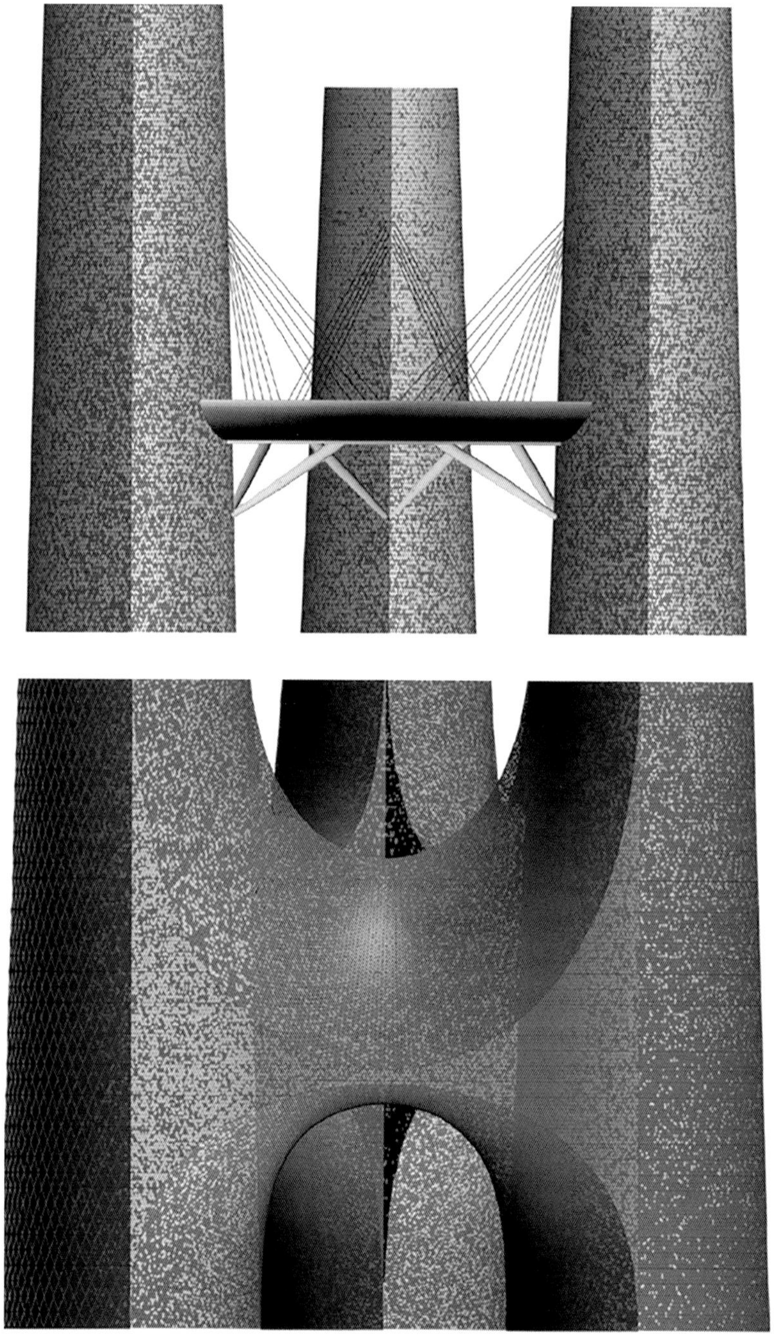

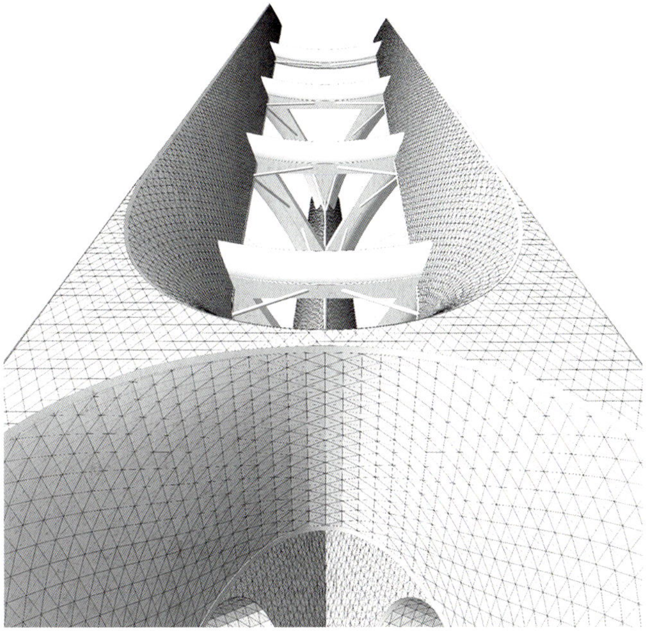

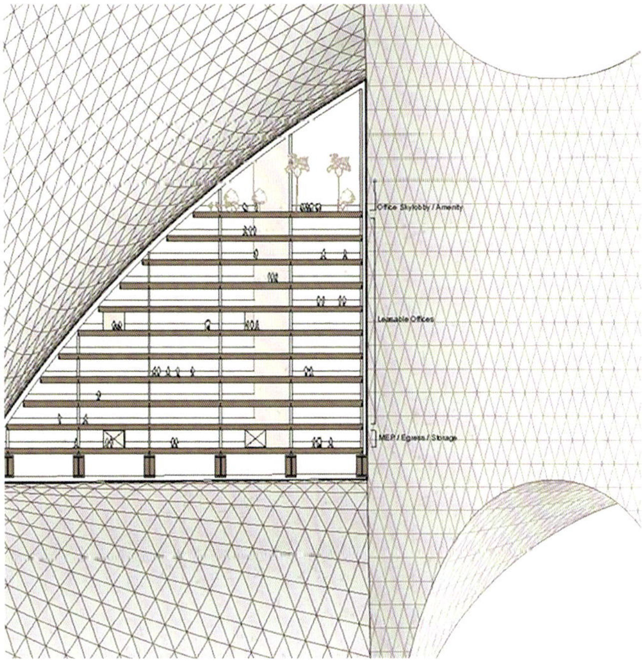

Office Skylobby / Amenity
Leasable Offices
MEP / Egress / Storage

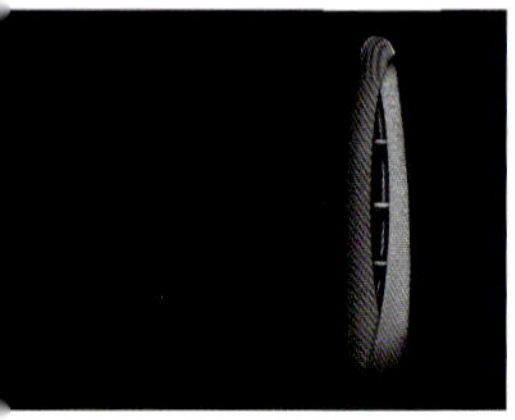

ZA'ABEEL SIGNATURE TOWER II

DUBAI, UAE, 2008

598M

Za'abeel Signature Tower II is part of the Za'abeel Energy City Master Plan in Dubai, which was completed in 2008. The tower was designed as the second of two schemes for the client, as the centerpiece for the new development.

The striking tower is comprised of a pair of towers that are structurally linked to each other, creating a mega building.

A driving design principle was to maintain the large center span that is connected by disc-like bridges. These openings allow wind to move through and give relief to the wind forces as they hit the broad face of a building.

The tower has prominent visual connections with the Burj Khalifa, Atrium City, and the waterfront. The tower oversees the entire Za'abeel Master Plan, including the Hotel and Commercial Towers.

- + CONTEXT
- + PROGRAM
- + PERFORMANCE
- + STRUCTURE

CONTEXT

The form of the tower is composed of two distinct halves that form a unified whole. Each facade is treated with a component-based wall system, which is informed by the tower's orientation to the sun. The components are derived from a common geometry while simultaneously reflecting an inverse relationship. The building's concept was drawn from three initial ideas:

Porosity: A distinctive central void maximizes the permeable surface area on its facade. Each facade opening is considered both as a portal affording vistas through and out of the building into the city of Dubai and an opportunity to optimize thermal control and natural light.

Intelligence: The tower represents an integration of technology and architecture. During the design phase, the complex geometries of the facade, which was inspired by Islamic patterning, are generated using parametric modeling techniques. LED screen tickers displaying local and global market information adorn the underside of the sky bridges through the buildings central void, reemphasize the union of technology and the architecture.

Gateway: The tower reasserts Za'abeel as a distinct focal point in Dubai. The building successfully competes with the visual and axial connections to the iconic structures of neighboring communities.

INITIAL SKETCHES, 2008

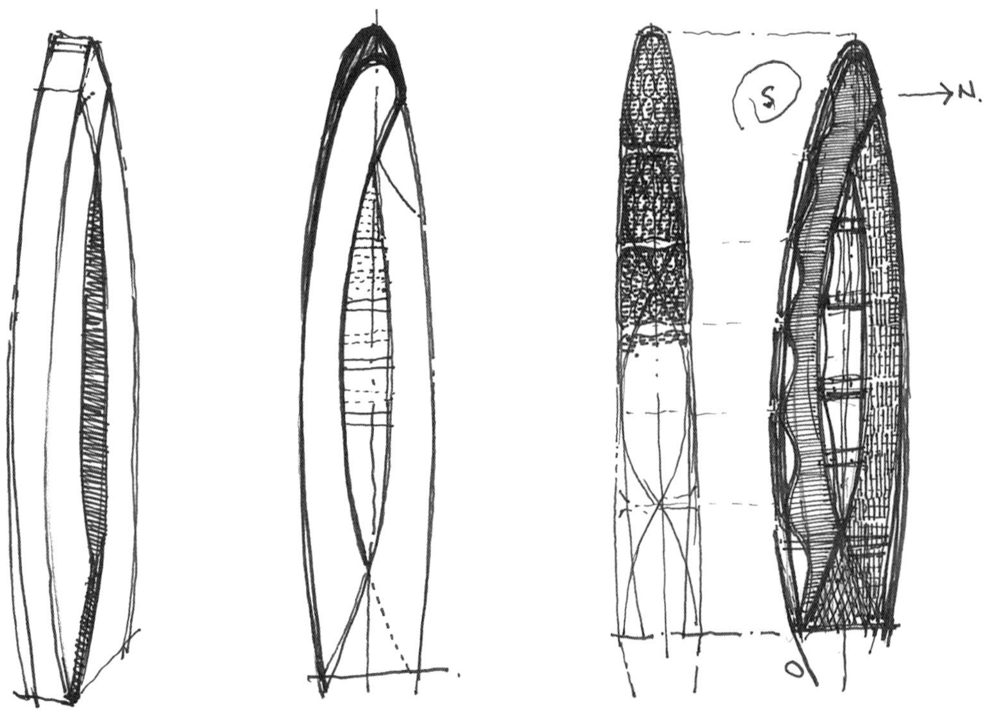

PROGRAM

The tower's program is mixed-use, consisting of office, residential, and hotel functions. As the floor plates become smaller at the top of the building, the residential program, which requires less lease span, is introduced. The bridge floors have sky-lobbies, community spaces, and amenities. Each tower has its own core which are interconnected structurally at the bridges.

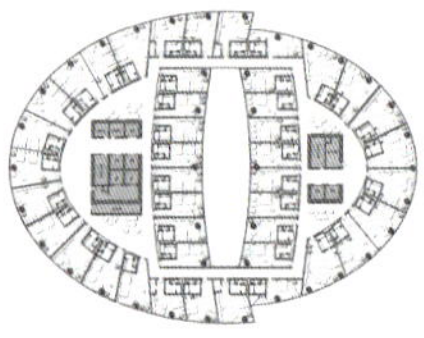

HOTEL

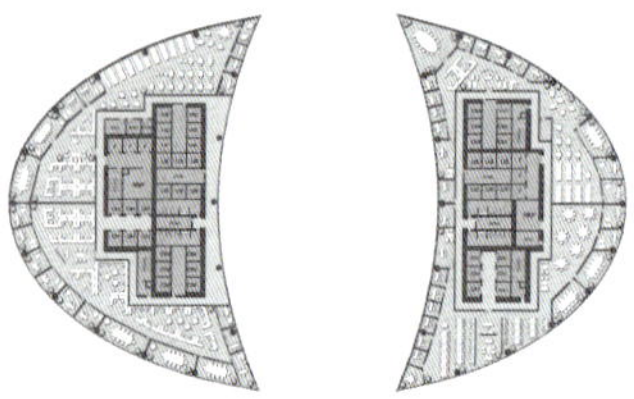

OFFICE

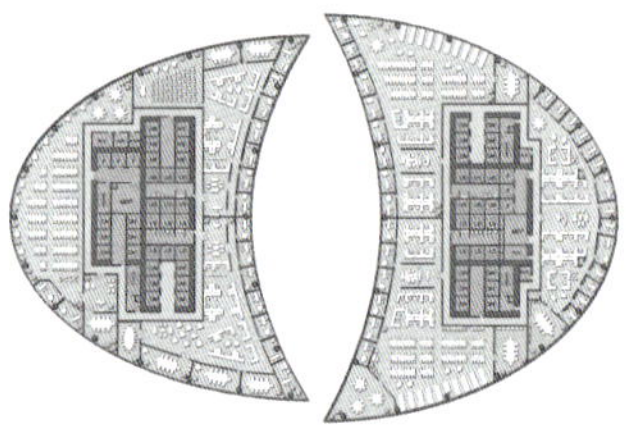

OFFICE

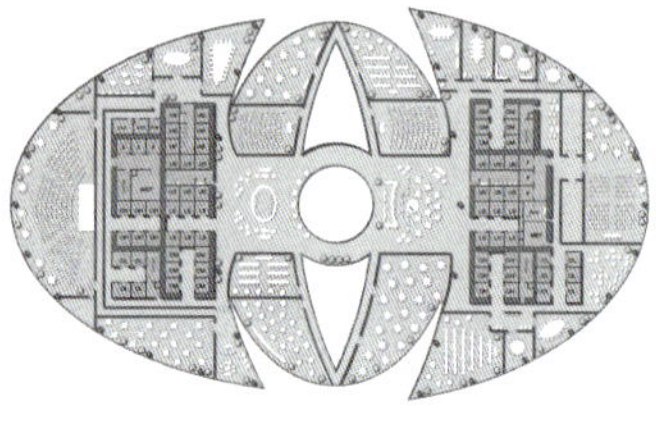

OFFICE

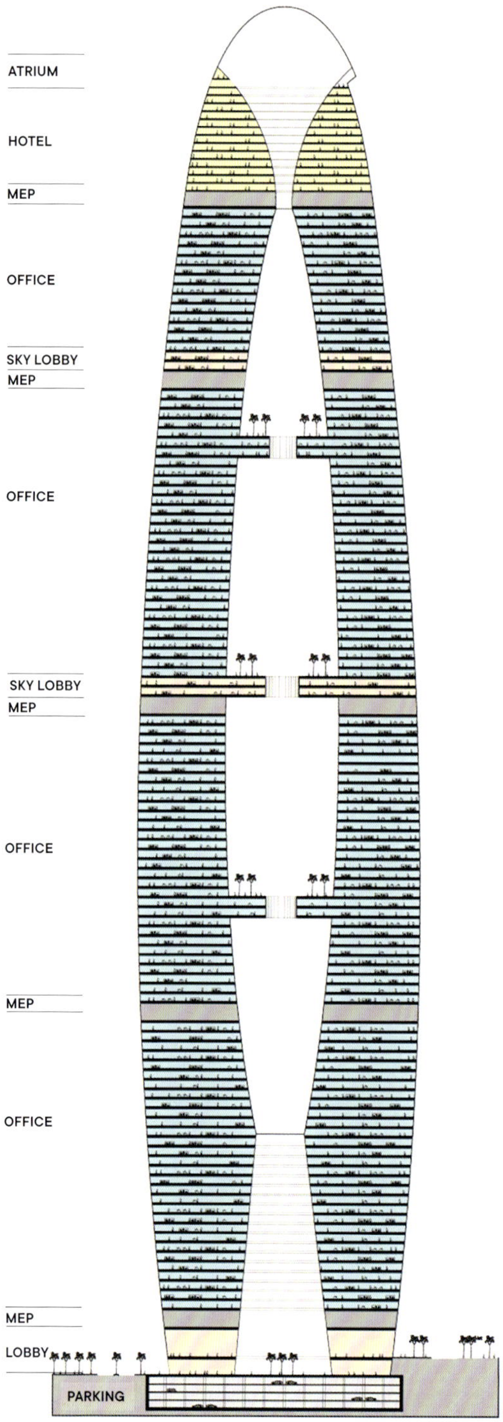

PERFORMANCE

The exterior wall design is divided by the two sides of the tower, creating a "positive" and "negative" side, in terms of their reaction to solar gain. Through a series of solar analysis studies, the design team discovered that one side of the tower has significantly more solar gain.

The exterior wall design responds by having more solid area on the western half of the tower and an increased glazed area on the east.

To provide additional function, the texture on the exterior wall reacts to the sun by angling to block direct sunlight. The inner portions, which do not have as much solar exposure due to self-shading of the building, are more generously glazed in a smooth surface.

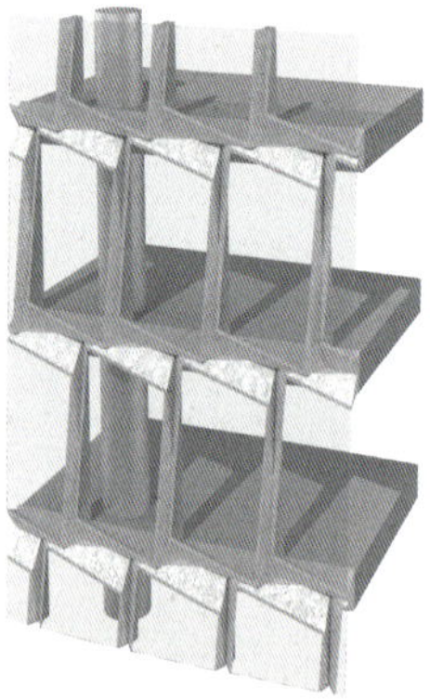

STRUCTURE

HYDER, STRUCTURAL ENGINEER

An internal truss, or outrigger, links the two cores, the inner frame, and the external frame. This provides stability in both the X and Y directions. The outrigger also creates an alternative path for the loads to transfer between the inner and external frames.

The loads created through the inner frame and the external frame are transmitted to a mega pyramid frame box at the lowest portion of the tower. This creates a still base to control lateral deflection at the tower's roof. The pyramid transmits loads directly to the foundation structure.

Lateral forces, such as wind and earthquake loads, are resisted by the inner frame's diagrid structure onto the perimeter columns and exterior frame. The force is transmitted to the ground through the pyramid frame at the base of the building.

While the jump form is utilized for the main tower's core walls, perimeter columns and the pyramid structure are constructed; tower slabs are constructed three to four floors behind the perimeter columns. The perimeter column's temporary bracing that was earlier installed becomes part of the slab construction.

These sequences continue past the first outrigger level. The embedment for the outrigger connection is constructed after the floor slabs have been constructed above the outrigger levels to prevent construction speed from slowing down.

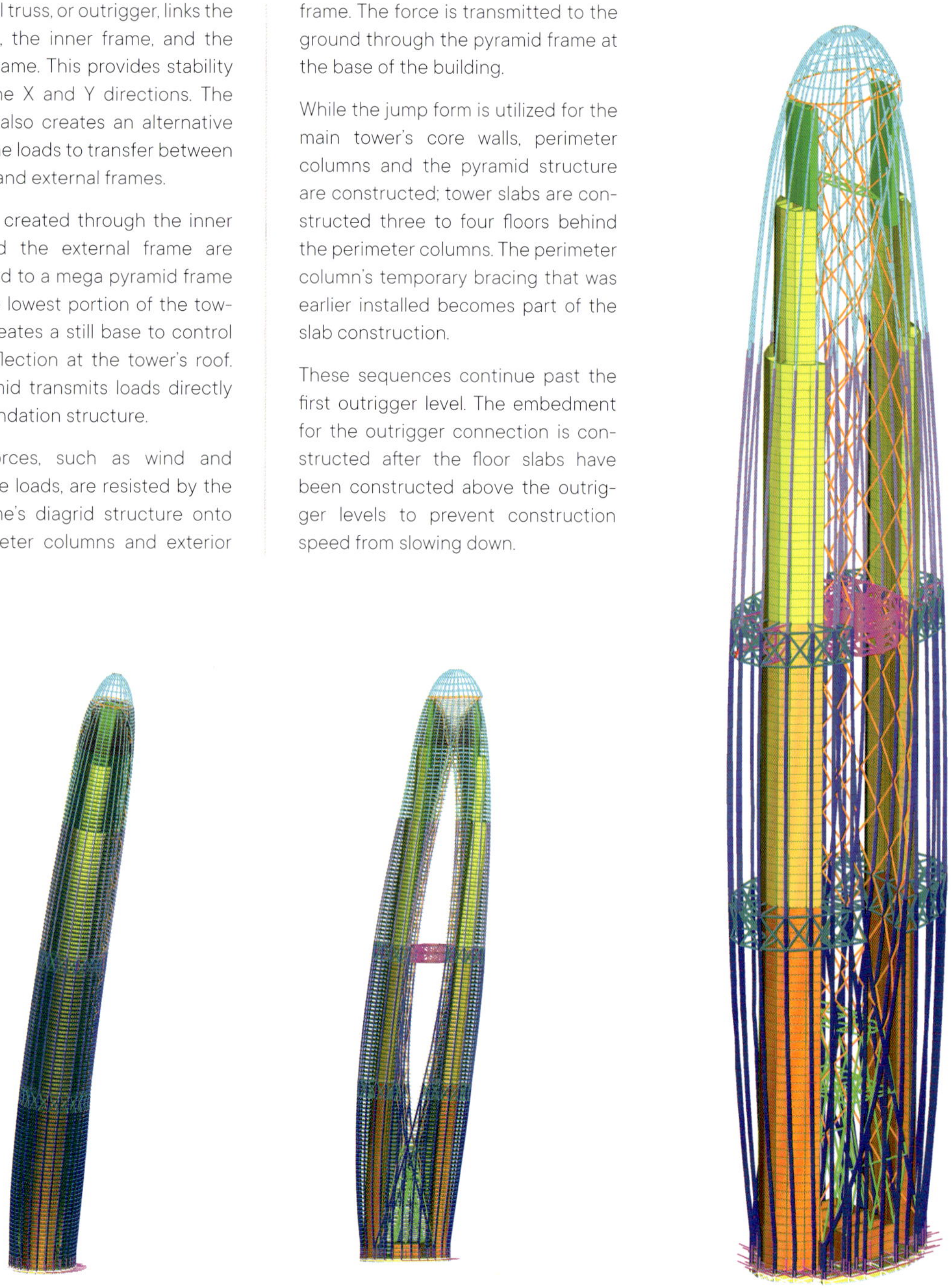

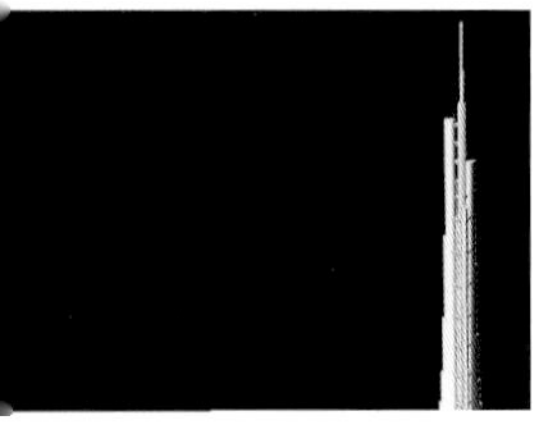

MILE HIGH TOWER PROTOTYPES

VARIOUS LOCATIONS 2008-2018

1600+M

Over the past 10 years, AS+GG has explored several concepts for a mile-high tower. Each prototype is design exercise that studies the structural and architectural viability of constructing a mixed-use, mile-high tower.

The first concept was designed for Chicago, Illinois and was designed for a specific site at the intersection of the north branch and the main stem of the Chicago River, on a plot known as Wolf Point. The design was completed with the idea that a megatall tower increases taxes, creates new employment opportunities, and increases economic activity in the area directly around the tower.

Although the design was presented to various potential developers, there was little interest. AS+GG maintains that the design would be an excellent opportunity to put a special building on a special site.

The second and third concepts were developed for a site in Mecca, Saudi Arabia. The client requested a building that honored the pilgrimage Muslim's strive to make at least once in their lifetime. The tower represents a triumph of modern technology, while paying homage to a holy tradition. Although unbuilt, the goal of building a Middle East mile-high tower may someday be realized.

- PROGRAM
- FORM
- PERFORMANCE
- STRUCTURE
- RESEARCH + DEVELOPMENT

PROGRAM

SCHEME 1

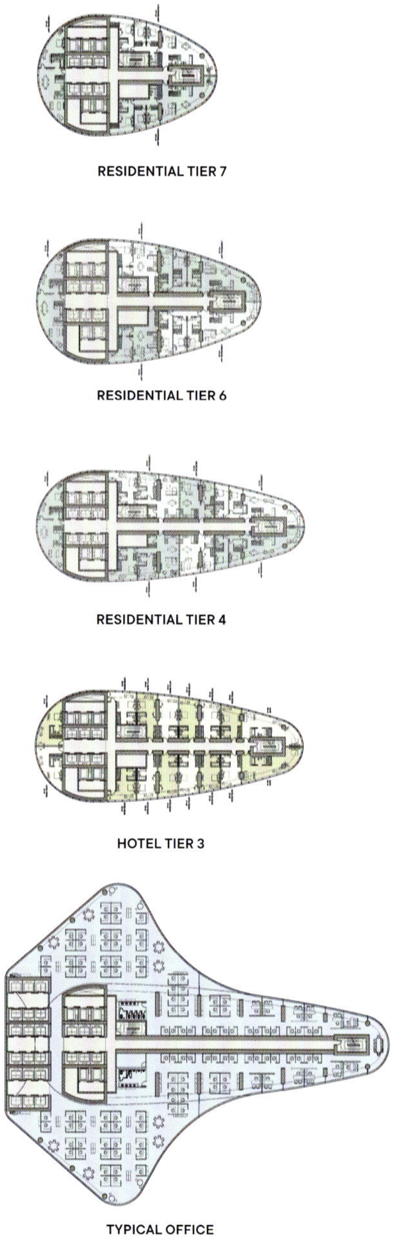

PROGRAM

SCHEME 2

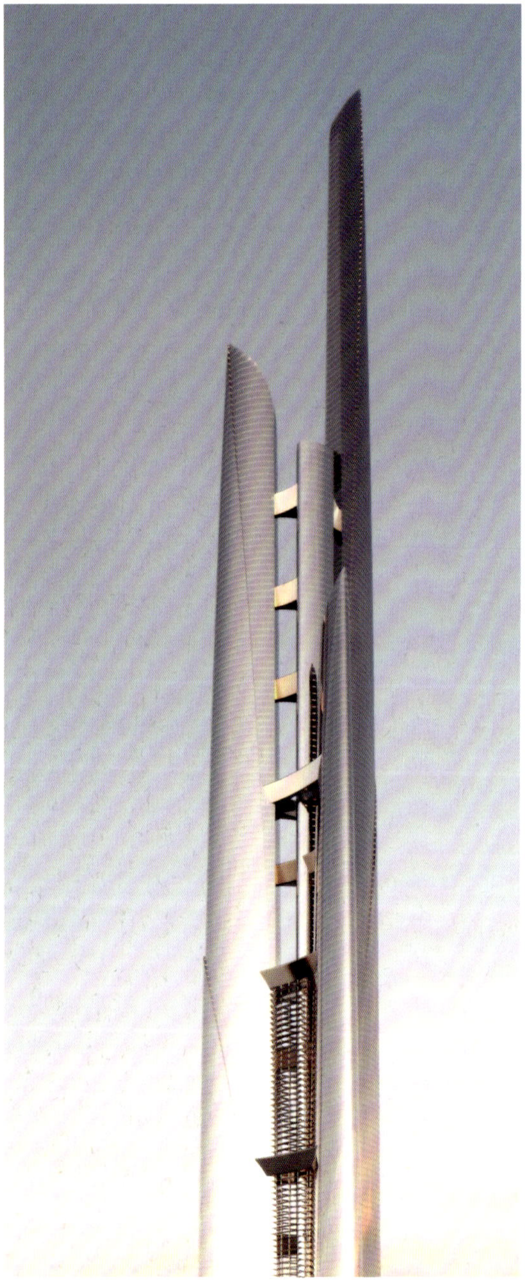

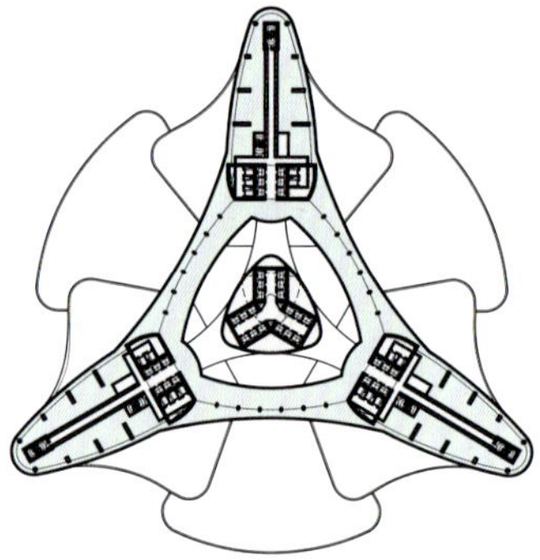

TIER 3
BRIDGE

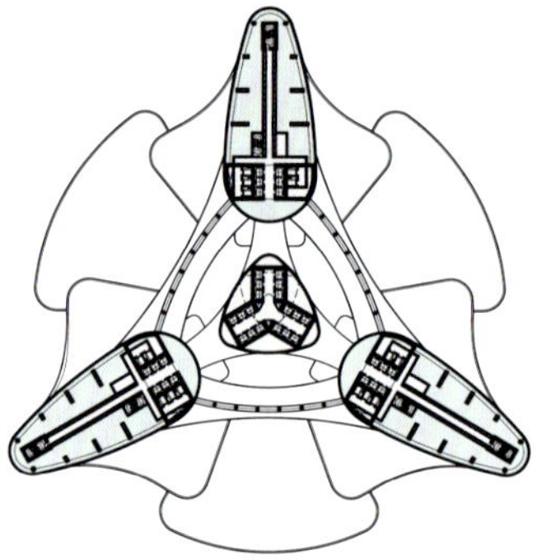

TIER 3

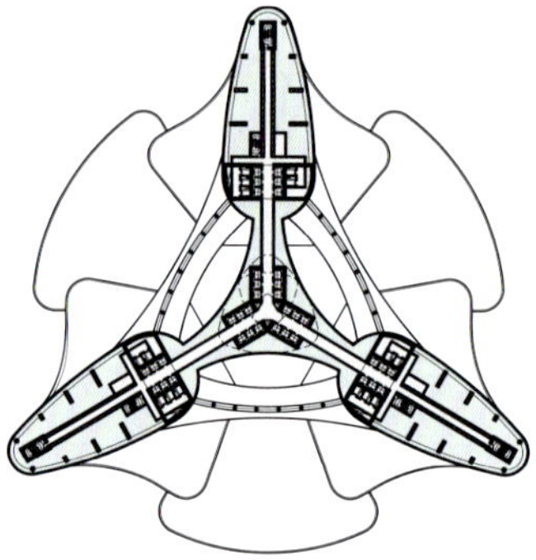

TIER 3
UMBILICAL

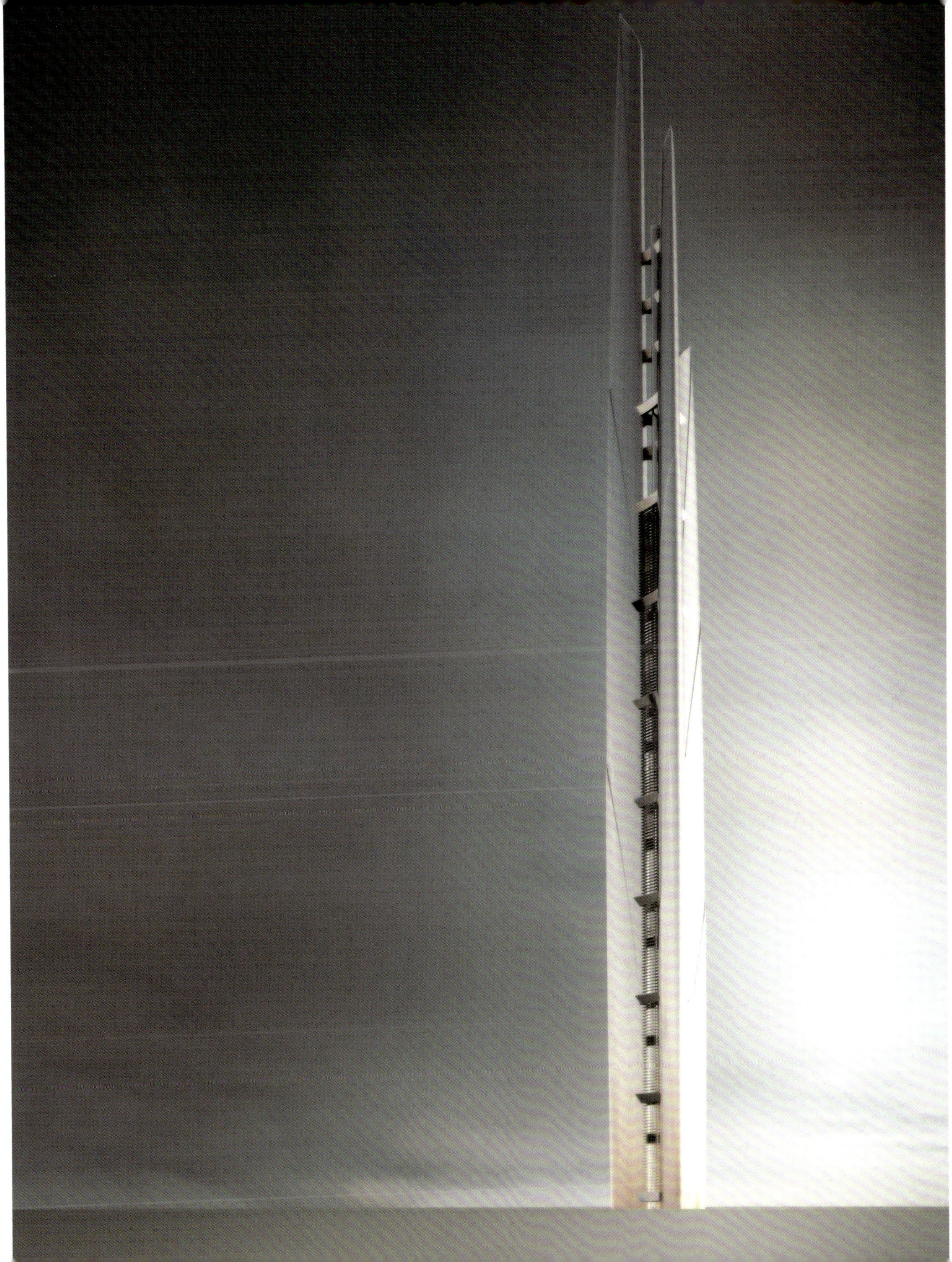

FORM

FLOOR PLATE
MATRIX

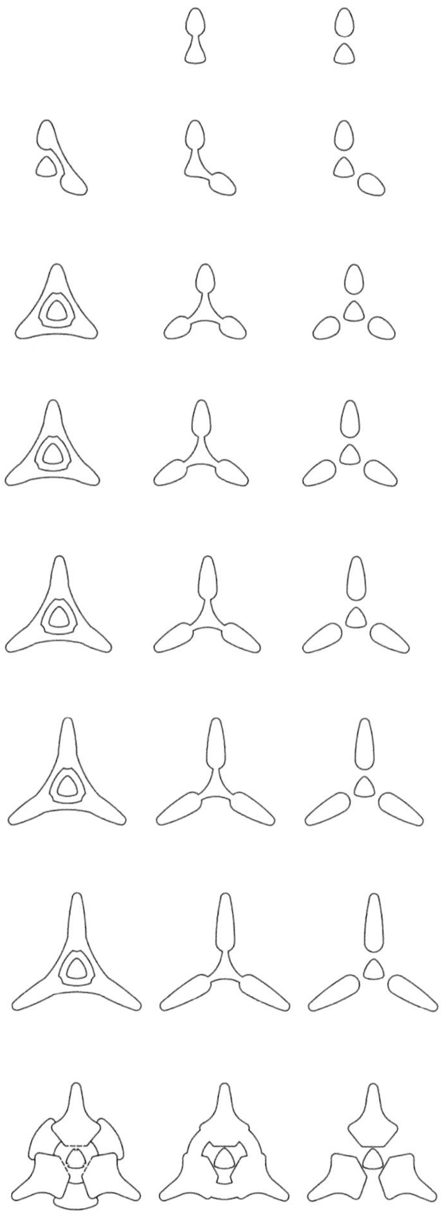

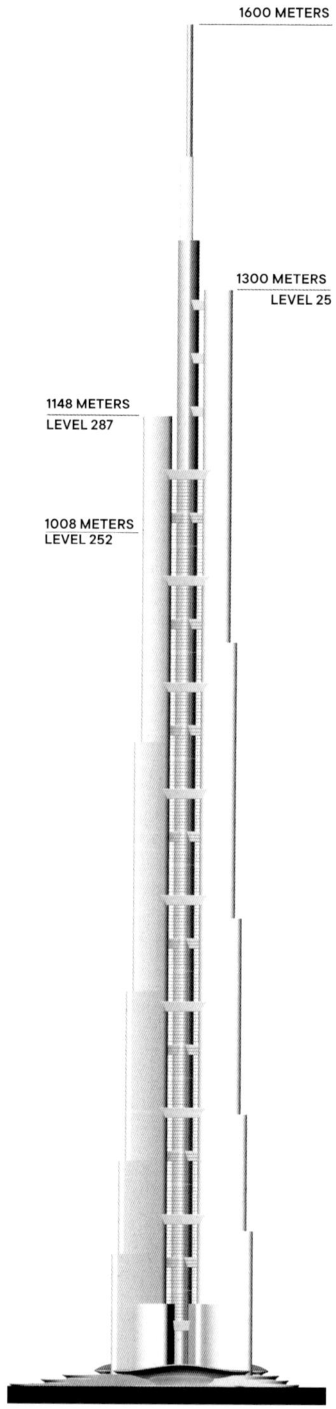

FORM

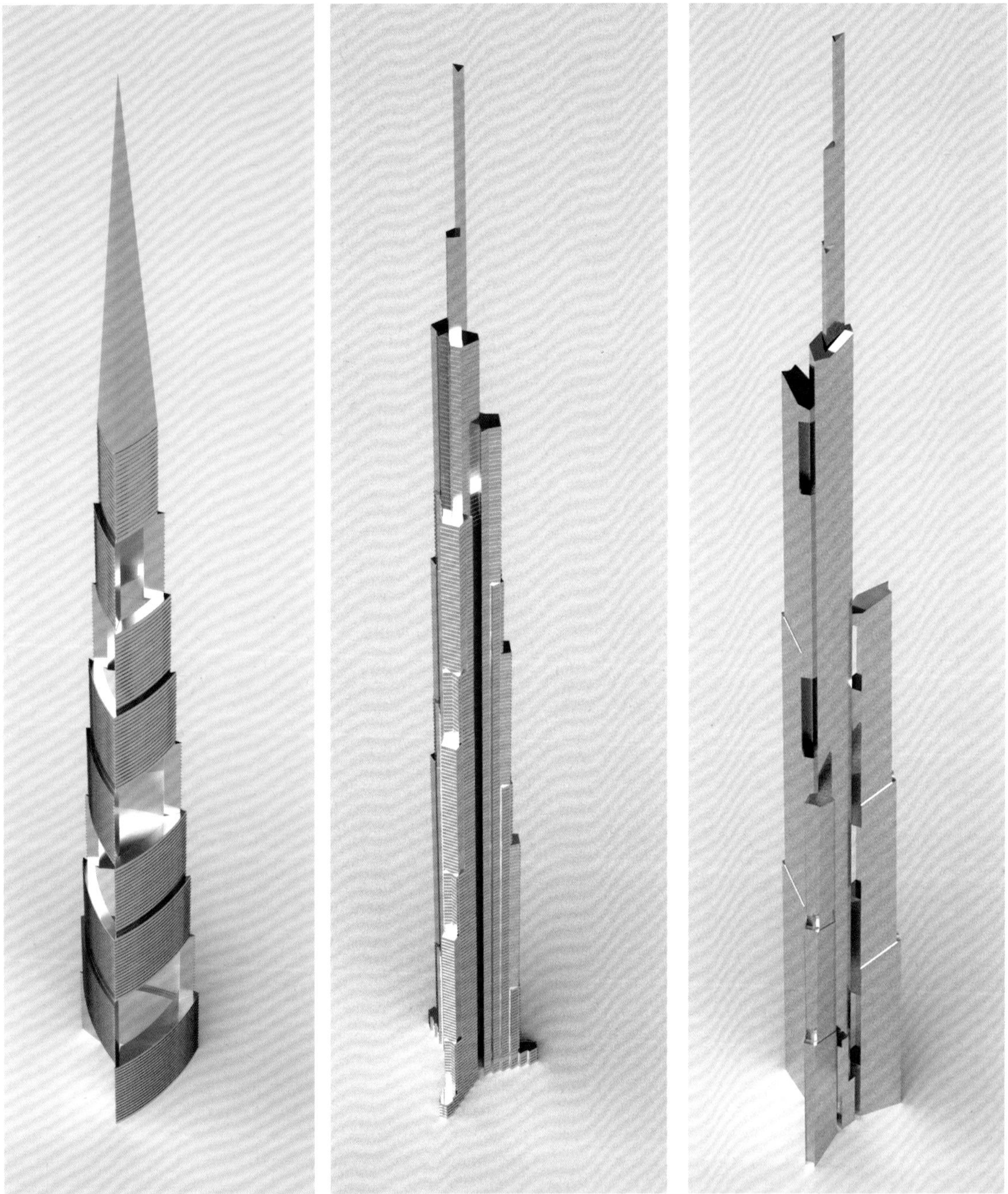

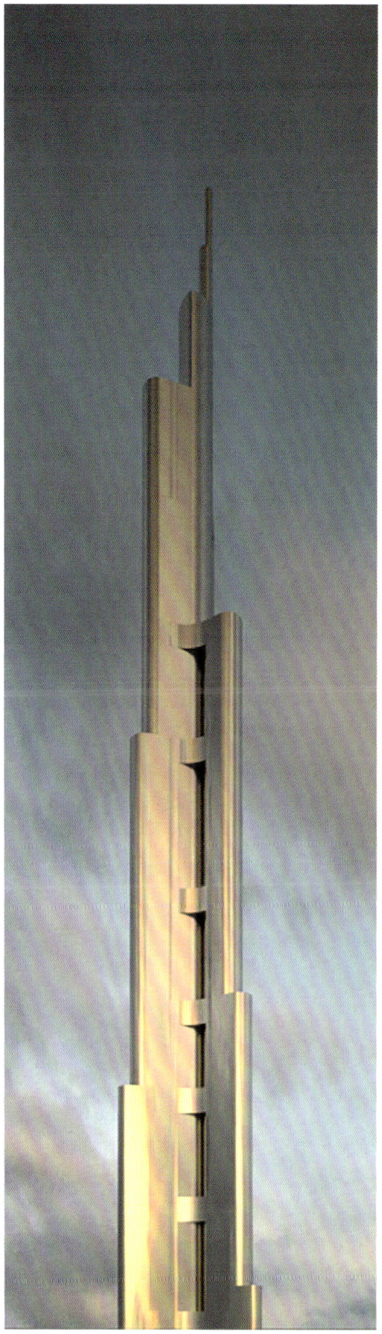

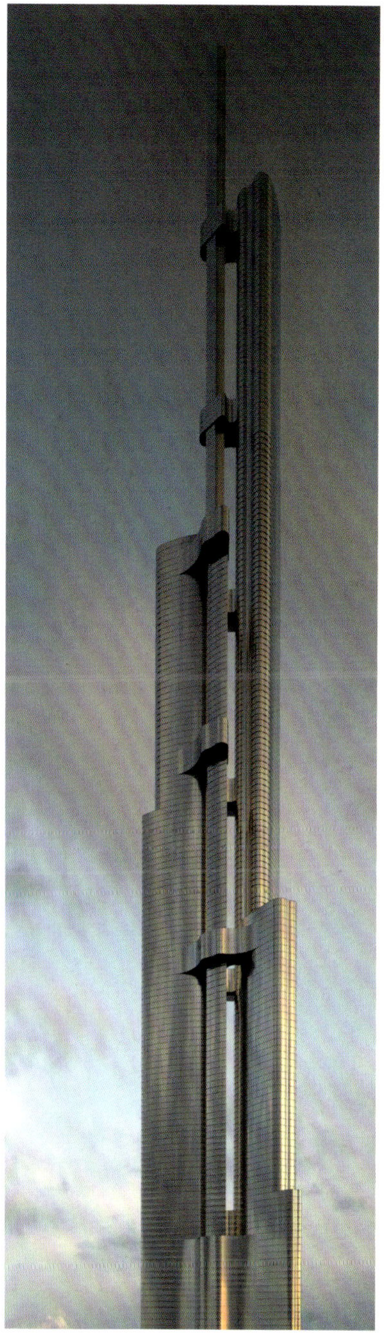

PERFORMANCE

Each prototype is comprised of three separate towers that are linked together with a central structural mast that encloses dozens of double-decker elevator shuttles. Further structural stability is achieved with a tubular structural lattice and three-story bridges every 32 floors, linking the towers together.

The central structural mast is also linked to the towers via a three-story umbilical every 32 floors. These linking elements combine to make a central atrium space between the towers, creating the opportunity for wind harvesting via vertical axis wind turbines.

The tower floor plates are shaped like tear drops that aerodynamically shape the mast, lattice, umbilical, and bridge elements to further channel wind dynamics through the turbine farm. The tower floor plates step up the building mass, decreasing in size in a spiral. These setbacks translate vertically up the building with expansive landscaped terraces integrated into the tower form.

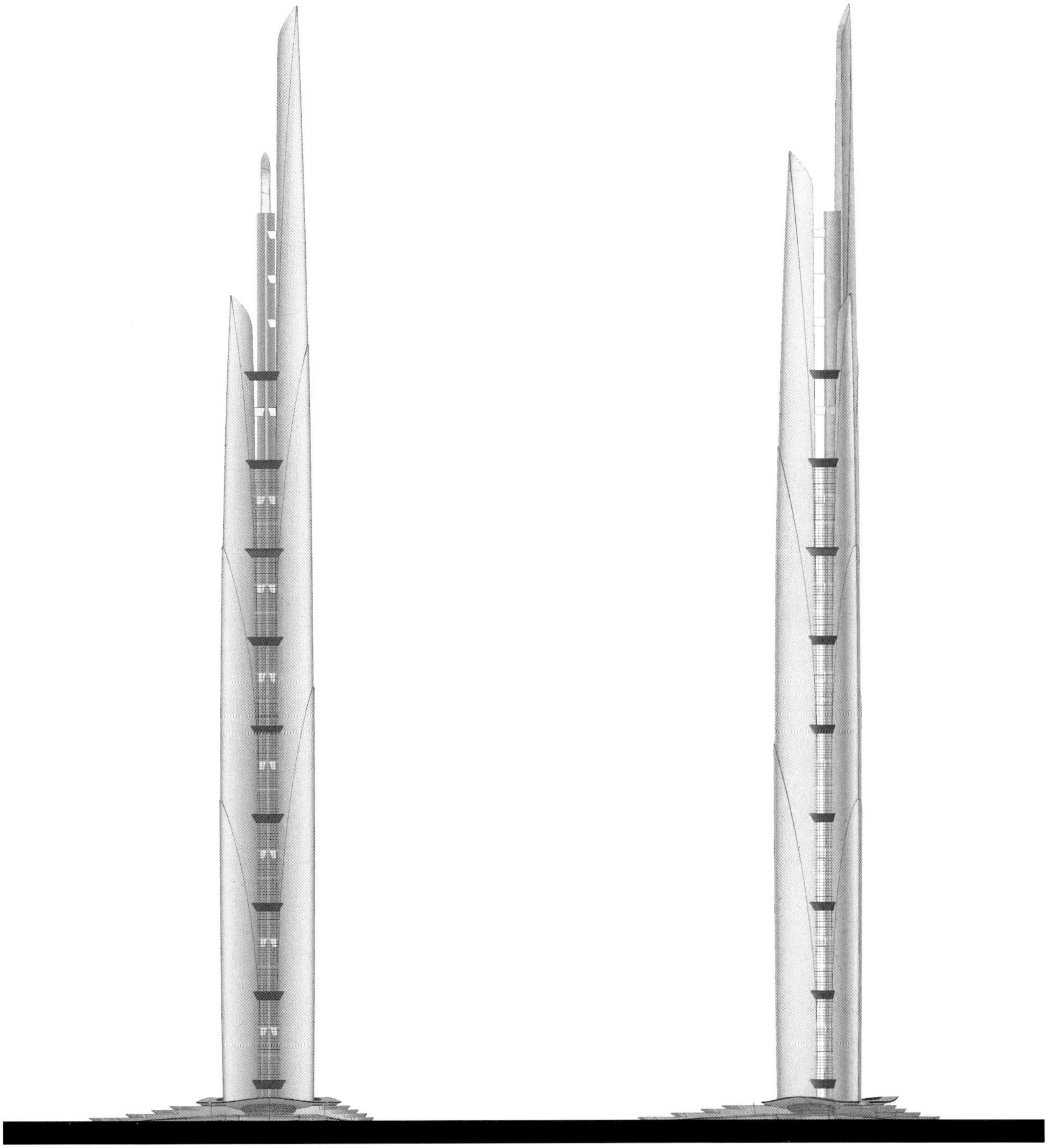

STRUCTURE

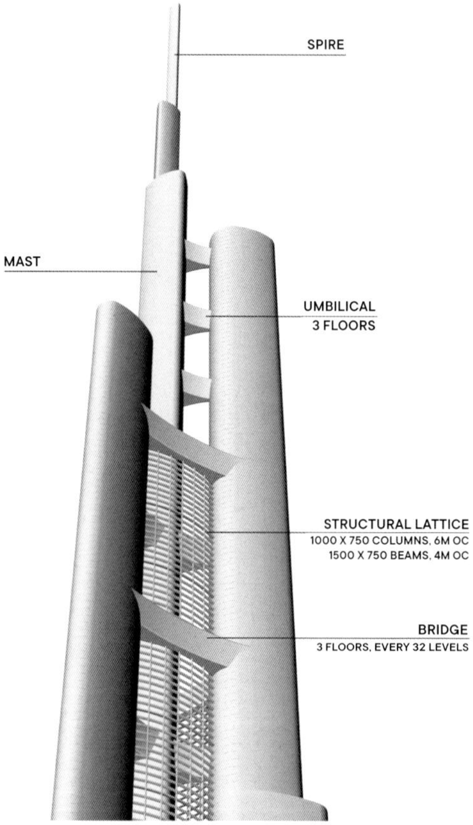
SPIRE
MAST
UMBILICAL
3 FLOORS
STRUCTURAL LATTICE
1000 X 750 COLUMNS, 6M OC
1500 X 750 BEAMS, 4M OC
BRIDGE
3 FLOORS, EVERY 32 LEVELS

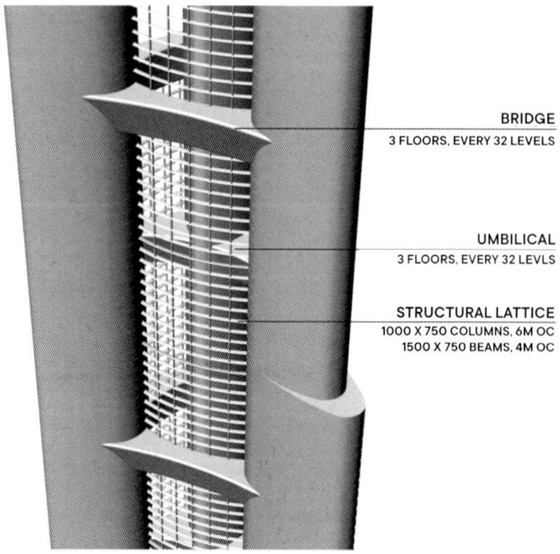
BRIDGE
3 FLOORS, EVERY 32 LEVELS
UMBILICAL
3 FLOORS, EVERY 32 LEVLS
STRUCTURAL LATTICE
1000 X 750 COLUMNS, 6M OC
1500 X 750 BEAMS, 4M OC

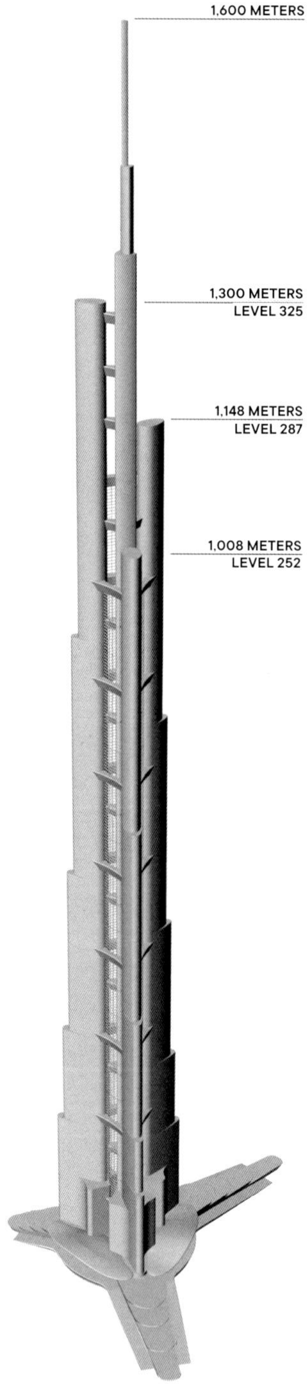
1,600 METERS
1,300 METERS
LEVEL 325
1,148 METERS
LEVEL 287
1,008 METERS
LEVEL 252

At AS+GG we are often asked how tall can we build? Is it possible to build a mile-high tower? We don't believe in saying "no" to design: you just have to figure out how to do it. If you ask the right questions, you can do anything.

Supertall towers are built for many different reasons: in celebration of a place or people, to create a symbol for an organization or individual, or to serve as a catalyst for future development. They also generate global publicity and spur economic development and tourism. This typology can represent a meaningful step forward and a symbol of success and optimism for the future. Considering this reasoning, what would be the impact of a Megatall tower? Would the reasons for building one be the same as a Supertall?

There are significant limiting factors when considering the design of a mile-high tower and these concerns need further study to determine the success of a building of this scale. One issue is that a mile-high tower would need an extremely large base to support its height. Therefore, land consideration is a top concern, along factors like infrastructure and transportation.

The actual size of the podium could also be a concern. Portions of the podium might be far from the perimeter of the actual building. How would you occupy that area? What function would it perform? And once that function is determined, would it make economic sense? The biggest challenge is the issue of elevators. To get to the top of the building, the occupant would transfer from one elevator to another at least two or three times, using current technologies. This is one of many challenges to solve, looking twoard the future of tall buildings.

HOW TALL CAN WE GO? A DISCUSSION WITH ADRIAN D. SMITH

HOW TALL CAN WE GO?

A DISCUSSION WITH ADRIAN D. SMITH, FAIA, RIBA

HOW IMPORTANT IS A TALL, ICONIC BUILDING IN ESTABLISHING A CITY AS A GLOBAL DESTINATION?

People create supertall buildings for a number of reasons: in celebration of a place or people, to create a symbol for an organization or individual, or to serve as a catalyst for future development. Supertall buildings also generate publicity and spur economic development and tourism. A supertall tower represents a meaningful step forward and a symbol of success and optimism for the future.

IS THERE A TECHNICAL LIMITATION? IS A 2000+ M PROJECT POSSIBLE IN THE COMING YEARS?

I'm often asked the question, "how tall can you go?" Specifically, people want to know if it's possible to build a mile-high tower. We have done some investigational work on a mile-high building, but it's purely speculative at this point. The biggest challenge for a building of that height is the issue with elevators. To get to the top, with current technology, you would have to transfer from one elevator to another at least two or three times, if not more, which would be extremely time-consuming. So that would be a significant limiting factor, and will have to be addressed by advances in elevator technology before a mile-high building is realistic.

Another issue in mile-high construction would be the very large footprint that would be needed to support a structure that tall. Also, within the cavity of that base would be a great deal of space, most of it nowhere near the perimeter of the building (i.e., near windows). How would you use all that area—as a giant atrium? And if you did use it that way, would it make economic sense? Those are questions that need to be answered satisfactorily before designing a building that tall.

SUPERTALL BUILDINGS HAVE AN APPEAL THAT EXCEEDS BUDGET OR PROFIT CONCERNS. SOME OF THEM BECOME TRADEMARKS OF A CITY OR EVEN A COUNTRY, THEY ARE LANDMARKS, ATTRACT TOURIST ETC., WILL YOU PLEASE COMMENT ON THAT?

That's absolutely right. One of the main reasons to build a supertall is to create a local, regional, or national landmark, bringing significant attention to its owner and location. The Petronas Towers in Malaysia are a great example of this approach. Petronas made little economic sense and sat two-thirds empty for several years after completion, but the worldwide attention it brought to Kuala Lumpur and to Petronas, as an oil and gas company, was very significant.

It established Kuala Lumpur as a tourist destination and enhanced its reputation as a location for business. It also showcased the attractive lifestyle of this part of the world and bolstered its economy. I think we're seeing a similar effect in Dubai with Burj Khalifa, and I believe the same thing will occur in Jeddah because of Jeddah Tower, formerly known as Kingdom Tower.

CONCLUSION

WHAT IS YOUR OPINION ON THE "RACE" TO THE TOP? ARE ARCHITECTS TRYING TO GO HIGHER AND HIGHER?

I think so, because the needs of our fast-urbanizing world demand it. More than any other typology, the tall building can address the needs of the future, while having the least environmental impact, particularly in terms of land use. Skyscrapers are inherently sustainable because they accommodate a large number of people on a comparatively small footprint of land. They also offer more efficient vertical transportation systems; elevators in skyscrapers are estimated to be forty times more energy efficient and ten times more materials efficient than an average automobile.

Skyscrapers also encourage the use of public transit by creating increasingly walkable cities. Studies have shown that the denser an urban population is, the lower the energy consumption per inhabitant for travel in cars. In fact, there is a direct relationship between the reduction of energy consumption through transportation and the increase in building density. Finally, tall buildings offer significant economies of scale compared to similar amounts of housing constructed in a low-rise form. With skyscrapers, you have one roof and one foundation rather than the multiple roofs and foundations that groups of buildings with the same cumulative area would require.

Tall buildings—including supertall and megatall buildings, which I would define as those which contain sixty stories or more—can also be designed to further decrease their environmental effect. They can take advantage of the fast wind speeds at higher altitudes and drive wind toward building-integrated turbines to generate power. Because they are less likely to have shadows cast on them, high-rises also make efficient use of photovoltaic systems to absorb solar power. And deep foundations make them ideal for geothermal heating and radiant cooling systems.

Supertall towers in particular can be a catalyst for growth and prosperity in cities around the world. Buildings are created for a number of reasons: in celebration of a place or people, as a symbol for an organization or individual, or to serve as the spark for future development.

Economically, a very tall tower makes sense as the centerpiece of a larger development. The central tower can increase the value of the adjacent land and the buildings around it, making the overall project financially feasible. This was the concept with Burj Khalifa, as seen below, where the tower itself made little or no profit but increased the value and desirability of the land around it, which made the overall development very profitable. In Shanghai, Jin Mao Tower, which I also designed while at SOM, was a similar example.

© Tim Griffith Photography

DO YOU EVER GET THE FEELING THAT THIS RACE FOR THE SKY BY BUILDING OWNERS MAY FIZZLE OUT IN THE FUTURE, OR WILL MAN ALWAYS STRIVE TO BUILD TALLER AND TALLER BUILDINGS?

Consistent with human nature and subject to business conditions, developers throughout the world will always look to architects to design taller buildings. Skyscrapers are inherently sustainable because they accommodate a large number of people on a small footprint of land. They also offer efficient vertical and horizontal transportation systems, encouraging the use of public transit and creating increasingly walkable cities.

ARE THE SKYSCRAPERS THE FUTURE OF THE CITIES?

I believe that supertall towers represent a meaningful step forward and a symbol of success and optimism for the future. I have seen the pride in people's eyes when they are involved in creating, owning, building, or operating such grand edifices. I believe that we must always strive for greatness and find the means to attain it. If not, we become irrelevant. Likewise, cities must continue to build and improve their conditions. When we lose the spirit to reach for glory, we lose our soul. But I think that tall buildings are just a piece of the future for cities. An important cog no doubt, but there are other factors in combination with supertalls that must be present.

What excites me are the satellite cities that we are designing at Adrian Smith + Gordon Gill Architecture. We have the opportunity to create new cities that are holistic, zero energy, and self-sustaining. The project plan is circular in form, about 1.3 kilometers in diameter, and is a live/work environment for about 100,000 people.

The prototypes we are designing can be replicated in China, India, Africa, and many underdeveloped countries. There are great benefits to this layout. For example, the city's compressed size and high density ensures that lives there can walk to work. If someone needs to get out of the city, they can hop on subway line.

The projects have also been designed to achieve a remarkable series of sustainable benchmarks. The city will use 48 percent less energy and 58 percent less water than a conventional development of similar population. It will also produce 89 percent less landfill waste and generate 60 percent less carbon dioxide.

Conserving existing farmland also becomes an economic and sustainable priority, with more than 60 percent of the 800-acre-site area preserved for agriculture and open space.

While tall towers are exciting to design, creating the entire district around a tall tower as a satellite city has the potential to make a difference for the greatest number of people, which is a goal for our firm in the future.

GREAT CITY CHENGDU BY AS+GG

APPENDIX: PROJECT CREDITS, AWARDS, PUBLICATIONS

A S
G G

PROJECT CREDITS

1 PARK AVENUE

Design Partners	Adrian Smith and Gordon Gill
Management Partner	Robert Forest
Project Manager	Ben Johnson
Senior Designer	Jeff Stafford and Fei Xu
Senior Technical	Peter Weismantle

Project Team

Leslie Baluga, Charles Collett, Joshua Cooper, Richard Cosgrove, Patrick Fitzpatrick, Brendan Gibbons, Simon Gore, Christopher Harvey, Jessica Hogue, Darren Hoppa, Zhya Jacobs, Matthew Nyweide, David Rariden, Bradley Riemann, Siddant Sinha, Teddy Slowik, Donald Stark, Rebecca Stewart, Abhijit Thenge, Bradley Wilkins

Client	Meraas
Structural Engineer	Halvorson and Partners
MEP Engineer	Syska Hennessy Group
Fire Life Safety	Rolf Jensen and Associates, Inc.
Vertical Transportation	Fortune Consulting, Ltd.
Wind Engineering	RWDI Consulting Engineers
LEED	Hilson Moran
Masterplan	Hyder, SOM, WSP
Soils	STS
Civil	Hyder, WSP
Façade Access	Lerch Bates

CHENGDU GREENLAND TOWER

Design Partners	Adrian Smith and Gordon Gill
Management Partner	Robert Forest
Project Manager	Ben Johnson
Senior Designer	Fei Xu
Senior Technical	Peter Weismantle

Project Team

Tyler Austin, Rustem Baishev, Mariela Bayer, Sara Beardsley, Rachael Bennett, Nicholas Berchtold, John Burcher, Jessica Butler, Ashley Byers, Sally Cathcart, Daniel Caven, Marc Cerone, Rebecca Cryder, Katherine Dailey, Michelle Dumont, Elliot Eakin, David Emmons, Keara Fanning, Sobieslaw Fedyk, Dian Feng, Patrick Fitzpatrick, Joshua Frank, Iris Gan, Natalya Ganyukova, Dimitra Gelagoti, Brendan Gibbons, Gail Goldstead, Felix Griggs, Kira Ho, DongSoo Jang, Tamara Jimshitashvili, Joel Kerner, Angela Khermouch, Changhoon Kim, Hyungwoo Kim, Alexander Knowles, Alison Lampier, Rebecca LeMaster, Randi Lesniewski, Mengxi Li, Yuchen Liu, Weiwei Luo, Jaclyn Marcus, Tashio Martinez, Christopher Miller, Jongpil Park, Benjamin Raines, Daniel Ramos, Yi Ren, Catherine Rogg, Matthew Simpson, Chad Smith, Jeff Snodgrass, Jiatuo Song, James Struthers, Anthony Trifiletti, Luis Villafane, Anthony Viola, Brent Watanabe

Client	Greenland Group Real Estate Dev. Co., Ltd
Structural Engineer	Thornton Tomasetti
MEP Engineer	Positivenergy Practice
Vertical Transportation	Fortune Shepler Consulting
Exterior Wall	PFT
Façade Access	Lerch Bates
Lighting	OVI Office for Visual Interaction
Local Design Institute	ECADI (East China Architecture Design and Research Institute)
Acoustic, Security	SMW
Fire Life Safety	Rolf Jensen and Associates, Inc
Landscape	SWA
Wind Engineering	RWDI Consulting Engineers

WUHAN GREENLAND CENTER

Design Partners	Adrian Smith and Gordon Gill
Management Partner	Robert Forest
Project Manager	Ben Johnson
Senior Designer	Juan Betancur
Senior Technical	Peter Weismantle

Project Team

Rachael Bennett, Jillian Blakey, Ana Blomeier, Nathan Bowman, John Burcher, Sally Cathcart, Marc Cerone, Raymond Coleman, Colin Craig, Rebecca Cryder, Emily Dones, Patrick Fitzpatrick, Joshua Frank, Iris Gan, Brendan Gibbons, Felix

PROJECT CREDITS

Griggs, Kira Ho, Brian Hubbard, Brooke Ingram, DongSoo Jang, Qi Jia, Robert Jillson, Laura Jimenez, Tamara Jimshitashvili, Trudie Kahler, Joshua Kuffner, Ryan Kukuraitis, Soeun Lee, David LeFevre, Rebecca Lemaster, Randi Lesniewski, Miaoqi Liu, Weiwei Luo, Takuya Mamada, Christopher Miller, Suncica Milosevic, Luis Palacio, Robert Perry, James Reisinger, Yi Ren, Catherine Rogg, Mario Romero, Rachel Sears, Daniel Segraves, Mohamed Sheriff, Matthew Simpson, Jason Smith, Joshua Smith, Matt Snoap, Jorge Soler, Michelle Swanson, Corey Thomas, Anthony Trifiletti, Chen-Han Tu, Anthony Viola, Perry Wreaks, Si Wu, Dong Yan, Margaret Yoo, Andrew Zell, Jing Zhang, Yueming Zhou

Client	Wuhan Greenland Property Co, Ltd
Civil	Prism Engineering, Inc
Structural Engineer	Thornton Tomasetti
MEP Engineer	Positivenergy Practice
Fire Life Safety	Rolf Jensen & Associates, Ltd
Architectural Lighting	Fisher Marantz Stone
Lighting	Aurora Lighting Design, Inc
Exterior Wall	PFT
Façade Access	Lerch Bates
Vertical Transportation	Fortune consulting, Ltd
Wind Engineering	RWDI Consulting Engineers
Landscape	SWA
Local Design Institute	ECADI (East China Architecture Design and Research Institute)

YONGSAN DANCING DRAGONS

Design Partners	Adrian Smith and Gordon Gill
Management Partner	Robert Forest
Project Manager	Brian M. Jack
Senior Designer	Sara Beardsley
Senior Technical	Sae Hwang Oh

Project Team

Miguel Alvarez, James Bayless, Frederik Berte, Brett Bridgeland, John Burcher, Ashley Byers, Sally Cathcart, Marc Cerone, Raymond Coleman, Rebecca Cryder, Christopher Drew, Sobieslaw Fedyk, Katrina Fernandez Nova, Patrick Fitzpatrick, Masumeh Geranpayeh, Brendan Gibbons, Felix Griggs, Kira Ho, Brooke Ingram, Qi Jia, Laura Jimenez, Tamara Jimshitashvili, Hyungwoo Kim, Lin Kim, Soo Hye Kim, Hans Koesters, June Hae Lee, Soeun Lee, Randi Lesniewski, Takuya Mamada, Jonathan Orlove, Michelle Pak, Jongpil Park, Catherine Rogg, Mostapha Roudsari, David Schweim, Chen-Han Tu, Brent Watanabe, Margaret Yoo

Client	Yongsan Development Co, Ltd
Structural Engineer	Werner Sobek
Wind Engineering	RWDI Consulting Engineers
Local Architect	Siaplan Architects and Planners
Local Structural Engineer	Dongyang
Façade Access	Lerch Bates
Fire Life Safety	AON
Landscape	Martha Schwartz Partners
Lighting	OVI Office for Visual Interaction
MEP Engineer	PositivEnergy Practice
Retail	Tanseisha

400 N. LAKESHORE

Design Partners	Adrian Smith and Gordon Gill
Management Partner	Robert Forest
Project Manager	Matthew Dumich
Urban Designer	Richard Wilson
Senior Designer	Alejandro Stochetti
Senior Technical	Peter Weismantle

Project Team

Tyler Austin, Nicholas Berchtold, Allison Conley, Nathan Diestelkamp, Joel Kerner, Hyungwoo Kim, Soeun Lee, Jennie Matusova, Andy Park, Jonathan Reyes, Jay Schairbaum, David Schweim, Jeff Snodgrass, Alejandro Stochetti, Michelle Swanson, Zilong Tan, Alex Valverde, Timothy Winstanley

Client	Related Midwest
Structural Engineer	Thornton Tomasetti
Wind Engineering	RWDI Consulting Engineers

SKY SAIL

Design Partners	Adrian Smith and Gordon Gill
Management Partner	Robert Forest
Project Manager	Ben Johnson
Senior Designer	Juan Betancur

Project Team

Rachael Bennett, Charles Harris, Travis Howe, Brooke Ingram, Hyungwoo Kim, Michelle Pak, Jongpil Park, Robert Perry, James Reisinger, Yi Ren, Anthony Viola

Client	Zhongnan Group
Structural Engineer	Thornton Tomasetti
MEP Engineer	Positivenergy Practice

BURJ 2020

Design Partners	Adrian Smith and Gordon Gill
Management Partner	Robert Forest
Project Manager	Ben Johnson
Urban Designer	Richard Wilson
Senior Designer	Alejandro Stochetti
Senior Technical	Peter Weismantle

Project Team

Rafi Al-Alim, Tyler Austin, George Baciu, Ryan Beemsterboer, Nicholas Berchtold, Ana Blomeier, Connor Borchardt, John Burcher, Marc Cerone, Wing Sum Cheng, Rebecca Cryder, Ryan Dalgaard, Stephen Dinnen, Christopher Drew, Elliot Eakin, Peter Eichberger, Rezvan Farahany, Kyle Faulkner, Sobieslaw Fedyk, Katrina Fernandez Nova, Natalya Ganyukova, Gail Goldstead, Felix Griggs, Travis Howe, Robert Jillson, Patrick Keeney, Joel Kerner, Changhoon Kim, Alexander Knowles, Sunghak Ko, Rebecca LeMaster, Mengxi Li, Liam Lowry, Jaclyn Marcus, Melissa Marrero, Christopher Miller, Mateusz Nosek, Michelle Pak, Andy Park, Jongpil Park, Shawn Phillips, Natalia Quintanilla, Daniel Ramos, Seychelle Reed, Yi Ren, Alyson Reuter, Jonathan Reyes, Lauren Sajek, Thomas Schneider, Myongki Seong, Jeff Snodgrass, Christopher Strasser, James Struthers, Maria Sturchio, Michelle Swanson, Zilong Tan, Jennie Tolfa, Anthony Viola, Ning Wang, Zhaochen Wang, Xueting Wei, Preston Welker, Jonathan Wilkinson, Timothy Winstanley, Jiajing Xie, Tianyu Xu, Jing Zhang, Ruoqi Zhong

Client	DMCC
Client Representative	Turner Middle East, Ltd.
Structural Engineer	Thornton Tomasetti
MEP Engineer	Positivenergy Practice
Architect of Record	BHNS
Traffic and Parking	Langan
Vertical Transportation	Fortune Shepler Consulting
Wind Engineering	RWDI Consulting Engineers
Lighting	Office for Visual Interaction
Landscape	SWA
Façade Access	Lerch Bates
Fire Life Safety	Jensen Hughes
Civil and Geotechnical	Langan
Acoustics	SMW

ZA'ABEEL COMMERCIAL TOWER

Design Partners	Adrian Smith and Gordon Gill
Management Partner	Robert Forest
Senior Designer	Juan Betancur

Project Team

Alexis Burson, Michael Newton, Josh Smith

Client	Meraas
Structural Engineer	Thornton Tomasetti

CLEAN TECHNOLOGY TOWER

Design Partners	Adrian Smith and Gordon Gill
Management Partner	Robert Forest
Senior Designer	Les Ventsch

Project Team

Ann Buckman, Jorge Soler, Brad Wilkins

PROJECT CREDITS

MERAAS TOWER

Design Partners	Adrian Smith and Gordon Gill
Management Partner	Robert Forest
Senior Designer	Fei Xu

Project Team

Olga Anaya, Megan Beidler, Gail Borthwick, Jeffrey Boyer, Brendan Gibbons, Kira Ho, Tyler Noblin, Brent Schuettpeltz, Les Ventsch, Nathan Woods

Client	Meraas
Structural Engineer	Thornton Tomasetti
Building Maintenance	Lerch Bates
Vertical Transportation	Fortune Consulting, Ltd
Wind Engineering	RWDI Consulting Engineers
Fire Life Safety	Rolf Jensen and Associates, Inc.
MEP Engineer	Environmental Systems Design

ZA'ABEEL SIGNATURE TOWER I

Design Partners	Adrian Smith and Gordon Gill
Management Partner	Robert Forest
Senior Designer	Juan Betancur

Project Team

Elyse Agnello, Alexis Burson, Ahmed Constable, Josh Hutchinson, Chung Rhee, Josh Smith

Client	Meraas
Structural Engineer	Thornton Tomasetti

XIAN GREENLAND TOWER

Design Partners	Adrian Smith and Gordon Gill
Management Partner	Robert Forest
Project Manager	Ben Johnson
Senior Designer	Juan Betancur
Senior Technical	Iris Gan

Project Team

Nora Ames, Jennie Tolfa, Anthony Viola, Jing Zhang

Client	Greenland Group Real Estate Development Company, Ltd.
Structural Engineer	Thornton Tomasetti

ZA'ABEEL HOTEL

Design Partners	Adrian Smith and Gordon Gill
Management Partner	Robert Forest
Senior Designer	Sara Beardsley

Project Team

Brian Kneesel, Chung Rhee, Anthony Viola

Client	Meraas
Structural Engineer	Thornton Tomasetti

JEDDAH TOWER

Design Partners	Adrian Smith and Gordon Gill
Management Partner	Robert Forest
Project Manager	Brian M. Jack
Senior Designer	Alejandro Stochetti
Senior Technical	Peter Weismantle

Project Team

Miguel Alvarez, Mohamad Araji, George Baciu, Ryan Bakke, Rachel Banach, Sara Beardsley, Frederik Berte, Juan Betancur, Jillian Blakey, Ana Blomeier, Gail Borthwick, Nathan Bowman, Brett Bridgeland, Hayes Brister, Sydney Brown, John Burcher, Alexis Burson, Jessica Butler, Ashley Byers, Sally Cathcart, Marc Cerone, Raymond Coleman, Charles Collett, Colin Craig, Rebecca Cryder, Katherine Dailey, Ryan Dalgaard, Thomas Demetrion, Christopher Drew, Michelle Dumont, Elliot Eakin, Kyle Faulkner, Sobieslaw Fedyk, Robert Finigan, Patrick Fitzpatrick, Robert Forest, Joshua Frank, Natalya Ganyukova, Krystian Gardula, Dimitra Gelagoti, Danielle Gharst,

Brendan Gibbons, Gordon Gill, Gail Goldstead, Felix Griggs, Christopher Harvey, Zachary Heaps, Jessica Hogue, Travis Howe, Stephen Hsueh, Brian Hubbard, London Huenefeld, Christopher Hurst, Brooke Ingram, Brian Jack, DongSoo Jang, Matthias Janikowski, Robert Jillson, Laura Jimenez, Tamara Jimshitashvili, Ben Johnson, Changhoon Kim, Lin Kim, Soo Hye Kim, Peter Kindel, Alexander Knowles, Hans Koesters, So Young Lee, Soeun Lee, David LeFevre, Rebecca Lemaster, Randi Lesniewski, Todd Mackinson, John Maher, Takuya Mamada, Jaclyn Marcus, Tashio Martinez, Rucha Mehendale, Olia Miho, Christopher Miller, Michael Newton, Vanessa Newton, Tyler Noblin, Matthew Nyweide, David Osmond, Luis Palacio, Griffin Pemberton, Michael Perez, Robert Perry, Benjamin Raines, David Rariden, Katie Rariden, Dennis Rehill, Yi Ren, Albert Rhee, Beumhyeung Rhee, Catherine Rogg, Mostapha Roudsari, Sean Satterfield, Thomas Schneider, David Schweim, Rachel Sears, Myongki Seong, Mohamed Sheriff, Matthew Simpson, Jason Smith, Donald Stark, Andrew Suszko, Michelle Swanson, Afaq Syed, Anthony Trifiletti, Chen-Han Tu, Les Ventsch, Anthony Viola, Michael Waldo, Christopher Walker, Brent Watanabe, Kirsten Weismantle, Preston Welker, Marc Woodcock, Margaret Yoo

Client	Jeddah Economic Company
Structural Engineer	Thornton Tomasetti
MEP Engineer, Acoustic, Technology Systems	Environmental Systems Design
Architect of Record	Dar Al Handashah
Fire Life Safety	Rolf Jensen Associates
Geotechnical, Civil, Traffic, Roads, Utilities	Langan International
Wind Engineering	RWDI Consulting Engineers
Vertical Transportation	Fortune Consulting, Ltd.
Façade Access	Lee Herzog Consulting
Materials Handling	Lerch Bates
Security	Sako
Cathodic Protection	AEGIS
Master Plan	HOK
Lighting	Aurora

SHENZHEN HONG KONG INTERNATIONAL CENTER

Design Partners	Adrian Smith and Gordon Gill
Management Partner	Robert Forest
Project Manager	Ben Johnson
Senior Designer	Fei Xu
Senior Technical	Iris Gan

Project Team

Tyler Austin, Alexander Bahr, Sara Beardsley, Nicholas Berchtold, Marc Cerone, Bintou Coulibaly, Rebecca Cryder, Christopher Drew, Sobieslaw Fedyk, Katrina Fernandez Nova, Liyuan Ge, Yongsan Huang, Nash Kennedy, Joel Kerner, Ryan Kukuraitis, Soeun Lee, Yuchen Liu, Weiwei Luo, Melissa Marrero, Luis Palacio, Natalia Quintanilla, Jonathan Reyes, Jeff Snodgrass, Maria Sturchio, Zilong Tan, Richard Wilson, Xi Yi, Jing Zhang, Yuxin Zheng, Ruoqi Zhong,

Client	Shimao Properties Holdings Ltd.
Structural Engineer	Thornton Tomasetti
MEP Engineer	WSP

CENTRAL PARK TOWER

Design Partners	Adrian Smith and Gordon Gill
Management Partner	Robert Forest
Project Manager	Brian M. Jack
Senior Designer	David Schweim

Project Team

Miguel Alvarez, George Baciu, Nicholas Berchtold, Frederik Berte, Jae Yun Cho, Allison Conley, Nathan Diestelkamp, Patrick Fitzpatrick, Marshall Ford, Brendan Gibbons, Richard Gnat, Gail Goldstead, Heng Gu, Charles Harris, Kira Ho, Robert Jillson, Changhoon Kim, Hyungwoo Kim, Paul Kim, Todd Mackinson, Jennie Matusova, Michelle Pak, Viorica Pisau, David Rariden, Yi Ren, Thomas Schneider, Myongki Seong, Jeff Snodgrass, Donald Stark, Alex Valverde, Les Ventsch, Timothy Winstanley, Jing Zhang

PROJECT CREDITS

Client	Extell Development Company
Structural Engineer	WSP Cantor Seinuk
MEP Engineer	AKF Group
Architect of Record	AAI Architects, PC
Acoustics	Cerami & Associates
Geotechnical	Langan Engineering
Fire Life Safety, Code	Construction Consulting Associates
Curtainwall	AJLP Consulting
Landmark, Preservation	Jan Hird Pokorny Associates, Inc
Interiors	Rottet Studio
Vertical Transportation	Van Duesen and Associates
Wind Engineering, Snow and Ice	RWDI
Lighting	Cline Bettridge Bernstein Lighting Design
AV / Security	The Clarient Group
Landscape	HM White
Façade Maintenance	Entek Engineering

AHKMAT TOWER

Design Partners	Adrian Smith and Gordon Gill
Management Partner	Robert Forest
Project Manager	Brian M. Jack
Senior Designer	Alejandro Stochetti
Senior Technical	Sae Hwang Oh Sara Beardsley

Project Team

Rustem Baishev, Ryan Beemsterboer, Nicholas Berchtold, Frederik Berte, Connor Borchardt, John Burcher, Jessica Butler, Marc Cerone, Wing Sum Cheng, Allison Conley, Rebecca Cryder, Nathan Diestelkamp, Iliana Doytcheva, Christopher Drew, Ryan Duncan, Elliot Eakin, Mihael Efremov, Rezvan Farahany, Natalya Ganyukova, Gail Goldstead, Felix Griggs, John Harmon, Joel Kerner, Hyungwoo Kim, Lin Kim, Sunghak Ko, Rebecca LeMaster, Mengxi Li, Yuchen Liu, Jaclyn Marcus, Christopher Miller, Mateusz Nosek, Andy Park, Natalia Quintanilla, Seychelle Reed, Thomas Schneider, Paul Schroeckenstein, Alexander Semochkin, Myongki Seong, Matthew Simpson, Matt Snoap, Jeff Snodgrass, Christopher Strasser, James Struthers, Maria Sturchio, Rachel Tobe, Luis Villafane, Kirsten Weismantle, Peter Weismantle, Preston Welker, Wei Yu

Client	MFC Akhmat Tower, LLC; Smart Building, LLC
Structural Engineer	Thornton Tomasetti
MEP Engineer	Positivenergy Practice
Architect of Record	GorProject
Civil, Geotechnical, Traffic	Langan International
Vertical Transportation	Fortune Shepler Saling, Inc
Wind Engineering	RWDI Consulting Engineers
Landscape	Garth A Wemmer
Façade Lighting	Office for Visual Interaction
Façade Access, Waste Management	Lerch Bates
Lighting	Aurora Lighting
Graphics	Forcade
Pool	Aqua Design
Kitchen, Laundry	Cini-Little International

RUNMAO TOWER

Design Partners	Adrian Smith and Gordon Gill
Management Partner	Robert Forest
Project Manager	Ben Johnson
Senior Designer	Fei Xu
Senior Technical	Iris Gan

Project Team

Nora Ames, Tyler Austin, Alexander Bahr, Nicholas Berchtold, Marc Cerone, Jennifer Cooper, Alexis Crates, Rebecca Cryder, Caitlin, Dashiell, Christopher Drew, Iris Gan, Gail Goldstead, Rebecca Greenberg, Felix Griggs, Wilson Harkhono, Yongsan Huang, Nash Kennedy, Ryan Kukuraitis, Soeun Lee, Miaoqi Liu, Yuchen Liu, Weiwei Luo, Melissa Marrero, Christian Newman, Luis Palacio, Joseph Peltier, Griffin Pemberton, Natalia Quintanilla, Jonathan Reyes, Thomas Schneider, Arham Siddiqui, Michaela Singson, Jeff Snodgrass, Mingjian Suo,

Zilong Tan, Jennie Tolfa, Anthony Viola, Richard Wilson, Perry Wreaks, Tianyu Xu, Dong Yan, Xi Yi, Ailing Zhang, Jing Zhang, Meng Zhang, Ruoqi Zhong, Yueming Zhou

Client	China Jinmao Nanjing Company
Local Design Insitute	ECADI (East China Architecture Design and Research Institute)
Structural Engineer	Thornton Tomasetti
MEP Engineer, Vertical Transportation	WSP
Landscape Architect	SWA
Architectural Lighting	Office for Visual Interaction
Exterior Wall, Façade Access	Alt Limited

ELPHINSTONE MILLS

Design Partners	Adrian Smith and Gordon Gill
Management Partner	Robert Forest
Senior Designer	Les Ventch

Project Team

Olga Anaya, Gail Borthwick, Nathan Bowman, April Chen, Joshua Cooper, Cara Ellis, David Ellis, Jeff Gibbon, Brendan Gibbons, Ryan Hayes, Jessica Hogue, Hrishikesh Madane, Alex Martinez, Luis Palacio, Carlo Parente, Nalin Ramkumar, Mario Romero, Kshitij Sawant, Teddy Slowik, Jorge Soler, Matthew Stewart

Client	Indiabulls Real Estate Ltd.
Structural Engineer	Y S Sane Associates
Vertical Transportation	Fortune Consulting Ltd
MEP Engineer	Eskayem Consultants Ltd

BIOPHILIC TOWER

Design Partners	Adrian Smith and Gordon Gill
Management Partner	Robert Forest
Project Manager	Ben Johnson
Senior Designer	Juan Betancur

Project Team

Rachael Bennett, Charles Harris, Travis Howe, Brooke Ingram, Hyungwoo Kim, Michelle Pak, Jongpil Park, Robert Perry, James Reisinger, Yi Ren, Anthony Viola

Client	Zhongnan Group
Structural Engineer	Thornton Tomasetti
MEP Engineer	Positivenergy Practice

KLIFD TOWER

Design Partners	Adrian Smith and Gordon Gill
Management Partner	Robert Forest
Senior Designer	Alejandro Stochetti
Urban Designer	Peter Kindel

Project Team

Frederik Berte, Marc Cerone, Christopher Drew, Keara Fanning, Katrina Fernandez Nova, Patrick Fitzpatrick, Brendan Gibbons, Alex Gormley, Qi Jia, Hyungwoo Kim, June Hae Lee, Andres Lopez Montoya, Tashio Martinez, Jonathan Orlove, Benjamin Raines, Dennis Rehill, Mostapha Sadeghipour Roudsari, David Schweim, Margaret Yoo

Client	1 Malaysian Development Berhad
Structural Engineer	Thornton Tomasetti
MEP Engineer	PositivEnergy Practice

DOHA TOWER

Design Partners	Adrian Smith and Gordon Gill
Management Partner	Robert Forest
Senior Designer	Alejandro Stochetti

Project Team

Fernando Alessandrini, April Chen, Ryan Hanlon, Jason Minor, Sean Satterfield, Nathaniel Woods

PROJECT CREDITS

IMPERIAL TOWER

Design Partners	Adrian Smith and Gordon Gill
Management Partner	Robert Forest
Project Manager	Jonathan Orlove
Senior Designer	Carlo Parente

Project Team

Rachel Bennett, Christopher Drew, Michelle Dumont, Patrick Fitzpatrick, Krystian Gardula, Brendan Gibbons, Matthias Janikowski, Michael Newton, Vanessa Newton, Tyler Noblin, Beumhyeung Rhee, Marc Woodcock

Client	SD Corporation

1 DUBAI ATRIUM CITY

Design Partners	Adrian Smith and Gordon Gill
Management Partner	Robert Forest
Project Manager	Brian M. Jack
Senior Designer	Jeff Stafford
Senior Technical	Peter Weismantle

Project Team

Nicholas Addison, Miguel Alvarez, Gabriel Ball, Ben Johnson, John Burcher, Anthony Cissell, Charles Collett, Joshua Cooper, Reinaldo Correa, Thomas Denney, Robert Finigan, Christina Halatsis, Christopher Harvey, Gregg Herman, Travis Howe, Brian Hubbard, Boyka Ivanova, Ben Johnson, Jeffrey Knapke, Phat Nguyen, Andrew Osvalds, Julia Robertson, Karen Rutherford, Kshitij Sawant, Mordecai Scheckter, Daniel Segraves, Siddant Sinha, Eric Snow, Brett Sterly, Rebecca Stewart, Anthony Trifiletti, Brent Watanabe

Client	Meraas
Structural Engineer	Halvorson and Partners
Civil Engineer	V3
Security	Sako
Façade Access	Lerch Bates
MEP Engineer, Sustainability	Environmental Systems Design
Wind Engineering	RWDI Consulting Engineers
Vertical Transportation	Fortune Consulting, Ltd
Fire Life Safety	Rolf Jensen Associates
Geotechnical	STS and AECOM
Masterplan	WSP
Parking	Walker
Graphics, Animation	Orphanage Animation Studios

ZA'ABEEL SIGNATURE TOWER II

Design Partners	Adrian Smith and Gordon Gill
Management Partner	Robert Forest
Senior Designer	Juan Betancur

Project Team

Elyse Agnello, Alexis Burson, Ahmed Constable, Josh Hutchinson, Chung Rhee, Josh Smith

MILE HIGH TOWER PROTOTYPES

Design Partners	Adrian Smith and Gordon Gill
Management Partner	Robert Forest
Senior Designer	Dennis Rehill and Anthony Viola

Project Team

Miguel Alvarez, Chris Harvey, Alejandro Stochetti, Matthew Nyweide, Brent Watanabe, Ashley Satterfield

AWARDS + PUBLICATIONS

1 PARK AVENUE

Publications

L'esspresso, "The new design is born," January 15, 2009

Identity, "The future is now," November 2008

Identity, "Green Giants," November 2008

Cityscape Magazine, "New look for old," November 2008

Chicago Tribune, "Chicago architects plan more towers in Dubai," October 7, 2008

The National, "Meraas tower to join Dubai's buildings in the sky," October 6, 2008

Crain's Chicago Business, "Smith + Gill wins Dubai deal," June 2, 2008

Gulf News, "Dubai gives the necessary freedom designers need," May 9, 2008

Gulf News, "Dubai will become city of supertowers," May 4, 2008

CHENGDU GREENLAND TOWER

Awards

Architizer A+ Awards, Architecture + Technology, Finalist, 2014

Publications

Tall Buildings Russia, "Chengdu Greenland," July 2015

Building Design + Construction, "Adrian Smith + Gordon Gill designed crystalline tower breaks ground in southwestern China," November 24, 2014

Architizer, "Why the High-Tech Chengdu Tower Represents the Future of Western Chinese Cities," May 6, 2014

Dezeen, "Construction Starts on Smith and Gill's Ice-Inspired Skyscraper for Chengdu," November 20, 2014

WUHAN GREENLAND CENTER

Awards

The Chicago Athenaeum, Green Good Design Award, Green Architecture, 2017

Re-Thinking the Future, Sustainability Award, First Award, Mixed-Use, 2016

Publications

Curbed, "10 tallest buildings under construction or in development around the world," February 21, 2017

Curbed, "New Buildings We are Looking Forward to in 2017," Patrick Sisson, December 11, 2016

World Architecture News, "Wuhan's Supertall Tower Heads for the Top," April 8, 2016

Hopsca III, "Wuhan Greenland Center," September 2014

The Architect's Newspaper, "Skyscraper Expert Gordon Gill Talks High Performance Facades," Anna Bergren Miller, March 28, 2014

Modern Green Structure and Architecture, "Wuhan Greenland Center," September 2013

Beyond, "Efficient Streamlined Design: Wuhan Greenland Center," December 18, 2012

CTBUH Journal, "The tallest in 2020: Entering the Era of MEgatall," Nathaniel Hollister and Dr. Antony Wood, March 2012

Bloomberg, "Chinese Tower May add Floors to Become World's Tallest after Burj Khalifa," February 27, 2012

China Daily, "Wuhan Greenland Center to be China's Tallest Building," February 27, 2012

Perspective, "High up in the Wind," September 2011

Civil Engineering Magazine, "Wuhan Tower," August 2011

Architectural Record, "On the boards: Wuhan Greenland Center," August 2011

World Architecture News, "Adrian Smith + Gordon Gill, Thornton Tomasetti and PositivEnergy Practice to Design World's Fourth Tallest Building," June 21, 2011

Inhabit, "AS+GG's Aerodynamic Wuhan Greenland Center to be World's 4th tallest Building," Bridgett Meinhold, June 21, 2011

Concept Magazine, "Wuhan Greenland Center," Summer 2011

Chicago Tribune, "Smith and Gill win competition for Supertall Tower in China," Blair Kamin, June 21, 2011

China Daily, "World's 3rd Tallest Building Design Unveiled," Yan Weijue, June 22, 2011

YONGSAN DANCING DRAGONS

Awards

The Chicago Athenaeum, Green Good Design Award, Green Architecture, 2015

The Chicago Athenaeum, International Architecture Award, 2014

The Chicago Athenaeum, American Architecture Award, 2013

Publications

World Architecture 9, "Dancing Dragons," 2015

Landmark Architecture (Korea), "Dancing Dragons," 2014

AWARDS + PUBLICATIONS

The Skycourt and the Skygarden, "Dancing Dragons," Jason Pomeroy, 2014

Evolo, "Dancing Dragons for Yongsan International Business District in Seoul," August, 2013

Beyond Magazine, "Dancing Dragons," Aug. 12, 2012

Architect Magazine, "Dancing Dragons," August 12, 2012

Civil Engineering, "Ancient Architecture inspires Contemporary Tower Complex," September 2012

World Architecture News, "AS+GG Unveils design for supertall mixed use towers in Seoul, South Korea," May 11, 2012

Architecture Source, "Breathing Life into Korean Architecture Feat," May 17, 2012

World Architecture News, "Year of the Dragon: AS+GG Unveils design for supertall mixed use towers for Seoul, South Korea," May 11, 2012

Inhabit, "Adrian Smith and Gordon Gill Unveil Dancing Dragons Towers with Scaly Breathable Skin," May 11, 2012

400 N. LAKESHORE

Awards

Architizer A+ Awards, Residential-Unbuilt -Multi-Unit Housing, Finalist, 2018

The Chicago Athenaeum, American Architecture Awards, (As Confidential Residential Development,) 2017

BURJ 2020

Publications

Arabian Business, "DMCC free zone hires U.S. Designer for Uptown Dubai Mega-project," January 10, 2018

Construction Week, "Construction begins on new Mixed-use district near Dubai's JLT," Jumana Abdel-Razzaq, September 25, 2017

Gulf News, "Dubai's Latest District Gets a Name," September 25, 2017

Design MENA, "Burj 2020 by Adrian Smith and Gordon Gill will be 'Diamond of Dubai'" September 8, 2016

The National, "Burj 2020: Architectural duo set their sights on Dubai," September 8, 2016

Construction Week, "Adrian Smith + Gordon Gill to Design Burj 2020," June 2016

ZA'ABEEL PROJECTS

Awards

Rethinking the Future, Global Architecture & Design Awards, First Award Commercial, Signature Tower 1, 2019

Publications

World Architecture Firm Selection, "Za'abeel Energy City Master Plan" October 29, 2013

CLEAN TECHNOLOGY TOWER

Publications

Voir Vert, "Le prototype de la Clean Technology

Tower," September 17, 2013

Riscaldamento Climatizzazione Idronica, "Biomimicry in building design," February 2009

Space, "Clean technology building," January 2009

Modern Design, "The 11th hour...and the carbon-conflict: smooth operator," May 2008

MERAAS TOWER

Publications

Vertical Density (China), "Meraas Tower," January, 2010

World Architecture News, "Meraas development taps Adrian Smith + Gordon Gill for megaproject," October 9, 2008

Chicago Tribune, "Chicago architects plan more towers in Dubai," October 7, 2008

The National, "Meraas Tower to join Dubai's buildings in the sky," Bradley Hope, October 6, 2008

Crain's Chicago Business, "Smith + Gill wins Dubai deal," June 2, 2008

Gulf News, "Dubai gives the necessary freedom designers need," May 9, 2008

Gulf News, "Dubai will become city of supertowers," May 4, 2008

JEDDAH TOWER

Awards

Middle East AIA, Non-Built Category, Merit Award, 2014

Publications

Forbes, "7 Supertall Buildings in the Works Around the Globe," July 22, 2018

The Architect's Newspaper, "Saudi Arabia is building a future for its millennial population," June 25, 2018

The Architect's Newspaper, "You Jeddah Believe It – Construction on World's Tallest Tower Moves Forward," Audrey Wachs, Feb 14, 2018

Fortune, "This is what the World's Tallest Tower Will Soon Look Like," Alex Schimecca, Feb 22, 2018

Architectural Record, "Jeddah Tower, Saudi Arabia," May 2017

International Journal of High-Rise Buildings, "Vertical Shortening Considerations for 1km Kingdom Tower," John Peronto, Robert Sinn, Matthew Huizinga, March 2017

Curbed, "10 tallest buildings under construction or in development around the world," February 21, 2017

Civil Engineering Magazine, " Learnings from Jeddah Tower," September 1, 2016

Structure Magazine, "Rising to the Clouds with Confidence," June, 2016

The Wall Street Journal, "Jeddah Aiming for Towering Height," Feb. 3, 2016

City Lab, "Can a skyscraper Soar Above the Clouds?," Dec 31, 2015

The Telegraph, "Onwards and upwards for the Skyscraper," Dec 6, 2015

Chicago Tribune, "Saudi Arabia Plans to building the world's tallest skyscraper," Dec 2, 2015

Engineering News Record, "Jeddah' Tower's Climb to one Kilometer Picks Up Speed," Nov. 11, 2015

The Observer, "Megastructures: 7 wonders of the modern world near completion," Douglas Murphy, Nov. 9, 2015

Time Magazine, "When it comes to the new Ultra Tall, The Sky is the Limit", July 2015

The Guardian, "Jeddah's Kingdom Tower: How much Higher can Skyscrapers Go?" June 4, 2015

New York Magazine, "The Rise of the Mile High Building," Justin Davidson, March 21, 2015

Fire Risk Management, "Tall Buildings Smoke Control," Peter Weismantle, July/August 2015

Architectural Record, "Big Bigger Biggest," March 2014

McGraw Hill Education, "Tall and Supertall Buildings: Kingdom Tower," 2014

CNN, "Real High Tech: How will Elevators work in the world's tallest building," Daisy Carrington, July 2, 2014

Dubai Chronicle, "Saudi Arabia and the UAE will soon be home to the two tallest buildings ever built," May 23, 2014

CNN, "Saudi Arabia to building world's tallest tower, reaching 1 kilometer into the sky," Daisy Carrington, April 18, 2014

Arab News, "Kingdom Tower Project in Jeddah progressing as planned," May 1, 2014

Bloomberg Businessweek, "Shedding the Vortex," Bryant Urstadt, April 8, 2014

International Construction, " Bauer Completes Foundation Construction on Kingdom Tower," Chris Sleight, Feb. 11, 2014

CTBUH Journal, "Case Study: Kingdom Tower: Jeddah," 2013 Issue I

Popular Science, "Rise of the Supertalls," Feb 15, 2013

Discovery Channel Magazine, "Reach for the Sky," April, 2012

LA Times, "Critic's Notebook: Skyscrapers Remain Powerful Symbols, Post 9/11" Christopher Hawthorne, Sept. 4, 2011

Arabian Business, " Kingdom Tower Architect grapples the wind at 3,000 ft," August 30, 2011

Gulf Daily, "A Bird? A Plane? It's Kingdom Tower!," August 11, 2011

Chicago Suntimes, "Chicago Firm Designing New Tallest Building," August 2, 2011

Chicago Tribune, "Chicago Firm's design towers over the rest," August 3, 2011

World Architecture News, "AS+GG Confirmed for Kingdom Tower," August 2, 2011.

Construction Week Online, "Kingdom Tower is next step in Skyscraper Design," August 3, 2011

Architecture Update, "Vertically Unlimited," interview with Adrian Smith, Sept, 2011

Chicago Tribune, "Saudi Mega-tower designed by Chicago Architects Moving Ahead," Blair Kamin, Oct. 22, 2010

AWARDS + PUBLICATIONS

SHENZHEN HONG KONG INTERNATIONAL CENTER

Publications

Design Boom, "China's Tallest Building: AS+GG reveals plans for 700m skyscraper," Jan 24, 2019

USA News Hub, "China's tallest building: AS+GG Reveals plans for 700m skyscraper," Jan 24, 2019

Building Design + Construction, "AS+GG Designed Tower will be the tallest in China," Jan 16, 2019

The Architect's Newspaper, "Adrian Smith + Gordon Gill Designs Tallest Building in China," Jan 16, 2019

Dezeen, "Adrian Smith + Gordon Gill reveals design for China's next skyscraper," Jan 14, 2018

Arch Daily, "Adrian Smith + Gordon Gill to Design China's Tallest Skyscraper," Jan 11, 2019

Archinect, "Adrian Smith + Gordon Gill to design Shimao Shenzhen Longgang Master Plan and 700m anthropomorphic tower," Jan 9, 2019

News Atlas, "There's a new contender for the World's Second Tallest Skyscraper," Adam Williams, Jan 9, 2019

CENTRAL PARK TOWER

Awards

CTBUH, Award of Excellence, Best Tall Building 400 meters and above, 2020

Publications

The New York Times, "Building a Cantilever," Tim McKeough, June 4, 2021

New York Magazine, "A Slide of the Sky: The Supertall 111 West 57th is what the ruling class buildings for itself", Justin Davidson, June 9, 2021

Architectural Digest, "The 11 Most Anticipated Buildings of 2020," Jan 14, 2020

The Architect's Newspaper, "Central Park Tower out to become the world's tallest residential building," Sept 19, 2019

New York Magazine, "The Challenges of Constructing New York's Tallest Apartment Building," Sept 16, 2019

Wall Street Journal, "The man Behind Billionaire's Row Battles to Sell the World's Tallest Condo," Katherine Clarke and Candace Taylor, Jan 17, 2019

Arch Daily, "The Tallest Residential Building in the World is Coming to New York City," Niall Patrick Walsh, Oct 18, 2018

Metropolis, "Take a Closer Look at the Design of the World's Tallest Residential Tower," Anna Fixsen, Oct. 18, 2018

Business Insider, "Extell Development Company Closes on a $1.135 Billion Financing package for Central Park Tower, the Tallest Residential Building in the World," Jan 2, 2018

Curbed New York, "Extell's Midtown supertall, Central Park Tower, is getting its façade," Tanay Warerkar, Dec 8, 2017

Building Design + Construction, "Size Matters in NYC," John Caulfield, April 23, 2015

The Atlantic, "The Newest, Tallest Supertall Tower in New York City," Kriston Capps, May 11, 2015

Archinect, "Adrian Smith Will Design NYC, North America's Tallest Building," Dec 17, 2012

The Architect's Newspaper, "Adrian Smith + Gordon Gill's First Manhattan Skyscraper Among the City's Tallest," Dec 18, 2012

New York Business Journal, "Get ready for city's next tallest residential tower, plus NYC's first Nordstrom - - in one building," Dec 17, 2012

AHKMAT TOWER

Publications

CTBUH Journal, "Technical Considerations for Akhmat Tower," Beardsley, Stochetti, Cerone, Peronto, 2018 Issue III

Tall Buildings (Russia), "Incarnating traditions of Vainakh Architecture," 2016

RUNMAO TOWER

Publications

Architect Magazine, "South HeXi Yuzui Financial District and Tower," Novemer 6th, 2019

News Atlas, "Sculpted supertall skyscraper will boast energy-efficient design," Adam Williams, November 13, 2019

The Nanjinger, "500 Metres High! Tallest Building in Nanjing set for Change," Frank Hossack, April 1, 2020

Arch Daily, "AS+GG Releases Design for New Financial District in China," Christele Harrouk, November 13, 2019

Architectural Record, "On the Boards," Josephine Minutillo, January 27, 2020

BIOPHILIC TOWER

Awards

Architectural Review, MIPIM Future Project Award, Tall Buildings, Commendation, 2015

The Chicago Athenaeum, American Architecture Award, 2013

IMPERIAL TOWER

Publications

Tall Buildings Russia, "Imperial Tower," Jan 5, 2015

World Architecture News, "400m Imperial Tower Designed by Adrian Smith + Gordon Gill," Pallavi, May 20, 2013

DNA India, "Design of Mumbai's Prospective Tallest building Unveiled," Payal Mohta, May 13, 2013

Building Design + Construction, "First look, Adrian Smith + Gordon Gill's skyscraper designed to 'confuse the wind'" May 7, 2013

1 DUBAI ATRIUM CITY

Publications

Superlative Emirates, "The New Dimension of Urban Design, Adrian Smith + Gordon Gill Architecture" March 23, 2012

Home and Lifestyle Magazine, "Dubai's Comeback," Helmut Melzer, Nov 16, 2011

Identity, "The Future is Now," Nov, 2008

Identity, "Green Giants," Nov 2008

Chicago Tribune, "Chicago Architects plan more towers in Dubai," Blair Kamin, Oct. 7, 2008

Crain's Chicago Business, "Smith + Gill wins Dubai deal," June 2, 2008

Gulf News, "Dubai gives the necessary freedom designers need," May 9, 2008

Gulf News, "Dubai will become city of supertowers," May 4, 2008

MILE HIGH TOWER PROTOTYPES

Big Think, "Is it possible to build a mile-high skyscraper," Mike Colagrossi, September 14, 2020

Stir World, "Adrian Smith and Gordon Gill on skyscraper architecture and energy-efficient buildings," Vladimir Belogolovsky, December 19, 2019

Trimble, "The Building Technology Behind a Mile High Skyscraper," Gary Wollenhaupt, November 13, 2018

CNN, "Tall building history: The making of the modern skyscraper," David Nicholson-Cole, December 21, 2017

Chicagoly, "From Up On High," Alan P. Henry, Summer 2017

Chicago Magazine, "The Man with His Head in the Clouds," Tom Chiarella, June 7, 2016

Curbed, "Supertalls and Sustainable Skyscrapers: Architect Adrian Smith on the Mile-High Building," Patrick Sisson, April 12, 2016

Wired, "How to Keep a 1,500-Foot Skyscraper From Falling Over," Sophia Chen, July 27, 2015

New York Magazine, "The Rise of the Mile-High Building," Justin Davidson, March 24, 2015

Business Insider, "Tallest Buildings of the Future," December 1, 2015

Popular Science, "The Rise of the Supertalls," Clay Risen, October 3, 2014

Chicago Architect, "A to Z with Adrian Smith," May-June 2014

Bloomberg Businessweek, "Shedding the Vortex," Brian Urstadt, March 24, 2014

Building, Design + Construction, "Are we on the brink of the first mile-high building?" October 10, 2013

Icon Magazine, "Adrian Smith: the world's tallest buildings," Owen Pritchard, March 21, 2013

The Smithsonian Magazine, "Better, Faster, Taller – How Big can Buildings Really Get?" Rose Eveleth, August 20, 2012

Popular Mechanics, "Taller: How Future Skyscrapers Will Beat the Burj Khalifa," Adam Hadhazy, May 16, 2012

Discovery Channel Magazine, "Reach for the Sky," Chris Wright, April 2012

The Big Project, "Icon under construction," August 2011

The Wall Street Journal, "Architect Q&A: The State of Super-Tall Towers," Maura Webber Sadovi, July 8, 2011

ACKNOWLEDGMENTS

Supertall/Megatall: How High Can We Go? represents a body of work that has been years in the making and has involved the contributions of hundreds of architects, engineers, and other building industry professionals. AS+GG partners Adrian Smith, Gordon Gill, and Robert Forest wish to thank every member of the project teams who have contributed to the designs that are documented in this publication.

A special thank you is extended to the AS+GG team who did the graphic design and layout, research, writing, and editing to produce such a comprehensive and unique publication: Jocelyn Moriarty, Sara Beardsley, Anthony Viola, Katrina Fernandez Nova, Peter Weismantle, Iris Gan, Fei Xu, Alejandro Stochetti, Marc Cerone, Juan Betancur, Ruoqi Zhong, Taylor Hess, and Jade Boudreaux.